MIXED

MIXED

PORTRAITS OF MULTIRACIAL KIDS

BY **KIP FULBECK**
FOREWORD BY **DR. MAYA SOETORO-NG**
AFTERWORD BY **CHER**

CHRONICLE BOOKS
SAN FRANCISCO

Library of Congress Cataloging-in-Publication Data available.

ISBN-: 978-0-8118-7408-3

Manufactured in China

Design by **ELOISE LEIGH**

10 9 8 7 6 5 4 3 2 1

Chronicle Books LLC
680 Second Street
San Francisco, CA 94107
www.chroniclebooks.com

for Heather and Jack

ACKNOWLEDGMENTS

I'd like to express my thanks to the many giving individuals who opened up their homes, businesses, and community centers to the pandemonium of these photo shoots, as well as the many people who helped this project come to life: Kris Andrews, George Avelino, B.J. Barclay, Jonathan Cecil, Cher, Kayla Coleman, Fanshen Cox, Veronica De La Cruz, Heidi Durrow, Stuart Gaffney, Manny Garcia, Colin Gardner, Jim Goldberg, Stephen Gong, Mariko Gordon, Jocelyn Gottesman, Morgan Harris, Robert Horsting, Yumi Kinoshita, Christian Kasseck, Stacey Kwon, Robert Lee, Naomi Melo, Dan "The Nazz" Nazzareta, Betty Nguyen, Ben Northover, Joannie Osato, Michella Rivera-Gravage, Jennifer Ruiz, Yasamin Salari, Katy Schwager, Joel Sherman, Karen Spector, Kellie Stoelting, Shannon Sun-Higginson, Ken Tanabe, Joshua Thomas, Derrick Velasquez, Charmaine Wash, Angela Williams, and Don Young.

Thanks again to the spectacular crew at Chronicle Books, with bonus thanks to Jessica Hulce, Eloise Leigh, Becca Cohen, Patti Quill, and my simpatico editor, Bridget Watson Payne. Thanks to my super assistants, Jill Carlson, Lindsay Castro, and Melissa Ortiz, who made up for my forgetfulness more times than I can count. Thanks to my literary agent, Faye Bender, and my booking agents, Andy Roth and Erica Langston, for believing in me as an artist. Thanks to the staff at the Japanese

American National Museum, especially Lisa Sasaki, Clement Hanami, and Koji Sakai; my colleagues in the UCSB Art Department; my fellow artists who continue to challenge and expand the definitions of who we are; and my many academic contemporaries advancing multiethnic research, particularly Paul Spickard, Reg Daniel, Wei Ming Dariotis, Rudy Guevarra, Velina Hasu Houston, Evelyn Hu-Dehart, Laura Kina, Cindy Nakashima, Darby Li Po Price, Curtiss Takada Rooks, Kieu Linh Valverde, and Teresa Kay Williams-León. Thanks to my teachers, especially Phel Steinmetz, David Antin, Eleanor Antin, Georgia Florentine, Allan Kaprow, Robyn Hunt, Jim Lin, Lisa Lowe, and Martha Rosler; and of course my students, who ground and check me on a daily basis.

Thanks to my family, especially my parents, who had the good sense to follow love above legality; to the hundreds of parents who allowed me the privilege of photographing their children; and to all the kids who cut loose and took part in this whole thing (you guys were the coolest part). Special thanks to my righthand man Michael Velasquez, whose artistic skills grace each of these pages, and to Maya Soetoro-Ng, for continuing to inspire people throughout the world. I could not have made this book without the strength, criticism, and support of my wonderful wife, Heather. And to my son, Jack—may the world continue to welcome you in more ways than you can imagine.

KIP FULBECK

SANTA BARBARA, CA

I could be anywhere, picking up some innocuous bureaucratic form on a clipboard, filling in lines and checking boxes.

NAME:

ADDRESS:

AGE:

GENDER:

And there it is, staring me in the face:

RACE (CHECK ONE)

☐

☐

☐

☐

☐

☐

☐

I'm amazed, on a regular basis, to find this query still printed. Like some old joke that's lost its humor and turned sour. A true anachronism, as out of place and completely out of bounds as smoking on airplanes, WMD fabrications, or actors wearing blackface. A textual solecism. A farce. Yet I constantly hear from people still confronted with it—on job questionnaires, school surveys, traffic violations, health forms, community and housing assessments. And I still come across it occasionally myself.

For millions of Americans, this question amounts to asking us to lie. It's asking us to choose one parent over another, or one great-great-grandparent over another, or one part of ourselves over another. And despite centuries of ignoring (or denying) the idea of racial mixing, multiracial heritage and multiracial identity are core ingredients of our society. Interracial unions have been part of America's history since its inception, yet only recently have these collective and individual histories begun to be recognized.

It was just ten years ago that the U.S. Census—for the first time—allowed participants to check more than one box to define their racial heritage, an option nearly seven million people chose to exercise and millions more will exercise in the coming years. Today, a decade later, a rapidly growing number of voices are demanding more. We want acknowledgment of all our heritages. We want to be recognized for who we are. We want to define ourselves rather than have our selves define us.

Full disclosure: I have a personal stake in this. For starters, as an artist, I've created work exploring personal identity for the better part of two decades. In many ways, I've bet my career on the fact that we all have a need to tell our own stories, to define ourselves, and I've been fortunate enough to share this work with audiences of all ages all over the world. But this book is something more significant. On March 21, 2009, I became a father. My son, Jack, was born—named after my own father. And in this one moment, my life, and the meaning behind my entire work as an artist, shifted significantly. After two decades making art that questions the very idea of race, that explores the complications and consequences of choosing sides or affiliations (or worse, having them chosen for you), that argues against the concepts of compartmentalization, categorization, and conceptual laziness, my stakes have suddenly been raised.

And while we can rehash the fact that race doesn't exist biologically, that the very idea of human beings being broken down into genetically discrete groups is scientifically unsound, that somewhere between 50,000 to 100,000 years ago our common ancestors migrated out of what is now Africa, we must also acknowledge that, for better or worse, in the reality of our daily lives, race exists. In the broadest sense, viewing others as inherently *different* has allowed our species to commit some of the worst atrocities in our young history—the enslavement of western African peoples, the decimation to near extermination of Native Americans, the genocides of the Ottoman Empire, Auschwitz, Rwanda, and Nanking—to name a few. But it is in the personal view that I want to focus, where seeing others as different, and being seen as different, affects us in the smallest and yet most profound ways.

My mother is Cantonese; my father an American-born mix of English, Irish, and Welsh descent. They wed at a time when their marriage would still have been illegal in many states, a fact I cherish since it tinges my own birth with a hint of defiance, of rebelliousness—qualities I've always prided myself on. And like with any past legalities we now look back at with disbelief, we silently pat ourselves on the back for our collective progress, our communal advancement. We point out to ourselves, proudly, that we no longer deny women the right to vote, force African Americans to the backs of buses, or limit citizenship based on race.

Advertising often co-ops this self-satisfaction, using it to sell products bearing social responsibility, marketing progressiveness by association. In the '70s, we came a long way, baby. In the '80s, we wore the United Colors of Benetton. In the '90s, girl power/riot grrrl music went onstage at

Lilith Fair with Daisy Rock Guitars following, and we saw the rise of female participants in previously male-dominated "extreme" sports like snowboarding and surfing (flanked by Roxy attire). Today we walk past the multiple multicolored, multiethnic, anonymously ecstatic silhouettes of iPod dancers with a distinct sense of *now*.

Let me state it clearly. Yes, we have made progress. But the pace has been dawdling, and we have not come far enough. As a culture, as a nation, as people, it's quite simple—we are nowhere remotely near where we need to be. I declare this statement publicly, hear the same responses, and feel returning frustrations. I hear *come-on-in-this-day-and-age* and I think of illegal immigration debates, prison populations, the number of female CEOs, and the thirty-one states where you can be fired for being gay. I hear *to-be-honest-I-don't-really-notice-race-myself* and I've got a lot of questions, as well as a lifetime of stories to share with you. How much time do you have? In response to my parents' marriage I hear *sure-but-that-was-back-in-the-'60s*

and I think about Bob Jones University banning interracial dating until 2000 (and Alabama not amending its state constitution until the same year). I think of how much more awareness, education, and acceptance we as a population must cultivate, how our priorities must be reset at both the individual and the global levels. This is the world my son inherits from me.

But in many ways, it is a world changing for the better. My son will not face the same questions I did. He will not be forced to choose sides. And while there are still those who may attempt it, he will never have to accept another person telling him who he is. My hope for him is more than an advertising campaign, just as he is more than an enormously untapped audience or some new demographic. No laws, no societal or familial expectations, no stagnant community mores nor trends of popular inertia will keep him from living where he wants, learning what he wants, or loving whom he wants. We will look back at disputes over the environment, gay marriage debates, the treatment of farm animals, and passionate anti-science sentiments with embarrassment. My Celtic, red-haired wife will not have to put up with questions about him being adopted from China, and I don't have to give him a Chinese name to prove his link to that part of his ancestry. He lives in a world of problems but also of promise. Where a warming planet is causing glacial changes but where societal changes—once also glacial—now move with ever-increasing speed. He is born into a generation of awareness and responsibility, already past due and with a full schedule ahead, led by a president of character, with millions of young adults embracing idealism and service.

Jack is beautiful. And the kids in this book are beautiful. But I didn't set out to make a book about beautiful ethnically mixed kids. All too often, mixed-race people are already perceived as beautiful-because-exotic. All too often, multiracial kids are fawned over by well-meaning strangers for that special something—the texture of their hair, their skin tone, the shape of their eyes, that slight touch of *flava*. And we must be conscious of oversimplification. We must be mindful that moving forward means not returning to making snap judgments about people based on factors that are only skin-deep. We must recognize that "exotic" can be a euphemism for "different." As an artist, I wanted to capture the beauty of these children beyond their physical attributes. I wanted to shoot their enthusiasms, their playfulness, their messiness, their crankiness, their imagination, and their hope. And most importantly, I wanted to photograph them *as them*, not as them getting photographed.

Racial mixing and being multiracial alone will not solve our society's problems. The fact that these kids are mixed is not what will make them our ambassadors for a better world. What will do that is the fact that they represent what we all are—unique, questioning, afraid, hopeful, angry, joyous . . . But more than this, these children, like all children, are honest and fearless in bringing themselves to the table, honest in showing without prejudice what many of us as adults choose to hide, or have forgotten how to show. What I learned from making these photographs, and from the birth of my son, is the importance of maintaining this clarity. Because doing this project, I got checked. I got reminded on a daily basis how much I've forgotten the basics. These kids don't just think pollution is wrong. They *know* pollution is wrong. And if you ask them about war, smoking, animals, money, recycling, or helping others in need, what they know becomes pretty obvious to you as well.

To be honest, when I started this book, I wasn't sure why I was doing it. I just knew I wanted to. I've been working with kids for twenty years now, driving down every summer to Solana Beach, where I sleep on a friend's extra bed, get up at 6:00 a.m. each day, and teach 25 ten-year-old Junior Lifeguards about lifesaving, surfing, oceanography, and teamwork. It's the college summer job I never really quit, the lifestyle I could never quite shed. And thinking about it now, I guess I began this project for the same reason. Each summer, on that first day with the kids, I'm reminded how exciting life is, how much discovery we have

before us, and how much how we treat each other really matters. The kids speak without filtering, laugh unselfconsciously, and value every minute of play they get. And they listen, with results showing the next day ("We went to the store, and I told them we didn't need a bag because they just go in a landfill!"). For a teacher, that's something special. It's nice to see proof education works sometimes.

Photographing each individual kid for this book was like that first summer day, over and over. Once we got past their holiday photo poses, past the strained smiles and attention-getting expressions, my job was essentially the same. Create a relationship between us without adult expectations and without adult barriers. Let them tell me who they are and show me who they are on their terms. And give them the opportunity to define themselves. Give them the opportunity I didn't have as a child, and an opportunity I want my son to always have.

Before this project, before writing this essay, really, I'd never put together the fact that I started working with kids at the same time I started making art, that both endeavors have continually intertwined, fed, and complemented each other, and that both have fueled me in ways I cannot repay. I'd never put together the fact that these careers—being an artist and being a teacher—aren't separate. They're just what I do. Whether you call that a career or profession, a lifestyle or calling, they can't be split any more than both my heritages can be separated within me; that fellow lifeguard questions of "Wait a minute—you're a professor?" and fellow faculty comments about "that *Baywatch* thing you do in the summer" only prove we might also need to check more than one box when asked *so-what-do-you-do?*

And when Jack is old enough to read this, I hope he'll feel I did the best job I could, that it was an effort made in sincerity, and perhaps even made out of love for him (though I didn't know him yet when I was doing it). Art doesn't often change the world. But this art, and this teaching and learning, has changed mine. For twenty years, I've made work woven around my own experiences growing up mixed, exploring the philosophical flexings of my own identity, and challenging others to do the same in telling their stories. As a child, I never knew other kids went through the same dilemmas I did. And as an adult, I'm learning other adults struggle as much as I do, and sometimes still feel as much like a kid as I do, whether we show it outwardly or not (I think we just hide it better). But in this amazing time we're living in, kids are getting better and better at checking us, at resetting the bar, at making us again realize the importance of the basics. And that's a good thing.

My mother was a white American and my father was a brown Indonesian.

When I was a preteen living in Jakarta, our mother transformed one corner

of one room in our house into a place of protection, filled with guardian

spirits. There she put objects and images that were intended to keep me

safe and to remind me of the spirits' continuing attentions.

There was a painted wooden totem from British Columbia; a banner of the Chinese Vaishravana, the Guardian King of the North; a bronze Mesopotamian bull; a feng shui mirror from Hong Kong; a Maori *hei-tiki*; a brightly painted Mexican cross; a jade necklace of an Olmec head; a Javanese Garuda; and a carving of Lakshmi, the Hindu goddess of fortune, harvest, and fertility. My mother, whom I always called "Mama Annie"—and who is also our President Obama's mama—wanted me to believe that these images, spirits, and deities would take care of me because I had been given a gift of belonging to more than one world, that I had a flexibility that she never had, an ability to shape-shift and move through doors or fences that for her were obstructions. Later, she took a picture of me with henna-streaked hair in a *shalwar kameez*, straddling the Karakoram border between China and Pakistan. This was the start of a collection of more than a dozen border pictures taken in

Europe, mainland South and Southeast Asia, North and Central America—collected the way another might collect pictures of themselves at mountain summits.

There are advantages and disadvantages to being mixed. Our world can be flexible, interesting, mobile, and unique. One can travel within one's own identity and be a sojourner without an airplane ticket. Or we can feel too different, untethered, and lonely. One of the major developmental tasks of childhood is to successfully learn the basic cultural rules of society, to internalize those principles and practices and use them. It feels important that we learn our cultures in order to know who we are, but what if we are of two different cultures and what if they clash or compete in some respects? On the one hand, mixed kids have an expanded worldview; on the other hand, they may feel torn by divided loyalties. Mixed kids may be more confident in social situations because of their internal flexibility; on the other hand, they may be fearful of making cultural mistakes.

I confess I've had my own issues. In Indonesia and the United States in my youth, I did feel as though I had to make a choice between my worlds. While I felt special when talking to village kids about faraway lands, I also had Indonesian family members who criticized my mother for raising me to be too irreverently American; in speaking Indonesian or preserving the rich cultural heritage of my family, I felt myself to be hopelessly inadequate. I was always missing the worlds I had left behind. I felt convinced that my dearest friends were incapable of understanding me because they seemed so firmly grounded in one place. Although as an adult I have seldom felt myself to be "less than" and have usually felt myself to be "more than" as a result of my mixed cultural inheritance, for many others the struggle to peacefully balance competing cultures continues well into adulthood.

Of course, Indonesia, Hawaii, and New York are all multicultural places with long histories of racial mixing without the largely negative attitudes toward mixed race evidenced elsewhere.

But I envied those around me who had a clear community. As many teenagers do, I worked to try on new identities, blending into surroundings with a desire to belong and be claimed. On the one hand, mixed kids are invisible or possess chameleon properties; on the other hand, they are visibly different. In Indonesia, people identified me as American. In the United States, people identified me as Indonesian. I began to define myself by my difference and expressed scorn towards (while desperately wishing for) a club or set or posse. I tried to talk to my mother about these confusing feelings, yet her response was always that I was special and beautiful specifically because I was multiracial.

Many things have changed since I was a child, and many things have stayed the same. Today, multiracial people can take pride in the symbol and visage of my brother, our president. Here is a man who, it has often been noted, feels very comfortable in his own skin. He is easygoing with everyone. He has developed an effective voice for helping people realize their common ground as well as a platform that was built between two shores and is more inclusive than most. He has developed a vision that includes all people in binding obligation to one another. I believe that he is aided in these efforts by the fact that he has such a wide range of cultural experiences and perspectives from which to draw. While he hasn't struggled or thrashed about in naming himself (he considers himself to be a black man), neither has he denied any part of his self. He has worked to know and honor all sides of his family. I believe that we can learn much from his example.

My own attitudes toward my multiracial heritage started to change when traveling with my maternal grandparents at the age of twenty. Everyone seemed to claim me as one of their own. In London, I was assumed to be Pakistani or Indian. In Turkey, I was Turkish. In Italy, I was Italian. In Egypt, I was Egyptian. Being told that I looked like I belonged everywhere and to everyone helped me feel my fledgling pride in my own multiracialism. I felt a little more interesting and worldly.

Although the way we look is indeed a superficial matter, the way that we feel about the way we look and the way that we are treated because of the way we look matters a great deal. There is great value in seeing ourselves reflected in others and knowing that there is some shared experience between us and others "out there." That is why Kip Fulbeck is important and why *Mixed* is a book that matters. It is important that we be given an opportunity to name ourselves. *Mixed* is a book I wish I'd had. It wasn't until my late twenties, after my mother had died of cancer, that I recalled and started to truly believe in the merit of Mom's advice that I more fully exploit (in the best sense of the word) my internal diversity—my biculturalism and my multilingualism and my well-traveled heels and my knowing how to plant rice as well as navigate the New York City subway system, rather than self-indulgently dwelling on the discomfort of my homelessness.

There are clear signs that fundamental things are in fact changing, not just in terms of our president and not just in the big cities and not just in the United States. Neighborhoods grow increasingly mixed. New immigrants occupy spaces near old immigrants. Tourism and high levels of mobility have led to an overall increase of cosmopolitanism. The number of interracial marriages has skyrocketed. Mixed-race children now number in the millions. And yet in the schools, their confusion often approximates my own from two decades ago. The newly visible and active presence of mixed-race youth offers interesting opportunities for discussions about identity. In addition to empowering youth of mixed heritage by giving them images with which to identify, books like *Mixed* can help society as a whole to explore and understand the increasingly common mixed-heritage experience. By promoting both reflection and discussion, *Mixed* can more broadly encourage appreciation for complex identities and thereby usher in a more truly inclusive understanding of "diversity."

Some of our kids will take pride in inheriting a long line of mixed-race ancestry, and others will prefer to claim traditional racial categories. Others still will spurn all labels. Clearly, mixed-heritage people vary widely in the way they choose to identify and interact with their background cultures, and they should have freedom in choosing. As a group, the mixed-heritage population is too diverse to be discussed in monolithic terms. New media, books, magazines, and schools have important roles to play in helping young people articulate their identities in new ways. Of course, while we can encourage a broadening of perspectives on race and ethnicity, people will need reliable communities, both tangible and intellectual, with which to identify. But, as young people explore and name their identities, the teacher in me begins to see the great need and potential for curriculum that deliberately grapples with more complex constructions of identity.

Ideally, young people should feel good about all parts of their heritage. Healthy multiracial identity requires that while we may never fully appreciate, love, and claim every part of our identities, at the very least we should not feel compelled to apologize for any of it. Adolescence is a crucial time to try on different identities. Shifting back and forth between ethnic groups is a natural part of trying to figure out where you fit, who you are, and what works. Trying on different styles and images is something that all children do, not only racially or ethnically mixed kids. We can use such narratives to change the way teachers talk about diversity and identity. We can work with teachers to discover how to better help their students grow more intellectually subtle, more tolerant of ambiguity, more adept at finding out who they are and can be, and better equipped to build bridges later in life.

While we must be wary of biracial and bicultural people being exoticized or being portrayed as the answer to racism and other troubling issues, books like *Mixed* allow more kids to recognize the abundant presence of other people who might be grappling with the same issues they grapple with. I hope that for our children, the pain of not belonging is lessened and the individual is given additional options beyond the either/or.

Not long ago, I had to get fingerprinted for a new job at a private school and I was told, when filling out the requisite forms, that I had neither the right to choose more than one racial category nor the right to abstain from designating my race. Being compelled to make such a choice in 2006 seemed to me an absurdity. I have a new optimism for my daughter, who will surely know that diversity, whether internal or external, is no danger to well-being. I feel great curiosity about the ways she will choose to identify herself. I wonder whether she will want to declare herself free from the racial categories that have affected previous generations. And if she does want to acknowledge the complexity of her parentage, will she live in a world that permits her to do so? I hope and trust that she will.

AUSTIN

African American
Mexican
Norwegian
German
Native American

FROM MOM

I think it's a tremendously exciting time. I'm biracial (black/white) and spent so many years answering the question "What are you?" and feeling the need to explain myself. It was thrilling for me when the term "multiracial" began to appear on forms—finally, no need to check "other" or just to "pick one." How could I do that when I truly felt that I was somehow different from either of my parents' identities? I feel lucky to be part of a group of people that is taking pride in self-definition. What does it mean for my boy? My hope for him is that this means that he will be free to choose for himself how he wants to identify, free of the insecurities of others. I believe that the reason that I was always asked "What are you?" is because my indefinability somehow made others feel uncomfortable. I was fine—felt myself to be the norm, in fact, until other people came along! I hope that Khaled will truly know that feeling: to be the "norm" with the freedom to explore his own racial, ethnic, and religious identity at the pace and in the ways that he, not society, chooses.

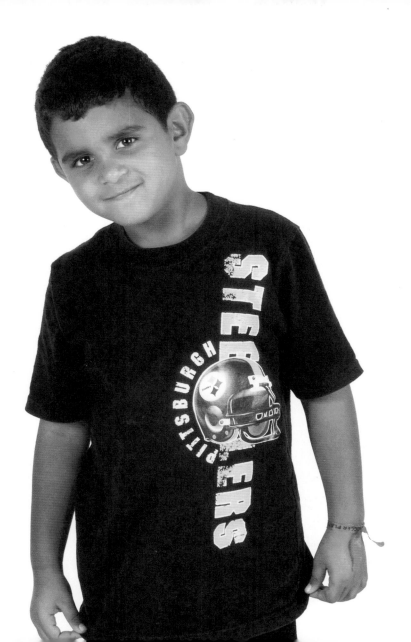

me and
my sister
Dylan.
camryn.

My sister is 3.
I am six
we love
each other.

CAMRYN & DYLAN
Hawaiian
Chinese
Swedish
English
Irish
Scottish
French
Native American

DANIEL
Filipino
Chinese
Italian
English
Portuguese

FROM MOM

It is so much fun teaching Daniel about his various ethnicities. Everywhere we go, people ask me what he is ethnically. We love sharing our cultures and our mixtures. Having two mixed parents is very special.

JACK

African American
Japanese
Scottish
Native American

FROM DAD

As a black man, you get used to being identified as the bad guy. I'm used to that. But what rubs me the wrong way is that I am dumb no matter how much education I've received. So having someone like President Barack Obama means my sons have no choice but to excel, because in some ways it's expected now for people mixed with black to win. Thanks, Mr. President.

Strangers say, "Aw cute. What are they?" In the black community, it's cool . . . just one look and move on. In the Asian community, it's walk a few steps . . . look . . . walk a few steps . . . look . . . walk a few steps . . . look. It's like my family has messed up the world. The first time my wife took my oldest son (who was at the time four months old) to her mom's house, her mother made her park halfway down the street like we had an alien in the car or something . . . something I will never forget. It's funny today, but then it was very painful nonsense.

OWEN
Vietnamese
Scottish
Mexican
Peruvian
Swiss

FROM DAD

Everyone asks about Owen, "Where does the red hair come from?" Sometimes my wife will be asked this question with a whisper on the side as if I'm not the father!

BROOKE

African American
Portuguese

JAKE & MILO
Spanish
Chinese
Malay
Irish
English

I am Ninjajake 👁

I AM ZOMBIE MI 👁

We are brothers

We battle Monsters of all kinds

KYLE

Japanese
Filipino
Spanish
Mexican
Native American
Greek
Armenian

SAMARA
Haitian
Russian
Polish

FROM MOM

Our four-year-old daughter has labeled her skin "cinnamon" and so we sing Neil Young's "Cinnamon Girl" to her.

I love christmas and paint balling, and i like to build things like a gocart. I also play as a quarter back in football.

FROM MOM

For me it is especially poignant for our family to participate in this project in this epic year with a "mixed kid" president! *Finally* a president that represents me (I'm also a mixed kid) and my family, a group of people that seemed not to exist in the political definition of America. Whenever being "an American" was upheld as a badge of honor the only face represented was a white, homogenous type. It is so wonderful to see that "mixed kids" is in actuality a huge group in the United States of America and we are finally being seen. Since I grew up all over the world (America, Iran, the Netherlands, Canada, the Netherlands again, and back to the States) I have never fully felt a citizen of one country or felt the need to pledge allegiance to only one. I consider myself and my family world citizens and think the world would be a better place if the Pledge of Allegiance was to one world. Borders only serve to divide and we see all the good that has done thus far.

SARAH
Caucasian
Chinese

CHLOE
African American
Caucasian
Creole

GABRIELA

Filipina
Dutch
Indonesian
Irish
Italian

FROM MOM

I love her Rasta-mullet hairstyle. Curly in the front, dread in the back. People can never quite figure out her ethnicity—which is just how I like it.

MILENA
Armenian
African American
Russian
Jewish
Scottish
English

DANIEL

Japanese
Swedish
Italian
Austrian
Slovakian

My name is Micah I like to go to my frens haos My friends is eli. I slep at my Name friends house a lot, and some times we roll down the stairs. for fun.

GRACE

Filipina
Scottish
Japanese
Chinese

MADISON

Japanese
French
Irish
English
Hungarian

FROM MOM

When my daughter was in second grade, her class did a geography activity
that involved listing and locating the countries where your family is from.
Madison marked Ireland, France, England, Hungary, and Japan. When it
was her turn to share, she stated that her grandmother was from Japan.
Her teacher, whom I'm friends with, looked at her and said, "I don't think so,
Madison. Are you sure?" Madison said "Yes, my mommy's mother is from
Japan." Her classmates acted surprised by this statement and many didn't
believe her. Her teacher looked at her in disbelief, but didn't argue because
my daughter is an excellent student, and she didn't want to contradict her
without knowing. Later that day, when I came to volunteer, her teacher told
me about the assignment and what had happened. I said, "Yes, she's right."
She said, "I'm glad I didn't contradict her. I had no idea. I never really thought
about it, but I would have guessed you were Italian." I found this amusing
because during my childhood being "different" and Asian was a source of
daily comment, yet now things had progressed to the point that most
people seemed unable to differentiate one's heritage when one is mixed.

NEVAEH

Filipina
Italian
African American
Native American
Spanish
Chinese

MAYA & SOLVEJ
Swedish
Korean
Chinese
Slovenian
Hungarian
Polish

I have many traditions in my blood.

MAYA

SOLVE

BEN
Japanese
Caucasian

FROM MOM

I grew up as the only hapa kid in an all white town and got picked on a lot. When I was pregnant, I worried so much about stupid things like what she would look like, whether she'd look "too Korean" or "too Jewish." I now realize she's just perfect!

TÉA & ZOE
Filipina
Spanish
Chinese
Korean
Syrian
Turkish

I am me.
I am a animal lover.
I am also a dream
but I am real,
I love New York, It
is a big plases.
I want to go to
China one day it
is a nice culture
I am me!
I am eight yea
old.

Jada

TRON

Japanese
Hawaiian
Italian
Greek
English
German

ALISON
Japanese
African American
Irish
French Canadian
English

FROM DAD

I grew up in a world that was not ready to understand my biracial background. People were confused that the color of my skin did not match that of my parents, and I endured questions and assumptions about my ethnicity throughout my childhood. Worse than that, I can only remember one peer who was biracial, and we were friends for only a few years. My children, however, are growing up in a different world, and I could not be more grateful. They are not novelties, they are merely a part of the fabric that makes up their community, as several of their friends are also biracial. Our children's multiracial background is viewed with interest instead of curiosity, and people seem to see similarities between them and their parents rather than differences. In fact, I cannot count the number of times that strangers have stopped us in public and told us how beautiful our family is. I struggled for years to come to terms with my racial identity, but I don't believe that my children will have that problem.

RYLAND
Korean
Slovakian
Ukrainian
Polish
Russian
Greek
Irish
Italian
German
Scottish
English

I'm 12.
Guitar and video games.
Period.

FROM DAD

Isabelle Oojin is such a *yentita*. She takes her *Shabbat* very seriously. She is also a little actress. She was in a school play on Purim. While every other girl wanted to be Esther, Isabelle volunteered to be Vashti, the queen who wasn't afraid to say "no" to the king when he demanded she do something she didn't want to do. That's Isabelle.

KAI & DAYLEN

Laotian
Cambodian
Chinese
Danish
French

ZADIE
Grenadian
Czech
Austrian
Hungarian
German

FROM MOM

Diego has days when he wants to be hugged
and called "Gunkers," although "KooKoo" is
his regular nickname. He is scared of cater-
pillars, just like his daddy. He loves reading
and math. When he grows up, he wants to
be a canoe pusher, astronaut, inventor, pilot,
policeman, and now a *teppanyaki* chef.

DIEGO
Scottish
Irish
Danish
Seminole
Cheyenne
Filipino

I am 50, 50. My hobby is soccer.
My dream is to enter the
olympics.
My mom saids it's always good to
dream. So I do.
God Bless

Trinity

MAXWELL
Japanese
French
Irish
English
Hungarian

FROM MOM

My children are often viewed as being "white." However, other Asians often recognize their ethnicity and "claim" them. I remember a particular incident of this when my son, Max, was about eighteen months old. He had blond, curly hair then, and was very fair, a true towhead. We were at a Japanese festival, and a kind, elderly Japanese woman approached him, playfully interacting. She looked up at me and said, "He's Japanese," nodding her head up and down. She smiled at me and her face was positively beaming. There was total acceptance. It felt like an embrace.

OLIVER

Indian
Korean
Scottish
Irish
Dutch
Portuguese

DERRICK

African American
Mexican
Irish

I am Dante, Jewpanese, and Jewish, Buddhist. I am always annoyed by my sister who calls me a fat nerd. I Play piano and violin, and am an A student. I have 3 dogs, and hate P.E. I'm 100% Dante.

Taja, thats me. I am the same ethnicities as my Brother, Jewish Japenese. My Favorite thing in the world is swimming witch I do every summer. I spend 24 hours with my nerdy brother, but I am an A student and good at what I do so my life i's very great. MY family and dogs help me through life and I would not trade my Family or life for any thing.

Me:

Taja, by Dante

Duh?

stains

Dante by Taja

FROM MOM

Kaliyah is Italian and black and because of her appearance some people will automatically assume that she is Spanish and will come up to us speaking Spanish. They mistake Kaliyah for any other race but what she really is.

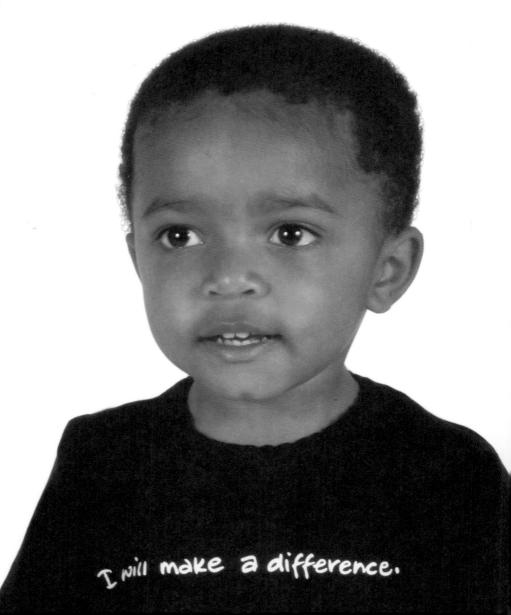

CHAYA

African American
Scottish
Irish
Portuguese
German
English
Japanese

FROM MOM

I constantly remind Emilio that he is a beautiful, bright, and talented boy. I was so happy when Emilio decided to grow out his hair and embrace it because for a long time he wanted it to be "yellow" and "straight." Letting his hair grow out affirms to the world that he is Blaxican and proud! I tell Emilio that he is Blaxican and comes from a beautiful heritage of oppressed people who have struggled in the United States, and for that he should be proud and find the strength that is within him.

DIEGO
Mexican
Spanish
African American
Native American
Caucasian

FIORABELLA
Filipina
Puerto Rican
Korean
Hawaiian
Irish
Italian

My name is Fiorabella. I am nine years old. I like drawing, painting, reading and writing. I am confident, powerful and strong. I am a person who expresses myself in many ways. Some ways I do that is to show facial expressions or to draw pictures. I like being a kid because you have a bigger mind to be different things. I dont want to be anyone else but me.

ANJU

Japanese
Hawaiian
Italian
Greek
English
German

FROM DAD

Since Asher's still a baby, we don't have talks about race or racial identity. We just do our best to expose him to all facets of his cultural heritage and make him feel loved from all directions. His maternal grandparents speak to him in Mandarin, his aunt speaks to him in Japanese, etc. He meets friends and family of all different races with one common trait to their faces: they are smiling for him.

I LOVE ♡
PAPL ANAMLS
MINERALS AND
PLANTS

O → ⚭ → 🐰 → 🐰 → 🧅 → 🧅 → JULIA

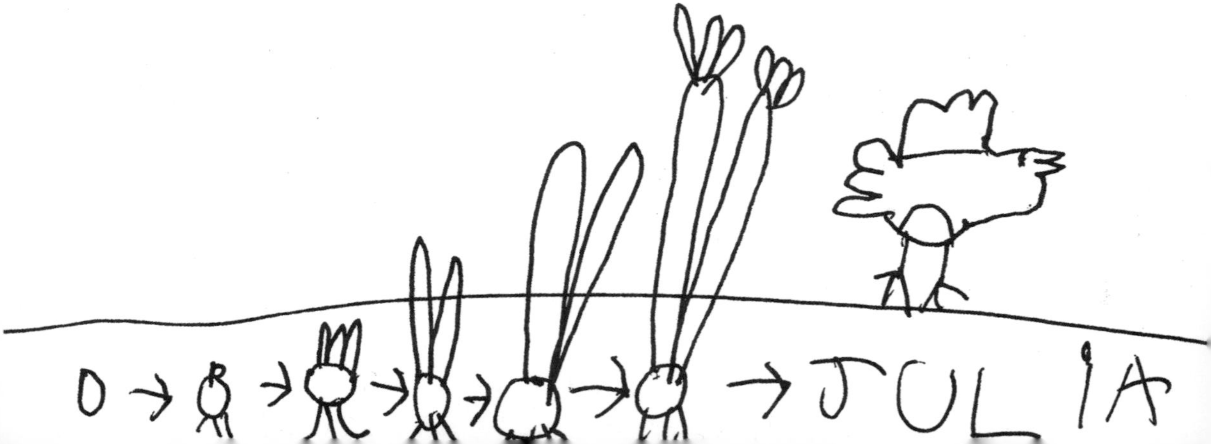

ZOË
Colombian
Portuguese
Irish
Italian
German

FROM MOM

One day when Kailani and daddy were together and he told someone in the elevator that she was "half Japanese." She said, "Daddy, I'm lots of Japanese!" Kailani may have an easier time accepting differences because she's exposed to so many cultures in New York. It was so different from how I was raised in Japan where there was only one race and ethnicity. I think she sees her friends as individuals rather than by their ethnicity. I've never been told by strangers that she's a mixed kid when I'm with her alone. But when I visited Japan with her, several people recognized her as "half" and complimented me. My husband has some different experiences. When Kailani was a baby, he was with her at the NYU bookstore. One lady asked him if he adopted her from China. To me, being a parent of a mixed kid is definitely easier in the U.S.

BEN
Filipino
German
Irish
English
Native American

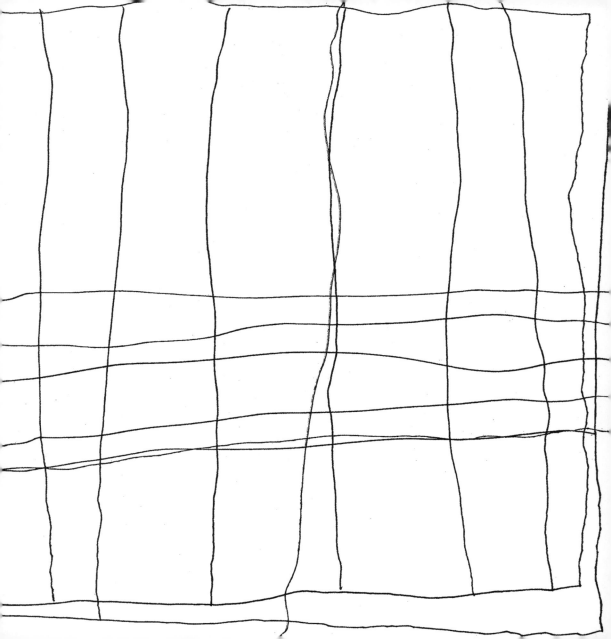

FROM MOM

We plan on telling Olivier that identifying with one race would be impossible. We hope that he embraces Bollywood, dessert wine, bagpipes and kilts, kimchi, four-leaf clovers, and wooden shoes.

FROM MOM

Our child already asked us a few times, "Mommy, Daddy, am I
Japanese, Filipino, or American?" Racial identity can sometimes be
confusing for a seven-year-old kid. So what did we tell him? We said,
"You will always be half-Japanese and half-Filipino because Daddy
is Japanese and Mommy is Filipino and you were born in America."
Then he said, "So am I more Japanese or more Filipino?" We know
the question will go on and on. So we told him, "All you have to know
is you are a hapa, a wonderful mixture of half-Japanese and half-
Filipino blood." He said, "Okay!" I guess he's got it clear now!

AVERI
Japanese
Irish
Jewish
English
Native American
Black Dutch

a girl who likes the beach

ELLIS
Filipina
Chinese
Spanish
Irish
Dutch
German
French

KASDEN
Chinese
African American
Native American

FROM MOM

Whenever someone asks, "What are they?" about my kids, I always reply, "The United Nations." My little Mexi-Peruvi-Scot-Swiss-Vietnamese kids attract a lot of attention wherever we go. I don't know if it's the red hair of my son or that my daughter looks Asian but has blue eyes. I love watching people trying to figure out our family dynamics, especially when we are eating *pho* at a Vietnamese restaurant and my son yells out, "*Noi!*" (grandma on the father's side, in Vietnamese). Or the expression on people's faces when they hear my daughter call my mom "*Gorda*" (her childhood nickname, "*Abuela*," sounded too old). At our kids' parties, people are munching on egg rolls and *nuc mam* alongside enchiladas, rice, and beans. My kids know both the joy of busting open a piñata at birthdays as well as opening a red envelope on Tet.

MORGAN
Vietnamese
Scottish
Mexican
Peruvian
Swiss

FROM MOM

Twins. Hope is the "older, more mature" sister.

HOPE & KAI
Hawaiian
Filipina/Filipino
English
German
French
Swedish

LULU

Filipina
German
Irish
English
Native American

KYLE
Japanese
Irish

FROM MOM

Kyle recently turned three. Whenever we say something about race, he says, "Ready . . . set . . . go"—and starts running!

My name is Maeve.
My mom is black, and my dad is
white. I like art and building
things. My dad is from Irelands
and my mom is from America.
When I grow up I want to
be an engineer. I enjoy drawing

SHAUN

Scottish
Irish
English
German
Cherokee
Seminole
Okinawan

BELLA
African American
Filipina

FROM MOM

I think we are going in a positive direction. My daughter is so happy and proud that she points out that our president and his family (mainly the daughters) are just like her. It's amazing to hear that from a five-year-old and how she related to them. Even at a young age, her multiracial heritage has become a part of her life without her knowing it. She was in total shock when we were in the Philippines at the hotel pool and all the kids were saying *kuya*—which means brother. I think it was a shock for her because she thought of it as her special word for her brother.

DAVIS

Chinese
Mexican
Danish

I play Soccer. I am amazing.
People Say you aren't asian.
Then I say I
not believe me. am. People still do

LUCAS
Japanese
German
Scottish
Irish
Russian

MIYA
Japanese
Irish
Italian
French

McGUIRE

Filipino
Japanese
Okinawan

HEATHER
Japanese
Russian Jew

FROM MOM

Heather is hapa not only in her ethnicity, but in everything she is. She has a wonderful mix of personal traits and of likes and dislikes. She is loving and sweet, but is not lacking in attitude. She loves dolls and dressing up, but also loves *Star Wars* and *Bakugan*. She loves chocolate ice cream, but not chocolate syrup. We love our little hapa girl!

NINA

Chinese
German
Spanish

I am Keyan. I am Brown Like Barack Obama. one Day I will Be a Pro foot Ball Player and the President.

MAILE
Scottish
Irish
Danish
Seminole
Cheyenne
Filipina

I like to swim
I like to eat

김윤재

I like to
fly.

piano
is fun

GRANT

Filipino
Scottish
Japanese
Chinese

FROM MOM

Suhaila is a storyteller. She narrates her day
with forceful imagination. She loves the moon
and she sees dragons and lions in the clouds.
She just started studying insects, but has been
a dinosaur lover since she was two. Now four,
she tells me she wants to be a paleontologist.
She also assures me that she will be my snuggle
bunny forever. I'm thinking I should make her
sign a contract. She is our love.

SUHAILA
Malay
Indonesian
Scottish
Irish
Hakka
Cantonese

KAMAKA

Hawaiian
Filipino
Portuguese
Spanish
Irish
German
Native American

A 9 year old girl. I am half Japanese, three fourths Mexican, and one fourth Philipino. In sports do basketball, softball, and karate.

NYLA
Japanese
Russian Jew

FROM MOM

Nyla is feisty (like her mom) and gentle and laid-back (like her dad). She is a mixture of us, yet her own individual self.

TAYLOR

African American
Native American
Haitian
Scottish

I LOVE
Family

FROM MOM

I think issues that pertain to race have come a long way historically. There is greater intermingling of races, to the point where what defines a person isn't their race; it's the culture that they choose to self-identify with. Being of multiethnic background teaches you to value diversity, because you are a living, breathing form of what diversity represents. There has been a clear shift towards the increased visibility of multiethnic children. Interracial relationships are definitely more accepted, and as a result more and more multiracial children are being born. This is great in terms of having a child see someone else that looks like them, and feel accepted, but what is interesting is also the increased idealism society has placed on looking "exotic." As for my child, I think that our society's evolution will only bring her greater opportunity. She is one of a kind. Unique.

ROSIE
Chinese
Mexican
Danish

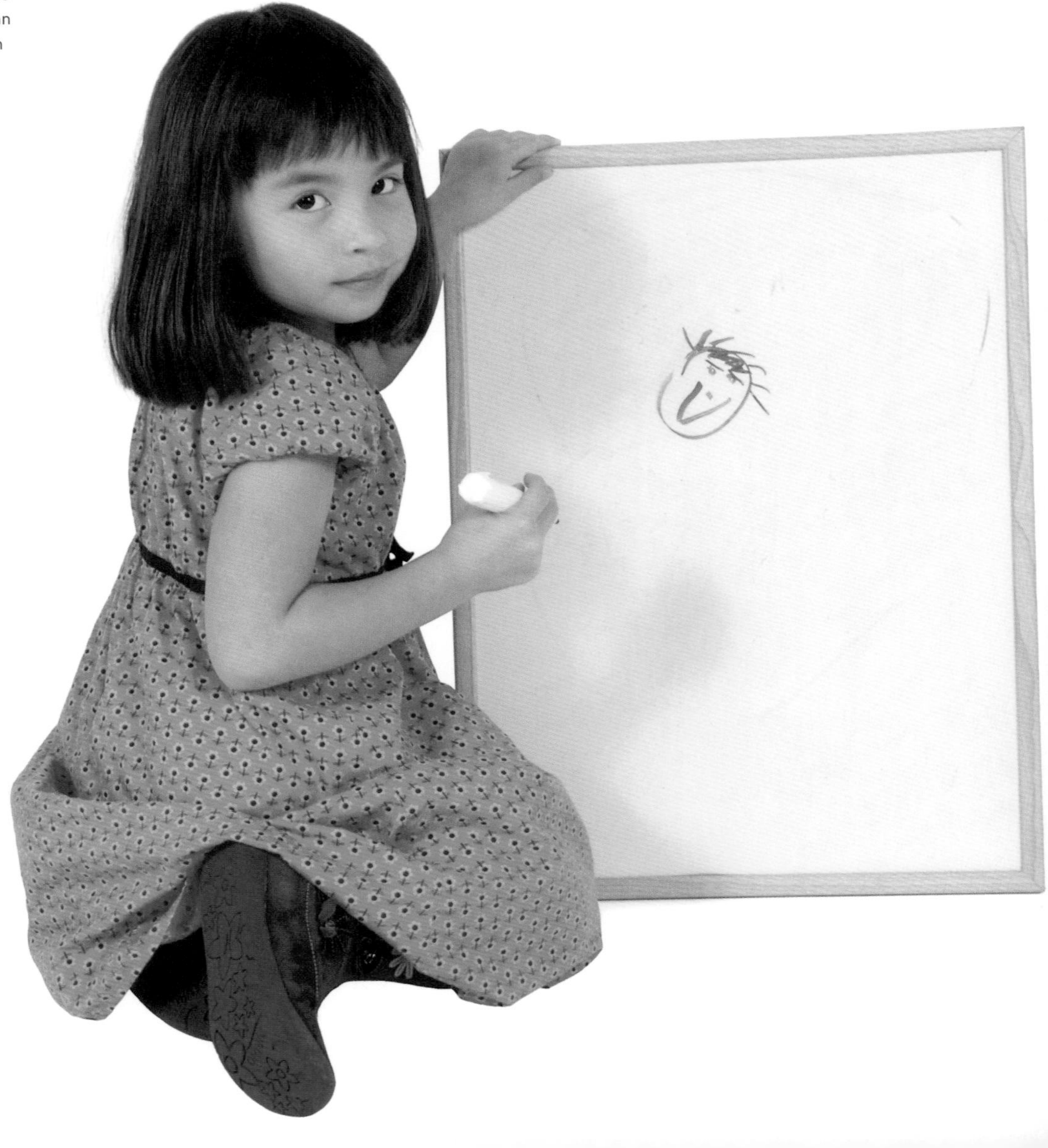

Chinese, Mexican, Danish

6 YEARS OLD

FROM MOM

Kaya is a very sweet girl who has empathy for all things. She loves all animals and wants to be a veterinarian when she grows up. She refuses to wear pink and likes to think of herself as a tomboy.

KAYA
Chinese
Spanish
English
Irish
Hawaiian

SETH
Laotian
Cambodian
Chinese
Danish
French

Getting my braces off was incredible, but now I have a retainer. It's a watern (I don't know how to spell it))

It's not as bad as braces, but when lose it I'm in al of trouble

COURTNEY
Japanese
Finnish
English
Irish
German

MEMPHIS LOU

Indian
Irish
African American

NOA
Hawaiian
Chinese
French
Austrian
Filipino
Spanish

FROM MOM

I tell my children that race is made-up, a term constructed by the government to categorize ethnicities in boxes that make it easier for them to think about ethnic differences. I tell my children to embrace the richness of their multiethnic and multicultural heritage. Historically, thinking about race as a means for categorizing difference (not to mention allocating government funds) has been submerged in negativity and discrimination. At this moment in history, multiracial issues are socio-politically thriving, but U.S. society still seems to misunderstand multiethnicity, seeking to reduce it to one race. Multiracials must continue to organize, create art, write books, and reach out in grassroots ways to ensure that the integrity of a multiracial identity isn't hampered by hypodescent/blood quantum methodologies. These are reductionist approaches meant to abbreviate identity for the convenience of government or the security of perceived monoraces who fear that their communities that they think of as monoracial will be fragmented by multirace. Still, my children do live in a time when they don't have to explain their identity constantly; they are freer to live it in all its beautiful complexities. DNA testing also allows us to learn even more about our cultural ties. That is exciting. Strangers think my children are Polynesian-European mixtures, thinking I'm the South Pacific woman who mated with European blood. But my children are chameleons even more so than I. They are assumed to be Hawaiian in Hawaii or on the West Coast. They are Latino to Latinos, Greeks to Greeks, South Americans to South Americans. It's splendid.

LEILANI
Japanese
English
Irish
Native American
African American

JULIA
Thai
French
Pakistani
German
Scottish
Irish
Czech

JADE

Hawaiian
Puerto Rican
Chinese
Italian
Scottish
Irish

am Ari. I am almost 13 years old & I
a boy. I am both Muslim & Jewish. I am a light
ownish color. My mom is brown & from Sri Lanka & my
d is white & from New York. I have travelled the
rld from Egypt to Sri Lanka, from rich to poor, from
mall to large. I know how to play 3 instruments:
he Middle Eastern drum, the Middle Eastern flute, &
he American violin.

My father is the head of the Middle Eastern
Ensemble at UCSB and I am in it. It is quite
un & I suggest that you watch its concerts.
am unusually tall for my age which I am
roud of. most kids think I am Indian.

ANNA
Filipina
German
Irish
English
Native American

I am Anna.
I have brown I don't like homewrok
eyes.

I have brownish skin.
I have brown hair.
I like to play gymnastix.
I am seven years old.

It's a crown
not a pope.

ANNIKA

Swedish
Peruvian
German
Polish
French Canadian

AFTERWORD

There is something fantastic that happens when people who come from different backgrounds meet and fall in love. The children who come from these unions are not mere mixtures; they are "magic potions"! When I look at them, I see exotic spices, fragrant herbs, lovely flowers, and colors that can overwhelm the senses. I see a vision of the future.

AMERICAN
GOVERNMENT

AMERICAN GOVERNMENT
Readings and Cases

FIFTH EDITION

PETER WOLL
Brandeis University

Little, Brown and Company
BOSTON · TORONTO

THIRD PRINTING

Published simultaneously in Canada
by Little, Brown & Company (Canada) Limited

PRINTED IN THE UNITED STATES OF AMERICA

This book is dedicated to
JOHN W. WOLL and
RUTH C. WOLL

Preface

This book is designed to provide students with key readings and cases that are central to an understanding of the governmental process. This edition contains up-to-date and relevant material designed to stimulate interest and discussion, and at the same time to show how our system functions. Basic material in this, as in the earlier editions, includes: theories on the political process; the nature and origins of constitutional theory and practice; the relationship between the national government, the states, and local communities; problems arising in connection with civil liberties and civil rights; the organization and functions of political parties, the role of elections, and electoral behavior; interest groups; the responsibilities, powers, and limitations of the President; the structure and functions of Congress and the environment of congressional decision making; the judicial process; and the structure, functions, and role of the bureaucracy.

Extraordinary political events have occurred in recent years. The resignation of President Richard M. Nixon on August 9, 1974 was without precedent in our history. Gerald Ford, appointed to the Vice Presidency by President Nixon and confirmed by Congress under the terms of the Twenty-fifth amendment, became the first president to occupy the White House who had not been elected by the people. In fourteen years the country had seen four presidents and a vacancy in the Vice Presidency three times. This turnover in leadership during such a short time span was unprecedented, as were the presidential nominations of two Vice Presidents, Nelson Rockefeller becoming the second when he was nominated to the Vice Presidency by President Ford on August 20, 1974.

This edition, with many new selections, will help students understand and analyze the causes and significance of the important political events of the 1970's. The important decision of the Supreme Court in *United States* v. *Richard M. Nixon* on the question of executive privilege is included in the section on separation of powers and checks and balances. A section on the role of impeachment in the constitutional system of checks and balances has been added to the discussion of constitutional government. The debate that took place between President Nixon's attorneys on the one hand, and the House

Judiciary Committee on the other, over what constitutes grounds for impeachment and conviction is included, along with the articles of impeachment passed by the Committee.

Selections dealing with the significance of Watergate are to be found throughout the book, with a special section dealing with Watergate and the Presidency, including relevant parts of the Nixon transcripts that were released in 1974, and which contain a verbatim account (with certain deletions made by the President and his staff) of Oval Office discussions of the Watergate break-in and cover-up. Relevant differences between the Nixon transcripts and the House Judiciary Committee's version of the same taped conversations are noted. These transcripts are used particularly to reveal the relationship between the President and his staff, as well as the way in which presidential character affects decision making in the White House.

In the field of civil liberties and civil rights the new edition contains additional and provocative materials on the busing issue including the 1974 Supreme Court decision in the Detroit case, as well as key cases dealing with the emerging doctrine of equal protection of the laws in relation to the delivery of public services. New selections in the area of political parties deal with the disintegration of parties in the 1970's, as well as with the issue of public financing of election campaigns. Other discussions of contemporary issues in the new edition include: congressional reform; the decline of the Senate "establishment"; judicial activism versus judicial self-restraint in relation to the Warren and Burger courts; the use of plea bargaining by federal prosecutors; the role of the bureaucracy as a check upon presidential power; and the dilemma of government officials who want to "get out and speak out" on public policy issues which they feel have been improperly handled by the President and other high level officials.

Numerous individuals have helped the author in the presentation of this and previous editions. I would particularly like to thank Henry J. Abraham, Charles O. Jones, and Everett C. Ladd for their excellent suggestions on this new edition.

Michèle Borgers gave me encouragement throughout the preparation of the book. Neil Sullivan made many valuable suggestions and tracked down the new selections. Trudi Rogers happily and efficiently did the necessary typing of the manuscript.

Contents

EQUAL PROTECTION OF THE LAWS: SCHOOL DESEGREGATION

EQUAL PROTECTION OF THE LAWS: PUBLIC SERVICES

ELECTORAL REAPPORTIONMENT

CONGRESS AND THE COMMITTEE SYSTEM

THE SENATE: FOLKWAYS AND FOLK WISDOM

CONSTITUTIONAL BACKGROUND: JUDICIAL INDEPENDENCE AND JUDICIAL REVIEW

AMERICAN GOVERNMENT

The Setting of the American System

CHAPTER 1

Theories on the Nature of the Political Process

The political process involves the nature, distribution, uses, and implications of political power. As one political scientist, Harold Lasswell, has stated, politics determines who gets what, when, and how. What is the character of the political process?

Elite Theory

Several theories attempt to explain the political process. These deal with how power is distributed and employed. A central premise of much democratic theory is that governmental decision making is based on the will of the people expressed through intermediaries, such as representatives in the legislature, and the leaders of political parties and interest groups. Belief in government of the people, by the people, and for the people is a key component in the folklore of American democracy. But how does our democratic system actually function? C. Wright Mills suggests that our political process and our society in general, far from being based upon the people's will, is ruled by an elite. Mills is a most important elite theorist, and his selection is representative of a broad school of thought.

1

C. Wright Mills

THE STRUCTURE OF POWER IN AMERICAN SOCIETY

I

Power has to do with whatever decisions men make about the arrangements under which they live, and about the events which make up the history of their times. Events that are beyond human decision do happen; social arrangements do change without benefit of explicit decision. But insofar as such decisions are made, the problem of who is involved in making them is the basic problem of power. Insofar as they could be made but are not, the problem becomes who fails to make them?

We cannot today merely assume that in the last resort men must always be governed by their own consent. For among the means of power which now prevail is the power to manage and to manipulate the consent of men. That we do not know the limits of such power, and that we hope it does have limits, does not remove the fact that much power today is successfully employed without the sanction of the reason or the conscience of the obedient.

Surely nowadays we need not argue that, in the last resort, coercion is the "final" form of power. But then, we are by no means constantly at the last resort. Authority (power that is justified by the beliefs of the voluntarily obedient) and manipulation (power that is wielded unbeknown to the powerless)—must also be considered, along with coercion. In fact, the three types must be sorted out whenever we think about power.

In the modern world, we must bear in mind, power is often not so authoritative as it seemed to be in the medieval epoch: ideas which justify rules no longer seem so necessary to their exercise of power. At least for many of the great decisions of our time—especially those of an international sort—mass "persuasion" has not been "necessary;" the fact is simply accomplished. Furthermore, such ideas as are available to the powerful are often neither taken up nor used by them. Such ideologies usually arise as a response to an effective debunking of power; in the United States such opposition has not been effective enough recently to create the felt need for new ideologies of rule.

There has, in fact, come about a situation in which many who have lost faith in prevailing loyalties have not acquired new ones, and so pay no attention to politics of any kind. They are not radical, not liberal, not conservative,

From *Power, Politics and People: The Collected Essays of C. Wright Mills*, edited by Irving Louis Horowitz. Reprinted by permission of Oxford University Press, Inc.

not reactionary. They are inactionary. They are out of it. If we accept the Greeks' definition of the idiot as an altogether private man, then we must conclude that many American citizens are now idiots. And I should not be surprised, although I do not know, if there were not some such idiots even in Germany. This—and I use the word with care—this spiritual condition seems to me the key to many modern troubles of political intellectuals, as well as the key to much political bewilderment in modern society. Intellectual "conviction" and moral "belief" are not necessary, in either the rulers or the ruled, for a ruling power to persist and even to flourish. So far as the role of ideologies is concerned, their frequent absences and the prevalence of mass indifference are surely two of the major political facts about the Western societies today.

How large a role any explicit decisions do play in the making of history is itself an historical problem. For how large that role may be depends very much upon the means of power that are available at any given time in any given society. In some societies, the innumerable actions of innumerable men modify their milieux, and so gradually modify the structure itself. These modifications —the course of history—go on behind the backs of men. History is drift, although in total "men make it." Thus, innumerable entrepreneurs and innumerable consumers by ten thousand decisions per minute may shape and reshape the free-market economy. Perhaps this was the chief kind of limitation Marx had in mind when he wrote, in *The 18th Brumaire:* that "Men make their own history, but they do not make it just as they please; they do not make it under circumstances chosen by themselves. . . ."

But in other societies—certainly in the United States and in the Soviet Union today—a few men may be so placed within the structure that by their decisions they modify the milieux of many other men, and in fact nowadays the structural conditions under which most men live. Such elites of power also make history under circumstances not chosen altogether by themselves, yet compared with other men, and compared with other periods of world history, these circumstances do indeed seem less limiting.

I should contend that "men are free to make history," but that some men are indeed much freer than others. For such freedom requires access to the means of decision and of power by which history can now be made. It has not always been so made; but in the later phases of the modern epoch it is. It is with reference to this epoch that I am contending that if men do not make history, they tend increasingly to become the utensils of history-makers as well as the mere objects of history.

The history of modern society may readily be understood as the story of the enlargement and the centralization of the means of power—in economic, in political, and in military institutions. The rise of industrial society has involved these developments in the means of economic production. The rise of the nation-state has involved similar developments in the means of violence and in those of political administration.

In the Western societies, such transformations have generally occurred gradually, and many cultural traditions have restrained and shaped them. In most of the Soviet societies, they are happening very rapidly indeed and without the great discourse of Western civilization, without the Renaissance and without the Reformation, which so greatly strengthened and gave political focus to the idea of freedom. In those societies, the enlargement and the coordination of all the means of power has occurred more brutally, and from the beginning under tightly centralized authority. But in both types, the means of power have now become international in scope and similar in form. To be sure, each of them has its own ups and downs; neither is as yet absolute; how they are run differs quite sharply.

Yet so great is the reach of the means of violence, and so great the economy required to produce and support them, that we have in the immediate past witnessed the consolidation of these two world centers, either of which dwarfs the power of Ancient Rome. As we pay attention to the awesome means of power now available to quite small groups of men we come to realize that Ceasar could do less with Rome than Napoleon with France; Napoleon less with France than Lenin with Russia. But what was Caesar's power at its height compared with the power of the changing inner circles of Soviet Russia and the temporary adminstrations of the United States? We come to realize—indeed they continually remind us—how a few men have access to the means by which in a few days continents can be turned into thermonuclear wastelands. That the facilities of power are so enormously enlarged and so decisively centralized surely means that the powers of quite small groups of men, which we may call elites, are now of literally inhuman consequence.

My concern here is not with the international scene but with the United States in the middle of the twentieth century. I must emphasize "in the middle of the twentieth century" because in our attempt to understand any society we come upon images which have been drawn from its past and which often confuse our attempt to confront its present reality. That is one minor reason why history is the shank of any social science: we must study it if only to rid ourselves of it. In the United States, there are indeed many such images and usually they have to do with the first half of the nineteenth century. At that time the economic facilities of the United States were very widely dispersed and subject to little or to no central authority.

The state watched in the night but was without decisive voice in the day.

One man meant one rifle and the militia were without centralized orders.

Any American, as old-fashioned as I, can only agree with R. H. Tawney that "whatever the future may contain, the past has shown no more excellent social order than that in which the mass of the people were the masters of the holdings which they ploughed and the tools with which they worked, and could boast . . . 'It is a quietness to a man's mind to live upon his own and to know his heir certain.' "

But then we must immediately add: all that is of the past and of little relevance to our understanding of the United States today. Within this society three broad levels of power may now be distinguished. I shall begin at the top and move downward.

II

The power to make decisions of national and international consequence is now so clearly seated in political, military, and economic institutions that other areas of society seem off to the side and, on occasion, readily subordinated to these. The scattered institutions of religion, education and family are increasingly shaped by the big three, in which history-making decisions now regularly occur. Behind this fact there is all the push and drive of a fabulous technology; for these three institutional orders have incorporated this technology and now guide it, even as it shapes and paces their development.

As each has assumed its modern shape, its effects upon the other two have become greater, and the traffic between the three has increased. There is no longer, on the one hand, an economy, and, on the other, a political order, containing a military establishment unimportant to politics and to money-making. There is a political economy numerously linked with military order and decision. This triangle of power is now a structural fact, and it is the key to any understanding of the higher circles in America today. For as each of these domains has coincided with the others, as decisions in each have become broader, the leading men of each—the high military, the corporation executives, the political directorate—have tended to come together to form the power elite of America.

The political order, once composed of several dozen states with a weak federal-center, has become an executive apparatus which has taken up into itself many powers previously scattered, legislative as well as administrative, and which now reaches into all parts of the social structure. The long-time tendency of business and government to become more closely connected has since World War II reached a new point of explicitness. Neither can now be seen clearly as a distinct world. The growth of executive government does not mean merely the "enlargement of government" as some kind of autonomous bureaucracy: under American conditions, it has meant the ascendency of the corporation man into political eminence. Already during the New Deal, such men had joined the political directorate; as of World War II they came to dominate it. Long involved with government, now they have moved into quite full direction of the economy of the war effort and of the post-war era.

The economy, once a great scatter of small productive units in somewhat automatic balance, has become internally dominated by a few hundred corporations, administratively and politically interrelated, which together hold the keys to economic decision. This economy is at once a permanent-war economy and a private-corporation economy. The most important relations of the corporation to the state now rest on the coincidence between military and corporate interests, as defined by the military and the corporate rich, and accepted by politicians and public. Within the elite as a whole, this coincidence of military domain and corporate realm strengthens both of them and further subordinates the merely political man. Not the party politician, but the corporation executive, is now more likely to sit with the military to answer the question: what is to be done?

The military order, once a slim establishment in a context of civilian distrust, has become the largest and most expensive feature of government; behind smiling public relations, it has all the grim and clumsy efficiency of a great and sprawling bureaucracy. The high military have gained decisive political and economic relevance. The seemingly permanent military threat places a premium upon them and virtually all political and economic actions are now judged in terms of military definitions of reality: the higher military have ascended to a firm position within the power elite of our time.

In part at least this is a result of an historical fact, pivotal for the years since 1939: the attention of the elite has shifted from domestic problems—centered in the thirties around slump—to international problems—centered in the forties and fifties around war. By long historical usage, the government of the United States has been shaped by domestic clash and balance; it does not have suitable agencies and traditions for the democratic handling of international affairs. In considerable part, it is in this vacuum that the power elite has grown.

(i) To understand the unity of this power elite, we must pay attention to the psychology of its several members in their respective milieux. Insofar as the power elite is composed of men of similar origin and education, of similar career and style of life, their unity may be said to rest upon the fact that they are of similar social type, and to lead to the fact of their easy intermingling. This kind of unity reaches its frothier apex in the sharing of that prestige which is to be had in the world of the celebrity. It achieves a more solid culmination in the fact of the interchangeability of positions between the three dominant institutional orders. It is revealed by considerable traffic of personnel within and between these three, as well as by the rise of specialized go-betweens as in the new style high-level lobbying.

(ii) Behind such psychological and social unity are the structure and the mechanics of those institutional hierarchies over which the political directorate, the corporate rich, and the high military now preside. How much of these hierarchies is shaped and what relations it has with the others determine in large part the relations of their rulers. Were these hierarchies scattered and disjointed, then their respective elites might tend to be scattered and disjointed; but if they have many interconnections and points of coinciding interests, then their elites tend to form a coherent kind of grouping. The unity of the elite is not a simple reflection of the unity of institutions, but men and institutions are always related; that is why we must understand the elite today in connection with such institutional trends as the development of a permanent-war establishment, alongside a privately incorporated economy, inside a virtual political vacuum. For the men at the top have been selected and formed by such institutional trends.

(iii) Their unity, however, does not rest solely upon psychological similarity and social intermingling, nor entirely upon the structural blending of commanding positions and common interests. At times it is the unity of a more explicit coordination.

To say that these higher circles are increasingly coordinated, that this is *one* basis of their unity, and that at times—as during open war—such coordination is quite wilful, is not to say that the coordination is total or continuous, or even that it is very surefooted. Much less is it to say that the power elite has emerged as the realization of a plot. Its rise cannot be adequately explained in any psychological terms.

Yet we must remember that institutional trends may be defined as opportunities by those who occupy the command posts. Once such opportunities are recognized, men may avail themselves of them. Certain types of men from each of these three areas, more farsighted than others, have actively promoted the liaison even before it took its truly modern shape. Now more have come to see that their several interests can more easily be realized if they work together, in informal as well as in formal ways, and accordingly they have done so.

The idea of the power elite is of course an interpretation. It rests upon and it enables us to make sense of major institutional trends, the social similarities and psychological affinities of the men at the top. But the idea is also based upon what has been happening on the middle and lower levels of power, to which I now turn.

III

There are of course other interpretations of the American system of power. The most usual is that it is a moving balance of many competing interests. The image of balance, at least in America, is derived from the idea of the economic market: in the nineteenth century, the balance was thought to occur between a great scatter of individuals and enterprises; in the twentieth century, it is thought to occur between great interest blocs. In both views, the politician is the key man of power because he is the broker of many conflicting powers.

I believe that the balance and the compromise in American society—the "countervailing powers" and the "veto groups," of parties and associations, of strata and unions—must now be seen as having mainly to do with the middle levels of power. It is these middle levels that the political journalist and the scholar of politics are most likely to understand and to write about—if only because, being mainly middle class themselves, they are closer to them. Moreover these levels provide the noisy content of most "political" news and gossip; the images of these levels are more or less in accord with the folklore of how democracy works; and, if the master-image of balance is accepted, many intellectuals, especially in their current patrioteering, are readily able to satisfy

such political optimism as they wish to feel. Accordingly, liberal interpretations of what is happening in the United States are now virtually the only
interpretations that are widely distributed.

But to believe that the power system reflects a balancing society is, I think,
to confuse the present era with earlier times, and to confuse its top and bottom
with its middle levels.

By the top levels, as distinguished from the middle, I intend to refer, first
of all, to the scope of the decisions that are made. At the top today, these
decisions have to do with all the issues of war and peace. They have also to
do with slump and poverty which are now so very much problems of international scope. I intend also to refer to whether or not the groups that struggle
politically have a chance to gain the positions from which such top decisions
are made, and indeed whether their members do usually hope for such top
national command. Most of the competing interests which make up the clang
and clash of American politics are strictly concerned with their slice of the
existing pie. Labor unions, for example, certainly have no policies of an international sort other than those which given unions adopt for the strict economic
protection of their members. Neither do farm organizations. The actions of
such middle-level powers may indeed have consequence for top-level policy;
certainly at times they hamper these policies. But they are not truly concerned
with them, which means of course that their influence tends to be quite
irresponsible.

The facts of the middle levels may in part be understood in terms of the
rise of the power elite. The expanded and centralized and interlocked hierarchies over which the power elite preside have encroached upon the old balance
and relegated it to the middle level. But there are also independent developments of the middle levels. These, it seems to me, are better understood as an
affair of entrenched and provincial demands than as a center of national
decision. As such, the middle level often seems much more of a stalemate than
a moving balance.

(i) The middle level of politics is not a forum in which there are debated
the big decisions of national and international life. Such debate is not carried
on by nationally responsible parties representing and clarifying alternative
policies. There are no such parties in the United States. More and more,
fundamental issues never come to any point or decision before the Congress,
much less before the electorate in party campaigns. In the case of Formosa,
in the spring of 1955 the Congress abdicated all debate concerning events and
decisions which surely bordered on war. The same is largely true of the 1957
crisis in the Middle East. Such decisions now regularly bypass the Congress,
and are never clearly focused issues for public decision.

The American political campaign distracts attention from national and
international issues, but that is not to say that there are no issues in these
campaigns. In each district and state, issues are set up and watched by organized interests of sovereign local importance. The professional politician is of
course a party politician, and the two parties are semifeudal organizations:

they trade patronage and other favors for votes and for protection. The differences between them, so far as national issues are concerned, are very narrow and very mixed up. Often each seems to be fifty parties, one to each state; and accordingly, the politician as campaigner and as Congressman is not concerned with national party lines, if any are discernible. Often he is not subject to any effective national party discipline. He speaks for the interests of his own constituency, and he is concerned with national issues only insofar as they affect the interests effectively organized there, and hence his chances of reelection. That is why, when he does speak of national matters, the result is so often such an empty rhetoric. Seated in his sovereign locality, the politician is not at the national summit. He is on and of the middle levels of power.

(ii) Politics is not an arena in which free and independent organizations truly connect the lower and middle levels of society with the top levels of decision. Such organizations are not an effective and major part of American life today. As more people are drawn into the political arena, their associations become mass in scale, and the power of the individual becomes dependent upon them; to the extent that they are effective, they have become larger, and to that extent they have become less accessible to the influence of the individual. This is a central fact about associations in any mass society: it is of the most consequence for political parties and for trade unions.

In the thirties, it often seemed that labor would become an insurgent power independent of corporation and state. Organized labor was then emerging for the first time on an American scale, and the only political sense of direction it needed was the slogan, "organize the unorganized." Now without the mandate of the slump, labor remains without political direction. Instead of economic and political struggles it has become deeply entangled in administrative routines with both corporation and state. One of its major functions, as a vested interest of the new society, is the regulation of such irregular tendencies as may occur among the rank and file.

There is nothing, it seems to me, in the make-up of the current labor leadership to allow us to expect that it can or that it will lead, rather than merely react. Insofar as it fights at all it fights over a share of the goods of a single way of life and not over that way of life itself. The typical labor leader in the United States of America today is better understood as an adaptive creature of the main business drift than as an independent actor in a truly national context.

(iii) The idea that this society is a balance of powers requires us to assume that the units in balance are of more or less equal power and that they are truly independent of one another. These assumptions have rested, it seems clear, upon the historical importance of a large and independent middle class. In the latter nineteenth century and during the Progressive Era, such a class of farmers and small businessmen fought politically—and lost—their last struggle for a paramount role in national decision. Even then, their aspirations seemed bound to their own imagined past.

This old, independent middle class has of course declined. On the most generous count, it is now 40 percent of the total middle class (at most 20 percent of the total labor force). Moreover, it has become politically as well as economically dependent upon the state, most notably in the case of the subsidized farmer.

The *new* middle class of white-collar employees is certainly not the political pivot of any balancing society. It is in no way politically unified. Its unions, such as they are, often serve merely to incorporate it as hanger-on of the labor interest. For a considerably period, the middle class *was* an independent base of power; the new middle class cannot be. Political freedom and economic security *were* anchored in small and independent properties; they are not anchored in the world of the white-collar job. Scattered property holders were economically united by more or less free markets; the jobs of the new middle class are integrated by corporate authority. Economically, the white-collar classes are in the same condition as wage workers; politically, they are in a worse condition, for they are not organized. They are no vanguard of historic change; they are at best a rear guard of the welfare state.

The agrarian revolt of the nineties, the small-business revolt that has been more or less continuous since the eighties, the labor revolt of the thirties—each of these has failed as an independent movement which could countervail against the powers that be; they have failed as politically autonomous third parties. But they have succeeded, in varying degree, as interests vested in the expanded corporation and state; they have succeeded as parochial interests seated in particular districts, in local divisions of the two parties, and in the Congress. What they would become, in short, are well-established features of the *middle* levels of balancing power, on which we may now observe all those strata and interests which in the course of American history have been defeated in their bids for top power or which have never made such bids.

Fifty years ago many observers thought of the American state as a mask behind which an invisible government operated. But nowadays, much of what was called the old lobby, visible or invisible, is part of the quite visible government. The "governmentalization of the lobby" has proceeded in both the legislative and the executive domain, as well as between them. The executive bureaucracy becomes not only the center of decision but also the arena within which major conflicts of power are resolved or denied resolution. "Administration" replaces electoral politics; the maneuvering of cliques (which include leading Senators as well as civil servants) replaces the open clash of parties.

The shift of corporation men into the political directorate has accelerated the decline of the politicians in the Congress to the middle levels of power; the formation of the power elite rests in part upon this relegation. It rests also upon the semiorganized stalemate of the interests of sovereign localities, into which the legislative function has so largely fallen; upon the virtually complete absence of a civil service that is a politically neutral but politically relevant, depository of brain-power and executive skill; and it rests upon the increased official secrecy behind which great decisions are made without benefit of public or even of Congressional debate.

IV

There is one last belief upon which liberal observers everywhere base their interpretations and rest their hopes. That is the idea of the public and the associated idea of public opinion. Conservative thinkers, since the French Revolution, have of course Viewed With Alarm the rise of the public, which they have usually called the masses, or something to that effect. "The populace is sovereign," wrote Gustave LeBon, "and the tide of barbarism mounts." But surely those who have supposed the masses to be well on their way to triumph are mistaken. In our time, the influence of publics or of masses within political life is in fact decreasing, and such influence as on occasion they do have tends, to an unknown but increasing degree, to be guided by the means of mass communication.

In a society of publics, discussion is the ascendant means of communication, and the mass media, if they exist, simply enlarge and animate this discussion, linking one face-to-face public with the discussions of another. In a mass society, the dominant type of communication is the formal media, and publics become mere markets for these media: the "public" of a radio program consists of all those exposed to it. When we try to look upon the United States today as a society of publics, we realize that it has moved a considerable distance along the road to the mass society.

In official circles, the very term, "the public," has come to have a phantom meaning, which dramatically reveals its eclipse. The deciding elite can identify some of those who clamor publicly as "Labor," others as "Business," still others as "Farmer." But these are not the public. "The public" consists of the unidentified and the nonpartisan in a world of defined and partisan interests. In this faint echo of the classic notion, the public is composed of these remnants of the old and new middle classes whose interests are not explicitly defined, organized, or clamorous. In a curious adaptation, "the public" often becomes, in administrative fact, "the disengaged expert," who, although never so well informed, has never taken a clear-cut and public stand on controversial issues. He is the "public" member of the board, the commission, the committee. What "the public" stands for, accordingly, is often a vagueness of policy (called "open-mindedness"), a lack of involvement in public affairs (known as "reasonableness"), and a professional disinterest (known as "tolerance").

All this is indeed far removed from the eighteenth-century idea of the public of public opinion. The idea parallels the economic idea of the magical market. Here is the market composed for freely competing entrepreneurs; there is the public composed of circles of people in discussion. As price is the result of anonymous, equally weighted, bargaining individuals, so public opinion is the result of each man's having thought things out for himself and then contributing his voice to the great chorus. To be sure, some may have more influence on the state of opinion than others, but no one group monopolizes the discussion, or by itself determines the opinions that prevail.

In this classic image, the people are presented with problems. They discuss them. They formulate viewpoints. These viewpoints are organized, and they compete. One viewpoint "wins out." Then the people act on this view, or their representatives are instructed to act it out, and this they promptly do.

Such are the images of democracy which are still used as working justifications of power in America. We must now recognize this description as more a fairy tale than a useful approximation. The issues that now shape man's fate are neither raised nor decided by any public at large. The idea of a society that is at bottom composed of publics is not a matter of fact; it is the proclamation of an idea, and as well the assertion of a legitimation masquerading as fact.

I cannot here describe the several great forces within American society as well as elsewhere which have been at work in the debilitation of the public. I want only to remind you that publics, like free associations, can be deliberately and suddenly smashed, or they can more slowly wither away. But whether smashed in a week or withered in a generation, the demise of the public must be seen in connection with the rise of centralized organizations, with all their new means of power, including those of the mass media of distraction. These, we now know, often seem to expropriate the rationality and the will of the terrorized or—as the case may be—the voluntarily indifferent society of masses. In the more democratic process of indifference the remnants of such publics as remain may only occasionally be intimidated by fanatics in search of "disloyalty." But regardless of that, they lose their will for decision because they do not possess the instruments for decision; they lose their sense of political belonging because they do not belong; they lose their political will because they see no way to realize it.

The political structure of a modern democratic state requires that such a public as is projected by democratic theorists not only exist but that it be the very forum within which a politics of real issues is enacted.

It requires a civil service that is firmly linked with the world of knowledge and sensibility, and which is composed of skilled men who, in their careers and in their aspirations, are truly independent of any private, which is to say, corporation, interests.

It requires nationally responsible parties which debate openly and clearly the issues which the nation, and indeed the world, now so rigidly confronts.

It requires an intelligentsia, inside as well as outside the universities, who carry on the big discourse of the Western world, and whose work is relevant to and influential among parties and movements and publics.

And it certainly requires, as a fact of power, that there be free associations standing between families and smaller communities and publics, on the one hand, and the state, the military, the corporation, on the other. For unless these do exist, there are no vehicles for reasoned opinion, no instruments for the rational exertion of public will.

Such democratic formations are not now ascendant in the power structure of the United States, and accordingly the men of decision are not men selected and formed by careers within such associations and by their performance before such publics. The top of modern American society is increasingly unified, and often seems wilfully coordinated: at the top there has emerged an elite whose power probably exceeds that of any small group of men in world history. The middle levels are often a drifting set of stalemated forces: the middle does not link the bottom with the top. The bottom of this society is politically fragmented, and even as a passive fact, increasingly powerless: at the bottom there is emerging a mass society.

These developments, I believe, can be correctly understood neither in terms of the liberal nor the Marxian interpretation of politics and history. Both these ways of thought arose as guidelines to reflection about a type of society which does not now exist in the United States. We confront there a new kind of social structure, which embodies elements and tendencies of all modern society, but in which they have assumed a more naked and flamboyant prominence.

That does not mean that we must give up the ideals of these classic political expectations. I believe that both have been concerned with the problem of rationality and of freedom: liberalism, with freedom and rationality as supreme facts about the individual; Marxism, as supreme facts about man's role in the political making of history. What I have said here, I suppose, may be taken as an attempt to make evident why the ideas of freedom and of rationality now so often seem so ambiguous in the new society of the United States of American.

The previous selection by C. Wright Mills clearly spells out the anti-democratic implications of elite theory. There is no doubt in Mills's mind that elite power is the antithesis of democracy. Classical democratic theory is predicated upon a belief in the ability and desire of people to govern themselves. Elite theory suggests that neither the ability nor desire for popular self-government exists. The democratic process, of necessity, must be limited to those actively interested in wielding political power either directly by controlling political offices or indirectly through active participation in electoral and pressure group politics. Many elite theorists have attempted to reconcile what they consider to be the inevitability of elite power with the classical theory of democracy. They have done this by proclaiming that elite control is not anti-democratic per se, but can fit into the classical theory of democracy and even make it more meaningful. If broad popular participation in politics is impossible, as elite theorists suggest, then democracy can be made meaningful only through "democratic elites." Such elites act in the interests of the people, and are kept responsive through competition from competing elites. The adherence of elites to democratic values and the circulation of elites provides effective and accountable democratic leadership. This theory of democracy is critically analyzed in the following selection.

2
Jack L. Walker

A CRITIQUE OF THE ELITIST
THEORY OF DEMOCRACY

During the last thirty years, there have been numerous attempts to revise or reconstitute the "classical" theory of democracy: the familiar doctrine of popular rule, patterned after the New England town meeting, which asserts that public policy should result from extensive, informed discussion and debate. By extending general participation in decision-making the classical theorists hoped to increase the citizen's awareness of his moral and social responsibilities, reduce the danger of tyranny, and improve the quality of government. Public officials, acting as agents of the public at large, would then carry out the broad policies decided upon by majority vote in popular assemblies.

Although it is seldom made clear just which of the classical democratic theorists is being referred to, contemporary criticism has focused primarily on the descriptive elements of the theory, on its basic conceptions of citizenship, representation, and decision-making. The concept of an active, informed, democratic citizenry, the most distinctive feature of the traditional theory, is the principal object of attack. On empirical grounds it is argued that very few such people can be found in Western societies. Public policy is not the expression of the common good as conceived of by the citizenry after widespread discussion and compromise. This description of policy making is held to be dangerously naive because it overlooks the role of demagogic leadership, mass psychology, group coercion, and the influence of those who control concentrated economic power. In short, classical democratic theory is held to be unrealistic; first because it employs conceptions of the nature of man and the operation of society which are utopian, and second because it does not provide adequate, operational definitions of its key concepts.

Since contemporary scholars have found the classical theory of democracy inadequate, a "revisionist" movement has developed, much as it has among contemporary Marxists, seeking to reconstitute the theory and bring it into closer correspondence with the latest findings of empirical reserach. One major restatement, called the "elitist theory of democracy" by Seymour Mar-

From Jack L. Walker, "A Critique of the Elitist Theory of Democracy," *American Political Science Review* 60, pp. 285–295. Footnotes omitted. Reprinted by permission.

tin Lipset, is now employed in many contemporary books and articles on American politics and political behavior and is fast becoming part of the conventional wisdom of political science.

The adequacy of the elitist theory of democracy, both as a set of political norms and as a guide to empirical research, is open to serious question. It has two major shortcomings: first, in their quest for realism, the revisionists have fundamentally changed the normative significance of democracy, rendering it a more conservative doctrine in the process; second, the general acceptance of the elitist theory by contemporary political scientists has led them to neglect almost completely some profoundly important developments in American society.

NORMATIVE IMPLICATIONS OF THE ELITIST THEORY

At the heart of the elitist theory is a clear presumption of the average citizen's inadequacies. As a consequence, democratic systems must rely on the wisdom, loyalty, and skill of their political leaders, not on the population at large. The political system is divided into two groups: the *elite,* or the "political entrepreneurs," who possess ideological commitments and manipulative skills; and the *citizens at large,* the masses or the "apolitical clay" of the system, a much larger class of passive, inert followers who have little knowledge of public affairs and even less interest. The factor that distinguished democratic and authoritarian systems, according to this view, is the provision for limited, peaceful competition among members of the elite for the formal positions of leadership within the system. As Joseph Schumpeter summarized the theory: "the democratic method is that institutional arrangement for arriving at political decisions in which individuals acquire the power to decide by means of a competitive struggle for the people's vote."

Democracy is thus conceived primarily in procedural terms; it is seen as a method of making decisions which insures efficiency in administration and policy making and yet requires some measure of responsiveness to popular opinion on the part of the ruling elites. The average citizen still has some measure of effective political power under this system, even though he does not initiate policy, because of his right to vote (if he chooses) in regularly scheduled elections. The political leaders, in an effort to gain support at the polls, will shape public policy to fit the citizens' desires. By anticipating public reaction the elite grants the citizenry a form of indirect access to public policy making, without the creation of any kind of formal institution and even in the absence of any direct communication. "A few citizens who are non-voters, and who for some reason have no influential contact with voters, have no indirect influence. Most citizens, however, possess a moderate degree of indirect influence, for elected officials keep the real or imagined preferences of constituents constantly in mind in deciding what policies to adopt or reject." An ambiguity is created here because obviously leaders sometimes create opinions as well as respond to them, but since the leaders are constantly being challenged by rivals seeking to gain the allegiance of the masses it is assumed that the individual citizen will receive information from several conflicting sources, making it extremely difficult for any one group to "engineer consent" by manipulating public opinion. As Lipset puts it: "Representation is neither simply a means of political adjustment to social pressures nor an instrument of manipulation. It involves both functions, since the purpose of representation is to locate the combinations of relationships between parties and social bases which make possible the operation of efficient government."

There has been extensive research and speculation about the prerequisites for a democratic system of this kind. There is general agreement that a well-developed social pluralism and an extensive system of voluntary groups or associations are needed along with a prevailing sense of psychological security, widespread education, and limited disparities of wealth. There must be no arbitrary barriers to political participation, and "enough people must participate in the governmental process so that political leaders compete for the support of a large and more or less representative cross section of the population."

Elitist theory departs markedly from the classical tradition at this point. Traditionally it was assumed that the most important prerequisite for a stable democracy was general agreement among the politically active (those who vote) on certain fundamental policies and basic values, and widespread acceptance of democratic procedures and restraints on political activity. Political leaders would not violate the basic consensus, or "democratic mold," if they wished to be successful in gaining their objectives, because once these fundamental restraints were broken the otherwise passive public would become aroused and would organize against the offending leaders. Elitist theorists argue instead that agreement on democratic values among the "intervening structure of elites," the very elements which had been seen earlier as potential threats to democracy, is the main bulwark against a breakdown in constitutionalism. Writing in 1959 David Truman discards his notion of "potential groups," a variation of the traditional doctrine of consensus, and calls instead for a "consensus of elites," a determination on the part of the leaders of political parties, labor unions, trade associations and other voluntary associations to defend the fundamental procedures of democracy in order to protect their own positions and the basic structure of society itself from the threat of an irresponsible demagogue. V. O. Key, in his *Public Opinion and the American Democracy,* concludes that "the critical element for the health of a democratic order consists in the beliefs, standards, and competence of those who constitute the influentials, the opinion-leaders, the political activists in the order." Similarly, Robert Dahl concludes in his study of New Haven that the skillful, active political leaders in the system are the true democratic "legitimists." Since democratic procedures regulate their conflicts and protect their privileged positions in the system the leaders can be counted on to defend the democratic creed even if a majority of the voters might prefer some other set of procedures.

It has also been suggested by several elitist theorists that democracies have good reason to fear increased political participation. They argue that a successful (that is, stable) democratic system depends on widespread apathy and general political incompetence. The ideal of democratic participation is thus transformed into a "noble lie" designed chiefly to insure a sense of responsibility among political leaders. As Lester Milbrath puts it: " . . . it is important to continue moral admonishment for citizens to become active in politics, not because we want or expect great masses of them to become active, but rather because the admonishment helps keep the system open and sustains a belief in the right of all to participate, which is an important norm governing the behavior of political elites." If the uninformed masses participate in large numbers, democratic self-restraint will break down and peaceful competition among the elites, the central element in the elitist theory, will become impossible.

The principal aim of the critics whose views we are examining has been to make the theory of democracy more realistic, to bring it into closer correspondence with empirical reality. They are convinced that the classical theory does not account for "much of the real machinery" by which the system operates, and they have expressed concern about the possible spread among Americans of either unwarranted anxiety or cynical disillusionment over the condition of democracy. But it is difficult to transform a utopian theory into a realistic account of political behavior without changing the theory's normative foundations. By revising the theory to bring it into closer correspondence with reality, the elitist theorists have transformed democracy from a radical into a conservative political doctrine, stripping away its distinctive emphasis on popular political activity so that it no longer serves as a set of ideals toward which society ought to be striving.

The most distinctive feature, and the principal orienting value, of classical democratic theory was its emphasis on individual participation in the development of public policy. By taking part in the affairs of his society the citizen would gain in knowledge and understanding, develop a deeper sense of social responsibility, and broaden his perspective beyond the narrow confines of his private life. Although the classical theorists accepted the basic framework of Lockean democracy, with its emphasis on limited government, they were *not* primarily concerned with the *policies* which might be produced in a democracy; above all else they were concerned with *human development*, the opportunities which existed in political activity to realize the untapped potentials of men and to create the foundations of a genuine human community. In the words of John Stuart Mill: " . . . the most important point of excellence which any form of government can possess is to promote the virtue and intelligence of the people themselves. The first question in respect to any political institutions is how far they tend to foster in the members of the community the various desirable qualities, . . . moral, intellectual, and active."

In the elitist version of the theory, however, emphasis has shifted to the needs and functions of the system as a whole; there is no longer a direct concern with human development. The central question is not how to design a political system which stimulates great individual participation and enhances the moral development of its citizens, but how "to combine a substantial degree of popular participation with a system of power capable of governing *effectively* and *coherently.*"

The elitist theory allows the citizen only a passive role as an object of political activity; he exerts influence on policy making only by rendering judgments after the fact in national elections. The safety of contemporary democracy lies in the high-minded sense of responsibility of its leaders, the only elements of society who are actively striving to discover and implement the common good. The citizens are left to "judge a world they never made, and thus to become a genteel counterpart of the mobs which sporadically unseated aristocratic governments in eighteenth- and nineteenth-century Europe."

The contemporary version of democratic theory has, it seems, lost much of the vital force, the radical thrust of the classical theory. The elitist theorists, in trying to develop a theory which takes account of the way the political system actually operates, have changed the principal orienting values of democracy. The heart of the classical theory was its justification of broad participation in the public affairs of the community; the aim was the production of citizens who were capable enough and responsible enough to play this role. The classical theory was not meant to describe any existing system of government; it was an outline, a set of prescriptions for the ideal polity which men should strive to create. The elitist theorists, in their quest for realism, have changed this distinctive prescriptive element in democratic theory; they have substituted stability and efficiency as the prime goals of democracy. If these revisions are accepted, the danger arises that in striving to develop more reliable explanations of political behavior, political scientists will also become sophisticated apologists for the existing political order. Robert Lane, in concluding his study of the political ideologies of fifteen "common men" in an Eastern city, observes that they lack a utopian vision, a well-defined sense of social justice that would allow them to stand in judgment on their society and its institutions. To some degree, the "men of Eastport" share this disability with much of the American academic elite.

THE ELITIST THEORY AS A GUIDE FOR RESEARCH

The shortcomings of the elitist theory are not confined to its normative implications. Serious questions also arise concerning its descriptive accuracy and its utility as a guide to empirical research. The most unsatisfactory element in the theory is its concept of the passive, apolitical, common man who pays allegiance to his governors and to the sideshow of politics while remaining primarily concerned with his private life, evenings of television with his family, or the demands of his job. Occasionally, when the average citizen finds his primary goals threatened by the actions or inactions of government, he may strive vigorously to influence the course of public policy, but "*homo civicus*" as Dahl calls him, "is not, by nature, a political animal."

It was the acceptance of this concept that led the elitist theorists to reject the traditional notion of consensus. It became implausible to argue that the citizenry is watchful and jealous of the great democratic values while at the same time suggesting that they are uninvolved, uninformed, and apathetic. Widespread apathy also is said to contribute to democratic stability by insuring that the disagreements that arise during campaigns and elections will not involve large numbers of people or plunge the society into violent disorders or civil war.

No one can deny that there is widespread political apathy among many sectors of the American public. But it is important to ask why this is so and not simply to explain how this phenomenon contributes to the smooth functioning of the system. Of course, the citizens' passivity might stem from their satisfaction with the operation of the political system, and thus they would naturally become aroused only if they perceived a threat to the system. Dahl, for one, argues that the political system operates largely through "inertia," tradition, or habitual responses. It remains stable because only a few "key" issues are the objects of controversy at any one time, the rest of public policy having been settled and established in past controversies which are now all but forgotten. Similarly, Nelson Polsby argues that it is fallacious to assume that the quiescent citizens in a community, especially those in the lower income groups, have grievances unless they actually express them. To do so is to arbitrarily assign "upper- and middle-class values to all actors in the community."

But it is hard to believe, in these days of protest demonstrations, of Black Muslims and the Deacons of Defense and Justice, that the mood of cynical apathy toward politics which affects so many American Negroes is an indication of their satisfaction with the political system and with the weak, essentially meaningless alternatives it usually presents to them. To assume that apathy is a sign of satisfaction in this case is to overlook the tragic history of the Negroes in America and the system of violent repression long used to deny them any entrance into the regular channels of democratic decision-making.

Students of race relations have concluded that hostile attitudes toward a racial group do not necessarily lead to hostile actions, and amicable feelings do not ensure amicable actions. Instead, "it is the social demands of the situation, particularly when supported by accepted authority figures, which are the effective determinants of individual action. . . ." This insight might apply to other areas besides race relations. It suggests that society's political culture, the general perceptions about the nature of authority and the prevailing expectations of significant reference groups, might be a major influence on the political behavior of the average citizen regardless of his own feelings of satisfaction or hostility. There have been sizable shifts in rates of political participation throughout American history which suggests that these rates are not rigidly determined. A recent analysis indicates that rates of voter participation are now *lower* than they were in the nineteenth century even though the population is now much better educated and the facilities for communication much better developed. Other studies indicate that there are marked differences in the political milieu of towns and cities which lead citizens of one area to exhibit much more cynicism and distrust of the political system than others. Although the studies showed no corresponding changes in feelings of political competence, cynical attitudes might inhibit many forms of participation and thus induce apathy.

Political apathy obviously has many sources. It may stem from feelings of personal inadequacy, from a fear of endangering important personal relationships, or from a lack of interest in the issues; but it may also have its roots in the society's institutional structure, in the weakness or absence of group stimulation or support, in the positive opposition of elements within the political system to wider participation; in the absence, in other words, of appropriate spurs to action or the presence of tangible deterrents. Before the causes of apathy can be established with confidence much more attention must be directed to the role of the mass media. How are the perceptions of individual citizens affected by the version of reality they receive, either directly or indirectly, from television, the national wire services, and the public schools—and how do these perceptions affect their motivations? Political scientists have also largely neglected to study the use of both legitimate and illegitimate sanctions and private intimidation to gain political ends. How do the activities of the police, social workers, or elements of organized crime affect the desires and the opportunities available for individual political participation?

Certainly the apparent calm of American politics is not matched by our general social life, which is marked by high crime rates, numerous fads and crazes, and much intergroup tension. One recent study showed that during the civil rights protests in Atlanta, Georgia, and Cambridge, Maryland, crime rates in the Negro communities dropped substantially. A finding of this kind suggests that there is some connection between these two realms of social conflict and that both may serve as outlets for individual distress and frustration. High crime (or suicide) rates and low rates of voting may very well be related; the former may represent "leakage" from the political system.

Once we admit that the society is not based on a widespread consensus, we must look at our loosely organized, decentralized political parties in a different light. It may be that the parties have developed in this way precisely because no broad consensus exists. In a fragmented society which contains numerous geographic, religious, and racial conflicts, the successful politician has been the man adept at negotiation and bargaining, the man best able to play these numerous animosities off against each other and thereby build *ad hoc* coalitions of support for specific programs. Success at this delicate business of coalition building depends on achieving some basis for communication among the leaders of otherwise antagonistic groups and finding a formula for compromise. To create these circumstances sharp conflicts must be avoided and highly controversial, potentially explosive issues shunned. Controversy is shifted to other issues or the public authorities simply refuse to deal with the question, claiming that they have no legitimate jurisdiction in the case or burying it quietly in some committee room or bureaucratic pigeonhole.

In other words, one of the chief characteristics of our political system has been its success in suppressing and controlling internal conflict. But the avoidance of conflict, the suppression of strife, is *not* necessarily the creation of satisfaction or consensus. The citizens may remain quiescent, the political system might retain its stability, but significant differences of opinion remain, numerous conflicts are unresolved, and many desires go unfulfilled. The frustrations resulting from such deprivations can create conflict in other, nonpolitical realms. Fads, religious revivals, or wild, anomic riots such as those which occurred in the Negro ghettos of several large American cities during the summers of 1964 and 1965, phenomena not directly related to the achievement of any clearly conceived political goals, may be touched off by unresolved tensions left untended by the society's political leaders.

The American political system is highly complex, with conflicting jurisdictions and numerous checks and balances. A large commitment in time and energy must be made, even by a well-educated citizen, to keep informed of the issues and personalities in all levels of government. Most citizens are not able or willing to pay this kind of cost to gain the information necessary for effective political participation. This may be especially true in a political system in which weak or unclear alternatives are usually presented to the electorate. For most citizens the world of politics is remote, bewildering, and meaningless, having no direct relation to daily concerns about jobs or family life. Many citizens have desires or frustrations with which public agencies might be expected to deal, but they usually remain unaware of possible solutions to their problems in the public sphere. This group within our political system are citizens only from the legal point of view. If a high degree of social solidarity and sense of community are necessary for true democratic participation, then these marginal men are not really citizens of the state. The polity has not been extended to include them.

For the elitist theorist widespread apathy is merely a fact of political life, something to be anticipated, a prerequisite for democratic stability. But for the classical democrat political apathy is an object of intense concern because the overriding moral purpose of the classical theory is to expand the boundaries of the political community and build the foundations for human understanding through participation by the citizens in the affairs of their government.

LEADERS AND FOLLOWERS

While most elitist theorists are agreed in conceiving of the average citizen as politically passive and uncreative, there seems to be a difference of opinion (or at least of emphasis) over the likelihood of some irrational, antidemocratic outburst from the society's common men. Dahl does not dwell on this possibility. He seemingly conceives of *homo civicus,* the average citizen, as a man who consciously chooses to avoid politics and to devote himself to the pleasures and problems of his job and family:

> Typically, as a source of direct gratifications political activity will appear to *homo civicus* as less attractive than a host of other activities; and, as a strategy to achieve his gratifications indirectly political action will seem considerably less efficient than working at his job, earning more money, taking out insurance, joining a club, planning a vacation, moving to another neighborhood or city, or coping with an uncertain future in manifold other ways.

Lipset, on the other hand, seems much more concerned with the danger that the common man might suddenly enter the political system, smashing democratic institutions in the process, as part of an irrational, authoritarian political force. He sees "profoundly antidemocratic tendencies in lower class groups," and he has been frequently concerned in his work with Hitler, McCarthy, and other demagogic leaders who have led antidemocratic mass movements.

Although there are obviously some important differences of opinion and emphasis concerning the political capacities of average citizens and the relative security of democratic institutions, the elitist theorists agree on the crucial importance of leadership in insuring both the safety and viability of representative government. This set of basic assumptions serves as a foundation for their explanation of change and innovation in American politics, a process in which they feel creative leadership plays the central role.

Running throughout the work of these writers is a vision of the "professional" politician as hero, much as he is pictured in Max Weber's essay, "Politics as a Vocation." Dahl's Mayor Lee, Edward Banfield's Mayor Daley, Richard Neustadt's ideal occupant of the White House all possess great skill and drive and are engaged in the delicate art of persuasion and coalition building. They are actively moving the society forward toward their own goals, according to their own special vision. All of them possess the pre-eminent qualities of Weber's ideal-type politician: "passion, a feeling of responsibility, and a sense of proportion." As in Schumpeter's analysis of capitalism, the primary source of change and innovation in the political system is the "political entrepreneur"; only such a leader can break through the inherent conservatism of organizations and shake the masses from their habitual passivity.

It is obvious that political leaders (especially chief executives) have played a very important role in American politics, but it is also clear that the American system's large degree of internal bargaining, the lack of many strong hierarchical controls and its numerous checks and balances, both constitutional and political, place powerful constraints on the behavior of political executives. American presidents, governors, and mayors usually find themselves caught in a web of cross pressures which prevent them from making bold departures in policy or firmly attaching themselves to either side of a controversy. The agenda of controversy, the list of questions which are recognized by the active participants in politics as legitimate subjects of attention and concern, is very hard to change.

Just as it can be argued that the common citizens have a form of indirect influence, so it can also be argued that the top leaders of other institutions in the society, such as the business community, possess indirect influence as well. As Banfield suggests in his study of Chicago, the top business leaders have great potential power: "if the twenty or thirty wealthiest men in Chicago acted as one and put all their wealth into the fight, they could easily destroy or capture the machine." The skillful politician, following Carl Friedrich's "rule of anticipated reactions," is unlikely to make proposals which would unite the business community against him. The aspiring politician learns early in his career, by absorbing the folklore which circulates among the politically active, which issues can and cannot be exploited successfully. It is this constellation of influences and anticipated reactions, "the peculiar mobilization of bias" in the community, fortified by a general consensus of elites, that determines the agenda of controversy. The American political system, above all others, seems to be especially designed to frustrate the creative leader.

But as rigid and inflexible as it is, the political system does produce new policies; new programs and schemes are approved; even basic procedural changes are made from time to time. Of course, each major shift in public policy has a great many causes. The elitist theory of democracy looks for the principal source of innovation in the competition among rival leaders and the clever maneuvering of political entrepreneurs, which is, in its view, the most distinctive aspect of a democratic system. Because so many political scientists have worn the theoretical blinders of the elitist theory, however, we have overlooked the importance of broadly based social movements, arising from the public at large, as powerful agents of innovation and change.

The primary concerns of the elitist theorists have been the maintenance of democratic stability, the preservation of democratic stability, the preservation of democratic procedures, and the creation of machinery which would produce efficient administration and coherent public policies. With these goals in mind, social movements (if they have been studied at all) have usually been pictured as threats to democracy, as manifestations of "political extremism." Lipset asserts that such movements typically appeal to the "disgruntled and the psychologically homeless, to the personal failures, the socially isolated, the economically insecure, the uneducated, unsophisticated, and authoritarian persons at every level of the society." Movements of this kind throw the political system out of gear and disrupt the mechanisms designed to maintain due process; if the elites were overwhelmed by such forces, democracy would be destroyed. This narrow, antagonistic view of social movements stems from the elitist theorists' suspicion of the political capacities of the common citizens, their fear of instability, and their failure to recognize the elements of rigidity and constraint existing in the political system. But if one holds that view and at the same time recognizes the tendency of the prevailing political system to frustrate strong leaders, it becomes difficult to explain how significant innovations in public policy, such as the social security system, the Wagner Act, the Subversive Activities Control Act of 1950, or the Civil Rights Bill of 1964, ever came about.

During the last century American society has spawned numerous social movements, some of which have made extensive demands on the political system, while others have been highly esoteric, mystical, and apolitical. These movements arise because some form of social dislocation or widespread sense of frustration exists within the society. But dissatisfaction alone is not a sufficient cause; it must be coupled with the necessary resources and the existence of potential leadership which can motivate a group to take action designed to change the offending circumstances. Often such movements erupt along the margins of the political system, and they sometimes serve the purpose of encouraging political and social mobilization, of widening the boundaries of the polity. Through movements such as the Negroes' drive for civil rights, or the Midwestern farmers' crusade for fair prices in the 1890's, or the Ku Klux Klan, or the "radical right" movements of the 1960's, "*prepolitical* people who have not yet found, or only begun to find, a specific language in which to express their aspirations about the world" are given new orientation, confidence, knowledge, sources of information, and leadership.

Social movements also serve, in Rudolf Heberle's words, as the "creators and carriers of public opinion." By confronting the political authorities, or by locking themselves in peaceful—or violent—conflict with some other element of the society, social movements provoke trials of strength between contending forces or ideas. Those trials of economic, political, or moral strength take place in the court of public opinion and sometimes place enormous strain on democratic institutions and even the social fabric itself. But through such trials, as tumultuous as they may sometimes be, the agenda of controversy, the list of acceptable, "key" issues may be changed. In an effort to conciliate and mediate, and political leaders fashion new legislation, create unique regulatory bodies, and strive to establish channels of communication and accommodation among the combatants.

Of course, members of the political elite may respond to the movement by resisting it, driving it underground, or destroying it; they may try to co-opt the movement's leaders by granting them privileges or by accepting parts of its program, or even by making the leaders part of the established elite; they may surrender to the movement, losing control of their offices in the political system in the process. The nature of the political leader's response is probably a prime determinant of the tactics the movement will adopt, the kind of leadership that arises within it, and the ideological appeals it develops. Other factors might determine the response of the leadership, such as the existence of competing social movements with conflicting demands, the resources available to the political leaders to satisfy the demands of the movement, the social status of the participants in the movement, the presence of competing sets of leaders claiming to represent the same movement, and many other elements peculiar to each particular situation. In this process social movements may be highly disruptive and some institutions may be completely destroyed; the story does not always have a happy ending. But one major consequence (function, if you will) of social movements is to break society's log jam, to prevent ossification in the political system, to prompt and justify major innovations in social policy and economic organization.

This relationship of challenge and response between the established political system and social movements has gone without much systematic study by political scientists. Sociologists have been concerned with social movements, but they have directed most of their attention to the causes of the movements, their "natural history," and the relationship between leaders and followers within them. Historians have produced many case studies of social movements but little in the way of systematic explanation. This would seem to be a fruitful area for investigation by political scientists. But this research is not likely to appear unless we revise our concept of the masses as politically inert, apathetic, and bound by habitual responses. We must also shift our emphasis from theories which conceive of the "social structure in terms of a functionally integrated system held in equilibrium by certain patterned and recurrent processes" to theories which place greater emphasis on the role of coercion and constraint in the political system and which concentrate on the influences within society which produce "the forces that maintain it in an unending process of change." The greatest contribution of Marx to the understanding of society was his realization that internal conflict is a major source of change and innovation. One need not accept his metaphysical assumptions to appreciate this important insight.

CONCLUSION

In a society undergoing massive social change, fresh theoretical perspectives are essential. Political theorists are charged with the responsibility of constantly reformulating the dogmas of the past so that democratic theory remains relevant to the stormy realities of twentieth century American society with its sprawling urban centers, its innumerable social conflicts, and its enormous bureaucratic hierarchies.

In restating the classical theory, however, contemporary political scientists have stripped democracy of much of its radical *élan* and have diluted its utopian vision, thus rendering it inadequate as a guide to the future. The elitist theorists generally accept the prevailing distribution of status in the society (with exceptions usually made for the American Negro) and find it "not only compatible with political freedom but even . . . a condition of it." They place great emphasis on the limitations of the average citizen and are suspicious of schemes which might encourage greater particpation in public affairs. Accordingly, they put their trust in the wisdom and energy of an active, responsible elite.

Besides these normative shortcomings the elitist theory has served as an inadequate guide to empirical research, providing an unconvincing explanation of widespread political apathy in American society and leading political scientists to ignore manifestations of discontent not directly related to the political system. Few studies have been conducted of the use of force, or informal, illegitimate coercion in the American political system, and little attention has been directed to the great social movements which have marked American society in the last one hundred years.

If political science is to be relevant to society's pressing needs and urgent problems, professional students of politics must broaden their perspectives and become aware of new problems which are in need of scientific investigation. They must examine the norms that guide their efforts and guard against the danger of uncritically accepting the values of the going system in the name of scientific objectivity. Political scientists must strive for heightened awareness and self-knowledge; they must avoid rigid presumptions which diminish their vision, destroy their capacities for criticism, and blind them to some of the most significant social and political developments of our time.

Group Theory

Group theory has been the keystone of democratic political theory for several decades. The essence of group theory is that in the democratic process interest groups interact naturally and properly to produce public policy. In American political thought, the origins of this theory can be found in the theory of concurrent majority in John C. Calhoun's *Disquisition on Government.*

It is very useful to discuss the operation of interest groups within the framework of what can best be described as a concurrent majority system. In contemporary usage the phrase "concurrent majority" means a system in which major government policy decisions must be approved by the dominant interest groups directly affected. The word *concurrent* suggests that each group involved must give its consent before policy can be enacted. Thus a concurrent majority is a majority of each group considered separately. If we take as an example an area such as agricultural policy, in which three or four major private interest groups can be identified, we can say that the concurrent majority is reached when each group affected gives its approval before agricultural policy is passed. The extent to which such a system of concurrent majority is actually functioning is a matter that has not been fully clarified by empirical research. Nevertheless, it does seem tenable to conclude that in many major areas of public policy, it is necessary at least to achieve a concurrent majority of the *major* or *dominant* interests affected.

The *theory* of concurrent majority originated with John C. Calhoun. Calhoun, born in 1781, had a distinguished career in public service at both the national and state levels. The idea of concurrent majority evolved from the concept of state nullification of federal law. Under this states' rights doctrine, states would be able to veto any national action. The purpose of this procedure was theoretically to protect states in a minority from encroachment by a national majority that could act through Congress, the President, and even the Supreme Court. Those who favored this procedure had little faith in the separation of powers doctrine as an effective device to prevent the arbitrary exercise of national power. At the end of his career Calhoun decided to incorporate his earlier views on state nullification into a more substantial theoretical treatise in political science; thus he wrote his famous *Disquisition on Government* (New York: D. Appleton & Co., 1853) in the decade between 1840 and 1850. He attempted to develop a general theory of constitutional (limited) government, the primary mechanism of which would be the ability of the major interest groups (states in Calhoun's time) to veto legislation adverse to their interests. Students should overlook some of the theoretical inconsistencies in Calhoun and concentrate upon the basic justification he advances for substituting his system of concurrent majority for the separation of powers device. Under the latter, group interests are not necessarily taken into account, for national laws can be passed on the basis of a numerical majority. And even though this majority may reflect the interests of some groups, it will not necessarily reflect the interests of all groups affected. Thus Calhoun is arguing that a system in which the major interest groups can dominate the policy process is really more in accord with constitutional democracy than the system established in our Constitution and supported in *Federalist 10.*

3
John C. Calhoun

A DISQUISITION ON GOVERNMENT

... What I propose is ... to explain on what principles government must be formed in order to resist by its own interior structure—or to use a single term, *organism*—the tendency to abuse of power. This structure ... is what is meant by constitution, in its strict and more usual sense; and it is this which distinguishes what are called "constitutional" governments from "absolute." ...

How government, then, must be constructed in order to counteract, through its organism, this tendency on the part of those who make and execute the laws to oppress those subject to their operation is the next question which claims attention.

There is but one way in which this can possibly be done, and that is by such an organism as will furnish the ruled with the means of resisting successfully this tendency on the part of the rulers to oppression and abuse. Power can only be resisted by power—and tendency by tendency. Those who exercise power and those subject to its exercise—the rulers and the ruled—stand in antagonistic relations to each other. The same constitution of our nature which leads rulers to oppress the ruled—regardless of the object for which government is ordained—will, with equal strength, lead the ruled to resist when possessed of the means of making peaceable and effective resistance. Such an organism, then, as will furnish the means by which resistance may be systematically and peaceably made on the part of the ruled to oppression and abuse of power on the part of the rulers is the first and indispensable step toward *forming* a constitutional government. And as this can only be effected by or through the right of suffrage—the right on the part of the ruled to choose their rulers at proper intervals and to hold them thereby responsible for their conduct—the responsibility of the rulers to be ruled, through the right of suffrage, is the indispensable and primary principle in the foundation of a constitutional government. When this right is properly guarded, and the people sufficiently enlightened to understand their own rights and the interests of the community and duly to appreciate the motives and conduct of those appointed to make and execute the laws, it is all-sufficient to give to those who elect effective control over those they have elected.

I call the right of suffrage the indispensable and primary principle, for it would be a great and dangerous mistake to suppose, as many do, that it is, of itself, sufficient to form constitutional governments. To this erroneous opinion may be traced one of the causes why so few attempts to form constitutional governments have succeeded, and why of the few which have, so small a number have had durable existence. It has led not only to mistakes in the attempts to form such governments, but to their overthrow when they have, by some good fortune, been correctly formed. So far from being, of itself, sufficient—however well guarded it might be and however enlightened the people—it would, unaided by other provisions, leave the government as absolute as it would be in the hands of irresponsible rulers; and with a tendency, at least as strong, toward oppression and abuse of its power, as I shall next proceed to explain.

. . . The right of suffrage . . . transfers, in reality, the actual control over the government from those who make and execute the laws to the body of the community and thereby places the powers of the government as fully in the mass of the community as they would be if they, in fact, had assembled, made, and executed the laws themselves without the intervention of representatives or agents. The more perfectly it does this, the more perfectly it accomplishes its ends; but in doing so, it only changes the seat of authority without counteracting, in the least, the tendency of the government to oppression and abuse of its powers.

If the whole community had the same interests so that the interests of each and every portion would be so affected by the action of the government that the laws which oppressed or impoverished one portion would necessarily oppress and impoverish all others—or the reverse—then the right of suffrage, of itself, would be all-sufficient to counteract the tendency of the government to oppression and abuse of its powers, and, of course, would form, of itself, a perfect constitutional government. . . .

But such is not the case. On the contrary, nothing is more difficult than to equalize the action of the government in reference to the various and diversified interests of the community; and nothing more easy than to pervert its powers into instruments to aggrandize and enrich one or more interests by oppressing and impoverishing the others. . . . The more extensive and populous the country, the more diversified the condition and pursuits of its population; and the richer, more luxurious, and dissimilar the people, the more difficult is it to equalize the action of the government, and the more easy for one portion of the community to pervert its powers to oppress and plunder the other.

Such being the case, it necessarily results that the right of suffrage, by placing the control of the government in the community, must, from the same constitution of our nature which makes government necessary to preserve society, lead to conflict among its different interests—each striving to obtain possession of its powers as the means of protecting itself against the others or of advancing its respective interests regardless of the interests of others. For this purpose, a struggle will take place between the various interests to obtain a majority in order to control the government. If no one interest be strong enough, of itself, to obtain it, a combination will be formed between those whose interests are most alike—each conceding something to the others until a sufficient number is obtained to make a majority. The process may be slow and much time may be required before a compact, organized majority can be thus formed, but formed it will be in time, even without preconcert or design, by the sure workings of that principle or constitution of our nature in which government itself originates. When once formed, the community will be divided into two great parties—a major and minor—between which there will be incessant struggles on the one side to retain, and on the other to obtain the majority and, thereby, the control of the government and the advantages it confers. . . .

Nor is it less certain . . . that the dominant majority . . . would have the same tendency to oppression and abuse of power which, without the right of suffrage, irresponsible rulers would have. No reason, indeed, can be assigned why the latter would abuse their power, which would not apply, with equal force, to the former. The dominant majority, for the time, would in reality, through the right of suffrage, be the rulers—the controlling, governing, and irresponsible power; and those who make and execute the laws would, for the time, be in reality but *their* representatives and agents.

Nor would the fact that the former would constitute a majority of the community counteract a tendency originating in the constitution of man and which, as such, cannot depend on the number by whom the powers of the government may be wielded. . . . Be it which it may, the minority, for the time, will be as much the governed or subject portion as are the people in an aristocracy or the subjects in a monarchy. The only difference in this respect is that in the government of a majority the minority may become the majority, and the majority the minority, through the right of suffrage, and thereby change their relative positions without the intervention of force and revolution. But the duration or uncertainty of the tenure by which power is held cannot, of itself, counteract the tendency inherent in government to oppression and abuse of power. On the contrary, the very uncertainty of the tenure, combined with the violent party warfare which must ever precede a change of parties under such governments, would rather tend to increase than diminish the tendency to oppression.

As, then, the right of suffrage, without some other provision, cannot counteract this tendency of government, the next question for consideration is, What is that other provision? . . .

From what has been said, it is manifest that this provision must be of a character calculated to prevent any one interest or combination of interests from using the powers of government to aggrandize itself at the expense of the others. . . . There is but one certain mode in which this result can be secured, and that is by the adoption of some restriction or limitation which shall so effectually prevent any one interest or combination of interests from obtaining the exclusive control of the government as to render hopeless all attempts directed to that end. There is, again, but one mode in which this can be effected, and that is by taking the sense of each interest or portion of the community which may be unequally and injuriously affected by the action of the government separately, through its own majority or in some other way by which its voice may be fairly expressed, and to require the consent of each interest either to put or to keep the government in action. This, too, can be accomplished only . . . by dividing and distributing the powers of government, giv[ing] to each division or interest, through its appropriate organ, either a concurrent voice in making and executing the laws or a veto on their execution. It is only by such an organism that the assent of each can be made necessary to put the government in motion, or the power made effectual to arrest its action when put in motion; and it is only by the one or the other that the different interests, orders, classes, or portions into which the community may be divided can be protected, and all conflict and struggle between them prevented—by rendering it impossible to put or to keep it in action without the concurrent consent of all.

Such an organism as this, combined with the right of suffrage, constitutes, in fact, the elements of constitutional government. The one, by rendering those who make and execute the laws responsible to those on whom they operate, prevents the rulers from oppressing the ruled; and the other, by making it impossible for any one interest or combination of interests, or class or order, or portion of the community to obtain exclusive control, prevents any one of them from oppressing the other. It is clear that oppression and abuse of power must come, if at all, from the one or the other quarter. . . . It follows that the two, suffrage and proper organism combined, are sufficient to counteract the tendency of government to oppression and abuse of power and to restrict it to the fulfillment of the great ends for which it is ordained.

In coming to this conclusion I have assumed the organism to be perfect and the different interests, portions, or classes of the community to be sufficiently enlightened to understand its character and object, and to exercise, with due intelligence, the right of suffrage. . . . Where the organism is perfect, every interest will be truly and fully represented, and of course the whole community must be so. It may be difficult, or even impossible, to make a perfect organism —but, although this be true, yet even when, instead of the sense of each and of all, *it takes that of a few great and prominent interests only,* it would still, in a great measure, if not altogether, fulfill the end intended by a constitution. For in such case it would require so large a portion of the community, compared with the whole, to concur or acquiesce in the action of the government that the number to be plundered would be too few and the number to be aggrandized too many to afford adequate notices to oppression and the abuse of its powers. . . .

It results, from what has been said, that there are two different modes in which the sense of the community may be taken: one, simply by the right of suffrage, unaided; the other, by the right through a proper organism. Each collects the sense of the majority. But one regards number only and considers the whole community as a unit having but one common interest throughout, and collects the sense of the great number of the whole as that of the community. The other, on the contrary, regards interests as well as numbers—considering the community as made up of different and conflicting interests, as far as the action of the government is concerned—and takes the sense of each through its majority or appropriate organ, and the united sense of all as the sense of the entire community. The former of these I shall call the numerical or absolute majority, and the latter, the concurrent or constitutional majority. . . .

What is an interest group? The typical picture painted of interest or pressure groups presents an evil-minded, crooked-nosed lobbyist attempting to corner a Congressman to get him to vote for some "selfish" proposal which is, of course, against the "public interest." Lobbyists and interest groups are generally considered to be bad, working for their own ends against a higher national purpose.

David Truman's selection, taken from *The Governmental Process* (1951), contains (1) a definition of the term "interest group" and (2) a brief outline of the frame of reference within which the operations of interest groups should be considered. A fairly articulate interest group theory of the governmental process is sketched by Truman. It will become evident to the student of American government that interest groups, like political parties, form an integral part of our political system. Further, interest group theory suggests an entirely new way of looking at government.

4
David B. Truman

THE GOVERNMENTAL PROCESS

INTEREST GROUPS

Interest group refers to any group that, on the basis of one or more shared attitudes, makes certain claims upon other groups in the society for the establishment, maintenance, or enhancement of forms of behavior that are implied by the shared attitudes. . . . [F]rom interaction in groups arise certain common habits of response, which may be called norms, or shared attitudes. These afford the participants frames of reference for interpreting and evaluating events and behaviors. In this respect all groups are interest groups because they are shared-attitude groups. In some groups at various points in time, however, a second kind of common response emerges, in addition to the frame of reference. These are shared attitudes toward what is needed or wanted in a given situation, as demands or claims upon other groups in the society. The term "interest group" will be reserved here for those groups that exhibit both aspects of the shared attitudes. . . .

Definition of the interest group in this fashion . . . permits the identification of various potential as well as existing interest groups. That is, it invites examination of an interest whether or not it is found at the moment as one of the characteristics of a particular organized group. Although no group that makes claims upon other groups in society will be found without an interest or interests, it is possible to examine interests that are not at a particular point in time the basis of interactions among individuals, but that may become such. . . .

GROUPS AND GOVERNMENT:
DIFFICULTIES IN A GROUP INTERPRETATION OF POLITICS

Since we are engaged in an effort to develop a conception of the political process in the United States that will account adequately for the role of groups, particularly interest groups, it will be appropriate to take account of some of the factors that have been regarded as obstacles to such a conception and that have caused such groups to be neglected in many explanations of the dynamics of government. Perhaps the most important practical reason for this neglect is that the significance of groups has only fairly recently been forced to the attention of political scientists by the tremendous growth in the number of formally organized groups in the United States within the last few decades. It is difficult and unnecessary to attempt to date the beginning of such attention, but Herring in 1929, in his groundbreaking book, *Group Representation Before Congress,* testified to the novelty of the observations he reported when he stated: "There has developed in this government an extra-legal machinery of as integral and of as influential a nature as the system of party government that has long been an essential part of the government. . . . " Some implications of this development are not wholly compatible with some of the proverbial notions about representative government held by specialists as well as laymen. . . . This apparent incompatibility has obstructed the inclusion of group behaviors in an objective description of the governmental process.

More specifically, it is usually argued that any attempt at the interpretation of politics in terms of group patterns inevitably "leaves something out" or "destroys something essential" about the processes of "our" government. On closer examination, we find this argument suggesting that two "things" are certain to be ignored: the individual, and a sort of totally inclusive unity designated by such terms as "society" and "the state."

The argument that the individual is ignored in any interpretation of politics as based upon groups seems to assume a differentiation or conflict between "the individual" and some such collectivity as the group. . . .

Such assumptions need not present any difficulties in the development of a group interpretation of politics, because they are essentially unwarranted. They simply do not square with . . . evidence concerning group affiliations and individual behavior. . . . We do not, in fact, find individuals otherwise than in groups; complete isolation in space and time is so rare as to be an almost hypothetical situation. It is equally demonstrable that the characteristics of any interest group, including the activities by which we identify it, are governed by the attitudes and the circumstances that gave rise to the interactions of which it consists. There are variable factors, and, although the role played by a particular individual may be quite different in a lynch mob from that of the same individual in a meeting of the church deacons, the attitudes and behaviors involved in both are as much a part of his personality as is his treatment of his family. "The individual" and "the group" are at most merely convenient ways of classifying behavior, two ways of approaching the same phenomena, not different things.

The persistence among nonspecialists of the notion of an inherent conflict between "the individual" and "the group" or "society" is understandable in view of the doctrines of individualism that have underlain various political and economic conflicts over the past three centuries. The notion persists also because it harmonizes with a view of the isolated and independent individual as the "cause" of complicated human events. The personification of events, quite apart from any ethical considerations, is a kind of shorthand convenient in everyday speech and, like supernatural explanations of natural phenomena, has a comforting simplicity. Explanations that take into account multiple causes, including group affiliations, are difficult. The "explanation" of a national complex like the Soviet Union wholly in terms of a Stalin or the "description" of the intricacies of the American government entirely in terms of a Roosevelt is quick and easy. . . .

The second major difficulty allegedly inherent in any attempt at a group interpretation of the political process is that such an explanation inevitably must ignore some greater unity designated as society or the state. . . .

Many of those who place particular emphasis upon this difficulty assume explicitly or implicitly that there is an interest of the nation as a whole, universally and invariably held and standing apart from and superior to those of the various groups included within it. This assumption is close to the popular dogmas of democratic government based on the familiar notion that if only people are free and have access to "the facts," they will all want the same thing in any political situation. It is no derogation of democratic preferences to state that such an assertion flies in the face of all that we know of the behavior of men in a complex society. Were it in fact true, not only the interest group but even the political party should properly be viewed as an abnormality. The differing experiences and perceptions of men not only encourage individuality but also . . . inevitably result in differing attitudes and conflicting group affiliations. "There are," says Bentley in his discussion of this error of the social whole, "always some parts of the nation to be found arrayed against other arts." [From *The Process of Government* (1908).] Even in war, when a totally inclusive interest should be apparent if it is ever going to be, we always find pacifists, conscientious objectors, spies, and subversives, who reflect interests opposed to those of "the nation as a whole."

There is a political significance in assertions of a totally inclusive interest within a nation. Particularly in times of crisis, such as an international war, such claims are a tremendously useful promotional device by means of which a particularly extensive group or league of groups tries to reduce or eliminate opposing interests. Such is the pain attendant upon not "belonging" to one's "own" group that if a normal person can be convinced that he is the lone dissenter to an otherwise universally accepted agreement, he usually will conform. This pressure accounts at least in part for the number of prewar pacifists who, when the United States entered World War II, accepted the draft or volunteered. Assertion of an inclusive "national" or "public interest" is an effective device in many less critical situations as well. In themselves, these claims are part of the data of politics. However, they do not describe any actual or possible political situation within a complex modern nation. In developing a group interpretation of politics, therefore, we do not need to account for a totally inclusive interest, because one does not exist.

Denying the existence of an interest of the nation as a whole does not completely dispose of the difficulty raised by those who insist that a group interpretation must omit "the state." We cannot deny the obvious fact that we are examining a going political system that is supported or at least accepted by a large proportion of the society. We cannot account for such a system by adding up in some fashion the National Association of Manufacturers, the Congress of Industrial Organizations, the American Farm Bureau Federation, The American Legion, and other groups that come to mind when "lobbies" and "pressure groups" are mentioned. Even if the political parties are added to the list, the result could properly be designated as "a view which seems hardly compatible with the relative stability of the political system. . . ." Were such the exclusive ingredients of the political process in the United States, the entire system would have torn itself apart long since.

If these various organized interest groups more or less consistently reconcile their differences, adjust, and accept compromises, we must acknowledge that we are dealing with a system that is not accounted for by the "sum" of the organized interest groups in the society. We must go farther to explain the operation of such ideals or traditions as constitutionalism, civil liberties, representative responsibility, and the like. These are not, however, a sort of disembodied metaphysical influence, like Mr. Justice Holmes's "brooding ominipresence." We know of the existence of such factors only from the behavior and the habitual interactions of men. If they exist in this fashion, they are interests. We can account for their operation and for the system by recognizing such interests as representing what . . . we called potential interest groups in the "becoming" stage of activity. "It is certainly true," as Bently has made clear, "that we must accept a . . . group of this kind as an interest group itself." It makes no difference that we cannot find the home office and the executive secretary of such a group. Organization in this formal sense, as we have seen, represents merely a stage or degree of interaction that may or may not be significant at any particular point in time. Its absence does not mean that these interests do not exist, that the familiar "pressure groups" do not operate as if such potential groups were organized and active, or that these interests may not move from the potential to the organized stage of activity.

It thus appears that the two major difficulties supposedly obstacles to a group interpretation of the political process are not insuperable. We can employ the fact of individuality and we can account for the existence of the state without doing violence to the evidence available from the observed behaviors of men and groups. . . .

INTEREST GROUPS AND THE NATURE OF THE STATE

Men, wherever they are observed, are creatures participating in those established patterns of interaction that we call groups. Excepting perhaps the most casual and transitory, these continuing interactions, like all such interpersonal relationships, involve power. This power is exhibited in two closely interdependent ways. In the first place, the group exerts power over its members; an individual's group affiliations largely determine his attitudes, values, and the frames of reference in terms of which he interprets his experiences. For a measure of conformity to the norms of the group is the price of acceptance within it. ... In the second place, the group, if it is or becomes an interest group, which any group in society may be, exerts power over other groups in the society when it successfully imposes claims upon them.

Many interest groups, probably an increasing proportion in the United States, are politicized. That is, either from the outset or from time to time in the course of their development they make their claims through or upon the institutions of government. Both the forms and functions of government in turn are a reflection of the activities and claims of such groups. ...

The institutions of government are centers of interest-based power; their connections with interest groups may be latent or overt and their activities range in political character from the routinized and widely accepted to the unstable and highly controversial. In order to make claims, political interest groups will seek access to the key points of decision within these institutions. Such points are scattered throughout the structure, including not only the formally established branches of government but also the political parties in their various forms and the relationships between governmental units and other interest groups.

The extent to which a group achieves effective access to the institutions of government is the resultant of a complex of interdependent factors. For the sake of simplicity these may be classified in three somewhat overlapping categories: (1) factors relating to a group's strategic position in the society; (2) factors associated with the internal characteristics of the group; and (3) factors peculiar to the governmental institutions themselves. In the first category are: the group's status or prestige in the society, affecting the ease with which it commands deference from those outside its bounds; the standing it and its activities have when measured against the widely held but largely unorganized interests or "rules of the game"; the extent to which government officials are formally or informally "members" of the group; and the usefulness of the group as a source of technical and political knowledge. The second category includes: the degree and appropriateness of the group's organization; the degree of cohesion it can achieve in a given situation, especially in the light of competing group demands upon its membership; the skills of the leadership; and the group's resources in numbers and money. In the third category are: the operating structure of the government institutions, since such established features involve relatively fixed advantages and handicaps; and the effects of the group life of particular units or branches of the government. ...

A characteristic feature of the governmental system in the United States is that it contains a multiplicity of points of access. The federal system establishes decentralized and more or less independent centers of power, vantage points from which to secure privileged access to the national government. Both a sign and a cause of the strength of the constituent units in the federal scheme is the peculiar character of our party system, which has strengthened parochial relationships, especially those of national legislators. National parties, and to a lesser degree those in the states, tend to be poorly cohesive leagues of locally based organizations rather than unified and inclusive structures. Staggered terms for executive officials and various types of legislators accentuate differences in the effective electorates that participate in choosing these officers. Each of these different, often opposite, localized patterns (constituencies) is a channel of independent access to the larger party aggregation and to the formal government. Thus, especially at the national level, the party is an electing-device and only in limited measure an integrated means of policy determination. Within the Congress, furthermore, controls are diffused among committee chairmen and other leaders in both chambers. The variety of these points of access is further supported by relationships stemming from the constitutional doctrine of separation of powers, from related checks and balances, and at the state and local level from the common practice of choosing an array of executive officials by popular election. At the federal level the formal simplicity of the executive branch has been complicated by a Supreme Court decision that has placed a number of administrative agencies beyond the removal power of the President. The position of these units, however, differs only in degree from that of many that are constitutionally within the Executive Branch. In consequence of alternative lines of access available through the legislature and the Executive and of divided channels for the control of administrative policy, many nominally executive agencies are at various times virtually independent of the Chief Executive.

. . . Within limits, therefore, organized interest groups, gravitating toward responsive points of decision, may play one segment of the structure against another as circumstances and strategic considerations permit. The total pattern of government over a period of time thus presents a protean complex of crisscrossing relationships that change in strength and direction with alternations in the power and standing of interests, organized and unorganized.

From Truman's definition *any* group, organized or unorganized, that has a shared attitude toward goals and methods for achieving them should be classified as an interest group. Truman is essentially saying that, since people generally function as members of groups, it is more useful and accurate for the political observer to view the governmental process as the interaction of political interest groups. If one accepts the sociologist's assumption that men act and interact only as members of groups, then it is imperative that the governmental process be viewed as one of interest group interaction.

Within the framework of Truman's definition it is possible to identifiy both *public* and *private* interest groups. In the political process, governmental groups sometimes act as interest groups in the same sense as private organizations. In many public policies, governmental groups may have more at stake than private organizations. Thus administrative agencies, for example, may lobby as vigorously as their private counterparts to advance their own interests.

Theodore Lowi refers to group theory as "interest group liberalism." The following selection is taken from his well-known book *The End of Liberalism*

(1969), in which he severely criticizes group theory and its pervasive influence upon governmental decision makers. In reading the following selection, remember that the author does not use the term "liberal" in its ordinary sense. The political "liberal" in Lowi's terminology is much like the "economic Liberal" of the early 19th century. Just as economic liberalism preached that the public good emerged automatically from the free clash of private interests, the political liberal (in Lowi's terms) supports group theory which holds that the public interest in government is automatically achieved through the interaction of pressure groups.

5
Theodore J. Lowi

THE END OF LIBERALISM: THE INDICTMENT

The corruption of modern democratic government began with the emergence of interest-group liberalism as the public philosophy. Its corrupting influence takes at least four important forms, four counts, therefore, of an indictment for which most of the foregoing chapters are mere documentation. Also to be indicted, on at least three counts, is the philosophic component of the ideology, pluralism.

SUMMATION I: FOUR COUNTS AGAINST THE IDEOLOGY

(1) Interest-group liberalism as public philosophy corrupts democratic government because it deranges and confuses expectations about democratic institutions. Liberalism promotes popular decision-making but derogates from the decisions so made by misapplying the notion to the implementation as well as the formulation of policy. It derogates from the processes by treating all values in the process as equivalent interests. It derogates from democratic rights by allowing their exercise in foreign policy, and by assuming they are being exercised when access is provided. Liberal practices reveal a basic disrespect for democracy. Liberal leaders do not wield the authority of democratic government with the resoluteness of men certain of the legitimacy of their positions, the integrity of their institutions, or the justness of the programs they serve.

(2) Interest-group liberalism renders government impotent. Liberal governments cannot plan. Liberals are copious in plans but irresolute in plan-

ning. Nineteenth-century liberalism was standard without plans. This was an anachronism in the modern state. But twentieth-century liberalism turned out to be plans without standards. As an anachronism it, too, ought to pass. But doctrines are not organisms. They die only in combat over the minds of men, and no doctrine yet exists capable of doing the job. All the popular alternatives are so very irrelevant, helping to explain the longevity of interest-group liberalism. Barry Goldwater most recently proved the irrelevance of one. The *embourgeoisement* of American unions suggests the irrelevance of others.

The Departments of Agriculture, Commerce, and Labor provide illustrations, but hardly exhaust illustrations, of such impotence. Here clearly one sees how liberalism has become a doctrine whose means are its ends, whose combatants are its clientele, whose standards are not even those of the mob but worse, are those the bargainers can fashion to fit the bargain. Delegation of power has become alienation of public domain—the gift of sovereignty to private satrapies. The political barriers to withdrawal of delegation are high enough. But liberalism reinforces these through the rhetoric of justification and often even permanent legal reinforcement: Public corporations—justified, oddly, as efficient planning instruments—permanently alienate rights of central coordination to the directors and to those who own the corporation bonds. Or, as Walter Adams finds, the "most pervasive method . . . for alienating public domain is the certificate of convenience and necessity, or some variation thereof in the form of an exclusive franchise, license or permit. . . . [G]overnment has become increasingly careless and subservient in issuing them. The net result is a general legalization of private monopoly. . . ." While the best examples still are probably the 10 self-governing systems of agriculture policy, these are obviously only a small proportion of all the barriers the interest-group liberal ideology has erected to democratic use of government.

(3) Interest-group liberalism demoralizes government, because liberal governments cannot achieve justice. The question of justice has engaged the best minds for almost as long as there have been notions of state and politics, certainly ever since Plato defined the ideal as one in which republic and justice were synonymous. And since that time philosophers have been unable to agree on what justice is. But outside the ideal, in the realms of actual government and citizenship, the problem is much simpler. We do not have to define justice at all in order to weight and assess justice in government, because in the case of liberal policies we are prevented by what the law would call a "jurisdictional fact." In the famous jurisdictional case of *Marbury v. Madison* Chief Justice Marshall held that even if all the Justices hated President Jefferson for refusing to accept Marbury and the other "midnight judges" appointed by Adams, there was nothing they could do. They had no authority to judge President Jefferson's action one way or another because the Supreme Court did not possess such jurisdiction over the President. In much the same way, there

is something about liberalism that prevents us from raising the question of justice at all, no matter what definition of justice is used.

Liberal governments cannot achieve justice because their policies lack the *sine qua non* of justice—that quality without which a consideration of justice cannot even be initiated. Considerations of the justice in or achieved by an action cannot be made unless a deliberate and conscious attempt was made by the actor to derive his action from a general rule or moral principle governing such a class of acts. One can speak personally of good rules and bad rules, but a homily or a sentiment, like liberal legislation, is not a rule at all. The best rule is one which is relevant to the decision or action in question and is general in the sense that those involved with it have no direct control over its operation. A general rule is, hence, *a priori*. Any governing regime that makes a virtue of avoiding such rules puts itself totally outside the context of justice.

Take the homely example of the bull and the china shop. Suppose it was an op art shop and that we consider op worthy only of the junk pile. That being the case, the bull did us a great service, the more so because it was something we always dreamed of doing but were prevented by law from entering and breaking. But however much we may be pleased, we cannot judge the act. We can only like or dislike the consequences. The consequences are haphazard; the bull cannot have intended them. The act was a thoughtless, animal act which bears absolutely no relation to any aesthetic principle. We don't judge the bull. We only celebrate our good fortune. Without the general rule, the bull can reenact his scenes of creative destruction daily and still not be capable of achieving, in this case, aesthetic justice. The whole idea of justice is absurd.

The general rule ought to be a legislative rule because the United States espouses the ideal of representative democracy. However, that is merely an extrinsic feature of the rule. All that counts is the character of the rule itself. Without the rule we can only like or dislike the consequences of the governmental action. In the question of whether justice is achieved, a government without good rules, and without acts carefully derived therefrom, is merely a big bull in an immense china shop.

(4)   Finally, interest-group liberalism corrupts democratic government in the degree to which it weakens the capacity of governments to live by democratic formalisms. Liberalism weakens democratic institutions by opposing formal procedure with informal bargaining. Liberalism derogates from democracy by derogating from all formality in favor of informality. Formalism is constraining; playing it "by the book" is a role often unpopular in American war films and sports films precisely because it can dramatize personal rigidity and the plight of the individual in collective situations. Because of the impersonality of formal procedures, there is inevitably a separation in the real world between the forms and the realities, and this kind of separation gives rise to cynicism, for informality means that some will escape their collective fate better than others. There

has as a consequence always been a certain amount of cynicism toward public objects in the United States, and this may be to the good, since a little cynicism is the father of healthy sophistication. However, when the informal is elevated to a positive virtue, and hard-won access becomes a share of official authority, cynicism becomes distrust. It ends in reluctance to submit one's fate to the governmental process under any condition, as is the case in the United States in the mid-1960's.

Public officials more and more frequently find their fates paradoxical and their treatment at the hands of the public fickle and unjust when in fact they are only reaping the results of their own behavior, including their direct and informal treatment of the public and the institutions through which they serve the public. The more government operates by the spreading of access, the more public order seems to suffer. The more public men pursue their constituencies, the more they seem to find their constituencies alienated. Liberalism has promoted concentration of democratic authority but deconcentration of democratic power. Liberalism has opposed privilege in policy formulation only to foster it, quite systematically, in the implementation of policy. Liberalism has consistently failed to recognize, in short, that in a democracy forms are important. In a medieval monarchy all formalisms were at court. Deomcracy proves, for better or worse, that the masses like that sort of thing too.

Another homely parable may help. In the good old days, everyone in the big city knew that traffic tickets could be fixed. Not everyone could get his ticket fixed, but nonetheless a man who honestly paid his ticket suffered in some degree a dual loss: his money, and his self-esteem for having so little access. Cynicism was widespread, violations were many, but perhaps it did not matter, for there were so few automobiles. Suppose, however, that as the automobile population increased a certain city faced a traffic crisis and the system of ticket fixing came into ill repute. Suppose a mayor, victorious on the Traffic Ticket, decided that, rather than eliminate fixing by universalizing enforcement, he would instead reform the system by universalizing the privileges of ticket fixing. One can imagine how the system would work. One can imagine that some sense of equality would prevail, because everyone could be made almost equally free to bargain with the ticket administrators. But one would find it difficult to imagine how this would make the total city government more legitimate. Meanwhile, the purpose of the ticket would soon have been destroyed.

Traffic regulation, fortunately, was not so reformed. But many other government activities were. The operative principles of interest-group liberalism possess the mentality of a world of universalized ticket fixing: Destroy privilege by universalizing it. Reduce conflict by yielding to it. Redistribute power by the maxim of each according to his claim. Reserve an official place for every major structure of power. Achieve order by worshipping the processes (as distinguished from the forms and the procedures) by which order is presumed to be established.

If these operative principles will achieve equilibrium—and such is far from proven—that is all they will achieve. Democracy will have disappeared, because all of these maxims are founded upon profound lack of confidence in democracy. Democracy fails when it lacks confidence in its own authority.

Democratic forms were supposed to precede and accompany the formulation of policies so that policies could be implemented authoritatively and firmly. Democracy is indeed a form of absolutism, but ours was fairly well contrived to be an absolutist government under the strong control of consent-building prior to taking authoritative action in law. Interest-group liberalism fights the absolutism of democracy but succeeds only in taking away its authoritativeness. Whether it is called "creative federalism" by President Johnson, "cooperation" by the farmers, "local autonomy" by the Republicans, or "participatory democracy" by the New Left, the interest-group liberal effort does not create democratic power but rather negates it.

Systems Theory

Both elite theory and group theory suggest that political power is held by a single, definable sector of society. In reality, however, the study of government must take into account a wider variety of environmental factors. It is impossible to understand the governmental process merely by examining the operation of elites or interest groups. The context in which government functions must be analyzed to find other forces that determine the sources, uses, distribution, and effects of political power. One fruitful way to analyze government is to think of it as a part of a broad *political system,* the components of which interconnect to produce varying results. A political system is shaped by more than elites and interest groups—nor is it merely a series of formal governmental institutions. All countries have political systems that can be categorized by their component parts, some of which are the demands made upon the system, the supports given to it, the governmental structures through which the demands pass (including the character and distribution of formal authority), and finally the "outputs" of the system—the public policy that is developed and applied.

A political system differs greatly from other social systems, such as business organizations, clubs, fraternities, labor unions, agricultural groups, and all *private* groups. Like a political system, each of these private or semi-private organizations is a social system possessing differing demands and governing structures; but in a political system, unlike other social systems, the outputs have a compulsory effect and are binding upon all members of the community. Political outputs derive their legitimacy from the fact that they are based upon the sovereignty of the state or, in democratic countries, of the people. The concept of sovereignty justifies and indeed necessitates making the decisions of government, arrived at through the interplay of the components of the political system, binding upon the citizenry. In addition to its formal authority, the state possesses a monopoly of force, and therefore can enforce its decisions. No private organization has this ability. Private organizations can enforce decisions only within the boundaries of the private group, which makes their decisions less compelling than those of a political system. Moreover, it is much easier to withdraw from a private system than from the jurisdiction of a government. The attributes of a political system are examined in the next selection.

6

David Easton

AN APPROACH TO THE ANALYSIS
OF POLITICAL SYSTEMS

SOME ATTRIBUTES OF POLITICAL SYSTEMS

In an earlier work I have argued for the need to develop general, empirically oriented theory as the most economical way in the long run to understand political life. Here I propose to indicate a point of view that, at the least, might serve as a springboard for discussion of alternative approaches and, at most, as a small step in the direction of a general political theory. I wish to stress that what I have to say is a mere orientation to the problem of theory; outside of economics and perhaps psychology, it would be presumptuous to call very much in social science "theory," in the strict sense of the term.

Furthermore, I shall offer only a Gestalt of my point of view, so that it will be possible to evaluate, in the light of the whole, those parts that I do stress. In doing this, I know I run the definite risk that the meaning and implications of this point of view may be only superficially communicated; but it is a risk I shall have to undertake since I do not know how to avoid it sensibly.

The study of politics is concerned with understanding how authoritative decisions are made and executed for a society. We can try to understand political life by viewing each of its aspects piecemeal. We can examine the operation of such institutions as political parties, interest groups, government, and voting; we can study the nature and consequences of such political practices as manipulation, propaganda, and violence; we can seek to reveal the structure within which these practices occur. By combining the results we can obtain a rough picture of what happens in any self-contained political unit.

From David Easton, "An Approach to the Analysis of Political Systems," *World Politics,* Vol. IX (April 1957). The framework outlined in this article has since its publication been elaborated in two books: *A Framework for the Analysis of Political Systems* (Prentice-Hall, 1965) and *A Systems Analysis of Political Life* (John Wiley and Sons, 1965). Reprinted by permission of Princeton University Press.

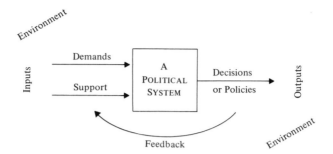

Figure 1

In combining these results, however, there is already implicit the notion that each part of the larger political canvas does not stand alone but is related to each other part; or, to put it positively, that the operation of no one part can be fully understood without reference to the way in which the whole itself operates. I have suggested in my book, *The Political System,* [1] that it is valuable to adopt this implicit assumption as an articulate premise for research and to view political life as a system of interrelated activities. These activities derive their relatedness or systemic ties from the fact that they all more or less influence the way in which authoritative decisions are formulated and executed for a society.

One we begin to speak of political life as a system of activity, certain consequences follow for the way in which we can undertake to analyze the working of a system. The very idea of a system suggests that we can separate political life from the rest of social activity, at least for analytical purposes, and examine it as though for the moment it were a self-contained entity surrounded by, but clearly distinguishable from, the environment or setting in which it operates. In much the same way, astronomers consider the solar system a complex of events isolated for certain purposes from the rest of the universe.

Furthermore, if we hold the system of political actions as a unit before our mind's eye, as it were, we can see that what keeps the system going are inputs of various kinds. These inputs are converted by the processes of the system into outputs and these, in turn, have consequences both for the system and for the environment in which the system exists. The formula here is very simple but, as I hope to show, also very illuminating: inputs—political system or processes—outputs. These relationships are shown diagrammatically in Figure 1. This diagram represents a very primitive "model"—to dignify it with a fashionable name—for approaching the study of political life.

Political systems have certain properties because they are systems. To present an overall view of the whole approach, let me identify the major

---

1. New York, 1953 [paperback edn., 1971].

attributes, say a little about each, and then treat one of these properties at somewhat greater length, even though still inadequately.

1. PROPERTIES OF IDENTIFICATION

To distinguish a political system from other social systems, we must be able to identify it by describing its fundamental units and establishing the boundaries that demarcate it from units outside the system.

a.   Units of a Political System. The units are the elements of which we say a system is composed. In the case of a political system, they are political actions. Normally it is useful to look at these as they structure themselves in political roles and political groups.

b.   Boundaries. Some of the most significant questions with regard to the operation of political systems can be answered only if we bear in mind the obvious fact that a system does not exist in a vacuum. It is always immersed in a specific setting or environment. The way in which a system works will be in part a function of its response to the total social, biological, and physical environment.

The special problem with which we are confronted is how to distinguish systematically between a political system and its setting. Does it even make sense to say that a political system has a boundary dividing it from its setting? If so, how are we to identify the line of demarcation?

Without pausing to argue the matter, I would suggest that it is useful to conceive of a political system as having a boundary in the same sense as a physical system. The boundary of a political system is defined by all those actions more or less directly related to the making of binding decisions for a society; every social action that does not partake of this characteristic will be excluded from the system and thereby will automatically be viewed as an external variable in the environment.

2. INPUTS AND OUTPUTS

Presumably, if we select political systems for special study, we do so because we believe that they have characteristically important consequences for society, namely, authoritative decisions. These consequences I shall call the outputs. If we judged that political systems did not have important outputs for society, we would probably not be interested in them.

Unless a system is approaching a state of entropy—and we can assume that this is not true of most political systems—it must have continuing inputs to keep it going. Without inputs the system can do no work; without outputs we cannot identify the work done by the system. The specific research tasks in this connection would be to identify the inputs and the forces that shape and change them, to trace the processes through which they are transformed into outputs, to describe the general conditions under which such processes can be maintained, and to establish the relationship between outputs and succeeding inputs of the system.

From this point of view, much light can be shed on the working of a political system if we take into account the fact that much of what happens within a system has its birth in the efforts of the members of the system to cope with the changing environment. We can appreciate this point if we consider a familiar biological system such as the human organism. It is subject to constant stress from its surroundings to which it must adapt in one way or another if it is not to be completely destroyed. In part, of course, the way in which the body works represents responses to needs that are generated by the very organization of its anatomy and functions; but in large part, in order to understand both the structure and the working of the body, we must also be very sensitive to the inputs from the environment.

In the same way, the behavior of every political system is to some degree imposed upon it by the kind of system it is, that is, by its own structure and internal needs. But its behavior also reflects the strains occasioned by the specific setting within which the system operates. It may be argued that most of the significant changes within a political system have their origin in shifts among the external variables. Since I shall be devoting the bulk of this article to examining some of the problems related to the exchange between political systems and their environments, I shall move on to a rapid description of other properties of political systems.

3. DIFFERENTIATION WITHIN A SYSTEM

As we shall see in a moment, from the environment come both energy to activate a system and information with regard to which the system uses this energy. In this way a system is able to do work. It has some sort of output that is different from the input that enters from the environment. We can take it as a useful hypothesis that if a political system is to perform some work for anything but a limited interval of time, a minimal amount of differentiation in its structure must occur. In fact, empirically it is impossible to find a significant political system in which the same units all perform the same activities at the same time. The members of a system engage in at least some minimal division of labor that provides a structure within which action takes place.

4. INTEGRATION OF A SYSTEM

This fact of differentiation opens up a major area of inquiry with regard to political systems. Structural differentiation sets in motion forces that are potentially disintegrative in their results for the system. If two or more units are performing different kinds of activity at the same time, how are these activities to be brought into the minimal degree of articulation necessary if the members of the system are not to end up in utter disorganization with regard to the production of the outputs of interest to us? We can hypothesize that if a structured system is to maintain itself, it must provide mechanisms whereby its members are integrated or induced to cooperate in some minimal degree so that they can make authoritative decisions.

INPUTS: DEMANDS

Now that I have mentioned some major attributes of political systems that I suggest require special attention if we are to develop a generalized approach, I want to consider in greater detail the way in which an examination of inputs and outputs will shed some light on the working of these systems.

Among inputs of a political system there are two basic kinds: demands and support. These inputs give a political system its dynamic character. They furnish it both with the raw material or information that the system is called upon to process and with the energy to keep it going.

The reason why a political system emerges in a society at all—that is, why men engage in political activity—is that demands are being made by persons or groups in the society that cannot all be fully satisfied. In all societies one fact dominates political life: scarcity prevails with regard to most of the valued things. Some of the claims for these relatively scarce things never find their way into the political system but are satisfied through the private negotiations of or settlements by the persons involved. Demands for prestige may find satisfaction through the status relations of society; claims for wealth are met in part through the economic system; aspirations for power find expression in educational, fraternal, labor, and similar private organizations. Only where wants require some special organized effort on the part of society to settle them authoritatively may we say that they have become inputs of the political system.

Systematic research would require us to address ourselves to several key questions with regard to these demands.

1.   How do demands arise and assume their particular character in a society? In answer to this question, we can point out that demands have their birth in two sectors of experience: either in the environment of a system or within the system itself. We shall call these the external and internal demands, respectively.

Let us look at the external demands first. I find it useful to see the environment not as an undifferentiated mass of events but rather as systems clearly distinguishable from one another and from the political system. In the environment we have such systems as the ecology, economy, culture, personality, social structure, and demography. Each of these constitutes a major set of variables in the setting that helps to shape the kind of demands entering a political system. For purposes of illustrating what I mean, I shall say a few words about culture.

The members of every society act within the framework of an ongoing culture that shapes their general goals, specific objectives, and the procedures that the members feel ought to be used. Every culture derives part of its unique quality from the fact that it emphasizes one or more special aspects of behavior and this strategic emphasis serves to differentiate it from other cultures with respect to the demands that it generates. As far as the mass of the people is concerned, some cultures, such as our own, are weighted heavily on the side of economic wants, success, privacy, leisure activity, and rational efficiency. Others, such as that of the Fox Indians, strive toward the maintenance of harmony, even if in the process the goals of efficiency and rationality may be sacrificed. Still others, such as the Kachins of highland Burma, stress the pursuit of power and prestige. The culture embodies the standards of value in a society and thereby marks out areas of potential conflict, if the valued things are in short supply relative to demand. The typical demands that will find their way into the political process will concern the matters in conflict that are labeled important by the culture. For this reason we cannot hope to understand the nature of the demands presenting themselves for political settlement unless we are ready to explore systematically and intensively their connection with the culture. And what I have said about culture applies, with suitable modifications, to other parts of the setting of a political system.

But not all demands originate or have their major locus in the environment. Important types stem from situations occurring within a political system itself. Typically, in every ongoing system, demands may emerge for alterations in the political relationships of the members themselves, as the result of dissatisfaction stemming from these relationships. For example, in a political system based upon representation, in which equal representation is an important political norm, demands may arise for equalizing representation between urban and rural voting districts. Similarly, demands for changes in the process of recruitment of formal political leaders, for modifications of the way in which constitutions are amended, and the like may all be internally inspired demands.

I find it useful and necessary to distinguish these from external demands because they are, strictly speaking, not inputs of the system but something that we can call "withinputs," if we can tolerate a cumbersome neologism, and because their consequences for the character of a political system are more direct than in the case of external demands. Furthermore, if we were not aware of this difference in classes of demands, we might search in vain for an explanation of the emergence of a given set of internal demands if we turned only to the environment.

2. How are demands transformed into issues? What determines whether a demand becomes a matter for serious political discussion or remains something to be resolved privately among the members of society? The occurrence of a demand, whether internal or external, does not thereby automatically convert it into a political *issue*. Many demands die at birth or linger on with the support of an insignificant fraction of the society and are never raised to the level of possible political decision. Others become issues, an issue being a demand that the members of a political system are

prepared to deal with as a significant item for discussion through the recognized channels in the system.

The distinction between demands and issues raises a number of questions about which we need data if we are to understand the processes through which claims typically become transformed into issues. For example, we would need to know something about the relationship between a demand and the location of its initiators or supporters in the power structures of the society, the importance of secrecy as compared with publicity in presenting demands, the matter of timing of demands, the possession of political skills or know-how, access to channels of communication, the attitudes and states of mind of possible publics, and the images held by the initiators of demands with regard to the way in which things get done in the particular political system. Answers to matters such as these would possibly yield a conversion index reflecting the probability of a set of demands being converted into live political issues.

If we assume that political science is primarily concerned with the way in which authoritative decisions are made for a society, demands require special attention as a major type of input of political systems. I have suggested that demands influence the behavior of a system in a number of ways. They constitute a significant part of the material upon which the system operates. They are also one of the sources of change in political systems, since as the environment fluctuates it generates new types of demand-inputs for the system. Accordingly, without this attention to the origin and determinants of demands we would be at a loss to be able to treat rigorously not only the operation of a system at a moment of time but also its change over a specified interval. Both the statics and historical dynamics of a political system depend upon a detailed understanding of demands, particularly of the impact of the setting on them.

INPUTS: SUPPORT

Inputs of demands alone are not enough to keep a political system operating. They are only the raw material out of which finished products called decisions are manufactured. Energy in the form of actions or orientations promoting and resisting a political system, the demands arising in it, and the decisions issuing from it must also be put into the system to keep it running. This input I shall call support. Without support, demands could not be satisfied or conflicts in goals composed. If demands are to be acted upon, the members of a system undertaking to pilot the demands through to their transformation into binding decisions and those who seek to influence the relevant processes in any way must be able to count on support from others in the system. Just how much support, from how many and which members of a political system, are separate and important questions that I shall touch on shortly.

What do we mean by support? We can say that A supports B either when A acts on behalf of or when he orients himself favorably toward B's goals, interests, and actions. Supportive behavior may thus be of two kinds. It may consist of actions promoting the goals, interests, and actions of another person. We may vote for a political candidate, or defend a decision by the highest court of the land. In these cases, support manifests itself through overt action.

On the other hand, supportive behavior may involve not external observable acts, but those internal forms of behavior we call orientations or states of mind. As I use the phrase, a supportive state of mind is a deep-seated set of attitudes or predispositions, or a readiness to act on behalf of some other person. It exists when we say that a man is loyal to his party, attached to democracy, or infused with patriotism. What such phrases as these have in common is the fact that they refer to a state of feelings on the part of a person. No overt action is involved at this level of description, although the implication is that the individual will pursue a course of action consistent with his attitudes. Where the anticipated action does not flow from our perception of the state of mind, we assume that we have not penetrated deeply enough into the true feelings of the person but have merely skimmed off his surface attitudes.

Supportive states of mind are vital inputs for the operation and maintenance of a political system. For example, it is often said that the struggle in the international sphere concerns mastery over men's minds. To a certain extent this is true. If the members of a political system are deeply attached to a system or its ideals, the likelihood of their participating in either domestic or foreign politics in such a way as to undermine the system is reduced by a large factor. Presumably, even in the face of considerable provocation, ingrained supportive feelings of loyalty may be expected to prevail.

We shall need to identify the typical mechanisms through which supportive attitudes are inculcated and continuously reinforced within a political system. But our prior task is to specify and examine the political objects in relation to which support is extended.

1. The Domain of Support

Support is fed into the political system in relation to three objects: the community, the regime, and the government. There must be convergence of attitude and opinion as well as some willingness to act with regard to each of these objects. Let us examine each in turn.

a. The Political Community. No political system can continue to operate unless its members are willing to support the existence of a group that seeks to settle differences or promote decisions through peaceful action in common. The point is so obvious—being dealt with usually under the heading of the growth of national unity—that it may well be overlooked; and yet it is a premise upon which the continuation of any political system depends. To refer to this phenomenon we can speak of the political community. At this level of support we are not concerned with whether a government exists or whether there is loyalty to a constitutional order. For the moment we only ask whether the members of the group that we are examining are sufficiently oriented toward each other to want to contribute their collective energies toward pacific settlement of their varying demands.

The American Civil War is a concrete illustration of the cessation of input of support for the political community. The war itself was definitive evidence that the members of the American political system could no longer contribute to the existence of a state of affairs in which peaceful solution of conflicting demands was the rule. Matters had come to the point where it was no longer a question of whether the South would support one or another alternative government, or whether it could envision its demands being satisfied through the normal constitutional procedures. The issue turned on whether there was sufficient mutual identification among the members of the system for them to be able to work together as a political community. Thus in any political system, to the extent that there is an in-group or we-group feeling and to the extent that the members of the system identify one another as part of this unit and exclude others according to some commonly accepted criteria, such as territoriality, kinship, or citizenship, we shall say that they are putting in support for the political community.

b.   The Regime. Support for a second major part of a political system helps to supply the energy to keep the system running. This aspect of the system I shall call the regime. It consists of all those arrangements that regulate the way in which the demands put into the system are settled and the way in which decisions are put into effect. They are the so-called rules of the game, in the light of which actions by members of the system are legitimated and accepted by the bulk of the members as authoritative. Unless there is a minimum convergence of attitudes in support of these fundamental rules—the constitutional principles, as we call them in Western society—there would be insufficient harmony in the actions of the members of a system to meet the problems generated by their support of a political community. The fact of trying to settle demands in common means that there must be known principles governing the way in which resolutions of differences of claims are to take place.

c.   The Government. If a political system is going to be able to handle the conflicting demands put into it, not only must the members of the system be prepared to support the settlement of these conflicts in common and possess some consensus with regard to the rules governing the mode of settlement; they must also be ready to support a government as it undertakes the concrete tasks involved in negotiating such settlements. When we come to the outputs of a system, we shall see the rewards that are available to a government for mobilizing support. At this point, I just wish to draw attention to this need on the part of a government for support if it is going to be able to make decisions with regard to demands. Of course, a government may elicit support in many ways: through persuasion, consent, or manipulation. It may also impose unsupported settlements of demands through threats of force. But it is a familiar axiom of political science that a government based upon force alone is not long for this world; it must buttress its position by inducing a favorable state of mind in its subjects through fair or foul means.

The fact that support directed to a political system can be broken down conceptually into three elements—support for the community, regime, and government—does not mean, of course, that in the concrete case support for each of these three objects is independent. In fact we might and normally do find all three kinds of support very closely intertwined, so that the presence of one is a function of the presence of one or both of the other types.

For example, withdrawal of support from the government of Louis XVI in effect also meant that members of the French monarchical system were challenging at least the regime; as it turned out in the ensuing revolution and civil war, there was even doubt whether the members of the system would continue to support a unified political community. In this case, what was initially opposition to the ruling sovereign—that is, to the government— quickly turned out to signify a lack of sufficient support for the regime and ultimately, to some extent, for the political community. But this is not always so and fortunately, from the point of view of social order, it is not typically the case. We are accustomed to calling for a change of government without thereby suggesting dissatisfaction with the regime or community. And at times, although this is less frequently true, the community shows sufficient intention to continue as a cooperating group to be able to accept a challenge to the regime. From 1832 to the 1880s England underwent a serious modification in its regime, introducing the basic elements of a system of popular democracy, without serious diminution of input of support at the community level. It is always a matter for empirical enquiry to discover the degree to which support at any one level is dependent upon support at the others.

This very brief discussion of support points up one major fact. If a system is to absorb a variety of demands and negotiate some sort of settlement among them, it is not enough for the members of the system to support only their own demands and the particular government that will undertake to promote these demands. For the demands to be processed into outputs it is equally essential that the members of the system stand ready to support the existence of a political community and some stable rules of common action that we call the regime.

2. Quantity and Scope of Support

How much support needs to be put into a system and how many of its members need to contribute such support if the system is to be able to do the job of converting demands to decisions? No ready answer can be offered. The actual situation in each case would determine the amount and scope required. We can, however, visualize a number of situations that will be helpful in directing our attention to possible generalizations.

Under certain circumstances very few members need to support a system at any level. The members might be dull and apathetic, indifferent to the general operations of the system, its progress or decisions. In a loosely connected system such as India has had, this might well be the state of mind of by far the largest segment of the membership. Either in fact they have not been affected by national decisions or they have not perceived that they were so affected. They may have little sense of identification with the present regime and government and yet, with regard to the input of demand, the system may be able to act on the basis of the support offered by the known 3 percent of the Western-oriented politicians and intellectuals who are politically active. In other words, we can have a small minority putting in quantitatively sufficient supportive energy to keep the system going. However, we can venture the hypothesis that where members of a system are putting in numerous demands, there is a strong probability that they will actively offer support or hostility at one of the three levels of the system, depending upon the degree to which these demands are being met through appropriate decisions.

Alternatively, we may find that all the members of a system are putting in support, but the amount may be so low as to place one or all aspects of the system in jeopardy. Modern France is perhaps a classic illustration. The input of support at the level of the political community is probably adequate for the maintenance of France as a national political unit. But for a variety of historical and contemporary reasons, there is considerable doubt as to whether the members of the French political system are putting in anything but a low order of support to the regime or any particular government. This low amount of support, even though spread over a relatively large segment of the population, leaves the French political system on somewhat less secure foundations than is the case with India. There support is less widespread but more active—that is, quantitatively greater—on the part of a minority. As this illustration indicates, the amount of support is not necessarily proportional to its scope.

It may seem from the above discussion as though the members of a political system either put in support or withhold it— that is, demonstrate hostility or apathy. In fact, members may and normally do simultaneously engage in supportive and hostile behavior. What we must be interested in is the net balance of support.

MECHANISMS OF SUPPORT

To this point I have suggested that no political system can yield the important outputs we call authoritative decisions unless, in addition to demands, support finds its way into the system. I have discussed the possible object to which support may be directed, and some problems with regard to the domain, quantity, and scope of support. We are now ready to turn to the main question raised by our attention to support as a crucial input: how do systems typically manage to maintain a steady flow of support? Without it a system will not absorb sufficient energy from its members to be able to convert demands to decisions.

In theory, there might be an infinite variety of means through which members could be induced to support a system; in practice, certain well-established classes of mechanisms are used. Research in this area needs to be directed to exploring the precise way in which a particular system utilizes these mechanisms and to refining our understanding of the way in which they contribute to the making of authoritative policy.

A society generates support for a political system in two ways: through outputs that meet the demands of the members of society; and through the processes of politicization. Let us look at outputs first.

Outputs as a Mechanism of Support

An output of a political system, it will be recalled, is a political decision or policy. One of the major ways of strengthening the ties of the members to their system is through providing decisions that tend to satisfy the day-to-day demands of these members. Fundamentally this is the truth that lies in the aphorism that one can fool some of the people some of the time but not all of them all of the time. Without some minimal satisfaction of demands, the ardor of all but the most fanatical patriot is sure to cool. The outputs, consisting of political decisions, constitute a body of specific inducements for the members of a system to support that system.

Inducements of this kind may be positive or negative. Where negative, they threaten the members of the system with various kinds of sanctions ranging from a small monetary fine to physical detention, ostracism, or loss of life, as in our own system with regard to the case of legally defined treason. In every system support stems in part from fear of sanctions or compulsion; in autocratic systems the proportion of coerced support is at a maximum. For want of space I shall confine myself to those cases where positive incentives loom largest.

Since the specific outputs of a system are policy decisions, it is upon the government that the final responsibility falls for matching or balancing outputs of decisions against input of demand. But it is clear that to obtain the support of the members of a system through positive incentives, a government need not meet all the demands of even its most influential and ardent supporters. Most governments, or groups such as political parties that seek to control governments, succeed in building up a reserve of support. This reserve will carry the government along even though it offends its followers, so long as over the extended short run these followers perceive the particular government as one that is in general favorable to their interests. One form that this reserve support takes in Western society is that of party loyalty, since the party is the typical instrument in a mass industrialized society for mobilizing and maintaining support for a government. However, continuous lack of specific rewards through policy decisions ultimately leads to the danger that even the deepest party loyalty may be shaken.

For example, labor has continued to support the Democratic Party even though much of the legislation promoted by members of that party has not served to meet labor's demands. In some measure, large sections of labor may continue to vote and campaign vigorously on behalf of the Democratic Party because they have no realistic alternative other than to support this party; but in addition the Democrats have built up in recent years, especially during the Roosevelt era, a considerable body of good will. It would take repeated neglect of labor's demands on the part of the Democratic Party to undermine the strong urban working-class support directed toward it and the government that the party dominates from time to time.

Thus a system need not meet *all the demands* of its members so long as it has stored up a reserve of support over the years. Nor need it satisfy even *some of the demands* of all its members. Just whose demands a system must seek to meet, how much of their demands, at what time, and under what conditions are questions for special research. We can say in advance that at least the demands of the most influential members require satisfaction. But this tells us little unless we know how to discover the influentials in a political system and how new sets of members rise to positions of influence.

The critical significance of the decisions of governments for the support of the other two aspects of a system—namely, the political community and the regime—is clear from what I have said above. Not all withdrawal of support from a government has consequences for the success or failure of a regime or community. But persistent inability of a government to produce satisfactory outputs for the members of a system may well lead to demands for changing of the regime or for dissolution of the political community. It is for this reason that the input-output balance is a vital mechanism in the life of a political system.

Politicization as a Mechanism of Support

It would be wrong to consider that the level of support available to a system is a function exclusively of the outputs in the form of either sanctions or rewards. If we did so conclude, we could scarcely account for the maintenance of numerous political systems in which satisfaction of demands has been manifestly low, in which public coercion is limited, and yet which have endured for epochs. Alternately, it might be difficult to explain how political systems could endure and yet manage to flout or thwart urgent demands, failing thereby to render sufficient *quid pro quo* for the input of support. The fact is that whatever reserve of support has been accumulated through past decisions is increased and reinforced by a complicated method for steadily manufacturing support through what I shall call the process of politicization. It is an awkward term, but nevertheless an appropriately descriptive one.

As each person grows up in a society, through a network of rewards and punishments the other members of society communicate to and instill in him the various institutionalized goals and norms of that society. This is well known in social research as the process of socialization. Through its operation a person learns to play his various social roles. Part of these goals and norms relate to what the society considers desirable in political life. The ways in which these political patterns are learned by the members of society constitute what I call the process of politicization. Through it a person learns to play his political roles, which include the absorption of the proper political attitudes.

Let us examine a little more closely something of what happens during the process of politicization. As members of a society mature, they must absorb the various orientations toward political matters that one is expected to have in that society. If the expectations of the members of society with regard to the way each should behave in specific political situations diverged beyond a certain range, it would be impossible to get common action with regard to the making of binding decisions. It is essential for the viability of an orderly political system that the members of the system have some common basic expectations with regard to the standards that are to be used in making political evaluations, to the way people will feel about various political matters, and to the way members of the system will perceive and interpret political phenomena.

The mechanism through which this learning takes place is of considerable significance in understanding how a political system generates and accumulates a strong reserve of support. Although we cannot pursue the details, we can mention a few of the relevant dimensions. In the first place, of course, the learning or politicization process does not stop at any particular period for the individual; it starts with the child and, in the light of our knowledge of learning, may have its deepest impact through the teen age. The study of the political experiences of and the influences operating on the child and the adolescent emerges as an important and neglected area of research.

In the second place, the actual process of politicization at its most general level brings in to operation a complex network of rewards and punishments. For adopting the correct political attitudes and performing the right political acts, for conforming to the generally accepted interpretations of political goals, and for undertaking the institutionalized obligations of a member of the given system, we are variously rewarded or punished. For conforming we are made to feel worthy, wanted, and respected and often obtain material advantages such as wealth, influence, improved opportunities. For deviating beyond the permissible range, we are made to feel unworthy, rejected, dishonored, and often suffer material losses.

This does not mean that the pattern of rewards and punishments is by any means always effective; if it were, we would never have changed from the Stone Age. A measure of nonconformity may at certain stages in the life history of a political system itself become a respected norm. Even where this is not the case, the most seductive rewards and the severest punishments will never succeed in preventing some of the members of a system from pursuing what they consider to be their inextinguishable interests and from seeking, with varying degrees of success, to change the goals and norms of the system. This is one of the important sources of political change closely associated with changes in the inputs of demands that are due to a changing environment. But we cannot pursue this crucial matter of the nature of political change, as it would lead us off in a new direction.

In the third place, the means used for communicating the goals and norms to others tend to be repetitive in all societies. The various political myths, doctrines, and philosophies transmit to each generation a particular interpretation of the goals and norms. The decisive links in this chain of transmission are parents, siblings, peers, teachers, organizations, and social leaders, as well as physical symbols such as flags or totems, ceremonies, and rituals freighted with political meaning.

These processes through which attachments to a political system become built into the maturing member of a society I have lumped together under the rubric of politicization. They illustrate the way in which members of a system learn what is expected of them. In this way they acquire knowledge about their political roles and a desire to perform them. In stable systems the support that accrues through these means adds to the reservoir of support being accumulated on a day-to-day basis through the outputs of decisions. The support obtained through politicization tends to be relatively—although, as we have seen, not wholly—independent of the vagaries of day-to-day outputs.

When the basic political attachments become deeply rooted or institutionalized, we say that the system has become accepted as legitimate. Politicization therefore effectively sums up the way in which legitimacy is created and transmitted in a political system. And it is an empirical observation that in those instances where political systems have survived the longest, support has been nourished by an ingrained belief in the legitimacy of the relevant governments and regimes.

What I am suggesting here is that support resting on a sense of the legitimacy of a government and regime provides a necessary reserve if the system is to weather those frequent storms when the more obvious outputs of the system seem to impose greater hardships than rewards. Answers to questions concerning the formation, maintenance, transmission, and change of standards of legitimacy will contribute generously to an understanding of the way in which support is sufficiently institutionalized so that a system may regularly and without excessive expenditure of effort transform inputs of demand into outputs of decisions.

That there is a need for general theory in the study of political life is apparent. The only question is how best to proceed. There is no one royal road that can be said to be either the correct one or the best. It is only a matter of what appears at the given level of available knowledge to be the most useful. At this stage it appears that system theory, with its sensitivity to the input-output exchange between a system and its setting offers a fruitful approach. It is an economical way of organizing presently disconnected political data and promises interesting dividends.

Constitutional Democracy: The Rule of Law

The Western political heritage has emphasized the importance of democracy and the rule of law. As early as Aristotle's *Politics,* the viability of democracy, provided there are sufficient checks upon unlimited popular rule, has been stressed.

The American constitutional tradition reflects the beliefs of many political philosophers. One of the most dominating figures is John Locke. It is not suggested that Locke was read by most of the colonists, but only that his ideas invariably found their way into many writings of eighteenth-century America, most importantly the Declaration of Independence. In a letter to Henry Lee in 1825, Thomas Jefferson wrote:

"When forced . . . to resort to arms for redress, an appeal to the tribunal of the world was deemed proper for our justification. This was the object of the Declaration of Independence. Not to find out new principles, or new arguments, never before thought of, not merely to say things which had never been said before; but to place before mankind the common sense of the subject, in terms so plain and firm as to command their assent, and to justify ourselves in the independent stand we are compelled to take. Neither aiming at originality of principle or sentiment, nor yet copied from any particular and previous writing, it was intended to be an expression of the American mind, and to give to that expression the proper tone and spirit called for by the occasion. All its authority rests then on the harmonizing sentiments of the day, whether expressed in conversation, in letters, printed essays, or in the elementary books of public right [such] as Aristotle, Cicero, Locke, Sidney, etc. . . . "

In May of 1790, Jefferson wrote: "Locke's little book on government is perfect as far as it goes." Although Jefferson's admiration of Locke was perhaps greater than that of many other colonists, his views did reflect a mood of eighteenth-century America. Locke's *Second Treatise, Of Civil Government* attempted to trace the reasons why men enter into political societies in the first place. The eighteenth century, no less than the twentieth, was an era characterized by attempts to be "scientific" in political formulations. Locke's *Second Treatise,* first published in 1690, reflected the scientific emphasis that was to prevail so widely beginning in the eighteenth century. To Locke, natural law was objectively valid, and therefore once ascertained, governments based upon it would have a superior claim to legitimacy. Locke is notable for his discussions of natural law, from which he derived the "best" form of government. In reading Locke, one should observe how much importance he placed upon property rights and the right of the people to dissolve government once it no longer meets their legitimate expectations.

7
John Locke

SECOND TREATISE, OF CIVIL GOVERNMENT

OF THE STATE OF NATURE

To understand political power aright, and derive it from its original, we must consider what estate all men are naturally in, and that is, a state of perfect freedom to order their actions, and dispose of their possessions and persons as they think fit, within the bounds of the laws of Nature, without asking leave or depending upon the will of any other man.

A state also of equality, wherein all the power and jurisdiction is reciprocal, no one having more than another, there being nothing more evident than that creatures of the same species and rank, promiscuously born to all the same advantages of Nature, and the use of the same faculties, should also be equal one amongst another, without subordination or subjection, unless the lord and master of them all should, by any manifest declaration of his will, set one above another, and confer on him, by an evident and clear appointment, an undoubted right to dominion and sovereignty. . . .

But though this be a state of liberty, yet it is not a state of license; though man in that state have an uncontrollable liberty to dispose of his person or possessions, yet he has not liberty to destroy himself, or so much as any creature in his possession, but where some nobler use than its bare preservation calls for it. The state of Nature has a law of Nature to govern it, which obliges every one, and reason, which is that law, teaches all mankind who will but consult it, that being all equal and independent, no one ought to harm another in his life, health, liberty or possessions. . . . And, being furnished with like faculties, sharing all in one community of Nature, there cannot be supposed any such subordination among us that may authorize us to destroy one another, as if we were made for one another's uses, as the inferior ranks of creatures are for ours. Every one as he is bound to preserve himself, and not to quit his station wilfully, so by the like reason, when his own preservation comes not in competition, ought he as much as he can to preserve the rest of mankind, and not unless it be to do justice on an offender, take away or impair the life, or what tends to the preservation of the life, the liberty, health, limb, or goods of another.

And that all men may be restrained from invading others' rights, and from doing hurt to one another, and the law of Nature be observed, which willeth the peace and preservation of all mankind, the execution of the law of Nature is in that state put into every man's hands, whereby every one has a right to punish the transgressors of that law to such a degree as may hinder its violation. For the law of Nature would, as all other laws that concern men in this world, be in vain if there were nobody that in the state of Nature had a power to execute that law, and thereby preserve the innocent and restrain offenders; and if any one in the state of Nature may punish another for any evil he has done, every one may do so. For in that state of perfect equality, where naturally there is no superiority or jurisdiction of one over another, what any may do in prosecution of that law, every one must needs have a right to do.

And thus, in the state of Nature, one man comes by a power over another, but yet no absolute or arbitrary power to use a criminal, when he has got him in his hands, according to the passionate heats or boundless extravagancy of his own will, but only to retribute to him so far as calm reason and conscience dictate, what is proportionate to his transgression, which is so much as may serve for reparation and restraint. . . .

Every offence that can be committed in the state of Nature may, in the state of Nature, be also punished equally, and as far forth, as it may, in a commonwealth. For-though it would be beside my present purpose to enter here into the particulars of the law of Nature, or its measures of punishment, yet it is certain there is such a law, and that too as intelligible and plain to a rational creature and a studier of that law as the positive laws of commonwealths, nay, possibly plainer; as much as reason is easier to be understood than the fancies and intricate contrivances of men, following contrary and hidden interests put into words. . . .

OF THE ENDS OF POLITICAL SOCIETY AND GOVERNMENT

If man in the state of Nature be so free as has been said, if he be absolute lord of his own person and possessions, equal to the greatest and subject to nobody, why will he part with his freedom, this empire, and subject himself to the dominion and control of any other power? To which it is obvious to answer, that though in the state of Nature he hath such a right, yet the enjoyment of it is very uncertain and constantly exposed to the invasion of others; for all being kings as much as he, every man his equal, and the greater part no strict observers of equity and justice, the enjoyment of the property he has in this state is very unsafe, very insecure. This makes him willing to quit this condition which, however free, is full of fears and continual dangers; and it is not without reason that he seeks out and is willing to join in society with others who are already united, or have a mind to unite for the mutual preservation of their lives, liberties, and estates, which I call by the general name—property.

The great and chief end, therefore, of men uniting into commonwealths, and putting themselves under government, is the preservation of their property; to which in the state of Nature there are many things wanting.

Firstly, there wants an established, settled, known law, received and allowed by common consent to be the standard or right and wrong, and the common measure to decide all controversies between them. For though the law of Nature be plain and intelligible to all rational creatures, yet men, being biased by their interest, as well as ignorant for want of study of it, are not apt to allow of it as a law binding to them in the application of it to their particular cases.

Secondly, in the state of Nature there wants a known and indifferent judge, with authority to determine all differences according to the established law. For every one in that state being both judge and executioner of the law of Nature, men being partial to themselves, passion and revenge is very apt to carry them too far, and with too much heat in their own cases, as well as negligence and unconcernedness, make them too remiss in other men's.

Thirdly, in the state of Nature there often wants power to back and support the sentence when right, and to give it due execution. They who by any injustice offended will seldom fail where they are able by force to make good their injustice. Such resistance many times makes the punishment dangerous, and frequently destructive to those who attempt it.

Thus mankind, notwithstanding all the privileges of the state of Nature, being but in an ill condition while they remain in it are quickly driven into society. Hence it comes to pass, that we seldom find any number of men live any time together in this state. The inconveniences that they are therein exposed to by the irregular and uncertain exercise of the power every man has of punishing the transgressions of others, make them take sanctuary under the established laws of government, and therein seek the preservation of their property. It is this makes them so willingly give up every one his single power of punishing to be exercised by such alone as shall be appointed to it amongst them, and by such rules as the community, or those authorised by them to that purpose, shall agree on. And in this we have the original right and rise of both the legislative and executive power as well as of the governments and societies themselves.

For in the state of Nature to omit the liberty he has of innocent delights, a man has two powers. The first is to do whatsoever he thinks fit for the preservation of himself and others within the permission of the law of Nature; by which law, common to them all, he and all the rest of mankind are one community, make up one society distinct from all other creatures, and were it not for the corruption and viciousness of degenerate men, there would be no need of any other, no necessity that men should separate from this great and natural community, and associate into lesser combinations. The other power a man has in the state of Nature is the power to punish the crimes committed against that law. Both these he gives up when he joins in a private, if I may so call it, or particular political society, and incorporates into any commonwealth separate from the rest of mankind.

The first power—viz., of doing whatsoever he thought fit for the preservation of himself and the rest of mankind, he gives up to be regulated by laws made by the society, so far forth as the preservation of himself and the rest of that society shall require; which laws of the society in many things confine the liberty he had by the law of Nature.

Secondly, the power of punishing he wholly gives up, and engages his natural force, which he might before employ in the execution of the law of Nature, by his own single authority, as he thought fit, to assist the executive power of the society as the law thereof shall require. For being now in a new state, wherein he is to enjoy many conveniences from the labor, assistance, and society of others in the same community, as well as protection from its whole strength, he is to part also with as much of his natural liberty, in providing for himself, as the good, prosperity, and safety of the society shall require, which is not only necessary but just, since the other members of the society do the like.

But though men when they enter into society give up the equality, liberty, and executive power they had in the state of Nature into the hands of the society, to be so far disposed of by the legislative as the good of the society shall require, yet it being only with an intention in every one the better to preserve himself, his liberty and property (for no rational creature can be supposed to change his condition with an intention to be worse), the power of the society or legislative constituted by them can never be supposed to extend farther than the common against those three defects above mentioned that made the state of Nature so unsafe and uneasy. And so, whoever has the legislative or supreme power of any commonwealth, is bound to govern by established standing laws, promulgated and known to the people, and not by extemporary decrees, by indifferent and upright judges, who are to decide controversies by those laws; and to employ the force of the community at home only in the execution of such laws, or abroad to prevent or redress foreign injuries and secure the community from inroads and invasion. And all this to be directed to no other end but the peace, safety, and public good of the people. . . .

OF THE EXTENT OF THE LEGISLATIVE POWER

The great end of men's entering into society being the enjoyment of their properties in peace and safety, and the great instrument and means of that being the laws established in that society, the first and fundamental positive law of all commonwealths is the establishing of the legislative power, as the first and fundamental natural law, which is to govern even the legislative itself, is the preservation of the society and (as far as will consist with the public good) of every person in it. This legislative is not only the supreme power of the commonwealth, but sacred and unalterable in the hands where the community have once placed it. Nor can any edict of anybody else, in what form soever conceived, or by what power soever backed, have the force and obligation of a law which has not its sanction from that legislative which the public has chosen and appointed; for without this the law could not have that which is absolutely necessary to its being a law, the consent of the society, over whom nobody can have a power to make laws but by their own consent and by authority received from them. . . .

These are the bounds which the trust that is put in them by the society and the law of God and Nature have set to the legislative power of every commonwealth, in all forms of government. First: They are to govern by promulgated established laws, not to be varied in particular cases, but to have one rule for rich and poor, for the favorite at Court and the countryman at plough. Secondly: These laws also ought to be designed for no other end ultimately but the good of the people. Thirdly: They must not raise taxes on the property of the people without the consent of the people given by themselves or their deputies. And this properly concerns only such governments where the legislative is always in being, or at least where the people have not reserved any part of the legislative to deputies, to be from time to time chosen by themselves. Fourthly: Legislative neither must nor can transfer the power of making laws to anybody else, or place it anywhere but where the people have. . . .

OF THE DISSOLUTION OF GOVERNMENT

The constitution of the legislative [authority] is the first and fundamental act of society, whereby provision is made for the continuation of their union under the direction of persons and bonds of laws, made by persons authorised thereunto, by the consent and appointment of the people, without which no one man, or number of men, amongst them can have authority of making laws that shall be binding to the rest. When any one, or more, shall take upon them to make laws whom the people have not appointed so to do, they make laws without authority, which the people are not therefore bound to obey; by which means they come again to be out of subjection, and may constitute to themselves a new legislative, as they think best, being in full liberty to resist the force of those who, without authority, would impose anything upon them. . . .

Whosoever uses force without right—as every one does in society who does it without law—puts himself into a state of war with those against whom he so uses it, and in that state all former ties are cancelled, all other rights cease, and every one has a right to defend himself, and to resist the aggressor. . . .

Here it is like the common question will be made: Who shall be judge whether the prince or legislative act contrary to their trust? This, perhaps, ill-affected and factious men may spread amongst the people, when the prince only makes use of his due prerogative. To this I reply, The people shall be judge; for who shall be judge whether his trustee or deputy acts well and according to the trust reposed in him, but he who deputes him and must, by having deputed him, have still a power to discard him when he fails in his trust? If this be reasonable in particular cases of private men, why should it be otherwise in that of the greatest moment, where the welfare of millions is concerned and also where the evil, if not prevented, is greater, and the redress very difficult, dear, and dangerous? . . .

To conclude. The power that every individual gave the society when he entered into it can never revert to the individuals again, as long as the society lasts, but will always remain in the community; because without this there can be no community—no commonwealth, which is contrary to the original agreement; so also when the society hath placed the legislative in any assembly of men, to continue in them and their successors, with direction and authority for providing such successors, the legislative can never revert to the people whilst that government lasts; because, having provided a legislative with power to continue for ever, they have given up their political power to the legislative, and cannot resume it. But if they have set limits to the duration of their legislative, and made this supreme power in any person or assembly only temporary; or else when, by the miscarriages of those in authority, it is forfeited; upon the forfeiture of their rulers, or at the determination of the time set, it reverts to the society, and the people have a right to act as supreme, and continue the legislative in themselves or place it in a new form, or new hands, as they think good.

The influence of John Locke goes far beyond his impact on the thinking of the founding fathers of the United States, such as Thomas Jefferson. Some scholars (among them, Louis Hartz, *The Liberal Tradition in America*) have interpreted the American political tradition in terms of the pervasive attachment to the ideas and values set forth in the writings of Locke. There is little question that American political life has been uniquely characterized by widespread adherence to the fundamental principles about the relations among men, society, and government expressed in Locke's writings.

It is not just that we have representative government, with institutions similar in structure and function to those of the constitutional democracy described in Locke's *Second Treatise,* but that through the years we have probably maintained, more than any other society, a widespread agreement about the fundamental human values cherished by Locke. His emphasis upon the sanctity of private property has been paramount in the American political tradition from the very beginning. Moreover, Locke's views on the nature of man are shared by most Americans. All our governmental institutions, processes, and traditions rest upon principles such as the primacy of the individual, man's inborn ability to exercise reason in order to discern truth and higher principles of order and justice, and a political and social equality among men in which no man shall count for more than another in determining the actions of government and their application. We may not have always practiced these ideals, but we have been *theoretically* committed to them.

CHAPTER 2

Constitutional Government

A remarkable fact about the United States government is that it has operated for over 180 years on the basis of a written Constitution. Does this suggest unusual sagacity on the part of the Founding Fathers, or exceptional luck? What was involved in framing the Constitution?

Framing the Constitution:
An Elitist or Democratic Process?

Charles Beard in his famous *Economic Interpretation of the Constitution* suggests that the framers of the Constitution were a small elite group who had substantial financial interests in the community, and who therefore were not representative of the broader political spectrum of that time. As they drafted the Constitution, their primary concern, according to Beard, was to limit the power of popular majorities and thus to protect their own property. The Constitution does contain many provisions that limit majority rule. Beard claims that the Constitution from initial adoption to final ratification was never supported by the majority of the people. Holding a Constitutional Convention in the first place was never submitted to a popular vote, nor was the Constitution that was finally agreed upon ratified by a popular referendum. A selection of delegates to ratifying conventions in the states was not done through a broad popular vote, but on the basis of suffrage qualifications that were within the discretion of state legislatures. Generally, voters qualified to vote for state legislatures were enfranchised to vote for delegates to ratifying conventions. Beard's thesis, much of which seems obvious to modern observers, was startling at the time it was published in 1913. Although those who framed the Constitution represented a very small segment of the public, nevertheless the instrument they drafted has endured and has been used to expand the democratic process to the farthest possible limits. However, as John P. Roche points out, the drafting of the Constitution itself was a highly political process in which numerous compromises among state factions and varying viewpoints were necessary.

8

John P. Roche

THE FOUNDING FATHERS:
A REFORM CAUCUS IN ACTION

Over the last century and a half, the work of the Constitutional Convention, and the motives of the Founding Fathers have been analyzed under a number of different ideological auspices. To one generation of historians, the hand of God was moving in the assembly; under a later dispensation, the dialectic (at various levels of philosophical sophistication) replaced the Deity: "relationships of production" moved into the niche previously reserved for Love of Country. Thus in counterpart to the Zeitgeist, the framers have undergone miraculous metamorphoses: at one time acclaimed as liberals and bold social engineers, today they appear in the guise of sound Burkean conservatives, men who in our time would subscribe to *Fortune,* look to Walter Lippmann for political theory, and chuckle patronizingly at the antics of Barry Goldwater. The implicit assumption is that if James Madison were among us, he would be President of the Ford Foundation, while Alexander Hamilton would chair the Committee for Economic Development.

The "Fathers" have thus been admitted to our best circles; the revolutionary ferocity which confiscated all Tory property in reach and populated New Brunswick with outlaws has been converted by the "Miltown School" of American historians into a benign dedication to "consensus" and "prescriptive rights." The Daughters of the American Revolution have, through the ministrations of Professors Boorstin, Hartz, and Rossiter, at last found ancestors worthy of their descendants. It is not my purpose here to argue that the "Fathers" were, in fact, radical revolutionaries; that proposition has been brilliantly demonstrated by Robert R. Palmer in his *Age of the Democratic Revolution.* My concern is with the future position that not only were they revolutionaries, but also they were democrats. Indeed, in my view, there is one fundamental truth about the Founding Fathers that *every* generation of Zeitgeisters has done its best to obscure: they were first and foremost superb democratic politicians. I suspect that in a contemporary setting, James Madison would be Speaker of the House of Representatives and Hamilton would be the *eminence grise* dominating (*pace* Theodore Sorensen or Sherman Adams) the Executive Office of the President. They were, with their colleagues, *political men*—not metaphysicians, disembodied conservatives or Agents of

From John P. Roche, "The Founding Fathers: A Reform Caucus in Action," *American Political Science Review* (December 1961). Reprinted by permission.

History—and as recent research into the nature of American politics in the 1780s confirms, they were committed (perhaps willy-nilly) to working within the democratic framework, within a universe of public approval. Charles Beard *and* the filiopietists to the contrary notwithstanding, the Philadelphia Convention was not a College of Cardinals or a council of Platonic guardians working within a manipulative, predemocratic framework; it was a *nationalist* reform caucus which had to operate with great delicacy and skill in a political cosmos full of enemies to achieve the one definitive goal—popular approbation.

Perhaps the time has come, to borrow Walton Hamilton's fine phrase, to raise the framers from immortality to mortality, to give them credit for their magnificent demonstration of the art of democratic politics. The point must be reemphasized; they *made* history and did it within the limits of consensus. There was nothing inevitable about the future in 1787; the *Zeitgeist,* that fine Hegelian technique of begging causal questions, could only be discerned in retrospect. What they did was to hammer out a pragmatic compromise which would both bolster the "National interest" and be acceptable to the people. What inspiration they got came from their collective experience as professional politicians in a democratic society. As John Dickinson put it to his fellow delegates on August 13, "Experience must be our guide. Reason may mislead us."

In this context, let us examine the problems they confronted and the solutions they evolved. The Convention has been described picturesquely as a counter-revolutionary junta and the Constitution as a coup d'état, but this has been accomplished by withdrawing the whole history of the movement for constitutional reform from its true context. No doubt the goals of the constitutional elite were "subversive" to the existing political order, but it is overlooked that their subversion could only have succeeded if the people of the United States endorsed it by regularized procedures. Indubitably they were "plotting" to establish a much stronger central government than existed under the Articles, but only in the sense in which one could argue equally well that John F. Kennedy was, from 1956 to 1960, "plotting" to become President. In short, on the fundamental *procedural* level, the Constitutionalists had to work according to the prevailing rules of the game. Whether they liked it or not is a topic for spiritualists—and is irrelevant: one may be quite certain that had Washington agreed to play the de Gaulle (as the Cincinnati once urged), Hamilton would willingly have held his horse, but such fertile speculation in no way alters the actual context in which events took place.

I

When the Constitutionalists went forth to subvert the Confederation, they utilized the mechanisms of political legitimacy. And the roadblocks which confronted them were formidable. At the same time, they were endowed with certain potent political assets. The history of the United States from 1786 to 1790 was largely one of a masterful employment of political expertise by the Constitutionalists as against bumbling, erratic behavior by the opponents of reform. Effectively, the Constitutionalists had to induce the states, by democratic techniques of coercion, to emasculate themselves. To be specific, if New York had refused to join the new Union, the project was doomed; yet before New York was safely in, the reluctant state legislature had *suasponte* to take the following steps: (1) agree to send delegates to the Philadelphia Convention; (2) provide maintenance for these delegates (these were distinct stages: New Hampshire was early in naming delegates, but did not provide for their maintenance until July); (3) set up the special ad hoc convention to decide on ratification; and (4) concede to the decision of the ad hoc convention that New York should participate. New York admittedly was a tricky state, with a strong interest in a status quo which permitted her to exploit New Jersey and Connecticut, but the same legal hurdles existed in every state. And at the risk of becoming boring, it must be reiterated that the *only* weapon in the Constitutionalist arsenal was an effective mobilization of public opinion.

The group which undertook this struggle was an interesting amalgam of a few dedicated nationalists with the self-interested spokesmen of various parochial bailiwicks. The Georgians, for example, wanted a strong central authority to provide military protection for their huge, underpopulated state against the Creek Confederacy; Jerseymen and Connecticuters wanted to escape from economic bondage to New York; the Virginians hoped to establish a system which would give that great state its rightful place in the councils of the republic. The dominant figures in the politics of these states therefore cooperated in the call for the Convention. In other states, the thrust towards national reform was taken up by opposition groups who added the "national interest" to their weapons system; in Pennsylvania, for instance, the group fighting to revise the Constitution of 1776 came out four-square behind the Constitutionalists, and in New York, Hamilton and the Schuyler *ambiance* took the same tack against George Clinton. There was, of course, a large element of personality in the affair: there is reason to suspect that Patrick Henry's opposition to the Convention and the Constitution was founded on his conviction that Jefferson was behind both, and a close study of local politics elsewhere would surely reveal that others supported the Constitution for the simple (and politically quite sufficient) reason that the "wrong" people were against it.

To say this is not to suggest that the Constitution rested on a foundation of impure or base motives. It is rather to argue that in politics there are no immaculate conceptions, and that in the drive for a stronger general government, motives of all sorts played a part. Few men in the history of mankind have espoused a view of the "common good" or "public interest" that militated against their private status; even Plato with all his reverence for disembodied reason managed to put philosophers on top of the pile. Thus it is not suprising that a number of diversified private interests joined to push the nationalist public interest; what would have been surprising was the absence of such a pragmatic united front. And the fact remains that, however motivated, these men did demonstrate a willingness to compromise their parochial interests in behalf of an ideal which took shape before their eyes and under their ministrations.

As Stanley Elkins and Eric McKitrick have suggested in a perceptive essay [76 *Political Science Quarterly* 181 (1961)], what distinguished the leaders of the Constitutionalist caucus from their enemies was a "Continental" approach to political, economic and military issues. To the extent that they shared an institutional base of operations, it was the Continental Congress (thirty-nine of the delegates to the Federal Convention had served in Congress), and this was hardly a locale which inspired respect for the state governments. Robert de Jouvenal observed French politics half a century ago and noted that a revolutionary Deputy had more in common with a nonrevolutionary Deputy than he had with a revolutionary non-Deputy; similarly one can surmise that membership in the Congress under the Articles of Confederation worked to establish a continental frame of reference, that a Congressman from Pennsylvania and one from South Carolina would share a universe of discourse which provided them with a conceptual common denominator vis-à-vis their respective state legislatures. This was particularly true with respect to external affairs: the average state legislator was probably about as concerned with foreign policy then as he is today, but Congressmen were constantly forced to take the broad view of American prestige, were compelled to listen to the reports of Secretary John Jay and to the dispatches and pleas from their frustrated envoys in Britain, France and Spain. From considerations such as these, a "Continental" ideology developed which seems to have demanded a revision of our domestic institutions primarily on the ground that only by invigorating our general government could we assume our rightful place in the international arena. Indeed, an argument with great force—particularly since Washington was its incarnation—urged that our very survival in the Hobbesian jungle of world politics depended upon a reordering and strengthening of our national sovereignty.

The great achievement of the Constitutionalists was their ultimate success in convincing the elected representatives of a majority of the white male population that change was imperative. A small group of political leaders with a Continental vision and essentially a consciousness of the United States' *international* impotence, provided the matrix of the movement. To their standard other leaders rallied with their own parallel ambitions. Their great assets were (1) the presence in their caucus of the one authentic American "father figure," George Washington, whose prestige was enormous; (2) the energy and talent of their leadership (in which one must include the towering intellectuals of the time, John Adams and Thomas Jefferson, despite their absence abroad), and their communications "network," which was far superior to anything on the opposition side; (3) the preemptive skill which made "their" issue The Issue and kept the locally oriented opposition permanently on the defensive; and (4) the subjective consideration that these men were spokesmen of a new and compelling credo: *American* nationalism, that ill-defined but nonetheless potent sense of collective purpose that emerged from the American Revolution.

Despite great institutional handicaps, the Constitutionalists managed in the mid-1780s to mount an offensive which gained momentum as years went by. Their greatest problem was lethargy, and paradoxically, the number of barriers in their path may have proved an advantage in the long run. Beginning with the initial battle to get the Constitutional Convention called and delegates appointed, they could never relax, never let up the pressure. In practical terms, this meant that the local "organizations" created by the Constitutionalists were perpetually in movement building up their cadres for the next fight. (The word *organization* has to be used with great caution: a political organization in the United States—as in contemporary England—generally consisted of a magnate and his following, or a coalition of magnates. This did not necessarily mean that it was "undemocratic" or "aristocratic," in the Aristotelian sense of the word: while a few magnates such as the Livingstons could draft their followings, most exercised their leadership without coercion on the basis of popular endorsement. The absence of organized opposition did not imply the impossibility of competition any more than low public participation in elections necessarily indicated an undemocratic suffrage.)

The Constitutionalists got the jump on the "opposition" (a collective noun: oppositions would be more correct) at the outset with the demand for a Convention. Their opponents were caught in an old political trap: they were not being asked to approve any specific program of reform, but only to endorse a meeting to discuss and recommend needed reforms. If they took a hard line at the first stage, they were put in the position of glorifying the status quo and of denying the need for *any* changes. Moreover, the Constitutionalists could go to the people with a persuasive argument for "fair play"—"How can you condemn reform before you know precisely what is involved?" Since the state legislatures obviously would have the final say on any proposals that might emerge from the Convention, the Constitutionalists were merely reasonable men asking for a chance. Besides, since they did not make any concrete proposals at that stage, they were in a position to capitalize on every sort of generalized discontent with the Confederation.

Perhaps because of their poor intelligence system, perhaps because of overconfidence generated by the failure of all previous efforts to alter the Articles, the opposition awoke too late to the dangers that confronted them in 1787. Not only did the Constitutionalists manage to get every state but Rhode Island (where politics was enlivened by a party system reminiscent of the "Blues" and the "Greens" in the Byzantine Empire) to appoint delegates to Philadelphia, but when the results were in, it appeared that they dominated the delegations. Given the apathy of the opposition, this was a natural phenomenon: in an ideologically nonpolarized political atmosphere those who get appointed to a special committee are likely to be the men who supported the movement for its creation. Even George Clinton, who seems to have been the first opposition leader to awake to the possibility of trouble, could not prevent the New York legislature from appointing Alexander Hamilton—though he did have the foresight to send two of his henchmen to dominate the delegation. Incidentally, much has been made of the fact that the delegates to Philadelphia were not elected by the people; some have adduced this fact as evidence of the "undemocratic" character of the gathering. But put in the context of the time, this argument is wholly specious: the central government under the Articles was considered a creature of the component states and in all the states but Rhode Island, Connecticut, and New Hampshire, members of the national Congress were chosen by the state legislatures. This was not a consequence of elitism or fear of the mob; it was a logical extension of states' rights doctrine to guarantee that the national institution did not end-run the state legislatures and make direct contact with the people.

II

With delegations safely named, the focus shifted to Philadelphia. While waiting for a quorum to assemble, James Madison got busy and drafted the so-called Randolph or Virginia Plan with the aid of the Virginia delegation. This was a political master-stroke. Its consequence was that once business got underway, the framework of discussion was established on Madison's terms. There was no interminable argument over agenda; instead the delegates took the Virginia Resolutions—"just for purposes of discussion"—as their point of departure. And along with Madison's proposals, many of which were buried in the course of the summer, went his major premise: a new start on a Constitution rather than piecemeal amendment. This was not necessarily revolutionary —a little exegesis could demonstrate that a new Constitution might be formulated as "amendments" to the Articles of Confederation—but Madison's proposal that this "lump sum" amendment go into effect after approval by nine states (the Articles required unanimous state approval for any amendment) was thoroughly subversive.

Standard treatments of the Convention divide the delegates into "nationalists" and "states' righters" with various improvised shadings ("moderate nationalists," etc.), but these are *a posteriori* categories which obfuscate more than they clarify. What is striking to one who analyzes the Convention as a case study in democratic politics is the lack of clear-cut ideological divisions in the Convention. Indeed, I submit that the evidence—Madison's *Notes,* the correspondence of the delegates, and debates on ratification—indicates that this was a remarkably homogeneous body on the ideological level. Yates and

Lansing, Clinton's two chaperones for Hamilton, left in disgust on July 10. (Is there anything more tedious than sitting through endless disputes on matters one deems fundamentally misconceived? It takes an iron will to spend a hot summer as an ideological *agent provocateur.*) Luther Martin, Maryland's bibulous narcissist, left on September 4 in a huff when he discovered that others did not share his self-esteem; others went home for personal reasons. But the hard core of delegates accepted a grinding regimen throughout the attrition of a Philadelphia summer precisely because they shared the Constitutionalist goal.

Basic differences of opinion emerged, of course, but these were not ideological; they were *structural.* If the so-called "states' rights" group had not accepted the fundamental purposes of the Convention, they could simply have pulled out and by doing so have aborted the whole enterprise. Instead of bolting, they returned day after day to argue and to compromise. An interesting symbol of this basic homogeneity was the initial agreement on secrecy: these professional politicians did not want to become prisoners of publicity; they wanted to retain that freedom of maneuver which is only possible when men are not forced to take public stands in the preliminary stages of negotiation. There was no legal means of binding the tongues of the delegates: at any stage in the game a delegate with basic principled objections to the emerging project could have taken the stump (as Luther Martin did after his exit) and denounced the convention to the skies. Yet Madison did not even inform Thomas Jefferson in Paris of the course of the deliberations and available correspondence indicates that the delegates generally observed the injunction. Secrecy is certainly uncharacteristic of any assembly marked by strong ideological polarization. This was noted at the time: the *New York Daily Advertiser,* August 14, 1787, commented that the "profound secrecy hitherto observed by the Convention [we consider] a happy omen, as it demonstrates that the spirit of party on any great and essential point cannot have arisen to any height."

Commentators on the Constitution who have read *The Federalist* in lieu of reading the actual debates have credited the Fathers with the invention of a sublime concept called "Federalism." Unfortunately *The Federalist* is probative evidence for only one proposition: that Hamilton and Madison were inspired propagandists with a genius for retrospective symmetry. Federalism, as the theory is generally defined, was an improvisation which was later promoted into a political theory. Experts on "federalism" should take to heart the advice of David Hume, who warned in his *Of the Rise and Progress of the Arts and Sciences* that "there is no subject in which we must proceed with more caution than in [history], lest we assign causes which never existed and reduce what is merely contingent to stable and universal principles." In any event, the final balance in the Constitution between the states and the nation must have come as a great disappointment to Madison, while Hamilton's unitary views are too well known to need elucidation.

It is indeed astonishing how those who have glibly designated James

Madison the "father" of Federalism have overlooked the solid body of fact which indicates that he shared Hamilton's quest for a unitary central government. To be specific, they have avoided examining the clear import of the Madison-Virginia Plan, and have disregarded Madison's dogged inch-by-inch retreat from the bastions of centralization. The Virginia Plan envisioned a unitary national government effectively freed from and dominant over the states. The lower house of the national legislature was to be elected directly by the people of the states with membership proportional to population. The upper house was to be selected by the lower and the two chambers would elect the executive and choose the judges. The national government would be thus cut completely loose from the states.

The structure of the general government was freed from state control in a truly radical fashion, but the scope of the authority of the national sovereign as Madison initially formulated it was breathtaking—it was a formulation worthy of the Sage of Malmesbury himself. The national legislature was to be empowered to disallow the acts of state legislatures, and the central government was vested, in addition to the powers of the nation under the Articles of Confederation, with plenary authority wherever "the separate States are incompetent or in which the harmony of the United States may be interrupted by the exercise of individual legislation." Finally, just to lock the door against state intrusion, the national Congress was to be given the power to use military force on recalcitrant states. This was Madison's "model" of an ideal national government, though it later received little publicity in *The Federalist.*

The interesting thing was the reaction of the Convention to this militant program for a strong autonomous central government. Some delegates were startled, some obviously leery of so comprehensive a project of reform, but nobody set off any fireworks and nobody walked out. Moreover, in the two weeks that followed, the Virginia Plan received substantial endorsement *en principe;* the initial temper of the gathering can be deduced from the approval "without debate or dissent," on May 31, of the Sixth Resolution which granted Congress the authority to disallow state legislation "contravening *in its opinion* the Articles of Union." Indeed, an amendment was included to bar states from contravening national treaties.

The Virginia Plan may therefore be considered, in ideological terms, as the delegates' Utopia, but as the discussions continued and became more specific, many of those present began to have second thoughts. After all, they were not residents of Utopia or guardians in Plato's Republic who could simply impose a philosophical ideal on subordinate strata of the population. They were practical politicians in a democratic society, and no matter what their private dreams might be, they had to take home an acceptable package and defend it—and their own political futures—against predictable attack. On June 14 the breaking point between dream and reality took place. Apparently realizing that under the Virginia Plan, Massachusetts, Virginia, and Pennsylvania could virtually dominate the national government—and probably appreciating that to sell this program to "the folks back home" would be impossible—the delegates from the small states dug in their heels and demanded time for a consideration of alternatives. One gets a graphic sense of the inner politics from John Dickinson's reproach to Madison: "You see the consequences of pushing things too far. Some of the members from the small States wish for two branches in the General Legislature and are friends to a good National Government; but we would sooner submit to a foreign power than . . . be deprived of an equality of suffrage in both branches of the Legislature, and thereby be thrown under the domination of the large States."

The bare outline of the *Journal* entry for Tuesday, June 14, is suggestive to anyone with extensive experience in deliberative bodies. "It was moved by Mr. Patterson [*sic,* Paterson's name was one of those consistently misspelled by Madison and everybody else] seconded by Mr. Randolph that the further consideration of the report from the Committee of the whole House [endorsing the Virginia Plan] be postponed til tomorrow and before the question for postponement was taken. It was moved by Mr. Randolph seconded by Mr. Patterson that the House adjourn." The House adjourned by obvious prearrangement of the two principals: since the preceding Saturday when Brearley and Paterson of New Jersey had announced their fundamental discontent with the representational features of the Virginia Plan, the informal pressure had certainly been building up to slow down the steamroller. Doubtless there were extended arguments at the Indian Queen between Madison and Paterson, the latter insisting that events were moving rapidly towards a probably disastrous conclusion, towards a political suicide pact. Now the process of accommodation was put into action smoothly—and wisely, given the character and strength of the doubters. Madison had the votes, but this was one of those situations where the enforcement of mechanical majoritarianism could easily have destroyed the objectives of the majority: the Constitutionalists were in quest of a qualitative as well as a quantitative consensus. This was hardly from deference to local Quaker custom; it was a political imperative if they were to attain ratification.

III

According to the standard script, at this point the "states' rights" group intervened in force behind the New Jersey Plan, which has been characteristically portrayed as a reversion to the status quo under the Articles of Confederation with but minor modifications. A careful examination of the evidence indicates that only in a marginal sense is this an accurate description. It is true that the New Jersey Plan put the states back into the institutional picture, but one could argue that to do so was a recognition of political reality rather than an affirmation of states' rights. A serious case can be made that the advocates of the New Jersey Plan, far from being ideological addicts of states' rights, intended to substitute for the Virginia Plan a system which would both retain

strong national power and have a chance of adoption in the states. The leading
spokesman for the project asserted quite clearly that his views were based more
on counsels of expediency than on principle; said Paterson on June 16: "I came
here not to speak my own sentiments, but the sentiments of those who sent
me. Our object is not such a Governmt. as may be best in itself, but such a
one as our Constituents have authorized us to prepare, and as they will
approve." This is Madison's version; in Yates's transcription, there is a crucial
sentence following the remarks above: "I believe that a little practical virtue
is to be preferred to the finest theoretical principles, which cannot be carried
into effect." In his preliminary speech on June 9, Paterson had stated "to the
public mind we must accommodate ourselves," and in his notes for this and
his later effort as well, the emphasis is the same. The *structure* of government
under the Articles should be retained:

    2. Because it accords with the Sentiments of the People
        [Proof:] 1. Coms. [Commissions from state legislatures defining the jurisdic-
                 tion of the delegates]
                 2. News-papers—Political Barometer. Jersey never would have sent
                    Delegates under the first [Virginia] Plan—
        Not here to sport Opinions of my own. Wt. [What] can be done. A little
        practicable Virtue preferrable to Theory.

This was a defense of political acumen, not of states' rights. In fact,
Paterson's notes of his speech can easily be construed as an argument for
attaining the substantive objectives of the Virginia Plan by a sound political
route, i.e., pouring the new wine in the old bottles. With a shrewd eye, Paterson
queried:

> Will the Operation, and Force of the [central] Govt. depend upon the mode of
> Representn.—No—it will depend upon the Quantum of Power lodged in the leg.
> ex. and judy. Departments—Give [the existing] Congress the same Powers that
> you intend to give the two Branches, [under the Virginia Plan] and I apprehend
> they will act with as much Propriety and more Energy. . . .

In other words, the advocates of the New Jersey Plan concentrated their fire
on what they held to be the *political liabilities* of the Virginia Plan—which
were matters of institutional structure—rather than on the proposed scope of
national authority. Indeed, the Supremacy Clause of the Constitution first saw
the light of day in Paterson's Sixth Resolution; the New Jersey Plan contemplated the use of military force to secure compliance with national law; and
finally Paterson made clear his view that under either the Virginia or the New
Jersey systems, the general government would ". . . act on individuals and not
on states." From the states' rights viewpoint, this was heresy: the fundament
of that doctrine was the proposition that any central government had as its
constituents the states, not the people, and could only reach the people through
the agency of the state government.

Paterson then reopened the agenda of the Convention, but he did so within a distinctly nationalist framework. Paterson's position was one of favoring a strong central government in principle, but opposing one which in fact *put the big states in the saddle.* (The Virginia Plan, for all its abstract merits, did very well by Virginia.) As evidence for this speculation, there is a curious and intriguing proposal among Paterson's preliminary drafts of the New Jersey Plan:

> Whereas it is necessary in Order to form the People of the U.S. of America in to a Nation, that the States should be consolidated, by which means all the Citizens thereof will become equally intitled to and will equally participate in the same Privileges and Rights ... it is therefore resolved, that all the Lands contained within the Limits of each state individually, and of the U.S. generally be considered as constituting one Body or Mass, and be divided into thirteen or more integral parts.
>
> Resolved, That such Divisions or integral Parts shall be styled Districts.

This makes it sound as though Paterson was prepared to accept a strong unified central government along the lines of the Virginia Plan if the existing states were eliminated. He may have gotten the idea from his New Jersey colleague Judge David Brearley, who on June 9 had commented that the only remedy to the dilemma over representation was "that a map of the U.S. be spread out, that all the existing boundaries be erased, and that a new partition of the whole be made into 13 equal parts." According to Yates, Brearley added at this point, "then a government on the present [Virginia Plan] system will be just."

This proposition was never pushed—it was patently unrealistic—but one can appreciate its purpose: it would have separated the men from the boys in the large-state delegations. How attached would the Virginians have been to their reform principles if Virginia were to disappear as a component geographical unit (the largest) for representational purposes? Up to this point, the Virginians had been in the happy position of supporting high ideals with that inner confidence born of knowledge that the "public interest" they endorsed would nourish their private interest. Worse, they had shown little willingness to compromise. Now the delegates from the small states announced that they were unprepared to be offered up as sacrificial victims to a "national interest" which reflected Virginia's parochial ambition. Caustic Charles Pinckney was not far off when he remarked sardonically that "the whole [conflict] comes to this": "Give N. Jersey an equal vote, and she will dismiss her scruples, and concur in the Natil. system." What he rather unfairly did not add was that the Jersey delegates were not free agents who could adhere to their private convictions; they had to take back, sponsor and risk their reputations on the reforms approved by the Convention—and in New Jersey, not in Virginia.

Paterson spoke on Saturday, and one can surmise that over the weekend there was a good deal of consultation, argument, and caucusing among the delegates. One member at least prepared a full length address: on Monday Alexander Hamilton, previously mute, rose and delivered a six-hour oration. It was a remarkably apolitical speech; the gist of his position was that *both* the

Virginia and New Jersey Plans were inadequately centralist, and he detailed a reform program which was reminiscent of the Protectorate under the Cromwellian *Instrument of Government* of 1653. It has been suggested that Hamilton did this in the best political tradition to emphasize the moderate character of the Virginia Plan, to give the cautious delegates something *really* to worry about; but this interpretation seems somehow too clever. Particularly since the sentiments Hamilton expressed happened to be completely consistent with those he privately—and sometimes publicly—expressed throughout his life. He wanted, to take a striking phrase from a letter to George Washington, a "strong well mounted government"; in essence, the Hamilton Plan contemplated an elected life monarch, virtually free of public control, on the Hobbesian ground that only in this fashion could strength and stability be achieved. The other alternatives, he argued, would put policy-making at the mercy of the passions of the mob; only if the sovereign was beyond the reach of selfish influence would it be possible to have government in the interests of the whole community.

From all accounts, this was a masterful and compelling speech, but (aside from furnishing John Lansing and Luther Martin with ammunition for later use against the Constitution) it made little impact. Hamilton was simply transmitting on a different wavelength from the rest of the delegates; the latter adjourned after his great effort, admired his rhetoric, and then returned to business. It was rather as if they had taken a day off to attend the opera. Hamilton, never a particularly patient man or much of a negotiator, stayed for another ten days and then left, in considerable disgust, for New York. Although he came back to Philadelphia sporadically and attended the last two weeks of the Convention, Hamilton played no part in the laborious task of hammering out the Constitution. His day came later when he led the New York Constitutionalists into the savage imbroglio over ratification—an arena in which his unmatched talent for dirty political infighting may well have won the day. For instance, in the New York Ratifying Convention, Lansing threw back into Hamilton's teeth the sentiments the latter had expressed in his June 18 oration in the Convention. However, having since retreated to the fine defensive positions immortalized in *The Federalist,* the Colonel flatly denied that he had ever been an enemy of the states, or had believed that conflict between states and nation was inexorable! As Madison's authoritative *Notes* did not appear until 1840, and there had been no press coverage, there was no way to verify his assertions, so in the words of the reporter, "a warm personal altercation between [Lansing and Hamilton] engrossed the remainder of the day [June 28, 1788]."

IV

On Tuesday morning, June 19, the vacation was over. James Madison led off with a long, carefully reasoned speech analyzing the New Jersey Plan which, while intellectually vigorous in its criticisms, was quite conciliatory in mood.

"The great difficulty," he observed, "lies in the affair of Representation; and if this could be adjusted, all others would be surmountable." (As events were to demonstrate, this diagnosis was correct.) When he finished, a vote was taken on whether to continue with the Virginia Plan as the nucleus for a new constitution: seven states voted "Yes"; New York, New Jersey, and Delaware voted "No"; and Maryland, whose position often depended on which delegates happened to be on the floor, divided. Paterson, it seems, lost decisively; yet in a fundamental sense he and his allies had achieved their purpose: from that day onward, it could never be forgotten that the state governments loomed ominously in the background and that no verbal incantations could exorcise their power. Moreover, nobody bolted the convention: Paterson and his colleagues took their defeat in stride and set to work to modify the Virginia Plan, particularly with respect to its provisions on representation in the national legislature. Indeed, they won an immediate rhetorical bonus; when Oliver Ellsworth of Connecticut rose to move that the word "national" be expunged from the Third Virginia Resolution ("Resolved that a *national* Government ought to be established consisting of a *supreme* Legislative, Executive and Judiciary"), Randolph agreed and the motion passed unanimously. The process of compromise had begun.

For the next two weeks, the delegates circled around the problem of legislative representation. The Connecticut delegation appears to have evolved a possible compromise quite early in the debates, but the Virginians and particularly Madison (unaware that he would later be acclaimed as the prophet of "federalism") fought obdurately against providing for equal representation of states in the second chamber. There was a good deal of acrimony and at one point Benjamin Franklin—of all people—proposed the institution of a daily prayer; practical politicians in the gathering, however, were meditating more on the merits of a good committee than on the utility of Divine intervention. On July 2, the ice began to break when through a number of fortuitous events—and one that seems deliberate—the majority against equality of representation was converted into a dead tie. The Convention had reached the stage where it was "ripe" for a solution (presumably all the therapeutic speeches had been made), and the South Carolinians proposed a committee. Madison and James Wilson wanted none of it, but with only Pennsylvania dissenting, the body voted to establish a working party on the problem of representation.

The members of this committee, one from each state, were elected by the delegates—and a very interesting committee it was. Despite the fact that the Virginia Plan had held majority support up to that date, neither Madison nor Randolph was selected (Mason was the Virginian) and Baldwin of Georgia, whose shift in position had resulted in the tie, was chosen. From the composition, it was clear that this was not to be a "fighting" committee: the emphasis in membership was on what might be described as "second-level political entrepreneurs." On the basis of the discussions up to that time, only Luther Martin of Maryland could be described as a "bitter-ender." Admittedly, some divination enters into this sort of analysis, but one does get a sense of the mood of the delegates from these choices—including the interesting selection of Benjamin Franklin, despite his age and intellectual wobbliness, over the brilliant and incisive Wilson or the sharp, polemical Gouverneur Morris, to represent Pennsylvania. His passion for conciliation was more valuable at this juncture than Wilson's logical genius, or Morris's acerbic wit.

There is a common rumor that the framers divided their time between philosophical discussions of government and reading the classics in political theory. Perhaps this is as good a time as any to note that their concerns were highly practical, that they spent little time canvassing abstractions. A number of them had some acquaintance with the history of political theory (probably gained from reading John Adams's monumental compilation *A Defense of the Constitutions of Government,* the first volume of which appeared in 1786), and it was a poor rhetorician indeed who could not cite Locke, Montesquieu, or Harrington *in support* of a desired goal. Yet up to this point in the deliberations, no one had expounded a defense of states' rights or the "separation of powers" on anything resembling a theoretical basis. It should be reiterated that the Madison model had no room either for the states or for the "separation of powers": effectively *all* governmental power was vested in the national legislature. The merits of Montesquieu did not turn up until *The Federalist;* and although a perverse argument could be made that Madison's ideal was truly in the tradition of John Locke's *Second Treatise of Government,* the Locke whom the American rebels treated as an honorary president was a pluralistic defender of vested rights, not of parliamentary supremacy.

It would be tedious to continue a blow-by-blow analysis of the work of the delegates; the critical fight was over representation of the states and once the Connecticut Compromise was adopted on July 17, the Convention was over the hump. Madison, James Wilson, and Gouverneur Morris of New York (who was there representing Pennsylvania!) fought the compromise all the way in a last-ditch effort to get a unitary state with parliamentary supremacy. But their allies deserted them and they demonstrated after their defeat the essentially opportunist character of their objections—using "opportunist" here in a nonpejorative sense, to indicate a willingness to swallow their objections and get on with the business. Moreover, once the compromise had carried (by five states to four, with one state divided), its advocates threw themselves vigorously into the job of strengthening the general government's substantive powers—as might have been predicted, indeed, from Paterson's early statements. It nourishes an increased respect for Madison's devotion to the art of politics, to realize that this dogged fighter could sit down six months later and prepare essays for *The Federalist* in contradiction to his basic convictions about the true course the Convention should have taken.

V

Two tricky issues will serve to illustrate the later process of accommodation. The first was the institutional position of the Executive. Madison argued for an executive chosen by the national legislature and on May 29 this had been adopted with a provision that after his seven-year term was concluded, the chief magistrate should not be eligible for reelection. In late July this was reopened and for a week the matter was argued from several different points of view. A good deal of desultory speech-making ensued, but the gist of the problem was the opposition from two sources to election by the legislature. One group felt that the states should have a hand in the process; another small but influential circle urged direct election by the people. There were a number of proposals: election by the people, election by state governors, by electors chosen by state legislatures, by the national legislature (James Wilson, perhaps ironically, proposed at one point that an Electoral College be chosen by lot from the national legislature!), and there was some resemblance to three-dimensional chess in the dispute because of the presence of two other variables, length of tenure and reeligibility. Finally, after opening, reopening, and re-reopening the debate, the thorny problem was consigned to a committee for absolution.

The Brearley Committee on Postponed Matters was a superb aggregation of talent and its compromise on the Executive was a masterpiece of political improvisation. (The Electoral College, its creation, however, had little in its favor as an *institution*—as the delegates well appreciated.) The point of departure for all discussion about the presidency in the Convention was that in immediate terms, the problem was nonexistent; in other words, everybody present knew that under any system devised, George Washington would be President. Thus they were dealing in the future tense and to a body of working politicians the merits of the Brearley proposal were obvious: everybody got a piece of cake. (Or to put it more academically, each viewpoint could leave the Convention and argue to its constituents that it had *really* won the day.) First, the state legislatures had the right to determine the mode of selection of the electors; second, the small states received a bonus in the Electoral College in the form of a guaranteed minimum of three votes while the big states got acceptance of the principle of proportional power; third, if the state legislatures agreed (as six did in the first presidential election), the people could be involved directly in the choice of electors; and finally, if no candidate received a majority in the College, the right of decision passed to the national legislature with each state exercising equal strength. (In the Brearley recommendation, the election went to the Senate, but a motion from the floor substituted the House; this was accepted on the ground that the Senate already had enough authority over the executive in its treaty and appointment powers.)

This compromise was almost too good to be true, and the framers snapped it up with little debate or controversy. No one seemed to think well of the College as an *institution;* indeed, what evidence there is suggests that there was an assumption that once Washington had finished his tenure as President, the electors would cease to produce majorities and the Chief Executive would usually be chosen in the House. George Mason observed casually that the selection would be made in the House nineteen times in twenty and no one seriously disputed this point. The vital aspect of the Electoral College was that it got the Convention over the hurdle and protected everybody's interests. The future was left to cope with the problem of what to do with this Rube Goldberg mechanism.

In short, the framers did not in their wisdom endow the United States with a college of Cardinals—the Electoral College was neither an exercise in applied Platonism nor an experiment in indirect government base on elitist distrust of the masses. It was merely a jerry-rigged improvisation which has subsequently been endowed with a high theoretical content. When an elector from Oklahoma in 1960 refused to cast his vote for Nixon (naming Byrd and Goldwater instead) on the ground that the Founding Fathers intended him to exercise his great independent wisdom, he was indulging in historical fantasy. If one were to indulge in counter-fantasy, he would be tempted to suggest that the Fathers would be startled to find the College still in operation—and perhaps even dismayed at their descendants' lack of judgment or inventiveness.

The second issue on which some substantial practical bargaining took place was slavery. The morality of slavery was, by design, not at issue; but in its other concrete aspects, slavery colored the arguments over taxation, commerce, and representation. The "Three-Fifths Compromise," that three-fifths of the slaves would be counted both for representation and for purposes of direct taxation (which was drawn from the past—it was a formula of Madison's utilized by Congress in 1783 to establish the basis of state contributions to the Confederation treasury) had allayed some Northern fears about Southern overrepresentation (no one then foresaw the trivial role that direct taxation would play in later federal financial policy), but doubts still remained. The Southerners, on the other hand, were afraid that Congressional control over commerce would lead to the exclusion of slaves or to their excessive taxation as imports. Moreover, the Southerners were disturbed over "navigation acts," i.e., tariffs, or special legislation providing, for example, that exports be carried only in American ships; as a section depending upon exports, they wanted protection from the potential voracity of their commercial brethren of the Eastern states. To achieve this end, Mason and others urged that the Constitution include a proviso that navigation and commercial laws should require a two-thirds vote in Congress.

These problems came to a head in late August and, as usual, were handed to a committee in the hope that, in Gouverneur Morris's words, "these things may form a bargain among the Northern and Southern States." The Committee reported its measures of reconciliation on August 25, and on August 29 the package was wrapped up and delivered. What occurred can best be described in George Mason's dour version (he anticipated Calhoun in his conviction that permitting navigation acts to pass by majority vote would put the South in economic bondage to the North—it was mainly on this ground that he refused to sign the Constitution):

The Constitution as agreed to till a fortnight before the Convention rose was such a one as he would have set his hand and heart to. . . . [Until that time] The 3 New England States were constantly with us in all questions . . . so that it was these three States with the 5 Southern ones against Pennsylvania, Jersey and Delaware. With respect to the importation of slaves, [decision-making] was left to Congress. This disturbed the two Southernmost States who knew that Congress would immediately suppress the importation of slaves. Those two States therefore struck up a bargain with the three New England States. If they would join to admit slaves for some years, the two Southern-most States would join in changing the clause which required the ⅔ of the Legislature in any vote [on navigation acts]. It was done.

On the floor of the Convention there was a virtual love-feast on this happy occasion. Charles Pinckney of South Carolina attempted to overturn the committee's decision, when the compromise was reported to the Convention, by insisting that the South needed protection from the imperialism of the Northern states. But his Southern colleagues were not prepared to rock the boat and General C. C. Pinckney arose to spread oil on the suddenly ruffled waters; he admitted that:

It was in the true interest of the S[outhern] States to have no regulation of commerce; but considering the loss brought on the commerce of the Eastern States by the Revolution, their liberal conduct towards the views of South Carolina [on the regulation of the slave trade] and the interests the weak Southn. States had in being united with the strong Eastern states, he thought it proper that no fetters should be imposed on the power of making commercial regulations; *and that his constituents, though prejudiced against the Eastern States, would be reconciled to this liberality.* He had himself prejudices agst the Eastern States before he came here, but would acknowledge that he had found them as liberal and candid as any men whatever. (Italics added.)

Pierce Butler took the same tack, essentially arguing that he was not too happy about the possible consequences, but that a deal was a deal. Many Southern leaders were later—in the wake of the "Tariff of Abominations"—to rue this day of reconciliation; Calhoun's *Disquisition on Government* was little more than an extension of the argument in the Convention against permitting a Congressional majority to enact navigation acts.

VI

Drawing on their vast collective political experience, utilizing every weapon in the politician's arsenal, looking constantly over their shoulders at their constituents, the delegates put together a Constitution. It was a makeshift affair; some sticky issues (for example, the qualification of voters) they ducked entirely; others they mastered with that ancient instrument of political sagacity, studied ambiguity (for example, citizenship), and some they just overlooked. In this last category, I suspect, fell the matter of the power of the federal courts to determine the constitutionality of acts of Congress. When the judicial article was formulated (Article III of the Constitution), deliberations were still in the stage where the legislature was endowed with broad power under the Randolph formulation, authority which by its own terms was scarcely amenable to judicial review. In essence, courts could hardly determine when "the separate States are incompetent or . . . the harmony of the United States may be interrupted"; the national legislature, as critics pointed out, was free to define its own jurisdiction. Later the definition of legislative authority was changed into the form we know, a series of stipulated powers, *but the delegates never seriously reexamined the jurisdiction of the judiciary under this new limited formulation.* All arguments on the intention of the framers in this matter are thus deductive and *a posteriori,* though some obviously make more sense than others.

The framers were busy and distinguished men, anxious to get back to their families, their positions, and their constituents, not members of the French Academy devoting a lifetime to a dictionary. They were trying to do an important job, and do it in such a fashion that their handiwork would be acceptable to very diverse constituencies. No one was rhapsodic about the final document, but it was a beginning, a move in the right direction, and one they had reason to believe the people would endorse. In addition, since they had modified the impossible amendment provisions of the Articles (the requirement of unanimity which could always be frustrated by "Rogues Island") to one demanding approval by only three-quarters of the states, they seemed confident that gaps in the fabric which experience would reveal could be rewoven without undue difficulty.

So with a neat phrase introduced by Benjamin Franklin (but devised by Gouverneur Morris) which made their decision sound unanimous, and an inspired benediction by the Old Doctor urging doubters to doubt their own infallibility, the Constitution was accepted and signed. Curiously, Edmund Randolph, who had played so vital a role throughout, refused to sign, as did his fellow Virginian George Mason and Elbridge Gerry of Massachusetts. Randolph's behavior was eccentric, to say the least—his excuses for refusing his signature have a factitious ring even at this late date; the best explanation seems to be that he was afraid that the Constitution would prove to be a liability in Virginia politics, where Patrick Henry was burning up the countryside with impassioned denunciations. Presumably, Randolph wanted to check the temper of the populace before he risked his reputation, and perhaps his job, in a fight with both Henry and Richard Henry Lee. Events lend some justification to this speculation: after much temporizing and use of the conditional subjunctive tense, Randolph endorsed ratification in Virginia and ended up getting the best of both worlds.

Madison, despite his reservations about the Constitution, was the campaign manager in ratification. His first task was to get the Congress in New York to light its own funeral pyre by approving the "amendments" to the

Articles and sending them on to the state legislatures. Above all, momentum had to be maintained. The anti-Constitutionalists, now thoroughly alarmed and no novices in politics, realized that their best tactic was attrition rather than direct opposition. Thus they settled on a position expressing qualified approval but calling for a second Convention to remedy various defects (the one with the most demagogic appeal was the lack of a Bill of Rights). Madison knew that to accede to this demand would be equivalent to losing the battle, nor would he agree to conditional approval (despite wavering even by Hamilton). This was an all-or-nothing proposition: national salvation or national impotence with no intermediate positions possible. Unable to get Congressional approval, he settled for second best: a unanimous resolution of Congress transmitting the Constitution to the states for whatever action they saw fit to take. The opponents then moved from New York and the Congress, where they had attempted to attach amendments and conditions, to the states for the final battle.

At first the campaign for ratification went beautifully: within eight months after the delegates set their names to the document, eight states had ratified. Only in Massachusetts had the result been close (187–168). Theoretically, a ratification by one more state convention would set the new government in motion, but in fact until Virginia and New York acceded to the new Union, the latter was a fiction. New Hampshire was the next to ratify; Rhode Island was involved in its characteristic political convulsions (the legislature there sent the Constitution out to the towns for decision by popular vote and it got lost among a series of local issues); North Carolina's convention did not meet until July and then postponed a final decision. This is hardly the place for an extensive analysis of the conventions of New York and Virginia. Suffice it to say that the Constitutionalists clearly outmaneuvered their opponents, forced them into impossible political positions, and won both states narrowly. The Virginia Convention could serve as a classic study in effective floor management: Patrick Henry had to be contained, and a reading of the debates discloses a standard two-stage technique. Henry would give a four-or five-hour speech denouncing some section of the Constitution on every conceivable ground (the federal district, he averred at one point, would become a haven for convicts escaping from state authority!); when Henry subsided, "Mr. Lee of Westmoreland" would rise and literally poleaxe him with sardonic invective (when Henry complained about the militia power, "Lighthorse Harry" really punched below the belt: observing that while the former Governor had been sitting in Richmond during the Revolution, *he* had been out in the trenches with the troops and thus felt better qualified to discuss military affairs). Then the gentlemanly Constitutionalists (Madison, Pendleton and Marshall) would pick up the matters at issue and examine them in the light of reason.

Indeed, modern Americans who tend to think of James Madison as a rather desiccated character should spend some time with this transcript. Probably Madison put on his most spectacular demonstration of nimble rhetoric in what might be called "The Battle of the Absent Authorities." Patrick Henry in the course of one of his harangues alleged that Jefferson was known to be opposed to Virginia's approving the Constitution. This was clever: Henry hated Jefferson, but was prepared to use any weapon that came to hand. Madison's riposte was superb: First, he said that with all due respect to the great reputation of Jefferson, he was not in the country and therefore could not formulate an adequate judgment; second, no one should utilize the reputation of an outsider—the Virginia Convention was there to think for itself; third, if there were to be recourse to outsiders, the opinions of George Washington should certainly be taken into consideration; and finally, he knew from privileged personal communications from Jefferson that in fact the latter *strongly favored* the Constitution. To devise an assault route into this rhetorical fortress was literally impossible.

VII

The fight was over; all that remained now was to establish the new frame of government in the spirit of its framers. And who were better qualified for this task than the framers themselves? Thus victory for the Constitution meant simultaneous victory for the Constitutionalists; the anti-Constitutionalists either capitulated or vanished into limbo—soon Patrick Henry would be offered a seat on the Supreme Court and Luther Martin would be known as the Federalist "bull-dog." And irony of ironies, Alexander Hamilton and James Madison would shortly accumulate a reputation as the formulators of what is often alleged to be our political theory, the concept of "federalism." Also, on the other side of the ledger, the arguments would soon appear over what the framers "really meant"; while these disputes have assumed the proportions of a big scholarly business in the last century, they began almost before the ink on the Constitution was dry. One of the best early ones featured Hamilton versus Madison on the scope of presidential power, and other framers characteristically assumed positions in this and other disputes on the basis of their political convictions.

Probably our greatest difficulty is that we know so much more about what the framers *should have meant* than they themselves did. We are intimately acquainted with the problems that their Constitution should have been designed to master; in short, we have read the mystery story backwards. If we are to get the right "feel" for their time and their circumstances, we must in Maitland's phrase, "think ourselves back into a twilight." Obviously, no one can pretend completely to escape from the solipsistic web of his own environment, but if the effort is made, it is possible to appreciate the past roughly on its own terms. The first step in this process is to abandon the academic premise that because we can ask a question, there must be an answer.

Thus we can ask what the framers meant when they gave Congress the power to regulate interstate and foreign commerce, and we emerge, reluctantly perhaps, with the reply that they may not have known what they meant, that there may not have been any semantic consensus. The Convention was not a seminar in analytic philosophy or linguistic analysis. Commerce was *commerce* —and if different interpretations of the word arose, later generations could worry about the problem of definition. The delegates were in a hurry to get a new government established; when definitional arguments arose, they characteristically took refuge in ambiguity. If different men voted for the same proposition for varying reasons, that was politics (and still is); if later generations were unsettled by this lack of precision, that would be their problem.

There was a good deal of definitional pluralism with respect to the problems the delegates did discuss, but when we move to the question of extrapolated intentions, we enter the realm of spiritualism. When men in our time, for instance, launch into elaborate talmudic exegesis to demonstrate that federal aid to parochial schools is (or is not) in accord with the intentions of the men who established the Republic and endorsed the Bill of Rights, they are engaging in historical Extra-Sensory Perception (If one were to join this E.S.P. contingent for a minute, he might suggest that the hard-boiled politicians who wrote the Constitution and Bill of Rights would chuckle scornfully at such an invocation of authority: obviously a politician would chart his course on the intentions of the living, not of the dead, and count the number of Catholics in his constituency.)

The Constitution, then, was not an apotheosis of "constitutionalism," a triumph of architectonic genuis; it was a patch-work sewn together under the pressure of both time and events by a group of extremely talented democratic politicians. They refused to attempt the establishment of a strong, centralized sovereignty on the principle of legislative supremacy for the excellent reason that the people would not accept it. They risked their political fortunes by opposing the established doctrines of state sovereignty because they were convinced that the existing system was leading to national impotence and probably foreign domination. For two years, they worked to get a convention established. For over three months, in what must have seemed to the faithful participants an endless process of give-and-take, they reasoned, cajoled, threatened, and bargained amongst themselves. The result was a Constitution which the people, in fact, by democratic processes, did accept, and a new and far better national government was established.

Beginning with the inspired propaganda of Hamilton, Madison and Jay, the ideological build-up got under way. *The Federalist* had little impact on the ratification of the Constitution, except perhaps in New York, but this volume had enormous influence on the image of the Constitution in the minds of future generations, particularly on historians and political scientists who have an innate fondness for theoretical symmetry. Yet, while the shades of Locke and Montesquieu *may* have been hovering in the background, and the delegates *may* have been unconscious instruments of a transcendent *telos,* the careful observer of the day-to-day work of the Convention finds no overarching principles. The "separation of powers" to him seems to be a by-product of suspicion, and "federalism" he views as a *pis aller,* as the farthest point the delegates felt they could go in the destruction of state power without themselves inviting repudiation.

To conclude, the Constitution was neither a victory for abstract theory nor a great practical success. Well over half a million men had to die on the battlefields of the Civil War before certain constitutional principles could be defined—a baleful consideration which is somehow overlooked in our customary tributes to the farsighted genius of the framers and to the supposed American talent for "constitutionalism." The Constitution was, however, a vivid demonstration of effective democratic political action, and of the forging of a national elite which literally persuaded its countrymen to hoist themselves by their own boot straps. American pro-consuls would be wise not to translate the Constitution into Japanese, or Swahili, or treat it as a work of semi-Divine origin; but when students of comparative politics examine the process of nation-building in countries newly freed from colonial rule, they may find the American experience instructive as a classic example of the potentialities of a democratic elite.

Limitation of Governmental Power and of Majority Rule

The most accurate and helpful way to characterize our political system is to call it a constitutional democracy. The term implies a system in which the government is regulated by laws that control and limit the exercise of political power. In a constitutional democracy people participate in government on a limited basis. A distinction should be made between an unlimited democratic government and a constitutional democracy. In the former, the people govern through the operation of a principle such as majority rule without legal restraint; in the latter, majority rule is curtailed and checked through various legal devices. A constitutional system is one in which the formal authority of government is restrained. The checks upon government in a constitutional society customarily include a division or fragmentation of authority that prevents government from controlling all sectors of human life.

Hamilton noted in *Federalist 1,* "It seems to have been reserved to the people of this country, to decide by their conduct and example, the important question, whether societies of men are really capable or not, of establishing good government from reflection and choice, or whether they are forever destined to depend, for their political constitutions, on accident and force." The framers of our Constitution attempted to structure the government in such a way that it would meet the needs and aspirations of the people and at the same time check the arbitrary exercise of political power. The doctrine of the separation of powers was designed to prevent any one group from gaining control of the national governmental apparatus. The selections reprinted here from *The Federalist,* which was written between October, 1787, and August, 1788, outline the theory and mechanism of the separation of powers.

9
Alexander Hamilton

FEDERALIST 1

I propose, in a series of papers to discuss the following interesting particulars . . . The utility of the UNION to your political prosperity . . . The insufficiency of the present confederation to preserve that Union . . . The necessity of a government, at least equally energetic with the one proposed, to the attainment of this object . . . The conformity of the proposed constitution to the true principles of republican government . . . Its analogy to your own state constitution . . . and lastly, The additional security, which its adoption will afford to the preservation of that species of government, to liberty, and to property.

10
James Madison

FEDERALIST 47

I proceed to examine the particular structure of this government, and the distribution of this mass of power among its constituent parts.

One of the principal objections inculcated by the more respectable adversaries to the constitution, is its supposed violation of the political maxim, that the legislative, executive, and judiciary departments, ought to be separate and distinct. In the structure of the federal government, no regard, it is said, seems to have been paid to this essential precaution in favor of liberty. The several departments of power are distributed and blended in such a manner, as at once to destroy all symmetry and beauty of form; and to expose some of the essential parts of the edifice to the danger of being crushed by the disproportionate weight of other parts.

No political truth is certainly of greater intrinsic value, or is stamped with the authority of more enlightened patrons of liberty, than that on which the objection is founded. The accumulation of all powers, legislative, executive, and judiciary, in the same hands, whether of one, a few, or many, and whether hereditary, self-appointed, or elective, may justly be pronounced the very definition of tyranny. Were the federal constitution, therefore, really chargeable with this accumulation of power, or with a mixture of powers, having a dangerous tendency to such an accumulation, no further arguments would be necessary to inspire a universal reprobation of the system. I persuade myself, however, that it will be made apparent to every one, that the charge cannot be supported, and that the maxim on which it relies has been totally misconceived and misapplied.

The oracle who is always consulted and cited on this subject, is the celebrated Montesquieu. If he be not the author of this invaluable precept in the science of politics, he has the merit of at least displaying and recommending it most effectually to the attention of mankind. . . .

From . . . facts, by which Montesquieu was guided, it may clearly be inferred, that in saying, "there can be no liberty, where the legislative and executive powers are united in the same person, or body of magistrates"; or "if the power of judging, be not separated from the legislative and executive powers," he did not mean that these departments ought to have no *partial agency* in, or no *control* over, the acts of each other. His meaning . . . can amount to no more than this, that where the *whole* power of one department is exercised by the same hands which possess the *whole* power of another department, the fundamental principles of a free constitution are subverted. . . .

If we look into the constitutions of the several states, we find, that notwithstanding the emphatical, and, in some instances, the unqualified terms in which this axiom has been laid down, there is not a single instance in which the several departments of power have been kept absolutely separate and distinct. . . .

The constitution of Massachusetts has observed a sufficient, though less pointed caution, in expressing this fundamental article of liberty. It declares, "that the legislative department shall never exercise the executive and judicial powers, or either of them: the executive shall never exercise the legislative and judicial powers, or either of them: the judicial shall never exercise the legislative and executive powers, or either of them." This declaration corresponds precisely with the doctrine of Montesquieu. . . . It goes no farther than to prohibit any one of the entire departments from exercising the powers of another department. In the very constitution to which it is prefixed, a partial mixture of powers has been admitted. . . .

FEDERALIST 48

. . . I shall undertake in the next place to show, that unless these departments be so far connected and blended, as to give to each a constitutional control over the others, the degree of separation which the maxim requires, as essential to a free government, can never in practice be duly maintained.

It is agreed on all sides, that the powers properly belonging to one of the departments ought not to be directly and completely administered by either of the other departments. It is equally evident, that neither of them ought to possess, directly or indirectly, an overruling influence over the others in the administration of their respective powers. It will not be denied, that power is of an encroaching nature, and that it ought to be effectually restrained from passing the limits assigned to it. After discriminating, therefore, in theory, the several classes of power, as they may in their nature be legislative, executive, or judiciary; the next, and most difficult task, is to provide some practical security for each, against the invasion of the others. What this security ought to be, is the great problem to be solved.

Will it be sufficient to mark, with precision, the boundaries of these departments, in the constitution of the government, and to trust to these parchment barriers against the encroaching spirit of power? This is the security which appears to have been principally relied on by the compilers of most American constitutions. But experience assures us, that the efficacy of the provision has been greatly overrated; and that some more adequate defense is indispensably necessary for the more feeble, against the more powerful members of the government. The legislative department is everywhere extending the sphere of its activity, and drawing all power into its impetuous vortex. . . .

In a government where numerous and extensive prerogatives are placed in the hands of an hereditary monarch, the executive department is very justly regarded as the source of danger, and watched with all the jealousy which a zeal for liberty ought to inspire. In a democracy, where a multitude of people exercise in person the legislative functions, and are continually exposed, by their incapacity for regular deliberation and concerted measures, to the ambitious intrigues of their executive magistrates, tyranny may well be apprehended on some favorable emergency, to start up in the same quarter. But in a representative republic, where the executive magistracy is carefully limited, both in the extent and the duration of its power; and where the legislative is exercised by an assembly, which is inspired by a supposed influence over the people, with an intrepid confidence in its own strength; which is sufficiently numerous to feel all the passions which actuate a multitude; yet not so numerous as to be incapable of pursuing the objects of its passions, by means which reason prescribes; it is against the enterprising ambition of this department, that the people ought to indulge all their jealousy and exhaust all their precautions.

The legislative department derives a superiority in our governments from other circumstances. Its constitutional powers being at once more extensive, and less susceptible of precise limits, it can, with the greater facility, mask, under complicated and indirect measures, the encroachment which it makes on the coordinate departments. It is not infrequently a question of real nicety in legislative bodies, whether the operation of a particular measure will, or will not extend beyond the legislative sphere. On the other side, the executive power being restrained within a narrower compass, and being more simple in its nature; and the judiciary being described by landmarks, still less uncertain, projects of usurpation by either of these departments would immediately betray and defeat themselves. Nor is this all: as the legislative department alone has access to the pockets of the people, and has in some constitutions full discretion, and in all a prevailing influence over the pecuniary rewards of those who fill the other departments; a dependence is thus created in the latter, which gives still greater facility to encroachments of the former. . . .

FEDERALIST 51

To what expedient then shall we finally resort, for maintaining in practice the necessary partition of power among the several departments, as laid down in the constitution? The only answer that can be given is, that as all these exterior provisions are found to be inadequate, the defect must be supplied, by so contriving the interior structure of the government, as that its several constit-uent parts may, by their mutual relations, be the means of keeping each other in their proper places. . . .

In order to lay a due foundation for that separate and distinct exercise of the different powers of government, which, to a certain extent, is admitted on all hands to be essential to the preservation of liberty, it is evident that each department should have a will of its own; and consequently should be so constituted, that the members of each should have as little agency as possible in the appointment of the members of the others. . . .

It is equally evident, that the members of each department should be as little dependent as possible on those of the others, for the emoluments annexed to their offices. Were the executive magistrate, or the judges, not independent of the legislature in this particular, their independence in every other, would be merely nominal.

But the great security against a gradual concentration of the several powers in the same department, consists in giving to those who administer each department, the necessary constitutional means, and personal motives, to resist encroachments of the others. The provision for defense must in this, as in all other cases, be made commensurate to the danger of attack. Ambition must be made to counteract ambition. The interest of the man must be connected with the constitutional rights of the place. It may be a reflection on human nature, that such devices should be necessary to control the abuses of government. But what is government itself, but the greatest of all reflections on human nature? If men were angels, no government would be necessary. If angels were to govern men, neither external nor internal controls on government would be necessary. In framing a government, which is to be administered by men over men, the great difficulty lies in this: You must first enable the government to control the governed; and in the next place, oblige it to control itself. A dependence on the people is, no doubt, the primary control on the government; but experience has taught mankind the necessity of auxiliary precautions.

This policy of supplying by opposite and rival interests, the defect of better motives, might be traced through the whole system of human affairs, private as well as public. We see it particularly displayed in all the subordinate distributions of power; where the constant aim is, to divide and arrange the several offices in such a manner, as that each may be a check on the other; that the private interest of every individual, may be a sentinel over the public rights. These inventions of prudence cannot be less requisite to the distribution of the supreme powers of the state.

But it is not possible to give to each department an equal power of self-defense. In republican government, the legislative authority necessarily predominates. The remedy for this inconvenience is, to divide the legislature into different branches; and to render them by different modes of election, and different principles of action, as little connected with each other, as the nature of their common functions, and their common dependence on the society will admit. It may even be necessary to guard against dangerous encroachments, by still further precautions. As the weight of the legislative authority requires that it should be thus divided, the weakness of the executive may require, on the other hand, that it should be fortified. An absolute negative on the legislature, appears, at first view, to be the natural defense with which the executive magistrate should be armed. But perhaps it would be neither altogether safe, nor alone sufficient. On ordinary occasions, it might not be exerted with the requisite firmness; and on extraordinary occasions, it might be perfidiously abused. May not this defect of an absolute negative be supplied by some qualified connection between this weaker department, and the weaker branch of the stronger department, by which the latter may be led to support the constitutional rights of the former, without being too much detached from the rights of its own department?

On July 24, 1974, the Supreme Court in *United States v. Richard M. Nixon* rendered a historic decision interpreting the meaning of the separation of powers. President Nixon had attempted to claim executive privilege in refusing to obey a district court order to turn over tape recordings and other data involving White House conversations pertaining to the Watergate coverup. Special Watergate Prosecutor Leon Jaworski had successfully sought from District Court Judge John Sirica a subpoena directing the President to produce the tapes and documents, to be used as evidence in the trial of six former Nixon aides who were accused of conspiring to conceal the burglary in 1972 of the Democratic National Headquarters in the Watergate complex. The court held unanimously (Justice Rehnquist, one of Nixon's four appointees to the court, disqualified himself) that the President is subject to the judicial process, and cannot claim executive privilege in refusing to turn over the subpoenaed material on the general grounds that the material contained "confidential conversations between a President and his close advisers that it would be inconsistent with the public interest to produce." The court stated that although the separation of powers requires that each branch give deference to the others, only the courts have the power to say what the law is with respect to the claim of executive privilege. The proper scope of judicial power in a particular case and controversy cannot in any way be subject to presidential control.

11
United States v. Richard M. Nixon
—U.S.—(1974)

Mr. Chief Justice Burger delivered the opinion of the Court:

These cases present for review the denial of a motion, filed on behalf of the President of the United States, in the case of United States v. Mitchell et al. (D.C. Crim. No. 74–110), to quash a third party subpoena duces tecum [requires the party who is summoned to appear in court to bring some document or piece of evidence to be used or inspected by the court] issued by the United States District Court for the District of Columbia, pursuant to Fed. Rule Crim. Proc. 17 (C). The subpoena directed the President to produce certain tape recordings and documents relating to his conversations with aides and advisers. The Court rejected the President's claims of absolute executive privilege, of lack of jurisdiction, and of failure to satisfy the requirements of Rule 17 (C) [that the evidence sought must be specific, relevant to the case, and admissible in court]. The President appealed to the Court of Appeals. We granted the United States petition for certiorari before judgment, and also the President's responsive cross-petition for certiorari before judgment, because of the public importance of the issues presented and the need for their prompt resolution.

On March 1, 1974, a grand jury of the United States District Court for the District of Columbia returned an indictment charging seven named individuals with various offenses, including conspiracy to defraud the United States and to obstruct justice. Although he was not designated as such in the indictment, the grand jury named the President, among others, as an unindicted co-conspirator. On April 18, 1974, upon motion of the special prosecutor . . . a subpoena duces tecum was issued pursuant to Rule 17 (C) to the President by the United States District Court and made returnable on May 2, 1974. This subpoena required the production, in advance of the September 9 trial date, of certain tapes, memoranda, papers, transcripts, or other writings relating to certain precisely identified meetings between the President and others. The Special Prosecutor was able to fix the time, place and persons present at these discussions because the White House daily logs and appointment records had been delivered to him.

Transcripts Were Released. On April 30, 1974, the President publicly released edited transcripts of forty-three conversations; portions of twenty conversations subject to subpoena in the present case were included. On May 1, 1974, the President's counsel filed a "special appearance" and a motion to quash the subpoena, under Rule 17 (C). This motion was accompanied by a formal claim of privilege. At a subsequent hearing, further motions to expunge the grand jury's action naming the President as an unindicted co-conspirator and for protective orders against the disclosure of that information were filed or raised orally by counsel for the President.

On May 20, 1974, the District Court denied the motion to quash and the motions to expunge and for protective orders. It further ordered "the President or any subordinate officer, official or employee with custody or control of the documents or objects subpoenaed," to deliver to the District Court, on or before May 31, 1974, the originals of all subpoenaed items, as well as an index and analysis of those items, together with tape copies of those portions of the subpoenaed recordings for which transcripts had been released to the public by the President on April 30. . . .

The District Court held that the judiciary, not the President, was the final arbiter of a claim of executive privilege. The court concluded that, under the circumstances of this case, the presumptive privilege was overcome by the Special Prosecutor's prima facie "demonstration of need sufficiently compelling to warrant judicial examination in chambers. . . ."

THE CLAIM OF PRIVILEGE

A

Having determined that the requirements of Rule 17 (e) were satisfied, we turn to the claim that the subpoena should be quashed because it demands "confidential conversations between a President and his close advisers that it would be inconsistent with the public interest to produce." . . . The first contention is a broad claim that the separation of powers doctrine precludes judicial review of a president's claim of privilege. The second contention is that if he does not prevail on the claim of absolute privilege, the Court should hold as a matter of constitutional law that the privilege prevails over the subpoena duces tecum.

In the performance of assigned constitutional duties each branch of the Government must initially interpret the Constitution, and the interpretation of its powers by any branch is due great respect from the others.

The President's counsel, as we have noted, reads the Constitution as providing an absolute privilege of confidentiality for all Presidential communications. Many decisions of this Court, however, have unequivocally reaffirmed the holding of Marbury v. Madison, 1 Cranch 137 (1803), that "it is emphatically the province and duty of the Judicial department to say what the law is." . . .

No holding of the Court has defined the scope of judicial power specifically relating to the enforcement of a subpoena for confidential Presidential communications for use in a criminal prosecution, but other exercises of powers by the executive branch and the legislative branch have been found invalid as in conflict with the Constitution. . . .

Our system of Government "requires that Federal courts on occasion interpret the Constitution in a manner at variance with the construction given the document by another branch." . . .

Notwithstanding the deference each branch must accord the others, the "judicial power of the United States" vested in the Federal courts by Art. 111, Section 1, of the Constitution can no more be shared with the executive branch than the chief executive, for example, can share with the judiciary the veto power, or the Congress share with the judiciary the power to override a Presidential veto. Any other conclusion would be contrary to the basic concept of separation of powers and the checks and balances that flow from the scheme of a tripartite Government. [See] the Federalist, No. 47, . . . We therefore reaffirm that it is "emphatically the province and the duty" of this court "to say what the law is" with respect to the claim of privilege presented in this case. Marbury v. Madison, supra, ...

B

In support of his claim of absolute privilege, the President's counsel urges two grounds one of which is common to all governments and one of which is peculiar to our system of separation of powers. The first ground is the valid need for protection of communications between high government officials and those who advise and assist them in the performance of their manifold duties; the importance of this confidentiality is too plain to require further discussion. Human experience teaches that those who expect public dissemination of their remarks may well temper candor with a concern for appearances and for their own interests to the detriment of the decision making process. Whatever the nature of the privilege of confidentiality of Presidential communications in the exercise of Art. 8 powers, the privilege can be said to derive from the supremacy of each branch within its own assigned area of constitutional duties. Certain powers and privileges flow from the nature of enumerated powers; the protection of the confidentiality of Presidential communications has similar constitutional underpinnings.

The second ground asserted by the President's counsel in support of the claim of absolute privilege rests on the doctrine of separation of powers. Here it is argued that the independence of the executive branch within its own sphere, Humphrey's Executor v. United States, 295 U.S. 602, 629–630 (1935): Kilbourn v. Thompson, 103 U.S. 168, 190–191 (1880), insulates a President from a judicial subpoena in an ongoing criminal prosecution, and thereby protects confidential Presidential communications.

However, neither the doctrine of separation of powers, nor the need for confidentiality of high level communications, without more, can sustain an absolute unqualified Presidential privilege of immunity from judicial process under all circumstances. The President's need for complete candor and objectivity from advisers calls for great deference from the courts. However, when the privilege depends solely on the broad, undifferentiated claim of public interest in the confidentiality of such conversations, a confrontation with other values arises. Absent a claim of need to protect military, diplomatic or sensitive national security secrets, we find it difficult to accept the argument that even the very important interest in confidentiality of Presidential communications is significantly diminished by production of such material for in camera inspection [in the judge's chambers] with all the protection that a District Court will be obliged to provide.

The impediment that an absolute, unqualified privilege would place in the way of the primary constitutional duty of the judicial branch to do justice in criminal prosecutions would plainly conflict with the function of the courts under Art. III. In designing the structure of our Government and dividing and allocating the sovereign power among three coequal branches, the framers of the Constitution sought to provide a comprehensive system, but the separate powers were not intended to operate with absolute independence.

"While the Constitution diffuses power the better to secure liberty, it also contemplates that practice will integrate the dispersed powers into a workable Government. It enjoins upon its branches separateness but interdependence, autonomy but reciprocity. Youngstown Sheet & Tube Co. v. Sawyer, 343 U.S. 579, 635 (1952) (Jackson, J., concurring)."

To read the Art. II powers of the President as providing an absolute privilege as against a subpoena essential to enforcement of criminal statutes on no more than a generalized claim of the public interest in confidentiality of nonmilitary and nondiplomatic discussions would upset the constitutional balance of "a workable government" and gravely impair the role of the courts under Art. III.

C

Since we conclude that the legitimate needs of the judicial process may outweigh Presidential privilege, it is necessary to resolve those competing interests in a manner that preserves the essential functions of each branch. The right and indeed the duty to resolve that question does not free the judiciary from according high respect to the representations made on behalf of the President. United States v. Burr, 25 Fed. Cas. 187, 190, 191–192 (No. 14,694) (1807).

The expectation of a President to the confidentiality of his conversations and correspondence, like the claim of confidentially of judicial deliberations, for example, has all the values to which we accord deference for the privacy of all citizens and added to those values the necessity for protection of the public interest in candid, objective, and even blunt or harsh opinions in Presidential decision-making. A President and those who assist him must be free to explore alternatives in the process of shaping policies and making decisions and to do so in a way many would be unwilling to express except privately. These are the considerations justifying a presumptive privilege for Presidential communications. The privilege is fundamental to the operation of government and inextricably rooted in the separation of powers under the Constitution. In Nixon v. Sirica, 487 F. 2d 700 (1973), the Court of Appeals held that such Presidential communications are "presumptively privileged," id., at 717, and this position is accepted by both parties in the present litigation.

We agree with Mr. Chief Justice Marshall's observation, therefore, that "in no case of this kind would a Court be required to proceed against the President as against an ordinary individual." United States v. Burr, 25 Fed. Cas. 187, 191 (No. 14,694) (CCD Va. 1807).

But this presumptive privilege must be considered in light of our historic commitment to the rule of law. This is nowhere more profoundly manifest than in our view that "the twofold aim [of criminal justice] is that guilt shall not escape or innocence suffer." Berger v. United States, 295 U.S. 18, 88 (1935). We have elected to employ an adversary system of criminal justice in which the parties contest all issues before a court of law. The need to develop all relevant facts in the adversary system is both fundamental and comprehensive. The ends of criminal justice would be defeated if judgments were to be founded on a partial or speculative presentation of the facts. The very integrity of the judicial system and public confidence in the system depend on full disclosure of all the facts, within the framework of the rules of evidence.

To ensure that justice is done, it is imperative to the function of courts that compulsory process be available for the production of evidence needed either by the prosecution or by the defense.

Only recently the Court restated the ancient proposition of law, albeit in the context of a grand jury inquiry rather than a trial,

" 'That the public . . . has a right to every man's evidence' except for those persons protected by a constitutional, common law, or statutory privilege, United States v. Bryan, 339 U.S., at 331 (1949); Blackmer v. United States, 284 U.S. 421, 438, Branzburg v. United States, 408 U.S. 665, 638 (1972)."

The privileges referred to by the Court are designed to protect weighty and legitimate competing interests. Thus, the Fifth Amendment to the Constitution provides that no man "shall be compelled in any criminal case to be a witness against himself."

And, generally, an attorney or a priest may not be required to disclose what has been revealed in professional confidence. These and other interests are recognized in law by privileges against forced disclosure, established in the Constitution, by statute, or at common law. Whatever their origins, these exceptions to the demand for every man's evidence are not lightly created nor expansively construed, for they are in derogation of the search for truth.

In this case the President challenges a subpoena served on him as a third party requiring the production of materials for use in a criminal prosecution on the claim that he has a privilege against disclosure of confidential communications. He does not place his claim of privilege on the ground they are military or diplomatic secrets. As to these areas of Art. II duties the courts have traditionally shown the utmost deference to Presidential responsibilities. In C. & S. Air Lines v. Waterman Steamship Corp., 333 U.S. 103, 111 (1948), dealing with Presidential authority involving foreign policy considerations, the Court said:

"The President, both as commander-in-chief and as the nation's organ for foreign affairs, has available intelligence services whose reports are not and ought not to be published to the world. It would be intolerable that courts, without the relevant information, should review and perhaps nullify actions of the executive taken on information properly held secret." id., at 111.

In United States v. Reynolds 345 U.S. 1 (1952), dealing with a claimant's demand for evidence in a damage case against the Government the Court said:

"It may be possible to satisfy the Court, from all the circumstances of the case, that there is a reasonable danger that compulsion of the evidence will expose military matters which, in the interest of national security, should not be divulged. When this is the case, the occasion for the privilege is appropriate, and the Court should not jeopardize the security which the privilege is meant to protect by insisting upon an examination of the evidence, even by the judge alone, in chambers."

No case of the Court, however, has extended this high degree of deference to a President's generalized interest in confidentiality. Nowhere in the Constitution as we have noted earlier, is there any explicit reference to a privilege of confidentiality, yet to the extent this interest relates to the effective discharge of a President's powers, it is constitutionally based.

The right to the production of all evidence at a criminal trial similarly has consitutional dimensions. The Sixth Amendment explicitly confers upon every defendant in a criminal trial the right "to be confronted with the witnesses against him" and "to have compulsory process for obtaining witnesses in his favor." Moreover, the Fifth Amendment also guarantees that no person shall be deprived of liberty without due process of law. It is the manifest duty of the courts to vindicate those guarantees and to accomplish that it is essential that all relevant and admissible evidence be produced.

In this case we must weigh the importance of the general privilege of confidentiality of Presidential communications in performance of his responsibilities against the inroads of such a privilege on the fair administration of criminal justice. The interest in preserving confidentiality is weighty indeed and entitled to great respect. However we cannot conclude that advisers will be moved to temper the candor of their remarks by the infrequent occasions of disclosure because of the possibility that such conversations will be called for in the context of a criminal prosecution.

On the other hand, the allowance of the privilege to withhold evidence that is demonstrably relevant in a criminal trial would cut deeply into the guarantee of due process of law and gravely impair the basic function of the courts. A President's acknowledged need for confidentiality in the communications of his office is general in nature, whereas the constitutional need for production of relevant evidence in a criminal proceeding is specific and central to the fair adjudication of a particular criminal case in the administration of justice.

Without access to specific facts a criminal prosecution may be totally frustrated. The President's broad interest in confidentiality of communications will not be vitiated by disclosure of a limited number of conversations preliminarily shown to have some bearing on the pending criminal cases.

We conclude that when the ground for asserting privilege as to subpoenaed materials sought for use in a criminal trial is based only on the generalized interest in confidentiality, it cannot prevail over the fundamental demands of due process of law in the fair administration of criminal justice. The generalized assertion of privilege must yield to the demonstrated, specific need for evidence in a pending criminal trial.

D

We have earlier determined that the District Court did not err in authorizing the issuance of the subpoena. If a President concludes that compliance with a subpoena would be injurious to the public interest he may properly, as was done here, invoke a claim of privilege on the return of the subpoena. Upon receiving a claim of privilege from the chief executive, it became the further duty of the District Court to treat the subpoenaed material as presumptively privileged and to require the Special Prosecutor to demonstrate that the Presidential material was "essential to the justice of the [pending criminal] case." United States v. Burr, Supra, at 192. Here the District Court treated the material as presumptively privileged, proceeded to find that the Special Prosecutor had made a sufficient showing to rebut the presumption and ordered an in camera examination of the subpoenaed material.

On the basis of our examination of the record we are unable to conclude that the District Court erred in ordering the inspection. Accordingly we affirm the order of the District Court that subpoenaed materials be transmitted to that court. We now turn to the important question of the District Court's responsibilities in conducting the in camera examination of Presidential materials or communications delivered under the compulsion of the subpoena duces tecum.

E

Enforcement of the subpoena duces tecum was stayed pending this Court's resolution of the issues raised by the petitions for certiorari. Those issues now having been disposed of, the matter of implementation will rest with the district court. "[T]he guard, furnished to [The President] to protect him from being harassed by vexations and unnecessary subpoenas, is to be looked for in the conduct of the [District] Court after the subpoenas have issued; not in any circumstances which is to precede their being issued." United States v. Burr, supra, at 34. Statements that meet the test of admissibility and relevance must be isolated; all other material must be excised. At this stage, the District Court is not limited to representations of the Special Prosecutor as to the evidence sought by the subpoena; the material will be available to the District Court. It is elementary that in camera inspection of evidence is always a procedure calling for scrupulous protection against any release or publication of material not found by the Court, at that stage, probably admissible in evidence and relevant to the issues of the trial for which it is sought. That being true of an ordinary situation, it is obvious that the District Court has a very heavy responsibility to see to it that Presidential conversations which are either not relevant or not admissible, are accorded that high degree of respect due the President of the United States. Mr. Chief Justice Marshall sitting as a trial judge in the Burr case, supra, was extraordinarily careful to point out that:

"[I]n no case of this kind would a court be required to proceed against the President as against an ordinary individual." United States v. Burr, 25 Fed. Cases 187, 191 (No. 14,694).

Marshall's statement cannot be read to mean in any sense that a President is above the law, but relates to the singularly unique role under Art. II of a President's communications and activities related to the performance of duties under that Article. Moreover, a President's communications and activities encompass a vastly wider range of sensitive material than would be true of any "ordinary individual." It is therefore necessary in the public interest to afford Presidential confidentiality the greatest protection consistent with the fair administration of justice. The need for confidentiality even as to idle conversations with associates in which casual reference might be made concerning political leaders within the country or foreign statesmen is too obvious to call for further treatment. We have no doubt that the District Judge will at all times accord to Presidential records that high degree of deference suggested in United States v. Burr, supra, and will discharge his responsibility to see to it that until released to the Special Prosecutor no in camera material is revealed to anyone. This burden applies with even greater force to excised material; once the decision is made to excise, the material is restored to its privileged status and should be returned under seal to its lawful custodian.

Since the matter came before the Court during the pendency of a criminal prosecution, and on representations that time is of the essence, the mandate shall issue forthwith.

Affirmed.

Mr. Justice Rehnquist took no part in the consideration or decision of these cases.

The Role of Impeachment in Checks and Balances

Article II, Section 4 of the Constitution provides that: ". . . The President, Vice President and all civil officers of the United States shall be removed from office on impeachment for, and conviction of, treason, bribery, or other high crimes and misdemeanors . . ."

Since the founding of the republic only 65 persons have ever been considered for impeachment by the House of Representatives. Of these, 12 have been impeached, eleven tried by the Senate (one Judge resigned after being impeached and charges were dropped against him), and four have been convicted. From these statistics it would seem that the impeachment process is little used and insignificant. The origins of the impeachment process date to British parliamentary practice in the 14th century. Impeachment developed because certain officers in government were, for various reasons, placed beyond the reach of ordinary criminal courts. High judicial and executive officers were not subject to the complaints of private individuals in the ordinary courts. Private persons, aggrieved by the actions of such officers, turned to Parliament for redress. The House of Commons became the accuser, and the House of Lords the body that tried cases of impeachment.

What is the meaning of the impeachment provisions of the Constitution? In particular, what does the phrase "high crimes and misdemeanors" mean? In order to bring impeachment proceedings against an official must he be accused of violation of criminal law, i.e., an indictable crime? Or, does the phrase "high crimes and misdemeanors" refer only to "crimes" against the nation and the public, political misdeeds or maladministration that would not be subject to ordinary criminal prosecution? These issues were raised in 1973 and 1974 as the House of Representatives began to investigate various actions of President Nixon, including those surrounding the Watergate affair, to determine if he should be impeached. The following selections deal with the impeachment process, beginning with the views of Alexander Hamilton in *Federalist 65,* and proceeding to an analysis by Raoul Berger.

12
Alexander Hamilton

FEDERALIST 65

The remaining powers which the plan of the convention allots to the Senate, in a distinct capacity, are comprised in their participation with the executive in the appointment to offices, and in their judicial character as a court for the trial of impeachments. As in the business of appointments the executive will be the principal agent, the provisions relating to it will most properly be discussed in the examination of that department. We will, therefore, conclude this head with a view of the judicial character of the Senate.

A well-constituted court for the trial of impeachments is an object not more to be desired than difficult to be obtained in a government wholly elective. The subjects of its jurisdiction are those offenses which proceed from the misconduct of public men, or, in other words, from the abuse or violation of some public trust. They are of a nature which may with peculiar propriety be denominated POLITICAL, as they relate chiefly to injuries done immediately to the society itself. The prosecution of them, for this reason, will seldom fail to agitate the passions of the whole community, and to divide it into parties more or less friendly or inimical to the accused. In many cases it will connect itself with the pre-existing factions, and will enlist all their animosities, partialities, influence, and interest on one side or on the other; and in such cases there will always be the greatest danger that the decision will be regulated more by the comparative strength of parties than by the real demonstrations of innocence or guilt.

The delicacy and magnitude of a trust which so deeply concerns the political reputation and existence of every man engaged in the administration of public affairs speak for themselves. The difficulty of placing it rightly in a government resting entirely on the basis of periodical elections will as readily be perceived, when it is considered that the most conspicuous characters in it will, from that circumstance, be too often the leaders or the tools of the most cunning or the most numerous faction, and on this account can hardly be expected to possess the requisite neutrality toward those whose conduct may be the subject of scrutiny.

The convention, it appears, thought the Senate the most fit depositary of this important trust. Those who can best discern the intrinsic difficulty of the thing will be the least hasty in condemning that opinion, and will be most inclined to allow due weight to the arguments which may be supposed to have produced it.

What, it may be asked, is the true spirit of the institution itself? Is it not designed as a method of NATIONAL INQUEST into the conduct of public men? If this be the design of it, who can so properly be the inquisitors for the nation as the representatives of the nation themselves? It is not disputed that the power of originating the inquiry, or, in other words, of preferring the impeachment, ought to be lodged in the hands of one branch of the legislative body. Will not the reasons which indicate the propriety of this arrangement strongly plead for an admission of the other branch of that body to a share of the inquiry? The model from which the idea of this institution has been borrowed pointed out that course to the convention. In Great Britain it is the province of the House of Commons to prefer the impeachment, and of the House of Lords to decide upon it. Several of the State constitutions have followed the example. As well the latter as the former seem to have regarded the practice of impeachments as a bridle in the hands of the legislative body upon the executive servants of the government. Is not this the true light in which it ought to be regarded?

Where else than in the Senate could have been found a tribunal sufficiently dignified, or sufficiently independent? What other body would be likely to feel *confidence enough in its own situation* to preserve, unawed and uninfluenced, the necessary impartiality between an *individual* accused and the *representatives of the people, his accusers?*

Could the Supreme Court have been relied upon as answering this description? It is much to be doubted whether the members of that tribunal would at all times be endowed with so eminent a portion of fortitude as would be called for in the execution of so difficult a task; and it is still more to be doubted whether they would possess the degree of credit and authority which might, on certain occasions, be indispensable towards reconciling the people to a decision that should happen to clash with an accusation brought by their immediate representatives. A deficiency in the first would be fatal to the accused; in the last, dangerous to the public tranquillity. The hazard, in both these respects, could only be avoided, if at all, by rendering that tribunal more numerous than would consist with a reasonable attention to economy. The necessity of a numerous court for the trial of impeachments is equally dictated by the nature of the proceeding. This can never be tied down by such strict rules, either in the delineation of the offense by the prosecutors or in the construction of it by the judges, as in common cases serve to limit the discretion of courts in favor of personal security. There will be no jury to stand between the judges who are to pronounce the sentence of law and the party who is to receive or suffer it. The awful discretion which a court of impeachments must necessarily have to doom to honor or to infamy the most confidential and the most distinguished characters of the community forbids the commitment of the trust to a small number of persons.

These considerations seem alone sufficient to authorize a conclusion, that the Supreme Court would have been an improper substitute for the Senate, as a court of impeachments. There remains a further consideration, which will not a little strengthen this conclusion. It is this: the punishment which may be the consequence of conviction upon impeachment is not to terminate the chastisement of the offender. After having been sentenced to a perpetual ostracism from the esteem and confidence and honors and emoluments of his country, he will still be liable to prosecution and punishment in the ordinary course of law. Would it be proper that the persons who had disposed of his fame, and his most valuable rights as a citizen, in one trial, should, in another trial, for the same offense, be also the disposers of his life and his fortune? Would there not be the greatest reason to apprehend that error, in the first sentence, would be the parent of error in the second sentence? That the strong bias of one decision would be apt to overrule the influence of any new lights which might be brought to vary the complexion of another decision? Those who know anything of human nature will not hesitate to answer these questions in the affirmative; and will be at no loss to perceive that by making the same persons judges in both cases, those who might happen to be the objects of prosecution would, in a great measure, be deprived of the double security intended them by a double trial. The loss of life and estate would often be virtually included in a sentence which, in its terms, imported nothing more than dismission from a present and disqualification for a future office. It may be said that the intervention of a jury, in the second instance, would obviate the danger. But juries are frequently influenced by the opinions of judges. They are sometimes induced to find special verdicts, which refer the main question to the decision of the court. Who would be willing to stake his life and his estate upon the verdict of a jury acting under the auspices of judges who had predetermined his guilt?

Would it have been an improvement of the plan to have united the

Supreme Court with the Senate in the formation of the court of impeachments? This union would certainly have been attended with several advantages; but would they not have been overbalanced by the signal disadvantage, already stated, arising from the agency of the same judges in the double prosecution to which the offender would be liable? To a certain extent, the benefits of that union will be obtained from making the chief justice of the Supreme Court the president of the court of impeachments, as is proposed to be done in the plan of the convention; while the inconveniences of an entire incorporation of the former into the latter will be substantially avoided. This was perhaps the prudent mean. I forbear to remark upon the additional pretext for clamor against the judiciary, which so considerable an augmentation of its authority would have afforded.

Would it have been desirable to have composed the court for the trial of impeachments of persons wholly distinct from the other departments of the government? There are weighty arguments, as well against as in favor of such a plan. To some minds it will not appear a trivial objection that it would tend to increase the complexity of the political machine, and to add a new spring to the government, the utility of which would at best be questionable. But an objection which will not be thought by any unworthy of attention is this: a court formed upon such a plan would either be attended with heavy expense, or might in practice be subject to a variety of casualties and inconveniences. It must either consist of permanent officers, stationary at the seat of government, and of course entitled to fixed and regular stipends, or of certain officers of the State governments, to be called upon whenever an impeachment was actually depending. It will not be easy to imagine any third mode materially different which could rationally be proposed. As the court, for reasons already given, ought to be numerous, the first scheme will be reprobated by every man who can compare the extent of the public wants with the means of supplying them. The second will be espoused with caution by those who will seriously consider the difficulty of collecting men dispersed over the whole Union; the injury to the innocent, from the procrastinated determination of the charges which might be brought against them; the advantage to the guilty, from the opportunities which delay would afford to intrigue and corruption; and in some cases the detriment to the State, from the prolonged inaction of men whose firm and faithful execution of their duty might have exposed them to the persecution of an intemperate or designing majority in the House of Representatives. Though this latter supposition may seem harsh and might not be likely often to be verified, yet it ought not to be forgotten that the demon of faction will, at certain seasons, extend his scepter over all numerous bodies of men.

But, though one or the other of the substitutes which have been examined or some other that might be devised should be thought preferable to the plan, in this respect reported by the convention, it will not follow that the Constitution ought for this reason to be rejected. If mankind were to resolve to agree in no institution of government, until every part of it had been adjusted to the most exact standard of perfection, society would soon become a general scene of anarchy, and the world a desert. Where is the standard of perfection to be found? Who will undertake to unite the discordant opinions of a whole community in the same judgment of it; and to prevail upon one conceited projector to renounce his *infallible* criterion for the *fallible* criterion of his more *conceited neighbor?* To answer the purpose of the adversaries of the Constitution, they ought to prove, not merely that particular provisions in it are not the best which might have been imagined, but that the plan upon the whole is bad and pernicious.

PUBLIUS

13
Raoul Berger

IMPEACHMENT AS AN INSTRUMENT OF REGENERATION

Impeachment, to most Americans today, seems to represent a dread mystery, an almost parricidal act, to be contemplated, if at all, with awe and alarm. It was not always so. Impeachment, said the House of Commons in 1679, was "the chief institution for the preservation of the government"; and chief among the impeachable offenses was "subversion of the Constitution." In 1641, the House of Commons charged that the Earl of Strafford had subverted the fundamental law and introduced an arbitrary and tyrannical government. By his trial, which merged into a bill of attainder and resulted in his execution, and by a series of other seventeenth-century impeachments, Parliament made the ministers accountable to it rather than to the King and stemmed a tide of absolutism that swept the rest of Europe. Thereafter, impeachment fell into relative disuse during the eighteenth century because a ministry could now be toppled by the House of Commons on a vote of no confidence.

Our impeachment, modeled on that of England, proceeds as follows: a committee of the House of Representatives may be instructed to investigate rumors or charges of executive misconduct. If the committee reports that it found impeachable offenses, it is directed by the House to prepare articles of impeachment, which are the analogue of the accusations contained in the several counts of an indictment by a grand jury. Strictly speaking, it is the

From Raoul Berger, "Impeachment: An Instrument of Regeneration," *Harper's* (January 1974). Reprinted by permission.

articles that constitute the impeachment. The articles, if approved by a majority of the House, are then filed with the Senate.

At that point, the articles are served by the Senate on the accused, who is given time within which to file an answer to the charges. At an appointed time, the Senate convenes as a court. If it is the President who is being tried, the Chief Justice of the Supreme Court acts as the presiding officer. Evidence is subject to the exclusionary rules applied by a court, and the accused is permitted by his counsel to cross-examine witnesses and to make arguments for acquittal. A vote of two-thirds of the Senators present is required for conviction.

When the Framers came to draft our Constitution, they might well have regarded impeachment as an outworn, clumsy institution, not particularly well-suited to a tripartite scheme of government protected by the separation of powers. Why, then, did they adopt it?

The reason lies in the fact that the Founders vividly remembered the seventeenth-century experience of the mother country. They remembered the absolutist pretensions of the Stuarts; they were haunted by the greedy expansiveness of power; they dreaded usurpation and tyranny. And so they adopted impeachment as a means of displacing a usurper—a President who exceeded the bounds of the executive's authority.

The colonists, after all, regarded the executive, in the words of Thomas Corwin, as "the natural enemy, the legislative assembly the natural friend of liberty." Throughout the colonial period, they had elected their own assemblies and trusted them as their own representatives. The governors, on the other hand, were often upper-class Englishmen with little understanding of American aspirations, who had been foisted on the colonists by the Crown. Hence, Congress was given the power to remove the President. This power, it must be emphasized, constitutes a deliberate breach in the doctrine of separation of powers, so that no arguments drawn from that doctrine (such as executive privilege) may apply to the preliminary inquiry by the House or the subsequent trial by the Senate.

The constitution adopts the old English formula: impeachment for and conviction of "treason, bribery, or other high crimes and misdemeanors." Because "crimes" and "misdemeanors" are familiar terms of criminal law, it is tempting to conclude that "high crimes and misdemeanors" is simply a grandiloquent version of ordinary "crimes and misdemeanors." Not so. As the terms "treason" and "bribery" suggest, these were offenses against the state, political crimes as distinguished from crimes against the person, such as murder. The association of "treason, bribery" with "other high crimes and misdemeanors" indicates that the latter also refer to offenses of a "political" nature. They were punishable by Parliament, whereas courts punished "misdemeanors," that is, lesser *private* wrongs. In short, "high crimes and misdemeanors" appears to be a phrase confined to impeachments, without roots in the ordinary English criminal law and which, so far as I could discover, had no relation to

whether a criminal indictment would lie in the particular circumstances.*
Certain political crimes—treason and bribery, for example—were also indictable crimes, but English impeachments did not require an indictable crime.
Nonetheless, the English impeachment was criminal because conviction was
punishable by death or imprisonment.

In fact, under English practice there were a number of impeachable
offenses that might not even be crimes under American criminal law. First and
foremost was subversion of the Constitution: for example, the usurpation of
power to which Parliament laid claim. Other impeachable offenses were abuse
of power, neglect of duty, corrupt practices that fell short of crimes, even the
giving of "bad advice" to the King by his ministers. Broadly speaking, these
categories outlined the boundaries of "high crimes and misdemeanors" at the
time the Constitution was adopted.

Let us now turn to Philadelphia in 1787. Article II, Section 4 of the
Constitution provides that "the President, Vice-President and all civil Officers
of the United States, shall be removed from Office on Impeachment for, and
Conviction of, Treason, Bribery, or other high Crimes and Misdemeanors."

There is good reason to conclude that the Framers consciously divorced
impeachment from the necessity of proving an indictable criminal offense. This
is because Article I, Section 3(7) provides that "judgment in Cases of Impeachment shall not extend further than to removal from Office, and disqualification
to hold and enjoy any Office . . . but the Party convicted shall nevertheless be
liable and subject to Indictment, Trial, Judgment and Punishment, according
to Law." Thus the Framers sharply separated removal from office from criminal punishment by indictment and conviction, in contrast to the English
practice, which joined criminal punishment and removal in one proceeding.
From the text of the Constitution there emerges a leading purpose: partisan
passions should not sweep an officer to the gallows.

The starting point, therefore, to borrow from Justice Story, is that impeachment "is not so much designed to punish as to secure the state against
gross official misdemeanors." It is prophylactic, designed to remove an unfit
officer from office, rather than punitive. Two important considerations persuade us to understand American impeachment in noncriminal terms, though

---

*The phrase "high crimes and misdemeanors" is first met, not in an ordinary
criminal proceeding, but in the impeachment of the Earl of Suffolk in 1386. At that
time there was no such crime as a misdemeanor. Lesser crimes were prosecuted as
"trespasses" well into the sixteenth century, and only then were trespasses supplanted
by "misdemeanors." As "trespass" itself suggests, "misdemeanors" derived from private wrongs, what lawyers call torts. Fitzjames Stephen stated that "prosecutions for
misdemeanors are to the Crown what actions for wrongs are to private persons."
Although "misdemeanors" entered into ordinary criminal law, they did not become the
criterion of the parliamentary "high" misdemeanors. Nor did "high misdemeanors"
find their way into the general criminal law. As late as 1757, Blackstone could say that
the "first and principal [high misdemeanor] is the *maladministration* of such high
officers, as are in the public trust and employment."

it may, of course, include offenses such as bribery and obstruction of justice, which are indictable "political" crimes. First, since Article I contemplates both indictment and impeachment, the issue of double jeopardy would be raised if impeachment were deemed criminal in nature. The Fifth Amendment, which embodies a centuries-old guarantee, provides that no person "shall be subject for the same offence to be twice put in jeopardy." This means that if a person were indicted and convicted he could not be impeached, or if he were impeached he could not be indicted. By providing that impeachment would not bar indictment, the Framers plainly indicated that impeachment was not criminal in nature. Therefore, criminal punishment may precede *or* follow impeachment.

A second consideration is the Sixth Amendment provision that "in all criminal prosecutions, the accused shall enjoy the right to a speedy and public trial by an impartial jury." If impeachment be deemed a "criminal prosecution," it is difficult to escape the requirement of trial by jury. Earlier, Article III, Section 2(3) had expressly exempted impeachment from the jury "trial of all crimes"; and with that exemption before them, the draftsmen of the Sixth Amendment extended trial by jury to "*all* criminal prosecutions" without exception, thereby exhibiting an intention to withdraw the former exemption. We must conclude either that the Founders felt no need to exempt impeachment from the Sixth Amendment because they did not consider it a "criminal prosecution," or that a jury trial is required if impeachment is in fact a "criminal proceeding."

Elsewhere* I have discussed the problems that arise from the Framers' employment of criminal terminology. I would only reiterate that if impeachment is indeed criminal in nature, it must comprehend the offenses considered grounds for impeachment at the adoption of the Constitution. On this score, the Senate, which tries impeachments, has on a number of occasions found officers guilty of nonindictable offenses, and to the Senate, at least initially, is left the construction of "high crimes and misdemeanors."

It does not follow that Rep. Gerald Ford was correct when he declared that an impeachable offense is whatever the House and Senate jointly "consider [it] to be." Still less can it be, as Mr. Nixon's then Attorney General Richard Kleindienst told the Senate, that "you don't need facts, you don't need evidence" to impeach the President, "all you need is votes." That would flout all requirements of due process, which must protect the President no less than the lowliest felon. The records of the Convention make quite plain that the Framers, far from proposing to confer illimitable power to impeach, intended only to confer a *limited* power.

When an early version of impeachment for "treason, bribery" came up for discussion, George Mason moved to add "maladministration," explaining that "treason as defined in the Constitution will not reach many great and

---

Impeachment: The Constitutional Problems (Harvard University Press, 1973).

dangerous offenses . . . Attempts to subvert the Constitution may not be Treason as above defined." Mark that Mason was bent on reaching "attempts to subvert the Constitution." But Madison demurred because "so vague a term [as maladministration] will be equivalent to a tenure during the pleasure of the Senate." In brief, Madison refused to leave the President at the mercy of the Senate. Thereupon, Mason suggested "high crimes and misdemeanors," which was adopted without objection.

Shortly before, the Convention had rejected "high misdemeanors" in another context because it "had a technical meaning too limited," so that adoption of "high crimes and misdemeanors" exhibits an intent to embrace the "limited," "technical meaning" of the words for purposes of impeachment. If "high crimes and misdemeanors" had an ascertainable content at the time the Constitution was adopted, that content marks the boundaries of the power. It is no more open to Congress to ignore those boundaries than it is to include "robbery" under the "bribery" offense, for "robbery" had a quite different common-law connotation.

Recent events are of surpassing interest, and it behooves us to weigh them in traditional common-law terms. It will be recalled that the first and foremost impeachable offense was subversion of the Constitution, of the fundamental law. Had Mr. Nixon persisted in his position that he could not be compelled by the courts to furnish the tapes of his conversations, that would have been a subversion of the Constitution. That issue may not yet be dead. In the wake of Mr. Nixon's dismissal of Special Prosecutor Archibald Cox, and the resignations of Attorney General Elliot Richardson and Deputy Attorney General William Ruckelshaus, the "fire storm," as a White House aide called it, that blew up across the country impelled President Nixon, by White House counsel, to advise Judge John Sirica, "This President does not defy the law. . . . he will comply in full with the orders of the court." Let the sober appraisal by *The Wall Street Journal* sum up the inferences we must draw from this event:

> In obeying the appeals court order requiring that the tapes be submitted to Judge Sirica, the President has indeed ceded, without a final Supreme Court test, some of the privilege to withhold information that he previously claimed for the Chief Executive. A precedent is being established whereby judges can demand White House evidence . . . The President tried to protect a presidential claim and lost. The claim may not have been entirely valid, but the loss is for real.

Nevertheless, during his press conference on the evening of October 26, 1973, Mr. Nixon stated, "We will not provide Presidential documents to a special prosecutor . . . if it is a document involving a conversation with the President. I would have to stand on the principle of confidentiality." Thus he renews the claim, lost before the Court of Appeals, to which he apparently yielded when he advised Judge Sirica that he would comply with the court's order. "Confidentiality," in short, still remains at issue. Were an independent prosecutor set up by Congressional enactment, and were he to insist on production of White House tapes and documents, a confrontation between the President and the courts would be replayed.

If Mr. Nixon were again to refuse to comply with a court order to produce tapes or documents, that would constitute subversion of the Constitution. Ours is a government of enumerated and limited powers, designed, in the words of the Founders, to "fence" the Congress and the executive about. To police these limits the courts were given the power of judicial review. On more than one occasion they have declared Acts of Congress, though signed by the President, unconstitutional. Although the House of Representatives was made the sole judge of the qualifications of its members, the Supreme Court held that in excluding Adam Clayton Powell for misappropriation of government funds, the House had exceeded its power, the sole qualifications for membership being age, residence, and citizenship. In short, it is the function of the courts finally to interpret the Constitution and to determine the scope of the powers conferred on either President or Congress. By what reasoning the President claims to be exempted from this judicial authority passes my comprehension. In disobeying a court order, the President would undermine a central pillar of the Constitution, and take a long step toward assertion of dictatorial power. Benign or otherwise, dictatorial power is utterly incompatible with our democratic system. Disobedience of a court order, I submit, would be subversion of the Constitution, the cardinal impeachable offense.

A second article of impeachment based on subversion of the Constitution could rest on the President's impoundment of appropriated funds. The Constitution gives Congress the sole power to provide for the general welfare; in so doing, it is entitled to select priorities. Nowhere in the Constitution is power given to the President to substitute his own priorities. Some twenty courts have held his impoundments to be unconstitutional, that is, in excess of his powers and an encroachment on the prerogatives of Congress.

The secret bombing of Cambodia in 1969–70 may also be viewed as a subversion of the Constitution. It is widely agreed among eminent historians that so far as the "original intention" of the Founders is concerned, the power to make war was exclusively vested by the Constitution in Congress. They intended, in the words of James Wilson, second only to Madison as an architect of the Constitution, to put it beyond the power of a "single man" to "hurry" us into war. The argument for a President powerful enough single-handedly to embroil the nation in war rests on comparatively recent Presidential assertions of power.

No President, or succession of Presidents, can by their own unilateral fiat rewrite the Constitution and reallocate to themselves powers purposely withheld from them and conferred on the Congress alone. On this reasoning, the Cambodian bombing, being a usurpation of Congressional power, constitutes a subversion of the Constitution, and is a clearly impeachable offense.

Although some twenty courts have gone against the President on the issue of impoundment, the Supreme Court has yet to speak. So too, although Presidential usurpation in the secret Cambodian bombing seems quite clear to me, the President has yet to have his day in court. Little as I attach to Presidential assertions of power plainly withheld from him by the Constitution, I am reluctant to have the Senate decide an issue of constitutional law, disputed by the President, in its own favor. That issue, the trial of Andrew Johnson teaches, is better left to the courts, removed from any suspicion of partisan bias, unclouded by conflict with the tradition that one should not sit in judgment on his own case.

There may well be other grounds of impeachment which the House Judiciary Committee will in due course consider. For example, thus far the implications of the Watergate coverup have been considered in terms of criminal complicity; but a statement by James Madison in the First Congress indicates that it may be viewed in wider perspective. Recall that Madison was the chief architect of the Constitution, and had a hand in the introduction of "high crimes and misdemeanors" in the impeachment provisions. Who would better know what scope the Founders intended to give those terms? Arguing for an exclusive Presidential power to remove his subordinates, Madison stated that this "will make him in a peculiar manner responsible for their conduct, and subject him to impeachment himself, if he . . . neglects to superintend their conduct, so as to check their excesses."

On March 22, 1973, Mr. Nixon stated, "It is clear that unethical as well as illegal activities took place in the course of [the reelection] campaign . . . to the extent that I failed to prevent them, I should have been more vigilant." This is little short of a confession of neglect; and that neglect is no less clear with respect to the ensuing cover-up launched by his subordinates, an obstruction of justice. Mr. Nixon stated, "I must and do assume responsibility for such [reelection] actions." Responsibility carries with it accountability, not, it is true, criminal responsibility, for no principal is responsible for the crimes of his agent. But he is civilly responsible for the wrongs he enabled them to commit; and impeachment, you will recall, is prophylactic, not criminal. President Nixon can be impeached, in Madison's words, for "neglect to superintend [his subordinates'] conduct, so as to check their excesses."

The Founders feared an excess of power in executive hands; they had just thrown off the shackles of one tyrant, George III, and were not minded to submit to another. Hence, they provided impeachment as an essential restraint against arbitrary one-man rule. The wisdom of the Founders has been abundantly confirmed by recent events. The time has come to regard impeachment, not as a clumsy, outworn apparatus, but rather as an instrument of regeneration for protection of our liberties and our constitutional system.

The views of Raoul Berger, which are supported by Hamilton in *Federalist 65,* clearly support the idea that impeachable conduct does not have to be criminal. In Great Britain, although impeachments did not require an indictable crime, the impeachment process was a criminal process because conviction resulted in the criminal penalties of death, imprisonment, or a heavy fine. However, in the United States the only penalty for impeachment and conviction is removal from office. Punishment, if it is to come at all, must come from separate criminal proceedings. By custom the President cannot be indicted while in office. Lower officials can have criminal actions brought against them when they are in office.

The following selections are excerpts first, from a memorandum issued by the staff of the House Judiciary Committee in February of 1974 on the Constitutional grounds for presidential impeachment. The second selection gives the position that was taken by President Nixon's attorneys, which stands in stark contrast to the views of the House Judiciary Committee staff as well as to those of Raoul Berger and Alexander Hamilton.

14
The House Judiciary Committee

SPELLING OUT THE GROUNDS

An excerpt from a memorandum on "Constitution Grounds for Presidential Impeachment" issued by the impeachment inquiry staff of the House Judiciary Committee.

The American experience with impeachment, reflects the principle that impeachable conduct need not be criminal. Of the 13 impeachments voted by the House since 1789, at least 10 involved one or more allegations that did not charge a violation of criminal law.

Impeachment and the criminal law serve fundamentally different purposes. Impeachment is the first step in a remedial process—removal from office and possible disqualification from holding future office. The purpose of impeachment is not personal punishment; its function is primarily to maintain constitutional government. Furthermore, the Constitution itself provides that impeachment is no substitute for the ordinary process of criminal law since it specifies that impeachment does not immunize the officer from criminal liability for his wrongdoing.

The general applicability of the criminal law also makes it inappropriate as the standard for a process applicable to a highly specific situation such as removal of a President. The criminal law sets a general standard of conduct which all must follow. It does not address itself to the abuses of presidential power. In an impeachment proceeding a President is called to account for abusing powers which only a President possesses.

From "The House Judiciary Committee—Spelling Out the Grounds," *The Washington Post* (February 25, 1974), p. A20. Reprinted by permission.

Other characteristics of the criminal law make criminality inappropriate as an essential element of impeachable conduct. While the failure to act may be a crime, the traditional focus of criminal law is prohibitory. Impeachable conduct, on the other hand, may include the serious failure to discharge the affirmative duties imposed on the President by the Constitution. Unlike a criminal case, the cause for the removal of a President may be based on his entire course of conduct in office. In particular situations, it may be a course of conduct more than individual acts that has a tendency to subvert constitutional government.

To confine impeachable conduct to indictable offenses may well be to set a standard so restrictive as not to reach conduct that might adversely affect the system of government. Some of the most grievous offenses against our constitutional form of government may not entail violations of the criminal law.

If criminality is to be the basic element of impeachable conduct, what is the standard of criminal conduct to be? Is it to be criminality as known to the common law, or as divined from the Federal Criminal Code, or from an amalgam of state criminal statutes? If one is to turn to state statutes, then which of those of the states is to obtain? If the present Federal Criminal Code is to be the standard, then which of those of the states is to obtain? If the present Federal Criminal Code is to be the standard, then which of its provisions is to apply? If there is to be new federal legislation to define the criminal standard, then presumably both the Senate and the President will take part in fixing that standard. How is this to be accomplished without encroachment upon the constitutional provision that "the sole power" of impeachment is vested in the House of Representatives?

A requirement of criminality would be incompatible with the intent of the framers to provide a mechanism broad enough to maintain the integrity of constitutional government. Impeachment is a constitutional safety valve; to fulfill this function, it must be flexible enough to cope with exigencies not now foreseeable. Congress has never undertaken to define impeachable offenses in the criminal code. Even respecting bribery, which is specifically identified in the Constitution as grounds for impeachment, the federal statute establishing the criminal offense for civil officers generally was enacted over 75 years after the Constitutional Convention.

In sum, to limit impeachable conduct to criminal offenses would be incompatible with the evidence concerning the constitutional meaning of the phrase "high Crimes and Misdemeanors" and would frustrate the purpose that the framers intended for impeachment. State and federal criminal laws are not written in order to preserve the nation against serious abuse of the presidential office. But this is the purpose of the constitutional provision for the impeachment of a President and that purpose gives meaning to "high Crimes and Misdemeanors."

Impeachment is a constitutional remedy addressed to serious offenses against the system of government. The purpose of impeachment under the Constitution is indicated by the limited scope of the remedy (removal from office and possible disqualification from future office) and by the stated grounds for impeachment (treason, bribery and other high crimes and misdemeanors). It is not controlling whether treason and bribery are criminal. More important, they are constitutional wrongs that subvert the structure of government, or undermine the integrity of office and even the Constitution itself, and thus are "high" offenses in the sense that word was used in English impeachments.

The framers of our Constitution consciously adopted a particular phrase from the English practice to help define the constitutional grounds for removal. The content of the phrase "high Crimes and Misdemeanors" for the framers is to be related to what the framers knew, on the whole, about the English practice—the broad sweep of English constitutional history and the vital role impeachment had played in the limitation of royal prerogative and the control of abuses of ministerial and judicial power.

Impeachment was not a remote subject for the framers. Even as they labored in Philadelphia, the impeachment trial of Warren Hastings, Governor-General of India, was pending in London, a fact to which George Mason made explicit reference in the Convention. Whatever may be said on the merits of Hastings' conduct, the charges against him exemplified the central aspect of impeachment—the parliamentary effort to reach grave abuses of governmental power.

The framers understood quite clearly that the constitutional system they were creating must include some ultimate check on the conduct of the executive, particularly as they came to reject the suggested plural executive. While insistent that balance between the executive and legislative branches be maintained so that the executive would not become the creature of the legislature, dismissable at its will, the framers also recognized that some means would be needed to deal with excesses by the executive. Impeachment was familiar to them. They understood its essential constitutional functions and perceived its adaptability to the American context.

While it may be argued that some articles of impeachment have charged conduct that consituted crime and thus that criminality is an essential ingredient, or that some have charged conduct that was not criminal and thus that criminality is not essential, the fact remains that in the English practice and in several of the American impeachments the criminality issue was not raised at all. The emphasis has been on the significant effects of the conduct— undermining the integrity of office, disregard of constitutional duties and oath of office, arrogation of power, abuse of the governmental process, adverse impact on the system of government. Clearly, these effects can be brought about in ways not anticipated by the criminal law. Criminal standards and criminal courts were established to control individual conduct. Impeachment was evolved by Parliament to cope with both the inadequacy of criminal standards and the impotence of courts to deal with the conduct of great public figures. It would be anomalous if the framers, having barred criminal sanctions from the impeachment remedy and limited it to removal and possible disqualification from office, intended to restrict the grounds for impeachment to conduct that was criminal.

The longing for precise criteria is understandable; advance, precise definition of objective limits would seemingly serve both to direct future conduct and to inhibit arbitrary reaction to past conduct. In private affairs the objective is the control of personal behavior, in part through the punishment of misbehavior. In general, advance definition of standards respecting private conduct works reasonably well. However, where the issue is presidential compliance with the constitutional requirements and limitations on the presidency, the crucial factor is not the intrinsic quality of behavior but the significance of its effect upon our consitutional system or the functioning of our government.

It is useful to note three major presidential duties of broad scope that are explicitly recited in the Constitution: "to take Care that the Laws be faithfully executed," to "faithfully execute the Office of President of the United States" and to "preserve, protect, and defend the Constitution of the United States" to the best of his ability. The first is directly imposed by the Constitution; the second and third are included in the constitutionally prescribed oath that the President is required to take before he enters upon the execution of his office and are, therefore, also expressly imposed by the Constitution.

The duty to take care is affirmative. So is the duty faithfully to execute the office. A President must carry out the obligations of his office diligently and in good faith. The elective character and political role of a President make it difficult to define faithful exercise of his powers in the abstract. A President must make policy and exercise discretion. This discretion necessarily is broad, especially in emergency situations, but the constitutional duties of a President impose limitations on its exercise.

The "take care" duty emphasizes the responsibility of a President for the overall conduct of the executive branch, which the Constitution vests in him alone. He must take care that the executive is so organized that this duty is performed.

The duty of a President to "preserve, protect, and defend the Constitution" to the best of his ability includes the duty not to abuse his powers or transgress their limits—not to violate the rights of citizens, such as those guaranteed by the Bill of Rights, and not to act in derogation of powers vested elsewhere by the Constitution.

Not all presidential misconduct is sufficient to constitute grounds for impeachment. There is a further requirement—substantiality. In deciding whether this further requirement has been met, the facts must be considered as a whole in the context of the office, not in terms of separate or isolated events. Because impeachment of a President is a grave step for the nation, it is to be predicated only upon conduct seriously incompatible with either the consitutional form and principles of our government or the proper performance of constitutional duties of the presidential office.

15
President Nixon's Attorneys

IMPEACHMENT STANDARDS

[Following are excerpts from an analysis of the constitutional standards for impeachment that was prepared by attorneys for President Nixon and submitted to members of the House Judiciary Committee's impeachment inquiry staff.]

The English impeachment precedents represent the context in which the framers drafted the constitutional impeachment provision. In understanding this context and what it implies two things should be remembered.

First, the framers rejected the English system of government that existed in 1776; namely, absolute parliamentary supremacy. Instead, they opted for limited government with a finely devised system of separated powers in different branches.

Second, throughout the history of English impeachment practice, (beginning in 1376 and ending in 1805) there were two distinct types of impeachment in England. One type represented a well-established criminal process for reaching great offenses committed against the government by men of high station —who today would occupy a high government office. The other type of impeachments used this well-established criminal process in the 17th and early 18th century for the political purpose of achieving the absolute political supremacy of Parliament over the executive.

It is clear from the context of the constitutional commitment to due process that the framers rejected the political impeachments. They included in the impeachment provisions the very safeguards that had not been present in the English practice . . .

The language of the impeachment clause is derived directly from the English impeachments. "High crimes and misdemeanors" was the standard phrase used by those impeachments from 1376 onwards . . .

In light of English and American history and usage from the time of Blackstone onwards, there is no evidence to attribute anything but a criminal meaning to the unitary phrase "other high crimes and misdemeanors."

The only debate at the Constitutional Convention that is relevant to the impeachment clause is that which occurred subsequent to agreement by the framers on a concept of the presidency. Before Sept. 8, 1787, the debates were general and did not focus on a conclusive plan for the Chief Executive . . .

From "Impeachment Standards," *The Washington Post* (March 6, 1974), p. A26. Reprinted by permission.

The Sept. 8 impeachment debate, the only one based on a clear concept of the actual presidency, emphatically rejected "maladministration" as a standard for impeachment. Madison and Morris vigorously noted the defects of "maladministration" as an impeachment standard. Maladministration would set a vague standard and would put the President's tenure at the pleasure of the Senate. Moreover, it could be limited by the daily check of Congress, and the adoption of a four-year term.

Colonel Mason then withdrew the term "maladministration" and substituted the current phrase in response to the criticisms of Madison and Morris. The debates clearly indicate a purely criminal meaning for "other high crimes and misdemeanors."

The words "treason, bribery, or other high crimes and misdemeanors," construed either in light of present usage or as understood by the framers in the late 18th century, mean what they clearly connote—criminal offenses. Not only do the words inherently require a criminal offense, but one of a very serious nature committed in one's governmental capacity.

This criminality requirement is reinforced by judicial construction and statutory penalty provisions. It is further evidenced by the criminal context of the language used in the other constitutional provisions concerning impeachment, such as Art. III, Sec. 2, Cl. 3, which provides in part, "the trial of all crimes, except in cases of impeachment, shall be by jury."

A careful examination of the American impeachment precedents reveals that the United States House of Representatives has supported different standards for the impeachment of judges and a President since 1804. This is consistent with judicial construction of the Constitution as defined by the United States Supreme Court, and the clear language of the Constitution which recognizes a distinction between a President who may be removed from office by various methods and a judge who may be removed only by impeachment.

In the case of a judge, the "good behavior" clause (Article III, Section 1) and the removal provision (Article III, Section 4) must be construed together, otherwise the "good behavior" clause is a nullity. Thus, consistent with House precedent, a judge who holds office for a life tenure may be impeached for less than an indictable offense. Even here, however, senatorial precedents have demonstrated a reluctance to convict a judge in the absence of criminal conduct, thus leaving the standard for judicial impeachment less than conclusive.

The use of a predetermined criminal standard for the impeachment of a President is also supported by history, logic, legal precedent and a sound and sensible public policy which demands stability in our form of government. Moreover, the constitutional proscription against ex post facto laws, the requirement of due process, and the separation of powers inherent in the very structure of our Constitution preclude the use of any standard other than "criminal" for the removal of a President by impeachment.

In the 197-year history of our nation, only one House of Representatives has ever impeached a President. A review of the impeachment trial of President Andrew Johnson, in 1868, indicates that the predicate for such action was a bitter political struggle between the executive and legislative branches of government.

The first attempt to impeach President Johnson failed because "no specific crime was alleged to have been committed." The Senate's refusal to convict Johnson after his impeachment by the House, has, of course, become legendary . . .

The most salient lesson to be learned from the widely criticized Johnson trial is that impeachment of a President should be resorted to only for cases of the gravest kind—the commission of a crime named in the Constitution or a criminal offense against the laws of the United States.

The English precedents clearly demonstrate the criminal nature and origin of the impeachment process. The framers adopted the general criminal meaning and language of those impeachments, while rejecting the 17th century aberration where impeachment was used as a weapon by Parliament to gain absolute political supremacy at the expense of the rule of law.

In light of legislative and judicial usage, American case law, and established rules of constitutional and statutory construction, the term "other high crimes and misdemeanors" can only have a purely "criminal" meaning. Finally, in our review of the American impeachment precedents, we have shown that while judges may be impeached for something less then indictable offenses —even here the standard is less than conclusive—all evidence points to the fact that a President may not.

Thus the evidence is conclusive on all points; a President may only be impeached for indictable crimes. That is the lesson of history, logic, and experience on the phrase "treason, bribery and other high crimes and misdemeanors."

During the summer of 1974 the House Judiciary Committee engaged in long and solemn debate over proposed articles of impeachment of President Nixon. The Committee rejected an impeachment proposal that accused President Nixon of usurping the war powers of Congress by secretly authorizing the bombing of Cambodia beginning in 1969. It also failed to pass an accusation that the President had demeaned and misused his office by underpaying his federal income taxes and accepting at government expense improvements on his homes in California and Florida. Three articles of impeachment finally emerged from the Committee, but because of President Nixon's resignation they did not reach the full House for debate. Article I, accusing the President of obstructing justice in the Watergate affair, passed the Committee by a 27 to 11 bipartisan vote, with six of the seventeen Republicans on the Committee supporting the proposal. Article II, an omnibus article that alleged a wide range of abuses of presidential power by Nixon, passed overwhelmingly by 28 to 10. Article III accused the President of impeding the impeachment process by defying Committee subpoenas for tapes and documents. Article III barely passed, 21 to 17. To what extent do the following articles of impeachment that were passed by the House Judiciary Committee contain justifiable and supportable causes for the removal of a President from office?

16

House Judiciary Committee

ARTICLES OF IMPEACHMENT

IMPEACHMENT ARTICLE I

In his conduct of the office of President of the United States, Richard M. Nixon, in violation of his constitutional oath faithfully to execute the office of President of the United States and, to the best of his ability, preserve, protect, and defend the Constitution of the United States, and in violation of his constitutional duty to take care that the laws be faithfully executed, has prevented, obstructed, and impeded the administration of justice, in that:

On June 17, 1972, and prior thereto, agents of the Committee for the Re-election of the President committed unlawful entry of the headquarters of the Democratic National Committee in Washington, District of Columbia, for the purpose of securing political intelligence. Subsequent thereto, Richard M. Nixon, using the powers of his high office, engaged personally and through his close subordinates and agents, in a course of conduct or plan designed to delay, impede, and obstruct the investigation of such unlawful entry; to cover up, conceal and protect those responsible; and to conceal the existence and scope of other unlawful covert activities.

The means used to implement this course of conduct or plan included one or more of the following:

(1) making false or misleading statements to lawfully authorized investigative officers and employees of the United States;

(2) withholding relevant and material evidence of information from lawfully authorized investigative officers and employees of the United States;

(3) approving, condoning, acquiescing in, and counseling witnesses with respect to the giving of false or misleading statements to lawfully authorized investigative officers and employees of the United States and false or misleading testimony in duly instituted judicial and congressional proceedings;

(4) interfering or endeavoring to interfere with the conduct of investigations by the Department of Justice of the United States, the Federal Bureau of Investigation, the Office of Watergate Special Prosecution Force, and Congressional Committees;

(5) approving, condoning, and acquiescing in, the surreptitious payment of substantial sums of money for the purpose of obtaining the silence of influencing the testimony of witnesses, potential witnesses or individuals who participated in such unlawful entry and other illegal activities;

(6) endeavoring to misuse the Central Intelligence Agency, an agency of the United States;

(7) disseminating information received from officers of the Department of Justice of the United States to subjects of investigations conducted by lawfully authorized investigative officers and employees of the United States, for the purpose of aiding and assisting such subjects in their attempts to avoid criminal liability;

(8) making or causing to be made false or misleading public statements for the purpose of deceiving the people of the United States into believing that a thorough and complete investigation had been conducted with respect to allegations of misconduct on the part of personnel of the executive branch of the United States and personnel of the Committee for the Re-election of the President, and that there was no involvement of such personnel in such misconduct; or

(9) endeavoring to cause prospective defendants, and individuals duly tried and convicted, to expect favored treatment and consideration in return for their silence or false testimony, or rewarding individuals for their silence or false testimony.

In all of this, Richard M. Nixon has acted in a manner contrary to his trust as President and subversive of constitutional government, to the great prejudice of the cause of law and justice and to the manifest injury of the people of the United States.

Wherefore Richard M. Nixon, by such conduct, warrants impeachment and trial, and removal from office.

IMPEACHMENT ARTICLE II

Using the powers of the office of President of the United States, Richard M. Nixon, in violation of his constitutional oath faithfully to execute the office of President of the United States, and to the best of his ability preserve, protect and defend the Constitution of the United States, and in disregard of his constitutional duty to take care that the laws be faithfully executed, has repeatedly engaged in conduct violating the constitutional right of citizens, impairing the due and proper administration of justice in the conduct of lawful inquiries, of contravening the law of governing agencies of the executive branch and the purposes of these agencies.

This conduct has included one or more of the following:

(1) He has, acting personally and through his subordinates and agents, endeavored to obtain from the Internal Revenue Service in violation of the constitutional rights of citizens, confidential information contained in income tax returns for purposes not authorized by law; and to cause, in violation of the constitutional rights of citizens, income tax audits or other income tax investigations to be initiated or conducted in a discriminatory manner.

(2) He misused the Federal Bureau of Investigation, the Secret Service and other executive personnel in violation or disregard of the constitutional rights of citizens by directing or authorizing such agencies or personnel to conduct or continue electronic surveillance or other investigations for purposes unrelated to national security, the enforcement of laws or any other lawful function of his office.

He did direct, authorize or permit the use of information obtained thereby for purposes unrelated to national security, the enforcement of laws or any other lawful function of his office. And he did direct the concealment of certain records made by the Federal Bureau of Investigation of electronic surveillance.

(3) He has, acting personally and through his subordinants and agents, in violation or disregard of the constitutional rights of citizens, authorized and permitted to be maintained a secret investigative unit within the office of the President, financed in part with money derived from campaign contributions which unlawfully utilized the resources of the Central Intelligence Agency, engaged in covert and unlawful activities, and attempted to prejudice the constitutional right of an accused to a fair trial.

(4) He has failed to take care that the laws were faithfully executed by failing to act when he knew or had reason to know that his close subordinates endeavored to impede and frustrate lawful inquiries by duly constituted executive, judicial and legislative entities concerning the unlawful entry into the headquarters of the Democratic National Committee and the cover-up thereof and concerning other unlawful activities including those relating to the confirmation of Richard Kleindienst as Attorney General of the United States, the electronic surveillance of private citizens, and break-in into the offices of Dr. Lewis Fielding and the campaign financing practices of the Committee to Re-Elect the President.

(5) In disregard of the rule of law he knowingly misused the executive power by interfering with agencies of the executive branch including the Federal Bureau of Investigation, the Criminal Division and the office of Watergate special prosecution force of the Department of Justice, and the Central

Intelligence Agency, in violation of his duty to take care that the laws be faithfully executed.

In all of this Richard M. Nixon has acted in a manner contrary to his trust as President and subversive of constitutional government to the great prejudice of the cause of law and justice and to the manifest injury of the people of the United States.

Wherefore, Richard M. Nixon by such conducts warrants impeachment and trial and removal from office.

IMPEACHMENT ARTICLE III

In this conduct of the office of President of the United States, Richard M. Nixon, contrary to his oath faithfully to execute the office of President of the United States and to the best of his ability to preserve, protect and defend the Constitution of the United States, and in violation of his constitutional duty to take care that the laws be faithfully executed, has failed without lawful cause or excuse to produce papers and things, as directed by duly authorized subpoenas issued by the Committee on the Judiciary of the House of Representatives on April 11, 1974, May 15, 1974, May 30, 1974, and June 24, 1974, and willfully disobeyed such subpoenas.

The subpoenaed papers and things were deemed necessary by the committee in order to resolve by direct evidence fundamental factual questions relating to Presidential direction, knowledge or approval of actions demonstrated by other evidence to be substantial grounds for impeachment of the President.

In refusing to produce these papers and things Richard M. Nixon, substituting his judgment as to what materials were necessary for the inquiry, interposed the powers of the Presidency against the lawful subpoenas of the House of Representatives, thereby assuming for himself functions and judgments necessary to the exercise of the sole power of impeachment vested by the Constitution in the House of Representatives.

In all this, Richard M. Nixon has acted in a manner contrary to his trust as President and subversive of constitutional government, to the great prejudice of the cause of law and justice, and to the manifest injury of the people of the United States.

Wherefore, Richard M. Nixon, by such conduct warrants impeachment and trial and removal from office.

Federalism

The United States government utilizes a "federal" form to secure certain political and economic objectives. This chapter identifies both the traditional and modern goals of American federalism from the writings of important theorists who have examined general and specific problems in national-state relationships. The validity of federalism is also analyzed.

Constitutional Background: National v. State Power

No subject attracted greater attention or was more carefully analyzed at the time of the framing of the Constitution than federalism. *The Federalist* devoted a great deal of space to proving the advantages of a federal form of government relative to a confederacy, since the Constitution was going to take some of the power traditionally within the jurisdiction of state governments and give it to a newly constituted national government. Once again it is necessary to return to the Constitution and *The Federalist* to ascertain the basis for the establishment of a federal system of government, in which state governments as well as the national government receive independent constitutional grants of authority in defined areas.

17

Alexander Hamilton

FEDERALIST 16

The . . . death of the confederacy . . . is what we now seem to be on the point of experiencing, if the federal system be not speedily renovated in a more substantial form. It is not probable, considering the genius of this country, that the complying states would often be inclined to support the authority of the union, by engaging in a war against the noncomplying states. They would always be more ready to pursue the milder course of putting themselves upon an equal footing with the delinquent members, by an imitation of their example. And the guilt of all would thus become the security of all. Our past experience has exhibited the operation of this spirit in its full light. There would, in fact, be an insuperable difficulty in ascertaining when force would with propriety be employed. In the article of pecuniary contribution, which would be the most usual source of delinquency, it would often be impossible to decide whether it had proceeded from disinclination, or inability. The pretense of the latter would always be at hand. And the case must be very flagrant in which its fallacy could be detected with sufficient certainty to justify the harsh expedient of compulsion. It is easy to see that this problem alone, as often as it should occur, would open a wide field to the majority that happened to prevail in the national council, for the exercise of factious views, of partiality, and of oppression.

It seems to require no pains to prove that the states ought not to prefer a national constitution, which could only be kept in motion by the instrumentality of a large army, continually on foot to execute the ordinary requisitions or decrees of the government. And yet this is the plain alternative involved by those who wish to deny it the power of extending its operations to individuals. Such a scheme, if practicable at all, would instantly degenerate into a military despotism; but it will be found in every light impracticable. The resources of the union would not be equal to the maintenance of any army considerable enough to confine the larger states within the limits of their duty; nor would the means ever be furnished of forming such an army in the first instance. Whoever considers the populousness and strength of several of these states singly at the present juncture, and looks forward to what they will become, even at the distance of half a century, will at once dismiss as idle and visionary any scheme which aims at regulating their movements by laws, to operate upon them in their collective capacities, and to be executed by a coercion applicable to them in the same capacities. A project of this kind is little less romantic than the monster-taming spirit attributed to the fabulous heroes and demigods of antiquity. . . .

The result of these observations to an intelligent mind must clearly be this, that if it be possible at any rate to construct a federal government capable of regulating the common concerns, and preserving the general tranquillity, it must be founded, as to the objects committed to its case, upon the reverse of the principle contended for by the opponents of the proposed constitution [i.e., a confederacy]. It must carry its agency to the persons of the citizens. It must stand in need of no intermediate legislations; but must itself be empowered to employ the arm of the ordinary magistrate to execute its own resolutions. The majesty of the national authority must be manifested through the medium of the courts of justice. The government of the union, like that of each state, must be able to address itself immediately to the hopes and fears of individuals; and to attract to its support, those passions which have the strongest influence upon the human heart. It must, in short, possess all the means, and have a right to resort to all the methods, of executing the powers with which it is entrusted, that are possessed and exercised by the governments of the particular states.

To this reasoning it may perhaps be objected, that if any state should be disaffected to the authority of the union, it could at any time obstruct the execution of its laws, and bring the matter to the same issue of force, with the necessity of which the opposite scheme is reproached.

The plausibility of this objection will vanish the moment we advert to the essential difference between a mere NONCOMPLIANCE and a DIRECT and ACTIVE RESISTANCE. If the interposition of the state legislatures be necessary to give effect to a measure of the union [as in a confederacy], they have only NOT TO ACT, or TO ACT EVASIVELY, and the measure is defeated. This neglect of duty may be disguised under affected but unsubstantial provisions so as not to appear, and of course not to excite any alarm in the people for the safety of the constitution. The state leaders may even make a merit of their surreptitious invasions of it, on the ground of some temporary convenience, exemption, or advantage.

But if the execution of the laws of the national government should not require the intervention of the state legislatures; if they were to pass into immediate operation upon the citizens themselves, the particular governments could not interrupt their progress without an open and violent exertion of an unconstitutional power. No omission, nor evasions, would answer the end. They would be obliged to act, and in such a manner, as would leave no doubt that they had encroached on the national rights. An experiment of this nature would always be hazardous in the face of a constitution in any degree competent to its own defense, and of a people enlightened enough to distinguish between a legal exercise and an illegal usurpation of authority. The success of it would require not merely a factious majority in the legislature, but the concurrence of the courts of justice, and of the body of the people. . . .

FEDERALIST 17

An objection, of a nature different from that which has been stated and answered in my last address, may, perhaps, be urged against the principle of legislation for the individual citizens of America. It may be said, that it would tend to render the government of the union too powerful, and to enable it to absorb those residuary authorities, which it might be judged proper to leave with the states for local purposes. Allowing the utmost latitude to the love of power, which any reasonable man can require, I confess I am at a loss to discover what temptation the persons entrusted with the administration of the general government could ever feel to divest the states of the authorities of that description. The regulation of the mere domestic police of a state, appears to me to hold out slender allurements to ambition. Commerce, finance, negotiation, and war, seem to comprehend all the objects which have charms for minds governed by that passion; and all the powers necessary to those objects, ought, in the first instance, to be lodged in the national depository. The administration of private justice between the citizens of the same state; the supervision of agriculture, and of other concerns of a similar nature; all those things, in short, which are proper to be provided for by local legislation, can never be desirable cares of a general jurisdiction. It is therefore improbable, that there should exist a disposition in the federal councils, to usurp the powers with which they are connected; because the attempt to exercise them would be as troublesome as it would be nugatory; and the possession of them, for that reason, would contribute nothing to the dignity, to the importance, or to the splendor, of the national government.

But let it be admitted, for argument's sake, that mere wantonness, and lust of domination, would be sufficient to beget that disposition; still, it may be safely affirmed, that the sense of the constituent body of the national representatives, or in other words, of the people of the several states, would control the indulgence of so extravagant an appetite. It will always be far more easy for the state governments to encroach upon the national authorities, than for the national government to encroach upon the state authorities. The proof of this proposition turns upon the greater degree of influence which the state governments, if they administer their affairs with uprightness and prudence, will generally possess over the people; a circumstance which at the same time teaches us, that there is an inherent and intrinsic weakness in all federal constitutions; and that too much pains cannot be taken in their organization, to give them all the force which is compatible with the principles of liberty.

The superiority of influence in favor of the particular governments, would result partly from the diffusive construction of the national government; but chiefly from the nature of the objects to which the attention of the state administrations would be directed.

It is a known fact in human nature, that its affections are commonly weak in proportion to the distance of diffusiveness of the object. Upon the same principle that a man is more attached to his family than to his neighborhood, to his neighborhood than to the community at large, the people of each state would be apt to feel a stronger bias towards their local governments, than towards the government of the union, unless the force of that principle should be destroyed by a much better administration of the latter.

This strong propensity of the human heart, would find powerful auxiliaries in the objects of state regulation.

The variety of more minute interests, which will necessarily fall under the superintendence of the local administrations, and which will form so many rivulets of influence, running through every part of the society, cannot be particularized, without involving a detail too tedious and uninteresting to compensate for the instruction it might afford.

There is one transcendent advantage belonging to the province of the state governments, which alone suffices to place the matter in a clear and satisfactory light—I mean the ordinary administration of criminal and civil justice. This, of all others, is the most powerful, most universal and most attractive source of popular obedience and attachment. It is this, which, being the immediate and visible guardian of life and property; having its benefits and its terrors in constant activity before the public eye; regulating all those personal interests, and familiar concerns, to which the sensibility of individuals is more immediately awake; contributes, more than any other circumstance, to impress upon the minds of the people affection, esteem, and reverence towards the government. This great cement of society, which will diffuse itself almost wholly through the channels of the particular governments, independent of all other causes of influence, would insure them so decided an empire over their respective citizens, as to render them at all times a complete counterpoise, and not infrequently dangerous rivals to the power of the union.

Tracing the historical development of national-state relationships, one finds that there has been constant strife over the determination of the boundaries of national power in relation to the reserved powers of the states. The Civil War did not settle once and for all the difficult question of national versus state power. The Supreme Court has played an important role in the development of the federal system, and some of its most historic opinions have upheld national power at the expense of the states. In the early period of the Court, Chief Justice John Marshall in *McCulloch* v. *Maryland,* 4 Wheaton 316 (1819), stated two doctrines that have had a profound effect upon the federal system: (1) the doctrine of implied powers; (2) the doctrine of the supremacy of national law. The former enables Congress to expand its power into numerous areas affecting states directly. By utilizing the commerce clause, for example, Congress may now regulate what is essentially *intrastate* commerce, for the Court has held that this is implied in the original clause giving Congress the power to regulate commerce among the several states. The immediate issues in *McCulloch v. Maryland* were, first, whether or not Congress had the power to incorporate, or charter, a national bank; second, if Congress did have such a power, although nowhere stated in the Constitution, did the existence of such a bank prevent state action that would interfere in its operation?

18

McCULLOCH v. MARYLAND
4 WHEATON 316 (1819)

Mr. Chief Justice Marshall delivered the opinion of the Court, saying in part:

In the case now to be determined, the defendant, a sovereign state, denies the obligation of a law enacted by the legislature of the Union; and the plaintiff, on his part, contests the validity of an act which has been passed by the legislature of that state. The Constitution of our country, in its most interesting and vital parts, is to be considered; the conflicting powers of the government of the Union and of its members, as marked in that Constitution, are to be discussed; and an opinion given, which may essentially influence the great operations of the government. . . .

If any one proposition could command the universal assent of mankind, we might expect it would be this: that the government of the Union, though limited in its powers, is supreme within its sphere of action. This would seem to result necessarily from its nature. It is the government of all; its powers are delegated by all; it represents all, and acts for all. Though any one state may be willing to control its operations, no state is willing to allow others to control them. The nation, on those subjects on which it can act, must necessarily bind its component parts. But this question is not left to mere reason: the people have, in express terms, decided it, by saying, "this Constitution, and the laws of the United States, which shall be made in pursuance thereof," "shall be the supreme law of the land," and by requiring that the members of the state legislatures, and the officers of the executive and judicial departments of the states, shall take the oath of fidelity to it. . . .

A constitution, to contain an accurate detail of all the subdivisions of which its great powers will admit, and of all the means by which they may be carried into execution, would partake of the prolixity of a legal code, and could scarcely be embraced by the human mind. It would probably never be understood by the public. Its nature, therefore, requires that only its great outlines should be marked, its important objects designated, and the minor ingredients which compose those objects be deduced from the nature of the objects themselves. That this idea was entertained by the framers of the American Constitution, is not only to be inferred from the nature of the instrument, but from the language. . . .

Although, among the enumerated powers of government, we do not find the word "bank," or "incorporation," we find the great powers to lay and collect taxes; to borrow money; to regulate commerce; to declare and conduct a war; and to raise and support armies and navies. The sword and the purse, all the external relations, and no inconsiderable portion of the industry of the nation, are entrusted to its government. It can never be pretended that these vast powers draw after them others of inferior importance, merely because they are inferior. Such an idea can never be advanced. But it may, with great reason, be contended, that a government, entrusted with such ample powers, on the due execution of which the happiness and prosperity of the nation so vitally depends, must also be entrusted with ample means for their execution. The power being given, it is the interest of the nation of facilitate its execution. It can never be their interest, and cannot be presumed to have been their intention, to clog and embarrass its execution by withholding the most appropriate means. Throughout this vast republic, from the St. Croix to the Gulf of Mexico, from the Atlantic to the Pacific, revenue is to be collected and expended, armies are to be marched and supported. The exigencies of the nation may require, that the treasure raised in the North should be transported to the South, that raised in the East conveyed to the West, or that this order should be reversed. Is that construction of the Constitution to be preferred which would render these operations difficult, hazardous, and expensive? Can we adopt that construction (unless the words imperiously require it) which would impute to the framers of that instrument, when granting these powers for the public good, the intention of impeding their exercise by withholding a choice of means? If, indeed, such be the mandate of the Constitution, we have only to obey; but that instrument does not profess to enumerate the means by which the powers it confers may be executed; nor does it prohibit the creation of a corporation, if the existence of such a being be essential to the beneficial exercise of those powers. It is, then, the subject of fair inquiry, how far such means may be employed. . . .

We admit, as all must admit, that the powers of the government are limited, and that its limits are not to be transcended. But we think the sound construction of the Constitution must allow to the national legislature that discretion, with respect to the means by which the powers it confers are to be carried into execution, which will enable that body to perform the high duties assigned to it, in the manner most beneficial to the people. Let the end be legitimate, let it be within the scope of the Constitution, and all means which are appropriate, which are plainly adapted to that end, which are not prohibited, but consist with the letter and spirit of the Constitution, are constitutional. . . .

It being the opinion of the court that the act incorporating the bank is constitutional; and that the power of establishing a branch in the state of Maryland might be properly exercised by the bank itself, we proceed to inquire:

Whether the state of Maryland may, without violating the Constitution, tax that branch? . . .

That the power of taxation is one of vital importance; that it is retained by the states; that it is not abridged by the grant of a similar power to the government of the Union; that it is to be concurrently exercised by the two governments: are truths which have never been denied. But, such is the paramount character of the Constitution, that its capacity to withdraw any subject from the action of even this power, is admitted. The states are expressly forbidden to lay any duties on imports or exports, except what may be absolutely necessary for executing their inspection laws. If the obligation of this prohibition must be conceded—if it may restrain a state from the exercise of its taxing power on imports and exports; the same paramount character would seem to restrain, as it certainly may restrain, a state from such other exercise of this power, as is in its nature incompatible with, and repugnant to, the constitutional laws of the Union. A law, absolutely repugnant to another, as entirely repeals that other as if express terms of repeal were used.

On this ground the counsel for the bank place its claim to be exempted from the power of a state to tax its operations. There is no express provision for the case, but the claim has been sustained on a principle which so entirely pervades the Constitution, is so intermixed with the materials which compose it, so interwoven with its web, so blended with its texture, as to be incapable of being separated from it, without rending it into shreds.

This great principle is, that the Constitution and the laws made in pursuance thereof are supreme; that they control the Constitution and laws of the respective states, and cannot be controlled by them. From this, which may be almost termed an axiom, other propositions are deduced as corollaries, on the truth or error of which, and on their application to this case, the cause has been supposed to depend. These are, 1. That a power to create implies a power to preserve. 2. That a power to destroy, if wielded by a different hand, is hostile to, and incompatible with, these powers to create and preserve. 3. That where this repugnancy exists, that authority which is supreme must control, not yield to that over which it is supreme. . . .

If we apply the principle for which the state of Maryland contends, to the Constitution generally, we shall find it capable of changing totally the character of that instrument. We shall find it capable of arresting all the measures of the government, and of prostrating it at the foot of the states. The American people have declared their Constitution, and the laws made in pursuance thereof, to be supreme; but this principle would transfer the supremacy, in fact, to the states. . . .

The court has bestowed on this subject its most deliberate consideration. The result is a conviction that the states have no power, by taxation or otherwise, to retard, impede, burden, or in any manner control, the operations of the constitutional laws enacted by Congress to carry into execution the powers vested in the general government. That is, we think, the unavoidable consequence of that supremacy which the Constitution has declared. . . .

Constitutional doctrine regarding the power of the national government to regulate commerce among the states to promote general prosperity has been clarified in a series of Supreme Court cases. At issue is the interpretation of the power to "regulate commerce with foreign nations, and among the several States," granted to Congress in Article 1. Some of these cases have emphasized the role of the national government as umpire, enforcing certain rules of the game within which the free enterprise system functions; others have emphasized the positive role of the government in regulating the economy.

A key case supporting the supremacy of the national government in commercial regulation is *Gibbons v. Ogden,* 9 Wheaton 1 (1824). The New York legislature, in 1798, granted Robert R. Livingston the exclusive privilege to navigate by steam the rivers and other waters of the state, provided he could build a boat that would travel at four miles an hour against the current of the Hudson River. A two-year time limitation was imposed, and the conditions were not met; however, New York renewed its grant for two years in 1803 and again in 1807. In 1807 Robert Fulton, who now held the exclusive license with Livingston, completed and put into operation a steamboat which met the legislative conditions. The New York legislature now provided that a five-year extension of their monopoly would be given to Livingston and Fulton for each new steamboat they placed into operation on New York waters. The monopoly could not exceed thirty years, but during that period anyone wishing to navigate New York waters by steam had first to obtain a license from Livingston and Fulton, who were given the power to confiscate unlicensed boats. New Jersey and Connecticut passed retaliatory laws, the former authorizing confiscation of any New York ship for each ship confiscated by Livingston and Fulton, the latter prohibiting boats licensed in New York from entering Connecticut waters. Ohio also passed retaliatory legislation. Open commercial warfare seemed a possibility among the states of the union.

In 1793 Congress passed an act providing for the licensing of vessels engaged in the coasting trade, and Gibbons obtained under this statute a license to operate boats between New York and New Jersey. Ogden was engaged in a similar operation under an exclusive license issued by Livingston and Fulton, and thus sought to enjoin Gibbons from further operation. The New York court upheld the exclusive grants given to Livingston and Fulton, and Gibbons appealed to the Supreme Court. Chief Justice Marshall, in the following opinion, makes it quite clear that (1) states cannot interfere with a power granted to Congress by passing conflicting state legislation, and (2) the commerce power includes anything affecting "commerce among the states" and thus may include *intrastate* as well as interstate commerce. In this way the foundation was laid for broad national control over commercial activity.

19
GIBBONS v. OGDEN
9 WHEATON 1 (1824)

Mr. Chief Justice Marshall delivered the opinion of the Court, saying in part:

The appellant contends that this decree [of the New York court enjoining Gibbons from further operation because of the exclusive nature of the New York law granting a monopoly to Fulton and Livingston] is erroneous, because the laws which purport to give the exclusive privilege it sustains, are repugnant to the Constitution and laws of the United States.

They are said to be repugnant—

1.   To that clause in the Constitution which authorizes Congress to regulate commerce.

2.   To that which authorizes Congress to promote the progress of science and useful arts. . . .

As preliminary to the very able discussions of the Constitution which we have heard from the bar, and as having some influence on its construction, reference has been made to the political situation of these states, anterior to its formation. It has been said that they were sovereign, were completely independent, and were connected with each other only by a league. This is true. But, when these allied sovereigns converted their league into a government, when they converted their congress of ambassadors, deputed to deliberate on their common concerns, and to recommend measures of general utility, into a legislature, empowered to enact laws on the most interesting subjects, the whole character in which the states appear underwent a change, the extent of which must be determined by a fair consideration of the instrument by which that change was effected.

This instrument contains an enumeration of powers expressly granted by the people to their government. It has been said that these powers ought to be construed strictly. But why ought they to be so construed? Is there one sentence in the Constitution which gives countenance to this rule? In the last of the enumerated powers, that which grants, expressly, the means for carrying all others into execution, Congress is authorized "to make all laws which shall be necessary and proper" for the purpose. But this limitation on the means which may be used, is not extended to the powers which are conferred; nor is there one sentence in the Constitution, which has been pointed out by the gentlemen of the bar, or which we have been able to discern, that prescribes this rule. We do not, therefore, think ourselves justified in adopting it. . . . If, from the imperfections of human language, there should be serious doubts respecting the extent of any given power, it is a well settled rule that the objects for which it was given, especially when those objects are expressed in the instrument itself, should have great influence in the construction. . . . We know of no rule for construing the extent of such powers, other than is given by the language of the instrument which confers them, taken in connection with the purposes for which they were conferred.

The words are: "Congress shall have power to regulate commerce with foreign nations, and among the several States, and with the Indian tribes."

The subject to be regulated is commerce; and our Constitution being, as was aptly said at the bar, one of enumeration, and not of definition, to ascertain the extent of the power, it becomes necessary to settle the meaning of the word. The counsel for the appellee would limit it to traffic, to buying and selling, or the interchange of commodities, and do not admit that it comprehends navigation. This would restrict a general term, applicable to many objects, to one of its significations. Commerce, undoubtedly, is traffic, but it is something more: it is intercourse. It describes the commercial intercourse between nations, and parts of nations, in all its branches, and is regulated by prescribing rules for carrying on that intercourse. The mind can scarcely conceive a system for regulating commerce between nations, which shall exclude all laws concerning navigation, which shall be silent on the admission of the vessels of the one nation into the ports of the other, and be confined to prescribing rules for the conduct of individuals, in the actual employment of buying and selling, or of barter.

If commerce does not include navigation, the government of the Union has no direct power over that subject, and can make no law prescribing what shall constitute American vessels, or requiring that they shall be navigated by American seamen. Yet this power has been exercised from the commencement of the government, has been exercised with the consent of all, and has been understood by all to be a commercial regulation. . . .

The word used in the Constitution, then, comprehends, and has been always understood to comprehend, navigation, within its meaning; and a power to regulate navigation is as expressly granted as if that term had been added to the word "commerce."

To what commerce does this power extend? The Constitution informs us, to commerce "with foreign nations, and among the several States, and with the Indian tribes."

It has, we believe, been universally admitted that these words comprehend every species of commercial intercourse between the United States and foreign nations. No sort of trade can be carried on between this country and any other, to which this power does not extend. It has been truly said that commerce, as the word is used in the Constitution, is a unit, every part of which is indicated by the term.

If this be the admitted meaning of the word, in its application to foreign nations, it must carry the same meaning throughout the sentence, and remain a unit, unless there be some plain intelligible cause which alters it.

The subject to which the power is next applied, is to commerce "among the several States." The word "among" means intermingled with. A thing which is among others, is intermingled with them. Commerce among the states, cannot stop at the external boundary line of each state, but may be introduced into the interior.

It is not intended to say that these words comprehend that commerce which is completely internal, which is carried on between man and man in a state, or between different parts of the same state, and which does not extend to or affect other states. Such a power would be inconvenient, and is certainly unnecessary.

Comprehensive as the word "among" is, it may very properly be restricted to that commerce which concerns more states than one. The phrase is not one which would probably have been selected to indicate the completely interior traffic of a state. . . . The completely internal commerce of a state, then, may be considered as reserved for the state itself.

But, in regulating commerce with foreign nations, the power of Congress does not stop at the jurisdictional lines of the several states. It would be a very useless power if it could not pass those lines. The commerce of the United States with foreign nations is that of the whole United States. Every district has a right to participate in it. The deep streams which penetrate our country in every direction pass through the interior of almost every state in the Union, and furnish the means of exercising this right. If Congress has the power to regulate it, that power must be exercised whenever the subject exists. If it exists within the states, if a foreign voyage may commence or terminate at a port within a state, then the power of Congress may be exercised within a state.

This principle is, if possible, still more clear when applied to commerce "among the several States." They either join each other, in which case they are separated by a mathematical line, or they are remote from each other, in which case other states lie between them. What is commerce "among" them; and how is it to be conducted? Can a trading expedition between two adjoining states commence and terminate outside of each? And if the trading intercourse be between two states remote from each other, must it not commence in one, terminate in the other, and probably pass through a third? Commerce among the states must, of necessity, be commerce with the states. In the regulation of trade with the Indian tribes, the action of the law, especially when the Constitution was made, was chiefly within a state. The power of Congress, then, whatever it may be, must be exercised within the territorial jurisdiction of the several states. . . .

We are now arrived at the inquiry, what is this power?

It is the power to regulate; that is, to prescribe the rule by which commerce is to be governed. This power, like all others vested in Congress, is complete in itself, may be exercised to its utmost extent, and acknowledges no limitations other than are prescribed in the Constitution. These are expressed in plain terms, and do not affect the questions which arise in this case, or which have been discussed at the bar. . . .

The power of Congress, then, comprehends navigation within the limits of every state in the Union, so far as the navigation may be, in any manner, connected with "commerce with foreign nations, or among the several States, or with the Indian tribes." It may, of consequence, pass the jurisdictional line of New York, and act upon the very waters to which the prohibition now under consideration applies.

But it has been urged with great earnestness that, although the power of Congress to regulate commerce with foreign nations, and among the several states, be coextensive with the subject itself, and have no other limits than are prescribed in the Constitution, yet the states may severally exercise the same power, within their respective jurisdictions. In support of this argument, it is said that they possessed it as an inseparable attribute of sovereignty, before the formation of the Constitution, and still retain it, except so far as they have surrendered it by that instrument; that this principle results from the nature of the government, and is secured by the Tenth Amendment; that an affirmative grant of power is not exclusive, unless in its own nature it be such that the continued exercise of it by the former possessor is inconsistent with the grant, and that this is not of that description.

The appellant, conceding these postulates, except the last, contends that full power to regulate a particular subject, implies the whole power, and leaves no *residuum;* that a grant of the whole is incompatible with the existence of a sight in another to any part of it. . . .

. . . The sole question is, can a state regulate commerce with foreign nations and among the states, while Congress is regulating it? . . .

In our complex system, presenting the rare and difficult scheme of one general government, whose action extends over the whole, but which possesses only certain enumerated powers; and of numerous state governments, which retain and exercise all powers not delegated to the Union, contests respecting power must arise. Were it even otherwise, the measures taken by the respective governments to execute their acknowledged powers, would often be of the same description, and might, sometimes, interfere. This, however, does not prove that the one is exercising, or has a right to exercise, the powers of the other. . . .

It has been contended, by the counsel for the appellant, that, as the word to "regulate" implies in its nature full power over the thing to be regulated, it excludes, necessarily, the action of all others that would perform the same operation on the same thing. That regulation is designed for the entire result, applying to those parts which remain as they were, as well as to those which are altered. It produces a uniform whole, which is as much disturbed and deranged by changing what the regulating power designs to leave untouched, as that on which it has operated.

There is great force in this argument, and the Court is not satisfied that it has been refuted.

Since, however, in exercising the power of regulating their own purely internal affairs, whether of trading or police, the states may sometimes enact laws, the validity of which depends on their interfering with, and being contrary to, an act of Congress passed in pursuance of the Constitution, the Court will enter upon the inquiry, whether the laws of New York, as expounded by the highest tribunal of that state, have, in their application to this case, come into collision with an act of Congress, and deprived a citizen of a right to which that act entitles him. Should the collision exist, it will be immaterial whether those laws were passed in virtue of a concurrent power "to regulate commerce with foreign nations, or among the several States," or, in virtue of a power to regulate their domestic trade and police. In one case and the other, the acts of New York must yield to the law of Congress; and the decision sustaining the privileges they confer, against a right given by a law of the Union, must be erroneous.

This opinion has been frequently expressed in this Court, and is founded as well on the nature of the government as on the words of the Constitution. In argument, however, it has been contended that, if a law passed by a state, in the exercise of its acknowledged sovereignty, comes into conflict with a law passed by Congress in pursuance of the Constitution, they affect the subject, and each other, like equal opposing powers.

But the framers of our Constitution foresaw this state of things, and provided for it by declaring the supremacy not only of itself, but of the laws made in pursuance of it. The nullity of any act, inconsistent with the Constitution, is produced by the declaration that the Constitution is the supreme law. The appropriate application of that part of the clause which confers the same supremacy on laws and treaties, is to such acts of the state legislatures as do not transcend their powers, but, though enacted in the execution of acknowledged state powers, interfere with, or are contrary to the laws of Congress, made in pursuance of the Constitution, or some treaty made under the authority of the United States. In every such case, the act of Congress, or the treaty, is supreme; and the laws of the state, though enacted in the exercise of powers not controverted, must yield to it. . . .

. . . The real and sole question seems to be, whether a steam machine, in actual use, deprives a vessel of the privileges conferred by a license. . . .

But all inquiry into this subject seems to the Court to be put completely at rest, by the act . . . entitled "An act for the enrolling and licensing of steam-boats." . . .

This act demonstrates the opinion of Congress, that steamboats may be enrolled and licensed, in common with vessels using sails. They are, of course, entitled to the same privileges, and can no more be restrained from navigating waters, and entering ports which are free to such vessels, than if they were wafted on their voyage by the winds, instead of being propelled by the agency of fire. The one element may be as legitimately used as the other, for every commercial purpose authorized by the laws of the Union; and the act of a state inhibiting the use of either to any vessel having a license under the act of Congress, comes, we think, in direct collision with that act.

As this decides the cause, it is unnecessary to enter in an examination of that part of the Constitution which empowers Congress to promote the progress of science and the useful arts. . . .

Congress has used its contitutional power to regulate "commerce among the several States" to justify broad regulatory programs. In *Champion* v. *Ames,* 188 U.S. 321 (1903), the Court stated that Congress could bar transportation of objectionable articles in interstate commerce. This was in reference to an 1895 lottery law prohibiting lottery tickets from being sent through the channels of interstate commerce. After this decision Congress prohibited transportation of numerous other "objectionable" articles in interstate commerce; e.g., impure food and drugs, uninspected meat and fabrics, stolen automobiles, kidnapped persons, and women for immoral purposes. In this way a national police power was developed similar to that of the states in intent—i.e., the power to protect the health, welfare, and morals of the community—initially within the "reserved" powers of the states.

In 1916 Congress attempted to regulate child labor conditions within states by preventing the transportation in interstate commerce of goods produced by children under conditions that violated the standards of the Child Labor Act of 1916. Although the initial attempt was declared unconstitutional in *Hammer* v. *Dagenhart,* 247 U.S. 251 (1918), the device of regulation through controlling the transportation of goods in interstate commerce is now an accepted constitutional practice. Furthermore, the regulatory power of Congress extends to all economic areas—production, distribution, etc.—that in any way affect interstate commerce. Thus labor disputes that burden or obstruct interstate commerce are controlled under the Wagner Labor Relations Act of 1935 and the Taft-Hartley Act of 1947. The radio and television industry, because it uses the channels of interstate commerce, is regulated by the Federal Communications Act of 1934. The same is true of banks, securities dealers and exchanges, railroads, telephone companies, petroleum firms and natural gas companies, and trucking firms. The list of industries subject to national regulation through the commcerce clause could be extended indefinitely. Marshall's decision in *Gibbons* v. Ogden set the stage for extensive national regulation through its broad and flexible interpretation of the commerce clause.

Both *McCulloch* v. *Maryland* and *Gibbons* v. *Ogden* clearly held that the states cannot take action that will impinge upon the legitimate authority of Congress. These opinions reflected judicial acceptance of the fact that when the federal government acts, it generally preempts the field. But this does not mean that the states can never legislate concurrently with the national government. It depends upon the circumstances. For example, in *Pennsylvania* v. *Nelson,* 350 U.S. 497 (1956), the Supreme Court found that the Smith Act superseded a Pennsylvania sedition statute under which Nelson had been convicted. The Pennsylvania law, like the Smith Act, made it a crime to advocate the violent overthrow of the government of the United States or the government of Pennsylvania. The Supreme Court found that the Smith Act, in combination with a number of other federal subversive control statutes such as the Internal Security Act of 1950 and the Communist Control Act of 1954, proscribed advocacy to overthrow any government, whether federal, state, or local. On the basis of the aggregate of federal statutes in the sedition field, the Court concluded: "Congress had intended to occupy the field of sedition. Taken as a whole, they [the statutes] evince a Congressional plan which makes it reasonable to determine that no room has been left for the state to supplement it. Therefore, a state's sedition statute is superseded regardless of whether it purports to supplement the federal law. . . ." Although the *Nelson* case apparently nullified more than forty state sedition statutes, the issue has not been finally resolved. Several cases since the *Nelson* decision reflect a judicial hesitancy to prevent state and local authorities from enforcing statutes controlling subversive activities. (See *Beilan* v. *Board of Education,* 357 U.S. 399 [1958], and *Lerner* v. *Casey,* 357 U.S. 468 [1958].) The real problems that arise concerning the doctrine of national supremacy do not develop where there is clear state defiance of a federal law or a federal court order, for in these situations the enforcement of the principle of the supremacy of the Constitution and of national law can easily and clearly be carried out. Thus in *Cooper* v. *Aaron,* 358 U.S. 1 (1958), a federal district court order to proceed with integration at Central High School in Little Rock was upheld by the Supreme Court in face of the defiance of the Governor of Arkansas. The supremacy of the national government was clear, and the opinion of the Court was not ambiguous.

Another example of the problem of concurrent jurisdiction arose in the case of *Colorado Anti-Discrimination Commission* v. *Continental Air Lines,* 372 U.S. 714 (1963). This case involved the constitutionality of the Colorado Anti-Discrimination Act, which made it an unfair employment practice to refuse to hire qualified individuals because of race, creed, color, national origin, or ancestry. Under the Act a commission was established to investigate complaints. Marlon D. Green, a Negro, applied for a job as a pilot with Continental Air Lines, a small interstate carrier whose route passes through Colorado. He was refused a position, and he filed a complaint with the Anti-Discrimination Commission, claiming that the only reason he was not hired was because he was a Negro. The Commission held extensive hearings to determine the validity of his charge, and finally upheld it. Continental Air Lines was ordered to cease and desist from this particular discrimination and from any other discriminatory practices. The Commission directed the air line to enroll the applicant for its first opening in its pilot training school.

The validity of the Commission's cease and desist order was immediately attacked by Continental, which secured a judgment vacating the order from a lower State District Court. On appeal, the Supreme Court of Colorado affirmed the judgment. Both state courts held that the Colorado statute placed an undue burden upon interstate commerce, which was within the exclusive juristiction of the national government. However, the Supreme Court found that the Colorado statute merely extended, rather than conflicted with, the federal laws dealing with the same subject.

Federalism Today:
Decentralization of Power

The problems involved in determining the constitutional division of authority between the federal and the state governments reflect the more formal aspects of our federal system. Contemporary federalism must be viewed not only in this way but also in relation to the broader political and economic dimensions of the division of powers between the national and state levels of government. Also, as the following selection points out, there are many factors in addition to federalism that decentralize the American political system. All kinds of interest groups, including state and local governments, have numerous access points at the national level through which they can influence policy-making. Our decentralized political parties, a major cause of disunity, are controlled more by state organizations than by the national leaders. Federalism has not caused the disunity in the American system, although it has contributed to it. What kind of balance should exist between the federal and state levels in the exercise of governmental functions? In essence, this is part of a broader problem of centralization versus decentralization in government. The next selection deals with the many facets of this problem.

20
Morton Grodzins

THE FEDERAL SYSTEM

Federalism is a device for dividing decisions and functions of government. As the constitutional fathers well understood, the federal structure is a means, not an end. The pages that follow are therefore not concerned with an exposition of American federalism as a formal, legal set of relationships. The focus, rather, is on the purpose of federalism, that is to say, on the distribution of power between central and peripheral units of government.

THE SHARING OF FUNCTIONS

The American form of government is often, but erroneously, symbolized by a three-layer cake. A far more accurate image is the rainbow or marble cake, characterized by an inseparable mingling of differently colored ingredients, the colors appearing in vertical and diagonal strands and unexpected whirls. As colors are mixed in the marble cake, so functions are mixed in the American federal system. Consider the health officer, styled "sanitarian," of a rural county in a border state. He embodies the whole idea of the marble cake of government.

The sanitarian is appointed by the state under merit standards established by the federal government. His base salary comes jointly from state and federal funds, the county provides him with an office and office amenities and pays a portion of his expenses, and the largest city in the county also contributes to his salary and office by virtue of his appointment as a city plumbing inspector. It is impossible from moment to moment to tell under which governmental hat the sanitarian operates. His work of inspecting the purity of food is carried out under federal standards; but he is enforcing state laws when inspecting commodities that have not been in interstate commerce; and somewhat perversely he also acts under state authority when inspecting milk coming into the county from producing areas across the state border. He is a federal officer when impounding impure drugs shipped from a neighboring state; a federal-state officer when distributing typhoid immunization serum; a state officer when enforcing standards of industrial hygiene; a state-local officer when inspecting the city's water supply; and (to complete the circle) a local officer when insisting that the city butchers adopt more hygienic methods of handling their

From Morton Grodzins, Editor, "The Federal System," *Goals for Americans,* pp. 265–282. © 1960 by the American Assembly, Columbia University, New York, New York. Reprinted by permission of Prentice-Hall, Inc., Englewood Cliffs, New Jersey.

garbage. But he cannot and does not think of himself as acting in these separate capacities. All business in the county that concerns public health and sanitation he considers his business. Paid largely from federal funds, he does not find it strange to attend meetings of the city council to give expert advice on matters ranging from rotten apples to rabies control. He is even deputized as a member of both the city and county police forces.

The sanitarian is an extreme case, but he accurately represents an important aspect of the whole range of governmental activities in the United States. Functions are not neatly parceled out among the many governments. They are shared functions. It is difficult to find any governmental activity which does not involve all three of the so-called "levels" of the federal system. In the most local of local functions—law enforcement or education, for example—the federal and state governments play important roles. In what, a priori, may be considered the purest central government activities—the conduct of foreign affairs, for example—the state and local governments have considerable responsibilities, directly and indirectly.

The federal grant programs are only the most obvious example of shared functions. They also most clearly exhibit how sharing serves to disperse governmental powers. The grants utilize the greater wealth-gathering abilities of the central government and establish nationwide standards, yet they are "in aid" of functions carried out under state law, with considerable state and local discretion. The national supervision of such programs is largely a process of mutual accommodation. Leading state and local officials, acting through their professional organizations, are in considerable part responsible for the very standards that national officers try to persuade all state and local officers to accept.

Even in the absence of joint financing, federal-state-local collaboration is the characteristic mode of action. Federal expertise is available to aid in the building of a local jail (which may later be used to house federal prisoners), to improve a local water purification system, to step up building inspections, to provide standards for state and local personnel in protecting housewives against dishonest butchers' scales, to prevent gas explosions, or to produce a land use plan. States and localities, on the other hand, take important formal responsibilities in the development of national programs for atomic energy, civil defense, the regulation of commerce, and the protection of purity in foods and drugs; local political weight is always a factor in the operation of even a post office or a military establishment. From abattoirs and accounting through zoning and zoo administration, any governmental activity is almost certain to involve the influence, if not the formal administration, of all three planes of the federal system.

ATTEMPTS TO UNWIND THE FEDERAL SYSTEM

Within the past dozen years there have been four major attempts to reform or reorganize the federal system: the first (1947–1949) and second (1953–1955)

Hoover Commissions on Executive Organization; the Kestnbaum Commission on Intergovernmental Relations (1953–1955); and the Joint Federal-State Action Committee (1957–1959). All four of these groups have aimed to minimize federal activities. None of them has recognized the sharing of functions as the characteristic way American governments do things. Even when making recommendations for joint action, these official commissions take the view (as expressed in the Kestnbaum report) that "the main tradition of American federalism [is] the tradition of separateness." All four have, in varying degrees, worked to separate functions and tax sources.

The history of the Joint Federal-State Action Committee is especially instructive. The committee was established at the suggestion of President Eisenhower, who charged it, first of all, "to designate functions which the States are ready and willing to assume and finance that are now performed or financed wholly or in part by the Federal Government." He also gave the committee the task of recommending "Federal and State revenue adjustments required to enable the States to assume such functions."[1]

The committee subsequently established seemed most favorably situated to accomplish the task of functional separation. It was composed of distinguished and able men, including among its personnel three leading members of the President's Cabinet, the director of the Bureau of the Budget, and ten state governors. It had the full support of the President at every point, and it worked hard and conscientiously. Excellent staff studies were supplied by the Bureau of the Budget, the White House, the Treasury Department, and, from the state side, the Council of State Governments. It had available to it a large mass of research data, including the sixteen recently completed volumes of the Kestnbaum Commission. There existed no disagreements on party lines within the committee and, of course, no constitutional impediments to its mission. The President, his Cabinet members, and all the governors (with one possible exception) on the committee completely agreed on the desirability of decentralization-via-separation-of-functions-and-taxes. They were unanimous in wanting to justify the committee's name and to produce action, not just another report.

The committee worked for more than two years. It found exactly two programs to recommend for transfer from federal to state hands. One was the federal grant program for vocational education (including practical-nurse training and aid to fishery trades); the other was federal grants for municipal waste treatment plants. The programs together cost the federal government

---

[1]. The President's third suggestion was that the committee "identify functions and responsibilities likely to require state or federal attention in the future and . . . recommend the level of state effort, or federal effort, or both, that will be needed to assure effective action." The committee initially devoted little attention to this problem. Upon discovering the difficulty of making separatist recommendations, i.e., for turning over federal functions and taxes to the states, it developed a series of proposals looking to greater effectiveness in intergovernmental collaboration. The committee was succeeded by a legislatively based, 26-member Advisory Commission on Intergovernmental Relations, established September 29, 1959.

less than $80 million in 1957, slightly more than two per cent of the total federal grants for that year. To allow the states to pay for these programs, the committee recommended that they be allowed a credit against the federal tax on local telephone calls. Calculations showed that this offset device, plus an equalizing factor, would give every state at least 40 percent more from the tax than it received from the federal government in vocational education and sewage disposal grants. Some states were "equalized" to receive twice as much.

The recommendations were modest enough, and the generous financing feature seemed calculated to gain state support. The President recommended to Congress that all points of the program be legislated. None of them was, none has been since, and none is likely to be.

A POINT OF HISTORY

The American federal system has never been a system of separated governmental activities. There has never been a time when it was possible to put neat labels on discrete "federal," "state," and "local" functions. Even before the Constitution, a statute of 1785, reinforced by the Northwest Ordinance of 1787, gave grants-in-land to the states for public schools. Thus the national government was a prime force in making possible what is now taken to be the most local function of all, primary and secondary education. More important, the nation, before it was fully organized, established by this action a first principle of American federalism: the national government would use its superior resources to initiate and support national programs, principally administered by the states and localities.

The essential unity of state and federal financial systems was again recognized in the earliest constitutional days with the assumption by the federal government of the Revolutionary War debts of the states. Other points of federal-state collaboration during the Federalist period concerned the militia, law enforcement, court practices, the administration of elections, public health measures, pilot laws, and many other matters.

The nineteenth century is widely believed to have been the preeminent period of duality in the American system. Lord Bryce at the end of the century described (in *The American Commonwealth*) the federal and state governments as "distinct and separate in their action." The system, he said, was "like a great factory wherein two sets of machinery are at work, their revolving wheels apparently intermixed, their bands crossing one another, yet each set doing its own work without touching or hampering the other." Great works may contain gross errors. Bryce was wrong. The nineteenth century, like the early days of the republic, was a period principally characterized by intergovernmental collaboration.

Decisions of the Supreme Court are often cited as evidence of nineteenth-century duality. In the early part of the century the Court, heavily weighted with Federalists, was intent upon enlarging the sphere of national authority;

in the later years (and to the 1930s) its actions were in the direction of paring down national powers and indeed all governmental authority. Decisions referred to "areas of exclusive competence" exercised by the federal government and the states; to their powers being "separated and distinct"; and to neither being able "to intrude within the jurisdiction of the other."

Judicial rhetoric is not always consistent with judicial action, and the Court did not always adhere to separatist doctrine. Indeed, its rhetoric sometimes indicated a positive view of cooperation. In any case, the Court was rarely, if ever, directly confronted with the issue of cooperation versus separation as such. Rather it was concerned with defining permissible areas of action for the central government and the states; or with saying with respect to a point at issue whether any government could take action. The Marshall Court contributed to intergovernmental cooperation by the very act of permitting federal operations where they had not existed before. Furthermore, even Marshall was willing to allow interstate commerce to be affected by the states in their use of the police power. Later courts also upheld state laws that had an impact on interstate commerce, just as they approved the expansion of the national commerce power, as in statutes providing for the control of telegraphic communication or prohibiting the interstate transportation of lotteries, impure foods and drugs, and prostitutes. Similar room for cooperation was found outside the commerce field, notably in the Court's refusal to interfere with federal grants-in-land or cash to the states. Although research to clinch the point has not been completed, it is probably true that the Supreme Court from 1800 to 1936 allowed far more federal-state collaboration than it blocked.

Political behavior and administrative action of the nineteenth century provide positive evidence that, throughout the entire era of so-called dual federalism, the many governments in the American federal system continued the close administrative and fiscal collaboration of the earlier period. Governmental activities were not extensive. But relative to what governments did, intergovernmental cooperation during the last century was comparable with that existing today.

Occasional presidential vetoes (from Madison to Buchanan) of cash and land grants are evidence of constitutional and ideological apprehensions about the extensive expansion of federal activities which produced widespread intergovernmental collaboration. In perspective, however, the vetoes are a more important evidence of the continuous search, not least by state officials, for ways and means to involve the central government in a wide variety of joint programs. The search was successful.

Grants-in-land and grants-in-services from the national government were of first importance in virtually all the principal functions undertaken by the states and their local subsidiaries. Land grants were made to the states for, among other purposes, elementary schools, colleges, and special educational institutions; roads, canals, rivers, harbors, and railroads; reclamation of desert and swamp lands; and veterans' welfare. In fact whatever was at the focus of state attention became the recipient of national grants. (Then, as today, national grants established state emphasis as well as followed it.) If Connecticut wished to establish a program for the care and education of the deaf and dumb, federal money in the form of a land grant was found to aid that program. If higher education relating to agriculture became a pressing need, Congress could dip into the public domain and make appropriate grants to states. If the need for swamp drainage and flood control appeared, the federal government could supply both grants-in-land and, from the Army's Corps of Engineers, the services of the only trained engineers then available.

Aid also went in the other direction. The federal government, theoretically in exclusive control of the Indian population, relied continuously (and not always wisely) on the experience and resources of state and local governments. State militias were an all-important ingredient in the nation's armed forces. State governments became unofficial but real partners in federal programs for homesteading, reclamation, tree culture, law enforcement, inland waterways, the nation's internal communications system (including highway and railroad routes), and veterans' aid of various sorts. Administrative contacts were voluminous, and the whole process of interaction was lubricated, then as today, by constituent-conscious members of Congress.

The essential continuity of the collaborative system is best demonstrated by the history of the grants. The land grant tended to become a cash grant based on the calculated disposable value of the land, and the cash grant tended to become an annual grant based upon the national government's superior tax powers. In 1887, only three years before the frontier was officially closed, thus signaling the end of the disposable public domain, Congress enacted the first continuing cash grants.

A long, extensive, and continuous experience is therefore the foundation of the present system of shared functions characteristic of the American federal system, what we have called the marble cake of government. It is a misjudgment of our history and our present situation to believe that a neat separation of governmental functions could take place without drastic alterations in our society and system of government.

DYNAMICS OF SHARING:
THE POLITICS OF THE FEDERAL SYSTEM

Many causes contribute to dispersed power in the federal system. One is the simple historical fact that the states existed before the nation. A second is in the form of creed, the traditional opinion of Americans that expresses distrust of centralized power and places great value in the strength and vitality of local units of government. Another is pride in locality and state, nurtured by the nation's size and by variations of regional and state history. Still a fourth cause of decentralization is the sheer wealth of the nation. It allows all groups, including state and local governments, to partake of the central government's largesse, supplies room for experimentation and even waste, and makes unnecessary the tight organization of political power that must follow when the support of one program necessarily means the deprivation of another.

In one important respect, the Constitution no longer operates to impede centralized government. The Supreme Court since 1937 has given Congress a relatively free hand. The federal government can build substantive programs in many areas on the taxation and commerce powers. Limitations of such central programs based on the argument, "it's unconstitutional," are no longer possible as long as Congress (in the Court's view) acts reasonably in the interest of the whole nation. The Court is unlikely to reverse this permissive view in the foreseeable future.

Nevertheless, some constitutional restraints on centralization continue to operate. The strong constitutional position of the states—for example, the assignment of two Senators to each state, the role given the states in administering even national elections, and the relatively few limitations on their lawmaking powers—establish the geographical units as natural centers of administrative and political strength. Many clauses of the Constitution are not subject to the same latitude of interpretation as the commerce and tax clauses. The simple, clearly stated, unambiguous phrases—for example, the President "shall hold his office during the term of four years"—are subject to change only through the formal amendment process. Similar provisions exist with respect to the terms of Senators and Congressmen and the amendment process. All of them have the effect of retarding or restraining centralizing action of the federal government. The fixed terms of the President and members of Congress, for example, greatly impede the development of nationwide, disciplined political parties that almost certainly would have to precede continuous large-scale expansion of federal functions.

The constitutional restraints on the expansion of national authority are less important and less direct today than they were in 1879 or in 1936. But to say that they are less important is not to say that they are unimportant.

The nation's politics reflect these decentralizing causes and add some of their own. The political parties of the United States are unique. They seldom perform the function that parties traditionally perform in other countries, the function of gathering together diverse strands of power and welding them into one. Except during the period of nominating and electing a President and for the essential but nonsubstantive business of organizing the houses of Congress, the American parties rarely coalesce power at all. Characteristically they do the reverse, serving as a canopy under which special and local interests are represented with little regard for anything that can be called a party program. National leaders are elected on a party ticket, but in Congress they must seek cross-party support if their leadership is to be effective. It is a rare President during rare periods who can produce legislation without facing the defection of substantial numbers of his own party. (Wilson could do this in the first session of the Sixty-Third Congress; but Franklin D. Roosevelt could not, even during the famous hundred days of 1933.) Presidents whose parties form the majority of the Congressional houses must still count heavily on support from the other party.

The parties provide the pivot on which the entire governmental system swings. Party operations, first of all, produce in legislation the basic division of functions between the federal government, on the one hand, and state and local governments, on the other. The Supreme Court's permissiveness with respect to the expansion of national powers has not in fact produced any considerable extension of exclusive federal functions. The body of federal law in all fields has remained, in the words of Henry M. Hart, Jr., and Herbert Wechsler, "interstitial in its nature," limited in objective and resting upon the principal body of legal relationships defined by state law. It is difficult to find any area of federal legislation that is not significantly affected by state law.

In areas of new or enlarged federal activity, legislation characteristically provides important roles for state and local governments. This is as true of Democratic as of Republican administrations and true even of functions for which arguments of efficiency would produce exclusive federal responsibility. Thus the unemployment compensation program of the New Deal and the airport program of President Truman's administration both provided important responsibilities for state governments. In both cases attempts to eliminate state participation were defeated by a cross-party coalition of pro-state votes and influence. A large fraction of the Senate is usually made up of ex-governors, and the membership of both houses is composed of men who know that their reelection depends less upon national leaders or national party organization than upon support from their home constituencies. State and local officials are key members of these constituencies, often central figures in selecting candidates and in turning out the vote. Under such circumstances, national legislation taking state and local views heavily into account is inevitable.

Second, the undisciplined parties affect the character of the federal system as a result of Senatorial and Congressional interference in federal administrative programs on behalf of local interests. Many aspects of the legislative involvement in administrative affairs are formalized. The Legislative Reorganization Act of 1946, to take only one example, provided that each of the standing committees "shall exercise continuous watchfulness" over administration of laws within its jurisdiction. But the formal system of controls, extensive as it is, does not compare in importance with the informal and extralegal network of relationships in producing continuous legislative involvement in administrative affairs.

Senators and Congressmen spend a major fraction of their time representing problems of their constituents before administrative agencies. An even larger fraction of Congressional staff time is devoted to the same task. The total magnitude of such "case work" operations is great. In one five-month period of 1943 the Office of Price Administration received a weekly average of 842 letters from members of Congress. If phone calls and personal contacts are added, each member of Congress on the average presented the OPA with a problem involving one of his constituents twice a day in each five-day work week. Data for less vulnerable agencies during less intensive periods are also impressive. In 1958, to take only one example, the Department of Agriculture estimated (and underestimated) that it received an average of 159 Congressional letters per working day. Special Congressional liaison staffs have been created to service this mass of business, though all higher officials meet it in one form or another. The Air Force in 1958 had, under the command of a major general, 137 people (55 officers and 82 civilians) working in its liaison office.

The widespread, consistent, and in many ways unpredictable character of legislative interference in administrative affairs has many consequences for the tone and character of American administrative behavior. From the perspective of this paper, the important consequence is the comprehensive, day-to-day, even hour-by-hour, impact of local views on national programs. No point of substance or procedure is immune from Congressional scrutiny. A substantial portion of the entire weight of this impact is on behalf of the state and local governments. It is a weight that can alter procedures for screening immigration applications, divert the course of a national highway, change the tone of an international negotiation, and amend a social security law to accommodate local practices or fulfill local desires.

The party system compels administrators to take a political role. This is a third way in which the parties function to decentralize the American system. The administrator must play politics for the same reason that the politician is able to play in administration: the parties are without program and without discipline.

In response to the unprotected position in which the party situation places him, the administrator is forced to seek support where he can find it. One ever-present task is to nurse the Congress of the United States, that crucial constituency which ultimately controls his agency's budget and program. From the administratior's view, a sympathetic consideration of Congressional requests (if not downright submission to them) is the surest way to build the political support without which the administrative job could not continue. Even the completely task-oriented administrator must be sensitive to the need for Congressional support and to the relationship between case work requests, on one side, and budgetary and legislative support, on the other. "You do a good job handling the personal problems and requests of a Congressman," a White House officer said, "and you have an easier time convincing him to back your program." Thus there is an important link between the nursing of Congressional requests, requests that largely concern local matters, and the most comprehensive national programs. The administrator must accommodate to the former as a price of gaining support for the latter.

One result of administrative politics is that the administrative agency may become the captive of the nationwide interest group it serves or presumably regulates. In such cases no government may come out with effective authority: the winners are the interest groups themselves. But in a very large number of cases, states and localities also win influence. The politics of administration is a process of making peace with legislators who for the most part consider themselves the guardians of local interests. The political role of administrators therefore contributes to the power of states and localities in national programs.

Finally, the way the party system operates gives American politics their overall distinctive tone. The lack of party discipline produces an openness in the system that allows individuals, groups, and institutions (including state and local governments) to attempt to influence national policy at every step of the legislative-administrative process. This is the "multiple-crack" attribute of the American government. "Crack" has two meanings. It means not only many fissures or access points; it also means, less statically, opportunities for wallops or smacks at government.

If the parties were more disciplined, the result would not be a cessation of the process by which individuals and groups impinge themselves upon the central government. But the present state of the parties clearly allows for a far greater operation of the multiple crack than would be possible under the conditions of centralized party control. American interest groups exploit literally uncountable access points in the legislative-administrative process. If legislative lobbying, from committee stages to the conference committee, does not produce results, a Cabinet secretary is called. His immediate associates are petitioned. Bureau chiefs and their aides are hit. Field officers are put under pressure. Campaigns are instituted by which friends of the agency apply a secondary influence on behalf of the interested party. A conference with the President may be urged.

To these multiple points for bringing influence must be added the multiple voices of the influencers. Consider, for example, those in a small town who wish to have a federal action taken. The easy merging of public and private interest at the local level means that the influence attempt is made in the name of the whole community, thus removing it from political partisanship. The Rotary Club as well as the City Council, the Chamber of Commerce and the mayor, eminent citizens and political bosses—all are readily enlisted. If a conference in a Senator's office will expedite matters, someone on the local scene can be found to make such a conference possible and effective. If technical information is needed, technicians will supply it. State or national professional organizations of local officials, individual Congressmen and Senators, and not infrequently whole state delegations will make the local cause their own. Federal field officers, who service localities, often assume local views. So may elected and appointed state officers. Friendships are exploited, and political mortgages called due. Under these circumstances, national policies are molded by local action.

In summary, then, the party system functions to devolve power. The American parties, unlike any other, are highly responsive when directives move from the bottom to the top, highly unresponsive from top to bottom. Congressmen and Senators can rarely ignore concerted demands from their home constituencies; but no party leader can expect the same kind of response from those below, whether he be a President asking for Congressional support or a Congressman seeking aid from local or state leaders.

Any tightening of the party apparatus would have the effect of strengthening the central government. The four characteristics of the system, discussed above, would become less important. If control from the top were strictly applied, these hallmarks of American decentralization might entirely disappear. To be specific, if disciplined and program-oriented parties were achieved: (1) It would make far less likely legislation that takes heavily into account the desires and prejudices of the highly centralized power groups and institutions of the country, including the state and local governments. (2) It would to a large extent prevent legislators, individually and collectively, from intruding themselves on behalf of non-national interests in national administrative programs. (3) It would put an end to the administrator's search for his own political support, a search that often results in fostering state, local, and other non-national powers. (4) It would dampen the process by which individuals and groups, including state and local political leaders, take advantage of multiple cracks to steer national legislation and administration in ways congenial to them and the institutions they represent.

Alterations of this sort could only accompany basic changes in the organization and style of politics which, in turn, presuppose fundamental changes at the parties' social base. The sharing of functions is, in fact, the sharing of power. To end this sharing process would mean the destruction of whatever measure of decentralization exists in the United States today.

GOALS FOR THE SYSTEM OF SHARING

The Goal of Understanding

Our structure of government is complex, and the politics operating that structure are mildly chaotic. Circumstances are ever-changing. Old institutions mask intricate procedures. The nation's history can be read with alternative glosses, and what is nearest at hand may be furthest from comprehension. Simply to understand the federal system is therefore a difficult task. Yet without understanding there is little possibility of producing desired changes in the system. Social structures and processes are relatively impervious to purposeful change. They also exhibit intricate interrelationships so that change induced at point "A" often produces unanticipated results at point "Z." Changes introduced into an imperfectly understood system are as likely to produce reverse consequences as the desired ones.

This is counsel of neither futility nor conservation for those who seek to make our government a better servant of the people. It is only to say that the first goal for those setting goals with respect to the federal system is that of understanding it.

Two Kinds of Decentralization

The recent major efforts to reform the federal system have in large part been aimed at separating functions and tax sources, at dividing them between the federal government and the states. All of these attempts have failed. We can now add that their success would be undesirable.

It is easy to specify the conditions under which an ordered separation of functions could take place. What is principally needed is a majority political party, under firm leadership, in control of both Presidency and Congress, and, ideally but not necessarily, also in control of a number of states. The political discontinuities, or the absence of party links, (1) between the governors and their state legislatures, (2) between the President and the governors, and (3) between the President and Congress clearly account for both the picayune recommendations of the Federal-State Action Committee and for the failure of even those recommendations in Congress. If the President had been in control of Congress (that is, consistently able to direct a majority of House and Senate votes), this alone would have made possible some genuine separation and devolution of functions. The failure to decentralize by order is a measure of the decentralization of power in the political parties.

Stated positively, party centralization must precede governmental decentralization by order. But this is a slender reed on which to hang decentralization. It implies the power to centralize. A majority party powerful enough to bring about ordered decentralization is far more likely to choose in favor of ordered centralization. And a society that produced centralized national parties would, by that very fact, be a society prepared to accept centralized government.

Decentralization by order must be contrasted with the different kind of decentralization that exists today in the United States. It may be called the decentralization of mild chaos. It exists because of the existence of dispersed power centers. This form of decentralization is less visible and less neat. It rests on no discretion of central authorities. It produces at times specific acts that many citizens may consider undesirable or evil. But power sometimes wielded even for evil ends may be desirable power. To those who find value in the dispersion of power, decentralization by mild chaos is infinitely more desirable than decentralization by order. The preservation of mild chaos is an important goal for the American federal system.

Oiling the Squeak Points

In a governmental system of genuinely shared responsibilities, disagreements inevitably occur. Opinions clash over proximate ends, particular ways of doing things become the subject of public debate, innovations are contested. These are not basic defects in the system. Rather, they are the system's energy-reflecting life blood. There can be no permanent "solutions" short of changing the system itself by elevating one partner to absolute supremacy. What can be done is to attempt to produce conditions in which conflict will not fester but be turned to constructive solutions of particular problems.

A long list of specific points of difficulty in the federal system can be easily identified. No adequate congressional or administrative mechanism exists to review the patchwork of grants in terms of national needs. There is no procedure by which to judge, for example, whether the national government is justified in spending so much more for highways than for education. The working force in some states is inadequate for the effective performance of some nationwide programs, while honest and not-so-honest graft frustrates efficiency in others. Some federal aid programs distort state budgets, and some are so closely supervised as to impede state action in meeting local needs. Grants are given for programs too narrowly defined, and overall programs at the state level consequently suffer. Administrative, accounting and auditing difficulties are the consequence of the multiplicity of grant programs. City officials complain that the states are intrusive fifth wheels in housing, urban redevelopment, and airport building programs.

Some differences are so basic that only a demonstration of strength on one side or another can solve them. School desegregation illustrates such an issue. It also illustrates the correct solution (although not the most desirable method of reaching it): in policy conflicts of fundamental importance, touching the nature of democracy itself, the view of the whole nation must prevail. Such basic ends, however, are rarely at issue, and sides are rarely taken with such passion that loggerheads are reached. Modes of settlement can usually be found to lubricate the squeak points of the system.

A pressing and permanent state problem, general in its impact, is the difficulty of raising sufficient revenue without putting local industries at a competitive disadvantage or without an expansion of sales taxes that press hardest on the least wealthy. A possible way of meeting this problem is to establish a state-levied income tax that could be used as an offset for federal taxes. The maximum level of the tax which could be offset would be fixed by federal law. When levied by a state, the state collection would be deducted from federal taxes. But if a state did not levy the tax, the federal government would. An additional fraction of the total tax imposed by the states would be collected directly by the federal government and used as an equalization fund, that is, distributed among the less wealthy states. Such a tax would almost certainly be imposed by all states since not to levy it would give neither political advantage to its public leaders nor financial advantage to its citizens. The net effect would be an increase in the total personal and corporate income tax.

The offset has great promise for strengthening state governments. It would help produce a more economic distribution of industry. It would have obvious financial advantages for the vast majority of states. Since a large fraction of all state income is used to aid political subdivisions, the local governments would also profit, though not equally as long as cities are under-represented in state legislatures. On the other hand, such a scheme will appear disadvantageous to some low-tax states which profit from the in-migration of industry (though it would by no means end all state-by-state tax differentials). It will probably excite the opposition of those concerned over governmental centralization, and they will not be assuaged by methods that suggest them-selves for making both state and central governments bear the psychological impact of the tax. Although the offset would probably produce an across-the-board tax increase, wealthier persons, who are affected more by an income tax than by other levies, can be expected to join forces with those whose fear is centralization. (This is a common alliance and, in the nature of things, the philosophical issue rather than financial advantage is kept foremost.)

Those opposing such a tax would gain additional ammunition from the certain knowledge that federal participation in the scheme would lead to some federal standards governing the use of the funds. Yet the political strength of the states would keep these from becoming onerous. Indeed, inauguration of the tax offset as a means of providing funds to the states might be an occasion for dropping some of the specifications for existing federal grants. One federal standard, however, might be possible because of the greater representation of urban areas in the constituency of Congress and the President than in the constituency of state legislatures: Congress might make a state's participation in the offset scheme dependent upon a periodic reapportionment of state legislatures.

The income tax offset is only one of many ideas that can be generated to meet serious problems of closely meshed governments. The fate of all such schemes ultimately rests, as it should, with the politics of a free people. But much can be done if the primary technical effort of those concerned with improving the federal system were directed not at separating its interrelated parts but at making them work together more effectively. Temporary commis-sions are relatively inefficient in this effort, though they may be useful for making general assessments and for generating new ideas. The professional organizations of government workers do part of the job of continuously scruti-nizing programs and ways and means of improving them. A permanent staff, established in the President's office and working closely with state and local officials, could also perform a useful and perhaps important role.

The Strength of the Parts

Whatever governmental "strength" or "vitality" may be, it does not consist of independent decision-making in legislation and administration. Federal-state interpenetration here is extensive. Indeed, a judgment of the relative domestic strength of the two planes must take heavily into account the influ-ence of one on the other's decisions. In such an analysis the strength of the states (and localities) does not weigh lightly. The nature of the nation's politics makes federal functions more vulnerable to state influence than state offices are to federal influence. Many states, as the Kestnbaum Commission noted, live with "self-imposed constitutional limitations" that make it difficult for them to "perform all of the services that their citizens require." If this has the result of adding to federal responsibilities, the states' importance in shaping and administering federal programs eliminates much of the sting.

The geography of state boundaries, as well as many aspects of state internal organization, are the products of history and cannot be justified on any grounds of rational efficiency. Who, today, would create major governmental subdivisions the size of Maryland, Delaware, New Jersey, or Rhode Island? Who would write into Oklahoma's fundamental law an absolute state debt limit of $500,000? Who would design (to cite only the most extreme cases) Georgia's and Florida's gross underrepresentation of urban areas in both houses of the legislature?

A complete catalogue of state political and administrative horrors would fill a sizeable volume. Yet exhortations to erase them have roughly the same effect as similar exhortations to erase sin. Some of the worst inanities—for example, the boundaries of the states, themselves—are fixed in the national constitution and defy alteration for all foreseeable time. Others, such as urban underrepresentation in state legislatures, serve the overrepresented groups, including some urban ones, and the effective political organization of the deprived groups must precede reform.

Despite deficiencies of politics and organizations that are unchangable or slowly changing, it is an error to look at the states as static anachronisms. Some of them—New York, Minnesota, and California, to take three examples spanning the country—have administrative organizations that compare favorably in many ways with the national establishment. Many more in recent years have moved rapidly towards integrated administrative departments, statewide budgeting, and central leadership. The others have models-in-existence to follow, and active professional organizations (led by the Council of State Governments) promoting their development. Slow as this change may be, the states move in the direction of greater internal effectiveness.

The pace toward more effective performance at the state level is likely to increase. Urban leaders, who generally feel themselves disadvantaged in state affairs, and suburban and rural spokesmen, who are most concerned about national centralization, have a common interest in this task. The urban dwellers want greater equality in state affairs, including a more equitable share of state financial aid; nonurban dwellers are concerned that city dissatisfactions should not be met by exclusive federal, or federal-local, programs. Antagonistic, rather than amiable, cooperation may be the consequence. But it is a cooperation that can be turned to politically effective measures for a desirable upgrading of state institutions.

If one looks closely, there is scant evidence for the fear of the federal octopus, the fear that expansion of central programs and influence threatens to reduce the states and localities to compliant administrative arms of the central government. In fact, state and local governments are touching a larger proportion of the people in more ways than ever before; and they are spending a higher fraction of the total national product than ever before. Federal programs have increased, rather than diminished, the importance of the governors; stimulated professionalism in state agencies; increased citizen interest and participation in government; and, generally, enlarged and made more effective the scope of state action.[2] It may no longer be true in any significant sense that the states and localities are "closer" than the federal government to the people. It is true that the smaller governments remain active and powerful members of the federal system.

Central Leadership: The Need for Balance

The chaos of party processes makes difficult the task of presidential leadership. It deprives the President of ready-made Congressional majorities. It may produce, as in the chairmen of legislative committees, power-holders relatively hidden from public scrutiny and relatively protected from presidential direction. It allows the growth of administrative agencies which sometimes escape control by central officials. These are prices paid for a wide dispersion of political power. The cost is tolerable because the total results of dispersed power are themselves desirable and because, where clear national supremacy is essential, in foreign policy and military affairs, it is easiest to secure.

Moreover, in the balance of strength between the central and peripheral governments, the central government has on its side the whole secular drift towards the concentration of power. It has on its side technical developments that make central decisions easy and sometimes mandatory. It has on its side potent purse powers, the result of superior tax-gathering resources. It has potentially on its side the national leadership capacities of the presidential office. The last factor is the controlling one, and national strength in the federal system has shifted with the leadership desires and capacities of the Chief Executive. As these have varied, so there has been an almost rhythmic pattern: periods of central strength put to use alternating with periods of central strength dormant.

Following a high point of federal influence during the early and middle years of the New Deal, the postwar years have been, in the weighing of central-peripheral strength, a period of light federal activity. Excepting the Supreme Court's action in favor of school desegregation, national influence by design or default has not been strong in domestic affairs. The danger now is that the central government is doing too little rather than too much. National deficiencies in education and health require the renewed attention of the na-

---

2. See the valuable report, *The Impact of Federal Grants-in-Aid on the Structure and Functions of State and Local Governments,* submitted to the Commission on Intergovernmental Relations by the Governmental Affairs Institute (Washington, 1955).

tional government. Steepening population and urbanization trend lines have produced metropolitan area problems that can be effectively attacked only with the aid of federal resources. New definitions of old programs in housing and urban redevelopment, and new programs to deal with air pollution, water supply, and mass transportation are necessary. The federal government's essential role in the federal system is that of organizing, and helping to finance, such nationwide programs.

The American federal system exhibits many evidences of the dispersion of power not only because of formal federalism but more importantly because our politics reflect and reinforce the nation's diversities-within-unity. Those who value the virtues of decentralization, which writ large are virtues of freedom, need not scruple at recognizing the defects of those virtues. The defects are principally the danger that parochial and private interests may not coincide with, or give way to, the nation's interest. The necessary cure for these defects is effective national leadership.

The centrifugal force of domestic politics needs to be balanced by the centripetal force of strong presidential leadership. Simultaneous strength at center and periphery exhibits the American system at its best, if also at its noisiest. The interests of both find effective spokesmen. States and localities (and private interest groups) do not lose their influence opportunities, but national policy becomes more than the simple consequence of successful, momentary concentrations of non-national pressures: it is guided by national leaders.

The revelations surrounding Watergate severely undermined public confidence in the federal government in 1973 and 1974. Watergate had a spill-over effect upon public attitudes toward state and local governments causing public confidence at these levels to deteriorate also. Moreover, there were a sufficient number of scandals surrounding government officials at the state and local levels to justify this lack of confidence. While the federal government struggled to pass legislation that would remedy some of the conditions that led to Watergate and its surrounding scandals, the states surpassed the federal government in the passage of remedial legislation. For example, almost half of the states by the end of 1973 had passed legislation to eliminate or reduce secrecy in government, buttress the ethics of governmental officials, and provide for controls over campaign funding. In none of these areas had the federal government gone as far as the states. The states were fulfilling what has long been considered to be one of their principal functions in a federal system, namely, experimentation in legislation. The following selection discusses the reactions of the states to pressing public concerns in the mid-1970s.

21
Advisory Commission on
Intergovernmental Relations

FEDERALISM IN 1973: THE SYSTEM UNDER STRESS

Nineteen hundred seventy three was a year of troubled questioning for this country and its federal system of shared powers, questioning which underscored the nation's yearning for certainty. It was also a year that forever laid to rest any notion that the fate and fortune of Federal, State and local governments and the private sector are not inextricably tied together. It also testified to the importance of initiative by individual governmental units at every level.

The year began with uncertainty over the budget and inflation; it ended with doubts about the impact of energy shortages. Throughout, there ran the question of the adequacy of governmental leadership at all levels.

Federalism survived this year of testing—as it has weathered previous crises—again demonstrating its adaptability and resilience.

All the dynamics of federalism were evident in 1973. The energy crisis necessitated centralization while State initiative in various topics could lead to decentralization. The legislatures, executives and judiciary at every level of government actively participated in the system of checks and balances. Despite the growing loss of confidence, the people appeared to have faith in our federal system of government. A comprehensive survey of the opinions of the public and of government leadership sponsored by the Senate Subcommittee on Intergovernmental Relations, stated that:

> ... Americans—and the officials who serve them—concur generally on the following recommendations:
>
> (1) The power of the Federal establishment should be reduced, while the autonomous authority of State and local government should be augmented;
>
> (2) A central range of social concerns—guarantees of opportunity and dignity to the least fortunate citizens—remain, within the context of shared responsibility, a predominantly Federal concern.

CONFIDENCE IN GOVERNMENT

It was a year of shocking revelations, political bombshells following one another at intervals that left the American public reeling. Former and incumbent, elected and appointed officials at local, State and Federal levels were convicted, tried or indicted for a variety of offenses.

In February, a former U.S. Senator was sentenced to prison for taking an "illegal gratuity" during his incumbency. A Federal judge—a former governor —was convicted of bribery and is awaiting an appeal decision. Throughout the year, other State and local officials were indicted and several brought to trial. Two former U.S. Cabinet officials and several key White House aides were indicted with some guilty pleas resulting.

The Vice President resigned.

The public's confidence in government officials plummeted, according to the opinion polls.

The Senate Intergovernmental Relations Subcommittee commissioned a thorough study by the Louis Harris firm of public opinion and the opinions of State and local leaders.

Generally, 55 percent of the respondents felt that "the people running the country don't really care what happens to you" compared with only 26 percent in a poll taken in 1966. Further, 53 percent of the public thought "there is something deeply wrong today"—compared with 37 percent in 1968. While 64 percent of those surveyed listed inflation as our major problem, 43 percent listed "lack of integrity in government."

The solution—as it reflects on the federal system—was less straightforward in the minds of the people. Forty-two percent, a clear plurality, called for stripping power from the Federal government and large majorities suggested reallocating it to State and local governments. On the other hand, 67 percent agreed with the statement that "It's about time we had a strong Federal government again to get this country moving."

A blue-ribbon government commission, the National Advisory Commission on Criminal Justice Standards and Goals, in a report released after Thanksgiving, said the public perceives official corruption as widespread at all levels of government—Federal, State and local.

In a section on "Integrity in Government," the report said, "Public corruption makes an especially sinister contribution to criminality by providing an excuse and rationalization for its existence among those who commit crime. . . . Simply put, official corruption breeds disrespect for the law."

It warned that "As long as official corruption exists, the war against crime will be perceived by many as a war of the powerful against the powerless; 'law and order' will be just a hypocritical rally cry, and 'equal justice under law' will be an empty phrase."

Direct response to the crisis of confidence came first from State and local governments, demonstrating that governments closest to the people are more sensitive to the feelings at the grass roots. In the course of the year, nearly half the States passed legislation dealing with campaign funding, ethics or secrecy in government.

At the Federal level, direct reaction to the startling events of the year was cautious and limited—consisting more of rhetoric than action. Most Congressional attempts to fill the leadership gap were in vain—despite the crippling of the policy-initiating sector of the executive branch—although some preliminary Congressional steps taken in 1973 might yield results in 1974. However, on November 15, the House of Representatives funded a Judiciary Committee investigation of the appropriateness of conducting impeachment proceedings against the President.

Openness of Financing—Freedom of Information. A key factor in many of the year's political scandals was the complex, intertwined issue of how candidates finance their campaigns and the financial interests of office holders once they are elected or appointed. At least one-third of the States took legislative or executive action to open this issue to public scrutiny.

The Texas legislature was the first to act on this subject in 1973. One novel provision that could render violations of the financial disclosure law too expensive to risk makes any candidate, political committee or contributor civilly liable to all other opposing candidates for attorneys' fees and for double the amount of any unlawful contribution or expenditures, and to the State for triple that amount.

The Alabama legislature adopted a comprehensive government ethics and financial disclosure law. It requires not only State, county and municipal officials to file disclosures of their economic interests but also all State employees earning over $12,000. Persons doing business with the State must also file; and lobbyists must register. Another provision requires news reporters to register with a newly formed Ethics Commission.

Florida, Hawaii, Maryland and Ohio also adopted stringent financial disclosure laws; the governors of Illinois, Michigan and Missouri promulgated executive orders for executive branch personnel. Several States, including New Jersey, placed rigid limits on the amount any candidate can spend on election. Iowa and Maine took initial steps toward public financing of campaigns to avoid heavy reliance on priviate contributions. They permit taxpayers to earmark $1 of State tax payments for contributions to a political party.

At the Federal level, throughout the year Congress was considering a comprehensive campaign finance measure to set limits on expenditures by candidates for Federal office. The Senate passed the bill in July, but hearings were still in progress in the House by mid–November. In December, an attempt in the Senate to attach a public financing amendment to "must" debt limit legislation lost because of a filibuster.

Existing Federal legislation permits taxpayers to "check off" a $1 donation for campaign financing on their income tax returns. However, for 1972 returns, a separate form was required. A place on the main form will be provided for 1973 returns.

The people's desire to open up government also was manifested in a series of "sun shine laws" so termed because they were aimed at "letting the sun shine in" by opening government meetings to the public and increasing access to public documents.

Vermont, Oregon, Florida, Missouri and Tennessee adopted explicit sun shine laws, forbidding State or local bodies from holding secret meetings except for certain highly circumscribed purposes—and then requiring that minutes be kept to be made public at a later date. Several of the campaign financing and ethics laws contained open meeting provisions. The Texas ethics package extended the State's 1967 open meetings law to cover legislative committees, for example. The New Hampshire legislature made officials who refuse access to public documents liable for the attorneys' fees and court costs spent to obtain them.

At the Federal level, the strain for access to government information was perhaps greatest, with the most meager results. Here the problem was not only the public's right to know but Congressional access to information held by the executive branch. During the summer, three Congressional committees held joint hearings on a bill to assure Congressional and public access to information, but nothing came of it.

The Federal government operates under a Freedom of Information Act, which has come under substantial criticism. About the only result of the summer hearings was an Interagency Symposium on Improved Administration of the Freedom of Information Act, held by the Justice Department in late November.

Mention should also be made of the televised Ervin Committee hearings which gave the public a firsthand look at the proceedings of a Congressional investigation.

Accountability. At the heart of the openness-in-government issue was a feeling that had been growing and spreading over the years that "government" had taken on a life of its own with the basic purpose of self-perpetuation rather than service to the people. The events of 1973 brought this vague feeling to a head —and a clear call for greater accountability of all branches of government at all levels could be heard from every quarter, both inside and outside of government.

The judiciary provides one example. A long-standing dilemma of government has been how to raise judges above the direct political process but still make them accountable to the people. The best selection system does not assure the continuation of high performance on the bench when the long period of tenure of most judges is considered. Impeachment and address—the traditional methods of censure and removal—have not worked well. But a solution that has been gathering momentum is the judicial qualifications commission—a body composed of members of the bench, lawyers as well as laymen —and courts of the judiciary, specially instituted judicial tribunals. These bodies investigate complaints of judicial misbehavior or incompetence and clear the judge or recommend censure or even removal. In 1973, five States created a review body, bringing to 41 the States with some form of judicial review unit.

Significant legislative and executive efforts to strengthen government accountability are discussed in the section on government capability.

Political Participation. A positive indication of the will of the people to make government accountable to all the governed is the increased activity in traditional political avenues of minority groups.

Black officials across the nation, in fall 1973, voted to form a National Conference of Black Mayors to fight for civil rights "based on an organization and a concept and not on an individual," as one of the mayors articulated the feeling.

Success at the polls for black candidates has accelerated in the last few years. In 1973, three large cities—Los Angeles, Detroit and Atlanta—elected black mayors. Blacks won election or re-election in smaller cities such as Raleigh, North Carolina and in towns from Maryland to Georgia to Michigan. Of course, blacks and other minority members lost elections across the country as well.

These developments would indicate a faith in the flexibility and adaptability of the system and the firm resolve to work for change through it.

Seven additional States ratified the Equal Rights Amendment to the U.S. Constitution, bringing the number to 29 or 30, depending on whether a Nebraska move to rescind ratification is permitted. At least 15 States took independent action to ban sex discrimination in employment, credit transactions and other areas.

Citizen Participation. Citizen participation in most governmental activities has been more myth and rhetoric than reality and practice. Decisions on Federal grant projects frequently were handled by bureaucrats in Washington. Decisions on State-aided programs often were made in legislative committees in the State capitol. And city decisions often were taken out of the hands of municipal leaders by financial emergencies. Frequently the local governments lacked the authority to make the decision themselves in the first place.

A direct answer to this situation is home rule. And a trend toward home rule charters for cities and counties has been noted over the past half dozen years. This continued in 1973, with, for example, home rule legislation in Florida, Minnesota and Wisconsin. At the local level, Detroit adopted a new city charter.

Just as important, however, may be some indirect movements at the Federal level to increase citizen participation in and foreknowledge of governmental decisions.

Federal general revenue sharing is designed to make the use of Federal aid funds more accountable to the people.

Trying to follow the spirit of this law, large cities such as Detroit as well as smaller localities have held public hearings on general revenue sharing. The State of West Virginia held public symposia throughout the State on the best uses for revenue sharing allocations. Local governments are required to inform the citizenry of how the money is to be used by publishing plans for intended use and then reports of actual use in the local newspapers.

However, officials of many smaller cities say the documents required to be published in newspapers are complex and confusing, sometimes presenting a distorted view of how the money actually is to be used. Other officials complain that the average person-on-the-street does not attend the public hearings, but only the already highly-organized lobbies. At least one mayor has noted that his city is in such desperate financial straits that it cannot afford the luxury of citizen participation in allocating revenue sharing money—but must use the funds just to keep the city running.

On balance, however, Federal general revenue sharing can increase the direct influence of the people by involving them in planning for the use of revenue sharing money. . . .

During 1973, Federal, State and local governments each took a few steps forward and several steps backward in the quest for government capability. In between the levels, in the multistate and substate regions, the chaotic status quo reigned. . . .

At the State Level. Movement toward more capable government at the State level . . . went both forward and backward. A controversial new Montana constitution went into effect in 1973 and an Alabama constitutional revision commission reported to the legislature. No States voted on new constitutions during the year, but constitutional conventions and revision commissions were meeting in several States to begin the process of organized constitutional change.

Legislative. All but one State legislature met in 1973—a positive sign of increasing legislative responsibility. In May, the Ohio voters approved regular annual sessions, but at the polls in November, the voters of Kentucky and Texas turned down constitutional amendments for annual sessions.

At least six States raised legislative pay and another eight increased legislators' expense allowances. However, voters of Texas and Rhode Island rejected proposed legislative pay increases and the people of Washington State, in an initiative at the November election, voided a 1973 pay raise, limiting raises to a 5.5 percent hike.

At the State level, several legislatures assumed greater fiscal control.

Maine went to "zero-based budgeting" wherein every program comes equally before the legislature, at "ground zero." Previously, established programs would be funded automatically. Under the new system, every department head must list each budget item with its priority and budget justification.

The Oklahoma legislature created a Subcommittee on Fiscal Operations to work year-round in examining budgets, expenditures and State programs, and set up a system of performance post auditing. The legislature strengthened its oversight function and its ability to insure that agency programs are carried out according to legislative intent.

The Mississippi legislature created a Joint Legislative Committee on Performance Evaluation and Expenditure Review to investigate the expenditures of State agencies to determine how well the agencies are administering their programs. The Virginia legislature created a Joint Legislative Audit and Review Commission and Rhode Island established the post of Auditor General to report to the legislature and have the power to audit the accounts of all agencies of government outside the legislative branch.

Executive. The continuing campaign over the past half decade to organize the State executive into a smoothly running operation, accountable to elected State officials, moved ahead in a few States in 1973. The South Dakota legislature approved a massive reorganization of the State executive, consolidating 160 agencies into 16 departments. The 1974 legislature must approve the move. The North Carolina legislature moved ahead on executive branch restructuring. Other States reorganized individual departments—the number of States with Departments of Transportation reached 22. On the other hand, the voters of Rhode Island rejected an amendment for four-year terms for State officials.

Local Action. Local governments also were taking steps to revitalize their structures. A new city charter was adopted in Detroit—after failing at the polls earlier in the year. In Rochester, New York, however, the voters turned down a new charter. And the electorate of Dallas approved 34 charter amendments at a mid-June election.

Intergovernmental Actions. Crucial to more capable government is better qualified personnel. One intergovernmental attempt to improve the quality of government workers is the Intergovernmental Personnel Act of 1970 (IPA), which among other provisions, operates a program of mobility assignments— temporary intergovernmental transfers to get qualified personnel to the level of government that needs them. In October, the number of mobility assignments passed the 1,000 mark. Sixty percent of those assigned came from Federal agencies and 40 percent, from States, local government and academic institutions.

In addition, the IPA Advisory Council recommended the abolition of all administratively established Federal personnel requirements imposed on State and local governments accepting Federal grants. Instead, a single Federal requirement would be applied.

The National Commission on Productivity in 1973 investigated ways to increase the productivity of State and local government. Evaluation of the effectiveness of government was a high priority item in New Jersey and Wisconsin during the year.

Regionalism—Multistate. No clear Federal intention regarding multistate regional bodies could be determined because of conflicting actions during the year. The Appalachian Regional Commission—the most powerful of the multistate development bodies—continued its separate existence. But the regional commissions created under Title V of the *Public Works and Economic Development Act* of 1965, led a storm-tossed life. In 1973, two more commissions had been created by the Administration pursuant to the act—an apparent vote of confidence in the procedure. But, in early 1973, the President proposed letting them die and folding their functions into special revenue sharing. In the end, Congress extended the life of these commissions for one year only.

Regionalism—Substate. The picture was similarly foggy at the substate level. Despite Federal expressions of reliance on State-drawn substate districts, one law was passed and another proposed that could create new district boundaries. Passed was the Older Americans Act, which requires statewide districting under a complex set of new guidelines. The Allied Services Act—itself an HEW proprosal to approach service delivery on a people-oriented rather than program-oriented basis—takes care to conform its districting arrangements with existing substate districts.

At the State level, some movement toward strengthening regional arrangements could be discerned, but basic nagging questions remained: how do you devolve government responsibility to the substate level, if no effective organization exists to do the job? And the most fundamental political dilemma of the subject remained: how do you match local boundaries with area needs and make areawide organizations adequately representative of local government constituents?

Official action to establish statewide systems of substate districts has now been taken by 44 States. This has created 517 districts, but about one-third of them are not yet served by active regional organizations.

At the local level, no city-county mergers were approved in 1973, but four proposals went down to defeat at the polls.

Opening Communications. Another intergovernmental aspect of improving the capability of government is the need to open up communications among the levels and between the branches within each level.

Governor Daniel Evans, Chairman of the National Governors' Conference, opened an initiative on this front, forming a New Coalition of the leadership of the general government interest groups: the governors, legislators, mayors and county officials. By year's end, the coalition had met with the President on State-local input into the Federal budget and on the energy crisis.

Another step toward opening up communications is a series of Forums on Federalism, scheduled around the country as part of the American Revolutionary Bicentennial celebration. These symposia are aimed at opening up a dialogue on the issues of federalism between the people and elected and appointed government officials at every level. These steps are barely toe-wriggling on the long road to open communications.

THE LESSONS OF 1973

Federalism survived the turmoil of 1973, as it has come through previous difficult periods and as it inevitably will endure other years of chaos and conflict.

That does not mean, however, that the system performs at its best under the kind of stresses and strains heaped upon it in 1973; despite the baling-wire and chewing-gum approach to mending its breaks; or because of the "muddle through" method of initiating change.

The lessons of 1973 are several: Federal, State and local government and private enterprise are so tightly interwoven that the end of one thread frequently is indistinguishable from the beginning of another. But each strand must carry its own weight, or the fabric will fall.

The people of this country demand efficiency and compassion in government, certainty in the economy, and integrity of the leadership.

The achievement of these goals will require openness of communications and the willingness to compromise in order to restore the confidence of the people and reestablish a feeling of cooperation and coordination.

Thomas Jefferson, writing in 1816, articulated what could be the lessons of 1973:

> If a nation expects to be ignorant and free in a state of civilization, it expects what never was and never will be. The functionaries of every government have propensities to command at will the liberty and property of their constituents. There is no safe deposit for these but with the people themselves, nor can they be safe with them without information.

CHAPTER 4

Civil Liberties and Civil Rights

Civil liberties and civil rights cover a very broad area. Among the most fundamental civil liberties are those governing the extent to which individuals can speak, write, and read what they choose. The democratic process requires the free exchange of ideas. Constitutional government requires the protection of minority rights and, above all, the right to dissent.

Freedom of Speech and Press

There are many reasons why we should support freedom of speech and press. One of these is the impossibility of proving the existence of an Absolute Truth. No person nor group can be infallible. The "best" decisions are those that are made on the basis of the most widespread information available pertaining to the subject at hand. Freedom of information is an integral part of the democratic process. In this selection from John Stuart Mill's famous essay *On Liberty,* published in 1859, the justifications for permitting liberty of speech and press are discussed.

22
John Stuart Mill

LIBERTY OF THOUGHT
AND DISCUSSION

The time, it is to be hoped, is gone by when any defence would be necessary of the "liberty of the press" as one of the securities against corrupt or tyrannical government. No argument, we may suppose, can now be needed, against permitting a legislature or an executive, not identified in interest with the people, to prescribe opinions to them, and determine what doctrines or what arguments they shall be allowed to hear. This aspect of the question, besides, has been so often and so triumphantly enforced by preceding writers, that it needs not be specially insisted on in this place. Though the law of England, on the subject of the press, is as servile to this day as it was in the time of the Tudors, there is little danger of its being actually put in force against political discussion, except during some temporary panic, when fear of insurrection drives ministers and judges from their propriety; and, speaking generally, it is not, in constitutional countries, to be apprehended, that the government, whether completely responsible to the people or not, will often attempt to control the expression of opinion, except when in doing so it makes itself the organ of the general intolerance of the public. Let us suppose, therefore, that the government is entirely at one with the people, and never thinks of exerting any power of coercion unless in agreement with what it conceives to be their voice. But I deny the right of the people to exercise such coercion, either by themselves or by their government. The power itself is illegitimate. The best government has no more title to it than the worst. It is as noxious, or more noxious, when exerted in accordance with public opinion, than when in opposition to it. If all mankind minus one, were of one opinion, and only one person were of the contrary opinion, mankind would be no more justified in silencing that one person, than he, if he had the power, would be justified in silencing mankind. Were an opinion a personal possession of no value except to the owner; if to be obstructed in the enjoyment of it were simply a private injury, it would make some difference whether the injury was inflicted only on a few persons or on many. But the peculiar evil of silencing the expression of an opinion is, that it is robbing the human race; posterity as well as the existing generation; those who dissent from the opinion, still more than those who hold it. If the opinion is right, they are deprived of the opportunity of exchanging error for truth: if wrong, they lose, what is almost as great a benefit, the clearer perception and livelier impression of truth, produced by its collision with error.

It is necessary to consider separately these two hypotheses, each of which has a distinct branch of the argument corresponding to it. We can never be sure that the opinion we are endeavoring to stifle is a false opinion; and if we were sure, stifling it would be an evil still.

First: the opinion which it is attempted to suppress by authority may possible by true. Those who desire to suppress it, of course deny its truth; but they are not infallible. They have no authority to decide the question for all mankind, and exclude every other person from the means of judging. To refuse a hearing to an opinion, because they are sure that it is false, is to assume that *their* certainty is the same thing as *absolute* certainty. All silencing of discussion is an assumption of infallibility. Its condemnation may be allowed to rest on this common argument, not the worse for being common.

Unfortunately for the good sense of mankind, the fact of their fallibility is far from carrying the weight in their practical judgment, which is always allowed to it in theory; for while every one well knows himself to be fallible, few think it necessary to take any precautions against their own fallibility, or admit the supposition that any opinion, of which they feel very certain, may be one of the examples of the error to which they acknowledge themselves to be liable. Absolute princes, or others who are accustomed to unlimited deference, usually feel this complete confidence in their own opinions on nearly all subjects. People more happily situated, who sometimes hear their opinions disputed, and are not wholly unused to be set right when they are wrong, place the same unbounded reliance only on such of their opinions as are shared by all who surround them, or to whom they habitually defer: for in proportion to a man's want of confidence in his own solitary judgment, does he usually repose, with implicit trust, on the infallibility of "the world" in general. And the world, to each individual, means the part of it with which he comes in contact; his party, his sect, his church, his class of society: the man may be called, by comparison, almost liberal and large-minded to whom it means anything so comprehensive as his own country or his own age. Nor is his faith in this collective authority at all shaken by his being aware that other ages, countries, sects, churches, classes, and parties have thought, and even now think, the exact reverse. He devolves upon his own world the responsibility of being in the right against the dissentient worlds of other people; and it never troubles him that mere accident has decided which of these numerous worlds is the object of his reliance, and that the same causes which make him a Churchman in London, would have made him a Buddhist or a Confucian in Peking. Yet it is as evident in itself, as any amount of argument can make it, that ages are no more infallible than individuals; every age having held many opinions which subsequent ages have deemed not only false but absurd; and it is as certain that many opinions, now general, will be rejected by future ages, as it is that many, once general, are rejected by the present.

The objection likely to be made to this argument, would probably take some such form as the following. There is no greater assumption of infallibility in forbidding the propagation of error, than in any other thing which is done by public authority on its own judgment and responsibility. Judgment is given to men that they may use it. Because it may be used erroneously, are men to be told that they ought not to use it at all? To prohibit what they think pernicious, is not claiming exemption from error, but fulfilling the duty incumbent on them, although fallible, of acting on their conscientious conviction. If we were never to act on our opinions, because those opinions may be wrong, we should leave all our interests uncared for, and all our duties unperformed. An objection which applies to all conduct, can be no valid objection to any conduct in particular. It is the duty of governments, and of individuals, to form the truest opinions they can; to form them carefully, and never impose them upon others unless they are quite sure of being right. But when they are sure (such reasoners may say), it is not conscientiousness but cowardice to shrink from acting on their opinions, and allow doctrines which they honestly think dangerous to the welfare of mankind, either in this life or in another, to be scattered abroad without restraint, because other people, in less enlightened times, have persecuted opinions now believed to be true. Let us take care, it may be said, not to make the same mistake: but governments and nations have made mistakes in other things, which are not denied to be fit subjects for the exercise of authority: they have laid on bad taxes, made unjust wars. Ought we therefore to lay on no taxes, and, under whatever provocation, make no wars? Men, and governments, must act to the best of their ability. There is no such thing as absolute certainty, but there is assurance sufficient for the purposes of human life. We may, and must, assume our opinion to be true for the guidance of our own conduct: and it is assuming no more when we forbid bad men to pervert society by the propagation of opinions which we regard as false and pernicious.

I answer, that it is assuming very much more. There is the greatest difference between presuming an opinion to be true, because, with every opportunity for contesting it, it has not been refuted, and assuming its truth for the purpose of not permitting its refutation. Complete liberty of contradicting and disproving our opinion, is the very condition which justifies us in assuming its truth for purposes of action; and on no other terms can a being with human faculties have any rational assurance of being right.

When we consider either the history of opinion, or the ordinary conduct of human life, to what is it to be ascribed that the one and the other are no worse than they are? Not certainly to the inherent force of the human understanding; for, on any matter not self-evident, there are ninety-nine persons totally incapable of judging of it, for one who is capable; and the capacity of the hundredth person is only comparative; for the majority of the eminent men of every past generation held many opinions now known to be erroneous, and did or approved numerous things which no one will now justify. Why is it, then, that there is on the whole a preponderance among mankind of rational opinions and rational conduct? If there really is this preponderance—which there must be, unless human affairs are, and have always been, in an almost desperate state—it is owing to a quality of the human mind, the source of everything respectable in man either as an intellectual or as a moral being, namely, that his errors are corrigible. He is capable of rectifying his mistakes, by discussion and experience. Not by experience alone. There must be discussion, to show how experience is to be interpreted. Wrong opinions and practices gradually yield to fact and argument: but facts and arguments, to produce any effect on the mind, must be brought before it. Very few facts are able to tell their own story, without comments to bring out their meaning. The whole strength and value, then, of human judgment, depending on the one property, that it can be set when it is wrong, reliance can be placed on it only when the means of setting it right are kept constantly at hand. In the case of any person whose judgment is really deserving of confidence, how has it become so? Because he has kept his mind open to criticism of his opinions and conduct. Because it has been his practice to listen to all that could be said against him; to profit by as much of it as was just, and expound to himself, and upon occasion to others, the fallacy of what was fallacious. Because he has felt, that the only way in which a human being can make some approach to knowing the whole of a subject, is by hearing what can be said about it by persons of every variety of opinion, and studying all modes in which it can be looked at by every character of mind. No wise man ever acquired his wisdom in any mode but this; nor is it in the nature of human intellect to become wise in any other manner. The steady habit of correcting and completing his own opinion by collating it with those of others, so far from causing doubt and hesitation in carrying it into practice, is the only stable foundation for a just reliance on it: for, being cognizant of all that can, at least obviously, be said against him, and having taken up his position against all gainsayers—knowing that he has sought for objections and difficulties, instead of avoiding them, and has shut out no light which can be thrown upon the subject from any quarter—he has a right to think his judgment better than that of any person, or any multitude, who have not gone through a similar process.

It is not too much to require that what the wisest of mankind, those who are best entitled to trust their own judgment, find necessary to warrant their relying on it, should be submitted to by that miscellaneous collection of a few wise and many foolish individuals, called the public. The most intolerant of churches, the Roman Catholic Church, even at the canonization of a saint, admits, and listens patiently to, a "devil's advocate." The holiest of men, it appears, cannot be admitted to posthumous honors, until all that the devil could say against him is known and weighed. If even the Newtonian philosophy were not permitted to be questioned, mankind could not feel as complete assurance of its truth as they now do. The beliefs which we have most warrant for, have no safeguard to rest on, but a standing invitation to the whole world to prove them unfounded. . . .

We have now recognized the necessity to the mental well-being of mankind (on which all their other well-being depends) of freedom of opinion, and freedom of the expression of opinion, on four distinct grounds; which we will now briefly recapitulate.

First, if any opinion is compelled to silence, that opinion may, for aught we can certainly know, be true. To deny this is to assume our own infallibility.

Secondly, though the silenced opinion be an error, it may, and very commonly does, contain a portion of truth; and since the general or prevailing opinion on any subject is rarely or never the whole truth, it is only by the collision of adverse opinions that the remainder of the truth has any chance of being supplied.

Thirdly, even if the received opinion be not only true, but the whole truth; unless it is suffered to be, and actually is, vigorously and earnestly contested, it will, by most of those who receive it, be held in the manner of a prejudice, with little comprehension or feeling of its rational grounds. And not only this, but, fourthly, the meaning of the doctrine itself will be in danger of being lost, or enfeebled, and deprived of its vital effect on the character and conduct: the dogma becoming a mere formal profession, inefficacious for good, but cumbering the ground, and preventing the growth of any real and heartfelt conviction from reason or personal experience.

Before quitting the subject of freedom of opinion, it is fit to take some notice of those who say, that the free expression of all opinions should be permitted, on condition that the manner be temperate, and do not pass the bounds of fair discussion. Much might be said on the impossibility of fixing where these supposed bounds are to be placed; for if the test be offence to those whose opinion is attacked, I think experience testifies that this offence is given whenever the attack is telling and powerful, and that every opponent who pushes them hard, and whom they find it difficult to answer, appears to them, if he shows any strong feeling on the subject, an intemperate opponent. But this, though an important consideration in a practical point of view, merges in a more fundamental objection. Undoubtedly the manner of asserting an opinion, even though it be a true one, may be very objectionable, and may justly incur severe censure. But the principal offences of the kind are such as it is mostly impossible, unless by accidental self-betrayal, to bring home to conviction. The gravest of them is, to argue sophistically, to suppress facts or arguments, to misstate the elements of the case, or misrepresent the opposite opinion. But all this, even to the most aggravated degree, is so continually done in perfect good faith, by persons who are not considered, and in many other respects may not deserve to be considered, ignorant or incompetent, that it is rarely possible on adequate grounds conscientiously to stamp the misrepresentation as morally culpable; and still less could law presume to interfere with this kind of controversial misconduct. With regard to what is commonly meant by intemperate discussion, namely, invective, sarcasm, personality, and the like, the denunciation of these weapons would deserve more sympathy if it were ever proposed to interdict them equally to both sides; but it is only desired to restrain the employment of them against the prevailing opinion: against the unprevailing they may not only be used without general disapproval, but will be likely to obtain for him who uses them the praise of honest zeal and righteous indignation. Yet whatever mischief arises from their use, is greatest when they are employed against the comparatively defenceless; and whatever unfair advantage can be derived by any opinion from this mode of asserting it, accrues almost exclusively to received opinions. The worst offence of this kind which can be committed by a polemic, is to stigmatize those who hold the contrary opinion as bad and immoral men. To calumny of this sort, those who hold any unpopular opinion are peculiarly exposed, because they are in general few and uninfluential, and nobody but themselves feels much interest in seeing justice done them; but this weapon is, from the nature of the case, denied to those who attack a prevailing opinion: they can neither use it with safety to themselves, nor, if they could, would it do anything but recoil on their own cause. In general, opinions contrary to those commonly received can only obtain a hearing by studied moderation of language, and the most cautious avoidance of unnecessary offence, from which they hardly ever deviate even in a slight degree without losing ground: while unmeasured vituperation employed on the side of the prevailing opinion, really does deter people from professing contrary opinions, and from listening to those who profess them. For the interest, therefore, of truth and justice, it is far more important to restrain this employment of vituperative language than the other; and, for example, if it were necessary to choose, there would be much more need to discourage offensive attacks on infidelity, than on religion. It is, however, obvious that law and authority have no business with restraining either, while opinion ought, in every instance, to determine its verdict by the circumstances of the individual case; condemning every one, on whichever side of the argument he places himself, in whose mode of advocacy either want of candor, or malignity, bigotry, or intolerance of feeling manifest themselves; but not inferring these vices from the side which a person takes, though it be the contrary side of the question to our own: and giving merited honor to every one, whatever opinion he may hold, who has calmness to see and honesty to state what his opponents and their opinions really are, exaggerating nothing to their discredit, keeping nothing back which tells, or can be supposed to tell, in their favor. This is the real morality of public discussion; and if often violated, I am happy to think that there are many controversialists who to a great extent observe it, and a still greater number who conscientiously strive towards it.

Mill does not justify absolute liberty of speech and press but implies that there are boundaries—although difficult to determine—to public debate. Democratic governments have always been faced with this dilemma: At what point can freedom of speech and press be curtailed? The Supreme Court has had difficulty in making decisions in areas involving censorship and loyalty and security. Freedom of speech and press cannot be used to destroy the very government that protects civil liberties.

Justice Holmes, in *Schenck* v. *United States,* 249 U.S. 47 (1919), stated his famous "clear and present danger" test, which subsequently was applied at both the national and state levels, for deciding whether or not Congress could abridge freedom of speech under the First Amendment:

"The most stringent protection of free speech would not protect a man in falsely shouting fire in a theatre and causing a panic. It does not protect a man from an injunction against uttering words that may have all the effects of force. ... The question in every case is whether the words used are used in such circumstances and are of such a nature as to create a clear and present danger that they will bring about the substantive evils that Congress has a right to prevent. It is a question of proximity and degree. When a nation is at war many things that might be said in time of peace are such a hindrance to its efforts that their utterance will not be endured so long as men fight and that no Court could regard them as protected by any constitutional right."

In 1940 Congress passed the Smith Act, Section 2 of which made it unlawful for any person:

"(1) to knowingly or willfully advocate, abet, advise, or teach the duty, necessity, desirability, or propriety of overthrowing or destroying any government in the United States by force or violence ...; (2) with intent to cause the overthrow or destruction of any government in the United States, to print, publish, edit, issue, circulate, sell, distribute, or publicly display any written or printed matter advocating, advising, or teaching the duty, necessity, desirability, or propriety of overthrowing or destroying any government in the United States by force or violence; (3) to organize or help to organize any society, group, or assembly of persons who teach, advocate, or encourage the overthrow or destruction of any government in the United States by force or violence; or to be or become a member of, or affiliate with, any such society ..., knowing the purposes thereof."

The constitutionality of this act was tested in *Dennis* v. *United States*, 341 U.S. 494 (1951), which contained five opinions. Vinson spoke for the Court, with Frankfurter and Jackson concurring; Black and Douglas dissented.

23
DENNIS v. UNITED STATES
341 U.S. 494 (1951)

Mr. Chief Justice Vinson announced the judgment of the Court, saying in part:

Petitioners were indicted in July, 1948, for violation of the conspiracy provisions of the Smith Act. . . . A verdict of guilty as to all the petitioners was returned by the jury on October 14, 1949. The Court of Appeals affirmed the convictions. . . . We granted certiorari. . . .

. . . Our limited grant of the writ of certiorari has removed from our consideration any question as to the sufficiency of the evidence to support the jury's determination that petitioners are guilty of the offense charged. Whether on this record petitioners did in fact advocate the overthrow of the government by force and violence is not before us, and we must base any discussion of this point upon the conclusions stated in the opinion of the Court of Appeals, which treated the issue in great detail. That court held that the record in this case amply supports the necessary finding of the jury that petitioners, the leaders of the Communist Party in this country, were unwilling to work within our framework of democracy, but intended to initiate a violent revolution whenever the propitious occasion appeared. . . .

I

It will be helpful in clarifying the issues to treat next the contention that the trial judge improperly interpreted the statute by charging that the statute required an unlawful intent before the jury could convict. More specifically, he charged that the jury could not find the petitioners guilty under the indictment unless they found that petitioners had the intent to "overthrow . . . the Government of the United States by force and violence as speedily as circumstances would permit."

. . . The structure and purpose of the statute demand the inclusion of intent as an element of the crime. Congress was concerned with those who advocate and organize for the overthrow of the government. Certainly those who recruit and combine for the purpose of advocating overthrow intend to bring about that overthrow. We hold that the statute requires as an essential element of the crime proof of the intent of those who are charged with its violation to overthrow the government by force and violence. . . .

II

The obvious purpose of the statute is to protect existing government, not from change by peaceable, lawful and constitutional means, but from change by violence, revolution, and terrorism. That it is within the *power* of the Congress to protect the government of the United States from armed rebellion is a proposition which requires little discussion. Whatever theoretical merit there may be to the argument that there is a "right" to rebellion against dictatorial governments is without force where the existing structure of the government provides for peaceful and orderly change. We reject any principle of governmental helplessness in the face of preparation for revolution, which principle, carried to its logical conclusion, must lead to anarchy. No one could conceive that it is within the power of Congress to prohibit acts intended to overthrow the government by force and violence. The question with which we are concerned here is not whether Congress has such *power,* but whether the *means* that it has employed conflict with the First and Fifth Amendments to the Constitution.

One of the bases for the contention that the means which Congress has employed are invalid takes the form of an attack on the face of the statute on the grounds that by its terms it prohibits academic discussion of the merits of Marxism–Leninism, that it stifles ideas and is contrary to all concepts of a free speech and a free press. Although we do not agree that the language itself has that significance, we must bear in mind that it is the duty of the federal courts to interpret federal legislation in a manner not inconsistent with the demands of the Constitution. . . . This is a federal statute which we must interpret as well as judge. . . .

The very language of the Smith Act negates the interpretation which petitioners would have us impose on that Act. It is directed at advocacy, not discussion. Thus, the trial judge properly charged the jury that they could not convict if they found that petitioners did "no more than pursue peaceful studies and discussions or teaching and advocacy in the realm of ideas." He further charged that it was not unlawful "to conduct in an American college or university a course explaining the philosophical theories set forth in the books which have been placed in evidence." Such a charge is in strict accord with the statutory language, and illustrates the meaning to be placed on those words. Congress did not intend to eradicate the free discussion of political theories, to destroy the traditional rights of Americans to discuss and evaluate ideas without fear of governmental sanction. Rather Congress was concerned with the very kind of activity in which the evidence showed these petitioners engaged.

III

But although the statute is not directed at the hypothetical cases which petitioners have conjured, its application in this case has resulted in convictions for the teaching and advocacy of the overthrow of the government by force and violence, which, even though coupled with the intent to accomplish that overthrow, contains an element of speech. For this reason, we must pay special heed to the demands of the First Amendment marking out the boundaries of speech.

We pointed out in *Douds, supra,* that the basis of the First Amendment is the hypothesis that speech can rebut speech, propaganda will answer propaganda, free debate of ideas will result in the wisest governmental policies. It is for this reason that this Court has recognized the inherent value of free discourse. An analysis of the leading cases in this Court which have involved direct limitations on speech, however, will demonstrate that both the majority of the Court and the dissenters in particular cases have recognized that this is not an unlimited, unqualified right, but that the societal value of speech must, on occasion, be subordinated to other values and considerations. . . .

The rule we deduce from these cases [*Schenck* and others] is that where an offense is specified by a statute in nonspeech or nonpress terms, a conviction relying upon speech or press as evidence of violation may be sustained only when the speech or publication created a "clear and present danger" of attempting or accomplishing the prohibited crime, e.g. interference with enlistment. The dissents . . . in emphasizing the value of speech, were addressed to the argument of the sufficiency of the evidence. . . .

In this case we are squarely presented with the application of the "clear and present danger" test, and must decide what that phrase imports. We first note that many of the cases in which this Court has reversed convictions by use of this or similar tests have been based on the fact that the interest which the state was attempting to protect was itself too insubstantial to warrant restriction of speech. . . . Overthrow of the government by force and violence is certainly a substantial enough interest for the government to limit speech. Indeed, this is the ultimate value of any society, for if a society cannot protect its structure from armed internal attack, it must follow that no subordinate value can be protected. If, then, this interest may be protected, the literal problem which is presented is what has been meant by the use of the phrase "clear and present danger" of the utterances bringing about the evil within the power of Congress to punish.

Obviously, the words cannot mean that before the government may act, it must wait until the *putsch* is about to be executed, the plans have been laid and the signal is awaited. If government is aware that a group aiming at its overthrow is attempting to indoctrinate its members and to commit them to a course whereby they will strike when the leaders feel the circumstances permit, action by the government is required. The argument that there is no need for government to concern itself, for government is strong, it possesses ample powers to put down a rebellion, it may defeat the revolution with ease needs no answer. For that is not the question. Certainly an attempt to overthrow the government by force, even though doomed from the outset because of inadequate numbers or power of the revolutionists, is a sufficient evil for Congress to prevent. The damage which such attempts create both physically and politically to a nation makes it impossible to measure the validity in terms of the probability of success, or the immediacy of a successful attempt. In the instant case the trial judge charged the jury that they could not convict unless they found that petitioners intended to overthrow the government "as speedily as circumstances would permit." This does not mean, and could not properly mean, that they would not strike until there was certainty of success. What was meant was that the revolutionists would strike when they thought the time was ripe. We must therefore reject the contention that success or probability of success is the criterion.

The situation with which Justices Holmes and Brandeis were concerned in *Gitlow* was a comparatively isolated event [involving a conviction for criminal anarchy in New York of one Gitlow for circulating Communist literature], bearing little relation in their minds to any substantial threat to the safety of the community. . . . They were not confronted with any situation comparable to the instant one—the development of an apparatus designed and dedicated to the overthrow of the government, in the context of world crisis after crisis.

Chief Justice Learned Hand, writing for the majority below, interpreted the phrase as follows: "In each case [courts] must ask whether the gravity of the 'evil,' discounted by its improbability, justifies such invasion of free speech as is necessary to avoid the danger." 183 F.2d at 212. We adopt this statement of the rule. . . .

Likewise, we are in accord with the court below, which affirmed the trial court's finding that the requisite danger existed. The mere fact that from the period 1945 to 1948 petitioners' activities did not result in an attempt to overthrow the government by force and violence is of course no answer to the fact that there was a group that was ready to make the attempt. The formation by petitioners of such a highly organized conspiracy, with rigidly disciplined members subject to call when the leaders, these petitioners, felt that the time had come for action, coupled with the inflammable nature of world conditions, similar uprisings in other countries, and the touch-and-go nature of our relations with countries with whom petitioners were in the very least ideologically attuned, convince us that their convictions were justified on this score. And this analysis disposes of the contention that a conspiracy to advocate, as distinguished from the advocacy itself, cannot be constitutionally restrained, because it comprises only the preparation. It is the existence of the conspiracy which creates the danger. . . . If the ingredients of the reaction are present, we cannot bind the government to wait until the catalyst is added. . . .

We hold that §§ 2(a) (1), 2(a) (2) and (3) of the Smith Act, do not inherently, or as construed or applied in the instant case, violate the First Amendment and other provisions of the Bill of Rights, or the First and Fifth Amendments because of indefiniteness. Petitioners intended to overthrow the government of the United States as speedily as the circumstances would permit. Their conspiracy to organize the Communist Party and to teach and advocate the overthrow of the government of the United States by force and violence created a "clear and present danger" of an attempt to overthrow the government by force and violence. They were properly and constitutionally convicted for violation of the Smith Act. The judgments of conviction are affirmed. . . .

Mr. Justice Black, dissenting, said in part:

. . . At the outset I want to emphasize what the crime involved in this case is, and what it is not. These petitioners were not charged with an attempt to overthrow the government. They were not charged with overt acts of any kind designed to overthrow the government. They were not even charged with saying anything or writing anything designed to overthrow the government. The charge was that they agreed to assemble and to talk and publish certain ideas at a later date: The indictment is that they conspired to organize the Communist Party and to use speech or newspapers and other publications in the future to teach and advocate the forcible overthrow of the government. No matter how it is worded, this is a virulent form of prior censorship of speech and press, which I believe the First Amendment forbids. . . .

But let us assume, contrary to all constitutional ideas of fair criminal procedure, that petitioners although not indicted for the crime of actual advocacy, may be punished for it. Even on this radical assumption, the other opinions in this case show that the only way to affirm these convictions is to repudiate directly or indirectly the established "clear and present danger" rule. This the Court does in a way which greatly restricts the protections afforded by the First Amendment. The opinions for affirmance indicate that the chief reason for jettisoning the rule is the expressed fear that advocacy of Communist doctrine endangers the safety of the Republic. Undoubtedly, a governmental policy of unfettered communication of ideas does entail dangers. To the Founders of this nation, however, the benefits derived from free expression were worth the risk. They embodied this philosophy in the First Amendment's command that "Congress shall make no law . . . abridging the freedom of speech, or of the press. . . ." I have always believed that the First Amendment is the keystone of our government, that the freedoms it guarantees provide the best insurance against destruction of all freedom. At least as to speech in the realm of public matters, I believe that the "clear and present danger" test does not "mark the furthermost constitutional boundaries of protected expression" but does "no more than recognize a minimum compulsion of the Bill of Rights.". . .

So long as this Court exercises the power of judicial review of legislation, I cannot agree that the First Amendment permits us to sustain laws suppressing freedom of speech and press on the basis of Congress's or our own notions of mere "reasonableness." Such a doctrine waters down the First Amendment so that it amounts to little more than an admonition to Congress. The Amendment as so construed is not likely to protect any but those "safe" or orthodox views which rarely need its protection. I must also express my objection to the holding because, as Mr. Justice Douglas's dissent shows, it sanctions the determination of a crucial issue of fact by the judge rather than by the jury. Nor can I let this opportunity pass without expressing my objection to the severely limited grant of certiorari in this case which precluded consideration here of at least two other reasons for reversing these convictions: (1) the record shows a discriminatory selection of the jury panel which prevented trial before a representative cross-section of the community; (2) the record shows that one member of the trial jury was violently hostile to petitioners before and during the trial.

Public opinion being what it now is, few will protest the conviction of these Communist petitioners. There is hope, however, that in calmer times, when present pressure, passions and fears subside, this or some later Court will restore the First Amendment liberties to the high preferred place where they belong in a free society.

Mr. Justice Douglas, dissenting, said in part:

. . . [N]ever until today has anyone seriously thought that the ancient law of conspiracy could constitutionally be used to turn speech into seditious conduct. Yet that is precisely what is suggested. I repeat that we deal here with speech alone, not with speech *plus* acts of sabotage or unlawful conduct. Not a single seditious act is charged in the indictment. . . .

Free speech has occupied an exalted position because of the high service it has given our society. Its protection is essential to the very existence of a democracy. The airing of ideas releases pressures which otherwise might become destructive. When ideas compete in the market for acceptance, full and free discussion exposes the false and they gain few adherents. Full and free discussion even of ideas we hate encourages the testing of our own prejudices and preconceptions. Full and free discussion keeps a society from becoming stagnant and unprepared for the stresses and strains that work to tear all civilizations apart.

Full and free discussion has indeed been the first article of our faith. We have founded our political system on it. It has been the safeguard of every religious, political, philosophical, economic, and racial group amongst us. We have counted on it to keep us from embracing what is cheap and false; we have trusted the common sense of our people to choose the doctrine true to our genius and to reject the rest. This has been the one single outstanding tenet that has made our institutions the symbol of freedom and equality. We have deemed it more costly to liberty to suppress a despised minority than to let them vent their spleen. We have above all else feared the political censor. We have wanted a land where our people can be exposed to all the diverse creeds and cultures of the world.

There comes a time when even speech loses its constitutional immunity. Speech innocuous one year may at another time fan such destructive flames that it must be halted in the interest of the safety of the Republic. That is the meaning of the clear and present danger test. When conditions are so critical that there will be no time to avoid the evil that the speech threatens, it is time to call a halt. Otherwise, free speech which is the strength of the nation will be the cause of its destruction.

Yet free speech is the rule, not the exception. The restraint to be constitutional must be based on more than fear, on more than passionate opposition against the speech, on more than a revolted dislike for its contents. There must be some immediate injury to society that is likely if speech is allowed. . . .

. . . This record . . . contains no evidence whatsoever showing that the acts charged, viz., the teaching of the Soviet theory of revolution with the hope that it will be realized, have created any clear and present danger to the nation. The Court, however, rules to the contrary. . . .

The political impotence of the Communists in this country does not, of course, dispose of the problem. Their numbers; their positions in industry and government; the extent to which they have in fact infiltrated the police, the armed services, transportation, stevedoring, power plants, munition works, and other critical places—these facts all bear on the likelihood that their advocacy of the Soviet theory of revolution will endanger the Republic. But the record is silent on these facts. If we are to proceed on the basis of judicial notice, it is impossible for me to say that the Communists in this country are so potent or so strategically deployed that they must be suppressed for their speech. I could not so hold unless I were willing to conclude that the activities in recent years of committees of Congress, of the Attorney General, of labor unions, of state legislatures, and of Loyalty Boards were so futile as to leave the country on the edge of grave peril. To believe that petitioners and their following are placed in such critical positions as to endanger the nation is to believe the incredible. It is safe to say that the followers of the creed of Soviet Communism are known to the FBI; that in case of war with Russia they will be picked up overnight as were all prospective saboteurs at the commencement of World War II; that the invisible army of petitioners is the best known, the most beset, and the least thriving of any fifth column in history. Only those held by fear and panic could think otherwise. . . .

. . . The political censor has no place in our public debates. Unless and until extreme and necessitous circumstances are shown, our aim should be to keep speech unfettered and to allow the processes of law to be invoked only when the provocateurs among us move from speech to action.

Vishinsky wrote in 1938 in the Law of the Soviet State, "In our state, naturally, there is and can be no place for freedom of speech, press, and so on for the foes of socialism."

Our concern should be that we accept no such standard for the United States. Our faith should be that our people will never give support to those advocates of revolution, so long as we remain loyal to the purposes for which our nation was founded.

Freedom of Religion

The Establishment Clause of the First Amendment states: "Congress shall make no law respecting an establishment of religion, or prohibiting the free exercise thereof." How does this affect the rights of the individual? First, every person is free to worship in his own way. In line with this meaning, the establishment of religion cannot be curtailed by government; that is, government cannot take action that would prevent religious groups from operating in accordance with their beliefs. There are, however, exceptions, and the meaning of the protection of religion in the First Amendment has varied from one case to another. In this area as in all others involving civil liberties and civil rights the Supreme Court has had to try to balance the needs of the state with the rights of the individual. Religious freedom is not absolute.

In 1962, the Court rendered one of its most controversial decisions, *Engel v. Vitale,* 370 U.S. 421 (1962), based upon the Establishment Clause. This opinion banned the recitation of prayers in public schools.

24
ENGEL v. VITALE
370 U.S. 421 (1962)

Mr. Justice Black delivered the opinion of the Court, saying in part:

The respondent Board of Education of Union Free School District No. 9, New Hyde Park, New York, acting in its official capacity under state law, directed the School District's principal to cause the following prayer to be said aloud by each class in the presence of a teacher at the beginning of each school day:

> Almighty God, we acknowledge our dependence upon Thee, and we beg Thy blesssings upon us, our parents, our teachers and our country.

This daily procedure was adopted on the recommendation of the State Board of Regents, a governmental agency created by the state Constitution to which the New York Legislature has granted broad supervisory, executive, and legislative powers over the state's public school system. These state officials composed the prayer which they recommended and published as a part of their "Statement on Moral and Spiritual Training in the Schools," saying: "We believe that this Statement will be subscribed to by all men and women of good will, and we call upon all of them to aid in giving life to our program."

Shortly after the practice of reciting the Regents' prayer was adopted by the School District, the parents of ten pupils brought this action in a New York State Court insisting that use of this official prayer in the public schools was contrary to the beliefs, religions, or religious practices of both themselves and their children. Among other things, these parents challenged the constitutionality of both the state law authorizing the School District to direct the use of prayer in public schools and the School District's regulation ordering the recitation of this particular prayer on the ground that these actions of official governmental agencies violate that part of the First Amendment of the federal Constitution which commands that "Congress shall make no law respecting an establishment of religion"—a command which was "made applicable to the state of New York by the Fourteenth Amendment of the said Constitution." The New York Court of Appeals, over the dissents of Judges Dye and Fuld, sustained an order of the lower state courts which had upheld the power of New York to use the Regents' prayer as a part of the daily procedures of its public schools so long as the schools did not compel any pupil to join in the prayer over his or his parents' objection. We granted certiorari to review this important decision involving rights protected by the First and Fourteenth Amendments.

We think that by using its public school system to encourage recitation of the Regents' prayer, the state of New York has adopted a practice wholly inconsistent with the Establishment Clause. There can, of course, be no doubt that New York's program of daily classroom invocation of God's blessings as prescribed in the Regents' prayer is a religious activity. It is a solemn avowal of divine faith and supplication for the blessings of the Almighty. The nature of such a prayer has always been religious, none of the respondents has denied this and the trial court expressly so found. . . .

The petitioners contend among other things that the state laws requiring or permitting use of the Regents' prayer must be struck down as a violation of the Establishment Clause because that prayer was composed by governmental officials as a part of a governmental program to further religious beliefs. For this reason, petitioners argue, the state's use of the Regents' prayer in its public school system breaches the constitutional wall of separation between church and state. We agree with that contention since we think that the constitutional prohibition against laws respecting an establishment of religion must at least mean that in this country it is no part of the business of government to compose official prayers for any group of the American people to recite as a part of a religious program carried on by government.

It is a matter of history that this very practice of establishing governmentally composed prayers for religious services was one of the reasons which caused many of our early colonists to leave England and seek religious freedom in America. The Book of Common Prayer, which was created under governmental direction and which was approval by Acts of Parliament in 1548 and 1549, set out in minute detail the accepted form and content of prayer and other religious ceremonies to be used in the established, tax-supported Church of England. The controversies over the Book and what should be its content repeatedly threatened to disrupt the peace of that country as the accepted forms of prayer in the established church changed with the views of the particular ruler that happened to be in control at the time. Powerful groups representing some of the varying religious views of the people struggled among themselves to impress their particular views upon the government and obtain amendments of the Book more suitable to their respective notions of how religious services should be conducted in order that the official religious establishment would advance their particular religious beliefs. Other groups, lacking the necessary political power to influence the government on the matter, decided to leave England and its established church and seek freedom in America from England's governmentally ordained and supported religion.

It is an unfortunate fact of history that when some of the very groups which had most strenuously opposed the established Church of England found themselves sufficiently in control of colonial governments in this country to write their own prayers into law, they passed laws making their own religion the official religion of their respective colonies. Indeed, as late as the time of the Revolutionary War, there were established churches in at least eight of the thirteen former colonies and established religions in at least four of the other five. But the successful Revolution against English political domination was shortly followed by intense opposition to the practice of establishing religion by law. . . .

By the time of the adoption of the Constitution, our history shows that there was a widespread awareness among many Americans of the dangers of a union of church and state. . . . The First Amendment was added to the Constitution to stand as a guarantee that neither the power nor the prestige of the federal government would be used to control, support or influence the kinds of prayer the American people can say—that the people's religions must not be subjected to the pressures of government for change each time a new political administration is elected to office. Under that amendment's prohibition against governmental establishment of religion, as reinforced by the provisions of the Fourteenth Amendment, government in this country, be it state or federal, is without power to prescribe by law any particular form of prayer which is to be used as an official prayer in carrying on any program of governmentally sponsored religious activity.

There can be no doubt that New York's state prayer program officially establishes the religious beliefs embodied in the Regents' prayer. The respondents' argument to the contrary, which is largely based upon the contention that the Regents' prayer is "nondenominational" and the fact that the program, as modified and approved by state courts, does not require all pupils to recite the prayer but permits those who wish to do so to remain silent or be excused from the room, ignores the essential nature of the program's constitutional defects. Neither the fact that the prayer may be denominationally neutral, nor the fact that its observance on the part of the students is voluntary can serve to free it from the limitations of the Establishment Clause, as it might from the Free Exercise Clause, of the First Amendment, both of which are operative against the states by virtue of the Fourteenth Amendment. Although these two clauses may in certain instances overlap, they forbid two quite different kinds of governmental encroachment upon religious freedom. The Establishment Clause, unlike the Free Exercise Clause, does not depend upon any showing of direct governmental compulsion and is violated by the enactment of laws which establish an official religion whether those laws operate directly to coerce nonobserving individuals or not. This is not to say, of course, that laws officially prescribing a particular form of religious worship do not involve coercion of such individuals. When the power, prestige and financial support of government is placed behind a particular religious belief, the indirect coercive pressure upon religious minorities to conform to the prevailing officially approved religion is plain. But the purposes underlying the Establishment Clause go much further than that. Its first and most immediate purpose rested on the belief that a union of government and religion tends to destroy government and to degrade religion. The history of governmentally established religion, both in England and in this country, showed that whenever government had allied itself with one particular form of religion, the inevitable result has been that it had incurred the hatred, disrespect and even contempt of those who held contrary beliefs. That same history showed that many people had lost their respect for any religion that had relied upon the support of government to spread its faith. The Establishment Clause thus stands as an expression of principle on the part of the Founders of our Constitution that religion is too personal, too sacred, too holy, to permit its "unhallowed perversion" by a civil magistrate. Another purpose of the Establishment Clause rested upon an awareness of the historical fact that governmentally established religions and religious persecutions go hand in hand. The founders knew that only a few years after the Book of Common Prayer became the only accepted form of religious services in the established Church of England, an Act of Uniformity was passed to compel all Englishmen to attend those services and to make it a criminal offense to conduct or attend religious gatherings of any other kind —a law which was consistently flouted by dissenting religious groups in England and which contributed to widespread persecutions of people like John Bunyan who persisted in holding "unlawful [religious] meetings . . . to the great disturbance and distraction of the good subjects of this kingdom. . . ." And they knew that similar persecutions had received the sanction of law in several of the colonies in this country soon after the establishment of official religions in those colonies. It was in large part to get completely away from this sort of systematic religious persecution that the Founders brought into being our Nation, our Constitution, and our Bill of Rights with its prohibition against any governmental establishment of religion. The New York laws officially prescribing the Regents' prayer are inconsistent with both the purposes of the Establishment Clause and with the Establishment Clause itself.

It has been argued that to apply the Constitution in such a way as to prohibit state laws respecting an establishment of religious services in public schools is to indicate a hostility toward religion or toward prayer. Nothing, of course, could be more wrong. The history of man is inseparable from the history of religion. And perhaps it is not too much to say that since the beginning of that history many people have devoutly believed that "More things are wrought by prayer than this world dreams of." It was doubtless largely due to men who believed this that there grew up a sentiment that cuased men to leave the cross-currents of officially established state religions and religious persecution in Europe and come to this country filled with the hope that they could find a place in which they could pray when they pleased to the God of their faith in the language they chose. And there were men of this same faith in the power of prayer who led the fight for adoption of our Constitution and also for our Bill of Rights with the very guarantees of religious freedom that forbid the sort of governmental activity which New York has attempted here. These men knew that the First Amendment, which tried to put an end to governmental control or religion and of prayer, was not written to destroy either. They knew rather that it was written to quite well-justified fears which nearly all of them felt arising out of an awareness that governments of the past had shackled men's tongues to make them speak only the religious thoughts that government wanted them to speak and to pray only to the God that government wanted them to pray to. It is neither sacrilegious nor antireligious to say that each separate government in this country should stay out of the business of writing or sanctioning official prayers and leave that purely religious function to the people themselves and to those the people choose to look to for religious guidance.

It is true that New York's establishment of its Regents' prayer as an officially approved religious doctrine of that state does not amount to a total establishment of one particular religious sect to the exclusion of all others— that, indeed, the governmental endorsement of that prayer seems relatively insignificant when compared to the governmental encroachments upon religion which were commonplace 200 years ago. To those who may subscribe to the view that because the Regents' official prayer is so brief and general there can be no danger to religious freedom in its governmental establishment, however, it may be appropriate to say in the words of James Madison, the author of the First Amendment:

> [I]t is proper to take alarm at the first experiment on our liberties. . . . Who does not see that the same authority which can establish Christianity, in exclusion of all other Religions, may establish with the same ease any particular sect of Christians, in exclusion of all other Sects? That the same authority which can force a citizen to contribute three pence only of his property for the support of any one establishment, may force him to conform to any other establishment in all cases whatsoever?

The judgment of the Court of Appeals of New York is reversed and the cause remanded for further proceedings not inconsistent with this opinion.

Reversed and remanded.

Mr. Justice Frankfurter took no part in the decision of this case.

Mr. Justice White took no part in the consideration or decision of this case.

Mr. Justice Douglas concurred in a separate opinion.

Mr. Justice Stewart, dissenting.

A local school board in New York has provided that those pupils who wish to do so may join in a brief prayer at the beginning of each school day, acknowledging their dependence upon God and asking His blessing upon them and upon their parents, their teachers, and their country. The court today decides that in permitting this brief nondenominational prayer the school board has violated the Constitution of the United States. I think this decision is wrong.

The Court does not hold, nor could it, that New York has interfered with the free exercise of anybody's religion. For the state courts have made clear that those who object to reciting the prayer must be entirely free of any compulsion to do so, including any "embarrassments and pressure." Cf. *West Virginia State Board of Education v. Barnette,* 319 U.S. 624. But the Court says that in permitting school children to say this simple prayer, the New York authorities have established "an official religion."

With all respect, I think the Court has misapplied a great constitutional principle. I cannot see how an "official religion" is established by letting those who want to say a prayer say it. On the contrary, I think that to deny the wish of these school children to join in reciting this prayer is to deny them the opportunity of sharing in the spiritual heritage of our nation.

The Court's historical review of the quarrels over the Book of Common Prayer in England throws no light for me on the issue before us in this case. England had then and has now an established church. Equally unenlightening, I think, is the history of the early establishment and later rejection of an official church in our own states. For we deal here not with the establishment of a state church, which would, of course, be constitutionally impermissible, but with whether school children who want to begin their day by joining in prayer must be prohibited from doing so. Moreover, I think that the Court's task, in this as in all areas of constitutional adjudication, is not responsibly aided by the uncritical invocation of metaphors like the "wall of separation," a phrase nowhere to be found in the Constitution. What is relevant to the issue here is not the history of an established church in sixteenth-century England or in eighteenth-century America, but the history of the religious traditions of our people, reflected in countless practices of the institutions and officials of our government.

At the opening of each day's session of this Court we stand, while one of our officials invokes the protection of God. Since the days of John Marshall our Crier has said, "God save the United States and this Honorable Court." Both the Senate and the House of Representatives open their daily sessions with prayer. Each of our Presidents, from George Washington to John F. Kennedy, has upon assuming his office asked the protection and help of God.

The Court today says that the state and federal governments are without constitutional power to prescribe any particular form of words to be recited by any group of the American people on any subject touching religion. The third stanza of "The Star-Spangled Banner," made our national anthem by Act of Congress in 1931, contains these verses:

> Blest with victory and peace, may the heav'n rescued land
> Praise the Pow'r that hath made and preserved us a nation!
> Then conquer we must, when our cause it is just,
> And this be our motto, "In God is our Trust."

In 1954 Congress added a phrase to the Pledge of Allegiance to the Flag so that it now contains the words "one Nation *under God* indivisible, with liberty and justice for all." In 1952 Congress enacted legislation calling upon the President each year to proclaim a Nation Day of Prayer. Since 1865 the words "IN GOD WE TRUST" have been impressed on our coins.

Countless similar examples could be listed, but there is no need to belabor the obvious. It was all summed up by this Court just ten years ago in a single sentence: "We are a religious people whose institutions presuppose a Supreme Being." *Zoarch v. Clauson,* 343 U.S. 306, 313.

I do not believe that this Court, or the Congress, or the President has by the actions and practices I have mentioned established an "official religion" in violation of the Constitution. And I do not believe the state of New York has done so in this case. What each has done has been to recognize and to follow the deeply entrenched and highly cherished spiritual traditions of our nation —traditions which come down to us from those who almost two hundred years ago avowed their "firm reliance on the Protection of Divine Providence" when they proclaimed the freedom and independence of this brave new world.

I dissent.

A storm of controversy arose over the Supreme Court's decision in *Engel v. Vitale.* Misunderstanding the intention of the Supreme Court, which was clearly to *increase* religious freedom rather than restrict it, opponents of the school prayer decision succeeded in introducing a proposed constitutional amendment in Congress, that would have overruled the Supreme Court's decision. Known as the Becker Amendment, it had the support of extremist groups throughout the country as well as many well-intentioned citizens who felt that the Court's decision unduly restricted their religious freedom and indeed implied a bias against religion. The proposed amendment, on which the key House Judiciary Committee refused to act, had virtually no chance of passing the first Congressional hurdle. It clearly overruled decisions of the Supreme Court that had prevented the use of public school facilities for religious exercises, as well as its opinion in the school prayer case. A similar amendment failed by only twenty-eight votes to pass the House in 1971.

The Supreme Court has long held that there must be a wall of separation between church and state, which means that government cannot discriminate among religious creeds. There has always been a controversy over federal aid to parochial schools. It has been virtually impossible for Congress to reach an agreement upon the extent to which private schools with religious affilations should receive federal aid. It is questionable how much aid can be given without jeopardizing the separation of church and state.

At the state and local level, separation between church and state has raised many questions. Should bus transportation be given to private school students as well as those attending the public schools? Should released time be given for religious exercises in the public schools? And, perhaps the most controversial of all, should public schools have officially sanctioned prayers?

In the case of *Everson v. Board of Education,* 330 U.S. 1 (1947), the Supreme Court had to face the issue of how far local government could go in aiding Roman Catholic parochial schools. New Jersey had authorized local boards of education to reimburse parents for money they spent on bus transportation without regard to the nature of the school attended. Both those going to public and private schools could receive reimbursement. When this statute was challenged as a violation of the wall of separation doctrine, the Supreme court upheld it. In its opinion the Court pointed out that secular education serves a public purpose, and therefore tax money can be spent on private nonprofit schools as well as on public education. Although reimbursement for bus transportation to parochial schools constituted a degree of aid to religion, it was not in this case considered sufficient to justify a holding that it violated the First Amendment. The state was not acting as an agent of any religion, but remained neutral. It was providing a public service for all school children, in much the same way as it provides policemen and traffic control to assist children in reaching school safely.

Another issue that has developed concerning freedom of religion is whether the public schools may institute a "released time" program to permit religious instruction during the school day. In *McCollum v. Board of Education,* 333 U.S. 203 (1948), the Court held that a board of education could not use tax-supported property for religious instruction. An Illinois program had been providing for released time for students while they received religious instruction on school property. In *Zorach v. Clauson,* 343 U.S. 306 (1952), the Court retreated slightly from its decision in *McCollum* when it upheld a New York program that permitted students to go to religious centers beyond school property for religious instruction during the school day.

The status of the wall of separation doctrine today is ambiguous. The Supreme Court has held that a religious oath for office requiring an expressed belief in God is unconstitutional. (See *Torcaso v. Watkins,* 367 U.S. 488 [1961].) But Sunday closing laws are not unconstitutional, for even though they may once have had a religious motivation, today they achieve secular goals. (See *McGowan v. Maryland,* 366 U.S. 420 [1961].) In the educational area, the Court held in *Tilton v. Richardson,* 403 U.S. 672 (1971) that Congress could give some aid to secular higher education, although in companion cases it barred state aid to elementary and secondary education.

Equal Protection of the Laws: School Desegregation

By now most students are thoroughly familiar with the evolution of the "separate but equal" doctrine first enunciated by the Supreme Court in *Plessy v. Ferguson,* 163 U.S. 537 (1896). Students should note that what is involved in cases in this area is legal interpretation of the provison in the Fourteenth Amendment that no state may deny "to any person within its jurisdiction the equal protection of the laws." The *Plessy* case stated that separate but equal accommodations, required by state law to be established on railroads in Louisiana, did not violate the equal protection of the laws clause of the Fourteenth Amendment. The Court went on to say that the object of the Fourteenth Amendment:

"was undoubtedly to enforce the absolute equality of the two races before the law, but in the nature of things it could not have been intended to abolish distinction based upon color, or to enforce social, as distinguished from political, equality, or a commingling of the two races upon terms unsatisfactory to either. Laws permitting, and even requiring, their separation in places where they are liable to be brought into contact do not necessarily imply the inferiority of either race to the other, and have been generally, if not universally, recognized as within the competency of the state legislatures in the exercise of their police power. The most common instance of this is connected with the establishment of separate schools for white and colored children, which has been held to be a valid exercise of the legislative power even by courts of States where the political rights of the colored race have been longest and most earnestly enforced."

Both the police power and education are within the reserved powers of the states; they are reserved, however, only insofar as they do not conflict with provisions of the Constitution. The Supreme Court, in *Brown* v. *Board of Education,* 347 U.S. 483 (1954), finally crystallized its interpretation of the equal protection of the laws clause in a way that resulted in a significant decrease in state power in an area traditionally reserved to states, viz., education. In addition, a general principle was established which extended far beyond the field of education.

25

BROWN v. BOARD OF EDUCATION OF TOPEKA
347 U.S. 483 (1954)

Mr. Chief Justice Warren delivered the opinion of the Court, saying in part:

These cases come to us from the states of Kansas, South Carolina, Virginia, and Delaware. They are premised on different facts and different local conditions, but a common legal question justifies their consideration together in this consolidated opinion.

In each of the cases, minors of the Negro race, through their legal representatives, seek the aid of the courts in obtaining admission to the public schools of their community on a nonsegregated basis. In each instance, they had been denied admission to schools attended by white children under laws requiring or permitting segregation according to race. This segregation was alleged to deprive the plaintiffs of the equal protection of the laws under the Fourteenth Amendment. In each of the cases other than the Delaware case, a three-judge federal district court denied relief to the plaintiffs on the so-called "separate but equal" doctrine announced by this Court in *Plessy v. Ferguson.* . . .

The plaintiffs contend that segregated public schools are not "equal" and cannot be made "equal," and that hence they are deprived of the equal protection of the laws. Because of the obvious importance of the question presented, the Court took jurisdication. . . .

In the first cases in this Court construing the Fourteenth Amendment, decided shortly after its adoption, the Court interpreted it as proscribing all state-imposed discriminations against the Negro race. The doctrine of "separate but equal" did not make its appearance in this Court until 1896 in the case of *Plessy v. Ferguson, supra,* involving not education but transportation. American courts have since labored with the doctrine for over half a century. In this Court, there have been six cases involving the "separate but equal" doctrine in the field of public education. . . . In more recent cases, all on the graduate school level, inequality was found in that specific benefits enjoyed by white students were denied to Negro students of the same educational qualifications. . . . In none of these cases was it necessary to reexamine the doctrine to grant relief to the Negro plaintiff. And in *Sweatt v. Painter* [339 U.S. 629 (1950)], the Court expressly reserved decision on the question whether *Plessy v. Ferguson* should be held inapplicable to public education.

In the instant cases, that question is directly presented. Here, unlike *Sweatt v. Painter,* there are findings below that the Negro and white schools involved have been equalized, or are being equalized, with respect to buildings, curricula, qualifications and salaries of teachers, and other "tangible" factors. Our decision, therefore, cannot turn on merely a comparison of these tangible factors in the Negro and white schools involved in each of the cases. We must look instead to the effect of segregation itself on public education.

In approaching this problem, we cannot turn the clock back to 1868 when the Amendment was adopted, or even to 1896 when *Plessy v. Ferguson* was written. We must consider public education in the light of its full development and its present place in American life throughout the Nation. Only in this way can it be determined if segregation in public schools deprives these plaintiffs of the equal protection of the laws.

Today, education is perhaps the most important function of state and local governments. Compulsory school attendance laws and the great expenditures for education both demonstrate our recognition of the importance of education to our democratic society. It is required in the performance of our most basic public responsibilities, even service in the armed forces. It is the very foundation of good citizenship. Today it is a principal instrument in awakening the child to cultural values, in preparing him for later professional training, and in helping him to adjust normally to his environment. In these days, it is doubtful that any child may reasonably be expected to succeed in life if he is denied the opportunity of an education. Such an opportunity, where the state has undertaken to provide it, is a right which must be made available to all on equal terms.

We come then to the question presented: Does segregation of children in public schools solely on the basis of race, even though the physical facilities and other "tangible" factors may be equal, deprive the children of the minority group of equal educational opportunities? We believe that it does.

In *Sweatt v. Painter, supra,* in finding that a segregated law school for Negroes could not provide them equal educational opportunities, this Court relied in large part on "those qualities which are incapable of objective measurement but which make for greatness in a law school." In *McLaurin* v. *Oklahoma State Regents, supra* [339 U.S. 637 (1950)], the Court, in requiring that a Negro admitted to a white graduate school be treated like all other students, again resorted to intangible considerations: "his ability to study, to engage in discussions and exchange views with other students, and, in general, to learn his profession." Such considerations apply with added force to children in grade and high schools. To separate them from others of similar age and qualifications solely because of their race generates a feeling of inferiority as to their status in the community that may affect their hearts and minds in a way unlikely ever to be undone. The effect of this separation of their educational opportunities was well stated by a finding in the Kansas case by a court which nevertheless felt compelled to rule against the Negro plaintiffs:

> Segregation of white and colored children in public schools has a detrimental effect upon the colored children. The impact is greater when it has the sanction of the law; for the policy of separating the races is usually interpreted as denoting the inferiority of the Negro group. A sense of inferiority affects the motivation of a child to learn. Segregation with the sanction of law, therefore, has a tendency to retard the educational and mental development of Negro children and to deprive them of some of the benefits they would receive in a racially integrated school system.

Whatever may have been the extent of psychological knowledge at the time of *Plessy* v. *Ferguson*, this finding is amply supported by modern authority. Any language in *Plessy* v. *Ferguson* contrary to this finding is rejected.

We conclude that in the field of public education the doctrine of "separate but equal" has no place. Separate educational facilities are inherently unequal. Therefore, we hold that the plaintiffs and others similarly situated for whom the actions have been brought are by reason of the segregation complained of, deprived of the equal protection of the laws guaranteed by the Fourteenth Amendment. This disposition makes unnecessary any discussion whether such segregation also violates the Due Process Clause of the Fourteenth Amendment.

Because these are class actions, because of the wide applicability of this decision, and because of the great variety of local conditions, the formulation of decrees in these cases presents problems of considerable complexity. On re-argument, the consideration of appropriate relief was necessarily subordinate to the primary question—the constitutionality of segregation in public education. We have now announced that such segregation is a denial of the equal protection of the laws. In order that we may have the full assistance of the parties in formulating decrees, the cases will be restored to the docket, and the parties are requested to present further argument on Questions 4 and 5 previously propounded by the Court for the re-argument this Term [which deal with the implementation of desegregation]. The Attorney General of the United States is again invited to participate. The Attorneys General of the states requiring or permitting segregation in public education will also be permitted to appear as *amici curiae* upon request to do so by September 15, 1954, and submission of briefs by October 1, 1954. It is so ordered.

On the same day the decision was announced in the *Brown* case (1954), the Court held that segregation in the District of Columbia was unconstitutional on the basis of the due process clause of the Fifth Amendment. (See *Bolling* v. *Sharpe,* 347 U.S. 497 [1954].) This situation reversed the normal one in that a protection explicitly afforded citizens of states was not expressly applicable against the national government, and could be made so only through interpreting it into the concept of due process of law.

After hearing the views of all interested parties in the *Brown* case the Court, on May 31, 1955, announced its decision concerning the implementation of desegregation in public schools.

26

BROWN v. BOARD OF EDUCATION OF TOPEKA
349 U.S. 294 (1955)

Mr. Chief Justice Warren delivered the opinion of the Court, saying in part:

These cases were decided on May 17, 1954. The opinions of that date, declaring the fundamental principle that racial discrimination in public education is unconstitutional, are incorporated herein by reference. All provsions of federal, state, or local law requiring or permitting such discrimination must yield to this principle. There remains for consideration the manner in which relief is to be accorded.

Because these cases arose under different local conditions and their disposition will involve a variety of local problems, we requested further argument on the question of relief. . . . The parties, the United States, and the states of Florida, North Carolina, Arkansas, Oklahoma, Maryland, and Texas filed briefs and participated in the oral argument.

These presentations were informative and helpful to the Court in its consideration of the complexities arising from the transition to a system of public education freed of racial discrimination. The presentations also demonstrated that substantial steps to eliminate racial discrimination in public schools have already been taken, not only in some of the communities in which these cases arose, but in some of the states appearing as *amici curiae,* and in other states as well. Substantial progress has been made in the District of Columbia and in the communities in Kansas and Delaware involved in this litigation. The defendants in the cases coming to us from South Carolina and Virginia are awaiting the decision of this Court concerning relief.

Full implementation of these constitutional principles may require solution of varied local school problems. School authorities have the primary responsibility for elucidating, assessing, and solving these problems; courts will have to consider whether the action of school authorities constitutes good faith implementation of the governing constitutional principles. Because of their proximity to local conditions and the possible need for further hearings, the courts which originally heard these cases can best perform this judicial appraisal. Accordingly, we believe it appropriate to remand the cases to those courts.

In fashioning and effectuating the decrees, the courts will be guided by equitable principles. Traditionally, equity has been characterized by a practical flexibility in shaping its remedies and by a facility for adjusting and reconciling public and private needs. These cases call for the exercise of these traditional attributes of equity power. At stake is the personal interest of the plaintiffs in admission to public schools as soon as practicable on a nondiscriminatory basis. To effectuate this interest may call for elimination of a variety of obstacles in making the transition to school systems operated in accordance with the constitutional principles set forth in our May 17, 1954, decision. Courts of equity may properly take into account the public interest in the elimination of such obstacles in a systematic and effective manner. But it should go without saying that the vitality of these constitutional principles cannot be allowed to yield simply because of disagreement with them.

While giving weight to these public and private considerations, the courts will require that the defendants make a prompt and reasonable start toward full compliance with our May 17, 1954, ruling. Once such a start has been made, the courts may find that additional time is necessary to carry out the ruling in an effective manner. The burden rests upon the defendants to establish such time is necessary in the public interest and is consistent with good faith compliance at the earliest praticable date. To that end, the courts may consider problems related to administration, arising from the physical condition of the school plant, the school transportation system, personnel, revision of school districts and attendance areas into compact units to achieve a system of determining admission to the public schools on a nonracial basis, and revision of local laws and regulations which may be necessary in solving the foregoing problems. They will also consider the adequacy of any plans the defendants may propose to meet these problems and to effectuate a transition to a racially nondiscriminatory school system. During this period of transition, the courts will retain jurisdiction of these cases.

The judgments below, except that in the Delaware case, are accordingly reversed and the cases are remanded to the District Courts to take such proceedings and enter such orders and decrees consistent with this opinion as are necessary and proper to admit to public schools on a racially nondiscriminatory basis with all deliberate speed the parties to these cases. The judgment in the Delaware case—ordering the immediate admission of the plaintiffs to schools previously attended only by white children—is affirmed on the basis of the principles stated in our May 17, 1954, opinion, but the case is remanded to the Supreme Court of Delaware for such further proceedings as that Court may deem necessary in the light of this opinion.

It is so ordered.

After the second decision of the Supreme Court in *Brown* v. *Board of Education* in 1955, it soon became clear that many Southern states would proceed with deliberate speed not to implement the desegregation of public schools but to obstruct the intent of the Supreme Court. The Southern Manifesto, signed by 101 Congressmen from 11 Southern states in 1956, clearly indicated the line that would be taken by many Southern Congressmen to justify defiance of the Supreme Court. The gist of the Manifesto was simply that the Supreme Court did not have the constitutional authority to interfere in an area such as education, which falls within the reserved powers of the states.

After the two *Brown* decisions in 1954 and 1955, the implementation for desegregation in the South was very slow. Ten years later, less than 10 percent of the black pupils in the lower educational levels in the Southern states that had had legally segregated education before were enrolled in integrated schools. It was not until 1970 that substantial progress was made in the South. Between 1968 and 1970 the percentage of black students in all-black schools in eleven Southern states decreased from 68.0 percent to 18.4 percent. One device used to circumvent the Supreme Court's decisions was to establish de facto dual school systems, similar to those that exist in most Northern cities, whereby students are assigned to schools on the basis of the neighborhoods in which they live. Such systems are not de jure segregation because they are not based upon a law requiring segregation per se, but simply upon school board regulations assigning pupils on the basis of where they live. De facto school systems can be as segregated as were the de jure systems previously existing in the South, but the question is to what extent can courts interfere to break up de facto segregation patterns since they are not based upon legal stipulations?

In the *Swann* case the Supreme Court held that in Southern states with a history of legally segregated education the District Courts have broad power to assure "unitary" school systems by requiring: (1) reassignment of teachers so that each school faculty will reflect a racial balance similar to that which exists in the community as a whole; (2) reassignment of pupils to reflect a racial ratio similar to that which exists within the total community; (3) the use of noncontiguous school zones and the grouping of schools for the purpose of attendance to bring about racial balance; and (4) the use of busing of elementary and secondary school students within the school system to achieve racial balance.

This case and companion cases were referred to at the time as school "busing" cases, and caused tremendous controversy within the South because communities felt they were not being treated on an equal basis with their Northern counterparts, where de facto segregation is for the most part not subject to judicial intervention. The Nixon Administration, which favored neighborhood schools, was firmly opposed to the transportation of students beyond normal geographic school zones to achieve racial balance. Democratic Senator Ribicoff of Connecticut attempted to attach an amendment to an administration-sponsored bill providing $1.5 billion to aid school districts in the South in the desegregation of facilities that would have required nationwide integration of pupils from intercity schools with children from the suburbs. The amendment was defeated on April 21, 1971, by a vote of 51 to 35, with most Republicans voting against it and 13 of 34 Northern Democrats opposed. Busing remains a highly controversial political issue.

27

SWANN v. CHARLOTTE-MECKLENBURG COUNTY BOARD OF EDUCATION
403 U.S. 912 (1971)

Mr. Chief Justice Burger delivered the opinion of the Court, saying in part:

We granted certiorari in this case to review important issues as to the duties of school authorities and the scope of powers of federal courts under this Court's mandates to eliminate racially separate public schools established and maintained by state action. *Brown* v. *Board of Education,* 347 U.S. 483 (1954).

This case and those argued with it arose in states having a long history of maintaining two sets of schools in a single school system deliberately operated to carry out a governmental policy to separate pupils in schools solely on the basis of race. That was what *Brown* v. *Board of Education* was all about. These cases present us with the problem of defining in more precise terms than heretofore the scope of the duty of school authorities and district courts in implementing *Brown I* and the mandate to eliminate dual systems and establish unitary systems at once. Meanwhile district courts and courts of appeals have struggled in hundreds of cases with a multitude and variety of problems under this Court's general directive. Understandably, in an area of evolving remedies, those courts had to improvise and experiment without detailed or specific guidelines. This Court, in *Brown I,* appropriately dealt with the large constitutional principles; other federal courts had to grapple with the flinty, intractable realities of day-to-day implementation of those constitutional commands. Their efforts, of necessity, embraced a process of "trial and error," and our effort to formulate guidelines must take into account their experience.

I

The Charlotte-Mecklenburg school system, the forty-third largest in the nation, encompasses the city of Charlotte and surrounding Mecklenburg County, North Carolina. The area is large—550 square miles—spanning roughly 22 miles east-west and 36 miles north-south. During the 1968–1969 school year the system served more than 84,000 pupils in 107 schools. Approximately 71 percent of the pupils were found to be white and 29 percent Negro. As of June, 1969, there were approximately 24,000 Negro students in the system, of whom 21,000 attended schools within the city of Charlotte. Two-thirds of those 21,000—approximately 14,000 Negro students—attended 21 schools which were either totally Negro or more than 99 percent Negro.

This situation came about under a desegregation plan approved by the District Court at the commencement of the present litigation in 1965 . . . based upon geographic zoning with a free transfer provision. The present proceedings were initiated in September, 1968 by Petitioner Swann's motion for further relief based on *Green* v. *County School Board,* 391 U.S. 430 (1968), and its companion cases. All parties now agree that in 1969 the system fell short of achieving the unitary school system that those cases require.

The District Court held numerous hearings and received voluminous evidence. In addition to finding certain actions of the school board to be discriminatory, the court also found that residential patterns in the city and county resulted in part from federal, state, and local government action other than school board decisions. School board action based on these patterns, for example, by locating schools in Negro residential areas and fixing the size of the schools to accommodate the needs of immediate neighborhoods, resulted in segregated education. These findings were subsequently accepted by the Court of Appeals. . . .

II

Nearly seventeen years ago this Court held, in explicit terms, that state-imposed segregation by race in public schools denies equal protection of the laws. At no time has the Court deviated in the slightest degree from that holding or its constitutional underpinnings. None of the parties before us challenges the Court's decision of May 17, 1954, that

> in the field of public education the doctrine of "separate but equal" has no place. Separate educational facilities are inherently unequal. Therefore, we hold that the plaintiffs and others similarly situated . . . are, by reason of the segregation com-

plained of, deprived of the equal protection of the laws guaranteed by the Fourteenth Amendment. . . .

Because these are class actions, because of the wide applicability of this decision, and because of the great variety of local conditions, the formulation of decrees in these cases presents problems of considerable complexity. (*Brown* v. *Board of Education,* supra. . . .)

None of the parties before us questions the Court's 1955 holding in *Brown II.* . . .

Over the fifteen years since *Brown II,* many difficulties were encountered in implementation of the basic constitutional requirement that the state not discriminate between public school children on the basis of their race. Nothing in our national experience prior to 1955 prepared anyone for dealing with changes and adjustments of the magnitude and complexity encountered since then. Deliberate resistance of some to the Court's mandates has impeded the good-faith efforts of others to bring school systems into compliance. The detail and nature of these dilatory tactics have been noted frequently by this Court and other courts.

By the time the Court considered *Green* v. *County School Board,* 391 U.S. 430, in 1968, very little progress had been made in many areas where dual school systems had historically been maintained by operation of state laws. In *Green,* the Court was confronted with a record of a freedom-of-choice program that the District Court had found to operate in fact to preserve a dual system more than a decade after *Brown II.* While acknowledging that a freedom-of-choice concept could be a valid remedial measure in some circumstances, its failure to be effective in *Green* required that

The burden on a school board today is to come forward with a plan that promises realistically to work . . . *now* . . . until it is clear that state-imposed segregation has been completely removed. . . .

This was plain language, yet the 1969 Term of Court brought fresh evidence of the dilatory tactics of many school authorities. . . .

The problems encountered by the district courts and courts of appeals make plain that we should now try to amplify guidelines, however incomplete and imperfect, for the assistance of school authorities and courts. The failure of local authorities to meet their constitutional obligations aggravated the massive problem of converting from the state-enforced discrimination of racially separate school systems. This process has been rendered more difficult by changes since 1954 in the structure and patterns of communities, the growth of student population, movement of families, and other changes, some of which had marked impact on school planning, sometimes neutralizing or negating remedial action before it was fully implemented. Rural areas accustomed for half a century to the consolidated school systems implemented by bus transportation could make adjustments more readily than metropolitan areas with dense and shifting population, numerous schools, congested and complex traffic patterns. . . .

V

The central issue in this case is that of student assignment, and there are essentially four problem areas:

1. to what extent racial balance or racial quotas may be used as an implement in a remedial order to correct a previously segregated system;

2. whether every all-Negro and all-white school must be eliminated as an indispensable part of a remedial process of desegregation;

3. what are the limits, if any, on the rearrangement of school districts and attendance zones, as a remedial measure; and

4. what are the limits, if any, on the use of transportation facilities to correct state-enforced racial school segregation.

Racial Balances or Racial Quotas. The constant theme and thrust of every holding from *Brown I* to date is that state-enforced separation of races in public schools is discrimination that violates the Equal Protection Clause. The remedy commanded was to dismantle dual school systems. . . .

In this case it is urged that the District Court has imposed a racial balance requirement of 71 percent—29 percent on individual schools. The fact that no such objective was actually achieved—and would appear to be impossible—tends to blunt that claim, yet in the opinion and order of the District Court of December 1, 1969, we find that court directing:

> that efforts should be made to reach a 71–29 ratio in the various schools so that there will be no basis for contending that one school is racially different from the others . . . , that no school [should] be operated with an all-black or predominantly black student body, [and] that pupils of all grades [should] be assigned in such a way that as nearly as practicable the various schools at various grade levels have about the same proportion of black and white students.

The District Judge went on to acknowledge that variation "from that norm may be unavoidable." This contains intimations that the "norm" is a fixed mathematical racial balance reflecting the pupil constituency of the system. If we were to read the holding of the District Court to require, as a matter of substantive constitutional right, any particular degree of racial balance or mixing, that approach would be disapproved and we would be obliged to reverse. The constitutional command to desegregate schools does not mean that every school in every community must always reflect the racial composition of the school system as a whole.

As the voluminous record in this case shows, the predicate for the District Court's use of the 71 percent–29 percent ratio was twofold: first, its express finding, approved by the Court of Appeals and not challenged here, that a dual school system had been maintained by the school authorities at least until 1969; second, its finding, also approved by the Court of Appeals, that the school board had totally defaulted in its acknowledged duty to come forward with an acceptable plan of its own, notwithstanding the patient efforts of the District Judge who, on at least three occasions, urged the board to submit plans. As the statement of facts shows, these findings are abundantly supported by the record. It was because of this total failure of the school board that the District Court was obliged to turn to other qualified sources, and Dr. Finger was designated to assist the District Court to do what the board should have done.

We see therefore that the use made of mathematical ratios was no more than a starting point in the process of shaping a remedy, rather than an inflexible requirement. From that starting point the District Court proceeded to frame a decree that was within its discretionary powers, an equitable remedy for the particular circumstances. . . .

One-Race Schools. The record in this case reveals the familiar phenomenon that in metropolitan areas minority groups are often found concentrated in one part of the city. In some circumstances certain schools may remain all or largely of one race until new schools can be provided or neighborhood patterns change. Schools all or predominately of one race in a district of mixed population will require close scrutiny to determine that school assignments are not part of state-enforced segregation.

In light of the above, it should be clear that the existence of some small number of one-race, or virtually one-race, schools within a district is not in and of itself the mark of a system which still practices segregation by law. The district judge or school authorities should make every effort to achieve the greatest possible degree of actual desegregation and will thus necessarily be concerned with the elimination of one-race schools. No per se rule can adequately embrace all the difficulties of reconciling the competing interests involved; but in a system with a history of segregation the need for remedial criteria of sufficient specificity to assure a school authority's compliance with its constitutional duty warrants a presumption against schools that are substantially disproportionate in their racial composition. Where the school authority's proposed plan for conversion from a dual to a unitary system contemplates the continued existence of some schools that are all or predominately of one race, they have the burden of showing that such school assignments are genuinely nondiscriminatory. The court should scrutinize such schools, and the burden upon the school authorities will be to satisfy the court that their racial composition is not the result of present or past discriminatory action on their part.

An optional majority-to-minority transfer provision has long been recognized as a useful part of every desegregation plan. Provision for optional transfer of those in the majority racial group of a particular school to other schools where they will be in the minority is an indispensable remedy for those students willing to transfer to other schools in order to lessen the impact on them of the state-imposed stigma of segregation. In order to be effective, such a transfer arrangement must grant the transferring student free transportation

and space must be made available in the school to which he desires to move.
. . . The court orders in this and the companion Davis case now provide such
an option.

Remedial Altering of Attendance Zones. The maps submitted in these cases
graphically demonstrate that one of the principal tools employed by school
planners and by courts to break up the dual school system has been a frank
—and sometimes drastic—gerrymandering of school districts and attendance
zones. An additional step was pairing, "clustering," or "grouping" of schools
with attendance assignments made deliberately to accomplish the transfer of
Negro students out of formerly segregated Negro schools and transfer of white
students to formerly all-Negro schools. More often than not, these zones are
neither compact nor contiguous; indeed they may be on opposite ends of the
city. As an interim corrective measure, this cannot be said to be beyond the
broad remedial powers of a court. . . .

Transportation of Students. The scope of permissible transportation of students as an implement of a remedial decree has never been defined by this
Court and by the very nature of the problem it cannot be defined with precision. No rigid guidelines as to student transportation can be given for application to the infinite variey of problems presented in thousands of situations. Bus
transportation has been an integral part of the public education system for
years, and was perhaps the single most important factor in the transition from
the one-room schoolhouse to the consolidated school. Eighteen million of the
nation's public school children, approximately 39 percent, were transported to
their schools by bus in 1969–1970 in all parts of the country.

The importance of bus transportation as a normal and accepted tool of
educational policy is readily discernible in this and the companion case. The
Charlotte school authorities did not purport to assign students on the basis of
geographically drawn zones until 1965 and then they allowed almost unlimited
transfer privileges. The District Court's conclusion that assignment of children
to the school nearest their home serving their grade would not produce an
effective dismantling of the dual system is supported by the record.

Thus the remedial techniques used in the District Court's order were
within that court's power to provide equitable relief; implementation of the
decree is well within the capacity of the school authority.

The decree provided that the buses used to implement the plan would
operate on direct routes. Students would be picked up at schools near their
homes and transported to the schools they were to attend. The trips for
elementary school pupils average about seven miles and the District Court
found that they would take "not over thirty-five minutes at the most." This
system compares favorably with the transportation plan previously operated
in Charlotte under which each day 23,600 students on all grade levels were
transported an average of fifteen miles one way for an average trip requiring
over an hour. In these circumstances, we find no basis for holding that the local

school authorities may not be required to employ bus transportation as one tool of school desegregation. Desegregation plans cannot be limited to the walk-in school.

An objection to transportation of students may have validity when the time or distance of travel is so great as to risk either the health of the children or significantly impinge on the educational process. . . .

VI

The Court of Appeals, searching for a term to define the equitable remedial power of the district courts, used the term "reasonableness." In *Green, supra,* this Court used the term "feasible" and by implication, "workable," "effective," and "realistic" in the mandate to develop "a plan that promises realistically to work, and . . . to work *now.*" On the facts of this case, we are unable to conclude that the order of the District Court is not reasonable, feasible and workable. However, in seeking to define the scope of remedial power or the limits on remedial power of courts in an area as sensitive as we deal with here, words are poor instruments to convey the sense of basic fairness inherent in equity. Substance, not semantics, must govern, and we have sought to suggest the nature of limitations without frustrating the appropriate scope of equity.

At some point, these school authorities and others like them should have achieved full compliance with this Court's decision in Brown I. The systems will then be "unitary" in the sense required by our decisions in *Green* and *Alexander.*

It does not follow that the communities served by such systems will remain demographically stable, for in a growing, mobile society, few will do so. Neither school authorities nor district courts are constitutionally required to make year-by-year adjustments of the racial composition of student bodies once the affirmative duty to desegregate has been accomplished and racial discrimination through official action is eliminated from the system. This does not mean that federal courts are without power to deal with future problems; but in the absence of a showing that either the school authorities or some other agency of the state has deliberately attempted to fix or alter demographic patterns to affect the racial composition of the schools, further intervention by a district court should not be necessary.

For the reasons herein set forth, the judgment of the Court of Appeals is affirmed as to those parts in which it affirmed the judgment of the District Court. The order of the District Court dated August 7, 1970, is also affirmed.

It is so ordered.

In the following selection Nathan Glazer discusses the implications of the *Swann* case and other court decisions that have supported the use of busing to achieve integration in public schools. He raises three fundamental questions: (1) Does the

Constitution require that every school be racially balanced in proportion to the ratios of different ethnic groups within school communities? (2) Does such forced integration improve the education of black children? (3) Does forced integration improve the relations between the races? These are the questions which the author feels confront the courts in the contemporary busing cases. What judges feel should be the law often depends upon their perceptions of what is good public policy. But should judges be able to enforce their public views upon the community?

28
Nathan Glazer

IS BUSING NECESSARY?

For ten years after the 1954 Supreme Court decision in *Brown,* little was done to desegregate the schools of the South. But professionals were at work on the problem. The NAACP Legal Defense Fund continued to bring case after case into court to circumvent the endless forms of resistance to a full and complete desegregation of the dual school systems of the South. The federal courts, having started on this journey in 1954, became educated in all the techniques of subterfuge and evasion, and in their methodical way struck them down one by one. The federal executive establishment, reluctant to enter the battle of school desegregation, became more and more involved.

The critical moment came with the passage of the Civil Rights Act in 1964, in the wake of the assassination of a President and the exposure on television of the violent lengths to which Southern government would go in denying constitutional rights to Negroes. Under Title IV of the Civil Rights Act, the Department of Justice could bring suits against school districts maintaining segregation. Under Title VI, no federal funds under any program were to go to districts that practiced segregation. With the passage of the Elementary and Secondary Education Act in 1965, which made large federal funds available to schools, the club of federal withdrawal of funds became effective. In the Department of Justice and in the Department of Health, Education and Welfare, bureaucracies rapidly grew up to enforce the law. Desegregation no longer progressed painfully from test case to test case, endlessly appealed. It moved rapidly as every school district in the South was required to comply with federal requirements. HEW's guidelines for compliance steadily tightened, as the South roared and the North remained relatively indifferent. The

From Nathan Glazer, "Is Busing Necessary?", *Commentary* (March 1972), pp. 39–52. Reprinted from *Commentary,* by permission; Copyright © 1972 by the American Jewish Committee.

Department of Justice, HEW, and the federal courts moved in tandem. What the courts declared was segregation became what HEW declared was segregation. After 1969, when the Supreme Court ordered, against the new administration's opposition, the immediate implementation of desegregation plans in Mississippi, no further delay was to be allowed.

The federal government and its agencies were under continual attack by the civil-rights organizations for an attitude of moderation in the enforcement of both court orders and legal requirements. Nevertheless, as compared with the rate of change in the years 1954 to 1964, the years since 1964 have seen an astonishing speeding-up in the process of desegregating the schools of the South. . . .

. . . [T]he Director of the HEW Office of Civil Rights, J. Stanley Pottinger, could summarize some of the key statistics as of 1970 in the following terms:

> When school opened in the fall of 1968, only 18 percent of the 2.9 million Negro children in the Southern states attended schools which were predominantly white in their student enrollments. In the fall of 1970, that figure had more than doubled to 39 percent . . . [and] the percentage of Negroes attending 100 percent black schools dropped . . . from 68 percent to 14 percent. In 1968, almost no districts composed of majority Negro (and other minority) children were the subject of federal enforcement action. It was thought . . . that the limited resources of government ought to be focused primarily on the districts which had a majority of white pupils, where the greatest educational gains might be made, and where actual desegregation was not as likely to induce white pupils to flee the system. . . . 40 percent of all the Negro children in the South live in [such] systems. . . . Obviously, the greater the amount of desegregation in majority black districts, the fewer will be the number of black children . . . who will be counted as "desegregated" under a standard which measures only those minority children who attend majority white schools.
>
> In order to account for this recent anomaly, HEW has begun to extract from its figures the number of minority children who live in mostly white districts and who attend mostly white schools. Last year, approximately 54 percent of the Negro children in the South who live in such districts attended majority white schools. Conversely, nearly 40 percent of the 2.3 million white children who live in mostly black (or minority) districts, now attend mostly black (or minority) schools.*

There has been further progress since, and if one uses as the measure the number of blacks going to schools with a majority of white children, the South is now considerably more integrated than the North.

Yet the desegregation of schools is once again the most divisive of American domestic issues. . . .

[T]here is the reality that the blacks of the North and West are also segregated, not to mention the Puerto Ricans, Mexican Americans, and others.

---

*In *Inequality in Education,* Center for Law and Education, Harvard University, Aug. 3, 1971.

The civil-rights movement sees that minorities are concentrated in schools that may be all or largely minority, sees an enormous agenda of desegregation before it, and cannot pause to consider a success which is already in its mind paltry and inconclusive. The struggle must still be fought, as bitterly as ever.

There is a second point of view as to why desegregation, despite its apparent success, is no success. This is the Southern point of view, and now increasingly the Northern point of view. It argues that a legitimate, moral, and Constitutional effort to eliminate the unconstitutional separation of the races (most Southerners now agree with this judgment of *Brown*), has been turned into something else—an intrusive, costly, painful, and futile effort to regroup the races in education by elaborate transportation schemes. The Southern Congressmen who for so long tried to get others to listen to their complaints now watch with grim satisfaction the agonies of Northern Congressmen faced with the crisis of mandatory, court-imposed transportation for desegregation. On the night of November 4, 1971, as a desperate House passed amendment after amendment in a futile effort to stop busing, Congressman Edwards of Alabama said:

> Mr. Chairman, this will come as a shock to some of my colleagues. I am opposing this amendment. I will tell you why. I look at it from a rather cold standpoint. We are busing all over the First District of Alabama, as far as you can imagine. Buses are everywhere . . . people say to me, "How in the world are we ever going to stop this madness?" I say, "It will stop the day it starts taking place across the country, in the North, in the East, in the West, and yes, even in Michigan."

And indeed, one of the amendments had been offered by Michigan Congressmen, long-time supporters of desegregation, because what had been decreed for Charlotte, North Carolina, Mobile, Alabama, and endless other Southern cities was now on the way to becoming law in Detroit and its suburbs.

As a massive wave of antagonism to transportation for desegregation sweeps the country, the liberal Congressmen and Democratic Presidential aspirants who have for so long fought for desegregation ask themselves whether there is any third point of view: whether they must join with the activists who say that the struggle is endless and they must not flag, even now; or whether they must join with the Southerners. To stand with the courts in their latest decisions is, for liberal Congressmen, political suicide. A Gallup survey last October revealed that 76 percent of respondents opposed busing, almost as many in the East (71 percent), Midwest (77 percent), and West (72 percent), as in the South (82 percent); a majority of Muskie supporters (65 percent) as well as a majority of Nixon supporters (85 percent). Even more blacks oppose busing than support it (47 to 45 percent). But if to stand with the further extension to all the Northern cities and suburbs of transportation for desegregation is suicide, how can the liberal Congressmen join with the South and with what they view as Northern bigotry in opposing busing? Is there a third position, something which responds to the wave of frustration at court orders, and which does not mean the abandonment of hope for an integrated society?

How have we come from a great national effort to repair a monstrous wrong to a situation in which the sense of right of great majorities is offended by policies which seem continuous with that once noble effort? In order to answer this question, it is necessary to be clear on how the Southern issue became a national issue.

After the passage of the Civil Rights Act of 1964, the first attempt of the South to respond to the massive federal effort to impose desegregation upon it was "freedom of choice." There still existed the black schools and the white schools of a dual school system. But now whites could go to black schools (none did) and the blacks could go to white schools (few dared). It was perfectly clear that throughout the South "freedom of choice" was a means of maintaining the dual school system. In 1966 HEW began the process of demanding statistical proof that substantially more blacks were going to school with whites each year. The screw was tightened regularly, by the courts and HEW, and finally, in 1968, the Supreme Court gave the *coup de grâce,* insisting that dual school systems be eliminated completely. There must henceforth be no identifiable black schools and white schools, only schools. . . .

Busing has often been denounced as a false issue. Until busing was decreed for the desegregation of Southern cities, it was. As has been pointed out again and again, buses in the South regularly carried black children past white schools to black schools, and white children past black schools to white schools. When "freedom of choice" failed to achieve desegregation and geographical zoning was imposed, busing sometimes actually declined. In any case, when the school systems were no longer allowed to have buses for blacks and buses for whites, certainly the busing system became more efficient. After 1970, busing for desegregation replaced the busing for segregation.

But this was not true when busing came to Charlotte, North Carolina, and many other cities of the South, in 1971, after the key Supreme Court decision in *Swann* v. *Charlotte-Mecklenburg County Board of Education.* The City of Charlotte is 64 square miles, larger than Washington, D.C., but it is a part of Mecklenburg County, with which it forms a single school district of 550 square miles, which is almost twice the size of New York City. Many other Southern cities (Mobile, Nashville, Tampa) also form part of exceptionally large school districts. While 29 percent of the schoolchildren of Mecklenburg County are black, almost all live in Charlotte. Owing to the size of the county, 24,000 of 84,500 children were bused, for the purpose of getting children to schools beyond walking distance. School zones were formed geographically, and the issue was, could all-black and all-white schools exist in Mecklenburg County, if a principle of neighborhood school districting meant they would be so constituted?

The Supreme Court ruled they could not, and transportation could be used to eliminate black and white schools. The Court did not argue that there was a segregative intent in the creation of geographical zones—or that there was not—and referred to only one piece of evidence suggesting an effort to maintain segregation, free transfer. There are situations in which free transfer is used by white children to get out of mostly black schools, but if this had been the problem, the Court could have required a majority-to-minority transfer only (in which one can only transfer from a school in which one's race is a majority, and to a school in which one's race is a minority), as is often stipulated in desegregation plans. Instead the Court approved a plan which involved the busing of some 20,000 additional children, some for distances of up to 15 miles, from the center of the city to the outer limits of the county, and vice versa.

Two implications of the decision remain uncertain, but they may lead to a reorganization of all American education. If Charlotte, because it is part of the school district of Mecklenburg County, can be totally desegregated with each school having a roughly 71–29 white-black proportion, should not city boundaries be disregarded in other places and larger school districts of the Mecklenburg County scale be created wherever such action would make integration possible? A district judge has already answered this question in the affirmative for Richmond, Virginia.

But the second implication is: If Charlotte is—except for the background of a dual school system—socially similar to many Northern cities, and if radical measures can be prescribed to change the pattern that exists in Charlotte, should they not also be prescribed in the North? And to that question also a federal judge, ruling in a San Francisco case, has returned an affirmative answer.

San Francisco has a larger measure of integration probably than most Northern cities. Nevertheless *de facto* segregation—the segregation arising not from formal decisions to divide the races as in the South, but from other causes, presumed to be social and demographic—has long been an issue in San Francisco. In 1962, the NAACP filed suit against the school board, charging it with "affording, operating, and maintaining a racially segregated school system within the San Francisco Unified School District, contrary to and in violation of the equal protection and due process clause of the Fourteenth Amendment of the Constitution of the United States." As John Kaplan has written:

The history of this suit is a short and strange one. The Board of Education retained for its defense a distinguished local attorney, Joseph Alioto [now the mayor], who was primarily an anti-trust specialist. Alioto started discovery proceedings and the heart seemed to go out of the plaintiffs.

In any case, after admitting in depositions that the Board had no intention to produce a condition of racial imbalance; that it took no steps to bring about such a condition; that its lines were not drawn for the purpose of creating or maintaining racial imbalance; that there was no gerrymandering; and finally that the Board was under no obligation to relieve the situation by transporting students from their neighborhoods to other districts, the plaintiffs' attorney allowed the suit to be dismissed for want of prosecution on December 2, 1964.

It was assumed that this disposed of the legal issue. Meanwhile the San Francisco school system continued to struggle with the problem. After a long series of censuses, disputes, and studies, the school board proposed to set up two new integrated complexes, using transportation to integrate, one North and one South of Golden Gate Park. They were to open in 1970. When, however, one was postponed because of money problems, suit was brought once again by integration-minded parents, this time charging *de jure* segregation on the ground that the school board's failure to implement the two integrated school complexes amounted to an official act maintaining the schools in their presently segregated state.

Judge Stanley Weigel, before whom the matter was argued, very sensibly decided to wait for the Supreme Court's ruling in the Charlotte Mecklenburg County case which, he and many others thought, might once and for all settle the question of whether *de facto* segregation was no less unconstitutional than *de jure* segregation. Although one may doubt from certain passages in the Charlotte-Mecklenburg decision that the Supreme Court did indeed mean to outlaw *de facto* segregation, Judge Weigel seems to have decided that it did. "The law is settled," he declared, "that school authorities violate constitutional rights of children by establishing school attendance boundary lines knowing that the result is to continue or increase substantial racial imbalance."

But in ordering the desegregation of the San Francisco schools by transportation, Judge Weigel did not simply rest the matter on *de facto* segregation; he also listed acts of commission and omission which he believed amounted to *de jure* school segregation.

Now one can well imagine that a school board which does not or did not recently operate under state laws that required or permitted segregation could nevertheless through covert acts—which are equally acts under state authority—foster segregation. It could, for example, change school-zone lines, so as to confine black children in one school and permit white children to go to another school. It could build schools and expand them so that they served an all-black or all-white population. It could permit a transfer policy whereby white children could escape from black schools while blacks could not. It could assign black teachers to black schools and white teachers to white schools.

Judge Weigel charged all these things. The record—a record made by a liberal school board, appointed by a liberal mayor, in a liberal city, with a black president of the school board—does not, in this layman's opinion, bear him out, unless one is to argue that any action of a school board in construction policy or zone-setting or teacher assignment that precedes a situation in which there are some almost all-black schools (there were no all-black schools in San Francisco) and some almost all-white schools (there were no all-white schools in San Francisco) can be considered *de jure* segregation.

Under Judge Weigel's interpretation, there is no such thing as *de facto* segregation. All racial imbalance is the result of state actions, either taken or not taken. If not taken, they should have been taken. *De facto* disappears as a category requiring any less action than *de jure*.

This is the position of many lawyers who are arguing these varied cases.

I have described the San Francisco case because it led to a legal order requiring desegregation by transportation of the largest Northern or Western system so far affected by such an order. But massive desegregation had also been required by a district judge in Denver, who had then had his judgment limited by the Circuit Court of Appeals. It is this Denver case [*Keyes* v. *Denver* (1973)] that will become the first case on Northern or Western *de facto* school segregation —if we still allow the term some meaning—to be heard by the Supreme Court. What the Supreme Court will have to decide is whether the historical difference between Charlotte and Denver permits Denver or any other city to do any less than Charlotte has been required to do in order to integrate its schools. [The Court decided in *Keyes* v. *Denver* (1973) that desegregation could be required if there existed de facto segregation that was deliberately intended by the school system.]

Simultaneously, Detroit and the surrounding counties and the state of Michigan are under court order to come up with a plan that permits the desegregation of the schoolchildren of Detroit by busing to the neighboring suburbs, and a federal judge is moving toward the same result in Indianapolis. If the Supreme Court should uphold the district judge's ruling in the Richmond case, it will then similarly have to decide whether anything in the history or practices of Detroit and Indianapolis justifies ordering less in those cities than has been ordered in the city of Richmond.

The hardy band of civil-rights lawyers now glimpses—or glimpsed, before the two latest appointments to the Supreme Court—a complete victory, based on the idea that there is no difference between *de facto* and *de jure* segregation, an idea which is itself based on the larger idea that there is no difference between North and South. What is imposed on the South must be imposed on the North. As Ramsey Clark, a former Attorney-General of the United States, puts it, echoing a widely shared view:

> In fact, there is no *de facto* segregation. All segregation reflects some past actions of our governments. The FHA itself required racially restrictive covenants until 1948. But, that aside, the consequences of segregated schooling are the same whatever the cause. Segregated schools are inherently unequal however they come to be and the law must prohibit them whatever the reason for their existence.

In other words, whatever exists is the result of state action. If what exists is wrong, state action must undo it. If segregated schools were not made so by official decisions directly affecting the schools, then they were made so by other official decisions—Clark, for example, points to an FHA policy in effect until 1948—that encouraged residential segregation. Behind this argument rests the assumption, now part of the liberal creed, that racism in the North is different, if at all, from racism in the South only in being more hypocritical. All segregation arises from the same evil causes, and all segregation must be struck down. This is the position that many federal judges are now taking in the North—even if, as Judge Weigel did, they try to protect themselves by pointing to *some* action by the school board that they think might make the situation *de jure* in the earlier sense as well.

II

I believe that three questions are critical here. First, do basic human rights, as guaranteed by the Constitution, require that the student population of every school be racially balanced according to some specified proportion, and that no school be permitted a black majority? Second, whether or not this is required by the Constitution, is it the only way to improve the education of black children? Third, whether or not this is required by the Constitution, and whether or not it improves the education of black children, is it the only way to improve relations between the races?

These questions are in practice closely linked. What the Court decides is constitutional is very much affected by what it thinks is good for the nation. If it thinks that the education of black children can only be improved in schools with black minorities, it will be very much inclined to see situations in which there are schools with black majorities as unconstitutional. If it thinks race relations can only be improved if all children attend schools which are racially balanced, it will be inclined to find constitutional a requirement to have racial balance.

This is not to say that the courts do not need authority in the Constitution for what they decide. But this authority is broad indeed and it depends on a doctrine of judicial restraint—which has not been characteristic of the Supreme Court and subordinate federal courts in recent years—to limit judges in demanding what they think is right as well as what they believe to be within the Constitution. Indeed, it was in part because the Supreme Court believed that Negro children *were* being deprived educationally that it ruled as it did in *Brown.* They were being deprived because the schools were very far from "separate and equal." But even if they were "equal," their being "separate" would have been sufficient to make them unconstitutional: "To separate them from others of similar age and qualifications solely because of their race generates a feeling of inferiority as to their status in the community that may affect their hearts and minds in a way unlikely ever to be undone."

While much has been made of the point that the Court ruled as it did because of the evidence and views of social scientists as to the effects of segregation on the capacity of black children to learn, the fact is that the basis of the decision was that distinctions by race had no place in American law and public practice, neither in the schools, nor, as subsequent rulings asserted, in any other area, whether in waiting rooms or golf courses. This was clearly a matter of the "equal protection of the laws." It was more problematic as to what should be done to insure the "equal protection of the laws" when such protection had been denied for so long by dual school systems. But remedies were eventually agreed upon, and the Court has continued to rule unanimously —as it did in *Brown*—on these remedies down through *Swann* v. *Charlotte-Mecklenburg County Board of Education.*

Inevitably, however, the resulting increase in the freedom of black children—the freedom to attend the schools they wished—entailed a restriction on the freedom of others. In "freedom of choice," the freedom of white children was in no way limited. In geographical zoning to achieve integration, it was limited, but no more than that of black children. But in busing to distant schools, white children were in effect being conscripted to create an environment which, it had been decided, was required to provide equality of educational opportunity for black children. It was perhaps one thing to do this when the whites in question were the children or grandchildren of those who had deprived black children of their freedom in the past. But when a district judge in San Francisco ruled that not only white children but Chinese children and Spanish-speaking children must be conscripted to create an environment which, he believed, would provide equality of educational opportunity for black children, there was good reason for wondering whether "equal protection of the laws" was once again being violated, this time from the other side.

We are engaged here in a great enterprise to determine what the "equal protection of the laws" should concretely mean in a multi-racial and multi-ethnic society, and one in which various groups have suffered differing measures of deprivation. The blacks have certainly suffered the most, but the Chinese have suffered too, as have the Spanish-speaking groups, and some of the white ethnic groups. Is it "equal protection of the laws" to prevent Chinese-American children from attending nearby schools in their own community, conveniently adjacent to the afternoon schools they also attend? Is it "equal protection of the laws" to keep Spanish-speaking children from attending school in which their numerical dominance has led to bilingual classes and specially trained teachers? Can the Constitution possibly mean that?

One understands that the people do not vote on what the Constitution means. The judges decide. But it is one thing for the Constitution to say that, despite how the majority feels, it must allow black children into the public schools of their choice; and it is quite another for the Constitution to say, in the words of its interpreters, that some children, owing to their race or ethnic group alone, may not be allowed to attend the schools of their choice, even if their choice has nothing to do with the desire to discriminate racially. When, starting with the first proposition, one ends up with the second, as one has in San Francisco, one wonders if the Constitution can possibly have been interpreted correctly.

Again and again, reading the briefs and the transcripts and the analyses, one finds the words "escape" and "flee." The whites must not escape. They must not flee. Constitutional law often moves through strange and circuitous paths, but perhaps the strangest yet has been the one whereby, beginning with an effort to expand freedom—no Negro child shall be excluded from any public school because of his race—the law has ended up with as drastic a restriction of freedom as we have seen in this country in recent years. No child, of any race or group, may "escape" or "flee" the experience of integration. No school district may facilitate such an escape. Nor may it even (in the Detroit decision) fail to take action to close the loopholes permitting anyone to escape.

Let me suggest that, even though the civil-rights lawyers may feel that in advocating measures like these they are in the direct line of *Brown,* something very peculiar has happened when the main import of an argument changes from an effort to expand freedom to an effort to restrict freedom. Admittedly the first effort concerned the freedom of blacks, the second in large measure concerns the freedom of whites (but not entirely, as we have seen from the many instances in the South where blacks have resisted the elimination of black schools, and in the North where they have fought for community-controlled schools). Nevertheless, the tone of civil-rights cases has turned from one in which the main note is the expansion of freedom, into one in which the main note is the imposition of restrictions. It is ironic to read in Judge Stanley Weigel's decision, following which every child in the San Francisco elementary schools was placed in one of four ethnic or racial categories and made subject to transportation to provide an average mix of each in every school, an approving quotation from Judge Skelly Wright:

> The problem of changing a people's mores, particularly those with an emotional overlay, is not to be taken lightly. It is a problem which will require the utmost patience, understanding, generosity, and forbearance from all of us, of whatever race. But the principle is that we are, all of us, freeborn Americans, with a right to make our way, unfettered by sanctions imposed by man because of the work of God.

That was the language of 1956. One finds very little "patience, understanding," etc., in Judge Weigel's own decision, which required the San Francisco School District to prepare a plan to meet the following objectives:

> Full integration of all public elementary schools so that the ratio of black children to white children will then be and thereafter continue to be substantially the same in each school. To accomplish these objectives the plans may include:
> a. Use of non-discriminatory busing if, as appears now to be clear, at least some busing will be necessary for compliance with the law.
> b. Changing attendance zones whenever necessary to head off racial segregation.

According to Judge Weigel, the law even requires:

> Avoidance of the use of tracking systems or other educational techniques or innovations without provision for safeguard against racial segregation as a consequence.

Can all this be in the Constitution too?

A second issue that would seem to have some constitutional bearing is whether those who are to provide the children for a minority black environment are being conscripted only on the basis of income. The prosperous and the rich can avail themselves of private schooling, or they can "flee" to the suburbs. And if the Richmond and Detroit rulings should be sustained, making it impossible to "escape" by going to the suburbs, the class character of the decisions would become even more pronounced. For while many working-class and lower-middle class people can afford to live in suburbs, very few can afford the costs of private education.

Some observers have pointed out that leading advocates of transportation for integration—journalists, political figures, and judges—themselves send their children to private schools which escape the consequences of these legal decisions. But even without being *ad hominem,* one may raise a moral question: if the judges who are imposing such decisions, the lawyers who argue for them (including brilliant young lawyers from the best law schools employed by federal poverty funds to do the arguing), would not themselves send their children to the schools their decisions bring into being, how can they insist that others poorer and less mobile than they are do so? Clearly those not subject to a certain condition are insisting that others submit themselves to it, which offends the basic rule of morality in both the Jewish and Christian traditions. I assume there must be a place for this rule in the Constitution. . . .

There is unfortunately a widespread feeling, strong among liberals who have fought so long against the evil of racial segregation, that to stop now—before busing and expanded school districts are imposed on every city in the country—would be to betray the struggle for an integrated society. They are quite wrong. They have been misled by the professionals and specialists—in this instance, the government officials, the civil-rights lawyers, and the judges—as to what integration truly demands, and how it is coming about. Professionals and specialists inevitably overreach themselves, and there is no exception here.

It would be a terrible error to consider opposition to the recent judicial decisions on school integration as a betrayal of the promise of *Brown.* The promise of *Brown* is being realized. Black children may not be denied admittance to any school on account of their race (except for the cases in which courts and federal officials insist that they are to be denied admittance to schools with a black majority simply because they are black). The school systems of the South are desegregated. But more than that, integration in general has made enormous advances since 1954. It has been advanced by the hundreds of thousands of blacks in Northern and Western colleges. It has been advanced by the hundreds of thousands of blacks who have moved into professional and white-collar jobs in government, in the universities, in the school systems, in business. It has been advanced by the steady rise in black income which offers many blacks the opportunity to live in integrated areas. Most significantly, it has been advanced because millions of blacks now vote—in the South as well as the North—and because hundreds of blacks have been elected to school committees, city councils, state legislatures, the Congress. This is what is creating an integrated society in the United States.

We are far from this necessary and desirable goal. It would be a tragedy if the progress we made in achieving integration in the 1960s were not continued through the seventies. We can now foresee within a reasonable time the closing of many gaps between white and black. But I doubt that mandatory transportation of schoolchildren for integration will advance this process.

For, so far as the schools in particular are concerned, the increase in black political power means that blacks—like all other groups—can now negotiate, on the basis of their own power, and to the extent of their own power, over what kind of school systems should exist, and involving what measure of transportation and racial balance. In the varied settings of American life there will be many different answers to these questions. What Berkeley has done is not what New York City has done, and there is no reason why it should be. But everywhere black political power is present and contributing to the development of solutions.

There is a third path for liberals now agonized between the steady imposition of racial and ethnic group quotas on every school in the country—a path of pointlessly expensive and destructive homogenization—and surrender to the South. It is a perfectly sound American path, one which assumes that groups are different and will have their own interests and orientations, but which insists that no one be penalized because of group membership, and that a common base of experience be demanded of all Americans. It is the path that made possible the growth of the parochial schools, not as a challenge to a common American society, but as one variant within it. It is a path that, to my mind, legitimizes such developments as community control of schools and educational vouchers permitting the free choice of schools. There are as many problems in working out the details of this path as of the other two, but it has one thing to commend it as against the other two: it expands individual freedom, rather than restricts it.

One understands that the Constitution sets limits to the process of negotiation and bargaining even in a multi-racial and multi-ethnic setting. But the judges have gone far beyond what the Constitution can reasonably be thought to allow or require in the operation of this complex process. The judges should now stand back, and allow the forces of political democracy in a pluralist society to do their proper work.

Swann v. Charlotte-Mecklenburg County Board (1971) held that the courts could order the busing of school children within the limits of the city school district if necessary to achieve desegrated educational facilities. In the case of Charlotte-Mecklenburg the limits of the city school district included the surrounding county. However, only eighteen of the country's 100 largest city school districts contain both the inner city and the surrounding county. In cities such as San Francisco, Denver, Pasadena, and Boston, court-ordered busing plans pertained only to the central city school district. In 1974 the Supreme Court reviewed a busing plan for Detroit ordered by a federal District Court and sustained by the Court of Appeals that would have required the busing of students among fifty-four separate school districts in the Detroit metropolitan area to achieve racially balanced schools. The decision of the lower federal court in the Detroit case set a new precedent that required busing among legally separate school districts. Proponents of the Detroit busing plan argued that the central city of Detroit was 70 percent black, and that the only way integration could be achieved would be to link the school district of Detroit with the surrounding white suburban school districts. In *Milliken v. Bradley,* (1974), the Supreme Court held that the court-ordered Detroit busing plan could not be sustained under the Equal Protection Clause of the 14th Amendment, which was the constitutional provision relied upon in the lower court's decision to require busing. The Supreme Court found that there was no evidence of disparate treatment of white and black students among the fifty-three outlying school districts that surround Detroit. The only evidence of discrimination was within the city limits of Detroit itself. Therefore, since the outlying districts did not violate the Equal Protection Clause they could not be ordered to integrate their systems with that of Detroit. Since discrimination was limited to Detroit, the court order to remedy the situation must be limited to Detroit also. The following opinion outlines the view of the majority, and the strong dissents that were registered. The effect of the decision is to leave standing court orders for busing within school districts, but to prevent the forced merger of inner city schools with legally separate suburban school districts.

29
MILLIKEN v. BRADLEY
—U.S.—(1974)

Mr. Chief Justice Burger delivered the opinion of the Court, saying in part:
. . . The action was commenced in August of 1970 by the respondents, the Detroit branch of the National Association for the Advancement of Colored People and individual parents and students, on behalf of a class later defined by order of the United States District Court, E.D. Michigan, dated Feb. 16, 1971, to include "all school children of the City of Detroit and all Detroit resident parents who have children of school age."

The named defendants in the District Court included the Governor of Michigan, the Attorney General, the State Board of Education, the State Superintendent of Public Instruction, and the Board of Education of the City of Detroit, its members and its former superintendent of schools.

The State of Michigan as such is not a party to this litigation and references to the state must be read as references to the public officials, state and local, through whom the state is alleged to have acted.

In their complaint respondents attacked the constitutionality of a statute of the State of Michigan known as Act 48 of the 1970 legislature on the ground that it put the State of Michigan in the position of unconstitutionally interfering with the execution and operation of a voluntary plan of partial high school desegregation, known as the April 7, 1970, plan, which had been adopted by the Detroit Board of Education to be effective beginning with the fall, 1970, semester.

The complaint also alleged that the Detroit public school system was and is segregated on the basis of race as a result of the official policies and actions of the defendants and their predecessors in office, and called for the implementation of a plan that would eliminate "the racial identity of every school in the [Detroit] system and maintain now and hereafter a unitary non-racial school system. . . ."

Ever since Brown v. Board of Education, 347 U.S. 483 (1954), judicial consideration of school desegregation cases has begun with the standard that:

"In the field of public education the doctrine of 'separate but equal' has no place. Separate educational facilities are inherently unequal." 347 U.S. at 495.

This has been reaffirmed time and again as the meaning of the Constitution and the controlling rule of law.

The target of the Brown holding was clear and forthright: the elimination of state mandated or deliberately maintained dual school systems with certain schools for Negro pupils and others for white pupils. This duality and racial segregation was held to violate the Constitution in the cases subsequent to 1954. . . .

Viewing the record as a whole, it seems clear that the district court and the court of appeals shifted the primary focus from a Detroit remedy to the metropolitan area only because of their conclusion that total desegregation of Detroit would not produce the racial balance which they perceived as desirable.

Both courts proceeded on an assumption that the Detroit schools could not be truly desegregated—in their view of what constituted desegregation—unless the racial composition of the student body of each school substantially reflected the racial composition of the population of the metropolitan area as a whole. The metropolitan area was then defined as Detroit plus fifty-three of the outlying school districts. . . .

. . . The court's analytical starting point was its conclusion that school district lines are no more than arbitrary lines on a map "drawn for political convenience." Boundary lines may be bridged where there has been a constitutional violation calling for interdistrict relief, but the notion that school district lines may be casually ignored is contrary to the history of public education in our country.

No single tradition in public education is more deeply rooted than local control over the operation of schools; local autonomy has long been thought essential both to the maintenance of community concern and support for public schools and to quality of the educational process. See Wright v. Council of the City of Emporia, 407 U.S. 451, 469.

Thus, in San Antonio School District v. Rodriguez, 411 U.S. 1, 50, we observed that local control over the educational process affords citizens an opportunity to participate in decision-making, permits the structuring of school programs to fit local needs and encourages "experimentation, innovation and a healthy competition for educational excellence."

The Michigan educational structure involved in this case, in common with most states, provides for a large measure of local control and a review of the scope and character of these local powers indicates the extent to which the interdistrict remedy approved by the two courts could disrupt and alter the structure of public education in Michigan.

The metropolitan remedy would require, in effect, consolidation of fifty-four independent school districts historically administered as separate units into a vast new super school district. Entirely apart from the logistical and other serious problems attending large-scale transportation of students, the consolidation would give rise to an array of other problems in financing and operating this new school system.

Some of the more obvious questions would be: What would be the status and authority of the present popularly elected school boards? Would the children of Detroit be within the jurisdiction and operating control of a school board elected by the parents and residents of other districts?

What board or boards would levy taxes for school operations in these fifty-four districts constituting the consolidated metropolitan area? What provisions could be made for assuring substantial equality in tax levies among the fifty-four districts, if this were deemed requisite?

What provisions would be made for financing? Would the validity of long-term bonds be jeopardized unless approved by all of the component districts as well as the state? What body would determine that portion of the curricula now left to the discretion of local school boards? Who would establish attendance zones, purchase school equipment, locate and construct new schools, and indeed attend to all the myriad day-to-day decisions that are necessary to school operations affecting potentially more than three quarters of a million pupils?

It may be suggested that all of these vital operational problems are yet to be resolved by the district court, and that this is the purpose of the Court of Appeals' proposed remand. But it is obvious from the scope of the interdistrict remedy itself that absent a complete restructuring of the laws of Michigan relating to school districts the district court will become first, a de facto "legislative authority" to resolve these complex questions, and then the "school superintendent" for the entire area. This is a task which few, if any, judges are qualified to perform and one which would deprive the people of control of schools through their elected representatives. . . .

. . . School district lines and the present laws with respect to local control are not sacrosanct and if they conflict with the 14th Amendment Federal courts have a duty to prescribe appropriate remedies.

But our prior holdings have been confined to violations and remedies within a single school district. We therefore turn to address, for the first time, the validity of a remedy mandating cross-district or inter-district consolidation to remedy a condition of segregation found to exist in only one district.

The record before us, voluminous as it is, contains evidence of de jure segregated conditions only in the Detroit schools; ... With no showing of significant violation by the fifty-three outlying school districts and no evidence of any interdistrict violation or effect, the court went beyond the original theory of the case as framed by the pleadings and mandated a metropolitan area remedy. ...

... [T]erms such as "unitary" and "dual" systems, and "racially identifiable schools," have meaning and the necessary Federal authority to remedy the constitutional wrong is firmly established. But the remedy is necessarily designed, as all remedies are, to restore the victims of discriminatory conduct to the position they would have occupied in the absence of such conduct.

Disparate treatment of white and Negro students occurred within the Detroit school system and not elsewhere, and on the record the remedy must be limited to that system.

The constitutional right of the Negro respondents residing in Detroit is to attend a unitary school system in that district. Unless petitioners drew the district lines in a discriminatory fashion, or arranged for white students residing in the Detroit district to attend schools in Oakland and Macomb counties, they were under no constitutional duty to make provisions for Negro students to do so. ...

We conclude that the relief ordered by the district court and affirmed by the Court of Appeals was based upon an erroneous standard and was unsupported by record evidence that acts of the outlying districts affected the discrimination found to exist in the schools of Detroit. Accordingly, the judgment of the Court of Appeals is vacated and the case is remanded for further proceedings consistent with this opinion leading to prompt formulation of a decree directed to eliminating the segregation found to exist in Detroit city schools, a remedy which has been delayed since 1970.

Reversed and remanded.

Mr. Justice Stewart, concurring, said in part:

In joining the opinion of the Court, I think it appropriate in view of some of the extravagant language of the dissenting opinions, to state briefly my understanding of what it is that the Court decides today. ...

This is not to say, however, that an interdistrict remedy of the sort approved by the court of appeals would not be proper, or even necessary, in other factual situations. Were it to be shown, for example, that state officials had contributed to the separation of the races by drawing or redrawing school district lines ... , or by purposeful, racially discriminatory use of state housing or zoning laws, then a decree calling for transfer of pupils across district lines or for restructuring of district lines might well be appropriate.

In this case, however, no such interdistrict violation was shown. Indeed, no evidence at all concerning the administration of schools outside the City of Detroit was presented other than the fact that these schools contained a higher proportion of white pupils than did the schools within the city. Since the mere fact of different racial compositions in contiguous districts does not itself imply or constitute a violation of the equal protection clause in the absence of a showing that such disparity was imposed, fostered, or encouraged by the state or its political subdivisions, it follows that no interdistrict violation was shown in this case. . . .

Mr. Justice Douglas, dissenting, said in part:

The Court of Appeals has acted responsibly in these cases, and we should affirm its judgment. . . .

. . . [A]s the Court of Appeals held there can be no doubt that as a matter of Michigan law the state herself has the final say as to where and how school district lines should be drawn.

When we rule against the metropolitan area remedy we take a step that will likely put the problems of the blacks and our society back to the period that antedated the "separate but equal" regime of Plessy v. Ferguson, 163 U.S. 537. The reason is simple.

The inner core of Detroit is now rather solidly black; and the blacks, we know, in many instances are likely to be poorer, just as were the Chicanos in San Antonio Independent School District v. Rodriguez, 411 U.S. 1. By that decision the poorer school districts must pay their own way. It is therefore a foregone conclusion that we have now given the states a formula whereby the poor must pay their own way.

Today's decision given Rodriguez means that there is no violation of the equal protection clause though the schools are segregated by race and though the black schools are not only "separate" but "inferior."

So far as equal protection is concerned we are now in a dramatic retreat from the 8 to 1 decision in 1896 that blacks could be segregated in public facilities provided they received equal treatment. . . .

Mr. Justice White, with whom Mr. Justice Douglas, Mr. Justice Brennan, and Mr. Justice Marshall join, dissenting, said in part:

. . . Regretfully, and for several reasons, I can join neither the Court's judgment nor its opinion. The core of my disagreement is that deliberate acts of segregation and their consequences will go unremedied, not because a remedy would be infeasible or unreasonable in terms of the usual criteria governing school desegregation cases, but because an effective remedy would cause what the Court considers to be undue administrative inconvenience to the state.

The result is that the State of Michigan, the entity at which the 14th Amendment is directed, has successfully insulated itself from its duty to provide effective desegregation remedies by vesting sufficient power over its public schools in its local school districts. If this is the case in Michigan, it will be the case in most states. . . .

I am surprised that the Court, sitting at this distance from the State of Michigan, claims better insight than the Court of Appeals and the district court as to whether an interdistrict remedy for equal protection violations practiced by the State of Michigan would involve undue difficulties for the state in the management of its public schools.

In the area of what constitutes an acceptable desegregation plan, "we must of necessity rely to a large extent, as this Court has for more than sixteen years, on the informed judgment of the district courts in the first instance and on courts of appeals. . . ."

Obviously, whatever difficulties there might be, they are surmountable; for the Court itself concedes that had there been sufficient evidence of an interdistrict violation, the district court could have fashioned a single remedy for the districts implicated rather than a different remedy for each district in which the violation had occurred or had an impact.

I am even more mystified how the Court can ignore the legal reality that the constitutional violations, even if occurring locally, were committed by governmental entities for which the state is responsible and that it is the state that must respond to the command of the 14th Amendment. . . .

The Court draws the remedial line at the Detroit School District boundary, even though the 14th Amendment is addressed to the state and even though the state denies equal protection of the laws when its public agencies, acting in its behalf, invidiously discriminate. . . .

The unwavering decisions of this Court over the past twenty years support the assumption of the Court of Appeals that the district court's remedial power does not cease at the school district line. The Court's first formulation of the remedial principles to be followed in disestablishing racially discriminatory school systems recognized the variety of problems arising from different local school conditions and the necessity for that "practical flexibility" traditionally associated with courts of equity. . . .

Until today, the permissible contours of the equitable authority of the district courts to remedy the unlawful establishment of a dual school system have been extensive, adaptable, and fully responsive to the ultimate goal of achieving "the greatest possible degree of actual desegregation. . . ."

Mr. Justice Marshall, with whom Mr. Justice Douglas, Mr. Justice Brennan and Mr. Justice White join, dissenting, said in part:

. . . After twenty years of small, often difficult steps toward the great end, the court today takes a giant step backward. Notwithstanding a record showing widespread and pervasive racial segregation in the educational system provided by the State of Michigan for children in Detroit, this Court holds that the district court was powerless to require the state to remedy its constitutional violation in any meaningful fashion.

Ironically purporting to base its result on the principle that the scope of the remedy in a desegregation case should be determined by the nature and the extent of the constitutional violation, the Court's answer is to provide no remedy at all for the violation proved in this case, thereby guaranteeing that

Negro children in Detroit will receive the same separate and inherently unequal education in the future as they have been unconstitutionally afforded in the past.

I cannot subscribe to this emasculation of our constitutional guarantee of equal protection of the laws and must respectfully dissent. Our precedents, in my view, firmly establish that where as here, state-imposed segregation has been demonstrated, it becomes the duty of the state to eliminate root and branch all vestiges of racial discrimination and to achieve the greatest possible degree of actual desegregation.

I agree with both the District Court and the Court of Appeals that, under the facts of this case, this duty cannot be fulfilled unless the State of Michigan involves outlying metropolitan area school districts in its desegregation remedy.

Furthermore, I perceive no basis either in law or in the practicalities of the situation to justify the state's interposition of school district boundaries as absolute barriers to the implementation of an effective desegregation remedy.

Under established and frequently used Michigan procedures, school district lines are both flexible and permeable for a wide variety of purposes, and there is no reason why they must now stand in the way of meaningful desegregation relief.

The rights at issue in this case are too fundamental to be abridged on grounds as superficial as those relied on by the majority today.

We deal here with the rights of all of our children, whatever their race, to an equal start in life and to an equal opportunity to reach their full potential as citizens. Those children who have been denied that right in the past deserve better than to see fences thrown up to deny them the right in the future.

Our nation, I fear, will be ill-served by the Court's refusal to remedy separate and unequal education, for unless our children begin to learn together, there is little hope that our people will ever learn to live together.

The great irony of the Court's opinion and, in my view, its most serious analytical flaw may be gleaned from its concluding sentence, in which the Court remands for "prompt formulation of a decree directed to eliminating the segregation found to exist in Detroit City schools, a remedy which has been delayed since 1970."

The majority, however, seems to have forgotten the district court's explicit finding that a Detroit-only decree, the only remedy permitted under today's decision, "would not accomplish desegregation."

Nowhere in the Court's opinion does the majority confront, let alone respond to, the district court's conclusion that a remedy limited to the City of Detroit would not effectively desegregate the Detroit city schools. I, for one, find the district court's conclusion well supported by the record and its analysis compelled by our prior cases. . . .

. . . [S]everal factors in this case coalesce to support the district court's ruling that it was the State of Michigan itself, not simply to Detroit Board of Education, which bore the obligation of curing the condition of segregation within the Detroit city schools. The actions of the state itself directly contributed to Detroit's segregation. Under the 14th Amendment, the state is ultimately responsible for the actions of its local agencies. And finally, given the structure of Michigan's educational system Detroit's segregation cannot be viewed as the problem of an independent and separate entity. Michigan operates a single statewide system of education, a substantial part of which was shown to be segregated in this case. . . .

The state must also bear part of the blame for the white flight to the suburbs which would be forthcoming from a Detroit-only decree and would render such a remedy ineffective. Having created a system where whites and Negroes were intentionally kept apart so that they could not become accustomed to learning together, the state is responsible for the fact that many whites will react to the dismantling of that segregated system by attempting to flee to the suburbs.

Indeed, by limiting the district court to a Detroit-only remedy and allowing that flight to the suburbs to succeed, the Court today allows the state to profit from its wrong and to perpetuate for years to come the separation of the races it achieved in the past by purposeful state action. . . .

Equal Protection of the Laws: Public Services

In the early 1970's both federal and state courts began to expand the concept of equal protection of the laws under the 14th Amendment to include a requirement that states provide equality in the delivery of public services to citizens under their jurisdiction. Under this emerging judicial doctrine state and local governments could not discriminate among particular groups of citizens in the delivery of public services. However, the question remained: What constitutes a definable group for the purposes of determining discrimination? Discrimination is defined by the courts as the unequal treatment of citizens because of their membership in a particular group. For example, a state law that prevents blacks from using public facilities separates blacks from other citizens and discriminates against them. In the absence of clear-cut legal discrimination (*de jure* discrimination) it is difficult to prove that the actions of government constitute premeditated discrimination (which is one type of *de facto* discrimination). Groups can be classified in innumerable ways, such as groups of students, college professors, business men, laborers, and so on. When the result of government action is that a class of persons is disadvantaged relative to other groups that class is called "suspect" by the courts, and the classification of the group is called a "suspect classification." For example, the classification of a minority group by race is a "suspect classification" because in the past the actions of government have not dealt with racial minorities on an equal basis with the white majority. Racial minorities are the most unambiguous "suspect classes" in our society. Where government action appears to treat members of a racial minority unequally the presumption is that this constitutes discrimination and is a violation of the Equal Protection Clause of the 14th Amendment.

In *Hawkins v. Shaw* the United States Court of Appeals for the Fifth Circuit confronted the question of whether a town could systematically refuse to provide public services to black neighborhoods that it provided to white neighborhoods. The group that was disadvantaged in this case was clearly a "suspect class." If the town of Shaw was not purposely discriminating against this class, and could demonstrate that its public service delivery system was based upon rational considerations that had nothing whatsoever to do with racial considerations, the court could find that discrimination did not exist. This was the decision of the lower District Court, that was reviewed in the following opinion.

30
HAWKINS V. TOWN OF SHAW, MISSISSIPPI
437 F. 2d 1286 (1971)

Circuit Judge Tuttle delivered the opinion of the court:

Referring to a portion of town or a segment of society as being "on the other side of the tracks" has for too long been a familiar expression to most Americans. Such a phrase immediately conjures up an area characterized by poor housing, overcrowded conditions and, in short, overall deterioration. While there may be many reasons why such areas exist in nearly all of our cities, one reason that cannot be accepted is the discriminatory provision of municipal services based on race. It is such a reason that is alleged at the basis of this action.

Appellants are Negro citizens of the Town of Shaw, Mississippi. They alleged that the town has provided various municipal services including street paving and street lighting, sanitary sewers, surface water drainage as well as water mains and fire hydrants in a discriminatory manner based on race. Appellants brought a class action seeking injunctive relief under 42 U.S.C. § 1983 against the town, the town's mayor, clerk and five aldermen. After a three-day trial, the trial court applied the traditional equal protection standard despite the presence of appellants' undisputed statistical evidence which we feel clearly showed a substantial qualitative and quantitative inequity in the level and nature of services accorded "white" and "black" neighborhoods in Shaw. The court stated:

> "If actions of public officials are shown to have rested upon rational considerations, irrespective of race or poverty, they are not within the condemnation of the Fourteenth Amendment, and may not be properly condemned upon judicial review. Persons or groups who are treated differently must be shown to be similarly situated and their unequal treatment demonstrated to be *without any rational basis* or based upon an invidious factor such as race." 303 F.Supp. 1162, 1168 (N. D. Miss. 1969). (Emphasis added.)

Because this court has long adhered to the theory that "figures speak and when they do, Courts listen," we feel that appellants clearly made out a prima facie case of racial discrimination. The trial court thus erred in applying the traditional equal protection standard, for as this Court and the Supreme Court have held: "Where racial classifications are involved, the Equal Protection and Due Process Clauses of the Fourteenth Amendment 'command a more stringent standard' in reviewing discretionary acts of state or local officers." In applying this test, defendants' actions may be justified only if they show a compelling state interest. We have thoroughly examined the evidence and conclude that no such compelling interests could possibly justify the gross disparities in services between black and white areas of town that this record reveals.

FACTS

The Town of Shaw, Mississsippi, was incorporated in 1886 and is located in the Mississippi Delta. Its population, which has undergone little change since 1930, consists of about 2,500 people—1,500 black and 1,000 white residents. Residential racial segregation is almost total. There are 451 dwelling units occupied by blacks in town, and, of these, 97% (439) are located in neighborhoods in which no whites reside. That the town's policies in administering various municipal services have led to substantially less attention being paid to the black portion of town is clear.

Nearly 98% of all homes that front on unpaved streets in Shaw are occupied by blacks. Ninety-seven percent of the homes not served by sanitary sewers are in black neighborhoods. Further, while the town has acquired a significant number of medium and high intensity mercury vapor street lighting fixtures, every one of them has been installed in white neighborhoods. The record further discloses that similar statistical evidence of grave disparities in both the level and kinds of services offered regarding surface water drainage, water mains, fire hydrants, and traffic control apparatus was also brought forth and not disputed. Finally, it was alleged that this disparity was the result of a long history of racial discrimination.

Surely, this was enough evidence to establish a prima facie case of racial discrimination. The only question that remains to be examined is whether or not these disparities can possibly be justified by any compelling state interests. As we have already indicated, an examination of the record reveals they cannot.

STREET PAVING

[1] The undisputed evidence is that 97% of all those who live in homes fronting on unpaved streets are black. In attempting to justify this, the trial

court stated:

> "Initially, concrete paving was afforded to those streets serving commercial and industrial interests and to the areas nearest the town's center. In some cases this resulted in more street paving in white than Negro neighborhoods, but the paving actually done in the municipality was on the basis of general usage, traffic needs and other objective criteria. Residential neighborhoods not facing principal streets or thoroughfares long remained unpaved, regardless of their character as white or black neighborhoods."

The record simply does not support the justification that streets were built according to traffic needs and usage. The town's one engineer who made recommendations to defendants as to the priority of street paving projects testified that he had never surveyed the town to determine which streets were used the most. Nor did he compare the usage of streets in black neighborhoods with the usage of those in white neighborhoods. He even admitted that he was not familiar with the usage of streets in the Promised Land Addition, which is one of the oldest and largest black neighborhoods in Shaw.

The finding that many streets were paved in the business areas and that this resulted, "in some cases", in providing more paving in white rather than black neighborhoods, also fails to justify the existing disparities. As appellants point out, in 1956 when the first residential streets in black neighborhoods were paved, 96% of the white residents of Shaw already lived on paved streets, most of which had been paved during the 1930's. Many of these streets, however, were solely residential, and could not possibly serve commercial, industrial or any public buildings.

The trial court also found that many of the streets on which blacks live were too narrow to pave. The town engineer had testified that streets in black neighborhoods had not been paved because they did not have the fifty foot right-of-way he considered necessary. However, as appellants point out, most of the streets in Shaw, in both black and white neighborhoods, have platted rights of way that range from 30 to 40 feet. Further, while most streets *under* 50 feet in white neighborhoods are paved, those in the black areas are not.

In short, even if we assume that such criteria as traffic usage, need and width constitute compelling state interests, they were not applied equally to both black and white neighborhoods. We are led to the inevitable conclusion that Shaw's policies, which have resulted in such significant disparities between the black and white portions of town, are, in no way, justifiable.

STREETS LIGHTS

[2] The record clearly shows that absolutely no high power mercury vapor street lights have been installed in black residential areas. Only the much weaker bare bulb fixtures are to be found. The trial court stated that there was no showing that the lighting was inadequate and, in any event:

> "The brighter lights are provided for those streets forming either a state highway, or serving commerical, industrial or special school needs, or otherwise carrying the heaviest traffic load."

The fact that there was no specific showing that lighting was not adequate is not significant. What is significant is that it is clear that all of the *better* lighting that exists in Shaw can be found *only* in the white parts of town. Surely, this cannot be justified merely on the ground that the bare bulb fixtures are not shown to be inadequate. One might readily assume, it seems, that the modern high intensity lights are *more* adequate from the fact of their use by the city. *Improvements* to existing facilities provided in a discriminatory manner may also constitute a violation of equal protection.

The other justifications accepted by the trial court again fail, for if the "special needs" criteria were applied equally for the benefit of both black and white citizens, all the high intensity lights would not be in only the white areas of town. For example, while streets with heavy traffic serving commercial and public centers, such as Gale Street, in black areas have only bare bulb fixtures, many little traveled streets in white neighborhoods have the high intensity variety. In short, we are again convinced that as with the paving of streets, the placement of new light fixtures only in the white portion of town, cannot be justified.

SANITARY SEWERS

[3] While 99% of white residents are served by a sanitary sewer system, nearly 20% of the black population is not so served. The trial court thought this was justified by noting that:

> Part of the problem in reaching all older unserved areas has been the necessity for bringing this service into newer subdivisions developed for both races and brought into the town, as it is the town's firm policy to make sewer installations for all such new areas.

It is not at all clear from the record that such a "firm policy" exists. However, even assuming that it does, the fact that extensions are now made to new areas in a non-discriminatory manner is not sufficient when the effect of such a policy is to "freeze–in" the results of past discrimination. As this court stated in Henry v. Clarksdale Municipal Separate School District, 409 F.2d 682, 688 (5th Cir., 1969), "a relationship otherwise rational may be insufficient in itself to meet constitutional standards—if its effect is to freeze-in past discrimination." We find that since over one-third of the black population was not served when the original sewer system was constructed and nearly 20% of this population remains unserved, a policy of serving only new areas would freeze in the results of past discrimination.

The trial court, however, also stated that:

> "While the complaint about less than 100% sanitary sewage for all residences is certainly a real one, that condition arises basically from the fact that local law does not yet require indoor plumbing. The lack of sanitary sewers in certain areas of

the town is not the result of racial discrimination in withholding a vital service; rather it is a consequence of not requiring through a proper housing code, certain minimal conditions for inhabited housing."

While we recognize that a proper housing code would help this situation, it is circular reasoning to argue that because indoor plumbing is not required, sewers are not provided. If sewers were provided, indoor plumbing could be more easily installed. Indeed, without it, black residents desiring such facilities are forced to incur the extra expense of installing individual sewage disposal apparatus. In short, the justifications offered for the disparities that exist in the town's sewerage system are not valid.

SURFACE WATER DRAINAGE

[4] We do not doubt that as the trial court notes: "Having flat nonporous soil with slow run-off conditions, Shaw suffers from drainage problems common to the Delta area." Indeed, there are serious drainage problems in both the black and white sections of town. However, the record reveals that the problems of the black community are far more serious. Whereas, the white community has been provided with either underground storm sewers or a continuous system of drainage ditches, the black neighborhoods have been provided with a poorly maintained system of drainage ditches and, on many streets, none at all. The following testimony concerning the black portion of town is illustrative:

Q. What is the shape of the actual drainage ditches or absence of them within the area?

A. These vary, so greatly. In one section, for example, of Canaan Street where within the last week someone has come along and cleared a ditch. The ditch is in the shape of a spade; that is, it's one shovel wide and one shovel deep and whatever was in what is now the ditch is now heaped in a pile along the side and this in that area serves as a ditch.

On Lampton Street, back in the Gale Street area, the ditch is a major excavation being three or four feet deep and the course of it, for example, negotiating a turn by automobile traveling from Lampton Street and attempting to turn into one of the short streets such as Johnson Street or Mose Street or Shaw Street is very precarious kind of undertaking that requires backing up and adjusting several times so as to get the car down the street without leaving the car in the ditch.

Then in the Elm Street area there is no visible form of drainage.

Appellees point to various impediments to justify this disparity including haphazard subdividing, the absence of zoning regulations and rights of way of insufficient width. We have already dealt with the claim that roads in the black area are of insufficient width. Regarding the other impediments, we only note that they have been substantially overcome in white neighborhoods. We see no acceptable reason why they should not have been overcome in the black community as well.

WATER MAINS, FIRE HYDRANTS AND TRAFFIC CONTROL SIGNS

[5] Although water is supplied to all residents of the town, the trial court found that "at all times water pressure is inadequate in certain localities, irrespective of their racial character." We agree that the record discloses inadequate water pressure, but disagree that it is not related to the racial make-up of the locality.

The record reveals that the two areas where water pressure is most inadequate are black and constitute 63% of the town's black population. As appellants note, in the Gale Street area, 211 homes are served by 4" water mains while in the Promised Land, most of the 74 homes are served by 2" or 1¼" mains. Most of the white community is served by 6" mains. The 4" mains that do exist in the white portion of town serve, however, far fewer homes than the 4" mains in the black section. In short, as with the previously examined municipal services, the town's policies have again created a situation in which the black portion of town is severely disadvantaged. An examination of the record regarding the placement of fire hydrants as well as the placement of any traffic control signs in black neighborhoods leads us to the same conclusion.

INTENT

[6] Yet, despite the fact that we conclude that no compelling state interests can justify the disparities that exist in the black and white portions of town, it may be argued that this result was not intended. That is to say, the record contains no direct evidence aimed at establishing bad faith, ill will or an evil motive on the part of the Town of Shaw and its public officials. We feel, however, that the law on this point is clear. In a civil rights suit alleging racial discrimination in contravention of the Fourteenth Amendment, actual intent or motive need not be directly proved, for:

> "'equal protection of the laws' means more than merely the absence of governmental action designed to discriminate; * * * we now firmly recognize that the arbitrary quality of thoughtlessness can be as disastrous and unfair to private rights and the public interest as the perversity of a willful scheme." Norwalk CORE v. Norwalk Redevelopment Agency, 395 F.2d 920, 931 (2d Cir., 1968). *See also,* United States ex rel. Seals v. Wiman, 304 F.2d 53 at 65 (5 Cir., 1962); Jackson v. Godwin, 400 F.2d 529 (1968).

Having determined that no compelling state interests can possibly justify the discriminatory *results* of Shaw's administration of municipal services, we conclude that a violation of equal protection has occurred.

RELIEF

In reaching this decision and in fashioning an appropriate remedy, we are not unaware of the fundamental institutional problems involved. The need for judicially discoverable and manageable standards as well as an awareness of the distinctions between the roles played by the coordinate branches of government must, of course, be foremost in our mind. Nevertheless, having carefully considered the problems involved, we feel this case warrants judicial intervention.

The Town of Shaw, indeed any town, is not immune to the mandates of the Constitution. As Mr. Justice White noted in Avery v. Midland County, 390 U.S. 474 at 480, (1967):

> "A city, town, or county may no more deny the equal protection of the laws than it may abridge freedom of speech, establish an official religion, arrest without probable cause, or deny due process of law."

In concluding that an equal protection violation has occurred, we have not, of course, been guided by a statutory set of standards or regulations clearly defining how many paved streets or what kind of sewerage system a town like Shaw should have. We have, however, been able to utilize what we consider a most reliable yardstick—namely, the quality and quantity of municipal services provided in the white area of town. As the record reveals, this is an area which, for the most part, does not significantly differ in need or expectations from the black portion of town. Making a comparison between these two areas is hardly an insuperable judicial task. Indeed, we are dealing with some of the most basic amenities of urban life and the disparities are by no means slight.

[7] Yet, it may also be argued that even though this court has adequate standards to determine fairly that municipal services have been allocated in a discriminatory manner, the correction of this problem is not a judical function. We disagree. The separation of powers principle assumes that we have a system of checks and balances. In Madisonian terms, each department or power center is to act as a curb on other departments or centers. Indeed, "unless these departments be so far connected and blended, as to give to each a constitutional control over the others, the degree of separation which the maxim requires as essential to a free government, can never in practice, be duly maintained." Madison, The Federalist, No. 48. Utilizing the power vested in this court to check an abuse of state or municipal power is, in effect, consistent with the separation of powers principle.

In so doing, however, we are, by no means, the first court to exercise such power as to municipal actions. When confronted with a similar case, the court in Hadnot v. City of Prattville, 309 F. Supp. 967 (D.C.Ala. 1970), found discrimination in the provision of various facilities in municipal parks. The court ordered the city to equalize the "equipment, facilities and services" provided in a park located in a black neighborhood with those provided in parks located in white neighborhoods. In Gautreaux v. Chicago Housing Authority, 304 F.Supp. 736 (N.D.Ill. 1969), the court found discrimination in the administration of a public housing program and assumed a major role in implementing desegregation by issuing a comprehensive and specific order for integrating the public housing system. See also, Kennedy Park Homes Assoc. v. City of Lackawanna, D.C., 318 F.Supp. 669.

We feel that issuing a specific order outlining exactly how the equalization of municipal services should occur is neither necessary nor proper in the context of this case. We do require, however, that the Town of Shaw, itself, submit a plan for the court's approval detailing how it proposes to cure the results of the long history of discrimination which the record reveals. We are confident that the municipal authorities can, particularly because they so staunchly deny any racial motivation, propose a program of improvements that will, within a reasonable time, remove the disparities that bear so heavily on the black citizens of Shaw.

The case is reversed and remanded for further proceedings not inconsistent with the above opinion.

The Circuit Court in *Hawkins v. Shaw* unequivocally decided that a town could not systematically deny public services to its black neighborhoods. Race was a "suspect classification," and every effort had to be made to assure equal treatment. No question was raised in *Hawkins v. Shaw* concerning whether or not citizens have a fundamental right to public services. The issues confronting the Supreme Court in *San Antonio School District v. Rodriguez* (1973) were more complex. The background was that federal and state courts, including a three-judge district court that rendered the initial *Rodriguez* decision (appeals from three-judge district courts are taken directly to the Supreme Court, bypassing the usual practice of appealing first to Circuit Courts of Appeals), had come to the conclusion that "poor people" constitute a "suspect classification," and that state and local government action that disadvantages the "poor" relative to middle and upper income groups is discrimination and therefore a violation of the Equal Protection Clause of the 14th Amendment. In particular, lower courts in many states had decided that the property tax could not be used as a basis for the financing of public education, because poor districts within states did not receive nearly as much money in this way as more affluent neighborhoods. Children within poor neighborhoods were therefore being treated unequally *by the state*, because it was the state that authorized the use of the property tax for financing of local education. These lower court decisions threatened, in the words of Justice Powell of the Supreme Court in *San Antonio School District v. Rodriguez,* an "unprecedented upheaval in public education." Moreover, if wealth is to be considered a suspect classification for the purposes of determining discrimination in the delivery of public services an endless series of cases could arise challenging the unequal distribution of such services as fire and police protection, garbage collection, street paving, public transportation, and so on. It appeared that the decision of the Supreme Court in the *Rodriguez* case might have an extraordinary impact upon society. It is not surprising, therefore, that the Burger Court exercised judicial self-restraint, holding that: (1) wealth is not a suspect classification; (2) education is not a fundamental right or liberty guaranteed by the Constitution; (3) deference must be given to local initiative in matters of taxation and fiscal planning for educational policy; (4) the Texas educational system is based upon a rational plan that encourages local initiative and participation. For all of these reasons the Supreme Court found that the San Antonio school system, which admittedly did not establish equal funding of education within its school districts, was not discriminatory and in violation of the Equal Protection Clause of the 14th Amendment.

31
SAN ANTONIO SCHOOL DISTRICT v. RODRIGUEZ
411 U.S. 1 (1973)

Mr. Justice Powell delivered the opinion of the Court, saying in part:

This suit attacking the Texas system of financing public education was initiated by Mexican-American parents whose children attend the elementary and secondary schools in the Edgewood Independent School District, an urban school district in San Antonio, Texas. They brought a class action on behalf of school children throughout the State who are members of minority groups or who are poor and reside in school districts having a low property tax base. Named as defendants were the State Board of Education, the Commissioner of Education, the State Attorney General, and the Bexar County (San Antonio) Board of Trustees. The complaint was filed in the summer of 1968 and a three-judge court was impaneled in January 1969. In December 1971 the panel rendered its judgment in a per curiam opinion holding the Texas school finance system unconstitutional under the Equal Protection Clause of the Fourteenth Amendment. The State appealed, and we noted probable jurisdiction to consider the far-reaching constitutional questions presented. For the reasons stated in this opinion we reverse the decision of the District Court. . . .

I

. . . [S]ubstantial interdistrict disparities in school expenditures found by the District Court to prevail in San Antonio and in varying degrees throughout the State still exist. And it was these disparities, largely attributable to differences in the amounts of money collected through local property taxation, that led the District Court to conclude that Texas' dual system of public school finance violated the Equal Protection Clause. The District Court held that the Texas system discriminates on the basis of wealth in the manner in which education is provided for its people. 337 F Supp, at 282. Finding that wealth is a "suspect" classification and that education is a "fundamental" interest, the District Court held that the Texas system could be sustained only if the State could show that it was premised upon some compelling state interest. On this issue the court concluded that "[n]ot only are defendants unable to demonstrate compelling state interests . . . they fail even to establish a reasonable basis for these classifications."

Texas virtually concedes that its historically rooted dual system of financing education could not withstand the strict judicial scrutiny that this Court has found appropriate in reviewing legislative judgments that interfere with fundamental constitutional rights or that involve suspect classifications. If, as previous decisions have indicated, strict scrutiny means that the State's system is not entitled to the usual presumption of validity, that the State rather than the complainants must carry a "heavy burden of justification," that the State must demonstrate that its educational system has been structured with "precision" and is "tailored" narrowly to serve legitimate objectives and that it has selected the "least drastic means" for effectuating its objectives, the Texas financing system and its counterpart in virtually every other State will not pass muster. The State candidly admits that "[n]o one familiar with the Texas system would contend that it has yet achieved perfection." Apart from its concession that educational finance in Texas has "defects" and "imperfections," the State defends the system's rationality with vigor and disputes the District Court's finding that it lacks a "reasonable basis."

This, then, establishes the framework for our analysis. We must decide, first, whether the Texas system of financing public education operates to the disadvantage of some suspect class or impinges upon a fundamental right explicitly or implicitly protected by the Constitution, thereby requiring strict judicial scrutiny. If so, the judgment of the District Court should be affirmed. If not, the Texas scheme must still be examined to determine whether it rationally furthers some legitimate, articulated state purpose and therefore does not constitute an invidious discrimination in violation of the Equal Protection Clause of the Fourteenth Amendment.

II

The District Court's opinion does not reflect the novelty and complexity of the constitutional questions posed by appellees' challenge to Texas' system of school finance. In concluding that strict judicial scrutiny was required, that court relied on decisions dealing with the rights of indigents to equal treatment in the criminal trial and appellate processes, and on cases disapproving wealth restrictions on the right to vote. Those cases, the District Court concluded, established wealth as a suspect classification. Finding that the local property tax system discriminated on the basis of wealth, it regarded those precedents as controlling. It then reasoned, based on decisions of this Court affirming the undeniable importance of education, that there is a fundamental right to education and that, absent some compelling state justification, the Texas system could not stand.

We are unable to agree that this case, which in significant aspects is sui generis, may be so neatly fitted into the conventional mosaic of constitutional analysis under the Equal Protection Clause. Indeed, for the several reasons that follow, we find neither the suspect classification nor the fundamental interest analysis persuasive.

A

The wealth discrimination discovered by the District Court in this case, and by several other courts that have recently struck down school financing laws in other States, [e.g., *Serrano* v. *Priest,* 96 Cal Rptr 601 (1971)] is quite unlike any of the forms of wealth discrimination heretofore reviewed by this Court. Rather than focusing on the unique features of the alleged discrimination, the courts in these cases have virtually assumed their findings of a suspect classification through a simplistic process of analysis: since, under the traditional systems of financing public schools, some poorer people receive less expensive educations than other more affluent people, these systems discriminate on the basis of wealth. This approach largely ignores the hard threshold questions, including whether it makes a difference for purposes of consideration under the Constitution that the class of disadvantaged "poor" cannot be identified or defined in customary equal protection terms, and whether the relative—rather than absolute—nature of the asserted deprivation is of significant consequence. Before a State's laws and the justifications for the classifications they create are subjected to strict judicial scrutiny, we think these threshold considerations must be analyzed more closely than they were in the court below.

The case comes to us with no definitive description of the classifying facts or delineation of the disfavored class. Examination of the District Court's opinion and of appellees' complaint, briefs, and contentions at oral argument suggests, however, at least three ways in which the discrimination claimed here might be described. The Texas system of school finance might be regarded as discriminating (1) against "poor" persons whose incomes fall below some identifiable level of poverty or who might be characterized as functionally "indigent," or (2) against those who are relatively poorer than others, or (3) against all those who, irrespective of their personal incomes, happen to reside in relatively poorer school districts. Our task must be to ascertain whether, in fact, the Texas system has been shown to discriminate on any of these possible bases and, if so, whether the resulting classification may be regarded as suspect.

The precedents of this Court provide the proper starting point. The individuals or groups of individuals who constituted the class discriminated against in our prior cases shared two distinguishing characteristics: because of their impecunity they were completely unable to pay for some desired benefit, and as a consequence, they sustained an absolute deprivation of a meaningful opportunity to enjoy that benefit. In Griffin v Illinois, 351 US 12 (1956), and its progeny, the Court invalidated state laws that prevented an indigent criminal defendant from acquiring a transcript, or an adequate substitute for a transcript, for use at several stages of the trial and appeal process. The payment requirements in each case were found to occasion de facto discrimination against those who, because of their indigency, were totally unable to pay for transcripts. And, the Court in each case emphasized that no constitutional violation would have been shown if the State had provided some "adequate substitute" for a full stenographic transcript.

Likewise, in Douglas v California, 372 US 353 (1963), a decision establishing an indigent defendant's right to court-appointed counsel on direct appeal, the Court dealt only with defendants who could not pay for counsel from their own resources and who had no other way of gaining representation. Douglas provides no relief for those on whom the burdens of paying for a criminal defense are, relatively speaking, great but not insurmountable. Nor does it deal with relative differences in the quality of counsel acquired by the less wealthy.

Williams v Illinois, 399 US 235 (1970), and Tate v Short, 401 US 395 (1971), struck down criminal penalties that subjected indigents to incarceration simply because of their inability to pay a fine. Again, the disadvantaged class was composed only of persons who were totally unable to pay the demanded sum. Those cases do not touch on the question whether equal protection is denied to persons with relatively less money on whom designated fines impose heavier burdens. The Court has not held that fines must be structured to reflect each person's ability to pay in order to avoid disproportionate burdens. Sentencing judges may, and often do, consider the defendant's ability to pay, but in such circumstances they are guided by sound judicial discretion rather than by constitutional mandate.

Finally, in Bullock v Carter, 405 US 134 (1972), the Court invalidated the Texas filing fee requirement for primary elections. Both of the relevant classifying facts found in the previous cases were present there. The size of the fee, often running into the thousands of dollars and, in at least one case, as high as $8,900, effectively barred all potential candidates who were unable to pay the required fee. As the system provided "no reasonable alternative means of access to the ballot", inability to pay occasioned an absolute denial of a position on the primary ballot.

Only appellees' first possible basis for describing the class disadvantaged by the Texas school finance system—discrimination against a class of definably "poor" persons—might arguably meet the criteria established in these prior cases. Even a cursory examination, however, demonstrates that neither of the two distinguishing characteristics of wealth classifications can be found here.

First, in support of their charge that the system discriminates against the "poor," appellees have made no effort to demonstrate that it operates to the peculiar disadvantage of any class fairly definable as indigent, or as composed of persons whose incomes are beneath any designated poverty level. Indeed, there is reason to believe that the poorest families are not necessarily clustered in the poorest property districts. A recent and exhaustive study of school districts in Connecticut concluded that "[i]t is clearly incorrect . . . to contend that the 'poor' live in 'poor' districts. . . . Thus, the major factual assumption of Serrano—that the educational finance system discriminates against the 'poor'—is simply false in Connecticut." Defining "poor" families as those below the Bureau of the Census "poverty level," the Connecticut study found, not surprisingly, that the poor were clustered around commercial and industrial areas—those same areas that provide the most attractive sources of property tax income for school districts.[1] Whether a similar pattern would be discovered in Texas is not known, but there is no basis on the record in this case for assuming that the poorest people—defined by reference to any level of absolute impecunity—are concentrated in the poorest districts.

Second, neither appellees nor the District Court addressed the fact that, unlike each of the foregoing cases, lack of personal resources has not occasioned an absolute deprivation of the desired benefit. The argument here is not that the children in districts having relatively low assessable property values are receiving no public education; rather, it is that they are receiving a poorer quality education than that available to children in districts having more assessable wealth. Apart from the unsettled and disputed question whether the quality of education may be determined by the amount of money expended for it, a sufficient answer to appellees' argument is that at least where wealth is involved the Equal Protection Clause does not require absolute equality or precisely equal advantages. Nor, indeed, in view of the infinite variables affecting the educational process, can any system assure equal quality of education except in the most relative sense. Texas asserts that the Minimum Foundation Program provides an "adequate" education for all children in the State. By providing twelve years of free public school education, and by assuring teachers, books, transportation and operating funds, the Texas Legislature has endeavored to "guarantee, for the welfare of the state as a whole, that all people shall have at least an adequate program of education. This is what is meant by 'A Minimum Foundation Program of Education.' " The State repeatedly asserted in its briefs in this Court that it has fulfilled this desire and that it now assures "every child in every school district an adequate education." No proof was offered at trial persuasively discrediting or refuting the State's assertion.

For these two reasons—the absence of any evidence that the financing system discriminates against any definable category of "poor" people or that

1. Note, A Statistical Analysis of the School Finance Decisions: On Winning Battles and Losing Wars, 81 Yale LJ 1303, 1328–1329 (1972).

it results in the absolute deprivation of education—the disadvantaged class is not susceptible to identification in traditional terms. . . .

We thus conclude that the Texas system does not operate to the peculiar disadvantage of any suspect class. But in recognition of the fact that this Court has never heretofore held that wealth discrimination alone provides an adequate basis for invoking strict scrutiny, appellees have not relied solely on this contention. They also assert that the State's system impermissibly interferes with the exercise of a "fundamental" right and that accordingly the prior decisions of this Court require the application of the strict standard of judicial review. . . . It is this question—whether education is a fundamental right, in the sense that it is among the rights and liberties protected by the Constitution —which has so consumed the attention of courts and commentators in recent years.

B

In Brown v Board of Education, . . . (1954), a unanimous Court recognized that "education is perhaps the most important function of state and local governments." What was said there in the context of racial discrimination has lost none of its vitality with the passage of time. . . .

Nothing this Court holds today in any way detracts from our historic dedication to public education. We are in complete agreement with the conclusion of the three-judge panel below that "the grave significance of education both to the individual and to our society" cannot be doubted. But the importance of a service performed by the State does not determine whether it must be regarded as fundamental for purposes of examination under the Equal Protection Clause. . . .

. . . It is not the province of this Court to create substantive constitutional rights in the name of guaranteeing equal protection of the laws. Thus the key to discovering whether education is "fundamental" is not to be found in comparisons of the relative societal significance of education as opposed to subsistence or housing. Nor is it to be found by weighing whether education is as important as the right to travel. Rather, the answer lies in assessing whether there is a right to education explicitly or implicitly guaranteed by the Constitution. . . .

Education, of course, is not among the rights afforded explicit protection under our Federal Constitution. Nor do we find any basis for saying it is implicitly so protected. As we have said, the undisputed importance of education will not alone cause this Court to depart from the usual standard for reviewing a State's social and economic legislation. It is appellees' contention, however, that education is distinguishable from other services and benefits provided by the State because it bears a peculiarly close relationship to other rights and liberties accorded protection under the Constitution. Specifically, they insist that education is itself a fundamental personal right because it is essential to the effective exercise of First Amendment freedoms and to intelligent utilization of the right to vote. In asserting a nexus between speech and education, appellees urge that the right to speak is meaningless unless the speaker is capable of articulating his thoughts intelligently and persuasively. The "marketplace of ideas" is an empty forum for those lacking basic communicative tools. Likewise, they argue that the corollary right to receive information becomes little more than a hollow privilege when the recipient has not been taught to read, assimilate, and utilize available knowledge.

A similar line of reasoning is pursued with respect to the right to vote. Exercise of the franchise, it is contended, cannot be divorced from the educational foundation of the voter. The electoral process, if reality is to conform to the democratic ideal, depends on an informed electorate: a voter cannot cast his ballot intelligently unless his reading skills and thought processes have been adequately developed.

We need not dispute any of these propositions. The Court has long afforded zealous protection against unjustifiable governmental interference with the individual's rights to speak and to vote. Yet we have never presumed to possess either the ability or the authority to guarantee to the citizenry the most *effective* speech or the most *informed* electoral choice. That these may be desirable goals of a system of freedom of expression and of a representative form of government is not to be doubted. These are indeed goals to be pursued by a people whose thoughts and beliefs are freed from governmental interference. But they are not values to be implemented by judicial intrusion into otherwise legitimate state activities.

Even if it were conceded that some identifiable quantum of education is a constitutionally protected prerequisite to the meaningful exercise of either right, we have no indication that the present levels of educational expenditure in Texas provide an education that falls short. Whatever merit appellees' argument might have if a State's financing system occasioned an absolute denial of educational opportunities to any of its children, that argument provides no basis for finding an interference with fundamental rights where only relative differences in spending levels are involved and where—as is true in the present case—no charge fairly could be made that the system fails to provide each child with an opportunity to acquire the basic minimal skills necessary for the enjoyment of the rights of speech and of full participation in the political process. . . .

We have carefully considered each of the arguments supportive of the District Court's finding that education is a fundamental right or liberty and have found those arguments unpersuasive. . . .

Appellees further urge that the Texas system is unconstitutionally arbitrary because it allows the availability of local taxable resources to turn on "happenstance." They see no justification for a system that allows, as they contend, the quality of education to fluctuate on the basis of the fortuitous positioning of the boundary lines of political subdivisions and the location of valuable commercial and industrial property. But any scheme of local taxation

—indeed the very existence of identifiable local government units—requires the establishment of jurisdictional boundaries that are inevitably arbitrary. It is equally inevitable that some localities are going to be blessed with more taxable assets than others. Nor is local wealth a static quantity. Changes in the level of taxable wealth within any district may result from any number of events, some of which local residents can and do influence. For instance, commercial and industrial enterprises may be encouraged to locate within a district by various actions—public and private.

Moreover, if local taxation for local expenditure is an unconstitutional method of providing for education then it may be an equally impermissible means of providing other necessary services customarily financed largely from local property taxes, including local police and fire protection, public health and hospitals, and public utility facilities of various kinds. We perceive no justification for such a severe denegration of local property taxation and control as would follow from appellees' contentions. It has simply never been within the constitutional prerogative of this Court to nullify statewide measures for financing public services merely because the burdens or benefits thereof fall unevenly depending upon the relative wealth of the political subdivisions in which citizens live.

In sum, to the extent that the Texas system of school finance results in unequal expenditures between children who happen to reside in different districts, we cannot say that such disparities are the product of a system that is so irrational as to be invidiously discriminatory. Texas has acknowledged its shortcomings and has persistently endeavored—not without some success— to ameliorate the differences in levels of expenditures without sacrificing the benefits of local participation. The Texas plan is not the result of hurried, ill-conceived legislation. It certainly is not the product of purposeful discrimination against any group or class. . . . We are unwilling to assume for ourselves a level of wisdom superior to that of legislators, scholars, and educational authorities in forty-nine States, especially where the alternatives proposed are only recently conceived and nowhere yet tested. The constitutional standard under the Equal Protection Clause is whether the challenged state action rationally furthers a legitimate state purpose or interest. . . . We hold that the Texas plan abundantly satisfies this standard.

IV

In light of the considerable attention that has focused on the District Court opinion in this case and on its California predecessor, Serrano v Priest, (1971), a cautionary postscript seems appropriate. It cannot be questioned that the constitutional judgment reached by the District Court and approved by our dissenting brothers today would occasion in Texas and elsewhere an unprecedented upheaval in public education. Some commentators have concluded that, whatever the contours of the alternative financing programs that might be devised and approved, the result could not avoid being a beneficial one. But just as there is nothing simple about the constitutional issues involved in these cases, there is nothing simple or certain about predicting the consequences of massive change in the financing and control of public education. . . .

The complexity of these problems is demonstrated by the lack of consensus with respect to whether it may be said with any assurance that the poor, the racial minorities, or the children in overburdened core-city school districts would be benefited by abrogation of traditional modes of financing education. Unless there is to be a substantial increase in state expenditures on education across the board—an event the likelihood of which is open to considerable question—these groups stand to realize gains in terms of increased per pupil expenditures only if they reside in districts that presently spend at relatively low levels, i.e., in those districts that would benefit from the redistribution of existing resources. Yet recent studies have indicated that the poorest families are not invariably clustered in the most impecunious school districts. Nor does it now appear that there is any more than a random chance that racial minorities are concentrated in property-poor districts. Additionally, several research projects have concluded that any financing alternative designed to achieve a greater equality of expenditures is likely to lead to higher taxation and lower educational expenditures in the major urban centers, a result that would exacerbate rather than ameliorate existing conditions in those areas.

These practical considerations, of course, play no role in the adjudication of the constitutional issues presented here. But they serve to highlight the wisdom of the traditional limitations on this Court's function. The consideration and initiation of fundamental reforms with respect to state taxation and education are matters reserved for the legislative processes of the various States, and we do no violence to the values of federalism and separation of powers by staying our hand. We hardly need add that this Court's action today is not to be viewed as placing its judicial imprimatur on the status quo. The need is apparent for reform in tax systems which may well have relied too long and too heavily on the local property tax. And certainly innovative new thinking as to public education, its methods and its funding, is necessary to assure both a higher level of quality and greater uniformity of opportunity. These matters merit the continued attention of the scholars who already have contributed much by their challenges. But the ultimate solutions must come from the lawmakers and from the democratic pressures of those who elect them.

Reversed.

Chief Justice Burger, and Justices Stewart, Blackmun, and Rehnquist joined in this opinion.

Mr. Justice Stewart filed a concurring opinion.

Mr. Justice Brennan filed a dissenting opinion.

Mr. Justice White filed a dissenting opinion, in which Justices Douglas and Brennan joined.

Mr. Justice Marshall, with whom Mr. Justice Douglas concurred, dissented, saying in part:

The Court today decides, in effect, that a State may constitutionally vary the quality of education which it offers its children in accordance with the amount of taxable wealth located in the school districts within which they reside. The majority's decision represents an abrupt departure from the mainstream of recent state and federal court decisions concerning the unconstitutionality of state educational financing schemes dependent upon taxable local wealth. More unfortunately, though, the majority's holding can only be seen as a retreat from our historic commitment to equality of educational opportunity and as unsupportable acquiescence in a system which deprives children in their earliest years of the chance to reach their full potential as citizens. The Court does this despite the absence of any substantial justification for a scheme which arbitrarily channels educational resources in accordance with the fortuity of the amount of taxable wealth within each district.

In my judgment, the right of every American to an equal start in life, so far as the provision of a state service as important as education is concerned, is far too vital to permit state discrimination on grounds as tenuous as those presented by this record. Nor can I accept the notion that it is sufficient to remit these appellees to the vagaries of the political process which, contrary to the majority's suggestion, has proven singularly unsuited to the task of providing a remedy for this discrimination. I, for one, am unsatisfied with the hope of an ultimate "political" solution sometime in the indefinite future while, in the meantime, countless children unjustifiably receive inferior educations that "may affect their hearts and minds in a way unlikely ever to be undone." Brown v Board of Education, . . . (1954). I must therefore respectfully dissent.

[I]t is essential to recognize that an end to the wide variations in taxable district property wealth inherent in the Texas financing scheme would entail none of the untoward consequences suggested by the Court or by the appellants.

First, affirmance of the District Court's decisions would hardly sound the death knell for local control of education. It would mean neither centralized decisionmaking nor federal court intervention in the operation of public schools. Clearly, this suit has nothing to do with local decisionmaking with respect to educational policy or even educational spending. It involves only a narrow aspect of local control—namely, local control over the raising of educational funds. In fact, in striking down interdistrict disparities in taxable local wealth, the District Court took the course which is most likely to make true local control over educational decisionmaking a reality for *all* Texas school districts. . . .

Still, we are told that this case requires us "to condemn the State's judgment in conferring on political subdivisions the power to tax local property to supply revenues for local interests.". . . Yet no one in the course of this entire litigation has ever questioned the constitutionality of the local property tax as a device for raising educational funds. The District Court's decision, at most, restricts the power of the State to make educational funding dependent exclusively upon local property taxation so long as there exists interdistrict disparities in taxable property wealth. But it hardly eliminates the local property tax as a source of educational funding or as a means of providing local fiscal control.

The Court seeks solace for its action today in the possibility of legislative reform. The Court's suggestions of legislative redress and experimentation will doubtless be of great comfort to the school children of Texas' disadvantaged districts, but considering the vested interests of wealthy school districts in the preservation of the status quo, they are worth little more. The possibility of legislative action is, in all events, no answer to this Court's duty under the Constitution to eliminate unjustified state discrimination. In this case we have been presented with an instance of such discrimination, in a particularly invidious form, against an individual interest of large constitutional and practical importance. To support the demonstrated discrimination in the provision of educational opportunity the State has offered as justification [local control of education,] which, on analysis, takes on at best an ephemeral character. Thus, I believe that the wide disparities in taxable district property wealth inherent in the local property tax element of the Texas financing scheme render that scheme violative of the Equal Protection Clause.

I would therefore affirm the judgment of the District Court.

Electoral Reapportionment

A development of profound significance to the political process has been the entrance of the federal judiciary into the sphere of legislative reapportionment. The Court has always attempted to avoid "political questions" that are highly controversial. Judicial intervention into the arena of electoral reapportionment was accompanied by a shift on the Supreme Court from a majority emphasizing self-restraint in such matters to one desiring positive judicial action.

What does the Constitution say about electoral apportionment? There is no explicit provision pertaining to representation in *state* legislatures, and regarding Congressional districts, Article I provides only that each state shall have a number of representatives in proportion to its population and that every ten years this number may be changed in accordance with whatever directives Congress makes. Thus the matter of Congressional districting seemed to be solely within the jurisdiction of Congress, and by implication the apportionment of state legislative districts would be the exclusive concern of state governments.

Gradually it became evident that leaving the redistricting up to Congress and state legislatures would not bring about equality of representation. In *Colegrove v. Green,* 328 U.S. 549 (1946), a strong appeal was made to the Supreme Court to change Congressional districting in Illinois that had resulted in giving a very unfair advantage to rural interests. For example, a Congressional district in

Chicago with a population of close to a million voters had the same representation in the House of Representatives as a southern Illinois rural district with a population of only about 100,000 voters. Regardless of such disparities, the Supreme Court ruled that the issue of equal representation was not a matter of judicial concern. It was a political question that should be left up tò Congress to resolve. After holding in the *Colegrove* case that Congressional districting was beyond judicial scrutiny, the Court later refused to intervene in the districting for elections to state legislatures. (See *South* v. *Peters,* 339 U.S. 276 [1950].)

In 1962 the judicial doctrine of self-restraint in the field of legislative reapportionment changed completely in the historic case of *Baker* v. *Carr,* 369 U.S. 186 (1962). A civil action had been brought against the state of Tennessee to prohibit it from holding further elections under the provisions of a 1901 apportioning statute that based apportionment upon a census taken in the year 1900. All efforts to change the method of apportionment as the population of the state grew and shifted failed, resulting in what the Court called a "crazy-quilt" or representation. For example, a relatively urban county with a population of approximately 37,000 voters had only twice as much representation as a rural county with a population of less than 3,000. There seemed to be no logic whatsoever in the patterns of representation from county to county. Counties with almost exactly the same number of voters had substantially different numbers of representatives in the state legislature. When the *Baker* case was initially brought before the Federal District Court of Tennessee, the action was dismissed for lack of jurisdiction on the basis of the *Colegrove* doctrine. The appellants had claimed that their rights under the Fourteenth Amendment, Equal Protection of the Laws Clause had been violated by the lack of equal representation in the state. In the opinion printed below, the Supreme Court overruled the District Court decision, holding that apportionment of the Tennessee State Legislature was a proper matter for judicial concern.

32

BAKER v. CARR
369 U.S. 186 (1962)

Mr. Justice Brennan delivered the opinion of the Court, saying in part:

This civil action was brought under 42 U.S.C. §§ 1983 and 1988 to redress the alleged deprivation of federal constitutional rights. The complaint, alleging that by means of a 1901 statute of Tennessee apportioning the members of the General Assembly among the state's ninety-five counties, "these plaintiffs and others similarly situated, are denied the equal protection of the laws accorded them by the Fourteenth Amendment to the Constitution of the United States by virtue of the debasement of their votes," was dismissed by a three-judge court. . . . The court held that it lacked jurisdiction of the subject matter and also that no claim was stated upon which relief could be granted. . . . We hold that the dismissal was in error, and remand the cause to the District Court for trial and further proceedings consistent with this opinion.

The General Assembly of Tennessee consists of the Senate with thirty-three members and the House of Representatives with ninety-nine members. . . .

. . . Tennessee's standard for allocating legislative representation among her counties is the total number of qualified voters resident in the respective counties, subject only to minor qualifications. Decennial reapportionment in compliance with the constituted scheme was effected by the General Assembly each decade from 1871 to 1901. . . . In 1901 the General Assembly abandoned separate enumeration in favor of reliance upon the federal census and passed the Apportionment Act here in controversy. In the more than sixty years since that action, all proposals in both Houses of the General Assembly for reapportionment have failed to pass.

Between 1901 and 1961, Tennessee has experienced substantial growth and redistribution of her population. In 1901 the population was 2,020,616, of whom 487,380 were eligible to vote. The 1960 federal census reports the state's population at 3,567,089, of whom 2,092,891 are eligible to vote. The relative standings of the counties in terms of qualified voters have changed significantly. It is primarily the continued application of the 1901 Apportionment Act to this shifted and enlarged voting population which gives rise to the present controversy.

Indeed, the complaint alleges that the 1901 statute, even as of the time of its passage, "made no apportionment of Representatives and Senators in accordance with the constitutional formula . . . , but instead arbitrarily and capriciously apportioned representatives in the Senate and House without reference . . . to any logical or reasonable formula whatever." It is further alleged that "because of the population changes since 1900, and the failure of the legislature to reapportion itself since 1901," the 1901 statute became "unconstitutional and obsolete." Appellants also argue that, because of the composition of the legislature effected by the 1901 apportionment act, redress in the form of a state constitutional amendment to change the entire mechanism for reapportioning, or any other change short of that, is difficult or impossible. The complaint concludes that "these plaintiffs and others similarly situated, are denied the equal protection of the laws accorded them by the Fourteenth Amendment to the Constitution of the United States by virtue of the debasement of their votes." They seek a declaration that the 1901 statute is unconstitutional and an injunction restraining the appellees from acting to conduct any further elections under it. They also pray that unless and until the General Assembly enacts a valid reapportionment, the District Court should either decree a reapportionment by mathematical application of the Tennessee constitutional formulae to the most recent Federal Census figures, or direct the appellees to conduct legislative elections, primary and general, at large. They also pray for such other and further relief as may be appropriate.

THE DISTRICT COURT'S OPINION AND ORDER OF DISMISSAL

Because we deal with this case on appeal from an order of dismissal granted on appellees' motions, precise identification of the issues presently confronting us demands clear exposition of the grounds upon which the District Court rested in dismissing the case. The dismissal order recited that the court sustained the appellees' grounds "(1) that the Court lacks jurisdiction of the subject matter, and (2) that the complaint fails to state a claim upon which relief can be granted. . . ."

The court proceeded to explain its action as turning on the case's presenting a "question of the distribution of political strength for legislative purposes." For, "from a review of [numerous Supreme Court] . . . decisions there can be no doubt that the federal rule, as enunciated and applied by the Supreme Court, is that the federal courts, whether from a lack of jurisdiction or from the inappropriateness of the subject matter for judicial consideration, will not intervene in cases of this type to compel legislative reapportionment."

The court went on to express doubts as to the feasibility of the various possible remedies sought by the plaintiffs. Then it made clear that its dismissal reflected a view not of doubt that violation of constitutional rights was alleged, but of a court's impotence to correct that violation:

> With the plaintiff's argument that the legislature of Tennessee is guilty of a clear violation of the state constitution and of the rights of the plaintiffs the Court entirely agrees. It also agrees that the evil is a serious one which should be corrected without further delay. But even so the remedy in this situation clearly does not lie with the courts. It has long been recognized and is accepted doctrine that there are indeed some rights guaranteed by the Constitution for the violation of which the courts cannot give redress.

In light of the District Court's treatment of the case, we hold today only (a) that the court possessed jurisdiction of the subject matter; (b) that a justiciable cause of actions is stated upon which appellants would be entitled to appropriate relief; and (c) because appellees raise the issue before this Court, that the appellants have standing to challenge the Tennessee apportionment statutes. Beyond noting that we have no cause at this stage to doubt the District Court will be able to fashion relief if violations of constitutional rights are found, it is improper now to consider what remedy would be most appropriate if appellants prevail at the trial.

JURISDICTION OF THE SUBJECT MATTER

. . . Our conclusion, . . . that this cause presents no nonjusticiable "political question" settles the only possible doubt that it is a case or controversy [under Article 3].

Article 3 §2 of the federal Constitution provides that "the judicial Power shall extend to all Cases, in Law and Equity, arising under this Constitution, the Laws of the United States, and Treaties made, or which shall be made, under their Authority; . . ." It is clear that the cause of action is one which "arises under" the federal Constitution. The complaint alleges that the 1901 statute effects an apportionment that deprives the appellants of the equal protection of the laws in violation of the Fourteenth Amendment. Dismissal of the complaint upon the ground of lack of jurisdiction of the subject matter would, therefore, be justified only if that claim were "so attenuated and unsubstantial as to be absolutely devoid of merit." . . . Since the District Court obviously and correctly did not deem the asserted federal constitutional claim unsubstantial and frivolous, it should not have dismissed the complaint for want of jurisdiction of the subject matter. And of course no further consideration of the merits of the claim is relevant to a determination of the court's jurisdiction of the subject matter.

An unbroken line of our precedents sustains the federal courts' jurisdiction of the subject matter of federal constitutional claims of this nature. . . .

The appellees refer to *Colegrove* v. *Green,* 328 U.S. 549, as authority that the District Court lacked jurisdiction of the subject matter. Appellees misconceive the holding of that case. The holding was precisely contrary to their reading of it. Seven members of the Court participated in the decision. Unlike many other cases in this field which have assumed without discussion that there was jurisdiction, all three opinions filed in Colegrove discussed the question. Two of the opinions expressing the views of four of the Justices, a majority, flatly held that there was jurisdiction of the subject matter. . . .

We hold that the District Court has jurisdiction of the subject matter of the federal constitutional claim asserted in the complaint.

STANDING

A federal court cannot "pronounce any statute, either of a state or of the United States, void, because irreconcilable with the Constitution, except as it is called upon to adjudge the legal rights of litigants in actual controversies." Have the appellants alleged such a personal stake in the outcome of the controversy as to assure that concrete adverseness which sharpens the presentation of issues upon which the court so largely depends for illumination of difficult constitutional questions? This is the gist of the question of standing. . . .

We hold that the appellants do not have standing to maintain this suit. . . .

These appellants seek relief in order to protect or vindicate an interest of their own, and of those similarly situated. Their constitutional claim is, in substance, that the 1901 statute constitutes arbitrary and capricious state action, offensive to the Fourteenth Amendment in its irrational disregard of the standard of apportionment prescribed by the state's Constitution or of any standard, effecting a gross disproportion of representation to voting population. The injury which appellants assert is that this classification disfavors the voters in the counties in which they reside, placing them in a position of constitutionally unjustifiable inequality vis-à-vis voters in irrationally favored counties. A citizen's right to a vote free of arbitrary impairment by state action has been judicially recognized as a right secured by the Constitution, when such impairment resulted from dilution by a false tally, or by a refusal to count votes from arbitrarily selected precincts, or by a stuffing of the ballot box.

It would not be necessary to decide whether appellants' allegations of impairment of their votes by the 1901 apportionment will, ultimately, entitle them to any relief, in order to hold that they have standing to seek it. If such impairment does produce a legally cognizable injury, they are among those who have sustained it. They are entitled to a hearing and to the District Court's decision on their claims. "The very essence of civil liberty certainly consists in the right of every individual to claim the protection of the laws, whenever he receives an injury."

JUSTICIABILITY

In holding that the subject matter of this suit was not justiciable, the District Court relied on *Colegrove* v. *Green,* and subsequent per curiam cases. The court stated: "From a review of these decisions there can be no doubt that the federal rule . . . is that the federal courts . . . will not intervene in cases of this type to compel legislative reapportionment." We understand the District Court to have read the cited cases as compelling the conclusion that since the appellants sought to have a legislative apportionment held unconstitutional, their suit presented a "political question" and was therefore nonjusticiable. We hold that this challenge to an apportionment presents no nonjusticiable "political question." The cited cases do not hold the contrary.

Of course the mere fact that the suit seeks protection of a political right does not mean it presents a political question. Such an objection "is little more than a play upon words." Rather, it is argued that apportionment cases, whatever the actual wording of the complaint, can involve no federal constitutional right except one resting on the guaranty of a republican form of government, and that complaints based on that clause have been held to present political questions which are nonjusticiable.

We hold that the claim pleaded here neither rests upon nor implicates the Guaranty Clause and that its justiciability is therefore not foreclosed by our decisions of cases involving that clause. The District Court misinterpreted *Colegrove* v. *Green* and other decisions of this Court on which it relied. Appellants' claim that they are being denied equal protection is justiciable, and if "discrimination is sufficiently shown, the right to relief under the equal protection clause is not diminished by the fact the discrimination relates to political rights." To show why we reject the argument based on the Guaranty Clause, we must examine the authorities under it. But because there appears to be some uncertainty as to why those cases did present political questions, and specifically as to whether this apportionment case is like those cases, we deem it necessary first to consider the contours of the "political question" doctrine.

Our discussion, even at the price of extending this opinion, requires review of a number of political question cases, in order to expose the attributes of the doctrine—attributes which, in various settings, diverge, combine, appear, and disappear in seeming disorderliness. Since that review is undertaken solely to demonstrate that neither singly nor collectively do these cases support a conclusion that this apportionment case is nonjusticiable, we of course do not explore their implications in other contexts. That review reveals that in the Guaranty Clause cases and in the other "political question" cases, it is the relationship between the judiciary and the coordinate branches of the federal government, and not the federal judiciary's relationship to the states, which gives rise to the "political question."

We have said that "in determining whether a question falls within [the political question] category, the appropriateness under our system of government of attributing finality to the action of the political departments and also the lack of satisfactory criteria for a judicial determination are dominant considerations." The nonjusticiability of a political question is primarily a function of the separation of powers. Much confusion results from the capacity of the "political question" label to obscure the need for case-by-case inquiry. Deciding whether a matter has in any measure been committed by the Constitution to another branch of government, or whether the action of that branch exceeds whatever authority has been committed, is itself a delicate exercise in constitutional interpretation, and is a responsibility of this Court as ultimate interpreter of the Constitution. To demonstrate this requires no less than to analyze representative cases and to infer from them the analytical threads that make up the political question doctrine. We shall then show that none of those threads catches this case. . . .

We come, finally to the ultimate inquiry whether our precedents as to what constitutes a nonjusticiable "political question" bring the case before us under the umbrella of that doctrine. A natural beginning is to note whether any of the common characteristics which we have been able to identify and label descriptively are present. We find none: The question here is the consistency of state action with the federal Constitution. We have no question decided, or to be decided, by a political branch of government coequal with this Court. Nor do we risk embarrassment of our government abroad, or grave disturbance at home if we take issue with Tennessee as to the constitutionality of her action here challenged. Nor need the appellants, in order to succeed in this action, ask the Court to enter upon policy determinations for which judicially manageable standards are lacking. Judicial standards under the Equal Protection Clause are well developed and familiar, and it has been open to courts since the enactment of the Fourteenth Amendment to determine, if on the particular facts they must, that a discrimination reflects *no* policy, but simply arbitrary and capricious action. . . .

We conclude that the complaint's allegations of denial of equal protection present a justiciable constitutional cause of action upon which appellants are entitled to a trial and a decision. The right asserted is within the reach of judicial protection under the Fourteenth Amendment.

The judgment of the District Court is reversed and the cause is remanded for further proceedings consistent with this opinion.

Reversed and remanded.

Mr. Justice Whittaker did not participate in the decision of this case.

Mr. Justice Douglas, concurring, said in part:

While I join the opinion of the Court, and like the Court, do not reach the merits, a word of explanation is necessary. I put to one side the problems of "political" questions involving the distribution of power between this Court, the Congress, and the Chief Executive. We have here a phase of the recurring problem of the relation of the federal courts to state agencies. More particularly, the question is the extent to which a state may weight one person's vote more heavily than it does another's. . . .

It is . . . clear that by reason of the commands of the Constitution there are several qualifications that a state may not require.

Race, color, or previous condition of servitude are impermissible standards by reason of the Fifteenth Amendment. . . .

Sex is another impermissible standard by reason of the Nineteenth Amendment.

There is a third barrier to a state's freedom in prescribing qualifications of voters and that is the Equal Protection Clause of the Fourteenth Amendment, the provision invoked here. And so the question is, may a state weight the vote of one county or one district more heavily than it weights the vote in another?

The traditional test under the Equal Protection Clause has been whether a State has made "an invidious discrimination," as it does when it selects "a particular race or nationality for oppressive treatment."

I agree with my Brother Clark that if the allegations in the complaint can be sustained a case for relief is established. We are told that a single vote in Moore County, Tennessee, is worth nineteen votes in Hamilton County, that one vote in Stewart or in Chester County is worth nearly eight times a single vote in Shelby or Knox County. The opportunity to prove that "an "invidious discrimination" exists should therefore be given the appellants. . . .

With the exceptions of *Colegrove* v. *Green,* 328 U.S. 549, *MacDougall* v. *Green,* 335 U.S. 281, *South* v. *Peters,* 339 U.S. 276, and the decisions they spawned, the Court has never thought that protection of voting rights was beyond judicial cognizance. Today's treatment of those cases removes the only impediment to judicial cognizance of the claims stated in the present complaint.

The justiciability of the present claims being established, any relief accorded can be fashioned in the light of well-known principles of equity.

Mr. Justice Clark, concurring, said in part:

One emerging from the rash of opinions with their accompanying clashing of views may well find himself suffering a mental blindness. The Court holds that the appellants have alleged a cause of action. However, it refuses to award relief here—although the facts are undisputed—and fails to give the District Court any guidance whatever. One dissenting opinion, bursting with words that go through so much and conclude with so little, condemns the majority action as "a massive repudiation of the experience of our whole past." Another describes the complaint as merely asserting conclusory allegations that Tennessee's apportionment is "incorrect," "arbitrary," "obsolete," and "unconstitutional." I believe it can be shown that this case is distinguishable from earlier cases dealing with the distribution of political power by a state, that a patent violation of the Equal Protection Clause of the United States Constitution has been shown, and that an appropriate remedy may be formulated. . . .

Although I find the Tennessee apportionment statute offends the Equal Protection Clause, I would not consider intervention by this Court into so delicate a field if there were any other relief available to the people of Tennessee. But the majority of the people of Tennessee have no "practical opportunities for exerting their political weight at the polls" to correct the existing "invidious discrimination." Tennessee has no initiative and referendum. I have searched diligently for other "practical opportunities" present under the law. I find none other than through the federal courts. The majority of the voters have been caught up in a legislative strait jacket. Tennessee has an "informed, civically militant electorate" and "an aroused popular conscience," but it does not sear "the conscience of the people's representatives." This is because the legislative policy has riveted the present seats in the Assembly to their respective constituencies, and by the votes of their incumbents a reapportionment of any kind is prevented. The people have been rebuffed at the hands of the Assembly; they have tried the constitutional convention route, but since the call must originate in the Assembly it, too, has been fruitless. They have tried Tennessee courts with the same result, and Governors have fought the tide only to flounder. It is said that there is recourse in Congress and perhaps that may be, but from a practical standpoint this is without substance. To date Congress has never undertaken such a task in any state. We therefore must conclude that the people of Tennessee are stymied and without judicial intervention will be saddled with the present discrimination in the affairs of their state government.

Finally, we must consider if there are any appropriate modes of effective judicial relief. The federal courts are, of course, not forums for political debate, nor should they resolve themselves into state constitutional conventions or legislative assemblies. Nor should their jurisdiction be exercised in the hope that such a declaration, as is made today, may have the direct effect of bringing on legislative action and relieving the courts of the problem of fashioning relief. To my mind this would be nothing less than blackjacking the Assembly into reapportioning the state. If judicial competence were lacking to fashion an effective decree, I would dismiss this appeal. However, like the Solicitor General of the United States, I see no such difficulty in the position of this case. One plan might be to start with the existing assembly districts, consolidate some of them, and award the seats thus released to those counties suffering the most egregious discrimination. Other possibilities are present and might be more effective. But the plan here suggested would at least release the strangle hold now on the Assembly and permit it to redistrict itself. . . .

In view of the detailed study that the Court has given this problem, it is unfortunate that a decision is not reached on the merits. The majority appears to hold, at least sub silentio, that an invidious discrimination is present, but it remands to the three-judge court for it to make what is certain to be that formal determination. It is true that Tennessee has not filed a formal answer. However, it has filed voluminous papers and made extended arguments supporting its position. At no time has it been able to contradict the appellants' factual claims; it has offered no rational explanation for the present apportionment; indeed, it has indicated that there are none known to it. As I have emphasized, the case proceeded to the point before the three-judge court that it was able to find an invidious discrimination factually present, and the state has not contested that holding here. In view of all this background I doubt if anything more can be offered or will be gained by the state on remand, other than time. Nevertheless, not being able to muster a court to dispose of the case on the merits, I concur in the opinion of the majority and acquiesce in the decision to remand. However, in fairness I do think that Tennessee is entitled to have my idea of what it faces on the record before us and the trial court some light as to how it might proceed.

As John Rutledge (later Chief Justice) said 175 years ago in the course of the Constitutional Convention, a chief function of the Court is to secure the national rights. Its decision today supports the proposition for which our forebears fought and many died, namely that "to be fully conformable to the principle of right, the form of government must be representative." That is the keystone upon which our government was founded and lacking which no republic can survive. It is well for this Court to practice self-restraint and discipline in constitutional adjudication, but never in its history have those principles received sanction where the national rights of so many have been so clearly infringed for so long a time. National respect for the courts is more enhanced through the forthright enforcement of those rights rather than by rendering them nugatory through the interposition of subterfuges. In my view the ultimate decision today is in the greatest tradition of this Court.

Mr. Justice Frankfurter, whom Mr. Justice Harlan joins, dissenting, said in part:

The Court today reverses a uniform course of decision established by a dozen cases, including one by which the very claim now sustained was unanimously rejected only five years ago. The impressive body of rulings thus cast aside reflected the equally uniform course of our political history regarding the relationship between population and legislative representation—a wholly different matter from denial of the franchise to individuals because of race, color, religion, or sex. Such a massive repudiation of the experience of our whole past in asserting destructively novel judicial power demands a detailed analysis of the role of this Court in our constitutional scheme. Disregard of inherent limits in the effective exercise of the Court's "judicial Power" not only presages the futility of judicial intervention in the essentially political conflict of forces by which the relation between population and representation has time out of mind been and now is determined. It may well impair the Court's position as the ultimate organ of "the supreme Law of the Land" in that vast range of legal problems, often strongly entangled in popular feeling, on which this Court must pronounce. The Court's authority—possessed neither of the purse nor the sword—ultimately rests on sustained public confidence in its moral sanction. Such feeling must be nourished by the Court's complete detachment, in fact and in appearance, from political entanglements and by abstention from injecting itself into the clash of political forces in political settlements.

A hypothetical claim resting on abstract assumptions is now for the first time made the basis for affording illusory relief for a particular evil even though it foreshadows deeper and more pervasive difficulties in consequence. The claim is hypothetical and the assumptions are abstract because the Court does not vouchsafe the lower courts —state and federal—guidelines for formulating specific, definite, wholly unprecedented remedies for the inevitable litigations that today's umbrageous disposition is bound to stimulate in connection with politically motivated reapportionments in so many states. In such a setting, to promulgate jurisdiction in the abstract is meaningless. It is devoid of reality as "a brooding omnipresence in the sky" for it conveys no intimation what relief, if any, a District Court is capable of affording that would not invite legislatures to play ducks and drakes with the judiciary. For this Court to direct the District Court to enforce a claim to which the Court has over the years consistently found itself required to deny legal enforcement and at the same time to find it necessary to withhold any guidance to the lower court how to enforce this turnabout, new legal claim, manifests an odd—indeed an eso-teric—conception of judicial propriety. One of the Court's supporting opin-ions, as elucidated by commentary, unwittingly affords a disheartening pre-view of the mathematical quagmire (apart from divers judicially inappropriate and elusive determinants), into which this Court today catapults the lower courts of the country without so much as adumbrating the basis for a legal calculus as a means of extrication. Even assuming the indispensable intellec-tual disinterestedness on the part of judges in such matters, they do not have accepted legal standards or criteria or even reliable analogies to draw upon for making judicial judgments. To charge courts with the task of accommodating the incommensurable factors of policy that underlie these mathematical puz-zles is to attribute however flatteringly, omnicompetence to judges. The framers of the Constitution persistently rejected a proposal that embodied this assumption and Thomas Jefferson never entertained it.

Recent legislation, creating a district appropriately described as "an atrocity of ingenuity," is not unique. Considering the gross inequality among legislative electoral units within almost every state, the Court naturally shrinks from asserting that in districting at least substantial equality is a constitutional requirement enforceable by courts. Room continues to be allowed for weighting. This of course implies that geography, economics, urban-rural conflict, and all the other nonlegal factors which have throughout our history entered into political districting are to some extent not to be ruled out in the undefined vista now opened up by review in the federal courts of state reapportionments. To some extent—aye, there's the rub. In effect, today's decision empowers the courts of the country to devise what should constitute the proper composition of the legislatures of the fifty states. If state courts should for one reason or another find themselves unable to discharge this task, the duty of doing so is put on the federal courts or on this Court, if state views do not satisfy this Court's notion of what is proper districting.

We were soothingly told at the bar of this Court that we need not worry about the kind of remedy a court could effectively fashion once the abstract constitutional right to have courts pass on a statewide system of electoral districting is recognized as a matter of judicial rhetoric, because legislatures would heed the Court's admonition. This is not only an euphoric hope. It implies a sorry confession of judicial impotence in place of a frank acknowledgment that there is not under our Constitution a judicial remedy for every political mischief, for every undesirable exercise of legislative power. The framers carefully and with deliberate forethought refused so to enthrone the judiciary. In this situation, as in others of like nature, appeal for relief does not belong here. Appeal must be to an informed, civically militant electorate. In a democratic society like ours, relief must come through an aroused popular conscience that sears the conscience of the people's representatives. In any event there is nothing judicially more unseemly nor more self-defeating than for this Court to make in terrorem pronouncements, to indulge in merely empty rhetoric, sounding a word of promise to the ear, sure to be disappointing to the hope. . . .

Mr. Justice Harlan, whom Mr. Justice Frankfurter joins, dissented, saying in part:

The dissenting opinion of Mr. Justice Frankfurter, in which I join, demonstrates the abrupt departure the majority makes from judicial history by putting the federal courts into this area of state concerns—an area which, in this instance, the Tennessee state courts themselves have refused to enter.

It does not detract from his opinion to say that the panorama of judicial history it unfolds, though evincing a steadfast underlying principle of keeping the federal courts out of these domains, has a tendency, because of variants in expression, to becloud analysis in a given case. With due respect to the majority, I think that has happened here.

Once one cuts through the thicket of discussion devoted to "jurisdiction," "standing," "justiciability" and "political question," there emerges a straight-forward issue which, in my view, is determinative of this case. Does the complaint disclose a violation of a federal constitutional right, in other words, a claim over which United States District Court would have jurisdiction . . . ? The majority opinion does not actually discuss this basic question, but, as one concurring Justice observes, seems to decide it "sub silentio." However, in my opinion, appellants' allegations, accepting all of them as true, do not, parsed down or as a whole, show an infringement by Tennessee of any rights assured by the Fourteenth Amendment. Accordingly, I believe the complaint should have been dismissed for "failure to state a claim upon which relief can be granted."

It is at once essential to recognize this case for what it is. The issue here relates not to a method of state electoral apportionment by which seats in the *federal* House of Representatives are allocated, but solely to the right of a state to fix the basis of representation in its *own* legislature. Until it is first decided to what extent that right is limited by the Federal Constitution, and whether what Tennessee has done or failed to do in this instance runs afoul of any such limitation, we need not reach the issues of "justiciability" or "political question" or any of the other considerations which in such cases as *Colegrove* v. *Green,* 328 U.S. 549, led the Court to decline to adjudicate a challenge to a state apportionment affecting seats in the federal House of Representatives, in the absence of a controlling Act of Congress.

The appellants' claim in this case ultimately rests entirely on the Equal Protection Clause of the Fourteenth Amendment. It is asserted that Tennessee has violated the Equal Protection Clause by maintaining in effect a system of apportionment that grossly favors in legislative representation the rual sections of the state as against its urban communities. . . .

I can find nothing in the Equal Protection Clause or elsewhere in the federal Constitution which expressly or impliedly supports the view that state legislatures must be so structured as to reflect with approximate equality the voice of every voter. Not only is that proposition refuted by history, as shown by my Brother Frankfurter, but it strikes deep into the heart of our federal system. Its acceptance would require us to turn our backs on the regard which this Court has always shown for the judgment of state legislatures and courts on matters of basically local concern.

In the last analysis, what lies at the core of this controversy is a difference of opinion as to the function of representative government. It is surely beyond argument that those who have the responsibility for devising a system of representation may permissibly consider that factors other than bare numbers should be taken into account. The existence of the United States Senate is proof enough of that. To consider that we may ignore the Tennessee Legislature's judgment in this instance because that body was the product of an asymmetrical electoral apportionment would in effect be to assume the very conclusion here disputed. Hence we must accept the present form of the Tennessee Legislature as the embodiment of the state's choice, or, more realistically, its compromise, between competing political philosophies. The federal courts have not been empowered by the Equal Protection Clause to judge whether this resolution of the state's internal political conflict is desirable or undesirable, wise or unwise. . . .

. . . [R]educed to its essentials, the charge of arbitrariness and capriciousness rests entirely on the consistent refusal of the Tennessee Legislature over the past sixty years to alter a pattern of apportionment that was reasonable when conceived.

A federal District Court is asked to say that the passage of time has rendered the 1901 apportionment obsolete to the point where its continuance becomes vulnerable under the Fourteenth Amendment. But is not this matter one that involves a classic legislative judgment? Surely it lies within the province of a state legislature to conclude that an existing allocation of Senators and Representatives constitutes a desirable balance of geographical and demographical representation, or that in the interest of stability of government it would be best to defer for some further time the redistribution of seats in the state legislature.

Indeed, I would hardly think it unconstitutional if a state legislature's expressed reason for establishing or maintaining an electoral imbalance between its rural and urban population were to protect the state's agricultural interests from the sheer weight of numbers of those residing in its cities. . . .

In conclusion, it is appropriate to say that one need not agree, as a citizen, with what Tennessee has done or failed to do, in order to deprecate, as a judge, what the majority is doing today. Those observers of the Court who see it primarily as the last refuge for the correction of all inequality or injustice, no matter what its nature or source, will no doubt applaud this decision and its break with the past. Those who consider that continuing national respect for the Court's authority depends in large measure upon its wise exercise of self-restraint and discipline in constitutional adjudication, will view the decision with deep concern.

I would affirm.

After the *Baker* decision the Supreme Court on February 17, 1964, rendered additional decisions affecting Congressional apportionment. In *Wesberry* v. *Sanders,* 376 U.S. 1 (1964), the Court relied on Article I, Section 2 of the Constitution, which provides that Congressmen must be chosen "by the people of the several states," as a basis for holding that Congressional districts must be as nearly as possible equal in population. The *Baker* case was used as precedent.

33
WESBERRY v. SANDERS
376 U.S. 1 (1964)

Mr. Justice Black delivered the opinion of the Court, saying in part:

Appellants are citizens and qualified voters of Fulton County, Georgia, and as such are entitled to vote in Congressional elections in Georgia's Fifth Congressional District. That district, one of ten created by a 1931 Georgia statute, includes Fulton, DeKalb, and Rockdale Counties and has a population according to the 1960 census of 823,680. The average population of the ten districts is 394,312 less than half that of the Fifth. One district, the Ninth, has only 272,154 people, less than one-third as many as the Fifth. Since there is only one Congressman for each district, this inequality of population means that the Fifth District's Congressman has to represent from two to three times as many people as do Congressmen from some of the other Georgia districts.

Claiming that these population disparities deprived them and voters similarly situated of a right under the federal Constitution to have their votes for Congressmen given the same weight as the votes of other Georgians, the appellants brought this action . . . asking that the Georgia statute be declared invalid and that the appellees, the Governor and Secretary of the state of Georgia, be enjoined from conducting elections under it. The complaint alleged that appellants were deprived of the full benefit of their right to vote, in violation of (1) Art. I, §2 of the Constitution of the United States, which provides that "The House of Representatives shall be composed of Members chosen every second year by the People of the several States . . . "; (2) the Due Process, Equal Protection, and Privileges and Immunities Clauses of the Fourteenth Amendment; and (3) that part of Section 2 of the Fourteenth Amendment which provides that "Representatives shall be apportioned among the several States according to their respective numbers. . . . "

The case was heard by a three-judge District Court, which found unanimously, from facts not disputed, that:

> It is clear by any standard . . . that the population of the Fifth District is grossly out of balance with that of the other nine congressional districts of Georgia and in fact, so much so that the removal of DeKalb and Rockdale Counties from the District, leaving only Fulton with a population of 556,326, would leave it exceeding the average by slightly more than forty per cent.

Notwithstanding these findings, a majority of the court dismissed the complaint, citing as their guide Mr. Justice Frankfurter's minority opinion in *Colegrove v. Green,* an opinion stating that challenges to apportionment of congressional districts raised only "political" questions, which were not justiciable. Although the majority below said that the dismissal here was based on "want of equity" and not on justiciability, they relied on no circumstances which were peculiar to the present case; instead, they adopted the language and reasoning of Mr. Justice Franfurter's Colegrove opinion in concluding that the appellants had presented a wholly "political" question. Judge Tuttle, disagreeing with the court's reliance on that opinion, dissented from the dismissal, though he would have denied an injunction at that time in order to give the Georgia Legislature ample opportunity to correct the "abuses" in the apportionment. He relied on *Baker v. Carr*, which, after full discussion of Colegrove and all the opinions in it, held that allegations of disparities of population in state legislative districts raise justiciable claims on which courts may grant relief. We noted probably jurisdiction. 374 U.S. 802. We agree with Judge Tuttle that in debasing the weight of appellants' votes the state has abridged the right to vote for members of Congress guaranteed them by the United States Constitution, that the District Court should have entered a declaratory judgment to that effect, and that it was therefore error to dismiss this suit. The question of what relief should be given we leave for further consideration and decision by the District Court in light of existing circumstances. . . .

This statement in Baker, which referred to our past decisions holding Congressional apportionment cases to be justiciable, we believe was wholly correct and we adhere to it. Mr. Justice Frankfurter's Colegrove opinion contended that Art. I, §4, of the Constitution had given Congress "exclusive authority" to protect the right of citizens to vote for Congressmen, but we made it clear in Baker that nothing in the language of that article gives support to a construction that would immunize state Congressional apportionment laws which debase a citizen's right to vote from the power of courts to protect the constitutional rights of individuals from legislative destruction. . . . The right to vote is too important in our free society to be stripped of judicial protection by such an interpretation of Article I. This dismissal can no more be justified on the ground of "want of equity" than on the ground of "nonjusticiability." We therefore hold that the District Court erred in dismissing the complaint.

This brings us to the merits. We agree with the District Court that the 1931 Georgia apportionment grossly discriminates against voters in the Fifth Congressional District. A single Congressman represents from two to three times as many Fifth District voters as are represented by each of the Congressmen from the other Georgia Congressional districts. The apportionment statute thus contracts the value of some votes and expands that of others. If the federal Constitution intends that when qualified voters elect members of Congress each vote be given as much weight as any other vote, than this statute cannot stand.

We hold that, construed in its historical context, the command of Art. I, §2, that Representatives be chosen "by the People of the several States" means that as nearly as is practicable one man's vote in a congressional election is to be worth as much as another's. This rule is followed automatically, of course, when Representatives are chosen as a group on a statewide basis, as was a widespread practice in the first fifty years of our nation's history. It would be extraordinary to suggest that in such statewide elections the votes of inhabitants of some parts of a state, for example, Georgia's thinly populated Ninth District, could be weighed at two or three times the value of the votes of people living in more populous parts of the state, for example, the Fifth District around Atlanta. We do not believe that the framers of the Constitution intended to permit the same vote-diluting discrimination to be accomplished through the device of districts containing widely varied numbers of inhabitants. To say that a vote is worth more in one district than in another would not only run counter to our fundamental ideas of democratic government, it would cast aside the principle of a House or Representatives elected "by the People," a principle tenaciously fought for and established at the Constitutional Convention. The history of the Constitution, particularly that part of it relating to the adoption of Art. I, §2, reveals that those who framed the Constitution meant that, no matter what the mechanics of an election, whether statewide or by districts, it was population which was to be the basis of the House of Representatives. . . .

The debates at the Convention make at least one fact abundantly clear: that when the delegates agreed that the House should represent "people" they intended that in allocating Congressmen the number assigned to each state should be determined solely by the number of the state's inhabitants. The Constitution embodied Edmund Randolph's proposal for a periodic census to ensure "fair representation of the people," an idea endorsed by Mason as assuring that "numbers of inhabitants" should always be the measure of representation in the House of Representatives. The Convention also overwhelmingly agreed to a resolution offered by Randolph to base future apportionment squarely on numbers and to delete any reference to wealth. And the delegates defeated a motion made by Elbridge Gerry to limit the number of Representatives from newer Western states so that it would never exceed the number from the original states.

It would defeat the principle solemnly embodied in the Great Compromise—equal representation in the House of equal numbers of people—for us to hold that, within the states, legislatures may draw the lines of Congressional districts in such a way as to give some voters a greater voice in choosing a Congressman than others. The House of Representatives, the Convention agreed, was to represent the people as individuals, and on a basis of complete equality for each voter. The delegates were quite aware of what Madison called the "vicious representation" in Great Britain whereby "rotten boroughs" with few inhabitants were represented in Parliament on or almost on a par with cities of greater population. Wilson urged that people must be represented as individuals, so that America would escape the evils of the English system under which one man could send two members to Parliament to represent the borough of Old Sarum while London's million people sent but four. The delegates referred to rotten borough apportionments in some of the state legislatures as the kind of objectionable governmental action that the Constitution should not tolerate in the election of congressional representatives. . . .

It is in the light of such history that we must construe Art. I, §2, of the Constitution, which, carrying out the ideas of Madision and those of like views, provides that Representatives shall be chosen "by the People of the several States" and shall be "apportioned among the several States . . . according to their respective numbers." It is not surprising that our Court has held that this Article gives persons qualified to vote a constitutional right to vote and to have their votes counted. *United States v. Mosley,* 238 U.S. 383; *Ex parte Yarbrough,* 110 U.S. 651. Not only can this right to vote not be denied outright, it cannot, consistently with Article I, be destroyed by alteration of ballots, see *United States v. Classic,* 313 U.S. 299, or diluted by stuffing of the ballot box, see *United States v. Saylor,* 322 U.S. 385. No right is more precious in a free country than that of having a voice in the election of those who make the laws under which, as good citizens, we must live. Other rights, even the most basic, are illusory if the right to vote is undermined. Our Constitution leaves no room for classification of people in a way that unnecessarily abridges this right. In urging the people to adopt the Constitution, Madison said in No. 57 of *The Federalist:*

> Who are to be the electors of the Federal Representatives? Not the rich more than the poor; not the learned more than the ignorant; not the haughty heirs of distinguished names, more than the humble sons of obscure and unpropitious fortune. The electors are to be the great body of the people of the United States.
> . . .

Readers surely could have fairly taken this to mean, "one person, one vote."

While it may not be possible to draw Congressional districts with mathematical precision, that is no excuse for ignoring our Constitution's plain objective of making equal representation for equal numbers of people the fundamental goal for the House of Representatives. That is the high standard of justice and common sense which the Founders set for us.

Reversed and remanded.

Mr. Justice Clark wrote a separate opinion, concurring in part and dissenting in part;

Mr. Justice Harlan dissented, saying in part:

I had not expected to witness the day when the Supreme Court of the United States would render a decision which cast grave doubt on the constitutionality of the composition of the House of Representatives. It is not an exaggeration to say that such is the effect of today's decision. The Court's holding that the Constitution requires states to select Representatives either by elections at large or by elections in districts composed "as nearly as is practicable" of equal population places in jeopardy the seats of almost all the members of the present House of Representatives.

In the last Congressional election, in 1962, Representatives from forty-two states were elected from Congressional districts. In all but five of those states, the difference between the populations of the largest and smallest districts exceeded 100,000 persons. A difference of this magnitude in the size of districts the average population of which in each state is less than 500,000 is presumably not equality among districts "as nearly as is practicable," although the Court does not reveal its definition of that phase. Thus, today's decision impugns the validity of the election of 398 Representatives from 37 states, leaving a "constitutional" House of 37 members now sitting.

Only a demonstration which could not be avoided would justify this Court in rendering a decision the effect of which, inescapably as I see it, is to declare constitutionally defective the very composition of a coordinate branch of the federal government. The Court's opinion not only fails to make such a demonstration. It is unsound logically on its face and demonstrably unsound historically. . . .

. . . [T]he language of Art. I, §§2 and 4, the surrounding text, and the relevant history are all in strong and consistent direct contradiction of the court's holding. The constitutional scheme vests in the states plenary power to regulate the conduct of elections for Representatives, and, in order to protect the federal government, provides for Congressional supervision of the states' exercise of their power. Within this scheme, the appellants do not have the right which they assert, in the absence of provision for equal districts by the Georgia Legislature or the Congress. The constitutional right which the Court creates is manufactured out of whole cloth.

The unstated premise of the Court's conclusion quite obviously is that the Congress has not dealt, and the Court believes it will not deal, with the problem of Congressional apportionment in accordance with what the Court believes to be sound political principles. Laying aside for the moment the validity of such a consideration as a factor in constitutional interpretation, it becomes relevant to examine the history of Congressional action under Art. I, § 4. This history reveals that the Court is not simply undertaking to exercise a power which the Constitution reserves to the Congress; it is also overruling Congressional judgment. . . .

Today's decision has portents for our society and the Court itself which should be recognized. This is not a case in which the Court vindicates the kind of individual rights that are assured by the Due Process Clause of the Fourteenth Amendment, whose "vague contours," *Rochin* v. *California*, 342 U.S. 165, of course leave much room for constitutional developments necessitated by changing conditions in a dynamic society. Nor is this a case in which an emergent set of facts requires the Court to frame new principles to protect recognized constitutional rights. The claim for judicial relief in this case strikes at one of the fundamental doctrines of our system of government, the separation of powers. In upholding that claim, the Court attempts to effect reforms in a field which the Constitution, as plainly as can be, has committed exclusively to the political process.

This Court, no less than all other branches of the government, is bound by the Constitution. The Constitution does not confer on the Court blanket authority to step into every situation where the political branch may be thought to have fallen short. The stability of this institution ultimately depends not only upon its being alert to keep the other branches of government within constitutional bounds but equally upon recognition of the limitations on the Court's own functions in the Constitutional system.

What is done today saps the political process. The promise of judicial intervention in matters of this sort cannot but encourage popular inertia in efforts for political reform through the political process, with the inevitable result that the process is itself weakened. By yielding to the demand for a judicial remedy in this instance, the Court in my view does a disservice both to itself and to the broader values of our system of government.

Believing that the complaint fails to disclose a constitutional claim, I would affirm the judgment below dismissing the complaint.

Mr. Justice Stewart.

I think it is established that "this Court has power to afford relief in a case of this type as against the objection that the issues are not justiciable," and I cannot subscribe to any possible implication to the contrary which may lurk in Mr. Justice Harlan's dissenting opinion. With this single qualification I join the dissent because I think Mr. Justice Harlan has unanswerably demonstrated that Art. I, § 2, of the Constitution gives no mandate to this Court or to any court to ordain that Congressional districts within each state must be equal in population.

APPENDIX[a]

State and number of representatives[b]	Largest district	Smallest district	Difference between largest and smallest districts
Alabama (8)	. . . . . .	. . . . . .	. . . . . .
Alaska (1)	. . . . . .	. . . . . .	. . . . . .
Arizona (3)	663,510	198,236	465,274
Arkansas (4)	575,385	332,844	242,541
California (38)	588,933	301,872	287,061
Colorado (4)	653,954	195,551	458,403
Connecticut (6)	689,555	318,942	370,613
Delaware (1)	. . . . . .	. . . . . .	. . . . . .
Florida (12)	660,345	237,235	423,110

APPENDIX (cont.)

State and number of representatives[b]	Largest district	Smallest district	Difference between largest and smallest districts
Georgia (10)	823,680	272,154	551,526
Hawaii (2)	. . . . . .	. . . . . .	. . . . . .
Idaho (2)	409,949	257,242	152,707
Illinois (24)	552,582	278,703	273,879
Indiana (11)	697,567	290,596	406,971
Iowa (7)	442,406	353,156	89,250
Kansas (5)	539,592	373,583	166,009
Kentucky (7)	610,947	350,839	260,108
Louisiana (8)	536,029	263,850	272,179
Maine (2)	505,465	463,800	41,665
Maryland (8)	711,045	243,570	467,475
Massachusetts (12)	478,962	376,336	102,626
Michigan (19)	802,994	177,431	625,563
Minnesota (8)	482,872	375,475	107,397
Mississippi (5)	608,441	295,072	313,369
Missouri (10)	506,854	378,499	128,355
Montana (2)	400,573	274,194	126,379
Nebraska (3)	530,507	404,695	125,812
Nevada (1)	. . . . . .	. . . . . .	. . . . . .
New Hampshire (2)	331,818	275,103	56,715
New Jersey (15)	585,586	255,165	330,421
New Mexico (2)	. . . . . .	. . . . . .	. . . . . .
New York (41)	471,001	350,186	120,815
North Carolina (11)	491,461	277,861	213,600
North Dakota (2)	333,290	299,156	34,134
Ohio (24)	726,156	236,288	489,868
Oklahoma (6)	552,863	227,692	325,171
Oregon (4)	522,813	265,164	257,649
Pennsylvania (27)	553,154	303,026	250,128
Rhode Island (2)	459,706	399,782	59,924
South Carolina (6)	531,555	302,235	229,320
South Dakota (2)	497,669	182,845	314,824
Tennessee (9)	627,019	223,387	403,632
Texas (23)	951,527	216,371	735,156
Utah (2)	572,654	317,973	254,681
Vermont (1)	. . . . . .	. . . . . .	. . . . . .
Virginia (10)	539,618	312,890	226,728
Washington (7)	510,512	342,540	167,972
West Virginia (5)	422,046	303,098	118,948
Wisconsin (10)	530,316	236,870	293,446
Wyoming (1)	. . . . . .	. . . . . .	. . . . . .

[a]The populations of the districts are based on the 1960 Census. The districts are those used in the election of the current 88th Congress. The populations of the districts are available in the biographical section of the Congressional Directory, 88th Cong., 2nd Sess.

[b]435 in all.

After the *Wesberry* decision the Supreme Court held, in a series of decisions in June, 1964, that the Equal Protection Clause of the Fourteenth Amendment required the equal opportionment of *both* houses of state legislatures. Obviously such a decision could not be made regarding Congress because of constitutional specifications requiring that the Senate represent states as units, with two Senators for each state, regardless of population. The precedent-setting decision in June, 1964, was *Reynolds* v. *Sims.* In holding that both houses of bicameral state legislatures must now be apportioned on a population basis, the Court nevertheless provided that some deviations might be permissible. In what can only be described as a mystical statement the Court held: "So long as the divergencies from a strict population standard are based on legitimate considerations incident to the effectuation of a rational state policy, some deviations from the equal-population principle are constitutionally permissible with respect to the apportionment of seats in either or both of the two houses of a bicameral state legislature." Thus political subdivisions of a state may be given some representation that is not directly related to population. But the Court made it abundantly clear that the states would not be permitted to stray very far from the equal-population principle.

In April, 1968, the Supreme Court extended its reapportionment doctrine by holding that a County Commissioner's Court in Texas, which was elected from single-member districts that were substantially unequal in population, violated the Equal Protection Clause of the Fourteenth Amendment. The Court held that since the County Commissioner's Court was a unit of local government with jurisdiction over the entire geographic area of the county, it was subject to the "one man— one vote" rule.

As a result of the *Baker, Reynolds,* and *Wesberry* decisions, in a majority of states attempts were made to equalize the populations of state and Congressional districts. Redistricting, however, was based upon 1960 census figures which were far out-of-date and inaccurate by the time of the 1970 census. In some cases, population variance between the largest and smallest district within a state even after redistricting was over 400,000 persons. The 1970 census figures are now being used as a basis for redistricting.

Without doubt, the Supreme Court's decisions affecting state legislatures as well as the requirements for equal populations in Congressional districts within states will have a profound effect upon the pattern of American politics. The long-felt power of the rural sections of the country will begin to fade. If the present trend toward the increment of *suburban* populations continues, these areas may begin to exercise important political power. In the final analysis the suburbs may be the biggest beneficiaries of equal apportionment. Therefore, although be reapportioned state legislatures may be more sympathetic to urban problems than their predecessors, there is no guarantee that urban issues will be emphasized unless a community of interest develops between the suburbs and the urban centers. Thus reapportionment will not necessarily bring about the renewed interest in the problems of the city hoped for by those who feel that in the past urban interests were lost in rural-dominated legislatures.

Are there any arguments that can be advanced against equal apportionment? Certainly it is important for any political system to take into account varied interests. The representation of equal numbers of people in different electoral districts may not by itself bring about this equality. As the suburbs grow in population it is entirely possible that with the advent of equal apportionment both the center city and the rural areas of the country will be underrepresented in relation to their importance. Public policy formulated by officials elected from constituencies whose boundaries are determined solely on the basis of equal population may not balance the interests of all sections of the country.

PART TWO

Political Parties, Electoral Behavior, and Interest Groups

CHAPTER 5

Political Parties and The Electorate

The political process involves the sources, distribution, and use of power in the state. All the institutions and processes of government relate to this area. The role of political parties and the electoral system in determining and controlling political power is examined in this chapter.

CONSTITUTIONAL BACKGROUND

Political parties and interest groups have developed outside of the original constitutional framework to channel political power in the community, and for this reason they deserve special consideration from students of American government. The Constitution was designed to structure power relationships in such as way that the arbitrary exercise of political power by any one group or individual would be prevented. One important concept held by the framers of the Constitution was that faction, i.e., parties and interest groups, is inherently dangerous to political freedom and stable government. This is evident from *Federalist 10*.

34

James Madison

FEDERALIST 10

Among the numerous advantages promised by a well constructed Union, none deserves to be more accurately developed than its tendency to break and control the violence of faction. The friend of popular governments never finds himself so much alarmed for their character and fate as when he contemplates their propensity to this dangerous vice. He will not fail, therefore, to set a due value on any plan which, without violating the principles to which he is attached, provides a proper cure for it. The instability, injustice, and confusion, introduced into the public councils, have, in truth, been the mortal diseases under which popular governments have everywhere perished; as they continue to be the favorite and fruitful topics from which the adversaries to liberty derive their most specious declamations. The valuable improvements made by the American constitutions on the popular models, both ancient and modern, cannot certainly be too much admired; but it would be an unwarrantable partiality, to contend that they have as effectually obviated the danger on this side, as was wished and expected. Complaints are everywhere heard from our most considerate and virtuous citizens, equally the friends of public and private faith, and of public and personal liberty, that our governments are too unstable; that the public good is disregarded in the conflicts of rival parties; and that measures are too often decided, not according to the rules of justice, and the rights of the minor party, but by the superior force of an interested and overbearing majority. However anxiously we may wish that these complaints had no foundation, the evidence of known facts will not permit us to deny that they are in some degree true. It will be found, indeed, on a candid review of our situation, that some of the distresses under which we labor, have been erroneously charged on the operation of our governments; but it will be found, at the same time, that other causes will not alone account for many of our heaviest misfortunes; and, particularly, for that prevailing and increasing distrust of public engagements, and alarm for private rights, which are echoed from one end of the continent to the other. These must be chiefly, if not wholly, effects of the unsteadiness and injustice, with which a factious spirit has tainted our public administrations.

By a faction, I understand a number of citizens, whether amounting to a majority or minority of the whole, who are united and actuated by some common impulse of passion, or of interest, adverse to the rights of other citizens, or to the permanent and aggregate interest of the community.

There are two methods of curing the mischiefs of faction: The one, by removing its causes; the other, by controlling its effects.

There are again two methods of removing the causes of faction: the one, by destroying the liberty which is essential to its existence; the other, by giving to every citizen the same opinions, the same passions, and the same interests.

It could never be more truly said, than of the first remedy, that it was worse than the disease. Liberty is to faction what air is to fire, an aliment, without which it instantly expires. But it could not be a less folly to abolish liberty, which is essential to political life because it nourishes faction, than it would be to wish the annihilation of air, which is essential to animal life, because it imparts to fire its destructive agency.

The second expedient is as impracticable, as the first would be unwise. As long as the reason of man continues fallible, and he is at liberty to exercise it, different opinions will be formed. As long as the connection subsists between his reason and his self-love, his opinions and his passions will have a reciprocal influence on each other; and the former will be objects to which the latter will attach themselves. The diversity in the faculties of men, from which the rights of property originate, is not less an insuperable obstacle to a uniformity of interests. The protection of those faculties is the first object of government. From the protection of different and unequal faculties of acquiring property, the possession of different degrees and kinds of property immediately results; and from the influence of these on the sentiments and views of the respective proprietors, ensues a division of the society into different interests and parties.

The latent causes of faction are thus sown in the nature of man; and we see them everywhere brought into different degrees of activity, according to the different circumstances of civil society. A zeal for different opinions concerning religion, concerning government, and many other points, as well of speculation as of practice; an attachment to different leaders, ambitiously contending for preeminence and power; or to persons of other descriptions, whose fortunes have been interesting to the human passions, have, in turn, divided mankind into parties, inflamed them with mutual animosity, and rendered them much more disposed to vex and oppress each other, than to cooperate for their common good. So strong is this propensity of mankind, to fall into mutual animosities, that where no substantial occasion presents itself, the most frivolous and fanciful distinctions have been sufficient to kindle their unfriendly passions, and excite their most violent conflicts. But the most common and durable source of factions has been the various and unequal distribution of property. Those who hold, and those who are without property, have even formed distinct interests in society. Those who are creditors, and those who are debtors, fall under a like discrimination. A landed interest, a manufacturing interest, a mercantile interest, a moneyed interest, with many lesser interests, grow up of necessity in civilized nations, and divide them into different classes, actuated by different sentiments and views. The regulation of these various and interfering interests forms the principal task of modern legislation, and involves the spirit of party and faction in the necessary and ordinary operations of government.

No man is allowed to be a judge in his own cause; because his interest will certainly bias his judgment, and, not improbably, corrupt his integrity. With equal, nay, with greater reason, a body of men are unfit to be both judges and parties at the same time; yet what are many of the most important acts of legislation, but so many judicial determinations, not indeed concerning the rights of single persons, but concerning the rights of large bodies of citizens? And what are the different classes of legislators, but advocates and parties to the cause which they determine? Is a law proposed concerning private debts? It is a question to which the creditors are parties on one side, and the debtors on the other. Justice ought to hold the balance between them. Yet the parties are, and must be, themselves the judges; and the most numerous party, or, in other words, the most powerful faction, must be expected to prevail. Shall domestic manufactures be encouraged, and in what degree, by restrictions on foreign manufactures? are questions which would be differently decided by the landed and the manufacturing classes; and probably by neither with a sole regard to justice and the public good. . . .

It is in vain to say, that enlightened statesmen will be able to adjust these clashing interests, and render them all subservient to the public good. Enlightened statesmen will not always be at the helm; nor, in many cases, can such an adjustment be made at all, without taking into view indirect and remote considersations, which will rarely prevail over the immediate interest which one party may find in disregarding the rights of another, or the good of the whole.

The inference to which we are brought is, that the *causes* of faction cannot be removed; and that relief is only to be sought in the means of controlling its *effects.*

If a faction consists of less than a majority, relief is supplied by the republican principle, which enables the majority to defeat its sinister views, by regular vote. It may clog the administration, it may convulse the society; but it will be unable to execute and mask its violence under the forms of the constitution. When a majority is included in a faction, the form of popular government, on the other hand, enables it to sacrifice to its ruling passion or interest, both the public good and the rights of other citizens. To secure the public good, and private rights, against the danger of such a faction, and at the same time to preserve the spirit and the form of popular government, is then the great object to which our inquiries are directed. Let me add, that it is the great desideratum, by which along this form of government can be rescued from the opprobrium under which it has so long labored, and be recommended to the esteem and adoption of mankind.

By what means is this object attainable? Evidently by one of two only. Either the existence of the same passion or interest in a majority, at the same time must be prevented; or the majority, having such coexistent passion or interest, must be rendered, by their number and local situation, unable to concert and carry into effect schemes of oppression. If the impulse and the opportunity be suffered to coincide, we well know, that neither moral nor religious motives can be relied on as an adequate control. They are not found to be such on the injustice and violence of individuals, and lose their efficacy in proportion to the number combined together; that is, in proportion as their efficacy becomes needful.

From this view of the subject, it may be concluded, that a pure democracy, by which I mean a society consisting of a small number of citizens, who assemble and administer the government in person, can admit of no cure from the mischiefs of faction. A common passion or interest will, in almost every case, be felt by a majority of the whole; a communication and concert, results from the form of government itself; and there is nothing to check the inducements to sacrifice the weaker party, or an obnoxious individual. Hence it is, that such democracies have ever been spectacles of turbulence and contention; have ever been found incompatible with personal security, or the rights of property; and have, in general, been as short in their lives, as they have been violent in their deaths. Theoretic politicians, who have patronized this species of government, have erroneously supposed that by reducing mankind to a perfect equality in their political rights, they would, at the same time, be perfectly equalized and assimilated in their possessions, their opinions, and their passions.

A republic, by which I mean a government in which the scheme of representation takes place, opens a different prospect, and promises the cure for which we are seeking. Let us examine the points in which it varies from pure democracy, and we shall comprehend both the nature of the cure and the efficacy which it must derive from the union.

The two great points of difference, between a democracy and a republic, are, first, the delegation of the government, in the latter, to a small number of citizens elected by the rest; secondly, the greater number of citizens, and greater sphere of country, over which the latter may be extended.

The effect of the first difference is, on the one hand, to refine and enlarge the public views, by passing them through the medium of a chosen body of citizens, whose wisdom may best discern the true interest in their country, and whose patriotism and love of justice, will be least likely to sacrifice it to temporary or partial considerations. Under such a regulation, it may well happen, that the public voice, pronounced by the representatives of the people, will be more consonant to the public good, than if pronounced by the people themselves, convened for the purpose. On the other hand, the effect may be inverted. Men of factious tempers, of local prejudices, or of sinister designs, may by intrigue, by corruption, or by other means, first obtain the suffrages, and then betray the interests of the people. The question resulting is, whether small or extensive republics are most favorable to the election of proper guardians of the public weal; and it is clearly decided in favor of the latter by two obvious considerations.

In the first place, it is to be remarked, that however small the republic may be, the representatives must be raised to a certain number, in order to guard against the cabals of a few; and that however large it may be, they must be limited to a certain number, in order to guard against the confusion of a multitude. Hence, the number of representatives in the two cases not being in proportion to that of the constituents, and being proportionally greatest in the small republic, it follows that if the proportion of fit characters be not less in the large than in the small republic, the former will present a greater option, and consequently a greater probability of a fit choice.

In the next place, as each representative will be chosen by a greater number of citizens in the large than in the small republic, it will be more difficult for unworthy candidates to practice with success the vicious arts, by which elections are too often carried; and the suffrages of the people being more free, will be more likely to center in men who possess the most attractive merit, and the most diffusive and established characters. . . .

The other point of difference is, the greater number of citizens, and extent of territory, which may be brought within the compass of republican, than of democratic government; and it is this circumstance principally which renders factious combinations less to be dreaded in the former, than in the latter. The smaller the society, the fewer probably will be the distinct parties and interests composing it; the fewer the distinct parties and interests, the more frequently will a majority be found of the same party; and the smaller the number of individuals composing a majority, and the smaller the compass within which they are placed, the more easily they will concert and execute their plans of oppression. Extend the sphere, and you take in a greater variety of parties and interests; you make it less probable that a majority of the whole will have a common motive to invade the rights of other citizens; or if such a common motive exists, it will be more difficult for all who feel it to discover their own strength, and to act in unison with each other. . . .

Hence, it clearly appears, that the same advantage, which a republic has over a democracy, in controlling the effects of faction, is enjoyed by a large over a small republic—is enjoyed by the union over the states composing it. Does this advantage consist in the substitution of representatives, whose enlightened views and virtuous sentiments render them superior to local prejudices, and to schemes of injustice? It will not be denied, that the representation of the union will be most likely to possess these requisite endowments. Does it consist in the greater security afforded by a greater variety of parties, against the event of any one party being able to outnumber and oppress the rest? In an equal degree does the increased variety of parties, comprised within the union, increase this security? Does it, in fine, consist in the greater obstacles opposed to the concert and accomplishment of the secret wishes of an unjust and interested majority? Here, again, the extent of the union gives it the most palpable advantage.

The influence of factious leaders may kindle a flame within their particular states, but will be unable to spread a general conflagration through the other states; a religious sect may degenerate into a political faction in a part of the confederacy; but the variety of sects dispersed over the entire fact of it, must secure the national councils against any danger from that source; a rage for paper money, for an abolition of debts, for an equal division of property, or for any other improper or wicked project, will be less apt to pervade the whole body of the union, than a particular member of it; in the same proportion as such a malady is more likely to taint a particular county or district, than an entire state.

In the extent and proper structure of the union, therefore, we behold a republican remedy for the diseases most incident to republican government. And according to the degree of pleasure and pride we feel in being republicans, ought to be our zeal in cherishing the spirit, and supporting the character of Federalists.

The following selection is taken from E. E. Schattschneider's well-known treatise, *Party Government.* In this material he examines both the implications of *Federalist 10* and counter-arguments to the propositions stated by Madison, with regard to political parties and interest groups.

35
E. E. Schattschneider

PARTY GOVERNMENT

The Convention at Philadelphia produced a constitution with a dual attitude: it was propartly in one sense and antiparty in another. The authors of the Constitution refused to suppress the parties by destroying the fundamental liberties in which parties originate. They or their immediate successors accepted amendments that guaranteed civil rights and thus established a system of party tolerance, i.e., the right to agitate and to organize. This is the propartly aspect of the system. On the other hand, the authors of the Constitution set up an elaborate division and balance of powers within an intricate governmental structure designed to make parties ineffective. It was hoped that the parties would lose and exhaust themselves in futile attempts to fight their way through the labyrinthine framework of the government, much as an attacking army is expected to spend itself against the defensive works of a fortress. This is the antiparty part of the constitutional scheme. To quote Madison, the "great object" of the Constitution was "to preserve the public good and private rights against the danger of such a faction [party] and at the same time to preserve the spirit and form of popular government."

In Madison's mind the difference between an autocracy and a free republic seems to have been largely a matter of the precise point at which parties are stopped by the government. In an autocracy parties are controlled (suppressed) at the source; in a republic parties are tolerated but are invited to strangle themselves in the machinery of government. The result in either case is much the same, sooner or later the government checks the parties but *never do the parties control the government.* Madison was perfectly definite and unmistakable in his disapproval of party government as distinguished from party tolerance. In the opinion of Madison, parties were intrinsically bad, and the sole issue for discussion was the means by which bad parties might be prevented from becoming dangerous. What never seems to have occurred to the authors of the Constituion, however, is that parties might be *used* as beneficient instruments of popular government. It is at this point that the distinction between the modern and the antique attitude is made.

The offspring of this combination of ideas was a constitutional system having conflicting tendencies. The Constitution made the rise of parties inevitable yet was incompatible with party government. This scheme, in spite of its subtlety, involved a miscalculation. Political parties refused to be content with the role assigned to them. The vigor and enterprise of the parties have therefore made American political history the story of the unhappy marriage of the parties and the Constitution, a remarkable variation of the case of the irresistible force and the immovable object, which in this instance have been compelled to live together in a permanent partnership. . . .

THE RAW MATERIALS OF POLITICS

People who write about interests sometimes seem to assume that all interests are special and exclusive, setting up as a result of this assumption a dichotomy in which the interests on the one side are perpetually opposed to the public welfare on the other side. But there are common interests as well as special interests, and common interests resemble special interests in that they are apt to influence political behavior. The raw materials of politics are not all antisocial. Alongside of Madison's statement that differences in wealth are the most durable causes of faction there should be placed a corollary that the common possessions of the people are the most durable cause of unity. To assume that people have merely conflicting interests and nothing else is to invent a political nightmare that has only a superficial relation to reality. The body of agreement underlying the conflicts of a modern society ought to be sufficient to sustain the social order provided only that the common interests supporting this unity are mobilized. Moreover, not all differences of interests are durable causes of conflict. Nothing is apt to be more perishable than a political issue. In the democratic process, the nation moves from controversy to agreement to forgetfulness; politics is not a futile exercise like football, forever played back and forth over the same ground. The government creates and destroys interests at every turn.

There are, in addition, powerful factors inhibiting the unlimited pursuit of special aims by any organized minority. To assume that minorities will stop at nothing to get what they want is to postulate a degree of unanimity and concentration within these groups that does not often exist in real life. If every individual were capable of having only one interest to the exclusion of all others, it might be possible to form dangerous unions of monomaniacs who would go to great extremes to attain their objectives. In fact, however, people have many interests leading to a dispersion of drives certain to destroy some of the unanimity and concentration of any group. How many interests can an individual have? Enough to make it extremely unlikely that any two individuals will have the same combination of interests. Anyone who has ever tried to promote an association of people having some special interest in common will realize, first, that there are marked differences of enthusiasm within the group and, second, that interests compete with interests for the attention and enthusiasm of every individual. Every organized special interest consists of a group of busy, distracted individuals held together by the efforts of a handful of specialists and enthusiasts who sacrifice other matters in order to concentrate on one. The notion of resolute and unanimous minorities on the point of violence is largely the invention of paid lobbyists and press agents.

The result of the fact that every individual is torn by the diversity of his own interests, the fact that he is a member of many groups, is *the law of the imperfect political mobilization of interests.* That is, it has never been possible to mobilize any interest 100 percent. . . .

It is only another way of saying the same thing to state that conflicts of interests are not cumulative. If it were true that the dividing line in every conflict (or in all major conflicts) split the community identically in each case so that individuals who are opposed on one issue would be opposed to each other on all other issues also, while individuals who joined hands on one occasion would find themselves on the same side on all issues, always opposed to the same combination of antagonists, the cleavage created by the cumulative effect of these divisions would be fatal. But actually conflicts are not cumulative in this way. In real life the divisions are not so clearly marked, and the alignment of people according to interests requires an enormous shuffling back and forth from one side to the other, tending to dissipate the tensions created.

In view of the fact, therefore, (1) that there are many interests, including a great body of common interests, (2) that the government pursues a multiplicity of policies and creates and destroys interests in the process, (3) that each individual is capable of having many interests, (4) that interests cannot be mobilized perfectly, and (5) that conflicts among interests are not cumulative, it seems reasonable to suppose that the government is not the captive of blind forces from which there is no escape. There is nothing wrong about the raw materials of politics.

FUNCTIONS AND TYPES OF ELECTIONS

Most people transmit their political desires to government through elections. Elections are a critical part of the democratic process, and the existence of *free* elections is a major difference between democracies and totalitarian or authoritarian forms of government. Because elections reflect popular attitudes toward governmental parties, policies, and personalities, it is useful to attempt to classify different types of elections on the basis of changes and trends that take place within the electorate. Every election is not the same. For example, the election of 1932 with the resulting Democratic landslide was profoundly different from the election of 1960, in which Kennedy won by less than 1 percent of the popular vote.

Members of the Survey Research Center at the University of Michigan, as well as V. O. Key, Jr., have developed a typology of elections that is useful in analyzing the electoral system. The most prevalent type of election can be classified as a "maintaining election," "one in which the pattern of partisan attachments prevailing in the preceding period persists and is the primary influence on the forces governing the vote."[1] Most elections fall into the maintaining category, a fact significant for the political system because such elections result in political continuity and reflect a lack of serious upheavals within the electorate and government. Maintaining elections result in the continuation of the majority political party.

At certain times in American history, what V. O. Key, Jr., has called "critical elections" take place. He discusses this type of election, which results in permanent realignment of the electorate and reflects basic changes in political attitudes.

Apart from maintaining and critical elections, a third type, in which only temporary shifts take place within the electorate, occurs, which can be called "deviating elections." For example, the Eisenhower victories of 1952 and 1956 were deviating elections for several reasons, including the personality of Eisenhower and the fact that voters could register their choice for President without changing their basic partisan loyalties at Congressional and state levels. Deviating elections, with reference to the office of President, are probable when popular figures are running for the office.

In "reinstating elections," a final category that can be added to a typology of elections, there is a return to normal voting patterns. Reinstating elections take place after deviating elections as a result of the demise of the temporary forces that caused the transitory shift in partisan choice. The election of 1960, in which most of the Democratic majority in the electorate returned to the fold and voted for John F. Kennedy,[2] has been classified as a reinstating election.

---

[1] Angus Campbell, Philip E. Converse, Warren E. Miller, and Donald E. Stokes, *The American Voter* (New York: John Wiley & Sons, 1960), Chap. 19.

[2] See Philip E. Converse, Angus Campbell, Warren E. Miller, and Donald E. Stokes, "Stability and Change in 1960: A Reinstating Election," *The American Political Science Review,* Vol. 55 (June 1961), pp. 269–80.

36
V. O. Key, Jr.

A THEORY OF
CRITICAL ELECTIONS

Perhaps the basic differentiating characteristic of democratic orders consists in the expression of effective choice by the mass of the people in elections. The electorate occupies, at least in the mystique of such orders, the position of the principal organ of governance; it acts through elections. An election itself is a formal act of collective decision that occurs in a stream of connected antecedent and subsequent behavior. Among democratic orders elections, so broadly defined, differ enormously in their nature, their meaning, and their consequences. Even within a single nation the reality of election differs greatly from time to time. A systematic comparative approach, with a focus on variations in the nature of elections would doubtless be fruitful in advancing understanding of the democratic governing process. In behavior antecedent to voting, elections differ in the proportions of the electorate psychologically involved, in the intensity of attitudes associated with campaign cleavages, in the nature of expectations about the consequences of the voting, in the impact of objective events relevant to individual political choice, in individual sense of effective connection with community decision, and in other ways. These and other antecedent variations affect the act of voting itself as well as subsequent behavior. An understanding of elections and, in turn, of the democratic process as a whole must rest partially on broad differentiations of the complexes of behavior that we call elections.

While this is not the occasion to develop a comprehensive typology of elections, the foregoing remarks provide an orientation for an attempt to formulate a concept of one type of election—based on American experience —which might be built into a more general theory of elections. Even the most fleeting inspection of American elections suggests the existence of a category of elections in which voters are, at least from impressionistic evidence, unusually deeply concerned, in which the extent of electoral involvement is relatively quite high, and in which the decisive results of the voting reveal a sharp alteration of the preexisting cleavage within the electorate. Moreover, and perhaps this is the truly differentiating characteristic of this sort of election, the realignment made manifest in the voting in such elections seems to persist for several succeeding elections. All these characteristics cumulate to the conception of an election type in which the depth and intensity of electoral involvement are high, in which more or less profound readjustments occur in

From V. O. Key, Jr., "A Theory of Critical Elections," *The Journal of Politics,* 17:1 (February 1955). Reprinted by permission.

the relations of power within the community, and in which new and durable electoral groupings are formed. These comments suppose, of course, the existence of other types of complexes of behavior centering about formal elections, the systematic isolation and identification of which, fortunately, are not essential for the present discussion.

I

The presidential election of 1928 in the New England states provides a specific case of the type of critical election that has been described in general terms. In that year Alfred E. Smith, the Democratic presidential candidate, made gains in all the New England states. The rise in Democratic strength was especially notable in Massachusetts and Rhode Island. When one probes below the surface of the gross election figures it becomes apparent that a sharp and durable realignment also occurred within the electorate, a fact reflective of the activation by the Democratic candidate of low-income, Catholic, urban voters of recent immigrant stock. In New England, at least, the Roosevelt revolution of 1932 was in large measure an Al Smith revolution of 1928, a characterization less applicable to the remainder of the country.

The intensity and extent of electoral concern before the voting of 1928 can only be surmised, but the durability of the realignment formed at the election can be determined by simple analyses of election statistics. An illustration of the new division thrust through the electorate by the campaign of 1928 is provided by the graphs in Figure A, which show the Democratic percentages of the presidential vote from 1916 through 1952 for the city of Somerville and the town of Ashfield in Massachusetts. Somerville, adjacent to Boston, had a population in 1930 of 104,000 of which 28 percent was foreign born and 41 percent was of foreign-born or mixed parentage. Roman Catholics constituted a large proportion of its relatively low-income population. Ashfield, a farming community in western Massachusetts with a 1930 population of 860, was predominantly native born (8.6 percent foreign born), chiefly rural-farm (66 percent), and principally Protestant.

The impressiveness of the differential impact of the election of 1928 on Somerville and Ashfield may be read from the graphs in Figure A. From 1920 the Democratic percentage in Somerville ascended steeply while the Democrats in Ashfield, few in 1920, became even less numerous in 1928. Inspection of the graphs also suggests that the great reshuffling of voters that occurred in 1928 was perhaps the final and decisive stage in a process that had been under way for some time. That antecedent process involved a relatively heavy support in 1924 for La Follette in those towns in which Smith was subsequently to find special favor. Hence, in Figure A, as in all the other charts, the 1924 figure is the percentage of the total accounted for by the votes of both the Democratic and Progressive candidates rather than the Democratic percentage of the two-party vote. This usage conveys a minimum impression of

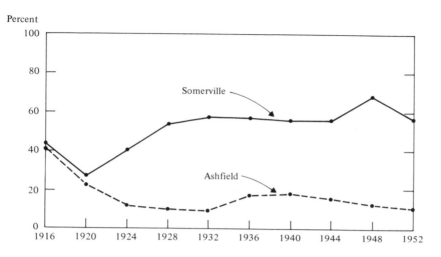

Figure A Democratic Percentages of Major-Party Presidential Vote, Somerville and Ashfield, Massachusetts, 1916–1952

the size of the 1924–1928 Democratic gain but probably depicts the nature of the 1920–1928 trend.

For present purposes, the voting behavior of the two communities shown in Figure A after 1928 is of central relevance. The differences established between them in 1928 persisted even through 1952, although the two series fluctuated slightly in response to the particular influences of individual campaigns. The nature of the process of maintenance of the cleavage is, of course, not manifest from these data. Conceivably the impress of the events of 1928 on individual attitudes and loyalties formed partisan attachments of lasting nature. Yet it is doubtful that the new crystallization of 1928 projected itself through a quarter of a century solely from the momentum given it by such factors. More probably subsequent events operated to reenforce and to maintain the 1928 cleavage. Whatever the mechanism of its maintenance, the durability of the realignment is impressive.

Somerville and Ashfield may be regarded more or less as samples of major population groups within the electorate of Massachusetts. Since no sample survey data are available for 1928, about the only analysis feasible is inspection of election returns for geographic units contrasting in their population composition. Lest it be supposed, however, that the good citizens of Somerville and Ashfield were aberrants simply unlike the remainder of the people of the Commonwealth, examination of a large number of towns and cities is in order. In the interest of both compression and comprehensibility, a mass of data is telescoped into Figure B. The graphs in that figure compare over the period 1916–1952 the voting behavior of the 29 Massachusetts towns and cities having

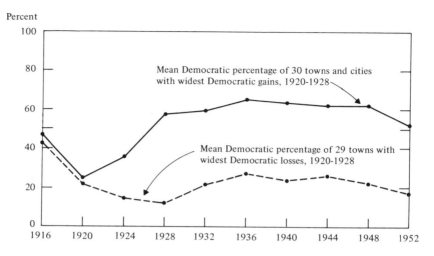

Figure B Persistence of Electoral Cleavage of 1928 in Massachusetts: Mean Democratic Percentage of Presidential Vote in Towns with Sharpest Democratic Gains, 1920–1928, and in Towns of Widest Democratic Losses, 1920–1928

the sharpest Democratic increases, 1920–1928, with that of the 30 towns and cities having the most marked Democratic loss, 1920–1928. In other words, the figure averages out a great many Ashfields and Somervilles. The data of Figure B confirm the expectation that the pattern exhibited by the pair of voting units in Figure A represented only a single case of a much more general phenomenon. Yet by virtue of the coverage of the data in the figure, one gains a stronger impression of the difference in the character of the election of 1928 and the other elections recorded there. The cleavage confirmed by the 1928 returns persisted. At subsequent elections the voters shifted to and fro within the outlines of the broad division fixed in 1928.

Examination of the characteristics of the two groups of cities and towns of Figure B—those with the most marked Democratic gains, 1920–1928, and those with the widest movement in the opposite direction—reveals the expected sorts of differences. Urban, industrial, foreign-born, Catholic areas made up the bulk of the first group of towns, although an occasional rural Catholic community increased its Democratic vote markedly. The towns with a contrary movement tended to be rural, Protestant, native born. The new Democratic vote correlated quite closely with a 1930 vote on state enforcement of the national prohibition law.

Melancholy experience with the eccentricities of data, be they quantitative or otherwise, suggests the prudence of a check on the interpretation of 1928. Would the same method applied to any other election yield a similar result, i.e., the appearance of a more or less durable realignment? Perhaps there can

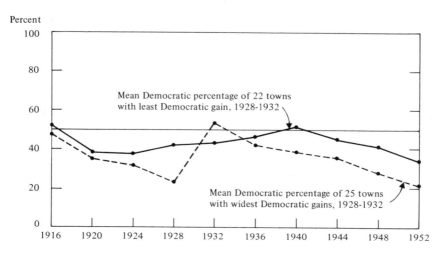

Percent

Figure C Impact of Election of 1932 in New Hampshire: Mean Democratic Percentage of Presidential Vote of Towns with Sharpest Democratic Gain, 1928–1932, Compared with Mean Vote of Towns at Opposite Extreme of 1928–1932 Change

be no doubt that the impact of the events of any election on many individuals forms lasting party loyalties; yet not often is the number so affected so great as to create a sharp realignment. On the other hand, some elections are characterized by a large-scale transfer of party affection that is quite short-term, a different sort of phenomenon from that which occurs in elections marked by broad and durable shifts in party strength. The difference is illustrated by the data on the election of 1932 in New Hampshire in Figure C. The voting records of the twenty-five towns with the widest Democratic gains from 1928 to 1932 are there traced from 1916 to 1952. Observe that Democratic strength in these towns shot up in 1932 but fairly quickly resumed about the same position in relation to other towns that it had occupied in 1928. It is also evident from the graph that this group of towns had on the whole been especially strongly repelled by the Democratic appeal of 1928. Probably the depression drove an appreciable number of hardened Republicans of these towns to vote for a change in 1932, but they gradually found their way back to the party of their fathers. In any case, the figure reflects a type of behavior differing markedly from that of 1928. To the extent that 1932 resembled 1928 in the recrystallization of party lines, the proportions of new Democrats did not differ significantly among the groups of towns examined. In fact, what probably happened to a considerable extent in New England was that the 1928 election broke the electorate into two new groups that would have been formed in 1932 had there been no realignment in 1928.

The Massachusetts material has served both to explain the method of analysis and to present the case of a single state. Examinations of the election of 1928 in other New England states indicate that in each a pattern prevailed similar to that of Massachusetts. The total effect of the realignment differed, of course, from state to state. In Massachusetts and Rhode Island the number of people affected by the upheaval of 1928 was sufficient to form a new majority coalition. In Maine, New Hampshire, and Vermont the same sort of reshuffling of electors occurred, but the proportions affected were not sufficient to overturn the Republican combination, although the basis was laid in Maine and New Hampshire for later limited Democratic successes. To underpin these remarks the materials on Connecticut, Maine, New Hampshire, and Rhode Island are presented in Figure D. The data on Vermont, excluded for lack of space, form a pattern similar to that emerging from the analysis of the other states.

In the interpretation of all these 1928 analyses certain limitations of the technique need to be kept in mind. The data and the technique most clearly reveal a shift when voters of different areas move in opposite directions. From 1928 to 1936 apparently a good deal of Democratic growth occurred in virtually all geographic units, a shift not shown up sharply by the technique. Hence, the discussion may fail adequately to indicate the place of 1928 as the crucial stage in a process of electoral change that began before and concluded after that year.

II

One of the difficulties with an ideal type is that no single actual case fits exactly its specifications. Moreover, in any system of categorization the greater the number of differentiating criteria for classes, the more nearly one tends to create a separate class for each instance. If taxonomic systems are to be of analytical utility, they must almost inevitably group together instances that are unlike at least in peripheral characteristics irrelevant to the purpose of the system. All of which serves to warn that an election is about to be classified as critical even though in some respects the behavior involved differed from that of the 1928 polling.

Central to our concept of critical elections is a realignment within the electorate both sharp and durable. With respect to these basic criteria the election of 1896 falls within the same category as that of 1928, although it differed in other respects. The persistence of the new division of 1896 was perhaps not so notable as that of 1928; yet the Democratic defeat was so demoralizing and so thorough that the party could make little headway in regrouping its forces until 1916. Perhaps the significant feature of the 1896 contest was that, at least in New England, it did not form a new division in which partisan lines became more nearly congruent with lines separating classes, religions, or other such social groups. Instead, the Republicans succeeded in drawing new support, in about the same degree, from all sorts of

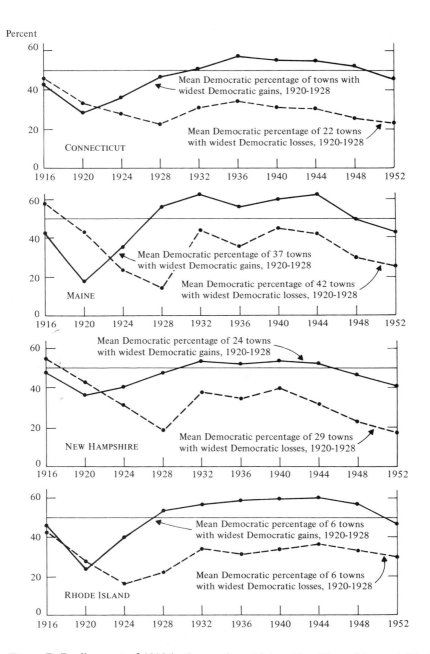

Figure D Realignment of 1928 in Connecticut, Maine, New Hampshire, and Rhode Island

economic and social classes. The result was an electoral coalition formidable in its mass but which required both good fortune and skill in political management for its maintenance, given its latent internal contradictions.

If the 1896 election is described in our terms as a complex of behavior preceding and following the formal voting, an account of the action must include the panic of 1893. Bank failures, railroad receiverships, unemployment, strikes, Democratic championship of deflation and of the gold standard, and related matters created the setting for a Democratic setback in 1894. Only one of the eight New England Democratic Representatives survived the elections of 1894. The two 1892 Democratic governors fell by the wayside and in all the states the Democratic share of the gubernatorial vote fell sharply in 1894. The luckless William Jennings Bryan and the free-silver heresy perhaps did not contribute as much as is generally supposed to the 1892–1896 decline in New England Democratic strength; New England Democrats moved in large numbers over to the Republican ranks in 1894.

The character of the 1892–1896 electoral shift is suggested by the data of Figure E, which presents an analysis of Connecticut and New Hampshire made by the technique used earlier in examining the election of 1928. The graphs make plain that in these states (and the other New England states show the same pattern) the rout of 1896 produced a basic realignment that persisted at least until 1916. The graphs in Figure E also make equally plain that the 1892–1896 realignment differed radically from that of 1928 in certain respects. In 1896 the net movement in all sorts of geographic units was toward the Republicans; towns differed not in the direction of their movement but only in the extent. Moreover, the persistence of the realignment of 1896 was about the same in those towns with the least Democratic loss from 1892 to 1896 as it was in those with the most marked decline in Democratic strength. Hence, the graphs differ from those on 1928 which took the form of opening scissors. Instead, the 1896 realignment appears as a parallel movement of both groups to a lower plateau of Democratic strength.

If the election of 1896 had had a notable differential impact on geographically segregated social groups, the graphs in Figure E of towns at the extremes of the greatest and least 1892–1896 change would have taken the form of opening scissors as they did in 1928. While the election of 1896 is often pictured as a last-ditch fight between the haves and the have-nots, that understanding of the contest was, at least in New England, evidently restricted to planes of leadership and oratory. It did not extend to the voting actions of the electorate. These observations merit some buttressing, although the inference emerges clearly enough from Figure E.

Unfortunately the census authorities have ignored the opportunity to advance demographic inquiry by publishing data of consequence about New England towns. Not much information is available on the characteristics of the populations of these small geographic areas. Nevertheless, size of total population alone is a fair separator of towns according to politically significant

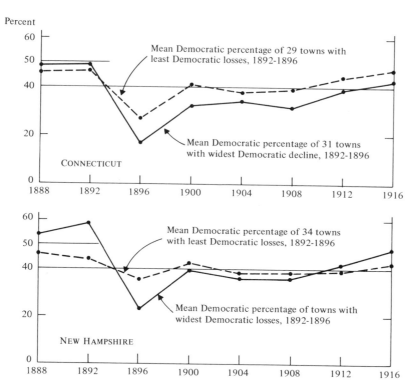

Figure E Realignment of 1896 in Connecticut and New Hampshire

characteristics. Classification of towns according to that criterion groups them roughly according to industrialization and probably generally also according to religion and national origin. Hence, with size of population of towns and cities as a basis, Table 1 contrasts the elections of 1896 and 1928 for different types of towns. Observe from the table that the mean shift between 1892 and 1896 was about the same for varying size groups of towns. Contrast this lack of association between size and political movement with the radically different 1920–1928 pattern which also appears in the table.

Table 1 makes clear that in 1896 the industrial cities, in their aggregate vote at least, moved toward the Republicans in about the same degree as did the rural farming communities. Some of the misinterpretations of the election of 1896 flow from a focus on that election in isolation rather than in comparison with the preceding election. In 1896, even in New England cities, the Democrats tended to be strongest in the poor, working-class, immigrant sections. Yet the same relation had existed, in a sharper form, in 1892. In 1896 the Republicans gained in the working-class wards, just as they did in the

Population size group	Mean Democratic percentage		Mean change 1892–96	Mean Democratic percentage		Mean change 1920–28
	1892	1896	1892–96	1920	1928	1920–28
1–999	34.0	14.7	−19.3	16.5	18.6	+ 2.1
2000–2999	38.8	18.3	−20.5	21.0	33.1	+12.1
10,000–14,999	46.7	26.9	−19.8	25.8	43.7	+17.9
50,000+	47.7	30.1	−17.6	29.5	55.7	+26.2

Table 1 Contrasts between Elections of 1896 and 1928 in Massachusetts: Shifts in Democratic Strength, 1892–1896 and 1920–1928, in Relation to Population Size of Towns

silk-stocking wards, over their 1892 vote. They were able to place the blame for unemployment upon the Democrats and to propagate successfully the doctrine that the Republican Party was the party of prosperity and the "full dinner pail." On the whole, the effect apparently was to reduce the degree of coincidence of class affiliation and partisan inclination. Nor was the election of 1896, in New England at least, a matter of heightened tension between city and country. Both city and country voters shifted in the same direction. Neither urban employers nor industrial workers could generate much enthusiasm for inflation and free trade; rather they joined in common cause. Instead of a sharpening of class cleavages within New England the voting apparently reflected more a sectional antagonism and anxiety, shared by all classes, expressed in opposition to the dangers supposed to be threatening from the West.

Other contrasts between the patterns of electoral behavior of 1896 and 1928 could be cited but in terms of sharpness and durability of realignment both elections were of roughly the same type, at least in New England. In these respects they seem to differ from most other elections over a period of a half century, although it may well be that each round at the ballot boxes involves realignment within the electorate similar in kind but radically different in extent.

III

The discussion points toward the analytical utility of a system for the differentiation of elections. A concept of critical elections has been developed to cover a type of election in which there occurs a sharp and durable electoral realignment between parties, although the techniques employed do not yield any information of consequence about the mechanisms for the maintenance of a new alignment, once it is formed. Obviously any sort of system for the gross characterization of elections presents difficulties in application. The actual election rarely presents in pure form a case fitting completely any particular concept. Especially in a large and diverse electorate a single polling may encompass radically varying types of behavior among different categories of voters; yet a dominant characteristic often makes itself apparent. Despite such difficulties, the attempt to move toward a better understanding of elections in the terms here employed could provide a means for better integrating the study of electoral behavior with the analysis of political systems. In truth, a considerable proportion of the study of electoral behavior has only a tenuous relation to politics.

The sorts of questions here raised, when applied sufficiently broadly on a comparative basis and carried far enough, could lead to a consideration of basic problems of the nature of democratic orders. A question occurs, for example, about the character of the consequences for the political system of the temporal frequency of critical elections. What are the consequences for public administration, for the legislative process, for the operation of the economy of frequent serious upheavals within the electorate? What are the correlates of that pattern of behavior? And, for those disposed to raise such questions, what underlying changes might alter the situation? Or, when viewed from the contrary position, what consequences flow from an electorate which is disposed, in effect, to remain largely quiescent over considerable periods? Does a state of moving equilibrium reflect a pervasive satisfaction with the course of public policy? An indifference about matters political? In any case, what are the consequences for the public order? Further, what are the consequences when an electorate builds up habits and attachments, or faces situations, that make it impossible for it to render a decisive and clear-cut popular verdict that promises not to be upset by caprice at the next round of polling? What are the consequences of a situation that creates recurring, evenly balanced conflict over long periods? On the other hand, what characteristics of an electorate or what conditions permit sharp and decisive changes in the power structure from time to time? Such directions of speculation are suggested by a single criterion for the differentiation of elections. Further development of an electoral typology would probably point to useful speculation in a variety of directions.

VOTING BEHAVIOR: RATIONAL OR IRRATIONAL?

Parties are supposed to bridge the gap between the people and their government. Theoretically they are the primary vehicles for translating the wishes of the electorate into public policy, sharing this role with interest groups and other governmental instrumentalities in varying degrees. If parties are to perform this aspect of their job properly, the party system must be conducive to securing meaningful debate and action. Party organization and procedure profoundly affect the ability of parties to act in a democratically responsible manner. It should also be pointed out, however, that the electorate has a responsibility in the political process—the responsibility to act rationally, debate the issues of importance, and record a vote for one party or the other at election time. These, at least, are electoral norms traditionally discussed. But does the electorate act in this manner? Is it desirable to have 100 percent electoral participation considering the characteristics of voting behavior? What are the determinants of electoral behavior? These questions are discussed in the following selection.

37

Bernard R. Berelson, Paul F. Lazarsfeld, and William N. McPhee

DEMOCRATIC PRACTICE AND DEMOCRATIC THEORY

REQUIREMENTS FOR THE INDIVIDUAL

Perhaps the main impact of realistic research on contemporary politics has been to temper some of the requirements set by our traditional normative theory for the typical citizen. "Out of all this literature of political observation and analysis, which is relatively new," says Max Beloff, "there has come to exist a picture in our minds of the political scene which differs very considerably from that familiar to us from the classical texts of democratic politics."

Experienced observers have long known, of course, that the individual voter was not all that the theory of democracy requires of him. As Bryce put it:

> How little solidity and substance there is in the political or social beliefs of nineteen persons out of every twenty. These beliefs, when examined, mostly resolve themselves into two or three prejudices and aversions, two or three prepossessions for a particular party or section of a party, two or three phrases or catch-words suggesting or embodying arguments which the man who repeats them has not analyzed.

While our data [from the Elmira study] do not support such an extreme statement, they do reveal that certain requirements commonly assumed for the successful operation of democracy are not met by the behavior of the "average" citizen. The requirements, and our conclusions concerning them, are quickly reviewed.

Interest, Discussion, Motivation. The democratic citizen is expected to be interested and to participate in political affairs. His interest and participation can take such various forms as reading and listening to campaign materials, working for the candidate or the party, arguing politics, donating money, and voting. In Elmira the majority of the people vote, but in general they do not give evidence of sustained interest. Many vote without real involvement in the election, and even the party workers are not typically motivated by ideological concerns or plain civic duty.

If there is one characteristic for a democratic system (besides the ballot itself) that is theoretically required, it is the capacity for and the practice of discussion. "It is as true of the large as of the small society," says Lindsay, "that its health depends on the mutual understanding which discussion makes possible; and that discussion is the only possible instrument of its democratic government." How much participation in political discussion there is in the community, what it is, and among whom—these questions have been given answers . . . earlier. . . . In this instance there was little true discussion between the candidates, little in the newspaper commentary, little between the voters and the official party representatives, some within the electorate. On the grass roots level there was more talk than debate, and, at least inferentially, the talk had important effects upon voting, in reinforcing or activating the partisans if not in converting the opposition.

An assumption underlying the theory of democracy is that the citizenry has a strong motivation for participation in political life. But it is a curious quality of voting behavior that for large numbers of people motivation is weak if not almost absent. It is assumed that this motivation would gain its strength from the citizen's perception of the difference that alternative decisions made to him. Now when a person buys something or makes other decisions of daily life, there are direct and immediate consequences for him. But for the bulk of the American people the voting decision is not followed by any direct, immediate, visible personal consequences. Most voters, organized or unorganized, are not in a position to foresee the distant and indirect consequences for themselves, let alone the society. The ballot is cast, and for most people that is the end of it. If their side is defeated, "it doesn't really matter."

Knowledge. The democratic citizen is expected to be well informed about political affairs. He is supposed to know what the issues are, what their history is, what the relevant facts are, what alternatives are proposed, what the party stands for, what the likely consequences are. By such standards the voter falls short. Even when he has the motivation, he finds it difficult to make decisions on the basis of full information when the subject is relatively simple and proximate; how can he do so when it is complex and remote? The citizen is not highly informed on details of the campaign, nor does he avoid a certain misperception of the political situation when it is to his psychological advantage to do so. The electorate's perception of what goes on in the campaign is colored by emotional feeling toward one or the other issue, candidate, party, or social group.

Principle. The democratic citizen is supposed to cast his vote on the basis of principle—not fortuitously or frivolously or impulsively or habitually, but with reference to standards not only of his own interest but of the common good as well. Here, again, if this requirement is pushed at all strongly, it becomes an impossible demand on the democratic electorate.

Many voters vote not for principle in the usual sense but "for" a group to which they are attached—their group. The Catholic vote or the hereditary vote is explainable less as principle than as a traditional social allegiance. The ordinary voter, bewildered by the complexity of modern political problems, unable to determine clearly what the consequences are of alternative lines of action, remote from the arena, and incapable of bringing information to bear on principle, votes the way trusted people around him are voting. . . .

On the issues of the campaign there is a considerable amount of "don't know"—sometimes reflecting genuine indecision, more often meaning "don't care." Among those with opinions the partisans *agree* on most issues, criteria, expectations, and rules of the game. The supporters of the different sides disagree on only a few issues. Nor, for that matter, do the candidates themselves always join the issue sharply and clearly. The partisans do not agree overwhelmingly with their own party's position, or, rather, only the small minority of highly partisan do; the rest take a rather moderate position on the political consideration involved in an election.

Rationality. The democratic citizen is expected to exercise rational judgment in coming to his voting decision. He is expected to have arrived at his principles by reason and to have considered rationally the implications and alleged consequences of the alternative proposals of the contending parties. Political theorists and commentators have always exclaimed over the seeming contrast here between requirement and fulfillment. . . . The upshot of this is that the usual analogy between the voting "decision" and the more or less carefully calculated decisions of consumers or businessmen or courts, incidentally, may be quite incorrect. For many voters political preferences may better be considered analogous to cultural tastes—in music, literature, recreational activities, dress, ethics, speech, social behavior. Consider the parallels between political preferences and general cultural tastes. Both have their origin in ethnic, sectional, class, and family traditions. Both exhibit stability and resistance to change for individuals but flexibility and adjustment over generations for the society as a whole. Both seem to be matters of sentiment and disposition rather than "reasoned preferences." While both are responsive to changed conditions and unusual stimuli, they are relatively invulnerable to direct argumentation and vulnerable to indirect social influences. Both are characterized more by faith than by conviction and by wishful expectation rather than careful prediction or consequences. The preference for one party rather than another must be highly similar to the preference for one kind of literature or music rather than another, and the choice of the same political party every four years may be parallel to the choice of the same old standards of conduct in new social situations. In short, it appears that a sense of fitness is a more striking feature of political preference than reason and calculation.

REQUIREMENTS FOR THE SYSTEM

If the democratic system depended solely on the qualifications of the individual voter, then it seems remarkable that democracies have survived through the centuries. After examining the detailed data on how individuals misperceive political reality or respond to irrelevant social influences, one wonders how a democracy ever solves its political problems. But when one considers the data in a broader perspective—how huge segments of the society adapt to political conditions affecting them or how the political system adjusts itself to changing conditions over long periods of time—he cannot fail to be impressed with the total result. Where the rational citizen seems to abdicate, nevertheless angels seem to tread. . . .

That is the paradox. *Individual voters* today seem unable to satisfy the requirements for a democratic system of government outlined by political theorists. But the *system of democracy* does meet certain requirements for a going political organization. The individual members may not meet all the standards, but the whole nevertheless survives and grows. This suggests that where the classic theory is defective is in its concentration on the *individual citizen.* What are undervalued are certain collective properties that reside in the electorate as a whole and in the political and social system in which it functions.

The political philosophy we have inherited, then, has given more consideration to the virtues of the typical citizen of the democracy than to the working of the *system* as a whole. Moreover, when it dealt with the system, it mainly considered the single constitutive institutions of the system, not those general features necessary if the institutions are to work as required. For example, the rule of law, representative government, periodic elections, the party system, and the several freedoms of discussion, press, association, and assembly have all been examined by political philosophers seeking to clarify and to justify the idea of political democracy. But liberal democracy is more than a political system in which individual voters and political institutions operate. For political democracy to survive, other features are required: the intensity of conflict must be limited, the rate of change must be restrained, stability in the social and economic structure must be maintained, a pluralistic social organization must exist, and a basic consensus must bind together the contending parties.

Such features of the system of political democracy belong neither to the constitutive institutions nor to the individual voter. It might be said that they form the atmosphere or the environment in which both operate. In any case, such features have not been carefully considered by political philosophers, and it is on these broader properties of the democratic political system that more reflection and study by political theory is called for. In the most tentative fashion let us explore the values of the political system, as they involve the electorate, in the light of the foregoing considerations.

Underlying the paradox is an assumption that the population is homogeneous socially and should be homogeneous politically: that everybody is about the same in relevant social characteristics; that, if something is a political virtue (like interest in the election), then everyone should have it; that there is such a thing as "the" typical citizen on whom uniform requirements can be imposed. The tendency of classic democratic literature to work with an image of "the" voter was never justified. For, as we will attempt to illustrate here, some of the most important requirements that democratic values impose on a system require a voting population that is not homogeneous but heterogeneous in its political qualities.

The need for heterogeneity arises from the contradictory functions we expect our voting system to serve. We expect the political system to adjust itself and our affairs to changing conditions; yet we demand too that it display a high degree of stability. We expect the contending interests and parties to pursue their ends vigorously and the voters to care; yet, after the election is over, we expect reconciliation. We expect the voting outcome to serve what is best for the community; yet we do not want disinterested voting unattached to the purposes and interests of different segments of that community. We want voters to express their own free and self-determined choices; yet, for the good of the community, we would like voters to avail themselves of the best information and guidance available from the groups and leaders around them. We expect a high degree of rationality to prevail in the decision; but were all irrationality and mythology absent, and all ends pursued by the most coldly rational selection of political means, it is doubtful if the system would hold together.

In short, our electoral system calls for apparently incompatible properties —which, although they cannot all reside in each individual voter, can (and do) reside in a heterogeneous electorate. What seems to be required of the electorate as a whole is a *distribution* of qualities along important dimensions. We need some people who are active in a certain respect, others in the middle, and still others passive. The contradictory things we want from the total require that the parts be different. This can be illustrated by taking up a number of important dimensions by which an electorate might be characterized.

Involvement and Indifference. How could a mass democracy work if all the people were deeply involved in politics? Lack of interest by some people is not without its benefits, too. True, the highly interested voters vote more, and know more about the campaign, and read and listen more, and participate more; however, they are also less open to persuasion and less likely to change. Extreme interest goes with extreme partisanship and might culminate in rigid fanaticism that could destroy democratic processes if generalized throughout the community. Low affect toward the election—not caring much—underlies the resolution of many political problems; votes can be resolved into a two-party split instead of fragmented into many parties (the splinter parties of the left, for example, splinter because their advocates are *too* interested in politics). Low interest provides maneuvering room for political shifts necessary for a complex society in a period of rapid change. Compromise might be based upon sophisticated awareness of costs and returns—perhaps impossible to demand of a mass society—but it is more often induced by indifference. Some people are and should be highly interested in politics, but not everyone is or needs to be. Only the doctrinaire would deprecate the moderate indifference that facilitates compromise.

Hence, an important balance between action motivated by strong sentiments and action with little passion behind it is obtained by heterogeneity within the electorate. Balance of this sort is, in practice, met by a distribution of voters rather than by a homogeneous collection of "ideal" citizens.

Stability and Flexibility. A similar dimension along which an electorate might be characterized is stability-flexibility. The need for change and adaptation is clear, and the need for stability ought equally to be (especially from observation of current democratic practice in, say, certain Latin American countries). . . . [I]t may be that the very people who are most sensitive to changing social conditions are those most susceptible to political change. For, in either case, the people exposed to membership in overlapping strata, those whose former life-patterns are being broken up, those who are moving about socially or physically, those who are forming new families and new friendships —it is they who are open to adjustments of attitudes and tastes. They may be the least partisan and the least interested voters, but they perform a valuable function for the entire system. Here again is an instance in which an individual "inadequacy" provides a positive service for society: The campaign can be a reaffirming force for the settled majority and a creative force for the unsettled minority. There is stability on both sides and flexibility in the middle.

Progress and Conservation. Closely related to the question of stability is the question of past versus future orientation of the system. In America a progressive outlook is highly valued, but, at the same time, so is a conservative one. Here a balance between the two is easily found in the party system and in the distribution of voters themselves from extreme conservatives to extreme liberals. But a balance between the two is also achieved by a distribution of political dispositions through time. There are periods of great political agitation (i.e., campaigns) alternating with periods of political dormancy. Paradoxically, the former—the campaign period—is likely to be an instrument of conservatism, often even of historical regression. . . .

Again, then, a balance (between preservation of the past and receptivity to the future) seems to be required of a democratic electorate. The heterogeneous electorate in itself provides a balance between liberalism and conservatism; and so does the sequence of political events from periods of drifting change to abrupt rallies back to the loyalties of earlier years.

Consensus and Cleavage. . . . [T]here are required *social* consensus and cleavage—in effect pluralism—in politics. Such pluralism makes for enough consensus to hold the system together and enough cleavage to make it move. Too much consensus would be deadening and restrictive of liberty; too much cleavage would be destructive of the society as a whole. . . . Thus again a requirement we might place on an electoral system—balance between total political war between segments of the society and total political indifference to group interests of that society—translates into varied requirements for different individuals. With respect to group or bloc voting, as with other aspects of political behavior, it is perhaps not unfortunate that "some do and some do not."

Individualism and Collectivism. Lord Bryce pointed out the difficulties in a theory of democracy that assumes that each citizen must himself be capable of voting intelligently:

> Orthodox democratic theory assumes that every citizen has, or ought to have, thought out for himself certain opinions, i.e., ought to have a definite view, defensible by argument, of what the country needs, of what principles ought to be applied in governing it, of the man to whose hands the government ought to be entrusted. There are persons who talk, though certainly very few who act, as if they believed this theory, which may be compared to the theory of some ultra-Protestants that every good Christian has or ought to have . . . worked out for himself from the Bible a system of theology.

In the first place, however, the information available to the individual voter is not limited to that directly possessed by him. True, the individual casts his own personal ballot. But, as we have tried to indicate . . . , that is perhaps the most individualized action he takes in an election. His vote is formed in the midst of his fellows in a sort of group decision—if, indeed, it may be called a decision at all—and the total information and knowledge possessed in the group's present and past generations can be made available for the group's choice. Here is where opinion-leading relationships, for example, play an active role.

Second, and probably more important, the individual voter may not have a great deal of detailed information, but he usually has picked up the crucial *general* information as part of his social learning itself. He may not know the parties' positions on the tariff, or who is for reciprocal trade treaties, or what are the differences on Asiatic policy, or how the parties split on civil rights, or how many security risks were exposed by whom. But he cannot live in an American community without knowing broadly where the parties stand. He has learned that the Republicans are more conservative and the Democrats more liberal—and he can locate his own sentiments and cast his vote accordingly. After all, he must vote for one or the other party, and, if he knows the big thing about the parties, he does not need to know all the little things. The basic role a party plays as an institution in American life is more important to his voting than a particular stand on a particular issue.

It would be unthinkable to try to maintain our present economic style of life without a complex system of delegating to others what we are not competent to do ourselves, without accepting and giving training to each other about what each is expected to do, without accepting our dependence on others in many spheres and taking responsibility for their dependence on us in some spheres. And, like it or not, to maintain our present political style of life, we may have to accept much the same interdependence with others in collective behavior. We have learned slowly in economic life that it is useful not to have everyone a butcher or a baker, any more than it is useful to have no one skilled in such activities. The same kind of division of labor—as repugnant as it may be in some respects to our individualistic tradition—is serving us well today in mass politics. There is an implicit division of political labor within the electorate.

THE ROLE OF PARTIES IN THE POLITICAL PROCESS

In the classical liberal democratic model of democracy political parties play a key role in bridging the gap between people and government. The purpose of parties is to develop meaningful programs and present choices to the electorate, and after the electorate has made its choice the parties are to implement programs in accordance with the wishes of the voters. The classical model of democracy can best be described as "government by discussion." Discussion proceeds in a sequential manner through three stages: (1) discussion within the parties on the formulation of issues that will be presented to the electorate; (2) discussion within the electorate of the party platforms that have been presented; (3) discussion within the legislature and the executive after the election to refine party programs in light of voter preferences. This model ideally presumes two-party government, a disciplined political party system, and a rational electorate. In the American political system, as the preceding selection indicates, the electorate does not always vote rationally in accordance with issue preferences. Moreover, as the following selection points out, a major development reaching fruition in the last decade is the decline in the role of political parties that may spell the "end of American party politics." If people cease to identify with political parties and no longer relate to government through parties then the usefulness of the electoral process as a vehicle of democratic participation is diminished.

38
Walter Dean Burnham

THE END OF AMERICAN PARTY POLITICS

American politics has clearly been falling apart in the past decade. We don't have to look hard for the evidence. Mr. Nixon is having as much difficulty controlling his fellow party members in Congress as any of his Democratic

From W. D. Burnham, "The End of American Party Politics," published by permission of Transaction, Inc., from *Society* 7:2, December 1969. Copyright © 1969 by Transaction, Inc.

predecessors had in controlling theirs. John V. Lindsay, a year after he helped make Spiro Agnew a household word, had to run for mayor as a Liberal and an Independent with the aid of nationally prominent Democrats. Chicago in July of 1968 showed that for large numbers of its activists a major political party can become not just a disappointment, but positively repellant. Ticket-splitting has become widespread as never before, especially among the young; and George C. Wallace, whose third-party movement is the largest in recent American history, continues to demonstrate an unusually stable measure of support.

Vietnam and racial polarization have played large roles in this breakdown, to be sure; but the ultimate causes are rooted much deeper in our history. For some time we have been saying that we live in a "pluralist democracy." And no text on American politics would be complete without a few key code words such as "consensus," "incrementalism," "bargaining" and "process." Behind it all is a rather benign view of our politics, one that assumes that the complex diversity of the American social structure is filtered through the two major parties and buttressed by a consensus of middle-class values which produces an electoral politics of low intensity and gradual change. The interplay of interest groups and public officials determines policy in detail. The voter has some leverage on policy, but only in a most diffuse way; and, anyway, he tends to be a pretty apolitical animal, dominated either by familial or local tradition, on one hand, or by the charisma of attractive candidates on the other. All of this is a good thing, of course, since in an affluent time the politics of consensus rules out violence and polarization. It pulls together and supports the existing order of things.

There is no doubt that this description fits "politics as usual," in the United States, but to assume that it fits the whole of American electoral politics is a radical oversimplification. Yet even after these past years of turmoil, few efforts have been made to appraise the peculiar rhythms of American politics in a more realistic way. This article is an attempt to do so by focusing upon two very important and little celebrated aspects of the dynamics of our politics: the phenomena of critical realignments of the electorate and of decomposition of the party in our electoral politics.

As a whole and across time, the reality of American politics appears quite different from a simple vision of pluralist democracy. It is shot through with escalating tensions, periodic electoral convulsions, and repeated redefinitions of the rules and general outcomes of the political game. It has also been marked repeatedly by redefinitions—by no means always broadening ones—of those who are permitted to play. One other very basic characteristic of American party politics that emerges from an historical overview is the profound incapacity of established political leadership to adapt itself to the political demands produced by the losers in America's stormy socioeconomic life. As is well known, American political parties are not instruments of collective purpose, but of electoral success. One major implication of this is that, as organizations, parties are interested in control of offices but not of government in any larger sense. It follows that once successful routines are established or re-established for office-winning, very little motivation exists among party leaders to disturb the routines of the game. These routines are periodically upset, to be sure, but not by adaptive change within the party system. They are upset by overwhelming external force.

It has been recognized, at least since the publication of V. O. Key's "A Theory of Critical Elections" in 1955, that some elections in our history have been far more important than most in their long-range consequences for the political system. Such elections seem to "decide" clusters of substantive issues in a more clear-cut way than do most of the ordinary varieties. There is even a consensus among historians as to when these turning points in electoral politics took place. The first came in 1800 when Thomas Jefferson overthrew the Federalist hegemony established by Washington, Adams, and Hamilton. The second came in 1828 and in the years afterward, with the election of Andrew Jackson and the democratization of the presidency. The third, of course, was the election of Abraham Lincoln in 1860, an election that culminated a catastrophic polarization of the society as a whole and resulted in civil war. The fourth critical election was that of William McKinley in 1896; this brought to a close the "Civil War" party system and inaugurated a political alignment congenial to the dominance of industrial capitalism over the American political economy. Created in the crucible of one massive depression, this "System of 1896" endured until the collapse of the economy in a second. The election of Franklin D. Roosevelt in 1932 came last in this series, and brought a major realignment of electoral politics and policy-making structures into the now familiar "welfare-pluralist" mode.

Now that the country appears to have entered another period of political upheaval, it seems particularly important not only to identify the phenomena of periodic critical realignments in our electoral politics, but to integrate them into a larger—if still very modest—theory of stasis and movement in American politics. For the realignments focus attention on the dark side of our politics, those moments of tremendous stress and abrupt transformation that remind us that "politics as usual" in the United States is not politics as always, and that American political institutions and leadership, once defined or redefined in a "normal phase" seem themselves to contribute to the building of conditions that threaten their overthrow.

To underscore the relevance of critical elections to our own day, one has only to recall that in the past, fundamental realignments in voting behavior have always been signaled by the rise of significant third parties: the Anti-Masons in the 1820s, the Free Soilers in the 1840s and 1850s, the Populists in the 1890s, and the LaFollette Progressives in the 1920s. We cannot know whether George Wallace's American Independent Party of 1968 fits into this series, but it is certain—as we shall see below—that the very foundations of American electoral politics have become quite suddenly fluid in the past few years, and that the mass base of our politics has become volatile to a degree unknown in the experience of all but the very oldest living Americans. The Wallace uprising is a major sign of this recent fluidity; but it hardly stands alone.

Third-party protests, perhaps by contrast with major-party bolts, point up the interplay in American politics between the inertia of "normal" established political routines and the pressures arising from the rapidity, unevenness and uncontrolled character of change in the country's dynamic socioeconomic system. All of the third parties prior to and including the 1968 Wallace movement constituted attacks by outsiders, who felt they were outsiders, against an elite frequently viewed in conspiratorial terms. The attacks were always made under the banner of high moralistic universals against an established political structure seen as corrupt, undemocratic, and manipulated by insiders for their own benefit and that of their supporters. All these parties were perceived by their activists as "movements" that would not only purify the corruption of the current political regime, but replace some of its most important parts. Moreover, they all telegraphed the basic clusters of issues that would dominate politics in the next electoral era: the completion of political democratization in the 1830s, slavery and sectionalism in the late 1840s and 1850s, the struggle between the industrialized and the colonial regions in the 1890s, and welfare liberalism vs. laissez-faire in the 1920s and 1930s. One may well view the American Independent Party in such a context.

The periodic recurrence of third-party forerunners of realignment—and realignments themselves, for that matter—are signficantly related to dominant peculiarities of polity and society in the United States. They point to an electorate especially vulnerable to breaking apart, and to a political system in which the sense of common nationhood may be much more nearly skin-deep than is usually appreciated. If there is any evolutionary scale of political modernization at all, the persistence of deep fault lines in our electoral politics suggests pretty strongly that the United States remains a "new nation" to this day in some important political respects. The periodic recurrence of these tensions may also imply that—as dynamically developed as our economic system is—no convincing evidence of political development in the United States can be found after the 1860s.

Nation-wide critical realignments can only take place around clusters of issues of the most fundamental importance. The most profound of these issues have been cast up in the course of the transition of our Lockeian-liberal commonwealth from an agrarian to an industrial state. The last two major realignments—those of 1893–1896 and 1928–1936—involved the two great transitional crises of American industrial-capitalism, the economic collapses of 1893 and 1929. The second of these modern realignments produced, of course, the broad coalition on which the New Deal's welfare-pluralist policy was ultimately based. But the first is of immediate concern to us here. For the 1896 adaptation of electoral politics to the imperatives of industrial-capitalism involved a set of developments that stand in the sharpest possible contrast to those occurring elsewhere in the Western world at about the same time. Moreover, they set in motion new patterns of behavior in electoral politics that were never entirely overcome even during the New Deal period, and which, as we shall see, have resumed their forward march during the past decade.

As a case in point, let me briefly sketch the political evolution of Pennsylvania—one of the most industrially developed areas on earth—during the 1890–1932 period. There was in this state a pre-existing, indeed. preindustrial, pattern of two-party competition, one that had been forged in the Jacksonian era and decisively amended, though not abolished, during the Civil War. Then came the realignment of the 1890s, which, like those of earlier times, was an abrupt process. In the five annual elections from 1888 through November 1892, the Democrats' mean percentage of the total two-party vote was 46.7 percent, while for the five elections beginning in February 1894 it dropped to a mean of 37.8 percent. Moreover, the greatest and most permanent Republican gains during this depression decade occurred where they counted most, numerically: in the metropolitan areas of Philadelphia and Pittsburgh.

The cumulative effect of this realignment and its aftermath was to convert Pennsylvania into a thoroughly one-party state, in which conflict over the basic political issues were duly transferred to the Republican primary after it was established in 1908. By the 1920s this peculiar process had been completed and the Democratic party had become so weakened that, as often as not, the party's nominees for major office were selected by the Republican leadership. But whether so selected or not, their general-election prospects were dismal: of the 80 state-wide contests held from 1894 through 1931, a candidate running with Democratic party endorsement won just one. Moreover, with the highly ephemeral exception of Theodore Roosevelt's bolt from the Republican party in 1912, no third parties emerged as general-election substitutes for the ruined Democrats.

The political simplicity which had thus emerged in this industrial heartland of the Northeast by the 1920s was the more extraordinary in that it occurred in an area whose socioeconomic division of labor was as complex and its level of development as high as any in the world. In most other regions of advanced industrialization the emergence of corporate capitalism was associated with the development of mass political parties with high structural cohesion and explicit collective purposes with respect to the control of policy and government. These parties expressed deep conflicts over the direction of public policy, but they also brought about the democratic revolution of Europe, for electoral participation tended to rise along with them. Precisely the opposit occurred in Pennsylvania and, with marginal and short-lived exceptions, the nation. It is no exaggeration to say that the political response to the collectivizing thrust of industrialism in this American state was the elimination of organized partisan combat, an extremely severe decline in electoral participation, the emergence of a Republican "coalition of the whole" and—by no means coincidentally—a highly efficient insulation of the controlling industrial-financial elite from effective or sustained countervailing pressures.

IRRELEVANT RADICALISM

The reasons for the increasing solidity of this "system of 1896" in Pennsylvania are no doubt complex. Clearly, for example, the introduction of the direct primary as an alternative to the general election, which was thereby emptied of any but ritualistic significance, helped to undermine the minority Democrats more and more decisively by destroying their monopoly of opposition. But nationally as well the Democratic party in and after the 1890s was virtually invisible to Pennsylvania voters as a usable opposition. For with the ascendency of the agrarian Populist William Jennings Bryan, the Democratic party was transformed into a vehicle for colonial, periphery-oriented dissent against the industrial-metropolitan center, leaving the Republicans as sole spokesmen for the latter.

This is a paradox that pervades American political history, but it was sharpest in the years around the turn of the century. The United States was so vast that it had little need of economic colonies abroad; in fact it had two major colonial regions within its own borders, the postbellum South and the West. The only kinds of attacks that could be made effective on a nation-wide basis against the emergent industrialist hegemony—the only attacks that, given the ethnic heterogeneity and extremely rudimentary political socialization of much of the country's industrial working class, could come within striking distance of achieving a popular majority—came out of these colonial areas. Thus "radical" protest in major-party terms came to be associated with the neo-Jacksonian demands of agrarian small-holders and small-town society already confronted by obsolescence. The Democratic party from 1896 to 1932, and in many respects much later, was the national vehicle for these struggles.

The net effect of this was to produce a condition in which—especially, but not entirely on the presidential level—the more economically advanced a state was, the more heavy were its normal Republican majorities likely to be. The nostalgic agrarian-individualist appeals of the national Democratic leadership tended to present the voters of this industrial state with a choice that was not a choice: between an essentially backward-looking provincial party articulating interests in opposition to those of the industrial North and East as a whole, and a "modernizing" party whose doctrines included enthusiastic acceptance of and co-operation with the dominant economic interests of region and nation. Not only did this partitioning of the political universe entail normal and often huge Republican majorities in an economically advanced state like Pennsylvania, but the survival of national two-party competition on such a basis helped to ensure that no local reorganization of electoral politics along class lines could effectively occur even within such a state. Such a voting universe had a tendency toward both enormous inbuilt stability and increasing entrenchment in the decades after its creation. Probably no force less overwhelming than the post-1929 collapse of the national economic system would have sufficed to dislodge it. Without such a shock, who can say how, or indeed whether, the "System of 1896" would have come to an end in Pennsylvania and the nation? To ask such a question is to raise yet another. For there is no doubt that in Pennsylvania, as elsewhere, the combination of trauma in 1929–1933 and Roosevelt's creative leadership provided the means for overthrowing the old order and for reversing dramatically the depoliticization of electoral politics which had come close to perfection under it. Yet might it not be the case that the dominant pattern of political adaptation to industrialism in the United States has worked to eliminate, by one means or another, the links provided by political parties between voters and rulers? In other words, was the post-1929 reversal permanent or only a transitory phase in our political evolution? And if transitory, what bearing would this fact have on the possible recurrence of critical realignments in the future?

WITHERING AWAY OF THE PARTIES

The question requires us to turn our attention to the second major dynamic of American electoral politics during this century: the phenomenon of electoral disaggregation, of the breakdown of party loyalty, which in many respects must be seen as the permanent legacy of the fourth party system of 1896–1932. One of the most conspicuous developments of this era, most notably during the 1900–1920 period, was a whole network of changes in the rules of the political game. This is not the place for a thorough treatment and documentation of these peculiarities. One can only mention here some major changes in the rules of the game, and note that one would have no difficulty in arguing that their primary latent function was to ease the transition from a preindustrial universe of competitive, highly organized mass politics to a depoliticized world marked by drastic shrinkage in participation or political leverage by the lower orders of the population. The major changes surely include the following:

- The introduction of the Australian ballot, which was designed to purify elections but also eliminated a significant function of the older political machines, the printing and distribution of ballots, and eased a transition from party voting to candidate voting.

- The introduction of the direct primary, which at once stripped the minority party of its monopoly of opposition and weakened the control of party leaders over nominating processes, and again hastened preoccupation of the electorate with candidates rather than parties.

- The movement toward nonpartisan local elections, often accompanied by a drive to eliminate local bases of representation such as wards in favor of at-large elections, which produced—as Samuel Hays points out—a shift of political pwer from the grass roots to city-wide cosmopolitan elites.

- The expulsion of almost all blacks, and a very large part of the poor-white population as well, from the Southern electorate by a series of legal and extralegal measures such as the poll tax.

- The introduction of personal registration requirements the burden of which, in faithful compliance with dominant middle-class values, was placed on the individual rather than on public authority, but which effectively disenfranchised large numbers of the poor.

BREAKDOWN OF PARTY LOYALTY

Associated with these and other changes in the rules of the game was a profound transformation in voting behavior. There was an impressive growth in the numbers of political independents and ticket-splitters, a growth accompanied by a sea-change among party elites from what Richard Jensen has termed the "militarist" (or ward boss) campaign style to the "mercantilist" (or advertising-packaging) style. Aside from noting that the transition was largely completed as early as 1916, and hence that the practice of "the selling of the president" goes back far earlier than we usually think, these changes too must be left for fuller exposition elsewhere.

Critical realignments, as we have argued, are an indispensable part of a stability-disruption dialectic which has the deepest roots in American political history. Realigning sequences are associated with all sorts of aberrations from the normal workings of American party politics, in the events leading up to nominations, the nature and style of election campaigning and the final outcome at the polls. This is not surprising, since they arise out of the collision of profound transitional crisis in the socioeconomic system with the immobility of a nondeveloped political system.

At the same time, it seems clear that for realignment to fulfill some of its most essential tension-management functions, for it to be a forum by which the electorate can participate in durable "consitution making," it is essential that political parties not fall below a certain level of coherence and appeal in the electorate. It is obvious that the greater the electoral disaggregation the less effective will be "normal" party politics as an instrument of countervailing influence in an industrial order. Thus, a number of indices of disaggregation significantly declined during the 1930s as the Democratic Party remobilized parts of American society under the stimulus of the New Deal. In view of the fact that political parties during the 1930s and 1940s were once again called upon to assist in a redrawing of the map of American politics and policy-making, this regeneration of partisan voting in the 1932–1952 era is hardly surprising. More than that, regeneration was necessary if even the limited collective purposes of the new majority coalition were to be realized.

Even so, the New Deal realignment was far more diffuse, protracted, and incomplete than any of its predecessors, a fact of which the more advanced New Dealers were only too keenly aware. It is hard to avoid the impression that one contributing element in this peculiarity of our last realignment was the much higher level of electoral disaggregation in the 1930s and 1940s than had existed at any time prior to the realignment of the 1890s. If one assumes that the end result of a long-term trend toward electoral disaggregation is the complete elimination of political parties as foci that shape voting behavior, then the possibility of critical realignment would, by definition, be eliminated as well. Every election would be dominated by TV packaging, candidate charisma, real or manufactured, and short-term, ad hoc influences. Every election, therefore, would have become deviating or realigning by definition, and American national politics would come to resemble the formless gubernatorial primaries that V. O. Key described in his classic *Southern Politics.*

The New Deal clearly arrested and reversed, to a degree, the march toward electoral disaggregation. But it did so only for the period in which the issues generated by economic scarcity remained central, and the generation traumatized by the collapse of 1929 remained numerically preponderant in the electorate. Since 1952, electoral disaggregation has resumed, in many measurable dimensions, and with redoubled force. The data on this point are overwhelming. Let us examine a few of them.

A primary aspect of electoral disaggregation, of course, is the "pulling apart" over time of the percentages for the same party but at different levels of election: this is the phenomenon of split-ticket voting. Recombining and reorganizing the data found in two tables of Milton Cummings' excellent study, *Congressmen and the Electorate,* and extending the series back and forward in time, we may examine the relationship between presidential and congressional elections during this century.

Such an array captures both the initial upward thrust of disaggregation in the second decade of this century, the peaking in the middle to late 1920s, the recession beginning in 1932, and especially the post-1952 resumption of the upward trend.

Other evidence points precisely in the same direction. It has generally been accepted in survey-research work that generalized partisan identification shows far more stability over time than does actual voting behavior, since the latter is subject to short-term factors associated with each election. What is not so widely understood is that this glacial measure of party identification has suddenly become quite volatile during the 1960s, and particularly during the last half of the decade. In the first place, as both Gallup and Survey Research Center data confirm, the proportion of independents underwent a sudden shift upward around 1966: while from 1940 to 1965 independents constituted about 20 percent to 22 percent of the electorate, they increased to 29 percent in 1966. At the present time, they outnumber Republicans by 30 percent to 28 percent.

Second, there is a clear unbroken progression in the share that independents have of the total vote along age lines. The younger the age group, the

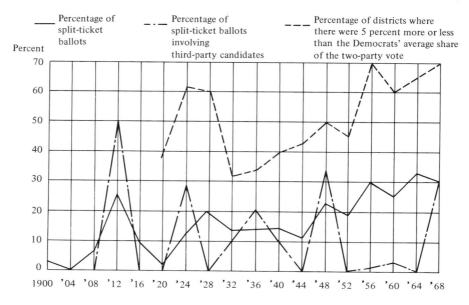

Figure A The Emergent Independent Majority, 1900–1968. Third-party candidates often inspire voters to split their tickets, but the overall trend has been for voters to ignore party labels.

larger the number of independents in it, so that among the 21–29 year olds, according to the most recent Gallup findings this year, 42 percent are independents—an increase of about 10 percent over the first half of the decade, and representing greater numbers of people than identify with either major party. When one reviews the June 1969 Gallup survey of college students, the share is larger still—44 percent. Associated with this quantitative increase in independents seems to be a major qualitative change as well. Examining the data for the 1950s, the authors of *The American Voter* could well argue that independents tended to have lower political awareness and political involvement in general than did identifiers (particularly strong identifiers) of either major party. But the current concentration of independents in the population suggests that this may no longer be the case. They are clearly and disproportionately found not only among the young, and especially among the college young, but also among men, those adults with a college background, people in the professional-managerial strata and, of course, among those with higher incomes. Such groups tend to include those people whose sense of political involvement and efficacy is far higher than that of the population as a whole. Even in the case of the two most conspicuous exceptions to this—the pile-up of independent identifiers in the youngest age group and in the South—it can be persuasively argued that this distribution does not reflect low political awareness and involvement but the reverse: a sudden, in some instances almost violent, increase in both awareness and involvement among southerners and young adults, with the former being associated both with the heavy increase in southern turnout in 1968 and the large Wallace vote polled there.

Third, one can turn to two sets of evidence found in the Survey Research Center's election studies. If the proportion of strong party identifiers over time is examined, the same pattern of long-term inertial stability and recent abrupt change can be seen. From 1952 through 1964, the proportion of strong Democratic and Republican party identifiers fluctuated in a narrow range between 36 percent and 40 percent, with a steep downward trend in strong Republican identifiers between 1960 and 1964 being matched by a moderate increase in strong Democratic identifiers. Then in 1966 the proportion of strong identifiers abruptly declined to 28 percent, with the defectors overwhelmingly concentrated among former Democrats. This is almost certainly connected, as is the increase of independent identifiers, with the Vietnam fiasco. While we do not as yet have the 1968 SRC data, the distribution of identifications reported by Gallup suggests the strong probability that this abrupt decline in party loyalty has not been reversed very much since. It is enough here to observe that while the ratio between strong identifiers and independents prior to 1966 was pretty stably fixed at between 1.6 to 1 and 2 to 1 in favor of the former, it is now evidently less than 1 to 1. Both Chicago and Wallace last year were the acting out of these changes in the arena of "popular theater."

Finally, both survey and election data reveal a decline in two other major indices of the relevance of party to voting behavior: split-ticket voting and the choice of the same party's candidates for President across time.

It is evident that the 1960s have been an era of increasingly rapid liquidation of pre-existing party commitments by individual voters. There is no evidence anywhere to support Kevin Phillips's hypothesis regarding an emergent Republican majority—assuming that such a majority would involve increases in voter identification with the party. More than that, one might well ask whether, if this process of liquidation is indeed a preliminary to realignment, the latter may not take the form of a third-party movement of truly massive and durable proportions.

The evidence lends some credence to the view that American electoral politics is undergoing a long-term transition into routines designed only to fill offices and symbolically affirm "the American way." There also seem to be tendencies for our political parties gradually to evaporate as broad and active intermediaries between the people and their rulers, even as they may well continue to maintain enough organizational strength to screen out the unacceptable or the radical at the nominating stage. It is certain that the significance of party as link between government and the governed has now come once again into serious question. Bathed in the warm glow of diffused affluence, vexed in spirit but enriched economically by our imperial military and space commitments, confronted by the gradually unfolding consequences of social

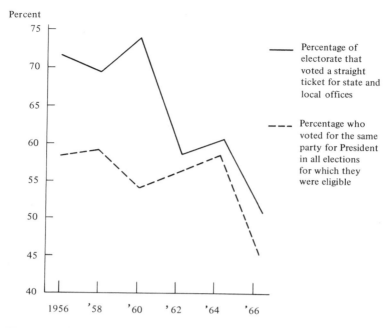

Figure B The Decline of Party Loyalty, 1956–1966.

change as vast as it is unplanned, what need have Americans of political parties? More precisely, why do they need parties whose structures, processes, and leadership cadres seem to grow more remote and irrelevant to each new crisis?

FUTURE POLITICS

It seems evident enough that if this long-term trend toward a politics without parties continues, the policy consequences must be profound. One can put the matter with the utmost simplicity: political parties, with all their well-known human and structural shortcomings, are the only devices thus far invented by the wit of Western man that can, with some effectiveness, generate countervailing collective power on behalf of the many individually powerless against the relatively few who are individually or organizationally powerful. Their disappearance as active intermediaries, if not as preliminary screening devices, would only entail the unchallenged ascendancy of the already powerful, unless new structures of collective power were somehow developed to replace them, and unless conditions in America's social structure and political culture came to be such that they could be effectively used. Yet neither of these contingencies, despite recent publicity for the term "participatory democracy," is likely to occur under immediately conceivable circumstances in the United States.

It is much more probable that the next chapter of our political history will resemble the metapolitical world of the 1920s.

But, it may be asked, may not a future realignment serve to recrystallize and revitalize political parties in the American system?

The present condition of America contains a number of what Marxists call "internal contradictions," some of which might provide the leverage for a future critical realignment if sufficiently sharp dislocations in everyday life should occur. One of the most important of these, surely, is the conversion—largely through technological change—of the American social stratification system from the older capitalist mixture of upper or "owning" classes, dependent white-collar middle classes, and proletarians into a mixture described recently by David Apter: the technologically competent, the technologically obsolescent, and the technologically superfluous. It is arguable, in fact, that the history of the Kennedy-Johnson Administrations on the domestic front could be written in terms of a coalition of the top and bottom of this Apter-ite mix against the middle, and the 1968 election as the first stage of a "counterrevolution" of these middle strata against the pressures from both of the other two. Yet the inchoate results of 1968 raise some doubts, to say the least, that it can yet be described as part of a realigning sequence: there was great volatility in this election, but also a remarkable and unexpectedly large element of continuity and voter stability.

It is not hard to find evidence of cumulative social disaster in our metropolitan areas. We went to war with Japan in 1941 over a destruction inflicted on us far less devastating in scope and intensity than that endured by any large American city today. But the destruction came suddenly, as a sharp blow, from a foreign power; while the urban destruction of today has matured as a result of our own internal social and political processes, and it has been unfolding gradually for decades. We have consequently learned somehow to adapt to it piecemeal, as best we can, without changing our lives or our values very greatly. Critical realignments, however, also seem to require sharp, sudden blows as a precondition for their emergence. If we think of realignment as arising from the spreading internal disarray in this country, we should also probably attempt to imagaine what kinds of events could produce a sudden, sharp, and general escalation in social tensions and threatened deprivations of property, status or values.

Conceivably, ghetto and student upheavals could prove enough in an age of mass communications to create a true critical realignment, but one may doubt it. Student and ghetto rebellions appear to be too narrowly defined socially to have a direct impact on the daily lives of the "vast middle," and thus produce transformations in voting behavior that would be both sweeping and permanent. For what happens in times of critical realignment is nothing less than an intense, if temporary, quasi revolutionizing of the vast middle class, a class normally content to be traditionalists or passive-participants in electoral politics.

Yet, even if students and ghetto blacks could do the trick, if they could even begin, with the aid of elements of the technological elite, a process of electoral realignment left-ward, what would be the likely consequences? What would the quasi revolutionizing of an insecure, largely urban middle class caught in a brutal squeeze from the top and the bottom of the social system look like? There are already premonitory evidences: the Wallace vote in both southern and nonsouthern areas, as well as an unexpected durability in his postelection appeal; the mayoral elections in Los Angeles and Minneapolis this year, and not least, Lindsay's narrow squeak into a second term as mayor of New York City. To the extent that the "great middle" becomes politically mobilized and self-conscious, it moves toward what has been called "urban populism," a stance of organized hostility to blacks, student radicals, and cosmopolitan liberal elites. The "great middle" remains, after all, the chief defender of the old-time Lockeian faith; both its material and cultural interests are bound up in this defense. If it should become at all mobilized as a major and cohesive political force in today's conditions, it would do so in the name of a restoration of the ancient truths by force if necessary. A realignment that directly involved this kind of mobilization—as it surely would, should it occur —would very likely have sinister overtones unprecedented in our political history.

Are we left, then, with a choice between the stagnation inplicit in the disaggregative trends we have outlined here and convulsive disruption? Is there something basic to the American political system, and extending to its electoral politics, which rules out a middle ground between drift and mastery?

The fact that these questions were raised by Walter Lippmann more than half a century ago—and have indeed been raised in one form or other in every era of major transitional crisis over the past century—is alone enough to suggest an affirmative answer. The phenomena we have described here provide evidence of a partly quantitative sort which seems to point in the same direction. For electoral disaggregation is the negation of party. Further, it is—or rather, reflects—the negation of structural and behavioral conditions in politics under which linkages between the bottom, the middle, and the top can exist and produce the effective carrying out of collective power. Critical realignments are evidence not of the presence of such linkages or conditions in the normal state of American electoral politics, but precisely of their absence. Correspondingly, they are not manifestations of democratic accountability, but infrequent and hazardous substitutes for it.

Taken together, both of these phenomena generate support for the inference that American politics in its normal state is the negation of the public order itself, as that term is understood in politically developed nations. We do not have government in our domestic affairs so much as "nonrule." We do not have political parties in the contemporary sense of that term as understood elsewhere in the Western world; we have anti-parties instead. Power centrifuges rather than power concentrators, they have been immensely important not as vehicles of social transformation but for its prevention through political means.

The entire setting of the critical realignment phenomenon bears witness to a deep-seated dialectic within the American political system. From the beginning, the American socioeconomic system has developed and transformed itself with an energy and thrust that has no parallel in modern history. The political system, from parties to policy structures, has seen no such development. Indeed, it has shown astonishingly little substantive transformation over time in its methods of operation. In essence, the political system of this "fragment society" remains based today on the same Lockeian formulation that, as Louis Hartz points out, has dominated its entire history. It is predicated upon the maintenance of a high wall of separation between politics and government on one side and the socioeconomic system on the other. It depends for its effective working on the failure of anything approximating internal sovereignty in the European sense to emerge here.

The Lockeian cultural monolith, however, is based upon a social assumption that has come repeatedly into collision with reality. The assumption, of course, is not only that the autonomy of socioeconomic life from political direction is the prescribed fundamental law for the United States, but that this autonomous development will proceed with enough smoothness, uniformity and generally distributed benefits that it will be entirely compatible with the usual functioning of our antique political structures. Yet the high (though far from impermeable) wall of separation between politics and society is periodically threatened with inundations. As the socioeconomic system develops in the context of unchanging institutions of electoral politics and policy formation, dysfunctions become more and more visible. Whole classes, regions or other major sectors of the population are injured or faced with an imminent threat of injury . Finally the triggering event occurs, critical realignments follow, the universe of policy and of electoral coalitions is broadly redefined, and the tensions generated by the crisis receive some resolution. Thus it can be argued that critical realignment as a periodically recurring phenomenon is as centrally related to the workings of such a system as is the archaic and increasingly rudimentary structure of the major parties themselves.

PARTY VS. SURVIVAL

One is finally left with the sense that the twentieth-century decomposition of partisan links in our electoral system also corresponds closely with the contemporary survival needs of what Samuel P. Huntington has called the American "Tudor polity." Electoral disaggregation and the concentration of certain forms of power in the hands of economic, technological, and administrative elites are functional for the short-term survival of nonrule in the United States. They may even somehow be related to the gradual emergence of internal sovereignty in this country—though to be sure under not very promising auspices for participatory democracy of any kind. Were such a development to occur, it would not necessarily entail the disappearance or complete suppression of subgroup tensions or violence in American social life, or of group bargaining and pluralism in the policy process. It might even be associated with increases in both. But it would, after all, reflect the ultimate sociopolitical consequences of the persistence of Lockeian individualism into an era of Big Organization: oligarchy at the top, inertia and spasms of self-defense in the middle, and fragmentation at the base. One may well doubt whether political parties or critical realignments need have much place in such a political universe.

POLITICAL CAMPAIGNING

V. O. Key, Jr., in *The Responsible Electorate* (Cambridge Mass.: The Belknap Press of Harvard University Press, 1966), suggests that the voice of the people is not capable of being manipulated by skillful politicians, nor is it apathetic. Rather, he suggests the sanguine view that individuals are indeed aware of government decisions affecting their lives and are capable of rendering rational judgments on the actions of political leaders. At the same time Key points out that voter rationality depends upon the rationality of political campaigns, although he argues that in many instances voters are clever enough to see through political propaganda. Joe McGinniss describes in his book *The Selling of the President 1968* how public relations experts and political propagandists view the electorate and also demonstrates how these views affected the management of President Nixon's campaign in 1968. Readers should ask themselves how a rational democratic electorate can be maintained if the political leadership holds voters in such low esteem.

39

Joe McGinniss

THE SELLING OF THE PRESIDENT
1968

Politics, in a sense, has always been a con game.

The American voter, insisting upon his belief in a higher order, clings to his religion, which promises another, better life; and defends passionately the illusion that the men he chooses to lead him are of finer nature than he.

It has been traditional that the successful politician honor this illusion. To succeed today, he must embellish it. Particularly if he wants to be President.

From Joe McGinniss, *The Selling of the President 1968,* Chapter 2. Copyright 1969, by Jocmac, Incorporated. Reprinted by permission of Trident Press, a division of Simon & Schuster, Inc.

"Potential presidents are measured against an ideal that's a combination of leading man, God, father, hero, pope, king, with maybe just a touch of the avenging Furies thrown in," an adviser to Richard Nixon wrote in a memorandum late in 1967. Then, perhaps aware that Nixon qualified only as father, he discussed improvements that would have to be made—not upon Nixon himself, but upon the image of him which was received by the voter.

That there is a difference between the individual and his image is human nature. Or American nature, at least. That the difference is exaggerated and exploited electronically is the reason for this book.

Advertising, in many ways, is a con game, too. Human beings do not need new automobiles every third year; a color television set brings little enrichment of the human experience; a higher or lower hemline no expansion of consciousness, no increase in the capacity to love.

It is not surprising, then, that politicians and advertising men should have discovered one another. And, once they recognized that the citizen did not so much vote for a candidate as make a psychological purchase of him, not surprising that they began to work together.

The voter, as reluctant to face political reality as any other kind, was hardly an unwilling victim. "The deeper problems connected with advertising," Daniel Boorstin has written in *The Image*, "come less from the unscrupulousness of our 'deceivers' than from our pleasure in being deceived, less from the desire to seduce than from the desire to be seduced. . . .

"In the last half-century we have misled ourselves . . . about men . . . and how much greatness can be found among them. . . . We have become so accustomed to our illusions that we mistake them for reality. We demand them. And we demand that there be always more of them, bigger and better and more vivid."

The presidency seems the ultimate extension of our error.

Advertising agencies have tried openly to sell Presidents since 1952. When Dwight Eisenhower ran for reelection in 1956, the agency of Batton, Barton, Durstine and Osborn, which had been on a retainer throughout his first four years, accepted his campaign as a regular account. Leonard Hall, national Republican chairman, said: "You sell your candidates and your programs the way a business sells its products."

The only change over the past twelve years has been that, as technical sophistication has increased, so has circumspection. The ad men were removed from the parlor but were given a suite upstairs.

What Boorstin says of advertising: "It has meant a reshaping of our very concept of truth," is particularly true of advertising on TV.

With the coming of television, and the knowledge of how it could be used to seduce voters, the old political values disappeared. Something new, murky, undefined started to rise from the mists. "In all countries," Marshall McLuhan writes, "the party system has folded like the organization chart. Policies and issues are useless for election purposes, since they are too specialized and hot. The shaping of a candidate's integral image has taken the place of discussing conflicting points of view."

Americans have never quite digested television. The mystique which should fade grows stronger. We make celebrities not only of the men who cause events but of the men who read reports of them aloud.

The televised image can become as real to the housewife as her husband, and much more attractive. Hugh Downs is a better breakfast companion, Merv Griffin cozier to snuggle with on the couch.

Television, in fact, has given status to the "celebrity" which few real men attain. And the "celebrity" here is the one described by Boorstin: "Neither good nor bad, great nor petty . . . the human pseudo-event . . . fabricated on purpose to satisfy our exaggerated expectations of human greatness."

This is, perhaps, where the twentieth century and its pursuit of illusion have been leading us. "In the last half-century," Boorstin writes, "the old heroic human mold has been broken. A new mold has been made, so that marketable human models—modern 'heroes'—could be mass-produced, to satisfy the market, and without any hitches. The qualities which now commonly make a man or woman into a 'nationally advertised' brand are in fact a new category of human emptiness."

The television celebrity is a vessel. An inoffensive container in which someone else's knowledge, insight, compassion, or wit can be presented. And we respond like the child on Christmas morning who ignores the gift to play with the wrapping paper.

Television seems particularly useful to the politician who can be charming but lacks ideas. Print is for ideas. Newspapermen write not about people but policies; the paragraphs can be slid around like blocks. Everyone is colored gray. Columnists—and commentators in the more polysyllabic magazines—concentrate on ideology. They do not care what a man sounds like; only how he thinks. For the candidate who does not, such exposure can be embarrassing. He needs another way to reach the people.

On television it matters less that he does not have ideas. His personality is what the viewers want to share. He need be neither statesman nor crusader, he must only show up on time. Success and failure are easily measured: How often is he invited back? Often enough and he reaches his goal—to advance from "politician" to "celebrity," a status jump bestowed by grateful viewers who feel that finally they have been given the basis for making a choice.

The TV candidate, then, is measured not against his predecessors—not against a standard of performance established by two centuries of democracy —but against Mike Douglas. How well does he handle himself? Does he mumble, does he twitch, does he make me laugh? Do I feel warm inside?

Style becomes substance. The medium is the massage and the masseur gets the votes.

In office, too, the ability to project electronically is essential. We were willing to forgive John Kennedy his Bay of Pigs; we followed without question the perilous course on which he led us when missiles were found in Cuba; we even tolerated his calling of reserves for the sake of a bluff about Berlin.

We forgave, followed, and accepted because we liked the way he looked.

And he had a pretty wife. Camelot was fun, even for the peasants, as long as it was televised to their huts.

Then came Lyndon Johnson, heavy and gross, and he was forgiven nothing. He might have survived the sniping of the displaced intellectuals had he only been able to charm. But no one taught him how. Johnson was syrupy. He stuck to the lens. There was no place for him in our culture.

"The success of any TV performer depends on his achieving a low-pressure style of presentation," McLuhan has written. The harder a man tries, the better he must hide it. Television demands gentle wit, irony, understatement: the qualities of Eugene McCarthy. The TV politician cannot make a speech; he must engage in intimate conversation. He must never press. He should suggest, not state; request, not demand. Nonchalance is the key word. Carefully studied nonchalance.

Warmth and sincerity are desirable but must be handled with care. Unfiltered, they can be fatal. Television did great harm to Hubert Humphrey. His excesses—talking too long and too fervently, which were merely annoying in an auditorium—became lethal in a television studio. The performer must talk to one person at a time. He is brought into the living room. He is a guest. It is improper for him to shout. Humphrey vomited on the rug.

It would be extremely unwise for the TV politican to admit such knowledge of his medium. The necessary nonchalance should carry beyond his appearance while *on* the show; it should rule his attitude *toward* it. He should express distaste for television; suspicion that there is something "phony" about it. This guarantees him good press, because newspaper reporters, bitter over their loss of prestige to the television men, are certain to stress anti-television remarks. Thus, the sophisticated candidate, while analyzing his own on-the-air technique as carefully as a golf pro studies his swing, will state frequently that there is no place for "public relations gimmicks" or "those show business guys" in his campaign. Most of the television men working for him will be unbothered by such remarks. They are willing to accept anonymity, even scorn, as long as the pay is good.

Into this milieu came Richard Nixon: grumpy, cold, and aloof. He would claim privately that he lost elections because the American voter was an adolescent whom he tried to treat as an adult. Perhaps. But if he treated the voter as an adult, it was as an adult he did not want for a neighbor.

This might have been excused had he been a man of genuine vision. An explorer of the spirit. Martin Luther King, for instance, got by without being one of the boys. But Richard Nixon did not strike people that way. He had, in Richard Rovere's words, "an advertising man's approach to his work," acting as if he believed "policies [were] products to be sold the public—this one today, that one tomorrow, depending on the discounts and the state of the market."

So his enemies had him on two counts: his personality, and the convictions—or lack of such—which lay behind. They worked him over heavily on both.

Norman Mailer remembered him as "a church usher, of the variety who would twist a boy's ear after removing him from church."

McLuhan watched him debate Kennedy and thought he resembled "the railway lawyer who signs leases that are not in the best interests of the folks in the little town."

But Nixon survived, despite his flaws, because he was tough and smart, and—some said—dirty when he had to be. Also, because there was nothing else he knew. A man to whom politics is all there is in life will almost always beat one to whom it is only an occupation.

He nearly became President in 1960, and that year it would not have been by default. He failed because he was too few of the things a President had to be—and because he had no press to lie for him and did not know how to use television to lie about himself.

It was just Nixon and John Kennedy and they sat down together in a television studio and a little red light began to glow and Richard Nixon was finished. Television would be blamed but for all the wrong reasons.

They would say it was makeup and lighting, but Nixon's problem went deeper than that. His problem was himself. Not what he said but the man he was. The camera portrayed him clearly. America took its Richard Nixon straight and did not like the taste.

The content of the programs made little difference. Except for startling lapses, content seldom does. What mattered was the image the viewers received, though few observers at the time caught the point.

McLuhan read Theodore White's *The Making of the President* book and was appalled at the section on the debates. "White offers statistics on the number of sets in American homes and the number of hours of daily use of these sets, but not one clue as to the nature of the TV image or its effects on candidates or viewers. White considers the 'content' of the debates and the deportment of the debaters, but it never occurs to him to ask why TV would inevitably be a disaster for a sharp intense image like Nixon's and a boon for the blurry, shaggy texture of Kennedy." In McLuhan's opinion: "Without TV, Nixon had it made."

What the camera showed was Richard Nixon's hunger. He lost, and bitter, confused, he blamed it on his beard.

He made another, lesser thrust in 1962, and that failed, too. He showed the world a little piece of his heart the morning after and then he moved East to brood. They did not want him, the hell with them. He was going to Wall Street and get rich.

He was afraid of television. He knew his soul was hard to find. Beyond that, he considered it a gimmick; its use in politics offended him. It had not been part of the game when he had learned to play, he could see no reason to bring it in now. He half suspected it was an eastern liberal trick: one more way to make him look silly. It offended his sense of dignity, one of the truest senses he had.

So his decision to use it to become President in 1968 was not easy. So much of him argued against it. But in his Wall Street years, Richard Nixon had traveled to the darkest places inside himself and come back numbed. He was, as in the Graham Greene title, a burnt-out case. All feeling was behind him; the machine inside had proved his hardiest part. He would run for President again and if he would have to learn television to run well, then he would learn it.

American still saw him as the 1960 Nixon. If he were to come at the people again, as candidate, it would have to be as something new; not this scarred, discarded figure from their past.

He spoke to men who thought him mellowed. They detected growth, a new stability, a sense of direction that had been lacking. He would return with fresh perspective, a more unselfish urgency.

His problem was how to let the nation know. He could not do it through the press. He knew what to expect from them, which was the same as he had always gotten. He would have to circumvent them. Distract them with coffee and doughnuts and smiles from his staff and tell his story another way.

Television was the only answer, despite its sins against him in the past. But not just any kind of television. An uncommitted camera could do irreparable harm. His television would have to be controlled. He would need experts. They would have to find the proper settings for him, or if they could not be found, manufacture them. These would have to be men of keen judgment and flawless taste. He was, after all, Richard Nixon, and there were certain things he could not do. Wearing love beads was one. He would need men of dignity. Who believed in him and shared his vision. But more importantly, men who knew television as a weapon: from broadest concept to most technical detail. This would be Richard Nixon, the leader, returning from exile. Perhaps not beloved, but respected. Firm but not harsh; just but compassionate. With flashes of warmth spaced evenly throughout.

Nixon gathered about himself a group of young men attuned to the political uses of television. They arrived at his side by different routes. One, William Gavin, was a thirty-one-year-old English teacher in a suburban high school outside Philadelphia in 1967, when he wrote Richard Nixon a letter urging him to run for President and base his campaign on TV. Gavin wrote on stationery borrowed from the University of Pennsylvania because he thought Nixon would pay more attention if the letter seemed to be from a college professor.

Dear Mr. Nixon:
    May I offer two suggestions concerning your plans for 1968?
    1. Run. You can win. Nothing can happen to you, politically speaking, that is worse than what has happened to you. Ortego y Gasset in his *The Revolt of the Masses* says: "These ideas are the only genuine ideas; the ideas of the shipwrecked. All the rest is rhetoric, posturing, farce. He who does not really feel himself lost, is lost without remission . . ." You, in effect, are "lost"; that is why you are the

only political figure with a vision to see things the way they are and not as Leftist or Rightist kooks would have them be. Run. You will win.

2. A tip for television: instead of those wooden performances beloved by politicians, instead of a glamorboy technique, instead of safety, be bold. Why not have live press conferences as your campaign on television? People will see you daring all, asking and answering questions from reporters, and not simply answering phony "questions" made up by your staff. This would be dynamic; it would be daring. Instead of the medium using you, you would be using the medium. Go on "live" and risk all. It is the only way to convince people of the truth: that you are beyond rhetoric, that you can face reality, unlike your opponents, who will rely on public relations. Television hurt you because you were not yourself; it didn't hurt the "real" Nixon. The real Nixon can revolutionize the use of television by dynamically going "live" and answering everything, the loaded and the unloaded question. Invite your opponents to this kind of a debate.

Good luck, and I know you can win if you see yourself for what you are; a man who had been beaten, humiliated, hated, but who can still see the truth.

A Nixon staff member had lunch with Gavin a couple of times after the letter was received and hired him.

William Gavin was brought to the White House as a speech writer in January of 1969.

Harry Treleaven, hired as creative director of advertising in the fall of 1967, immediately went to work on the more serious of Nixon's personality problems. One was his lack of humor.

"Can be corrected to a degree," Treleaven wrote, "but let's not be too obvious about it. Romney's cornball attempts have hurt him. If we've going to be witty, let a pro write the words."

Treleaven also worried about Nixon's lack of warmth, but decided that "he can be helped greatly in this respect by how he is handled. . . . Give him words to say that will show his *emotional* involvement in the issues. . . . Buchanan wrote about RFK talking about the starving children in Recife. *That's* what we have to inject. . . .

"He should be presented in some kind of 'situation' rather than cold in a studio. The situation should look unstaged even if it's not."

Some of the most effective ideas belonged to Raymond K. Price, a former editorial writer for the *New York Herald Tribune,* who became Nixon's best and most prominent speech writer in the campaign. Price later composed much of the inaugural address.

In 1967, he began with the assumption that, "The natural human use of reason is to support prejudice, not to arrive at opinions." Which led to the conclusion that rational arguments would "only be effective if we can get the people to make the *emotional* leap, or what theologians call [the] 'leap of faith.' "

Price suggested attacking the "personal factors" rather than the "historical factors" which were the basis of the low opinion so many people had of Richard Nixon.

"These tend to be more a gut reaction," Price wrote, "unarticulated, non-analytical, a product of the particular chemistry between the voter and the *image* of the candidate. *We have to be very clear on this point: that the response is to the image, not to the man.* . . . It's not what's *there* that counts, it's what's projected—and carrying it one step further, it's not what *he* projects but rather what the voter receives. It's not the man we have to change, but rather the *received impression.* And this impression often depends more on the medium and its use than it does on the candidate himself."

So there would not have to be a "new Nixon." Simply a new approach to television.

"What, then, does this mean in terms of our uses of time and of media?" Price wrote.

"For one thing, it means investing whatever time RN needs in order to work out firmly in his own mind that vision of the nation's future that he wants to be identified with. This is crucial. . . ."

So, at the age of fifty-four, after twenty years in public life, Richard Nixon was still felt *by his own staff* to be in need of time to "work out firmly in his own mind that vision of the nation's future that he wants to be identified with."

"Secondly," Price wrote, "it suggests that we take the time and the money to experiment, in a controlled manner, with film and television techniques, with particular emphasis on pinpointing those *controlled* uses of the television medium that can *best* convey the *image* we want to get across . . .

"The TV medium itself introduces an element of distortion, in terms of its effect on the candidate and of the often subliminal ways in which the image is received. And it inevitably is going to convey a partial image—thus ours is the task of finding how to control its use so the part that gets across is the part we want to have gotten across. . . .

"Voters are basically lazy, basically uninterested in making an *effort* to understand what we're talking about . . .," Price wrote. "Reason requires a high degree of discipline, of concentration; impression is easier. Reason pushes the viewer back, it assaults him, it demands that he agree or disagree; impression can envelop him, invite him in, without making an intellectual demand. . . . When we argue with him we demand that he make the effort of replying. We seek to engage his intellect, and for most people this is the most difficult work of all. The emotions are more easily roused, closer to the surface, more malleable. . . ."

So, for the New Hampshire primary, Price recommended "saturation with a film, in which the candidate can be shown better than he can be shown in person because it can be edited, so only the best moments are shown; then a quick parading of the candidate in the flesh so that the guy they've gotten intimately acquainted with on the screen takes on a living presence—not saying anything, just being seen. . . .

"[Nixon] has to come across as a person larger than life, the stuff of legend. People are stirred by the legend, including the living legend, not by the man himself. It's the aura that surrounds the charismatic figure more than it is the figure itself, that draws the followers. Our task is to build that aura. . . .

"So let's not be afraid of television gimmicks . . . get the voters to like the guy and the battle's two-thirds won."

So this was how they went into it. Trying, with one hand, to build the illusion that Richard Nixon, in addition to his attibutes of mind and heart, considered, in the words of Patrick K. Buchanan, a speech writer, "communicating with the people . . . one of the great joys of seeking the Presidency"; while with the other they shielded him, controlled him, and controlled the atmosphere around him. It was as if they were building not a President but an Astrodome, where the wind would never blow, the temperature never rise or fall, and the ball never bounce erratically on the artificial grass.

They could do this, and succeed, because of the special nature of the man. There was, apparently, something in Richard Nixon's character which sought this shelter. Something which craved regulation, which flourished best in the darkness, behind clichés, behind phalanxes of antiseptic advisers. Some part of him that could breathe freely only inside a hotel suite that cost a hundred dollars a day.

And it worked. As he moved serenely through his primary campaign, there was new cadence to Richard Nixon's speech and motion; new confidence in his heart. And, a new image of him on the television screen.

TV both reflected and contributed to his strength. Because he was winning he looked like a winner on the screen. Because he was suddenly projecting well on the medium he had feared, he went about his other tasks with assurance. The one fed upon the other, building to an astonishing peak in August as the Republican convention began and he emerged from his regal isolation, traveling to Miami not so much to be nominated as coronated. On live, but controlled, TV.

Ideal democratic theory assumes not only that the public participates in the political process by making rational judgments at election time, but also that individual members of the public will have access to political office should they choose to run. Presumably the qualifications of office-seekers should be up to the public that elects them, and should not be circumscribed by law or by other factors except where the public has decided through its elected representatives that those involved, for example, in fraud and corruption should be barred from office. In reality, however, one severe limitation on candidates is the necessity to spend large sums of money, primarily for television coverage. Those who run for office must either be wealthy themselves or have access to ample funds. This usually cannot be raised by small donors. Candidates without family wealth must rely on donations from wealthy individuals and indirectly from interest groups. Corporations and labor unions are by law barred from making direct financial contributions to political candidates; however, there are indirect ways in which they can aid financially.

In the Fall of 1974 Congress enacted a campaign finance bill that limited contributions and expenditures in federal elections, including primaries, and for the first time provided for the use of public funds for presidential primary and general election campaigns. The bill was a compromise between a liberal public financing law passed by the Senate and more limited legislation enacted by the House. The Senate bill provided for public financing not only of presidential elections, but also for Congressional contests. The House voted against public financing for Congressional elections 228-187 on August 8, 1974, perhaps fearing incumbents would lose their advantage over challengers in raising funds if public money was made available to all legitimate candidates. The effect of the campaign finance bill will be to reduce the reliance of presidential primary and general election candidates on private contributions. Acceptance of public money for the general presidential election contest is optional. Major party candidates qualify for full funding, and if they accept full public financing no private contributions are allowed. Minor party candidates and independent candidates will receive a portion of full funding based on the number of votes they have received in a past or current election. Although the 1974 legislation goes a long way to cure money abuses in political campaigns, a major gap is the failure to provide public funding for Congressional campaigns. In the following selection a United States Senator discusses the problems of financing Congressional campaigns under the current system. The statement is taken from testimony before the Senate Rules and Administration Subcommittee on Privileges and Elections on proposals to establish public funding of federal election campaigns, Sept. 18–21, 1973.

40
Joseph R. Biden, Jr.

THE HIGH PRICE CANDIDATES PAY FOR CAMPAIGN FUNDS

I've heard it mentioned here that we better go softly on public financing of elections because we need to preserve the two-party system. Well, I think unless we go very heavily on public financing of elections, we are going to lose the two-party system. One of the reasons I think the two parties are in such jeopardy is not because the small contributor is worried about being pushed out of the picture, but because the small contributor, in my opinion, feels what in the hell difference does it make whether I make the small contribution,

From "Senator Joe Biden: The High Price Candidates Pay for Campaign Funds," *The Washington Post* (October 1, 1973). Reprinted by permission.

because those Democrats are the product of big labor, and those Republicans are the product of big business. And what difference does it make if I contribute $5, $10, $50 or $100? And I think, if anything, a significant step toward public financing would increase the two-party system effort.

I also heard it pointed out that maybe we'd better not take a chance on financing someone who can't even raise enough money in the district to make a serious challenge, because his party, in fact, may not want to mount a serious challenge. Well, I sort of say, the party be damned. If I waited on the party in my state which did not contribute one single cent to my campaign, I would still be waiting in Delaware. I am sure it disappoints many that I didn't wait, but the fact remains that my party, for example, decided that the incumbent, who was clearly vulnerable, was not at all vulnerable, that there was no need to mount a race against him. And, quite frankly, the only reason they gave me the nomination was it was one way to get rid of the 30-year old kid. And, you know, "Let him run and it'll be the last we'll hear of him," and I am sure that exists in many other parts of the nation.

And in my neighboring state, Pennsylvania, I don't know for a fact, but if what I've heard for the last 10 years has any shred of truth to it, there are many, many congressional districts or some congressional districts, where there aren't candidates because the party cuts a deal, not because the people don't want a viable opponent but because they cut a deal, Republican or Democratic Party, for a judgeship or members on a planning commission instead of running a candidate against the incumbent. They say, "We won't run anybody if you in fact give us a piece of the pie." And that happens—we all know that happens—and so I'm not so in love with the fact, the concept that if the party doesn't think it merits the race, that that should really color whether or not a race is merited. And I'm not talking about my party or our party, the Democratic Party, I'm talking about both parties, I'm talking about any challenging party, any third party, some of which are strong in some states.

The other thing, I heard someone testify here earlier that the data is skimpy, on whether or not we should move forward in this direction. Well look, every one of us who are voting on this, even inexperienced Joe Biden, if you've been through it once, you know what you've got to do to raise money. And it's the most degrading damn thing in the world to go out and have to raise money unless you happen to be in a position where you are so strong you don't have to ask, or you have enough backing, either from your personal background or family that you need not ask and we've limited that . . . As a practical matter, we know what it takes to go out and raise money, we know we've got to go out with our hat in our hand whether it be to a labor union, some of whom are sitting here in the audience, or whether it be to big business interests. And how the devil am I going to pay a Matt Reese—who sits back there—$40,000 or $10,000 to come up and help me get elected?

. . . We talk about the fact that we don't have enough data. We all know, we may not have the specifics, we may not know exactly which way we are to go, but we all know the effect of what happens in raising money, and we all know how tough it is to raise money and we all know what we have to do to raise that money. Now, I am not implying we have to sell ourselves, that's not true, but in some instances if you had to go you'd probably have to sell yourself.

Let me give you a couple of examples, and since I'm likely to be not only one of the youngest one-term senators in history, I may regret having said this later on, but I am going to say it now. I can recall in one instance going to a labor union who I knew was contributing $5,000 to a Senate campaign—to anyone they endorse—all above board, all honest, you know, by the numbers and it was a check, the full works. And we walk in and sit down and we start off the discussion very polite. He said, "Mr. Biden would you like a cup of coffee?" We go through that routine, we have a cup of coffee and my brother who was my chief fund raiser with great experience at age 24, sitting next to me, and, he . . . goes through the social niceties with my brother, then he says "Well, what are your chances of winning?" and I go through the litany that I've gone through, as everyone else has who has run, a hundred times, and you go through and you do that by the numbers, and then you really get down to it. Then, no one asks you to buy your vote or to promise a vote but they say things like this to me anyway, . . . "Well Joe, had you been in the 92nd Congress how would you have voted on the SST and while you're at it how would you have voted on bailing out Lockheed?" Now, I may be a naive young feller, but I knew the right answer for $5,000. I knew what had to be said to get that money.

The same thing occurred again when it looked like the polls started to narrow and Joe Biden is going to win—all the "fat cat" Republicans from Greenville and Delaware—13 multimillionaires—invite me out to cocktails. Before that they wouldn't even let me park the car in front of their house, but they invite me to cocktails. We sit down and we start off, only the only difference is they offer me a Bloody Mary instead of a coke or a cup of coffee, and they're a little more frank about it. The spokesman for the group said, "Well Joe, let's get right to it, looks like you may win this damn thing and we underestimated it. Now Joe, I'd like to ask you a few questions. We know everybody running for public office has to talk about tax reform, and we know you've been talking about tax reform Joe, and it's particularly capital gains (and all these guys were millionaires as a consequence of unearned income)." One fellow leans over and sort of pats me on the knee in a fatherly fashion and, as if to say "It's just among us," says to me, "Joe, you really don't mean what you say about capital gains, do you?" Now I knew the right answer to that one for $20,000 and quite frankly, were it not for the fact that I had a Scotch Presbyterian wife who had a backbone like a ramrod and you had to cajole and who I was more afraid of than those people I was talking to, I would have said on both occasions "No, I didn't mean what I said about capital gains and yep I would have gone for the SST." Only because of her I didn't and I thought I lost it. You know I walked out of those meetings thinking my God it's all over, the second mortgage on the house is gone, really and truly, some of these people may think I am kidding. But I mean I literally put a second mortgage on my home to run for the office, like a lot of people have to do in order to run.

And when you put, as you well know and this is sort of rhetorical, but for the record, for people who've never run before, when you put your sweat, your blood, your time, your energies into a lifetime ambition to reach the second highest office in the land, United State Senate, a goal I would have been satisfied reaching at 60 and I had a chance of doing it at 30, at 29, I thought it was a matter of life and death. Senator, I mean I could see a direct correlation between how much money I was getting and how much that was doing for me in terms of where we are and I won't belabor the point, but lest any of the people who read this record later or any of the people who are listening to this, think that they are better than we or me, ask them the rhetorical question— how many of them want to appear in the second edition of Profiles in Courage. How many of them are in a position that they are willing to say, "Throw it to the wind, I don't need it" when they know that could be the margin?

And so the essence of what I'm trying to say here is, that I think it's not so much that the politician is ripping off the public but we politicians are ripped off by the system. We politicians are put in a position where at least there is a great deal of pressure in the one particular area, at least to prostitute our ideas, if not our integrity and maybe they're the same. At least to compromise . . . I know I said to myself, time and again, "Well it's much better that I get elected with 80 percent of my ideas intact than with a 100 percent and, you know, so maybe I should go ahead and do it . . ."

The other point that was made about incumbency, I mention in the statement. Let me just suffice it to say that if the limits that are now in effect in the bill that I voted for on the Senate floor, which is an improvement over what we have in my opinion, were those limits in effect, I would not be here testifying before you as a senator, because as an unknown 29-year old attorney, who's a county councilman running against a two-term congressman, two-term governor and two-term senator I *had* to spend more than the $150,000 I would be limited to . . . Now that I'm an incumbent, you know, when I go home it doesn't sound like such a bad idea, gee you know that sounds like a pretty good idea, to limit that kind of money. But in all candor, I think we are going to have an inhibiting effect on bringing people out and opening up the process and it was pointed out that 90 percent of the incumbents get reelected. I hope that figure holds up . . . but I hope we don't have to do it in the way that I think the bill may have the unintended effect of doing it . . . The chairman pointed out that there are a number of serious problems that we'll have with this bill, with any bill that has public financing as a major part or even a minor part. I agree with him, that's true. But the only thing I would like to say, in response to his worry about having to move in the direction of financing a candidate who couldn't raise more than $1,200 and wasting the taxpayers' money on that or on balloons or on billboards, I think that we would be better off to waste that money if it is truly a waste, than to let the corrupt system which we now have, the implicitly corrupt system which we now have continue in its form. Nothing is ever perfect. We are never going to pass a perfect law, we're never going to pass a law that isn't going to be broken, but I think if we move in the direction of significant public financing . . . unless we make a serious effort in the direction of making a significant part of it public financing, I think that the system is in serious trouble. You know my wife used to say something that I think is true, she said, "You should never burden an elected public official with too much responsibility." I think she's right.

CHAPTER 6

Interest Groups

Interest groups are vital cogs in the wheels of the democratic process. Although *Federalist 10* suggests that one major purpose of the separation of powers system is to break and control the "evil effects" of faction, modern political theorists take a much more sanguine view of the role that political interest groups as well as parties play in government. No longer are interest groups defined as being opposed to the "public interest." They are vital channels through which particular publics participate in the governmental process. This chapter examines the nature of interest groups and shows how they function.

THE NATURE AND FUNCTIONS OF INTEREST GROUPS

The discussion by V. O. Key, Jr., concentrates on private pressure groups and the extent to which they are links between public opinion and government. One interesting conclusion is that the elites of interest groups are not able to influence their members' attitudes to anywhere near the degree commonly thought possible. Pressure group participation in government more often than not reflects highly limited participation by the active elements of the groups. Public policy is often hammered out by very small numbers of individuals both in the government and in the private sphere. Political leaders can never stray too far beyond the boundaries of consent, but these are often very broad.

41
V. O. Key, Jr.

PRESSURE GROUPS

Pressure groups occupy a prominent place in analyses of American politics. In a regime characterized by official deference to public opinion and by adherence to the doctrine of freedom of association, private organizations may be regarded as links that connect the citizen and government. They are differentiated in both composition and function from political parties. Ordinarily they concern themselves with only a narrow range of policies, those related to the peculiar interests of the group membership. Their aim is primarily to influence the content of public policy rather than the results of elections. Those groups with a mass membership, though, may oppose or support particular candidates; in that case they are treated as groups with power to affect election results and, thereby, with capacity to pressure party leaders, legislators, and others in official position to act in accord with their wishes. . . .

PUZZLES OF PRESSURE POLITICS

. . . [There are] a series of puzzles as we seek to describe the role of pressure groups as links between opinion and government. Clearly the model of the lobbyist who speaks for a united following, determined in its aims and prepared to reward its friends and punish its enemies at the polls, does not often fit reality. Nor is it probable that the unassisted effort of pressure organizations to mold public opinion in support of their position has a large effect upon mass opinion. Yet legislators listen respectfully to the representations of the spokesmen of private groups, which in turn spend millions of dollars every year in propagandizing the public. Leaders of private groups articulate the concerns of substantial numbers of persons, even though they may not have succeeded in indoctrinating completely the members of their own groups. All this activity must have some functional significance in the political system. The problem is to identify its functions in a manner that seems to make sense. In this endeavor a distinction of utility is that made . . . between mass-membership organizations and nonmass organizations, which far outnumber the former.

Representation of Mass-Membership Groups. Only the spokesmen for mass-membership organizations can give the appearance of representing voters in sufficient numbers to impress (or intimidate) government. The influence of

Reprinted by permission of the publishers from V. O. Key, Jr., *The Responsible Electorate* (Cambridge, Mass.: The Belknap Press of Harvard University Press), Chapter 1, pp. 1–8. Copyright 1966, by the President and Fellows of Harvard College.

nonmass groups, which often have only a few hundred or a few thousand members, must rest upon something other than the threat of electoral retribution. As has been seen, the reality of the behavior of members of mass organizations is that in the short run they are not manipulable in large numbers by their leaders. Their party identification anchors many of them to a partisan position, and over the longer run they seem to be moved from party to party in presidential elections by the influences that affect all types and classes of people.

The spokesmen of mass-membership groups also labor under the handicap that they may be made to appear to be unrepresentative of the opinions of their members. When the president of an organization announces to a Congressional committee that he speaks for several million people, the odds are that a substantial proportion of his members can be shown to have no opinion or even to express views contrary to those voiced by their spokesmen. This divergency is often explained as a wicked betrayal of the membership or as a deliberate departure from the mass mandate. Yet it is not unlikely that another type of explanation more often fits the facts. Opinions, as we have seen in many contexts, do not fall into blacks and whites. It may be the nature of mass groups that attachment to the positions voiced by the peak spokesmen varies with attachment to and involvement in the group. At the leadership level the group position is voiced in its purest and most uncompromising form. A substantial layer of group activists subscribes to the official line, but among those with less involvement the faith wins less general acceptance. At the periphery of the group, though, the departure from the official line may be more a matter of indifference than of dissent. Leadership policy is often pictured as the consequence of interaction between leadership and group membership, which may be only partially true. Leaders may be more accurately regarded as dedicated souls who bid for group support of their position. Almost invariably they receive something less than universal acquiescence. This may be especially true in mass organizations in which political endeavor is to a degree a side issue—as, for example, in trade unions and farm organizations. As one traces attitudes and opinions across the strata of group membership, the clarity of position and the extremeness of position become more marked at the level of high involvement and activism.

If it is more or less the nature of mass organizations to encompass a spectrum of opinion rather than a single hue, much of the discussion of the representativeness of group leadership may be beside the point. However that may be, circumstances surrounding the leadership elements of mass organizations place them, in their work of influencing government, in a position not entirely dissimilar to that of leaders of nonmass groups. They must rely in large measure on means not unlike those that must be employed by groups with only the smallest membership. The world of pressure politics becomes more a politics among the activists than a politics that involves many people. Yet politics among the activists occurs in a context of concern about public opinion, a concern that colors the mode of action if not invariably its substance.

Arenas of Decision and Norms of Action. The maneuvers of pressure-group politics thus come ordinarily to occur among those highly involved and immediately concerned about public policy; the connection of these maneuvers with public opinion and even with the opinions of mass-membership organizations tends to be tenuous. Many questions of policy are fought out within vaguely bounded arenas in which the activists concerned are clustered. A major factor in the determination of the balance of forces within each arena is party control of the relevant governmental apparatus. Included among the participants in each issue-cluster of activists are the spokesmen for the pressure groups concerned, the members of the House and Senate committees with jurisdiction, and the officials of the administrative departments and agencies concerned. In the alliances of pressure politics those between administrative agencies and private groups are often extremely significant in the determination of courses of action. The cluster of concerned activists may include highly interested persons, firms, and organizations scattered over the country, though the boundaries delimiting those concerned vary from question to question, from arena to arena. In short, pressure politics among the activitists takes something of the form that it would take if there were no elections or no concern about the nature of public opinion; that is, those immediately concerned make themselves heard in the process of decision.

In the give and take among the activists, norms and values with foundations in public opinion are conditioning factors. The broad values of the society determine to a degree who will be heard, who can play the game. Those who claim to speak for groups that advocate causes outside the range of consensus may be given short shrift. Some groups advocating perfectly respectable causes may be heard with less deference than others. Subtle standards define what David Truman calls "access" to the decision makers. To some extent this is a party matter: an AFL-CIO delegation does not expect to be heard with much sympathy by a committee dominated by right-wing Republicans. The reality of access, too, may provide an index to the tacit standards in definition of those interests regarded as having a legitimate concern about public policy. The spokesmen of groups both large and small are often heard with respect, not because they wield power, but because they are perceived as the representatives of interests entitled to be heard and to be accorded consideration as a matter of right.

Within the range of the permissible, the process of politics among the activists is governed to some extent by the expectation that all entitled to play the game shall get a fair deal (or at least a fair hearing before their noses are rubbed in the dirt). Doubtless these practices parallel a fairly widespread set of attitudes within the population generally. Probably those attitudes could be characterized as a disposition to let every group—big business and labor unions as well—have its say, but that such groups should not be permitted to dominate the government. In the implementation of these attitudes the legalism of American legislators plays a role. Frequently Congressional committeemen regard themselves as engaged in a judicial role of hearing the evidence and of arriving at decisions based on some sort of standards of equity.

Rituals of the Activists. The maneuvers of group spokesmen, be they spokesmen for mass or nonmass organizations, are often accompanied by rituals in obeisance to the doctrine that public opinion governs. The belief often seems to be that Congressmen will be impressed by a demonstration that public opinion demands the proposed line of action or inaction. Hence, groups organize publicity campaigns and turn up sheaves of editorials in support of their position. They stimulate people to write or to wire their Congressmen; if the labor of stimulation is too arduous, they begin to sign to telegrams names chosen at random from the telephone directory. They solicit the endorsement of other organizations for their position. They lobby the American Legion and the General Federation of Women's Clubs for allies willing to permit their names to be used. On occasion they buy the support of individuals who happen to hold official positions in other organizations. They form fraudulent organizations with impressive letterheads to advance the cause. They attempt to anticipate and to soften the opposition of organizations that might be opposed to their position. Groups of similar ideological orientation tend to "run" together or to form constellations in confederation for mutual advantage.

All these maneuvers we have labelled "rituals"; that is, they are on the order of the dance of the rainmakers. That may be too brutal a characterization, for sometimes these campaigns have their effects—just as rain sometimes follows the rainmakers' dance. Yet the data make it fairly clear that most of these campaigns do not affect the opinion of many people and even clearer that they have small effect by way of punitive or approbative feedback in the vote. Their function in the political process is difficult to divine. The fact that organizations engage in these practices, though, is in itself a tribute to the importance of public opinion. To some extent, too, these opinion campaigns are not so much directed to mass opinion as to other activists who do not speak for many people either but have access to the arena of decision-making and perhaps have a viewpoint entitled to consideration. In another direction widespread publicity, by its creation of the illusion of mass support, may legitimize a position taken by a legislator. If a legislator votes for a measure that seems to arouse diverse support, his vote is not so likely to appear to be a concession to a special interest.

Barnums Among the Businessmen. An additional explanation that apparently accounts for a good deal of group activity is simply that businessmen (who finance most of the campaigns of public education by pressure groups) are soft touches for publicity men. The advertising and public-relations men have demonstrated that they can sell goods; they proceed on the assumption that the business of obtaining changes in public policy is analogous to selling soap. They succeed in separating businessmen from large sums of money to propagate causes, often in a manner that sooner or later produces a boomerang effect.

Professional bureaucrats of the continuing and well-established organizations practice restraint in their public-relations campaigns. They need to gain the confidence of Congressmen and other officials with whom they also need to be able to speak the next time they meet. The fly-by-night organization or the business group that falls into the clutches of an unscrupulous public-relations firm is more likely to indulge in the fantastic public relations and pressure campaign. Thus the National Tax Equality Association raised some $600,000 to finance a campaign against the tax exemptions of cooperatives, the most important of which are farm coops. Contributions came from concerns as scattered as the Central Power & Light Co., of Corpus Christi, Texas; Fairmont Foods Co., of Omaha, Nebraska; Central Hudson Gas Electric Corporation, of Poughkeepsie, New York; and the Rheem Manufacturing Co., of San Francisco. The late Representative Reed, of New York, who was not one to attack business lightly, declared:

> Mr. Speaker, an unscrupulous racket, known as the National Tax Equality Association, has been in operation for some time, directing its vicious propaganda against the farm co-operatives. To get contributions from businessmen, this racketeering organization has propagandized businessmen with false statements to the effect that if farm co-operatives were taxed and not exempted the revenue to the government would mount annually to over $800,000,000. [The treasury estimate was in the neighborhood of $20,000,000.] This is, of course, absolutely false and nothing more nor less than getting money under false pretenses. ... This outfit of racketeers known as the Tax Equality Association has led honest businessmen to believe that their contributions were deductible from gross income as ordinary and necessary business expense with reference to their Federal income-tax return.

The Tax Equality Association provided its subscribers with the following form letter to send to their Congressmen:

> Dear Mr. Congressman: You raised my income taxes. Now I hear you are going to do it again. But you still let billions in business and profits escape. How come you raise my taxes, but let co-ops, mutuals, and other profit-making corporations get off scot free, or nearly so? I want a straight answer—and I want these businesses fully taxed before you increase my or anyone else's income taxes again.

Letters so phrased are not well designed to produce favorable Congressional response. The ineptness of this sort of campaign creates no little curiosity about the political judgment of solvent businessmen who put their money or their corporation's money into the support of obviously stupidly managed endeavors.

Autonomous Actors or Links? This review of the activities of pressure groups may raise doubts about the validity of the conception of these groups as links between public opinion and government. The reality seems to be that the conception applies with greater accuracy to some groups than to others. Certainly group spokesmen may represent a shade of opinion to government even though not all their own members share the views they express. Yet to a considerable degree the work of the spokesmen of private groups, both large and small, proceeds without extensive involvement of either the membership or a wider public. Their operations as they seek to influence legislation and administration, though, occur in a milieu of concern about opinion, either actual or latent. That concern also disposes decision-makers to attend to shades of opinion and preference relevant to decision though not necessarily of great electoral strength—a disposition of no mean importance in the promotion of the equitable treatment of people in a democratic order. The chances are that the effects of organized groups on public opinion occur mainly over the long run rather than in short-run maneuvers concerned with particular congressional votes. Moreover, group success may be governed more by the general balance of partisan strength than by the results of group endeavors to win friends in the mass public. An industry reputed to be led by swindlers may not expect the most cordial reception from legislative committees, especially at times when the balance of strength is not friendly to any kind of business. If the industry can modify its public image, a task that requires time, its position as it maneuvers on particulars (about which few of the public can ever know anything) may be less unhappy. That modification may be better attained by performance than by propaganda.

CASE STUDIES IN PRESSURE GROUP POLITICS

Administrative agencies often are the focal point of government policy-making, and therefore pressure groups concentrate upon the bureaucracy in order to achieve their objectives. Public policy often emerges from administrative agency-pressure group interaction, for together such an alliance of public and private interest is very difficult to overcome. The following selection illustrates the way in which such a combination of interests has developed in the defense policy field, causing concern to proponents of greater presidential and Congressional control independent of the Pentagon and private contractors' interests.

42

THE "MILITARY LOBBY": ITS IMPACT ON CONGRESS AND THE NATION

What led President Eisenhower, on the eve of his retirement, to warn the nation of "unwarranted influence" by what he called "the military-industrial complex"?

What is this complex, what is the nature and extent of its influence, and how is it exercised?

What dangers—if any—are implicit in the situation described by the former President?

These were the principal questions raised by the President's parting words (for text, see below). In an attempt to answer them, *Congressional Quarterly* culled the record of presidential press conferences, Congressional hearings, and other public documents. In addition, extensive off-the-record interviews were conducted with members of Congress, representatives of defense contractors, former government officials, and other persons with pertinent information. Results of this survey of fact and opinion are summarized on the following pages.

EISENHOWER'S WARNING

In his final address to the Nation on January 17, President Eisenhower noted that the United States has been compelled to "create a permanent armaments industry of vast proportions" and to maintain a defense establishment employing 3.5 million persons and spending huge sums. He continued as follows:

> This conjunction of an immense military establishment and a large arms industry is new in American experience. The total influence—economic, political, even spiritual—is felt in every city, every state house, every office of the federal government. We recognize the imperative need for this development. Yet we must not fail to comprehend its grave implications. Our toil, resources and livelihood are all involved; so is the very structure of our society.
>
> In the councils of government, we must guard against the acquisition of unwarranted influence, whether sought or unsought, by the military-industrial complex. The potential for the disastrous rise of misplaced power exists and will persist. We must never let the weight of this combination endanger our liberties or democratic processes. We should take nothing for granted. Only an alert and knowledgeable

From the Congressional Quarterly, March 24, 1961, Copyright © 1961 by the Congressional Quarterly Service. Reprinted by permission. This article appeared in the *Congressional Record,* March 26, 1961, pp. 4557 ff.

citizenry can compel the proper meshing of the huge industrial and military machinery of defense with our peaceful methods and goals, so that security and liberty may prosper together.

EISENHOWER'S VIEWS

The President's warning of January 17 was his first public reference to a "military-industrial complex." But the concept was in the making for eight years, during which the President had touched on most of the major components of his final declaration. These were the principal elements of his thinking, as seen by his associates and partially reflected in the record:

National survival, he stated in 1953 and repeatedly thereafter, rested on "security with solvency." To achieve this required maximum effort to counter the inherent tendency of federal expenditures in general, and defense spending in particular, to rise. The key to success lay in "balance"—not, as he said April 25, 1958, during his battle with Congress over reorganization, in "overindulging sentimental attachments to outmoded military machines and concepts," nor, as he put it January 27, 1960, in heeding the "noisy trumpeting about dazzling military schemes or untrustworthy programs."

Ranged against this view, the President realized, was a host of special interests—the armed services and their civilian allies in business and in Congress. Beginning in 1953, when he cut the Air Force budget by $5 billion, the services had repeatedly carried their fight for more funds to Congress and the press. (More than one member had called him to say they were changing their votes in response to local pressures generated by the Pentagon.) "Obviously political and financial considerations" rather than "strict military needs" were influencing the situation, he said June 3, 1959. If such forces were allowed to prevail, he said March 11, 1959, "everybody with any sense knows that we are finally going to a garrision state."

Revered by the nation as its chief military hero, and respected as its Commander in Chief, the President was confident of his ability to "put need above pressure-group inducement, before local argument, before every kind of any pressure except that that America needs," as he put it February 11, 1960. The star-studded brass of the Pentagon awed him not a bit; "there are too many of these generals who have all sorts of ideas," he said February 3, 1960. Knowing how they "operated," however, he feared that his successor—whether Nixon or Kennedy—would be unable to withstand their pressures.

This, according to a close associate, was what impelled the President to speak out as he prepared to leave office. Deeply committed to the goal of disarmament, he was sensitive to the counterinfluence of the "military-industrial complex." The extent of his concern was indicated when, at his final press conference, January 18, he described the impact of widespread advertising by missile manufacturers as "almost an insidious penetration of our own minds that the only thing this country is engaged in is weaponry and missiles." This, he said, was something "we just can't afford."

BACKGROUND

Defense spending reached its postwar low of $11.1 billion in fiscal 1948. By 1953, the cold war and a hot war in Korea had boosted spending to its postwar high of $43.7 billion. President Eisenhower cut that to $35.5 billion in 1955; thereafter, defense outlays climbed each year, to reach a projected $42.9 billion in fiscal 1962. At no time during his eight years in office did military spending amount to less than one-half of the federal budget or less than 8 percent of the nation's gross national product. All told, the armed services spent $313 billion during the eight years, fiscal 1954–1961; when the costs of military aid, atomic energy, and stockpiling are added, that total mounts to $354 billion.

There is no yardstick by which to measure with precision the economic impact of these expenditures, but there is no question that it has been considerable. According to a 1960 study by the Defense Procurement Subcommittee of the Joint Economic Committee, there were 38 million procurement transactions with a dollar volume of $228 billion from 1950 through 1959. Few areas of the economy were untouched by these purchases of goods and services.

The largest portion of defense spending, however, is allocated to the development, production, and deployment of major weapons systems. In fiscal 1960, when military prime contract awards of $10,000 or more totaled $21 billion, $15.4 billion or 73.4 percent of the total went to 100 companies (or their subsidiaries) of which 65 were engaged primarily in "research, development, test or production of aircraft, missiles, or electronics." . . .

Despite the heavy concentration of prime contract awards among a small number of companies (in 1960 five companies accounted for 25 percent of the dollar volume, twenty one companies for 50 percent), extensive subcontracting helps to spread procurement expenditures, employment and profits throughout the country—although not as evenly as some states would like it. In addition, some 1.5 million members of the armed services and almost 1 million civilian employees of the Defense Department are spread throughout the fifty states, with payrolls that totaled $11.4 billion in fiscal 1960. Another $650 million was paid to more than one million members of the National Guard and other Reserve groups. . . .

A further indication of the extent of defense-related activities is the wide distribution of facilities. From lists furnished by the military services, Atomic Energy Commission, and National Aeronautics and Space Administration, CQ determined the location of 738 separate installations by Congressional district. According to this list, there are one or more installations in 282 of the country's 437 districts. . . .

Taken together, these data suggest the sweeping extent of the defense establishment and its economic impact, and provide the background against which to examine the concept of a "military-industrial complex."

HÉBERT PROBE

In mid-1959, the House Armed Services Special Investigations Subcommittee, headed by Representative F. Edward Hébert, Democrat of Louisiana, questioned seventy-five witnesses over twenty-five days regarding the employment of retired officers by defense industries. The public, and Hébert as the hearings began, was alarmed by reports "about the alleged conduct of some military men who depart the ranks of defense for lush places on the payrolls of defense contractors." As it turned out, no real evidence of misconduct was produced. But the hearings shed considerable light on the ramifications of military-industrial relations.

Retired Officers. More than 1,400 retired officers in the rank of major or higher—including 261 of general or flag rank—were found to be employed by the top 100 defense contractors. The company employing the largest number (187, including 27 retired generals and admirals) was General Dynamics Corp., headed by former Secretary of the Army Frank Pace, which also received the biggest defense orders of any company in 1960. Duties of these officers, according to the testimony of their employers, encompassed a wide range of technical, management, and "representation" functions. But in no case, it appeared, was the officer involved in "selling" or the negotiation of defense contracts.

"Influence." With little variation, retired officers told the Hébert subcommittee that they were "has-beens" without influence upon the decisions of their former colleagues still on active duty. None had experienced "pressure" of this kind while still in the service; if any retired officers had asked him for a favor, "I would throw them out on their ear," said Lt. Gen. C. S. Irvine (retired), director of planning for Avco Corp. No one, however, took issue with the statement of Vice Adm. H. G. Rickover that the former jobs of retired officers often were filled "by people who are their dear friends, or even by people whom they have been influential in appointing, and naturally they will be listened to."

Illustrative of this point was the testimony of Adm. William M. Fechteler, retired, former Chief of Naval Operations and a consultant to General Electric Atomic Products Division. He told of arranging appointments for a GE vice-president: "I took him in to see Mr. Gates, the Secretary of the Navy. I took him in to see Admiral Burke. He had not met Admiral Burke before. And then I made appointments with him with the Chief of the Bureau of Ships. But I did not accompany him there, because those are materiel bureaus which make contracts. And I studiously avoid even being in the room when anybody talks about a contract."

Entertainment. Two instances of entertainment by defense contractors came before the Hébert subcommittee. George Bunker, chairman of the Martin Co., acknowledged that his firm had entertained at least twenty-six active-duty officers at a weekend retreat in the Bahamas. Bunker denied there was any impropriety involved, saying "a man could neither operate nor compete effectively unless he had a close personal relationship." But spokesmen for the Secretaries of the three services agreed that such chumminess "doesn't look well" and could not be condoned.

The second case concerned an invitation to a "small off-the-record party" to discuss the plans and problems of the Air Research and Development Command with its newly promoted Chief, Lt. Gen. Bernard S. Schriever. The invitation, sent to Representative Hébert and nine other members of Congress (all but two of whom were members and of the Armed Services or Appropriations Committees), was issued by three Air Force contractors: Aerojet-General President Dan A. Kimball (onetime Secretary of the Navy), General Dynamics' Pace, and Martin's Bunker. All three men defended the propriety of the proposed party (which was called off because of the "publicity") as being in Pace's words, "a means of advancing the interests of the United States of America."

Advertising. Shortly before the Hébert hearings began, a major controversy developed in and out of Congress over the respective merits of two competing antiaircraft missile systems—the Army's Nike-Hercules and the Air Force's Bomarc. Advertisements extolling the virtues of the two systems were inserted in Washington, D.C., newspapers by their prime contractors—Western Electric Co. and Boeing Airplane Co., respectively—while the issue was before Congress. Questioned by the Hébert subcommittee about the timing and purpose of the ads, spokesmen for the companies insisted that they were parts of long-term "information" programs.

However, Boeing's Harold Mansfield acknowledged that his company was fighting against a "campaign" of "misinformation" about the Bomarc, while Western Electric's W. M. Reynolds said the Nike ads had been suggested to the company by the Army. Both companies also acknowledged discussing proposed cutbacks in the Nike and Bomarc programs with members of Congress from areas where employment would be affected. Said Mansfield: "Many of the most important decisions in the defense of our country are not made by military technicians. They are made in the Congress of the United States. And the Bomarc-Nike decision is one such decision."

Associations. Also questioned by the Hébert subcommittee were representatives of six organizations engaged in promoting the mutual interests of the armed services and their contractors in national security matters. All headquartered in Washington, they are the—

Association of the U.S. Army, with about 63,000 members (including military personnel on active duty) and 1958 income of $290,000, of which $143,000 was revenue from advertising in *Army* magazine. One of its aims: "To foster public understanding and support of the U.S. Army." Executive vice president: Lt. Gen. W. L. Weible, USA (retired). Among those on its advisory board: Donald Douglas, Jr., president of Douglas Aircraft Co.; Frank Pace, chairman of General Dynamics Corp.; Senators John J. Sparkman, Democrat, of Alabama, and Strom Thurmond, Democrat, of South Carolina.

Navy League, with about 38,000 members (no active duty personnel) and 1958 income of $179,000 plus $32,000 from advertising in *Navy—The Maga-*

zine of Sea Power. Self-description: "The civilian arm of the Navy." President: Frank Gard Jameson. Among those on its advisory council: Dan Kimball, president of Aerojet-General and former Secretary of the Navy; Adm. Robert B. Carney (retired), chairman of Bath Iron Works Shipbuilding Corp., and former Chief of Naval Operations.

Air Force Association, with about 60,000 members (including about 30,000 Air Force personnel) and 1958 income of $1.2 million, including $527,-000 from advertising in *Air Force and Space Digest.* Its aim: "To support the achievement of such airpower as is necessary" for national security. Executive director: James H. Straubel. Among its directors: 14 employees of defense contractors, including Lt. Gen. James H. Doolittle, USAF (retired) of Space Technology Laboratories.

American Ordnance Association, formerly the Army Ordnance Association, with about 42,000 members and 1958 income of $474,000, of which subscriptions and advertisements in the magazine *Ordnance* furnished $253,-000. Its aim: "Armament preparedness." Executive vice president: Col. Leo A. Codd, USAR (retired).

Aerospace Industries Association, formerly the Aircraft Industries Association, a trade association with 79 member companies and 1958 income of $1.4 million in dues ranging up to $75,000 per member. Its aim: To promote the manufacture and sale of "aircraft and astronautical vehicles of every nature and description." President: Gen. Orval R. Cook, USAF (retired).

National Security Industrial Association, formerly the Navy Industrial Association, with 502 member companies and 1958 income $238,000, mostly from dues. Its aim: "To establish a close working relationship between industrial concerns" and national security agencies. Executive director: Capt. R. N. McFarlane, USN (retired).

According to the testimony of their representatives, none of these groups had anything to do with procurement; all were ignorant of any "pressure" in behalf of one or another manufacturer. The three service groups acknowledged their interest in building up grassroots support for the respective branches of the armed forces; they also maintained that they were fully independent of the services they represented, although the testimony showed that, for the most part, Army, Navy, and Air Force doctrines and weapon systems received enthusiastic support in their respective publications.

All of the groups insisted that their primary function was to inform and educate. Only the Aerospace Industries Association has registered under the lobby law, but General Cook said "we believe we do not operate according to the classic definition of a lobbyist. . . . We don't even dream of buying any influence of any kind." Asked whether the best interests of the industry would be served by an increase or decrease in defense spending, Cook said: "From a selfish point of view, the best interest of the industry would be served by an increase, of course, but from a patriotic and national point of view, it might not be."

Peter J. Schenck, then president of the Air Force Association and an official of Raytheon Corp., described the basis for close military-industrial relations as follows: "The day is past when the military requirement for a major weapons system is set up by the military and passed on to industry to build the hardware. Today it is more likely that the military requirement is the result of joint participation of military and industrial personnel, and it is not unusual for industry's contribution to be a key factor. Indeed there are highly placed military men who sincerely feel that industry currently is setting the pace in the research and development of new weapons systems."

Conclusion

In its report filed January 18, 1960, the Hébert subcommittee said it was "impressed by several obvious inconsistencies in testimony" relating to the influence enjoyed by retired officers in the employment of defense contractors. Said the report: "The better grade and more expensive influence is a very subtle thing when being successfully applied. . . . The 'coincidence' of contract and personal contacts with firms represented by retired officers and retired civilian officials sometimes raises serious doubts as to the complete objectivity of some of these decisions." The subcommittee proposed, among other steps, a much tighter law regarding "sales" to the government by retired personnel; the House later passed a watered-down version of the proposal. (1959 Almanac, p. 727; 1960 Almanac, p. 279.)

ROLE OF CONGRESS

Charged with the responsibility of appropriating more than $40 billion each year for defense—and in the process deciding how to meet the conflicting claims of competing services for a larger share of the pie—Congress is up to its ears in the military-industrial issue. Collectively, the record shows, the members strive to sift fact from fancy, and to point up and root out instances of waste and duplication in the defense program. The record also shows that, individually, the members are zealous in representing the interests of their districts and states. Here are some examples:

"Fair Share." Documenting his case with facts and figures, Representative Hechler, Democrat, of West Virginia, told the House on June 1, 1959: "I am firmly against the kind of logrolling which would subject our defense program to narrowly sectional or selfish pulling and hauling. But I am getting pretty hot under the collar about the way my state of West Virginia is shortchanged in Army, Navy, and Air Force installations. I am going to stand up on my hind legs and roar until West Virginia gets the fair treatment she deserves." (Hechler plans to resume his campaign shortly.)

In the same vein, members of the New York delegation, led by Senators Kenneth B. Keating, Republican, and Jacob K. Javits, Republican, have long complained about the overconcentration of prime contract awards placed with

California firms. Asking only for a "fair share," they want defense procurement officials to consider "the strategic and economic desirability of allocating purchases to different geographic areas" of the country. . . .

Installations. The opening, expansion, cutback, or closing of any military installation is of vital interest to the Member whose area is affected. In recent years, with reductions in the size of the Army and other changes in the composition of defense forces, there have been more closings than openings, and the affected members have been quick to take issue. Some recent instances: Senator Albert Gore, Democrat, of Tennessee, said Febraury 15 that he had written Secretary of the Air Force Eugene M. Zuckert about reports that Stewart Air Force Base at Smyrna, Tennessee, might be closed, and had been assured that "as of now no change is contemplated which should cause any concern."

Senator Olin D. Johnston, Democrat, of South Carolina, after calling on President Kennedy February 20, said he had been assured that careful consideration would be given to the future of Fort Jackson at Columbia, South Carolina, and Donaldson Air Force Base at Greenville, South Carolina.

Representative Samuel S. Stratton, Democrat, of New York, said March 3 that he had wired Secretary Zuckert about reports of a plan to transfer certain operations from Griffiss Air Force Base at Rome, New York. Said Stratton: "It is fantastic to learn that one more defense department is considering recommendations which would have the effect of increasing unemployment in upstate New York, already hard hit by lay-offs."

Representative Emanuel Celler, Democrat, of New York, said March 6 that Secretary of Defense Robert S. McNamara had assured him he had no knowledge "of any plans or proposals to shut down the operations" at the Brooklyn Navy Yard.

Procurement. Decisions to begin, accelerate, reduce, or stop production of various weapons and weapon systems are also of major interest to members in whose districts or states the manufacturers involved are located. Here are examples of Representatives at work:

When the House Appropriations Committee chopped the Air Force's 1959 request for the Bomarc by $162.7 million, Representative Don Magnuson, Democrat, of Washington, charged that few members were aware of "the incredible lengths to which the adherents of the Nike defense system have gone in their attempt to discredit the Bomarc. . . . Of course, this is Army inspired." (Contractor for Bomarc was Boeing Airplane Co., headquartered in Seattle, Washington.)

Also in 1959, Representative John R. Foley, Democrat, of Maryland, offered an amendment to the defense bill to add $10 million to Air Force funds to buy 10 F—27 transports from the Fairchild Aircraft Co. of Hagerstown, Maryland, in Foley's district. This failed, but the Senate obliged with $11 million. When House conferees refused to go along, Senator J. Glenn Beall, Republican, of Maryland, begged the Senate to insist, saying that, of the $4 billion to be spent on aircraft, "all we ask for Fairchild is $11 million."

Recent reports that the Pentagon was thinking of cutting back the B—70 program led Representative Edgar W. Hiestand, Republican, of California, to write Secretary McNamara February 27 to assure him of "the strong congressional support for this valued program." North American Aviation, Inc., prime contractor for the B—70, is located in Heistand's district.

Reserves. The well-known solicitude shown by Congress for the National Guard and other Reserve forces reflects to some degree a widespread local interest in the payrolls, armories, and other benefits involved, as well as effective work by the National Guard Association and the Reserve Officers Association. Among the forty Reserve officers in Congress are ... [four] generals: Howard W. Cannon, Democrat, of Nevada, brigadier general, USAFR; Strom Thurmond, Democrat, of South Carolina, major general, USAR; and Representatives James Roosevelt, Democrat, of California, brigadier general, USMCR; and Robert L. F. Sikes, Democrat, of Florida, brigadier general, USAR; Cannon and Thurmond are members of the Armed Services Committee; Sikes, of the Defense Appropriations Subcommittee. ...

President Eisenhower made no headway whatsoever in his three-year campaign to reduce National Guard and Army Reserve manpower levels to "conform to the changing character and missions" of the active forces; Congress responded with a mandatory floor of 400,000 for the Guard, and funds to maintain both the Guard and the Reserve at full strength. These actions, said the President in his final budget message, "are unnecessarily costing the American people over $80 million annually and have been too long based on other than strictly military needs." Even at the lower strengths he again proposed, the Reserves would cost "well over $1 billion in 1962," he said.

Summing up the cumulative impact of these varied expressions of Congressional interest, Representative Jamie L. Whitten, Democrat, of Mississippi, a member of the House Appropriations Defense Subcommittee, testified as follows January 29, 1960, before the Joint Economic Committee's Defense Procurement Subcommittee:

> I am convinced defense is only one of the factors that enter into our determinations for defense spending. The others are pump priming, spreading the immediate benefits of defense spending, taking care of all services, giving all defense contractors a fair share, spreading the military bases to include all sections, etc. There is no state in the Union and hardly a district in a state which doesn't have defense spending, contracting, or a defense establishment. We see the effect in public and Congressional insistance on continuing contracts, or operating military bases, though the need has expired.

CASE OF THE ZEUS

The confluence of service, contractor, and Congressional pressures is illustrated by the current revival of a campaign to launch production of the Army's Nike-Zeus anti-missile system, although final tests are more than a year away. Congress added $137 million to the budget in 1958 to start production, but the President refused to spend it; in his final budget, providing about $287 million for further development of Nike-Zeus, he said, "funds should not be committed to production until development tests are satisfactorily completed." Subsequently, these things happened.

On February 1 the magazine *Army* appeared with seven articles lauding the Nike-Zeus—four of them by Army commanders on active duty. Also in the issue: full-page advertisements by Western Electric Co., prime contractor for Nike-Zeus, and eight of its major subcontractors, together with a map showing how much of the $410 million contract was being spent in each of thirty-seven states (but $111 million in California, $110 million in New Jersey). The general message: It's time to start production.

On February 2, Senator Thurmond told the Senate that "we must start production of the Nike-Zeus now." Extolling the "experienced Army-industry team" that developed the system, he argued that "by spending money now to provide a capability for the production of components in quantity, we will save money in the long run." Rising to support his arguments were Senators B. Everett Jordon, Democrat, of North Carolina, and Frank Carlson, Republican, of Kansas. (*Army's* map showed spending of $36 million in North Carolina and $8.5 million in Kansas.)

On February 7, Representative George P. Miller, Democrat, of California, urged every Member of the House to "read the current issue of *Army* magazine" and to "support immediate action for limited component production of the Nike-Zeus system." Miller, a member of the Science and Astronautics Committee, said this could be done, "with the addition of less than $175 million to the present Army budget."

On February 13, Representative Daniel J. Flood, Democrat, of Pennsylvania, gave the House substantially the same speech delivered February 2 by Senator Thurmond, and also concluded that "we must start production of the Nike-Zeus now." Flood appended an article on the subject published by the Sperry Rand Corp., a subcontractor for Nike-Zeus. (*Army's* figure for spending in Pennsylvania: $10 million.)

On February 23, Representative John W. McCormack, Democrat, of Massachusetts, House majority leader, asked every Member to read Flood's "prescient address" of February 13. McCormack's conclusion: "Close the gap in our military posture; muzzle the mad-dog missile threat of the Soviet Union; loose the Zeus through America's magnificent production lines now." (*Army's* figure for Massachusetts: $1.5 million.)

On March 6, the press reported that President Kennedy was expected to approve a Defense Department compromise plan calling for an additional $100 million to $200 million to start tooling up. Eventual costs were estimated at from $5 billion to $20 billion.

EXTENT OF INFLUENCE

Proponents of the Nike-Zeus, it should be noted, base their case squarely on the national interest—the touchstone of debate, pro and con, concerning the merits of every proposal made in the name of defense. It is never clear, however, where the national interest begins and self-interest leaves off.

All of the persons questioned by CQ agreed that an element of self-interest pervades relationships among the services, their contractors and members of Congress. There was no consensus, however, regarding the extent to which decisions affecting the national interest are influenced by the self-interest of persons and organizations involved. Here is the gist of these views.

The Services. Locked in competition for larger shares of a defense budget that has not kept pace with the soaring costs of new weapon systems, the services toil constantly to "sell" their particular doctrines, programs, and requirements to the public, industry, and Congress. Recent examples: television programs on the Navy's Polaris and "The New Marine," an Army-Industry Liaison Seminar in New Orleans, an Air Force tour of Strategic Air Command headquarters in Omaha for 35 new Members of Congress.

The services are especially careful of their relations with Congress, particularly with members of the Armed Services and Appropriations Committees. When a senior member of the House Armed Services Committee complained of rumors that a Marine Corps installation might be removed from his district, the Commandant came in person to assure him that no change would be made "so long as I am in the job." A junior committee member, on learning that an unsolicited Army training center was to be located in his district, concluded that "someone" in the Pentagon was looking out for his interests.

There is some truth, all agree, in Representative Whitten's statement to the Defense Procurement Subcommittee that "you can look at some of our key people in the key places in Congress and go see how many military establishments are in their districts." One oft-cited example: the state of Georgia, home of the chairmen of both Senate and House Armed Services Committees. (To the proposal that a new Air Force installation be placed in Georgia, one brave General is credited with replying that "one more base would sink the state.")

But Congressmen accustomed to the prevalence of "logrolling" in many other areas see nothing sinister in this situation. The services are generally credited with being "correct" in their dealings with members; none of those questioned by CQ complained of "pressure" by the services.

The Contractors. For many of the major defense contractors, their only client of any importance is the United States government and the bulk of their business is obtained through negotiated contracts with one or more of the armed services. It is a highly competitive field, by all accounts, in which a considerable premium is placed on "good personal relations" with the client. Even those companies doing business exclusively with one service will be found supporting all three service sounding boards: the Air Force Association, Navy League, and Association of the U.S. Army. Entertainment practices vary widely throughout the industry, but no one denies that personal friendships play an important part in shaping working relationships between client and vendor. Two episodes serve to illustrate the point.

In one "competition" for a new weapon system, Navy technicians decided to throw out one proposal on grounds it was based on faulty data. Warned by a Navy friend of the impending decision, the contractor promptly went to the admiral in charge and persuaded him to order a thirty-day delay to permit all bidders to submit additional data. (The well-informed contractor failed to win in the end, however.)

An Air Force "competition" for a new missile ended with a top-level decision to award the contract to Company A. Learning of this, the president of Company B went straight to the Secretary and persuaded him to order a complete review of the decision. Result: the contract went to Company B.

Sometimes helped and sometimes hurt by such manifestations of "influence," contractors generally accept it as "part of the game," recognizing that to some degree the outcome reflects a tendency on the part of all three services to take care of companies with whom they have been doing business for some time, before admitting any "outsiders." (Some companies have nevertheless managed to secure important prime contracts from all three services.)

Defense contractors vary in their attitudes toward relations with Congress. Small, new companies, trying to gain a foothold in the defense business, are quick to seek the aid of their Congressmen; established contractors recognize that such intercession may backfire, especially in an attempt to reverse an essentially technical decision by the services. As the Hébert hearings demonstrated, however, contractors are not at all reluctant to solicit the aid of interested members when (as in the Nike-Bomarc dispute) it is in the mutual interest of all concerned.

Congress. As the elected representatives of their states and districts, members of Congress take a keen political interest in the economic impact of defense activities in their areas, and are the first to admit it. But few believe that such considerations exert any significant influence over the course of defense spending or the shape of national strategy. The major complaint of some members is their lack of influence!

Certain members of the Armed Services Committees admit seeking the assignment because of large military installations and defense industries in their states or districts. Others consider themselves fortunate that they do not have such activities—and the local pressures that go along with them—in their own areas. Recognizing that changing military requirements may produce a "boom and bust" effect on any given community, they try to dissuade local enthusiasts who clamor for a new installation.

Outsiders detect a Navy bias in the makeup of the House Armed Services Committee and to a lesser extent, the Senate Armed Services Committee. (Of the former's thirty-seven members, twenty-five come from coastal states.) Committee members acknowledge that some of their colleagues reflect a service point of view (ten members of the House Committee are active reservists) and that the Navy's position is amply represented; they also contend, however, that there is a minimum of service-oriented partisanship in the work of the Committees.

As for dealings with contractors, most members express doubt concerning both the desirability and feasibility of intervening in procurement decisions. One Senator who did go to bat for one of his constituents (to no avail) found himself under fire from a competitor in the same state. His conclusion: it doesn't pay to get involved.

PROS AND CONS

Does the evidence support President Eisenhower's warning against "the acquisition of unwarranted influence, whether sought or unsought, by the military-industrial complex"? The answer varies with the individual.

"There is no question that the services and their contractors have an interest in maintaining a high degree of tension in the country," says a senior member of the House Defense Appropriations Subcommittee. But he foresees no threat to the democratic process, although admitting the need to guard against overly intimate relations between soldier, salesman, and legislator.

"There is a real danger that we may go the way of prewar Japan and Germany," says one member of the House Armed Service Committee, who objects to the presence of reserve officers on the Committee and sees the appointment of industrialists to top Defense Department posts as a bad practice.

"I don't know what Eisenhower was talking about," says a former Defense Department official. Strong civilian control over the military services can be maintained, he believes, by the selection of a sufficient number of able presidential appointees, regardless of their industrial background.

"The trouble is that national security has become popular—and the record of Congressional appropriations proves it," says a former Eisenhower associate. He sees the military-industrial complex as a "floating power" largely free of any restraint.

Several of those questioned by CQ ascribed the President's concern to over-preoccupation with the budget. Believing that the nation needs and can afford an even larger defense effort, they were inclined to dismiss his warning as misdirected. This point of view was reflected in *Air Force* magazine, which characterized reaction to the President's statement as a "flap" and deplored the "small wave of learned essays rehashing all of the irresponsible charges and insinuations that have been bandied around in Congressional hearings for the past few years." The great danger, it concluded, was that "an exercise of misdirected caution . . . could menace national security."

The first moves of the Kennedy Administration suggest little sympathy with the Eisenhower viewpoint. Orders have been placed for large numbers of additional transport planes. Steps have been taken to speed up defense purchases and "spread the business" in the interests of stimulating the lagging economy. Other proposals under consideration would add substantially to defense spending in the future.

At the same time, the new administration stands pledged to seek an agreement with the Soviets on banning nuclear tests and to pursue the goal of arms control. As yet, the chances of achieving either appear to be so remote as to preclude serious consideration of the possible opposition to any agreement by a "military-industrial complex." It may be worth noting, however, that the American Ordnance Assn. is calling for the "immediate resumption . . . of nuclear tests for both small and large weapons," and that *Ordnance* magazine argues that until the communist "goal of world dominion . . . is abandoned, there can be no lessening of our armament preparedness."

An important premise of group theory is that individuals do not count in the political process except as they operate through interest groups. The example of Ralph Nader might suggest the contrary, because there is little doubt that on an individual basis he has been able to gain many concessions from government in areas in which he is interested, such as automobile safety. Although he represents "consumer" interests, only in recent years has he attempted to organize his support in any formal way; originally he operated largely alone. Although Congressmen may have thought that a potential interest group was behind him and therefore they should pay attention to his demands, the fact is that until recently he stood alone against powerful private interests and was able to persuade Congressional committees and administrative agencies to enact policies more protective of the public interest as he conceived it. Richard Armstrong reviews Nader's activities and illustrates his influence upon the political process.

43
Richard Armstrong

THE PASSION THAT RULES
RALPH NADER

On a recent visit to Marymount College in Arlington, Virginia, Ralph Nader arrived at the school gymnasium an hour late. But he then proceeded to pacify an overflowing crowd of restless students—and earn a lecture fee of $2,500—

From Richard Armstrong, "The Passion that Rules Ralph Nader," reprinted from the May, 1971, issue of *Fortune* Magazine by special permission; © 1971 Time, Inc.

by denouncing America's big corporations in venomous language. Afterward one question from the audience brought a rousing and spontaneous burst of applause. When, the questioner asked, did he plan to run for President?

A slightly more measured assessment of the Nader phenomenon came from Bess Myerson, New York City's commissioner of consumer affairs, when she introduced him as star witness at a recent hearing on deceptive advertising. "Mr. Nader," she said, "is a remarkable man who, in the last six years, has done more as a private citizen for our country and its people than most public officials do in a lifetime."

The remarkable thing about this tribute is that it is literally true. In the seven years since he moved to Washington from Winsted, Connecticut—without funds and with a narrow base of expert knowledge in a single subject, automobile safety—Nader has created a flourishing nationwide movement, known as consumerism. He is chiefly responsible for the passage of at least six major laws, imposing new federal safety standards on automobiles, meat and poultry products, gas pipelines, coal mining, and radiation emissions from electronic devices. His investigations have led to a strenuous renovation at both the Federal Trade Commission and the Food and Drug Administration. And if the quality and convenience of American life do not seem dramatically improved after all that furious crusading, Nader can point to at least one quite tangible result. Last year, for the first time in nine years, traffic fatalities in the United States declined, to 55,300 from 56,400 in 1969. Unless the decline was a fluke (and officials at the Highway Traffic Safety Administration do not think it was), then for those 1,100 living Americans, whoever they may be, Nader can be said to have performed the ultimate public service.

MORE THAN TEN KREMLINS

And yet, despite all this, it is easy to conclude after a conversation with Nader that he is not primarily interested in protecting consumers. The passion that rules in him—and he is a passionate man—is aimed at smashing utterly the target of his hatred, which is corporate power. He thinks, and says quite bluntly, that a great many corporate executives belong in prison—for defrauding the consumer with shoddy merchandise, poisoning the food supply with chemical additives, and willfully manufacturing unsafe products that will maim or kill the buyer. In his words, the law should "pierce the corporate veil" so that individual executives could be jailed when their companies misbehaved. He emphasizes that he is talking not just about "fly-by-night hucksters" but the top management of "blue-chip business firms."

The lawyers who provide legal cover for all these criminal acts are, to Nader, nothing but "high-priced prostitutes." As for the advertising profession, Nader recently served up the following indictment: "Madison Avenue is engaged in an epidemic campaign of marketing fraud. It has done more to subvert and destroy the market system in this country than ten Kremlins ever dreamed of." With the certainty of the visionary, Nader would sweep away that shattered market system and replace it by various eccentric devices of his own, such as a government rating system for every consumer product.

If, on the one hand, Nader has advanced the cause of consumer protection by his skillful marshaling of facts in support of specific reforms, he has, on the other hand, made reform more difficult through his habit of coating his facts with invective and assigning the worst possible motives to almost everybody but himself. By some peculiar logic of his own, he has cast the consumer and the corporation as bitter enemies, and he seems to think that no reform is worth its salt unless business greets it with a maximum of suspicion, hostility, and fear.

Nader is a strange apparition in the well-tailored world of the Washington lawyer. His suits hang awkwardly off his lanky frame, all of them apparently gray and cut about a half size too large. His big brown eyes in their deep sockets have a permanent expression of hurt defiance, and before a crowd he blinks them nervously. The eyes, the bony face, and a small, set chin give him, a thirty-seven, the look of an underfed waif.

Nobody has been able to explain the deep personal anger that erupts when Nader begins to speak about corporations. He himself simply denies that he is anti-business. "People who make that charge are escalating the abstration," he told an interviewer recently, his long hands clasped together, his brown eyes flashing. "They don't dare face the issues." But anger of some kind is unmistakably there. It seems to spring out of some profound alienation from the comfortable world he sees around him, and perhaps dates back to his early days in the conservative little town of Winsted, where he was something of an oddball, the son of a Lebanese immigrant, the boy who read the Congressional Record. He recalls proudly that his father, who kept a restaurant and assailed customers with his political views, "forecast the corporate takeover of the regulatory agencies back in the 1930s." Princeton and Harvard Law School trained Nader's brilliant mind, but their social graces never touched his inner core. There seems something of the desert in him still, the ghost of some harsh prophet from his ancestral Lebanon.

According to one old friend, Nader has always had a conspiratorial view of the world, and when General Motors put private detectives on his trail in 1965 just before the publication of *Unsafe at Any Speed* that view was strongly reinforced. "He thought somebody was following him around," says the friend, "and then, by gosh, somebody *was* following him around." Apparently, at the time, Nader was convinced that GM planned to have him bumped off. He still moves about Washington in great secrecy from one rendezvous to the next.

THE FIFTH BRANCH OF GOVERNMENT

In his role as scourge of the regulatory agencies, Nader is aggressive and ill-mannered as a matter of calculated policy. "Rattle off a few facts so they will know you can't be bluffed," he tells his teams of young investigators setting out to interview government officials. "Get on the offensive and stay there." Says Lowell Dodge, who runs Nader's Auto Safety Center: "If somebody is messing up, Ralph wants to embarrass them."

But Nader can be an engaging fellow when he chooses. He takes care to maintain good relations with Washington journalists—parceling out news tips with an even hand—and many of them pay him the ultimate tribute of calling him the best reporter they know. To these men he seems to serve as a sort of ghost of conscience past, a reminder of investigations not pursued and stables left uncleansed. Both reporters and professional politicians find him extremely useful. "Nader has become the fifth branch of government, if you count the press as fourth," says a Senate aide who has worked with Nader often in drafting legislation. "He knows all the newspaper deadlines and how to get in touch with anybody any time. By his own hard work he has developed a network of sources in every arm of government. And believe me, no Senator turns down those calls from Ralph. He will say he's got some stuff and it's good, and the Senator can take the credit. Any afternoon he's in town you still see him trudging along the corridors here with a stack of documents under his arm, keeping up his contacts."

What Nader gets out of the intercourse is power—not the trappings but the substance—more of it by now than most of the Senators and Congressmen on whom he calls. When an important bill is pending he is quite capable of playing rough, threatening to denounce a Representative to the press unless he goes along on a key amendment. "Does Ralph like power?" The Senate aide laughed at such a naive question. "Good gracious, yes. He loves it." Compared to other powerful men in Washington, Nader enjoys a rare freedom of action, flourishing as a sort of freebooter who is able to pick his targets at will, unconstrained by an electorate or any judgment but his own. "You will find sensitive people around town who are saying it's time to take a second look at this guy," says the Senate aide. "There are people who wonder whether he ought to be the final arbiter of safety in autos or in the food supply. Nader has something the companies don't have—credibility—especially with the press. There is a danger that people will be afraid to go up against him for that reason alone."

REGRETS TO DAVID SUSSKIND

By any measure, Nader's power is still growing. He remains absolute master of his own movement, but he is no longer alone. "When I think of all the lean years Ralph spent knocking on doors—" says Theodore Jacobs, who was Nader's classmate at both Princeton and Harvard Law School and now serves as a sort of chief of staff. Jacobs had just concluded a telephone call that, from his end, had consisted only of various expressions of regret. "That was Susskind. He's got a new show, he wants Ralph, and I had to turn him down. Ralph hates New York—all that traffic and pollution—and I can't get him up there unless it's imperative. I spend a lot of my time saying no. Among other problems, he's got two people on his tail right now who are writing full-length biographies. He has to husband his time. He's down for the *Today* show next Tuesday, but that's right here in town. If there is an important bill pending in committee and they need some input, he'll be there. He'll duck anthing else for that."

Jacobs presides, loosely, over a modern suite of offices in downtown Washington housing the Center for the Study of Responsive Law. This is home base for the seven most senior of Nader's "raiders" and is one of the three organizations through which Nader now operates. The other two are located a few blocks away: the five-man Auto Safety Center and the Public Interest Research Group, staffed by twelve bright young graduates of top law schools, three of them women. In addition, there are the summertime student raiders, who this year will number about fifty, only one-quarter as many as last year. The program is being cut back, Jacobs explains, because the students are a mixed blessing, requiring a good deal of nursemaiding by the full-time staff. "But we still think it's useful for the regulatory agencies to see a fresh batch of faces wafting through."

One of the center's main functions is to handle a flood of crank calls. "No, I'm afraid Mr. Nader isn't here," says the young girl at the switchboard. "Can you tell me what it's about?" After a protracted conversation, she explains with a grin: "He said it was something so big he didn't dare put a word on paper. No name either, but still he wants to speak to Ralph." Nader drops by for a few minutes every day or so, and the other raiders emulate his casual example; by the switchboard, message boxes improvised out of brown paper are filled to overflowing with notices of calls never returned.

The Center for the Study of Responsive Law is tax-exempt, supported by well-known foundations, such as Field, Carnegie, and Stern, and by wealthy benefactors such as Midas muffler heir Gordon Sherman and Robert Townsend, author of *Up the Organization.* (Townsend gave $150,000.) On a budget of $300,000 a year, the center is able to pay its raiders a stipend of up to $15,000 each. "A far cry from five years ago," says one of the veteran raiders, Harrison Wellford, thirty-one, "when Ralph was being trailed by GM gumshoes and we would meet at night at the Crystal City hamburger joint on Connecticut Avenue to compare notes. We'd work our heads off and then get gunned down by someone from Covington & Burling [a large Washington law firm] who had been on an issue for a corporate client for ten years."

Consumers Union is the biggest single donor to the Auto Safety Center, which operates on a slender budget of $30,000 a year. The Public Interest Research Group, or PIRG as it is called, is Nader's own nonprofit law firm, and he pays all the bills out of his own pocket, including the stipends of $4,500 a year to the twelve young lawyers. It is an irony that must warm Nader's heart that the money comes out of the $270,000 he netted in the settlement of his lawsuit against GM for invasion of privacy. Since PIRG's budget is $170,000 a year, Nader is obviously going through his windfall at an unsustainable clip.

CONSCIOUSNESS III DOESN'T GIVE A DAMN

Nader calls his own organization "a big joke really, a drop in the bucket compared to the size of the problem." It is in his nature to conceive of the enemy as being enormous, pervasive, and exceedingly powerful. "How many public-interest lawyers would it take to oversee the Pentagon? A hundred? Multiply that by the number of departments and agencies. This country needs 50,000 full-time citizens, including 10,000 public-interest lawyers. And I could get that many applicants if I had the money." Last month Nader began a campaign to raise $750,000 from students in two states, Connecticut and Ohio, where the money would be used to set up Nader-like centers for investigating state and local government. Students in two other states, Oregon and Minnesota, have voted to donate $3 each from their college activities funds to finance similar organizations. Nader hopes that one plan or another will spread across the country.

To the young, Nader is a hero of great stature. Thousands of students in law, medicine, engineering, and every other field want to "conform their careers and their ideals," as he puts it, by going to work for him. They are the mass base of his movement, and he is able to pick and choose among them for his staff. (They say on campus that getting a job with Nader is "tougher than getting into Yale Law School.") And yet this appeal is in many ways hard to fathom. Nader has no use at all for the "counterculture," and he abhors drugs. "There's a conflict between living life on a level of feeling on the one hand and Ralph's product ethic on the other," admits Lowell Dodge. "To produce, to have an impact—that's what Ralph admires. Consciousness III doesn't give a damn about the FTC. Ralph does." Dodge thinks Nader is growing ever stronger on campus as revolutionary ideas begin to fade. "There's more interest in change *within* the system, and Ralph is the most effective example of an agent for change."

Nader hectors students mercilessly about their public duties, about their "anemic imaginations," about their "thousands of hours on the beach or playing cards." And they seem to love it. "Suppose students would engage in one of history's greatest acts of sacrifice and go without Coke and tobacco and alcohol, on which they spend $250 each a year?" he asked a student audience at Town Hall in New York. "They could develop the most powerful lobby in the country. Write to us! We'll tell you how to do it." Hands dived for pens as he called out his address in Washington.

It is possible to question, nevertheless, whether this enthusiasm would survive a close association with Nader. Although most of the members of his full-time staff plan to stay in public-interest legal work, many of them talk with enthusiasm about the day when they will be leaving Nader. One reason, of course, is money. "On $4,500 a year, it's tough," says Christopher White, one of the young lawyers at the Public Interest Research Group. And then these young people are blither spirits than Nader and have a spontaneity and graciousness he lacks. Although they refrain from criticizing him directly, the picture that emerges is of a boss at least as dictatorial as any they would find in a private law firm. "The emphasis is on production," one of them says. "Ralph thinks that if a brief is 90 percent right, it's a waste of time to polish it." Nader tells them that a work week of 100 hours is "about right." He lectures them about smoking, refuses to ride in their Volkswagens, and never has time to waste socializing. Lowell Dodge got a call from Nader last Christmas Eve, but only because Nader had a question to ask about work in progress.

NOTCHES ON NADER'S GUN

THE AUTOMOBILE. An auto-safety enthusiast while at Princeton and Harvard Law School, Nader went to Washington in 1964 to work on his pet subject as an aide to Daniel Patrick Moynihan, then Assistant Secretary of Labor, who happened to be interested in a field far removed from his assigned duties. Bored with office routine, Nader quit the following year and wrote *Unsafe at Any Speed* in ten weeks. During the Senate hearings on auto safety, he came out a clear winner in a much-publicized confrontation with James Roche, president (now chairman) of General Motors. The publicity assured passage of the Motor Vehicle Safety Act of 1966, establishing a government agency to set mandatory vehicle-safety standards, of which there are now thirty-four.

UNSANITARY MEAT. For his second campaign. Nader found ready-made evidence in a study done by the Department of Agriculture of state-regulated packing plants, considered to be in intrastate commerce and so not covered by federal law. Many of the plants were filthy and rodent infested, but apparently nobody of any consequence had ever bothered to read the study's report. Nader did. The result was the Wholesome Meat Act of 1967, giving states the option of bringing their inspection programs up to federal standards or having them supplanted by federal inspection. In 1968 the provisions of the act were applied to poultry products.

FEDERAL TRADE COMMISSION. A team of student raiders assigned by Nader to the FTC in 1968 found one official at the agency literally asleep on the job, others frequenting nearby saloons during working hours, and still others who seldom bothered to come to work at all. President Nixon commissioned a study of the FTC by an American Bar Association panel, which confirmed the major findings of the Nader report: low morale, lack of planning, preoccupation with trivial cases and timidity in pursuing important ones. Outcome: New faces and new vigor at the FTC.

FOOD AND DRUG ADMINISTRATION. Student raiders studying the FDA in the summer of 1969 compiled evidence on two important regulatory blunders: approval of cyclamates and monosodium glutamate for unristricted use in the food supply. Alerted by the raiders, the news media covered both stories with unrestrained enthusiasm until the FDA banned cyclamates from soft drinks and manufacturers voluntarily stopped putting monosodium glutamate in baby food. In December, President Nixon fired the three top officials at the FDA.

OTHER DOINGS. Legislation inspired by Nader: Natural Gas Pipeline Safety Act (1968), Radiation Control for Health and Safety Act (1968), Coal Mine Health and Safety Act (1969), Comprehensive Occupational Safety and Health Act (1970). Published reports: *The Chemical Feast* (On the FDA); *The Interstate Commerce Omission* (It recommends abolishing the ICC); *Vanishing Air* (a critical look at air-pollution-control laws and industry compliance); *What to do with Your Bad Car* ("an action manual for lemon owners"); *One Life—One Physician* (On the medical profession). Reports in progress on: the Department of Agriculture, nursing homes, water pollution, Du Pont, First National City Bank of New York, the Washington law firm of Covington & Burling, land-use policies in California, supermarkets, and "brown lung" disease in the textile industry.

The warmth and empathy so important to the young are not to be found in any relationship with Nader. Robert Townsend's daughter Claire, a pretty blonde student at Princeton, says with unblushing candor that she became a raider last summer partly because "I had a terrible crush on Ralph. All the girls have crushes on Ralph." But Nader apparently never has crushes on them. He still lives monklike in a rented room. His most pronounced concession to cravings of the flesh comes in appeasing a voracious although picky appetite. He is leery of most meats but often tops off a meal with two desserts. It is somehow typical of the man that when the soon-to-be-famous blonde detective tried to pick him up, back during his fight with GM, she found him in a supermarket buying a package of cookies.

TRYING TO FIND FREE ENTERPRISE

What young people admire in Nader is a dark and uncompromising idealism, coupled with a system of New Left economics that he is able to shore up with all sorts of impressive-sounding facts. They think he has got the goods on "the system." And he is completely free of any humdrum sense of proportion. A conversation with Nader makes the consumer society sound as gory as a battlefield: motorists "skewered like shish kebab on non-collapsible steering wheels"; babies burned to death by flammable fabrics improperly labeled; a little girl decapitated because a glove-compartment door popped open in a low-speed collision; "thousands of people poisoned and killed every year through the irresponsible use of pesticides and chemicals."

The corporate criminals responsible for this slaughter always go unpunished. "If we were as lenient toward individual crime as we are toward big-business crime we would empty the prisons, dissolve the police forces, and subsidize the criminals." The regulatory agencies are "chatteled to business and indifferent to the public," and Congress is "an anachronism, although a good investment for corporations." As for the market economy, it is rapidly being destroyed by the same corporate executives who are always "extolling it at stockholder meetings."

"Where is the free-enterprise system?" Nader asks, a sly smile lighting up his face. "I'm trying to find it. Is it the oil oligopoly, protected by import quotas? The shared monopolies in consumer products? The securities market, that bastion of capitalism operating on fixed commisions and now provided with socialized insurance? They call me a radical for trying to restore power to the consumer, but businessmen are the true radicals in this country. They are taking us deeper and deeper into corporate socialism—corporate power using government power to protect it from competition."

DOWN TO ZERO PROFITS

Nader is not exactly the first social critic to be astonished at the functions— and malfunctions—of a market economy, and to render them in overtones of darkest evil. But sinister tales of this sort, while they go down well enough with college crowds, throw no light at all on the issues Nader claims to want to face. It is true enough that unless consumers themselves are concerned about product safety, corporations have no particular bias in its favor. This is due, however, not to corporate depravity but rather to the economics of the case: an extra margin of safety is an invisible benefit that usually increases costs. When products, automobiles for example, are too complicated for consumers to make independent judgments as to safety, government must usually set standards if there are to be any—and it is a measure not just of business power but also of consumer indifference that safety standards for autos came so late.

Government must also counter the ceaseless efforts of corporations to escape from the rigors of competition through the acquisition of monopoly power, through tariff protection, import quotas, and the like. Granted that government hasn't done a very good job of this. All the same, most corporate executives, obliged to immerse themselves daily in what feels very much like competition, would be surprised to learn from Nader how free of it they are supposed to have become.

Given Nader's own diagnosis, it might be thought that he has been spending his time battling restraints on trade, but this is far from the case. He has instead been devoting his considerable ingenuity to devision new schemes for regulating and "popularizing" business, by such means as a federal charter for all corporations, "which would be like a constitution for a country," publication of corporate tax returns, and the election of public members to corporate boards. He would require an attack on pollution "with maximum use of known technology and down to zero profits."

Nader denies any desire to take the country into socialism, and in this he is apparently sincere. One of his raiders, Mark Green, told *The New York Times* recently that when Nader thinks of socialism "he doesn't think of Lenin but of Paul Rand Dixon," former Chairman of the FTC and, in Nader's mind, the quintessential bureaucrat. Yet Nader seems never to have grasped that when he talks about operating on "zero profits" he is talking not about a market economy but about a confiscatory, state-imposed system that would inevitably bring in train a host of other controls.

In his "consumer democracy" of the future, as he outlines it, everybody could order business around. Tightly controlled from above by the federal government, business would be policed at the local level by what would amount to consumer soviets. Nader thinks it will be easy to organize them, by handing out application forms in the parking lots of shopping centers. "Then collectively you can bargain with the owners of the center. You can say, 'Here are 18,000 families. We want a one-room office where we can have our staff within the center that will serve as a liaison between us and you. And we're going to develop certain conditions of our continuing patronage on a mass basis.' It might take the form of banning detergents with phosphates, improving service under a warranty, or holding down prices." Nader's product-rating system, including a telephone data bank for easy reference, would force manufacturers, he says, to abandon their present policy of "severe protective imitation" for one of "competition on price and quality." (Nobody has been able to explain just how such a system would make the millions of decisions the market makes now, many of them involving subjective judgments as to quality or value.)

While otherwise holding business in low esteem, Nader seems to have a blind faith in instant technology, insisting that if corporations are given tough enough deadlines, on antipollution devices or on proving the safety of food additives, they will somehow manage to comply. While it is true that some corporations plead ignorance as a convenient alibi for doing nothing about pollution, it is also true that feasible systems have not yet been developed to control a number of crucial pollutants, including sulphur dioxide. On the question of food additives, James Grant, deputy commissioner of the Food and Drug Administrations says, "Scientific advances solve problems but also raise new questions. We can prove that certain chemicals are unsafe, but we can never prove, once and for all, that *anything* in the food supply is safe. We frequently are obliged to make absolute decisions on the basis of partial knowledge. If I have one criticism to level at the consumer advocates, it's that they're unwilling to take scientific uncertainty into account."

DOES SEARS, ROEBUCK CHEAT?

Economics, clearly, is not Nader's strong suit. He seems to think of figures as weapons, to be tossed around for maximum effect. To cite one of his current favorite examples of business fraud, he says that the orange-juice industry is watering its product by 10 percent, and thus bilking the public out of $150 million a year. And he adds: "You may wish to compare that with what bank robbers took last year in their second most successful performance to date: $8 million." Nader says he arrived at the 10 percent figure on the basis of "insider information." He applied it to total sales of the citrus industry and, lo, another "statistic" on business fraud. Even if the industry were watering, which it strenuously denies, it does not follow that the public is being gypped out of $150 million. On a watering job of that scale, the price would reflect the water content, and if water were eliminated the price would have to go up.

Another of Nader's current favorite target is Sears, Roebuck & Co. "Nobody thinks Sears, Roebuck cheats people. But they charge interest from the date the sales contract is signed rather than from the date of delivery—a few pennies, millions of times a year." But Sears no longer has ownership or use of the merchandise once the contract is signed, and could not, for example, apply any price increase that might subsequently be decided upon. The contract is perfectly open and aboveboard and should be considered in the context of the total transaction, price versus values received.

Nader quotes and endorses an estimate by Senator Philip Hart of Michigan that the whole gamut of business fraud and gouging, from shoddy merchandise to monopoly pricing, costs the consumer some $200 billion a year, "or 25 percent of all personal income." That utterly fantastic figure is also more than four times as large as all corporate profits in 1970. For a clipping of that magnitude to be possible, even theoretically, it would have to run as a sort of inflationary factor through the whole economy—wages as well as prices—and thus the argument becomes something of a wash, but a grossly misleading one all the same.

Like reformers before him, Nader is extremely reluctant to admit that any progress at all has been made in any area of consumer protection, even where he has helped write new legislation. "Very little progress, really," he sums it up. "It's a push-and-shove situation." He still refers to the nation's meat supply as "often diseased or putrescent, contaminated by rodent hairs and other assorted debris, its true condition disguised by chemical additives." This is the identical language he used three years ago to arouse Congress and propel passage of the Wholesale Meat Act. Since then the Department of Agriculture has declared 289 packing plants "potentially hazardous to human health," and has told state authorities to clean them up or shut them down. The department says "much remains to be done" to eliminate unsanitary conditions—but perhaps not as much as Nader seems to think. Similarly, despite the thirty-four automobile safety standards enforced by law and 701 recall campaigns, Nader says that "the changes are purely cosmetic."

SHOCK WAVES AT THE AGENCIES

The most impressive documents to come out of the Nader movement are the reports on the regulatory agencies. In most respects they are detailed and thoughtful, written with surprising skill by various groups of amateurs working under Nader's direction. And they have sent shock waves through Washington's bureaucracy. Since their publication, agency awareness of the public interest has greatly increased, and a certain distance has crept into the previously cozy relations between the regulators and the regulated. That distance, however, is still not nearly great enough to please Nader, who wants industry policed with eternal suspicion. "Sharpness" is one word he uses to describe the proper attitude. Jail terms for executives, he says, would be far more effective than the voluntary compliance on which the agencies now mostly rely. "Jail is a great stigma to a businessman, and even a short sentence is a real deterrent," explains James Turner, who wrote the FDA report. "You would get maximum compliance with a minimum of prosecutions."

That may well be so. But in the atmosphere of hostility that would result, regulation might actually be less effective than at present. The agencies can now make sweeping judgments—that a rate is "discriminatory" or a trade practice "deceptive"—on the basis of a simple hearing. "If criminal penalties were involved, our statutes would be interpreted in a much less flexible way," says Robert Pitofsky, the new head of FTC's Bureau of Consumer Protection. Most regulatory matters are exceedingly complex, and the agencies have trusted the industries concerned to furnish the data. If this system were replaced by a program of independent government research on countless topics, the sums expended could be huge enough to dent the federal budget. "It has to be a cooperative effort," argues Administrator Douglas Toms of the National Highway Traffic Safety Administration, which sets auto safety standards. "We're not going to get anywhere with an ugly, persistent confrontation, where the two sides try to outshout each other. We'd be pitting a tiny government agency against the worldwide auto industry."

At the FDA, a new leadership is attempting to stay on cordial terms with the $125-billion food industry while attacking the two key problems documented in great detail in the Nader report, *The Chemical Feast*. First, the FDA is undertaking a comprehensive review of the hundreds of chemicals added to the food supply as preservatives, colorings, or flavorings. "None of these chemicals, perhaps, has been put to the most rigorous testing that present-day science could muster," admits Deputy Commissioner Grant, one of the new men at the agency. Second, the FDA has also acted on mounting evidence that many prepared foods are deficient in nutritional values, and is now setting guidelines for their fortification with vitamins and minerals. "In many ways the FDA was a bar to progress," says Grant, "and we are attempting to turn that around."

CONFESSIONAL FOR SINNERS

Among the agencies Nader has investigated, the FTC comes closest to the tough, pro-consumer point of view that he is pushing for. Under its new leadership the FTC has filed a flurry of complaints on deceptive advertising, and in a number of these cases it has gone far beyond the traditional cease-and-desist order (known around the FTC as "go and sin no more"). To the dismay of the advertising profession, the FTC now seeks what it calls "affirmative disclosure"—that is, an admission in future advertising, for a specific period, that previous ads were deceptive. Howard Bell, president of the American Advertising Federation, says this amounts to "public flogging."

"Somebody is going to take us to court on affirmative disclosure, and they should," Pitofsky cheerfully admits. "It is a substantial expansion of FTC power." The FTC is also insisting that claims be based on evidence. "We're not after something that 'tastes better.'" Pitofsky says. "That's just puffery. But if you say it's twice as fast or 50 percent stronger, we will take that to mean faster or stronger than your competitor's product, and it better be so."

By swinging to "a fairly stiff enforcement of the law," as Pitofsky puts it, the FTC hopes to encourage self-regulation by industry. "Voluntary compliance comes when companies see that they are better off cleaning house themselves than letting government do it for them." And that is what seems to be happening. Warning of "the regulatory tidal wave which threatens to envelop us," the American Advertising Federation is trying to establish a National Advertising Review Board, which would set standards for ads, seek voluntary compliance with the standards, and refer ads it finds deceptive to the FTC for action.

In all this unaccustomed bustle, the agencies are, of course, just doing what they were supposed to be doing all along. To say only that, however, is to ignore the extraordinary difficulty of the regulatory function when there is no counterpressure to the steady, case-by-case intervention of skilled lawyers with specific and valuable corporate interests to protect. Congress, like the agencies, responds to the pressures applied—it's a case of "who's banging on the door," in Nader's words. Yet the pressures applied by individual corporations in individual cases can work to subvert the larger interests of the business community as a whole. "Intriguingly enough," says the FDA's Grant, "the overwhelming majority of the food industry believes that it is better off with a strong FDA, because all get balanced treatment." It is Nader's accomplishment, and no small one, that he has given the agencies the other constituency they need, the public. "Until we came along," says Nader, "the people at the agencies had forgotten what citizens looked like."

Nader will bend all of his lobbying skill this year to persuade Congress to pass a bill that would give the consumer permanent representation before regulatory bodies. The consumer agency to be established by the bill would, in fact, attempt to do just the sort of thing that Nader is doing now, but with the help of government funds and powers. A number of other consumer bills have broad support this year, including regulation of warranties and power for the FTC to seek preliminary injunctions against deceptive advertising. But Nader says, "I'd trade them all for the consumer agency."

THE PROBLEM OF MAINTAINING CLOUT

But can a movement like consumerism, powerful and yet amorphous, really be institutionalized? Certainly the passion and craft of a Nader cannot be. Nor would the director of a consumer agency enjoy Nader's complete freedom of action. A Senate aide who helped draft the bill predicts that the new office might "have its time in the sun, like the Peace Corps or OEO. Then it will carve out a rather cautious domain of its own and become part of the bureaucracy."

That being so, there will still be opportunities for Nader, always provided that he can stay in the sun himself. His support is volatile, a matter of vague tides of public opinion. "His problem is maintaining clout," says Douglas Toms, the Traffic Safety Administrator. "He has a strange kind of constituency, people with a burr under their saddle for one reason or another. He has to constantly find vehicles to keep him in the public eye." Financing will continue to be a problem. Nader himself is well aware of all these difficulties. He says that a basic error of reform movements is expecting to succeed. "You will never succeed. All you're trying to do is reduce problems to the level of tolerability."

Nader's answer to that question about the presidency is: "I find that I am less and less interested in who is going to become President. A far more interesting question is, who's going to be the next president of General Motors?" Despite any such disclaimers, it is easy to imagine the movement going political and Nader running in some future year as, say, a candidate for the United States Senate from Connecticut. Nader might do well in politics, as a sort of latter-day Estes Kefauver. A recent Harris survey revealed that 69 percent of the people think "it's good to have critics like Nader to keep industry on its toes," while only 5 percent think he is "a troublemaker who is against the free enterprise system." This is the sort of public response that most politicians, including Presidents, yearn for in vain.

Judging Nader on the basis of the specific reforms he has brought about, it would be hard to disagree with this public verdict. There has been some cost, however, and this cannot be measured. He has visited his own suspicions and fears upon a whole society, and in the end his hyperbole may prove to be a dangerous weapon. But this year at least, the public apparently expects its crusaders to be twice as fast and 50 percent stronger.

Because administrative agencies are often the focal point of the policy process, interest groups exert intense pressure upon them to gain favorable policy outputs. During the latter part of the 1960s and early 1970s the FCC changed its previous policy of virtually automatic license renewal for radio and television broadcast stations to a policy of careful scrutiny of the programming and ownership of stations before granting license renewals. The FCC looked particularly closely at stations owned by newspapers for possible antitrust violations. Under the law broadcast stations are limited to a three-year licensing period. The FCC issued rules which stated that there was no presumption that a broadcast license was the property of the licensee, and the Commission encouraged challenges to licensees at renewal time. All of this greatly stirred up the industry, which in addition to putting pressure upon the FCC to change its policy, also lobbied Congress to pass a law which would extend the broadcaster's license from three to five years, and more-over would require groups challenging a license renewal to establish that the licensee had operated against the public interest before the FCC would be permit-ted to hold a hearing. Under present rules the FCC automatically holds hearings on all license renewals. Under intense industry pressure the FCC finally backed down and accepted the substance of the legislation regarding criteria for license renewal which has not yet passed Congress.

The following case study deals with the struggle between the broadcasting industry and the FCC on the issue of standards for broadcast licenses, and particu-larly government policy regarding media monopolies. Also revealed are the posi-tions on the antitrust issue taken by the FCC, Justice Department, Congress, the courts, and the White House. The contrasting constituencies and orientations of different parts of the government can produce different policy viewpoints. Apart from these substantive policy issues, the case discusses the two procedural meth-ods by which regulatory policy is made: general rule making, or on a case-by-case basis through adjudication. Which method produces the best policy is a matter of much debate.

44
Stephen R. Barnett

THE FCC'S NONBATTLE
AGAINST MEDIA MONOPOLY

Consolidation of ownership is one of the dominant facts of mass media opera-tions in this country. Newspaper chains now control more than 60 percent of the nation's daily newspaper circulation and are fast acquiring the rest. At the local level, daily newspaper monopoly prevails almost everywhere. And there are some ninety-three instances in some eighty-five American cities where the owner of the daily paper also owns a local TV station.

The existing anti-trust laws, even assuming the Department of Justice enforced them against the media, would have a limited effect in deterring concentration. They do not apply to newspaper chains, since newspapers in different cities are not in competition with one another, and they do not reach newspaper monopolies, unless the monopoly is created or maintained by im-proper means. Their impact on newspaper-TV combinations has never been tested; it would probably have to be fought out, in any event, through lengthy trials on a city-by-city basis.

From Stephen R. Barnett, "The FCC's Nonbattle Against Media Monopoly," reprinted from the *Columbia Journalism Review,* January/February 1973. ©.

The Federal Communications Commission, however, almost certainly does have authority to decline to license TV stations to the owners of daily papers in the same city. In fact, for more than four years the FCC has been considering a proposed rule to require the breakup of these combinations. This is the most significant attempt to deal with media concentration in this country since 1941–1944, when the FCC similarly examined newspaper ownership of radio stations (and ultimately declined to adopt a rule prohibiting such ownership, promising instead to deal with the problem on a case-by-case basis—which it generally has not done). The handling of the newspaper-TV issue by the FCC deserves attention, and so does the treatment of the story by the news media.

In the thirty years since the FCC last made a broad-scale inquiry into newspaper-broadcast combinations, two developments have transformed the media landscape. The rise of TV and the near-total development of newspaper monopoly have made it clear that any concern over media concentration must focus on newspaper-TV combinations. FCC Chairman Dean Burch, concurring in the FCC rule-making proposal (but without indicating how he would eventually vote), has put the problem succinctly: "There are only a few daily newspapers in each large city and their numbers are declining. There are only a few powerful VHF stations in these cities and their numbers cannot be increased. Equally important, the evidence shows that the very large majority of people get their news information from these two limited sources. Here then are the guts of the matter."

Concern over media concentration, and newspaper-TV combinations in particular, was not a bureaucratic figment of the FCC. Vice President Agnew, his political motivation notwithstanding, raised a real issue when he declared in November, 1969, "The American people should be made aware of the trend toward monopolization of the great public information vehicles and the concentration of more and more power over public opinion in fewer and fewer hands." He then went on to attack newspaper broadcast combinations in particular (albeit only those of the Washington *Post* and New York *Times*).

The President's Commission on Violence recommended in its 1969 report that "private and governmental institutions encourage the development of competing news media and discourage increased concentration of control over existing media." Hubert Humphrey—who, like Spiro Agnew, has since dropped the subject—wrote in a syndicated newspaper column in December, 1969, that "the really serious questions involving the media should be continually raised," and included among those questions, "Is there too much concentration of media ownership?" and "Should newspapers be prevented from owning broadcast stations in the same city?" Congress itself, in passing the Newspaper Preservation Act in 1970, espoused a policy designed to preserve separate ownership of the two newspapers in a city in order to provide "separate and independent voices"; that policy applies at least as strongly in favor of separate ownership of a newspaper and a TV station where there is no need to sacrifice economic competition through an anti-trust exemption.

The most potent expressions of concern have come from the Department of Justice and, in response, from the FCC. In August, 1968, the Department, in a filing with the FCC, pointed to "the existing concentration of media ownership in many ... cities" and recommended that the Commission do something about it, namely adopt a rule divorcing the ownership of daily newspapers and TV stations within the same city. The FCC entertained "comments" on the proposal for a prolonged period—four times extending the deadline at the request of the National Association of Broadcasters. Finally, in April, 1970, instead of making a decision, the Commission simply repeated the proposal, this time as its own, for more comments.

Specifically, the FCC proposed to adopt a rule requiring the owners of daily newspapers and TV stations in the same city—and also of daily newspapers and radio stations, of which there are some 230 instances—to sell either the station or the newspaper within five years. Citing a wide variety of surveys, the FCC declared: "In view of the primary position of the daily newspaper of general circulation and the television broadcast station as sources of news and other information, and discussion of public affairs, particularly with respect to local matters, it is not desirable that these two organs of mass communication should be under the same control in any community."

Far from being Draconian, the proposed rule would have a gentle, cushioned impact. By allowing divestiture in five years, it would "forfeit" no broadcast licenses. By banning only *local* combinations it would produce a trading process between combination owners in different cities. A special dispensation from the tax laws would waive the payment of capital-gains tax on sales or exchanges resulting from the rule. In addition, the rule would be subject to waiver in individual cases, specifically if it was shown that the newspaper or TV station as in the case of UHF could not survive without subsidies from its local cross-media affiliate. (Few if any of the affected newspapers, however, will need such subsidies; of the approximately ninety-three newspaper-TV combinations, some sixty-three involve the only daily newspaper publisher in town. In eight others, the TV licensee is one of two publishers who share a monopoly of the local newspaper market by virtue of a joint-operating agreement. In all the remaining cases except New York City—where the paper involved is the *Daily News,* which seems solvent—there are now only two competing publishers, each of which typically has the morning or evening market to himself, a situation in which the paper should be profitable if it even remotely deserves to be.)

Thus the rule would do little to bring new or independent owners into the mass media, but it would at least diversify the control of the dominant media outlets in each city. The result would be greater diversity and competition in local news coverage, in editorial points of view on local issues, in concepts of media service, and of course in the economic sphere. There would be a freer flow of news, commentary, and criticism on the many stories in which one of the local media outlets, or its owner, was interested or involved. One can see advantages on both ends, for example, if the Washington *Post* were to swap its TV station in Washington for the one in Chicago owned by the Chicago *Tribune,* or for one of the newspaper-owned stations in Dallas or Houston.

After reiterating in April, 1970, the proposal made by the Justice Department in 1968, the FCC started all over again with another protracted process of receiving comments. This included four more extensions of time granted at the request of the NAB and the American Newspaper Publishers Assn. before the process finally came to an end in August, 1971. It is now more than a year since then, more than two and a half years since the FCC proposed the rule, and more than four years since the original proposal by the Justice Department. Yet the FCC still has not acted. And according to a report in *Television Digest* in mid-September, 1972, the Commission has put the newspaper-broadcast proposal "on the back burner."

The reasons for the delay are not hard to find. The FCC's proposal has been the target of all-out opposition by the newspaper and broadcast industries. The NAB alone has raised and spent more than $300,000 in the fight. It has hired Lee Loevinger, who resigned as an FCC commissioner in 1968 to represent broadcast interests, as special counsel to present its case to the FCC. "Studies" opposing the rule have been commissioned from the academic world and elsewhere, and scores of opposing comments prepared by Washington lawyers have descended on the FCC. (ANPA told the Commission that opposing comments have come from "more than 150 responsible and informed publishers, broadcasters, press associations, and other spokesmen for the nation's newspapers and broadcast stations" while the proposed rules "have been supported so far by a *total* of only five pleadings.") Meanwhile, the industries have lobbied extensively to arouse opposition to the proposal from Congress and the White House. And through it all the nation's news media, with only the barest exceptions, have somehow overlooked the story.

Under cover of the media blackout, the industry's lobbying campaign has paid off handsomely at the White House. The Administration's two chief spokesmen on media matters, communications director Herbert Klein and Clay T. Whitehead, director of the Office of Telecommunications Policy, have made the circuit of broadcasters' and publishers' conventions expressing White House opposition to the FCC's proposal. At an NAB convention in 1970, for example, Klein praised "newspaper ownership of stations." Whitehead told the ANPA convention last April that adoption of the proposal "would be a great mistake," adding: "We are much more concerned about performance than who gets to own what." President Nixon himself may have conveyed the same message during the private meeting he held with thirty broadcast executives at the White House on June 22. (In supporting the industry's position, the White House repudiates the public stance of its own Justice Department, which has continued to urge the FCC to adopt the proposed rule.)

The net result of all this has been to keep the issue of local media concentration in suspension—to preserve the status quo—by a game of legal badminton between the Commission and the courts. With the unique exception of the case of WHDH in Boston the Commission and the courts have taken the position on challenges to renewal of broadcast licenses held by the local daily newspapers that the issue of "undue concentration" should not be considered on a case-by-case basis since nonrenewal would mean "forfeiture of the license." Instead, they have said, concentration should be considered in the context of an across-the-board rule such as the FCC has proposed, since that would allow for sale or exchange of the licenses involved (or of the newspapers).

In February, 1970, for example, the Federal Court of Appeals in Washington upheld the FCC's renewal of one of the broadcast licenses held by the media empire of the Mormon Church in Salt Lake City, but only because the FCC in the rule-making proceeding "is seriously engaged in a sweeping policy review" of local media concentration. Judge Edward Tamm, concurring in the decision, pointed to the "disheartening statistics describing the marked trend toward concentration of media ownership," warned that "the risk inherent in allowing these accretions of power to persist unchecked is clear," and emphasized that he was voting to sustain the renewal "solely because" of the "single, crucial fact" that the FCC was considering the issue in rule-making proceedings—proceedings which he thought "offer some hope that the Commission will finally come to grips with the grave problems inherent in the rising concentration of ownership in the mass media. . . ."

Last June—more than two years later—another panel of the same court similarly upheld the FCC's action in renewing, without a hearing on the concentration issue, the TV license held by the *Evening Star* in Washington. Again the court relied on the fact that "the FCC is currently investigating—in the context of the rule-making proceeding—whether it should adopt ruled which would require divestiture by newspapers or other multiple owners in a given market." But the FCC, after more than four years, continues to stall the proceeding.

The objective of those who oppose the rule, both within and outside the Commission, is apparently to keep the proceeding on ice at least until next summer. By then the FCC will have lost Commissioner Nicholas Johnson, who strongly favors the rule (his term ends in June).

Meanwhile, opponents of the proposed rule urge the FCC to reject it primarily on the ground that the subject should be handled by a case-by-case approach. Until recently, this was easy because that approach had never been tried. The approach may now be examined, however, in light of one application of it. This is the case of KRON-TV, the San Francisco TV station owned by the Chronicle Publishing Co., publisher of the city's only morning newspaper (and partner, since 1965, in a joint-operating agreement with the city's only evening newspaper, the Hearst-owned *Examiner*). The case involves charges of distortion of news on the TV station to promote the owner's newspaper interests; of distortion of the newspaper's contents to promote the owner's TV interests; and of distortion of TV news to promote the owner's interest in obtaining cable-TV franchises in the San Francisco area.

Ordinarily, allegations that a broadcast licensee has engaged in self-interested news distortion will not be given a hearing by the FCC. This is not because the Commission condones such conduct; on the contrary, it has declared that "slanting of the news amounts to a fraud upon the public and is patently inconsistent with the licensee's obligation to operate his facilities in the public interest." The reason lies, rather, in the FCC's declaration that it will "eschew a censor's role, including efforts to establish news distortion in situations where Government intervention would constitute a worse danger than the possible rigging itself." The FCC therefore will not inquire into alleged news distortion unless presented with a special sort of evidence. Nor will it hold up renewal of a broadcast license on this ground unless there is "substantial extrinsic evidence of motives inconsistent with the public interest," and "unless the extrinsic evidence of possible deliberate distortion or staging of the news which is brought to our attention involves the licensee, including its principals, top management, or news management."

To illustrate the kind of "substantial extrinsic evidence" that would meet this test, the FCC has regularly offered one example: "testimony of a station employee concerning his instructions from management," or documentary evidence of such instructions—"For example, if it is asserted by a newsman that he was directed by the licensee to slant the news, that would raise serious questions as to the character qualifications of the licensee. . . . " Not many newsmen will be willing to blow the whistle on their employers by presenting the FCC with the required evidence of news-distortion directives from the station's management, an act that must be done publicly and is very likely to ruin the career of the newsman who does it.

The KRON case is uniquely significant because that is what happened. Albert Kihn, a news cameraman who worked for KRON for eight years, became disenchanted with the events in the newsroom, kept a diary and collected evidence, and in the fall of 1968, when the station's license was up for renewal, told his story to the FCC. (Kihn has not since been regularly employed in broadcast journalism.) On the basis of Kihn's allegations, the FCC held up renewal of the license and ordered a hearing to determine whether "the licensee has attempted to slant news and public affairs programs to serve its business interests."

The hearing was held in San Francisco for thirty-seven days in 1970. On March 1, 1971, the FCC's hearing examiner, Chester F. Naumowicz, Jr., resolved all the issues in favor of the KRON management and recommended renewal of the license. The FCC must review this recommendation and make the final decision (subject to court appeal), but as yet has not done so. Meanwhile, KRON continues to operate on the license issued in 1965 and not renewed in 1968.

The facts in the KRON case, as determined by the hearing examiner, have a good deal of relevance to the FCC's proposed rule on newspaper-broadcast combinations. Notwithstanding his conclusion in favor of the station owner, the examiner's report demonstrates two things: 1) common ownership of more than one media outlet in the same city, and of a daily newspaper and TV station in particular, does have harmful effects; and 2) the case-by-case approach is ill-suited to dealing with them.

The hearing examiner, even while exonerating the KRON management of any "abuse" resulting from common ownership of the newspaper and TV station, determined that the public had been harmed in one important instance. This occurred in September, 1965, when the *Chronicle* and Hearst were about to put into effect the joint-operating agreement between their San Francisco newspapers. The agreement, signed in October, 1964, but kept secret, provided not only for joint publication of the *Chronicle* in the morning and Hearst's *Examiner* in the afternoon (with a 50–50 split of all profits from either paper), but also for elimination of what was then San Francisco's third daily, the *News-Call Bulletin,* also published by Hearst.

As the hearing examiner found, the story of the upcoming "merger" began to break in the week before the eventual announcement by the two publishers on Sept. 10, 1965. During this period two San Francisco TV stations and various radio stations covered the story, reporting "such things as meetings of unions which might be affected, and alterations on the physical plants of the newspapers involved." But there was no coverage in any of San Francisco's three newspapers prior to the Sept. 10 announcement, except that on Sept. 5 "the *Chronicle* published a reference to it based on a story from the New York *Times* wire service." Meanwhile, "no mention of the matter was made on KRON-TV" before the publishers' announcement.

The examiner found, as indeed was admitted, that KRON's lack of coverage resulted from orders by the station's chief executive. He found that when the story began to break on the other stations, KRON newsmen had "importuned their superiors for permission to cover the story," but were denied such permission. The station's chief executive, although a vice president of Chronicle Publishing Co., was unaware of the joint-operating agreement and telephoned the publisher of the *Chronicle* "to ascertain the validity of the rumors." But the publisher "refused to comment," whereupon the station chief "issued the instructions which blocked the KRON newsmen from broadcasting the story until the newspapers issued a statement on the matter."

The examiner concluded this was a "reasonable reaction to a unique and delicate situation, rather than an attempt to suppress news"; while "obviously a local newspaper merger was highly newsworthy," any coverage by KRON "would be publicly regarded as based on 'inside' information," and since the station actually had no inside information, the public would have been misled. It was a situation "where neither course was free of hazards," and therefore "a decision to say nothing was not unreasonable."

Accepting this, it follows that the newspaper broadcast tie was harmful to the public's interest in the news. Whichever course the station took, the public would suffer—either through not hearing of a "highly newsworthy" story, or through being misled into thinking it was getting inside information when it was not. Such a situation, moreover, was not in fact unique to the 1965 merger in San Francisco. While that story was especially newsworthy, a similar problem arises whenever a broadcast station is confronted with a potential news story involving a commonly owned newspaper, or vice versa—occasions by no means rare in these days of heightened public awareness of the mass media and frequent controversies involving them. It is inherent in common ownership of more than one significant media outlet in a city.

Another incident involved the municipality of South San Francisco at a time when the *Chronicle* was competing for the CATV franchise there. KRON newsmen were told, in a memo from the news director dated Dec. 20, 1966:

> Between now and the first of February, let us concentrate a little heavier on SOUTH San Francisco—if warranted. HPS would like to make those people happy. . . . ["HPS" was Harold P. See, president of KRON-TV and also of the *Chronicle*-owned cable-TV company.]

A second memo from the news director, dated Feb. 6. 1967, ordered coverage of a library dedication in South San Francisco and added:

> HPS wants to make sure that the mayor of South SF is prominent in any film we do!

KRON covered the dedication, but most of the film it took was ruined by the laboratory—a fact that led See to write a letter of explanation to the mayor of South San Francisco. See admitted the letter "was motivated by CATV considerations," but denied that "the dedication coverage was related to a CATV interest."

Weighing this evidence, the examiner found that it demonstrated "an unusual interest in a political figure" on See's part, but did not prove that his motives in ordering the coverage arose from the CATV interest. See denied such a motive, and there was "no direct evidence in contradiction" the examiner said. "While such an intention might be inferred from . . . [the] Feb. 6 memo, the inference could only be based on a conjectural choice of possible motives for See's interest in South San Francisco. If KRON is to be convicted on circumstantial evidence, the circumstances should be considerably less ambiguous."

As this incident and a number of others indicate, necessary proof of improper motive in questions of abuse of media power is very difficult to come by. Even after the initial hurdle is surmounted by employee testimony of questionable news orders from management the case turns on the subjective motive for those orders. The executive who gave the orders will deny that his motive was improper, and proving him a liar may well be impossible—even assuming the FCC may be conducting such an inquiry in the first place.

Still another example involved alleged distortion of *Chronicle* editorial material to promote the owner's interest in the TV station. The FCC, in its hearing order, had cited an allegation that a *Chronicle* column by Charles

McCabe "had been censored because the article urged 'citizens to contact the FCC about violence on television'." At the hearing, McCabe testified that in his ten years of writing a daily column for the *Chronicle,* "perhaps a total of less than 100 words has ever been censored from the content of my column, with one exception": a column on TV violence, written upon the death of Robert Kennedy, which urged readers to complain to the FCC and which the newspaper had "killed outright." McCabe's entire testimony was striken from the record by the hearing examiner—notwithstanding inclusion of the item in the FCC's hearing order—on the ground that inquiry into what a newspaper prints would be inconsistent with the First Amendment.

If this ruling was correct, it may be asked how the FCC, using the case-by-case approach, can ever protect the public against the various possible abuses of newspaper-broadcast cross-ownership that may affect the content of the newspaper. The FCC has not hesitated to denounce in principle the slanting of content to promote an owner's ancillary interests, and has considered newspaper content in a number of such cases. For instance, it has frequently considered (but never found proven) charges that a newspaper disciminates in favor of its own broadcast stations in TV and radio listings and related material.

Yet in refusing to hear such testimony, the examiner had a point. Even though a newspaper's right to publish does not include the right to hold a broadcast license, and even though the FCC correctly insists that distortion by a newspaper to promote the interests of the station would be improper action by the licensee, and even though the FCC will nonetheless refuse to hold a hearing except in the rare case presenting "extrinsic evidence" of such an abuse, a governmental inquiry into a newspaper's motive for what it prints or fails to print must cause discomfort. Whether or not it would be unconstitutional, such an inquiry should not be undertaken unless there is no alternative way of protecting the public's interest in an undistorted flow of news (an interest sharpened, of course, by the absence of competing newspapers in the city).

The objection to such a proceeding is not limited, however,, to issues involving the content of the newspaper. If it is undesirable for the FCC to probe the news decisions and underlying motives of a newspaper, it is no less undesirable in principle for it to be doing the same thing with respect to a broadcast station. Yet that is what the KRON hearing mainly consisted of. Whatever one thinks of the facts of the KRON case or of the hearing examiner's decision, this kind of inquiry into alleged abuses of media ownership is at best awkward and very possibly unconstitutional. Yet this is the case-by-case approach so strongly touted by opponents of the FCC's proposed rule. Under it, hearings of this kind are the only protection the public has against the most flagrant abuses of power by the owners of dominant media outlets in cities throughout the country.

What we have, then, is a shell game. Outraged by the WHDH case, where the FCC lifted a TV license from a newspsper through a case-by-case approach to media concentration, broadcasters and publishers have persuaded the FCC to renounce the case-by-case approach in favor of rule-making. Accordingly, the Commission and the Court of Appeals have refused, in view of the pending rule-making proceedings, to consider the concentration issue when licenses come up for renewal—and this has now gone on for more than four years, with no rule-making decision yet in sight.

One may wonder whether the Court of Appeals, which has tolerated the FCC's inaction in renewal cases out of deference to the rule-making proposal, will continue to do so indefinitely. But the industry has a solution to this danger, too. It is pushing for Congressional passage of a license-renewal bill —for which NAB already claims the support of forty-nine Senators and 256 Congressmen—that would extend the license period from three to five years and require renewal, regardless of any challenges or competing applications, as long as the incumbent licensee has made a "good faith effort" to serve the public. The bill would prevent the FCC from considering media concentration in such circumstances and would thus knock out permanently the case-by-case approach. It would leave a compliant FCC free to abandon the rule-making proceeding and walk away from the problem of local media concentration.

White waiting for the bill to pass, the industry can comfortably support keeping the rule-making proceeding alive to preserve its shield against case-by-case action, and the FCC can be expected to accommodate this desire. And the odds are that the bill will pass. Few lobbies are more powerful than broadcasters and publishers united. And there are *no* other lobbies that can back up their efforts to get what they want in Washington with an information blackout in the nation's newspapers and TV media.

PART THREE

National Governmental Institutions

CHAPTER 7

The Presidency

The American presidency is the only unique political institution that the United States has contributed to the world. It developed first in this country and later was imitated, usually unsuccessfully, in many nations. In no country and at no time has the institution of the presidency achieved the status and power that it possesses in the United States. This chapter will analyze the basis, nature, and implications of the power of this great American institution.

CONSTITUTIONAL BACKGROUND: SINGLE v. PLURAL EXECUTIVE

The change that has taken place in the presidency since the office was established in 1789 is dramatic and significant. The Framers of the Constitution were primarily concerned with the control of the arbitrary exercise of power by the legislature; thus they were willing to give the President broad power since he was not to be popularly elected and would be constantly under attack by the coordinate legislative branch. Although the framers were not afraid of establishing a vigorous presidency, there was a great deal of opposition to a potentially strong executive at the time the Constitution was drafted. In the *Federalist 70* Alexander Hamilton attempts to persuade the people of the desirability of a strong presidential office, and while persuading, he sets forth the essential constitutional basis of the office.

45

Alexander Hamilton

FEDERALIST 70

There is an idea, which is not without its advocates, that a vigorous executive is inconsistent with the genius of republican government. The enlightened well-wishers to this species of government must at least hope that the supposition is destitute of foundation; since they can never admit its truth, without, at the same time, admitting the condemnation of their own principles. Energy in the executive is a leading character in the definition of good government. It is essential to the protection of the community against foreign attacks; it is not less essential to the steady administration of the laws, to the protection of property against those irregular and high-handed combinations, which sometimes interrupt the ordinary course of justice, to the security of liberty against the enterprises and assaults of ambition, of faction, and of anarchy. Every man, the least conversant in Roman story, knows how often that republic was obliged to take refuge in the absolute power of a single man, under the formidable title of dictator, as well as against the intrigues of ambitious individuals, who aspired to the tyranny, and the seditions of whole classes of the community, whose conduct threatened the existence of all government, as against the invasions of external enemies, who menaced the conquest and destruction of Rome.

There can be no need, however, to multiply arguments or examples on this head. A feeble executive implies a feeble execution of the government. A feeble execution is but another phrase for a bad execution; and a government ill executed, whatever it may be in theory, must be, in practice, a bad government.

Taking it for granted, therefore, that all men of sense will agree in the necessity of an energetic executive, it will only remain to inquire, what are the ingredients which constitute this energy? How far can they be combined with those other ingredients, which constitute safety in the republican sense? And how far does this combination characterize the plan which has been reported by the convention?

The ingredients which constitute energy in the executive are, unity; duration; and adequate provision for its support; competent powers.

The ingredients which constitute safety in the republican sense are, a due dependence on the people; a due responsibility.

Those politicians and statesmen, who have been the most celebrated for the soundness of their principles, and for the justness of their views, have declared in favor of a single executive, and a numerous legislature. They have, with great propriety, considered energy as the most necessary qualification of the former, and have regarded this as most applicable to power in a single hand; while they have, with equal propriety, considered the latter as best adapted to deliberation and wisdom, and best calculated to conciliate the confidence of the people, and to secure their privileges and interests.

That unity is conducive to energy will not be disputed. Decision, activity, secrecy, and dispatch, will generally characterize the proceedings of one man, in a much more eminent degree than the proceedings of any greater number; and in proportion as the number is increased, these qualities will be diminished.

This unity may be destroyed in two ways; either by vesting the power in two or more magistrates, of equal dignity and authority; or by vesting it ostensibly in one man, subject, in whole or in part, to the control and cooperation of others, in the capacity of counsellors to him. . . .

The experience of other nations will afford little instruction on this head. As far, however, as it teaches anything, it teaches us not to be enamoured of plurality in the executive. . . .

Wherever two or more persons are engaged in any common enterprise or pursuit, there is always danger of difference of opinion. If it be a public trust of office, in which they are clothed with equal dignity and authority, there is peculiar danger of personal emulation and even animosity. From either, and especially from all these causes, the most bitter dissentions are apt to spring. Whenever these happen, they lessen the respectability, weaken the authority, and distract the plans and operations of those whom they divide. If they should unfortunately assail the supreme executive magistracy of a country, consisting of a plurality of persons, they might impede or frustrate the most important measures of the government, in the most critical emergencies of the state. And what is still worse, they might split the community into violent and irreconcilable factions, adhering differently to the different individuals who composed the magistracy. . . .

Upon the principles of a free government, inconveniences from the source just mentioned, must necessarily be submitted to in the formation of the legislature; but it is unnecessary, and therefore unwise, to introduce them into the constitution of the executive. It is here, too, that they may be most pernicious. In the legislature, promptitude of decision is oftener an evil than a benefit. The differences of opinion, and the jarrings of parties in that department of the government, though they may sometimes obstruct salutary plans, yet often promote deliberation and circumspection; and serve to check excesses in the majority, When a resolution, too, is once taken, the opposition must be at an end. That resolution is a law, and resistance to it punishable. But no favorable circumstances palliate, or atone for the disadvantages of dissention in the executive department. Here they are pure and unmixed. There is no point at which they cease to operate. They serve to embarrass and weaken the execution of the plan or measure to which they relate, from the first step to the final conclusion of it. They constantly counteract those qualities in the executive, which are the most necessary ingredients in its composition—vigor and expedition; and this without any counterbalancing good. In the conduct of war, in which the energy of the executive is the bulwark of the national security, everything would be to be apprehended from its plurality.

It must be confessed, that these observations apply with principal weight to the first case supposed, that is, to a plurality of magistrates of equal dignity and authority, a scheme, the advocates for which are not likely to form a numerous sect; but they apply, though not with equal, yet with considerable weight, to the project of a council, whose concurrence is made constitutionally necessary to the operations of the ostensible executive. An artful cabal in that council would be able to distract and to enervate the whole system of administration. If no such cabal should exist, the mere diversity of views and opinions would alone be sufficient to tincture the exercise of the executive authority with the spirit of habitual feebleness and dilatoriness.

But one of the weightiest objections to a plurality in the executive, and which lies as much against the last as the first plan, is, that it tends to conceal faults, and destroy responsibility. . . . It often becomes impossible, amidst mutual accusations, to determine on whom the blame or the punishment of a pernicious measure . . . ought really to fall. It is shifted from one to another with so much dexterity, and under such plausible appearances, that the public opinion is left in suspense about the real author. . . .

A little consideration will satisfy us, that the species of security sought for in the multiplication of the executive, is unattainable. Numbers must be so great as to render combination difficult; or they are rather a source of danger than of security. The united credit and influence of several individuals must be more formidable to liberty than the credit and influence of either of them separately. When power, therefore, is placed in the hands of so small a number of men, as to admit of their interests and views being easily combined in a common enterprise, by an artful leader, it becomes more liable to abuse, and more dangerous when abused, than if it be lodged in the hands of one man; who, from the very circumstances of his being alone, will be more narrowly watched and more readily suspected, and who cannot unite so great a mass of influence as when he is associated with others. . . .

I will only add, that prior to the appearance of the constitution, I rarely met with an intelligent man from any of the states, who did not admit as the result of experience, that the unity of the executive of this state was one of the best of the distinguishing features of our constitution.

THE NATURE OF THE PRESIDENCY: POWER AND PERSUASION

What is the position of the presidential office today? There is little doubt that it has expanded far beyond the expectations of the framers of the Constitution. The presidency is the only governmental branch with the necessary unity and energy to meet many of the most crucial problems of twentieth-century government in the United States; people have turned to the President in times of crisis to supply the central direction necessary for survival. In the next selection Clinton Rossiter, one of the leading American scholars of the presidency, gives his view of the role of the office.

46
Clinton Rossiter

THE PRESIDENCY—
FOCUS OF LEADERSHIP

No American can contemplate the presidency . . . without a feeling of solemnity and humility—solemnity in the face of a historically unique concentration of power and prestige, humility in the thought that he has had a part in the choice of a man to wield the power and enjoy the prestige.

Perhaps the most rewarding way to grasp the significance of this great office is to consider it as a focus of democratic leadership. Free men, too, have need of leaders. Indeed, it may well be argued that one of the decisive forces in the shaping of American democracy has been the extraordinary capacity of the presidency for strong, able, popular leadership. If this has been true of our past, it will certainly be true of our future, and we should therefore do our best to grasp the quality of this leadership. Let us do this by answering the essential question: For what men and groups does the President provide leadership?

First, the President is *leader of the Executive Branch.* To the extent that our federal civil servants have need of common guidance, he alone is in a position to provide it. We cannot savor the fullness of the President's duties unless we recall that he is held primarily accountable for the ethics, loyalty, efficiency, frugality, and responsiveness to the public's wishes of the two and one-third million Americans in the national administration.

Both the Constitution and Congress have recognized his power to guide the day-to-day activities of the Executive Branch, strained and restrained though his leadership may often be in practice. From the Constitution, explicitly or implicitly, he receives the twin powers of appointment and removal, as well as the primary duty, which no law or plan or circumstances can ever take away from him, to "take care that the laws be faithfully executed."

From Congress, through such legislative mandates as the Budget and Accounting Act of 1921 and the succession of Reorganization Acts, the Presi-

From Clinton Rossiter, "The Presidency—Focus of Leadership," *The New York Times Magazine,* (November 11, 1956). © 1956 by The New York Times Company. Reprinted by permission.

dent has received further acknowledgment of his administrative leadership. Although independent agencies such as the Interstate Commerce Commission and the National Labor Relations Board operate by design outside his immediate area of responsibility, most of the government's administrative tasks are still carried on within the fuzzy-edged pyramid that has the President at its lonely peak; the laws that are executed daily in his name and under his general supervision are numbered in the hundreds.

Many observers, to be sure, have argued strenuously that we should not ask too much of the President as administrative leader, lest we burden him with impossible detail, or give too much to him, lest we inject political considerations too forcefully into the steady business of the civil service. Still, he cannot ignore the blunt mandate of the Constitution, and we should not forget the wisdom that lies behind it. The President has no more important tasks than to set a high personal example of integrity and industry for all who serve the nation, and to transmit a clear lead downward through his chief lieutenants to all who help shape the policies by which we live.

Next, the President is *leader of the forces of peace and war.* Although authority in the field of foreign relations is shared constitutionally among three organs—President, Congress, and, for two special purposes, the Senate—his position is paramount, if not indeed dominant. Constitution, laws, customs, the practice of other nations and the logic of history have combined to place the President in a dominant position. Secrecy, dispatch, unity, continuity, and access to information—the ingredients of successful diplomacy—are properties of his office, and Congress, needless to add, possesses none of them. Leadership in foreign affairs flows today from the President—or it does not flow at all.

The Constitution designates him specifically as "Commander in Chief of the Army and Navy of the United States." In peace and war he is the supreme commander of the armed forces, the living guarantee of the American belief in "the supremacy of the civil over military authority."

In time of peace he raises, trains, supervises and deploys the forces that Congress is willing to maintain. With the aid of the Secretary of Defense, the Joint Chiefs of Staff and the National Security Council—all of whom are his personal choices—he looks constantly to the state of the nation's defenses. He is never for one day allowed to forget that he will be held accountable by the people, Congress and history for the nation's readiness to meet an enemy assault.

In time of war his power to command the forces swells out of all proportion to his other powers. All major decisions of strategy, and many of tactics as well, are his alone to make or to approve. Lincoln and Franklin Roosevelt, each in his own way and time, showed how far the power of military command can be driven by a President anxious to have his generals and admirals get on with the war.

But this, the power of command, is only a fraction of the vast responsibility the modern President draws from the Commander in Chief clause. We need only think back to three of Franklin D. Roosevelt's actions in World War II —the creation and staffing of a whole array of emergency boards and offices, the seizure and operation of more than sixty strike-bound or strike-threatened plants and industries, and the forced evacuation of 70,000 American citizens of Japanese descent from the West Coast—to understand how deeply the President's authority can cut into the lives and liberties of the American people in time of war. We may well tremble in contemplation of the kind of leadership he would be forced to exert in a total war with the absolute weapon.

The President's duties are not all purely executive in nature. He is also intimately associated, by Constitution and custom, with the legislative process, and we may therefore consider him as *leader of Congress*. Congress has its full share of strong men, but the complexity of the problems it is asked to solve by a people who still assume that all problems are solvable has made external leadership a requisite of effective operation.

The President alone is in a political, constitutional, and practical position to provide such leadership, and he is therefore expected, within the limits of propriety, to guide Congress in much of its lawmaking activity. Indeed, since Congress is no longer minded or organized to guide itself, the refusal or inability of the President to serve as a kind of prime minister results in weak and disorganized government. His tasks as leader of Congress are difficult and delicate, yet he must bend to them steadily or be judged a failure. The President who will not give his best thoughts to leading Congress, more so the President who is temperamentally or politically unfitted to "get along with Congress," is now rightly considered a national liability.

The lives of Jackson, Lincoln, Wilson, and the two Roosevelts should be enough to remind us that the President draws much of his real power from his position as *leader of his party*. By playing the grand politician with unashamed zest, the first of these men gave his epic administration a unique sense of cohesion, the second rallied doubting Republican leaders and their followings to the cause of the Union, and the other three achieved genuine triumphs as catalysts of Congressional action. That gifted amateur, Dwight D. Eisenhower, has also played the role for every drop of drama and power in it. He has demonstrated repeatedly what close observers of the presidency know well: that its incumbent must devote an hour or two of every working day to the profession of Chief Democrat or Chief Republican.

It troubles many good people, not entirely without reason, to watch the President dabbling in politics, distributing loaves and fishes, smiling on party hacks, and endorsing candidates he knows to be unfit for anything but immediate delivery to the county jail. Yet if he is to persuade Congress, if he is to achieve a loyal and cohesive administration, if he is to be elected in the first place (and reelected in the second), he must put his hand firmly to the plow of politics. The President is inevitably the nation's No. 1 political boss.

Yet he is, at the same time, if not in the same breath, *leader of public opinion*. While he acts as political chieftain of some, he serves as moral spokesman for all. It took the line of Presidents some time to sense the nation's need for a clear voice, but since the day when Andrew Jackson thundered against the Nullifiers of South Carolina, no effective President has doubted his prerogative to speak the people's mind on the great issues of his time, to serve, in Wilson's words, as "the spokesman for the real sentiment and purpose of the country."

Sometimes, of course, it is no easy thing, even for the most sensitive and large-minded Presidents, to know the real sentiment of the people or to be bold enough to state it in defiance of loudly voiced contrary opinion. Yet the President who senses the popular mood and spots new tides even before they start to run, who practices shrewd economy in his appearances as spokesman for the nation, who is conscious of his unique power to compel discussion on his own terms and who talks the language of Christian morality and the American tradition, can shout down any other voice or chorus of voices in the land. The President is the American people's one authentic trumpet, and he has no higher duty than to give a clear and certain sound.

The President is easily the most influential leader of opinion in this country principally because he is, among all his other jobs, our Chief of State. He is, that is to say, the ceremonial head of the government of the United States, the *leader of the rituals of American democracy*. The long catalogue of public duties that the Queen discharges in England and the Governor General in Canada is the President's responsibility in this country, and the catalogue is even longer because he is not a king, or even the agent of one, and is therefore expected to go through some rather undignified paces by a people who think of him as a combination of scoutmaster, Delphic oracle, hero of the silver screen, and father of the multitudes.

The role of Chief of State may often seem trivial, yet it cannot be neglected by a President who proposes to stay in favor and, more to the point, in touch with the people, the ultimate support of all his claims to leadership. And whether or not he enjoys this role, no President can fail to realize that his many powers are invigorated, indeed are given a new dimension of authority, because he is the symbol of our sovereignty, continuity and grandeur as a people.

When he asks a Senator to lunch in order to enlist his support for a pet project, when he thumps his desk and reminds the antagonists in a labor dispute of the larger interests of the American people, when he orders a general to cease caviling or else be removed from his command, the Senator and the disputants and the general are well aware—especially if the scene is laid in the White House—that they are dealing with no ordinary head of government. The framers of the Constitution took a momentous step when they fused the dignity of a king and the power of a Prime Minister in one elective office— when they made the President a national leader in the mystical as well as the practical sense.

Finally, the President has been endowed—whether we or our friends abroad like it or not—with a global role as *a leader of the free nations.* His leadership in this area is not that of a dominant executive. The power he exercises is in a way comparable to that which he holds as a leader of Congress. Senators and Congressmen can, if they choose, ignore the President's leadership with relative impunity. So, too, can our friends abroad; the action of Britain and France in the Middle East is a case in point. But so long as the United States remains the richest and most powerful member of any coalition it may enter, then its President's words and deeds will have a direct bearing on the freedom and stability of a great many other countries.

Having engaged in this piecemeal analysis of the categories of Presidential leadership, we must now fit the pieces back together into a seamless unity. For that, after all, is what the presidency is, and I hope this exercise in political taxonomy has not obscured the paramount fact that this focus of democratic leadership is a single office filled by a single man.

The President is not one kind of leader one part of the day, another kind in another part—leader of the bureaucracy in the morning, of the armed forces at lunch, of Congress in the afternoon, of the people in the evening. He exerts every kind of leadership every moment of the day, and every kind feeds upon and into all the others. He is a more exalted leader of ritual because he can guide opinion, a more forceful leader in diplomacy because he commands the armed forces personally, a more effective leader of Congress because he sits at the top of his party. The conflicting demands of these categories of leadership give him trouble at times, but in the end all unite to make him a leader without any equal in the history of democracy.

I think it important to note the qualification: "the history of democracy." For what I have been talking about here is not the Fuehrerprinzip of Hitler or the "cult of personality," but the leadership of free men. The presidency, like every other instrument of power we have created for our use, operates within a grand and durable pattern of private liberty and public morality, which means that the President can lead successfully only when he honors the pattern—by working toward ends to which a "persistent and undoubted" majority of the people has given support, and by selecting means that are fair, dignified and familiar.

The President, that is to say, can lead us only in the direction we are accustomed to travel. He cannot lead the gentlemen of Congress to abdicate their functions; he cannot order our civil servants to be corrupt and slothful; he cannot even command our generals to bring off a coup d'état. And surely he cannot lead public opinion in a direction for which public opinion is not prepared—a truth to which our strongest Presidents would make the most convincing witnesses. The leadership of free men must honor their freedom. The power of the presidency can move as a mighty host only with the grain of liberty and morality.

The President, then, must provide a steady focus of leadership—of administrators, Ambassadors, generals, Congressmen, party chieftains, people and men of good will everywhere. In a constitutional system compounded of diversity and antagonism, the presidency looms up as the countervailing force of unity and harmony. In a society ridden by centrifugal forces, it is the only point of reference we all have in common. The relentless progress of this continental republic has made the presidency our truly national political institution.

There are those, to be sure, who would reserve this role to Congress, but, as the least aggressive of our Presidents, Calvin Coolidge, once testified, "It is because in their hours of timidity the Congress becomes subservient to the importunities of organized minorities that the President comes more and more to stand as the champion of the rights of the whole country." The more Congress becomes, in Burke's phrase, "a confused and scuffling bustle of local agency" the more the presidency must become a clear beacon of national purpose.

It has been such a beacon at most great moments in our history. In this great moment, too, we may be confident it will burn brightly.

The constitutional and statutory *authority* of the President is indeed extraordinary. However, it is important to point out that the actual power of the President depends upon his political abilities. The President must act within the framework of a complex and diversified political constituency. He can use the authority of his office to buttress his strength, but this alone is not sufficient. Somehow he must be able to persuade those with whom he deals to follow him; otherwise, he will be weak and ineffective.

47

Richard E. Neustadt

PRESIDENTIAL POWER

In the United States we like to "rate" a President. We measure him as "weak" or "strong" and call what we are measuring his "leadership." We do not wait until a man is dead; we rate him from the moment he takes office. We are quite right to do so. His office has become the focal point of politics and policy in our political system. Our commentators and our politicians make a speciality of taking the man's measurements. The rest of us join in when we feel "government" impinging on our private lives. In the third quarter of the twentieth century millions of us have that feeling often.

From Richard E. Neustadt, *Presidential Power,* pp. 1–2, 6–8, 186–187. Reprinted by permission of John Wiley & Sons, Inc. Copyright © 1960 by John Wiley & Sons, Inc.

. . . Although we all make judgments about presidential leadership, we often base our judgments upon images of office that are far removed from the reality. We also use those images when we tell one another whom to choose as President. But it is risky to appraise a man in office or to choose a man for office on false premises about the nature of his job. When the job is the presidency of the United States the risk becomes excessive. . . .

We deal here with the President himself and with his influence on governmental action. In institutional terms the presidency now includes 2,000 men and women. The President is only one of them. But *his* performance scarcely can be measured without focusing on *him*. In terms of party, or of country, or the West, so-called, his leadership involves far more than governmental action. But the sharpening of spirit and of values and of purposes is not done in a vacuum. Although governmental action may not be the whole of leadership, all else is nurtured by it and gains meaning from it. Yet if we treat the presidency as the President, we cannot measure him as though he were the government. Not action as an outcome but his impact on the outcome is the measure of the man. His strength or weakness, then, turns on his personal capacity to influence the conduct of the men who make up government. His influence becomes the mark of leadership. To rate a President according to these rules, one looks into the man's own capabilities as seeker and as wielder of effective influence upon the other men involved in governing the country. . . .

"Presidential" . . . means nothing but the President. "Power" means *his* influence. It helps to have these meanings settled at the start.

There are two ways to study "presidential power." One way is to focus on the tactics, so to speak, of influencing certain men in given situations: how to get a bill through Congress, how to settle strikes, how to quiet Cabinet feuds, or how to stop a Suez. The other way is to step back from tactics on those "givens" and to deal with influence in more strategic terms: what is its nature and what are its sources? What can *this* man accomplish to improve the prospect that he will have influence when he wants it? Strategically, the question is not how he masters Congress in a peculiar instance, but what he does to boost his chance for mastery in any instance, looking toward tomorrow from today. The second of these two ways has been chosen for this [selection]. . . .

In form all Presidents are leaders, nowadays. In fact this guarantees no more than that they will be clerks. Everybody now expects the man inside the White House to do something about everything. Laws and customs now reflect acceptance of him as the Great Initiator, an acceptance quite as widespread at the Capitol as at his end of Pennsylvania Avenue. But such acceptance does not signify that all the rest of government is at his feet. It merely signifies that other men have found it practically impossible to do *their* jobs without assurance of initiatives from him. Service for themselves, not power for the President, has brought them to accept his leadership in form. They find his actions useful in their business. The transformation of his routine obligations testifies to their dependence on an active White House. A President, these days, is an invaluable clerk. His services are in demand all over Washington. His influence, however, is a very different matter. Laws and customs tell us little about leadership in fact.

Why have our Presidents been honored with this clerkship? The answer is that no one else's services suffice. Our Constitution, our traditions, and our politics provide no better source for the initiatives a President can take. Executive officials need decisions, and political protection, and a referee for fights. Where are these to come from but the White House? Congressmen need an agenda from outside, something with high status to respond to or react against. What provides it better than the program of the President? Party politicians need a record to defend in the next national campaign. How can it be made except by "their" Administration? Private persons with a public axe to grind may need a helping hand or they may need a grinding stone. In either case who gives more satisfaction than a President? And outside the United States, in every country where our policies and postures influence home politics, there will be people needing just the "right" thing said and done or just the "wrong" thing stopped *in Washington.* What symbolizes Washington more nearly than the White House?

A modern President is bound to face demands for aid and service from five more or less distinguishable sources: from Executive officialdom, from Congress, from his partisans, from citizens at large, and from abroad. The presidency's clerkship is expressive of these pressures. In effect they are constituency pressures and each President has five sets of constituents. The five are not distinguished by their membership; membership is obviously an overlapping matter. And taken one by one they do not match the man's electorate; one of them, indeed, is outside his electorate. They are distinguished, rather, by their different claims upon him. Initiatives are what they want, for five distinctive reasons. Since government and politics have offered no alternative, our laws and customs turn those wants into his obligations.

Why, then, is the President not guaranteed an influence commensurate with services performed? Constituent relations are relations of dependence. Everyone with any share in governing this country will belong to one (or two, or three) of his "constituencies." Since everyone depends on him why is he not assured of everyone's support? The answer is that no one else sits where he sits, or sees quite as he sees; no one else feels the full weight of his obligations. Those obligations are a tribute to his unique place in our political system. But just because it is unique they fall on him alone. *The same conditions that promote his leadership in form preclude a guarantee of leadership in fact.* No man or group at either end of Pennsylvania Avenue shares his peculiar status in our government and politics. That is why his services are in demand. By the same token, though, the obligations of all other men are different from his own. His Cabinet officers have departmental duties and constituents. His legislative leaders head *Congressional* parties, one in either House. His national party organization stands apart from his official family. His political allies in the states need not face Washington, or one another. The private groups that seek him out are not compelled to govern. And friends abroad are not compelled to run in our elections. Lacking his position and prerogatives, these men cannot regard his obligations as their own. They have their jobs to do; none is the same as his. As they perceive their duty they may find it right to follow him, in fact, or they may not. Whether they will feel obliged *on their responsibility* to do what he wants done remains an open question. . . .

There is reason to suppose that in the years immediately ahead the power problems of a President will remain what they have been in the decades just behind us. If so there will be equal need for presidential expertise of the peculiar sort . . . that has [been] stressed [i.e., political skill]. Indeed, the need is likely to be greater. The President himself and with him the whole government are likely to be more than ever at the mercy of his personal approach.

What may the sixties do to politics and policy and to the place of Presidents in our political system? The sixties may destroy them as we know them; that goes without saying. But barring deep depression or unlimited war, a total transformation is the least of likelihoods. Without catastrophes of those dimensions nothing in our past experience suggests that we shall see either consensus of the sort available to F.D.R. in 1933 and 1942, or popular demand for institutional adjustments likely to assist a President. Lacking popular demand, the natural conservatism of established institutions will keep Congress and the party organizations quite resistant to reforms that could give him a clear advantage over them. Four-year terms for Congressmen and Senators might do it, if the new terms ran with his. What will occasion a demand for that? As for crisis consensus it is probably beyond the reach of the next President. We may have priced ourselves out of the market for "productive" crises on the pattern Roosevelt knew—productive in the sense of strengthening his chances for sustained support *within* the system. Judging from the fifties, neither limited war nor limited depression is productive in those terms. Anything unlimited will probably break the system.

In the absence of productive crises, and assuming that we manage to avoid destructive ones, nothing now foreseeable suggests that our next President will have assured support from any quarter. There is no use expecting it from the bureaucracy unless it is displayed on Capitol Hill. Assured support will not be found in Congress unless contemplation of their own electorates keeps a majority of members constantly aligned with him. In the sixties it is to be doubted . . . that pressure from electors will move the same majority of men in either House toward consistent backing for the President. Instead the chances are that he will gain majorities, when and if he does so, by ad hoc coalition-building, issue after issue. In that respect the sixties will be reminiscent of the fifties; indeed, a closer parallel may well be in the late forties. As for "party discipline" in English terms—the favorite cure-all of political scientists since Woodrow Wilson was a youth—the first preliminary is a party link between the White House and the leadership on both sides of the Capitol. But even this preliminary has been lacking in eight of the fifteen years since the Second World War. If ballot-splitting should continue through the sixties it will soon be "un-American" for President and Congress to belong to the same party.

Even if the trend were now reversed, there is no short-run prospect that behind each party label we would find assembled a sufficiently like-minded bloc of voters, similarly aligned in states and districts all across the country, to negate the massive barriers our institutions and traditions have erected against "discipline" on anything like the British scale. This does not mean that a reversal of the ballot-splitting trend would be without significance. If the White House and the legislative leadership were linked by party ties again, a real advantage would accrue to both. Their opportunities for mutually productive bargaining would be enhanced. The policy results might surprise critics of our system. Bargaining "within the family" has a rather different quality than bargaining with members of the rival clan. But we would still be a long way from "party government." Bargaining, not "discipline," would still remain the key to Congressional action on a President's behalf. The critical distinctions between presidential party and Congressional party are not likely to be lost in the term of the next President.

THE PRESIDENTIAL ESTABLISHMENT

The expansion of the Executive Office of the President is a major development of the modern presidency. Created in 1939 by an executive order of President Roosevelt under reorganization authority granted to him by Congress, the Executive Office has expanded over the years and now occupies a pivotal position in government. The Executive Office was devised originally to act as a staff arm of the presidency. It was to consist of his closest personal advisors, as well as a small number of agencies, such as the Bureau of the Budget (now the Office of Management and Budget) that were to aid him in carrying out his presidential responsibilities.

The Executive Office was not to be an independent bureaucracy, but was to be accountable to the President and to act in accordance with his wishes. However, the tremendous expansion that has occurred in the Executive Office has raised the question of whether or not it has become an "invisible presidency," not accountable to anyone within or without government. The relationships between President Nixon and the Executive Office particularly raised this question. President Nixon's emphasis upon managerial techniques led him to expand very significantly the number of agencies within the Executive Office. Moreover, he delegated to his personal staff a wide range of responsibilities over which he failed to exercise continuous supervision. Ehrlichman and Haldeman, before they resigned because of their involvement in events surrounding the Watergate affair, ruthlessly wielded power around Washington in the name of the President. It was the lack of presidential supervision over his own staff that may have accounted for the Watergate break-in in the first place, as well as other questionable activities, including the burglary of Daniel Ellsberg's psychiatrist's office and the solicitation of unreported funds during the 1972 presidential election year. The following selection by Thomas E. Cronin describes the contemporary Executive Office of the President and its role within the governmental process.

48
Thomas E. Cronin

THE SWELLING OF THE PRESIDENCY

The advent of Richard Nixon's second term in the White House is marked by an uncommon amount of concern, in Congress and elsewhere, about the expansion of presidential power and manpower. Even the President himself is ostensibly among those who are troubled. Soon after his re-election, Mr. Nixon announced that he was planning to pare back the presidential staff. And in recent days, the President has said he is taking action to cut the presidential workforce in half and to "substantially" reduce the number of organizations that now come under the White House. Mr. Nixon's announcements have no doubt been prompted in part by a desire to add drama and an aura of change to the commencement of his second term. But he also seems genuinely worried that the presidency may have grown so large and top-heavy that it now weakens rather than strengthens his ability to manage the federal government. His fears are justified.

The presidency has, in fact, grown a full 20 percent in the last four years alone in terms of the number of people who are employed directly under the President. It has swelled to the point where it is now only a little short of the State Department's sprawling domestic bureaucracy in size.

This burgeoning growth of the presidency has, in the process, made the traditional civics textbook picture of the executive branch of our government nearly obsolete. According to this view, the executive branch is more or less neatly divided into Cabinet departments and their secretaries, agencies and their heads, and the President. A more contemporary view takes note of a few prominent presidential aides and refers to them as the "White House staff." But neither view adequately recognizes the large and growing coterie that surrounds the President and is made up of dozens of assistants, hundreds of

From Thomas E. Cronin, "The Swelling of the Presidency," *Saturday Review* (February 1973).

presidential advisers, and thousands of members of an institutional amalgam called the Executive Office of the President. While the men and women in these categories all fall directly under the President in the organizational charts, there is no generally used term for their common terrain. But it has swelled so much in size and scope in recent years, and has become such an important part of the federal government, that it deserves its own designation. Most apt perhaps is the Presidential Establishment.

The Presidential Establishment today embraces more than twenty support staffs (the White House Office, National Security Council, and Office of Management and Budget, etc.) and advisory offices (Council of Economic Advisers, Office of Science and Technology, and Office of Telecommunications Policy, etc.). It has spawned a vast proliferation of ranks and titles to go with its proliferation of functions (Counsel to the President, Assistant to the President, Special Consultant, Director, Staff Director, etc). "The White House now has enough people with fancy titles to populate a Gilbert and Sullivan comic opera," Congressman Morris Udall has reasonably enough observed.

There are no official figures on the size of the Presidential Establishment, and standard body counts vary widely depending on who is and who is not included in the count, but by one frequently used reckoning, between five and six thousand people work for the President of the United States. Payroll and maintenance costs for this staff run between $100 million and $150 million a year. (These figures include the Office of Economic Opportunity (OEO), which is an Executive Office agency and employs two thousand people, but not the roughly fifteen thousand-man Central Intelligence Agency, although that, too, is directly responsible to the Chief Executive.) These "White House" workers have long since outgrown the White House itself and now occupy not only two wings of the executive mansion but three nearby high-rise office buildings as well.

The expansion of the Presidential Establishment, it should be emphasized, is by no means only a phenomenon of the Nixon years. The number of employees under the President has been growing steadily since the early 1900s when only a few dozen people served in the White House entourage, at a cost of less than a few hundred thousand dollars annually. Congress's research arm, the Congressional Research Service, has compiled a count that underlines in particular the accelerated increase in the last two decades. This compilation shows that between 1954 and 1971 the number of presidential advisers has grown from 25 to 45, the White House staff from 266 to 600, and the Executive Office staff from 1,175 to 5,395.

But if the growth of the Presidential Establishment antedates the current administration, it is curious at least that one of the largest expansions ever, in both relative and absolute terms, has taken place during the first term of a conservative, management-minded President who has often voiced his objection to any expansion of the federal government and its bureaucracy.

Under President Nixon, in fact, there has been an almost systematic bureaucratization of the Presidential Establishment, in which more new coun-

cils and offices have been established, more specialization and division of labor
and layers of staffing have been added, than at any time except during World
War II. Among the major Nixonian additions are the Council on Environmental Quality, Council on International Economic Policy, Domestic Council, and
Office of Consumer Affairs.

The numbers in the White House entourage may have decreased somewhat since November when the President announced his intention to make
certain staff cuts. They may shrink still more if, as expected, the OEO is shifted
from White House supervision to Cabinet control, mainly under the Department of Health, Education, and Welfare. Also, in the months ahead, the
President will probably offer specific legislative proposals, as he has done
before, to reprogram or repackage the upper reaches of the executive.

Even so, any diminution of the Presidential Establishment has so far been
more apparent than real, or more incidental than substantial. Some aides, such
as former presidential counselor Robert Finch, who have wanted to leave
anyway, have done so. Others, serving as scapegoats on the altar of Watergate,
are also departing.

In addition, the President has officially removed a number of trusted
domestic-policy staff assistants from the White House rolls and dispersed them
to key sub-Cabinet posts across the span of government. But this dispersal can
be viewed as not so much reducing as creating yet another expansion—a
virtual setting up of White House outposts (or little White Houses?) throughout the Cabinet departments. The aides that are being sent forth are notable
for their intimacy with the President, and they will surely maintain direct links
to the White House, even though these links do not appear on the official
organizational charts.

Then too, one of the most important of the President's recent shifts of
executive branch members involves an unequivocal addition to the Presidential
Establishment. This is the formal setting up of a second office—with space and
a staff in the White House—for Treasury Secretary George Shultz as chairman
of yet another new presidential body, the Council on Economic Policy. This
move makes Shultz a member of a White House inner cabinet. He will now
be over-secretary of economic affairs alongside Henry Kissinger, over-secretary for national security affairs, and John Ehrlichman, over-secretary for
domestic affairs.

In other words, however the names and numbers have changed recently
or may be shifted about in the near future, the Presidential Establishment does
not seem to be declining in terms of function, power, or prerogative; in fact,
it may be continuing to grow as rapidly as ever.

Does it matter? A number of political analysts have argued recently that
it does, and I agree with them. Perhaps the most disturbing aspect of the
expansion of the Presidential Establishment is that it has become a powerful
inner sanctum of government, isolated from traditional, constitutional checks
and balances. It is common practice today for anonymous, unelected, and
unratified aides to negotiate sensitive international commitments by means of

executive agreements that are free from congressional oversight. Other aides in the Presidential Establishment wield fiscal authority over billions of dollars in funds that Congress has appropriated, yet the President refuses to spend, or that Congress has assigned to one purpose and the administration routinely redirects to another—all with no semblance of public scrutiny. Such exercises of power pose an important, perhaps vital, question of governmental philosophy: Should a political system that has made a virtue of periodic electoral accountability accord an ever-increasing policy-making role to White House counselors who neither are confirmed by the U.S. Senate nor, because of the doctrine of "executive privilege," are subject to questioning by Congress?

Another disquieting aspect of the growth of the Presidential Establishment is that the increase of its powers has been largely at the expense of the traditional sources of executive power and policy-making—the Cabinet members and their departments. When I asked a former Kennedy-Johnson Cabinet member a while ago what he would like to do if he ever returned to government, he said he would rather be a presidential assistant than a Cabinet member. And this is an increasingly familiar assessment of the relative influence of the two levels of the executive branch. The Presidential Establishment has become, in effect, a whole layer of government between the President and the Cabinet, and it often stands above the Cabinet in terms of influence with the President. In spite of the exalted position that Cabinet members hold in textbooks and protocol, a number of Cabinet members in recent administrations have complained that they could not even get the President's ear except through an assistant. In his book *Who Owns America?,* former Secretary of the Interior Walter Hickel recounts his combat with a dozen different presidential functionaries and tells how he needed clearance from them before he could get to talk to the President, or how he frequently had to deal with the assistants themselves because the President was "too busy." During an earlier administration, President Eisenhower's chief assistant, Sherman Adams, was said to have told two Cabinet members who could not resolve a matter of mutual concern: "Either make up your mind or else tell me and I will do it. We must not bother the President with this. He is trying to keep the world from war." Several of President Kennedy's Cabinet members regularly battled with White House aides who blocked them from seeing the President. And McGeorge Bundy, as Kennedy's chief assistant for national security affairs, simply sidestepped the State Department in one major area of department communications. He had all important incoming State Department cables transmitted simultaneously to his office in the White House, part of an absorption of traditional State Department functions that visibly continues to this day with presidential assistant Henry Kissinger. Indeed, we recently witnessed the bizarre and telling spectacle of Secretary of State William Rogers insisting that he *did* have a role in making foreign policy.

In a speech in 1971, Sen. Ernest Hollings of South Carolina plaintively noted the lowering of Cabinet-status. "It used to be," he said, "that if I had a problem with food stamps, I went to see the Secretary of Agriculture, whose department had jurisdiction over that problem. Not anymore. Now, if I want to learn the policy, I must go to the White House to consult John Price [a special assistant]. If I want the latest on textiles, I won't get it from the Secretary of Commerce, who has the authority and responsibility. No, I am forced to go to the White House and see Mr. Peter Flanigan. I shouldn't feel too badly. Secretary Stans [Maurice Stans, then Secretary of Commerce] has to do the same thing."

If Cabinet members individually have been downgraded in influence, the Cabinet itself as a council of government has become somewhat of a relic, replaced by more specialized comminglings that as often as not are presided over by White House staffers. The Cabinet's decline has taken place over several administrations. John Kennedy started out his term declaring his intentions of using the Cabinet as a major policy-making body, but his change of mind was swift, as his Postmaster General, J. Edward Day, has noted. "After the first two or three meetings," Day has written, "one had the distinct impression that the President felt that decisions on major matters were not made—or even influenced—at Cabinet sessions, and that discussion there was a waste of time. . . . When members spoke up to suggest or to discuss major administration policy, the President would listen with thinly disguised impatience and then postpone or otherwise bypass the question."

Lyndon Johnson was equally disenchanted with the Cabinet as a body and characteristically held Cabinet sessions only when articles appeared in the press talking about how the Cabinet was withering away. Under Nixon, the Cabinet is almost never convened at all.

Not only has the Presidential Establishment taken over many policy-making functions from the Cabinet and its members, it has also absorbed some of the operational functions. White House aides often feel they should handle any matters that they regard as ineptly administered, and they tend to intervene in internal departmental operations at lower and lower levels. They often feel underemployed, too, and so are inclined to reach out into the departments to find work and exercise authority for themselves.

The result is a continuous undercutting of Cabinet departments—and the cost is heavy. These intrusions can cripple the capacity of Cabinet officials to present policy alternatives, and they diminish self-confidence, morale, and initiative within the departments. George Ball, a former undersecretary of state, noted the effects on the State Department: "Able men, with proper pride in their professional skills, will not long tolerate such votes of no-confidence, so it should be no surprise that they are leaving the career service, and making way for mediocrity with the result that, as time goes on it may be hopelessly difficult to restore the Department. . . ."

The irony of this accretion of numbers and functions to the Presidential Establishment is that the presidency is finding itself increasingly afflicted with the very ills of the traditional departments that the expansions were often

Figure A

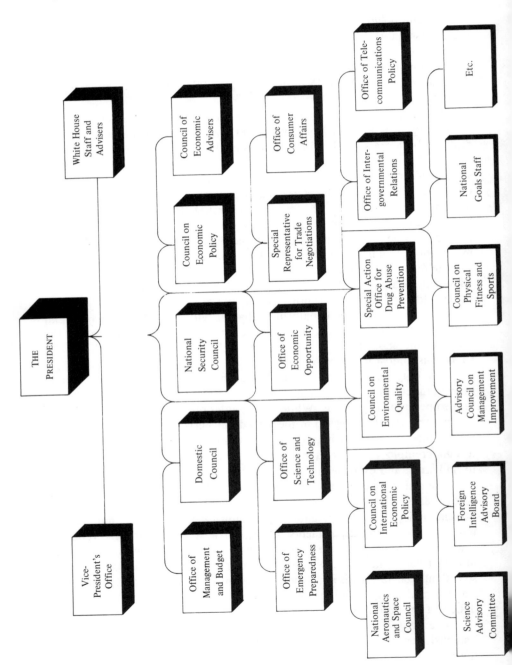

intended to remedy. The presidency has become a large, complex bureaucracy itself, rapidly acquiring many dubious characteristics of large bureaucracies in the process: layering, overspecialization, communication gaps, interoffice rivalries, inadequate coordination, and an impulse to become consumed with short-term, urgent operational concerns at the expense of thinking systematically about the consequences of varying sets of policies and priorities and about important long-range problems. It takes so much of the President's time to deal with the members of his own bureaucracy that it is little wonder he has little time to hear counsel from Cabinet officials.

Another toll of the burgeoning Presidential Establishment is that White House aides, in assuming more and more responsibility for the management of government programs, inevitably lose the detachment and objectivity that is so essential for evaluating new ideas. Can a lieutenant vigorously engaged in implementing the presidential will admit the possibility that what the President wants is wrong or not working? Yet a President is increasingly dependent on the judgment of these same staff members, since he seldom sees his cabinet members.

Why has the presidency grown bigger and bigger? There is no single villain or systematically organized conspiracy promoting this expansion. A variety of factors is at work. The most significant is the expansion of the role of the presidency itself—an expansion that for the most part has taken place during national emergencies. The reason for this is that the public and Congress in recent decades have both tended to look to the President for the decisive responses that were needed in those emergencies. The Great Depression and World War II in particular brought sizable increases in presidential staffs. And once in place, many stayed on, even after the emergencies that brought them had faded. Smaller national crises have occasioned expansion in the White House entourage, too. After the Russians successfully orbited *Sputnik* in 1957, President Eisenhower added several science advisers. After the Bay of Pigs, President Kennedy enlarged his national security staff.

Considerable growth in the Presidential Establishment, especially in the post-World War II years, stems directly from the belief that critical societal problems require that wise men be assigned to the White House to alert the President to appropriate solutions and to serve as the agents for implementing these solutions. Congress has frequently acted on the basis of this belief, legislating the creation of the National Security Council, the Council of economic Advisers, and the Council on Environmental Quality, among others. Congress has also increased the chores of the presidency by making it a statutory responsibility for the President to prepare more and more reports associated with what are regarded as critical social areas—annual economic and manpower reports, a biennial report on national growth, etc.

Most recently, President Nixon responded to a number of troublesome problems that defy easy relegation to any one department—problems like international trade and drug abuse—by setting up special offices in the Executive Office with sweeping authority and sizable staffs. Once established, these units rarely get dislodged. And an era of permanent crisis ensures a continuing accumulation of such bodies.

Another reason for the growth of the Presidential Establishment is that occupants of the White House frequently distrust members of the permanent government, Nixon aides, for example, have viewed most civil servants not only as Democratic but as wholly unsympathetic to such objectives of the Nixon administration as decentralization, revenue sharing, and the curtailment of several Great Society programs. Departmental bureaucracies are viewed from the White House as independent, unresponsive, unfamiliar, and inaccessible. They are suspected again and again of placing their own, congressional, or special-interest priorities ahead of those communicated to them from the White House. Even the President's own Cabinet members soon become viewed in the same light; one of the strengths of Cabinet members, namely their capacity to make a compelling case for their programs, has proved to be their chief liability with Presidents.

Presidents may want this type of advocacy initially, but they soon grow weary and wary of it. Not long ago, one White House aide accused a former Labor Secretary of trying to "out-Meany Meany." Efforts by former Interior Secretary Hickel to advance certain environmental programs and by departing Housing and Urban Development Secretary George Romney to promote innovative housing construction methods not only were unwelcome but after a while were viewed with considerable displeasure and suspicion at the White House.

Hickel writes poignantly of coming to this recognition during his final meeting with President Nixon, in the course of which the President frequently referred to him as an "adversary." "Initially," writes Hickel, "I considered that a compliment because, to me, an adversary is a valuable asset. It was only after the President had used the term many times and with a disapproving inflection that I realized he considered an adversary an enemy. I could not understand why he would consider me an enemy."

Not only have recent Presidents been suspicious about the depth of the loyalty of those in their Cabinets, but they also invariably become concerned about the possibility that sensitive administration secrets may leak out through the departmental bureaucracies, and this is another reason why Presidents have come to rely more on their own personal groups, such as task forces and advisory commissions.

Still another reason that more and more portfolios have been given to the presidency is that new federal programs frequently concern more than one federal agency, and it seems reasonable that someone at a higher level is required to fashion a consistent policy and to reconcile conflicts. Attempts by Cabinet members themselves to solve sensitive jurisdictional questions frequently result in bitter squabbling. At times, too, Cabinet members themselves have recommended that these multi-departmental issues be settled at the White House. Sometimes new presidential appointees insist that new offices for program coordination be assigned directly under the President. Ironically, such was the plea of George McGovern, for example, when President Kennedy offered him the post of director of the Food-for-Peace program in 1961. McGovern attacked the buildup of the Presidential Establishment in his campaign against Nixon, but back in 1961 he wanted visibility (and no doubt celebrity status) and he successfully argued against his being located outside the White House—either in the State or Agriculture departments. President Kennedy and his then campaign manager Robert Kennedy felt indebted to McGovern because of his efforts in assisting the Kennedy presidential campaign in South Dakota. Accordingly, McGovern was granted not only a berth in the Executive Office of the President but also the much-coveted title of special assistant to the President.

The Presidential Establishment has also been enlarged by the representation of interest groups within its fold. Even a partial listing of staff specializations that have been grafted onto the White House in recent years reveals how interest-group brokerage has become added to the more traditional staff activities of counseling and administration. These specializations form a veritable index of American society:

Budget and management, national security, economics, congressional matters, science and technology, drug abuse prevention, telecommunications, consumers, national goals, intergovernmental relations, environment, domestic policy, international economics, military affairs, civil rights, disarmament, labor relations, District of Columbia, cultural affairs, education, foreign trade and tariffs, past Presidents, the aged, health and nutrition, physical fitness, volunteerism, intellectuals, blacks, youth, women, "the Jewish community," Wall Street, governors, mayors, "ethnics," regulatory agencies and related industry, state party chairmen, Mexican-Americans.

It is as if interest groups and professions no longer settle for lobbying Congress, or having one of their number appointed to departmental advisory boards or sub-Cabinet positions. It now appears essential to "have your own man right there in the White House." Once this foothold is established, of course, interest groups can play upon the potential political backlash that could arise should their representation be discontinued.

One of the more disturbing elements in the growth of the Presidential Establishment is the development, particularly under the current administration, of a huge public-relations apparatus. More than 100 presidential aides are now engaged in various forms of press-agentry or public relations, busily selling and reselling the President. This activity is devoted to the particular occupant of the White House, but inevitably it affects the presidency itself, by projecting or reinforcing images of the presidency that are almost imperial in their suggestions of omnipotence and omniscience. Thus the public-relations apparatus not only has directly enlarged the presidential workforce but has expanded public expectations about the presidency at the same time.

Last, but by no means least, Congress, which has grown increasingly critical of the burgeoning power of the presidency, must take some blame itself for the expansion of the White House. Divided within itself and ill-equipped, or simply disinclined to make some of the nation's toughest political decisions in recent decades, Congress has abdicated more and more authority to the presidency. The fact that the recent massive bombing of North Vietnam was ordered by the President without even a pretense of consultation with Congress buried what little was left of the semblance of that body's war-making power. Another recent instance of Congress's tendency to surrender authority to the presidency, an extraordinary instance, was the passage by the House (though not the Senate) of a grant to the President that would give him the right to determine which programs are to be cut whenever the budget goes beyond $250 billion ceiling limit—a bill which, in effect, would hand over to the President some of Congress's long-cherished "power of the purse."

What can be done to bring the Presidential Establishment back down to size? What can be done to bring it to a size that both lightens the heavy accumulation of functions that it has absorbed and allows the Presidential Establishment to perform its most important functions more effectively and wisely?

First, Congress should curb its own impulse to establish new presidential agencies and to ask for yet additional reports and studies from the President. In the past Congress has been a too willing partner in the enlargement of the presidency. If Congress genuinely wants a leaner presidency, it should ask more of itself. For instance, it could well make better use of its own General Accounting Office and Congressional Research Service for chores that are now often assigned to the President.

Congress should also establish in each of its houses special committees on Executive Office operations. Most congressional committees are organized to deal with areas such as labor, agriculture, armed services, or education, paralleling the organization of the Cabinet. What we need now are committees designed explicitly to oversee the White House. No longer can the task of overseeing persidential operations be dispersed among dozens of committees and subcommittees, each of which can look at only small segments of the Presidential Establishment.

Some will complain that adding yet another committee to the already overburdened congressional system is just like adding another council to the overstuffed Presidential Establishment. But the central importance of what the presidency does (and does not do) must rank among the most critical tasks of the contemporary Congress. As things are organized now, the presidency escapes with grievously inadequate scrutiny. Equally important, Congress needs these committees to help protect itself from its own tendency to relinquish to the presidency its diminishing resources and prerogatives. Since Truman, Presidents have had staffs to oversee Congress; it is time Congress reciprocated.

Similar efforts to let the salutary light of public attention shine more brightly on the presidency should be inaugurated by the serious journals and newspapers of the nation. For too long, publishers and editors have believed that covering the presidency means assigning a reporter to the White House press corps. Unfortunately, however, those who follow the President around on his travels are rarely in a position to do investigative reporting on what is going on inside the Presidential Establishment. Covering the Executive Office of the President requires more than a President watcher; it needs a specialist who understands the arcane language and highly complex practices that have grown up in the Presidential Establishment.

Finally, it is time to reverse the downgrading of the Cabinet. President Nixon ostensibly moved in this direction with his designation several days ago of three Cabinet heads—HEW's Casper W. Weinberger, Agriculture's Earl L. Butz, and HUD's James T. Lynn—as, in effect, super-secretaries of "human resources," "natural resources," and "community development" respectively. The move was expressly made in the name of Cabinet consolidation, plans for which Mr. Nixon put forward in 1971 but which Congress has so far spurned.

The three men will hold onto their Cabinet Posts, but they have been given White House offices as well—as presidential counselors—and so it may be that the most direct effect of the appointments is a further expansion of the Presidential Establishment, rather than a counter-bolstering of the Cabinet. But if the move does, in fact, lead to Cabinet consolidation under broader divisions, it will be a step in the right direction.

Reducing the present number of departments would strengthen the hand of Cabinet members vis-à-vis special interests, and might enable them to serve as advisers, as well as advocates, to the President. Cabinet consolidation would also have another very desirable effect: it would be a move toward reducing the accumulation of power within the Presidential Establishment. For much of the power of budget directors and other senior White House aides comes from their roles as penultimate referees of interdepartmental jurisdictional disputes. Under consolidated departments, a small number of strengthened Cabinet officers with closer ties to the President would resolve these conflicts instead. With fewer but broader Cabinet departments, there would be less need for many of the interest-group brokers and special councils that now constitute so much of the excessive baggage in the overburdened presidency.

Meanwhile, the presidency remains sorely overburdened—with both functions and functionaries—and needs very much to be cut back in both. Certainly, the number of presidential workers can and should be reduced. Harry Truman put it best, perhaps, when he said with characteristic succinctness: "I do not like this present trend toward a huge White House staff. . . . Mostly these aides get in each other's way." But while the number of functionaries is the most tangible and dramatic measure of the White House's expansion, its increasing absorption of governmental functions is more profoundly disturbing. The current White House occupant may regard cutting down (or transferring) a number of his staff members as a way of mollifying critics who charge that the American presidency has grown too big and bloated, but it is yet another thing to reduce the President's authority or his accumulated prerogatives. As the nation's number-one critic of the swelling of government, President Nixon will, it is hoped, move—or will continue to move if he has truly already started—to substantially deflate this swelling in one of the areas where it most needs to be deflated—at home, in the White House.

THE PRESIDENCY AND WATERGATE: ISSUES AND ANSWERS

Although everyone would agree that the personality and character of the President profoundly affects the way in which the affairs of the White House are conducted, attempting to analyze presidential character is an extraordinarily difficult undertaking. It essentially involves psychoanalyzing the President, and unless he is placed on the couch (and perhaps even if he were to be placed on the couch) conclusions that must be reached from secondary sources are tenuous at best. Nevertheless, James D. Barber feels that it is both necessary and possible to deal with the question of presidential character, and to assess the character of presidential candidates before voting for them. In his well-known book *The Presidential Character: Predicting Performance in the White House* (Englewood Cliffs, New Jersey: Prentice-Hall, 1972) he develops a typology of presidential characters. Within the typology the most significant types are "active-positive," and "active-negative." The active-positive President is a man who is achievement oriented, productive, and has well-defined goals. He is rational "using his brain to move his feet," and above all is flexible and capable of changing his goals and methods as he perceives reasons for altering his course of action. Barber cites John F. Kennedy as an active-positive President. Above all, because he feels sure of himself, has a highly developed self-image which gives him the necessary personal security to direct himself rationally from within rather than simply letting events and the opinions of others sway him, the active-positive President does not allow himself to be locked into a position.

The active-negative President, on the other hand, is psychologically mixed up. He has a compulsive need to work because of personal problems and a misguided "Puritan-ethic." He is ambitious, power hungry, but lacks goals beyond that of rising to power. He can be politically amoral. His great energy often is directed in irrational ways, and once set in a course of action the active-negative President can become very rigid, especially in the face of opposition and criticism from the outside. Barber suggests that the active-negative President does not welcome criticism, and tends to surround himself by yes-men to fortify him in his preconceived notions of what is right. Unlike the active-positive President, the active-negative President needs artificial boosting because of his lack of a well-developed self-image. Professor Barber has classified President Nixon as an active-negative type. In the following selection he assesses the effects of President Nixon's character and personality on the Watergate Affair.

49

James David Barber

THE PRESIDENCY AFTER WATERGATE

For a long time before he became President, Nixon had been making clear his view of the world as an untrustworthy place where the only way to win was never to count on anyone but himself. The public, for example, he saw as a weak reed: "Frankly, most people are mentally and physically lazy. They believe they can get places by luck alone." The press he saw as fundamentally craven: "You know very well that whether you are on page one or page thirty depends on whether they fear you. It's as simple as that." One could not even trust one's friends in politics: "The rarest of all commodities is a political friendship that lasts through times of failure as well as success. . . . I was not unprepared for this reaction because I had already gained that experience during my mercurial career." These feelings of distrust were and are combined with an extraordinarily strong drive for power and victory. "I have never had much sympathy," Nixon wrote in *Six Crises,* "for the point of view, 'it isn't whether you win or lose that counts, but how you play the game:' How you play the game does count. But one must put top consideration on the will, the desire, and the determination to win." Politics as sportsmanship, as a system more valuable than its products, fades out; politics as a Hobbesian war of all against all fades in. His longtime attitude toward winning and the rules of the game is consistent with this report by Daniel Ellsberg of a conversation that occurred between Nixon and an American team in Vietnam working on election procedures:

> The opening moments of that visit have often come back to me. After shaking hands with each of us, Nixon asked: "Well, Ed, what are you up to?"
>
> [General] Lansdale replied: "We want to help General Thang make this the most honest election that's ever been held in Vietnam."
>
> "Oh sure, honest, yes, honest, that's right"-Nixon was sitting himself in an armchair next to Lansdale's— "*so long as you win!*" With the last words he winked, drove his elbow hard into Lansdale's arm, and, in a return motion, slapped his own knee. My teammates turned to stone.

Such episodes are clues to a resonance between Nixon's view of the political world and the win-at-any-price world of Watergate. How is a man who thinks that way likely to act and react as the scandal spreads? Here, some

---

From James David Barber, "The Presidency After Watergate," *World* (July 31, 1973).

understanding of his presidential character and its analogies to those of past Presidents may be instructive. And beyond explanation comes the question of the future: Do we want and need a new presidential system? Or are there other lines of reform more likely to serve the purpose of restoring the legitimacy of the office?

Judging from Nixon's own past, his course as he seeks to weather this umpteenth crisis in his political life will be to try to move past it quickly, on to yet another crisis. This method has helped him time and again; mired down in the defeat of Haynesworth and Carswell, he made a bitter speech about it on April 9, 1970, put the case behind him, and plunged into the Cambodian crisis, announcing the invasion on April 30. Three years to the day later, on April 30, 1973, Nixon tried to put Watergate behind him by making a speech and moving on to more important business. But this time the technique did not work. Watergate lingers on and on, even despite additional presidential explanations. At this writing, however, the most likely Nixonian response would appear to be continued efforts at diversion—the search for some highly newsworthy line of action on inflation control, foreign adventure, or whatever.

A darker prediction springs from the catch-22 bind of the Watergate crisis: If Nixon knew, he was a party to the corruption; if he did not know, he was incompetent. Judging from the histories of three Presidents who, I think, shared Nixon's basic political character type—Wilson, Hoover, and Lyndon Johnson—such a double threat to virtue and to power could trigger a process of rigid adherence to a failing policy. In my book *The Presidential Character* I suggested how that process might develop, as seen from the perspective of the Nixon type:

> Battered from all sides with demands that he yield yard after yard of his territory, that he conform to ignorant and selfish demands, he begins to feel his integrity slipping away from him. In doubt about his personal strength, he experiences compromise as a steady diminution of "the most powerful man in the world" to a mere clerk, ordered about by his supposed subordinates. At the same time, he is being harassed by critics who, unaware of the problems he faces, attribute his actions to low motives, adding insult to injury. At long last, after enduring all this for longer than any mortal should, he rebels and stands his ground. Masking his decision in whatever rhetoric is necessary, he rides the tiger to the end.

In just that fashion, Wilson killed his dream by rigidly insisting on the letter of his League treaty draft, Hoover hung onto his opposition to "the dole" long after national disaster, and Lyndon Johnson turned a minor commitment into a major war. The process of rigidification was, in each case, the outgrowth of a situation directly and simultaneously challenging the President's sense of self-righteousness and his sense of power.

That could happen to Nixon. The main hope for preventing it in the short run rests with the few confidants the President has some trust in—those few advisers who are also his friends. Short of the radical surgery of impeachment or resignation, genuine consultation of this sort is the best hope for the rest of his term. The public memory is short; if he stays in office, Nixon, by 1975–76, might have managed to rescue some of his presidential reputation.

But, again, the question is larger than Nixon's individual fate. Already the public is groggy with disillusionment—from the Kennedy assassinations through urban riots, Vietnam, campus rebellion, the credibility gap, the bombing, and now presidential police-state tactics. Naturally enough, attention turns to what we can do to ward off future traumas from the White House.

What should be the thrust of our thinking in the wake of Watergate? The easiest out is the moralistic focus: Nixon as a bad person. But Watergate is undoubtedly a painful and dramatic personal crisis for Richard Nixon; as a human being up against a terrible situation, he merits understanding, even sympathy. It does no good to hate the man or to wallow in glee over his comeuppance. As Harry Truman said, the President is a man like the rest of us—he puts his pants on one leg at a time. Neither Richard Nixon nor any other normal person gets up in the morning and says, "Today I'm going to be evil." The President means well—now, as when he ordered a rain of death and destruction on Southeast Asia. To cast the President as some sort of moral leper, a Caligula in the White House, is as unfair as it is inaccurate.

But the issue is the nation's course, not Nixon's fate. As long as discussion centers on the little details of who-said-what-to-whom, and especially just exactly what the President said, we are going to miss the forest for the trees. As long as we concentrate on the question of Nixon's precise degree of guilt, perhaps hoping that the whole ugly story will reach a cathartic denouement when he is "convicted" in some sense, we will miss the point. Nor will it do much good to lapse into the paranoia of conspiracy theories or the masochism of "What-has-happened-to-America?" We have been all these places before—in the backwash of the Kennedy assassination, for example—and they lead nowhere.

At this point in time (to use the Ervin witnesses' new cliché), it is obvious that we are dealing, not with a few idiosyncratic miscreants, but with a somewhat disorganized host of ethically indifferent Nixon enthusiasts operating in many different directions from coast to coast and beyond. Their crime was at least a threefold subversion: of the judicial, electoral, and free-speech processes. Whatever Nixon actually said, he is the one who decided whom to trust in his administration, and he is the one who set the political climate for his campaign. If he had made it perfectly clear that such things were not to happen, they would not have happened—not, at least, on anything like the scale of the actual operations. One can contrast the casual flow of hundreds of thousands of dollars in cash for shady purposes in the Nixon campaign with the outrage Eisenhower conveyed over a mere $18,000 fund his vice-presidential candidate was thought to have taken from a group of California businessmen. In the Eisenhower days a White House aide's acceptance of a coat or a rug was cause for scandal. That President also set a climate, one capsulized in the phrase "clean as a hound's tooth." Harding and Wilson, Coolidge and

Truman—each President sets a tone, a climate, a culture if you will (not always the one intended), from which his minions take their cues.

The Nixon campaign culture, it now appears, was permeated with distrust. The press could not be trusted to get across the President's message in sufficiently favorable light; therefore the press had to be intimidated and lied to and kept away from the administration's inner life. Despite the President's great advantages as a popular incumbent, the electoral process could not be trusted to produce the necessary victory; therefore the weapons of international espionage and sabotage had to be wheeled into action. The old processes of judge and jury could not be trusted to damn protesters and leakers; therefore the special operations, the *agents provocateurs,* the manufacturing of evidence, the dangling of the FBI directorship before Judge William M. Byrne, Jr.

In that context Nixon communicated his go-get-'em message to those who worked with and for him in the campaign. He did not have to elaborate the details as to how his purposes were to be executed: The subordinates got the point. His extreme isolation (a longtime element in his political style) added to the problem. Staffers in doubt about the limits could easily read into his cryptic comments about winning in an untrustworthy world a license to go the whole distance—beyond custom, beyond truth, beyond the law.

Thus Watergate traces to the Oval Office. The more realistic proposals for preventing future Watergates fall in two directions. The first stresses new law and a restructuring of the presidency as an institution. The threat of Watergate, from this perspective, is a threat to the office itself, a symptom that the presidential system is out of hand and in need of control. The powers of the presidency should be cut back. Congress should recapture the territory it has lost with respect to war and peace, funding and implementing domestic programs, controlling executive secrecy and emergency powers. If necessary, this argument goes, the Constitution should be changed to approximate more closely the British Cabinet system, to ensure the chief executive's dependence on congressional majorities. The President as political candidate would also be curtailed in the degree to which he could use his official resources as advantages in campaigning. And perhaps the burgeoning bureaucracy in the executive office of the President needs radical pruning. As for changes in law, they run the gamut from tighter definitions of "national security" and closer congressional supervision of the CIA and FBI to new legislation on campaign finance.

Necessary some of these changes may be, but none of them are, I believe, likely to be sufficient; some could be down-right harmful. Presidents have turned out to be the least law-controllable actors in the upper reaches of American government. Lincoln managed to suspend habeas corpus; Franklin Roosevelt got around the requirement for Senate advice and consent on treaties by inventing the "executive agreement." Nixon broadens his authority regarding national security to include spying on his domestic political competitors. By closing off access to presidential news (not to mention fakery and distortion), a President can make a mockery of the freedom of the press. Hypothetically a subject of the law, the President is also, in an important sense, a law-maker. The pathetic plea Nixon subordinates offer as justification for these Watergate crimes—that they assume what the President wants must be all right—illustrates that point.

Nor is the behavior of Presidents easy to contain in some organizational structure. Short of adopting Cabinet government, schemes for ensuring presidential consultation (with Congress, with his officially designated Cabinet, with the press) cannot ensure the genuineness of such consultation. Lyndon Johnson, for example, kept George Ball around for a good while as a kind of official dissenter, as Johnson escalated the war in Vietnam; the President would hear him out, congratulate himself for taking the other side into account, and march on in the same direction. John Kennedy could have organized his advising machinery for the Bay of Pigs as effectively as he later did for the Cuban missile crisis. The fact that Richard Nixon occasionally has conversations with congressmen says nothing about the quality or content or style of those conversations, which, it appears were not effective in helping him understand the realities of his situation. In short, you can perhaps bring a President to a roomful of knowledgeable people but you can't make him think differently as a result. So far no magical organization chart has been invented capable of preventing a determined President from seeing the world in his own peculiar way.

The temptation for reformers in this crisis, as Elizabeth Drew has observed perceptively, is "to confuse ad hocs with eternal truths." Not long ago the main thrust of reform sentiment was to strengthen a presidency in need of help; Vietnam and Watergate swing the pendulum in the opposite direction. Meanwhile, the traditional machinery is sitting there, waiting to be used. For it is as clear now as it was years ago that Congress could, through its regular powers of legislating and appropriating, take care of such immediate problems as stopping the bombing in Cambodia and mopping up the Watergate scandal. None of that requires a new Constitution or even a radical reorganization of the present, readily accessible mechanism for decision making.

Those basic institutional arrangements have proved remarkably enduring, for better or worse. The collapse of the Nixon presidency through impeachment or resignation would not collapse the presidency as such; indeed, it might make it easier for a new President to establish his legitimacy and authority against the background of Nixon's failure. Herbert Hoover's failure to cope with the Depression paved the way for FDR's remarkable exercise of presidential power. Scandals in the Harding and Truman administrations did not prevent their successors from picking up the reins and plowing on. Certainly Nixon's hand was strengthened in foreign policy—permitting him extraordinary departures regarding China and the Soviet Union—by the fact that he succeeded a President who had led us into disaster. Further back in history the presidency has survived its Grants and Pierces and Andrew Johnsons. We do not, then, seem in dire danger of a *constitutional* failure, whatever happens to Nixon.

Diagnosis and prescription would be on solider ground, I contend, if we looked beyond structures and processes to cultures and persons—the second direction of proposals for preventing future Watergates. There are types of reform other than "reorganization"—reform that reaches the substance of belief, the criteria of character, reform of values directly relevant to the Watergates and Vietnams. For in a very real sense, we Americans can make the government do what we want it to do—if we know what that is—and we can find Presidents who will lead us effectively—if we know how to find them.

Both Watergate and Vietnam grew out of fear and distrust, reinforced in large measure by what Richard Hofstadter used to call the paranoid style in American politics. The "tough-minded" characters in the Johnson and Nixon administrations did not just happen to appear; they grew out of a political culture in which the stakes of international and domestic politics had been vastly exaggerated by dramatic rhetoric. In fact Vietnam was just not all that important. In fact defeat for Nixon in 1972 would not have been the end of the world. The public, and those who educate publics through the media and the schools, should have known better. They should have been able to see how toughness can get in the way of vision. Part of the public mind knows that the tough guys in politics are as often as not trying to distract attention from their clay feet. Part of the public mind understands the difference between courage and bullying, between shrewdness and skulduggery. But those distinctions tend to get blurred when a civil fracas far away is translated into a threat to our way of life, or when an ordinary political campaign is turned into a life-or-death struggle. Then American humaneness, hope, and confidence erode; candidates and Presidents are encouraged to stress, not their concern for human welfare, but their readiness for mortal combat.

On the other hand, our culture values persuasion—the core value that sustains political life. Don't *tread* on me, we say: *Show* me. Persuasion in politics has at least three opposites: force, fraud, and secrecy. Genuine persuasion is possible only in an atmosphere of trust, such as the trust that the other person means what he is saying, that there can be at least rough agreement on the facts, and that both parties share enough common philosophy to live with the result. Most of what goes on in politics—for Presidents as for other politicans—is, in fact, persuasive behavior of this sort. There are other values in need of political restoration, but restoring the politics of persuasion, of meaningful public dialogue, is a first priority. That will take fostering, by those who try to communicate the realities of politics and by those who are bent on changing those realities.

In the Presidency the politics of persuasion can be made to work only by a President who believes in it, practices it—*likes* it. Before we start reorganizing the presidency, we ought to devote far more effort and attention to choosing the person who will do the reorganizing, who will determine whether or not any form of White House organization will work. The President's character, his political style, his way of looking at the world—these turn out to be the qualities we should have been attending to in the case of Mr. Nixon, not his long-forgotten stands on issues or his ideological postures on such matters as anticommunism or free enterprise. We wound up with a President whose personality feeds on the turmoil of crisis, whose extraordinary isolation cuts him off from political reality, and whose world view has little place in it for constitutional verities. Who now believes we should have taken more seriously Nixon's expressed intentions in 1968 to begin "realistic programs that restore self-respect to the poor and open up opportunity for the jobless man who wants to work," not to wait "until inflation backs us to the wall to start to get our economic house in order," to ensure that each Cabinet member would "have the stature and power to function effectively" and that "publicity would not center at the White House alone"? Nixon, like other candidates, says a lot of things in campaigns, intentions perhaps meant seriously and sincerely but that contradict egregiously the theme and thrust of his political habits that have become ingrained.

Next time around we will again have an opportunity to take a long and careful look at the candidates being brought forward for the presidency—well before the lists are made up. Then we will, if we are wise, assess the contenders as presidential characters, persons of extraordinary confidence and energy, flexible and open in style, experientially devoted to the politics of persuasion.

The thesis of the following selection is that Watergate is not an isolated event in American history. The author feels that the events of Watergate have many precedents in the last decade. Moreover, in contrast to the thesis of James Barber, Philip Kurland feels that the problem of Watergate did not arise because of the President's personal characteristics. One of the main institutional reasons for Watergate was the power of the President's staff as well as of top-level bureaucrats beholden to the President. Watergate was caused in part, the author feels, by the "arrogance of power" within the presidency and parts of the Executive Branch. The only way to prevent future Watergates is to reduce the influence of the White House staff—the invisible presidency—as well as other executive officials who work for the President. It is not the character of the men who occupy the office, but the institution of the presidency that must be changed.

50

Philip B. Kurland

THE ISSUES BEYOND WATERGATE

For me Watergate is not a place, not a series of recent events, not a point in time. Watergate is a compendium whose most important element is a state of mind, an attitude about how American government should function. Watergate is also a question whether these United States can survive as a constitutional democracy.

Is it erroneous to suggest that the immediate events of Watergate began with the Pentagon Papers leak? Is it heresy to suggest that the evils that were revealed by the Pentagon Papers were wrongdoings of Presidents Kennedy and Johnson and their advisers rather than those of President Nixon and his advisers? Is it inappropriate to notice that the "Plumbers" were President Nixon's contribution to the scandals of the Pentagon Papers? Is it irrelevant to notice that the Bay of Pigs and the CIA are integral parts of the Watergate scandal? Is it improper to suggest that President Truman's Korean venture is the direct precedent for the illegal war initiated by President Kennedy, stepped up by President Johnson and continued to a delayed end by President Nixon? Is it bad taste to assert that the secret bombings of Cambodia were no more secret than the original use of advisers in Vietnam or the use of CIA mercenaries in Southeast Asia at an earlier date?

For me, all these questions and more are necessary to the understanding of Watergate. Watergate did not occur as a biological sport. It is not a matter of yesterday, but of many yesterdays. Even the election methods that were the direct subject for study by the Watergate committee have their antecedents. Were Muskie's tears worse than Nixon's makeup in his first debate with Kennedy? Did money play a different role in the 1972 campaign than in the 1960 Democratic primaries and the contest that followed? Were the tactics that secured the nomination for the Democratic candidate in 1972, a candidacy that assured a Republican victory, more wholesome for our democratic institutions than those indulged by the Nixon campaign forces?

TWO PROPOSITIONS

Enough of the questions that I think are relevant to the Watergate problem. Let me turn to my two propositions.

From Philip B. Kurland, "The Issues Beyond Watergate," *The Wall Street Journal* (December 12, 1973). Reprinted with the permission of *The Wall Street Journal.* © Dow Jones & Company, Inc., 1973.

My first is that we are unduly concerned with the sensational and trivial aspects of Watergate and that neither the President, the Congress, the Judiciary, the press, nor the public have addressed the fundamental problems that the Watergate scandals have revealed. In no small measure, I submit, this trivialization of Watergate is due to the invocation of the judicial process to resolve what are essentially minor aspects of the basic issues. The Judiciary is incapable of resolving the broad constitutional problems reached by Watergate. Its function is limited to minor constitutional changes not structural constitutional reorganization.

The Judiciary has undertaken to decide—or has had imposed upon it— two kinds of questions. First, there are the series of questions of guilt or innocence of all those charged with criminal acts in the events immediately preceding, during and after the Watergate break-in. Admittedly, these cases are not, on an absolute scale, matters of small moment. But comparatively, they are flyspecks. We know without further judicial proceedings what was done. Indeed, we know who was responsible for what was done. The responsibility rests on that entity called the White House, regardless of whether any particular act was done by Haldeman or Ehrlichman, by Dean or Magruder, by Mitchell or Stans, or even by President Nixon himself. I submit that the judicial identification of individual culprits will not take us closer to solution of our basic problems but only farther away from such solutions. For we are likely to assume that all that is needed is punishment for the illegal acts by highly placed office holders.

I submit, too, that President Nixon understands this to be the case as he, at one and the same time, decries concentration on the Watergate problem and suggests that the matter be left to the courts, while he arrogantly warns Congress not to attempt to reduce the powers of the presidential office. With the shift to the courts of the trial of individual former officials of the administration will go all the attention of the press and the public.

Even the lawsuit involving the President himself ought to be considered of little importance. Even if the President were to be impeached and convicted or to resign, Watergate will be unresolved, except in the minds of the American public.

The basic questions are how we arrived at this stage and what can be done to ameliorate and diminish the danger. But the question how we came to be here is of importance only if it helps us move towards a solution. Here, as with the criminal trials that have been spewed up by the Watergate investigation, I should say that assignment of fault is not the first priority.

One thing that is clear to me, the problem does not derive from the President's personal characteristics, however much those character traits have exacerbated the problem. I was happy to find agreement with this conclusion in a recent column by Tom Wicker in The New York Times, for Mr. Wicker, as everybody knows, is a fully accredited, card-carrying Liberal, with a capital "L." And I am not. He wrote in the conclusion of his column, "Liberal Democrats will not automatically end the threat to liberty inherent in the imperial presidency merely by coming back to power in 1976. Their own doctrines need as much reexamination as the perversions of them sponsored by the Nixon administration."

This brings me to my second point. The constitutional crisis in which we are immersed is different in kind rather than in degree from those that have occurred before. The issue in the Agnew case, for example, was an issue of the old-fashioned kind of corruption. Watergate is of a different magnitude. In part this difference is shown by the fact that money was only a means and not an end for the Watergate capers.

In the midst of the Dreyfus scandal in France—and I regard the Dreyfus crisis as the closest parallel to the Watergate affair that comes within my narrow ken of history—William James wrote a letter to Mrs. Morse in which he said:

"Talk of corruption. We don't know what corruption means at home, with our improvised and shifting agencies of crude pecuniary bribery, compared with the solidly entrenched and permanently organized corruptive geniuses of monarchy, nobility, church, army, that penetrate the bosom of the higher kind as well as the lower kind of people in all European states."

To my mind, we have now arrived at that stage that James described as the condition of the European governments at the turn of the century. Certainly "crude pecuniary bribery" remains with us. But that is not nearly so threatening as the corruption that becomes rampant when we substitute a king and his court—even within the limits of an eight-year presidency—for the presidency as we once knew it, before the days of the CIA, the National Security Council, the Council of Economic Advisers, and the Office of Management and Budget.

The danger to American democracy and freedom rests not so much in the presidency itself but in the court [staff] that surrounds the presidency. In the Kennedy, Johnson and Nixon administrations we have gone back in history to the time when the king and his council wielded all national governmental authority. I don't know yet when the euphemism "The White House" first came into use as a description of something other than the presidential mansion at 1600 Pennsylvania Avenue. But it was exactly when the White House became what it now is, a fourth branch of government, that we started down the road to Watergate.

PROFESSOR BAILYN'S PERCEPTIONS

I am supported in my position by the history of the American colonies that led to the American Revolution, whose 200th anniversary we are about to celebrate. A startlingly perceptive and insightful work, Professor Bernard Bailyn's "The Ideological Origins of the American Revolution," published in 1967, demonstrates that the case for the American Revolution was based not so much on those simplifications that are taught in our history courses, as on the notion that the English constitutional system on which all men's liberties depended had been perverted by the men around the crown together with the king rather than by the king himself.

At the outset of this volume, Mr. Bailyn wrote:

"For the primary goal of the American revolution, which transformed American life and introduced a new era in human history, was not the overthrow or even the alteration of the existing social order but the preservation of political liberty threatened by the apparent corruption of the constitution."

"Corruption of the constitution" is exactly the disease of which Watergate is the symptom. Listen again to Mr. Bailyn's words, and his use of the words of those who lived in the era that gave birth to our nation, and ask yourselves whether the explanation of the corruption does not fit our day equally well:

"The most common explanation, however, an explanation that rose from the deepest sources of British political thought—located the spring and cause of all the distresses and complaints of the people in England or in America' in 'a kind of fourth power that the constitution knows nothing of, or has not provided against.' This 'overruling arbitrary power, which absolutely controls the King, Lords, and Commons' was composed, it was said, of the 'ministers and favorites' of the King, who, in defiance of God and man alike, 'extend their usurped authority infinitely too far,' and 'throwing off the balance of the constitution, make their despotic will' the authority of the nation."

The American Revolution, according to Mr. Bailyn, was a political revolution, not a social or economic revolution. It was fought to restore the constitutional balance that Englishmen and Americans thought essential to the liberties they claimed. In the two centuries that have elapsed, the "corruption of the constitution" has once again occurred. And, if our liberties are to be preserved, we should be looking to the means to restore the constitutional balance among the three branches of government. The first step, I repeat, should be the abolition of the fourth branch, "The White House."

THE POWER OF ARROGANCE

The American body politic is suffering not from what Senator Fulbright once described as "The Arrogance of Power," but rather from the power of arrogance, an arrogance whose visage we have all witnessed at the Watergate hearings through the testimony of those who spoke for, worked in, or worked for "The White House." An arrogance that permits Roger Helms to tell the Watergate committee that he made no representations to the FBI to limit the scope of its investigation, even as he was already on record before the Senate Armed Services Committee of having done just that. An arrogance that permits Attorney General Kleindienst to tell the Judiciary Committee that there was no presidential pressure to approve the ITT settlement, when he knew of presidential pressure to inhibit taking the case to the Supreme Court.

I cannot assure you that my prescribed first step toward the restoration of constitutional democracy is surely the right one. I do confidently assert that the proposed—albeit partial—answer at least addresses the right question. And I am equally confident that nothing contained either in the hearings or the judicial proceedings touches on the fundamental issue of how to restore the government's structural balance on which the Constitution rests. The spirit of liberty, of which Judge Learned Hand once spoke so eloquently, which is the necessary condition of American freedom, has no representatives at the councils that are directly concerned with Watergate, not in the Congress, not in the courts, not in the press, and certainly not in "The White House." It is in 1974 that we must take steps to avoid "1984." If the Watergate crisis passes from the public scene without the effectuation of the reforms so patently needed, it will soon be too late.

The preceding two selections have concluded respectively that the relationship between the President and the Watergate Affair was shaped by the character of President Nixon and the role of the President's staff. In April, 1974, President Nixon released transcripts of Oval Office discussions about Watergate and related matters. The President released the transcripts to the public in a last ditch attempt to gain support. He gave the original tapes of the conversations to the House Judiciary Committee. Instead of producing the kind of favorable public reaction that the President inscrutably expected, the transcripts caused a public outcry of unprecedented proportions and a rapid withdrawal of what little support the President had in Congress before the text of the transcripts was revealed.

The Nixon transcripts were bad enough for the President, but even worse were transcripts of the same tapes that were released in July, 1974, by the House Judiciary Committee that revealed discrepancies, alterations and omissions in the White House version of Oval Office conversations. The Committee account pictured a President actively involved in the Watergate cover-up. Finally, after the Supreme Court ruling in *United States* v. *Richard M. Nixon* (see selection 11, chapter two), President Nixon was essentially forced to reveal to the public the fact that he had been involved in the Watergate cover-up only six days after the break-in occurred. The following selection contains portions of the Nixon transcripts, and part of the June 23, 1972 tape released by President Nixon before his resignation on August 9, 1974. There are no meaningful differences between the White House and the House Judiciary Committee on what was said in the following selections. Each speaker is identified by an initial: the President (P.), White House counsel John Dean (D.), Presidential advisers H. R. Haldeman (H.) and John Ehrlichman (E.), and former Attorney General John Mitchell (M.).

In reading the transcripts students should keep in mind the two previous selections and attempt to assess the ways in which the transcripts support or detract from the conclusions of Barber and Kurland.

51
THE NIXON TRANSCRIPTS

JUNE 23, 1972

H. You know the Democratic break-in thing, we're back in the problem area because the FBI is not under control . . . the way to handle this now is for us to have Walters call Pat Gray and just say, "stay to hell out of this—this is, ah, business here we don't want you to go any further on it."

P. What about Pat Gray—you mean Pat Gray doesn't want to?

H. Pat does want to. He doesn't know how to, and he doesn't have, he doesn't have any basis for doing it. . . .

H. And you seem to think the thing to do is get them to stop?

P. Right, fine. . . .

P. Play it tough. That's the way they play it and that's the way we are going to play it. . . .

P. When you get in [to the CIA] people say, "Look, the problem is that this will open the whole Bay of Pigs thing, and the President just feels that ah," without going into the details—don't, don't lie to them to the extent to say there is no involvement, but just say this is a comedy of errors . . . they should call the FBI in and (unintelligible) don't go any further into this case period!

SEPTEMBER 15, 1972

This transcript begins as Haldeman and Ehrlichman enter the Oval Office.

P. Hi, how are you? You had quite a day today didn't you. You got Watergate on the way didn't you?

D. We tried.

H. How did it all end up?

D. Ah, I think we can say well at this point. The press is playing it just as we expect.

H. Whitewash?

D. No, not yet—the story right now—

P. It is a big story

H. Five indicted plus the WH former guy and all that.

D. Plus two White House fellows.

H. That is good that takes the edge off whitewash really that was the thing Mitchell kept saying that to people in the country [Watergate defendants G. Gordon] Liddy and [Howard] Hunt were big men. Maybe that is good.

P. How did [Mitchell's successor as head of CRP, Clark] MacGregor handle himself?

Newsweek, May 13, 1974; and Newsweek, August 19, 1974.

D. I think very well. He had a good statement which said that the Grand Jury had met and that it was now time to realize that some apologies may be due.

H. Fat chance . . .

P. Just remember, all the trouble we're taking, we'll have a chance to get back one day. How are you doing on your other investigations?

H. What has happened on the bug?

P. What bug?

D. The second bug there was a bug found in the telephone of one of the men at the [Democratic National Committee].

P. You don't think it was left over from the other time?

D. Absolutely not, the Bureau has checked and re-checked the whole place after that night. The man had specifically checked and rechecked the telephone and it was not there.

P. What the hell do you think was involved?

D. I think DNC was planted.

P. You think they did it?

D. Uh huh

P. (Expletive deleted)—do they really want to believe that we planted that?

H. Did they get anything on the finger prints?

D. No, nothing at all—either on the telephone or on the bug. The FBI has unleashed a full investigation . . . at the DNC starting with [Democratic chairman Lawrence] O'Brien right now.

H. Laughter. Using the same crew—

D. The same crew—the Washington Field Office.

P. What kind of questions are they asking him?

D. Anything they can think of because O'Brien is charging them with failing to find all the bugs.

H. Good, that will make them mad.

D. So [acting FBI Director L. Patrick] Gray is pissed and his people are pissed off. So maybe they will move in because their reputation is on the line. I think that is a good development.

P. I think that is a good development because it makes it look so (adjective deleted) funny. Am I wrong?

D. No, no, sir. It looks silly. If we can find that the DNC planted that, the whole story will reverse.

* * *

After a few minutes, the meeting is interrupted by a telephone call from John Mitchell. Only the President's side of the conversation is recorded. The Mitchell talk ends this way:

P. Well I tell you just don't let this keep you or your colleagues from concentrating on the big game. This thing is just one of those side issues and a month later everybody looks back and wonders what all the shooting was about. OK, John. Good night. Get a good night's sleep. And don't bug anybody without asking me? OK? Yeah. Thank you.

D. Three months ago I would have had trouble predicting there would be a day when this would be forgotten, but I think I can say that 54 days from now nothing is going to come crashing down to our surprise.

P. That what?

D. Nothing is going to come crashing down to our surprise.

P. Oh well, this is a can of worms as you know a lot of this stuff that went on. And the people who worked this way are awfully embarrassed. But the way you have handled all this seems to me has been very skillful putting your fingers in the leaks that have sprung here and sprung there . . . We are all in it together. This is a war. We take a few shots and it will be over. We will give them a few shots and it will be over . . . Don't worry. I wouldn't want to be on the other side right now. Would you?

D. Along that line, one of the things I've tried to do, I have begun to keep notes on a lot of people who are emerging as less than our friends because this will be over some day and we shouldn't forget the way some of them have treated us.

P. I want the most comprehensive notes on all those who tried to do us in. They didn't have to do it. If we had had a very close election and they were playing the other side I would understand this. No—they were doing this quite deliberately and they are asking for it and they are going to get it. We have not used the power in this first four years as you know. We have never used it. We have not used the Bureau and we have not used the Justice Department but things are going to change now. And they are either going to do it right or go.

D. What an exciting prospect.

P. Thanks. It has to be done. We have been (adjective deleted) fools for us to come into this election campaign and not do anything with regard to the Democratic Senators who are running, et cetera. And who the hell are they after? They are after us. It is absolutely ridiculous. It is not going to be that way any more.

H. Really, it is ironic that we have gone to extremes. You and your damn regulations. Everybody worries about not picking up a hotel bill.

D. I think you can be proud of the White House staff. It really has had no problems of that sort. And I love this [General Accounting Office] audit that is going on now. I think they have some suspicion that even a cursory investigation is going to discover something here. I don't think they can find a thing. I learned today, incidentally, and have not confirmed it, that the GAO auditor who is down here is here at the Speaker of the House's request.

P. That surprises me.

H. Well, (expletive deleted) the Speaker of the House. Maybe we better put a little heat on him.

P. I think so too.

H. Because he has a lot worse problems than he is going to find down here.

D. That's right.

H. That is the kind of thing that, you know, we really ought to do is call the Speaker and say, "I regret to say your calling the GAO down here because of what it is going to cause us to do to you."

P. Why don't you see if [Presidential aide Bryce] Harlow will tell him that.

H. Because he wouldn't do it—he would just be pleasant and call him Mr. Speaker . . .

P. You really can't sit and worry about it all the time. The worst may happen but it may not. So you just try to button it up as well as you can and hope for the best, and remember basically the damn business is unfortunately trying to cut our losses.

D. Certainly that is right and certainly it has had no effect on you.

H. No, it has been kept away from the White House and of course completely from the President.

FEBRUARY 28, 1973

The President meets with Dean in the Oval Office. The conversation turns to the planned hearings by the Senate Watergate Committee:

D. I would suspect if we are going to get any insight to what that Committee is going to do, it is going to be through [GOP Sen. Edward] Gurney. I don't know about [GOP Sen. Lowell] Weicker . . .

P. Weicker, I think the line to Weicker is through [Pat] Gray. Gray has to shape up here and handle himself well too. Do you think he will?

D. I do. I think Pat has had it tough. He goes up this morning as you know. He is ready. He is very comfortable in all of the decisions he has made, and I think he will be good.

P. But he is close to Weicker—that is what I meant.

D. Yes, he is.

P. And so, Gray . . .

D. He has a lead in there—yes.

P. One amusing thing about the Gray thing, and I knew this would come. They say Gray is a political crony and a personal crony of the President's. Did you know that I have never seen him socially?

D. Is that correct? No, I didn't.

P. I think he has been to a couple White House events, but I have never seen him separately.

D. The Press has got him meeting you at a social function. And, back in 1947, (inaudible) is something I have read.

P. Maybe at a [Adm. Arthur] Radford party or something like that. That's all. I don't know. But Gray is somebody that I know only—He was Radford's Assistant, used to attend [National Security Council] meetings. He has never been a social friend. Edgar Hoover, on the other hand, I have seen socially at least a hundred times. He and I were very close friends.

D. This is curious the way the press—

P. (expletive deleted)—Hoover was my crony. He was closer to me than Johnson, actually although Johnson used him more. But as for Pat Gray, (expletive deleted) I never saw him.

D. While it might have been a lot of blue chips to the late Director, I think we would have been a lot better off during this whole Watergate thing if he had been alive. Because he knew how to handle that Bureau—knew how to keep them in bounds.

P. Well, Hoover performed. He would have fought. That was the point. He would have defied a few people. He would have scared them to death. He has a file on everybody.

* * *

Later, the President speculates about the motives of the Democrats on the Watergate committee:

P. I frankly say that I would rather they would be partisan—rather than for them to have a façade of fairness and all the rest. [Sam] Ervin always talks about his being a great Constitutional lawyer. (expletive deleted) He's got [Howard] Baker totally toppled over to him. Ervin works harder than most of our Southern gentlemen. They are great politicians. They are just more clever than the minority . . .

D. I am convinced that he has shown that he is merely a puppet for Kennedy in this whole thing. The fine hand of the Kennedys' is behind this whole hearing . . .

P. Uh, huh.

D. He has kept this quiet and constant pressure on this thing. I think this fellow Sam Dash, who has been selected Counsel, is a Kennedy choice. I think this is also something we will be able to quietly and slowly document. Leak this to the press, and the parts and cast become much more apparent.

P. Yes, I guess the Kennedy crowd is just laying in the bushes waiting to make their move. I had forgotten, by the way, we talk about Johnson using the FBI. Did your friends tell you what Bobby did?

D. I haven't heard but I wouldn't be—

P. Johnson believed that Bobby bugged him.

D. That wouldn't surprise me.

P. Bobby was a ruthless (characterization omitted.) But the FBI does blatantly tell you that—or [former FBI assistant director William] Sullivan told you about the New Jersey thing. He did use a bug up there for intelligence work. (inaudible)

* * *

Dean informs the President that William Sullivan has information that the agency bugged Mr. Nixon during his 1968 campaign. The President is intrigued. Dean suggests that another former FBI official, Mark Felt, could make the details of that bugging operation public. This prompts the President to reminisce about Whittaker Chambers, who was the chief witness against Alger Hiss in the celebrated investigation that Mr. Nixon helped conduct when he was a young congressman:

P. Let's face it. Suppose Felt comes out now and unwraps. What does it do to him?

D. He can't do it.

P. How about (unintelligible)? Who is going to hire him? Let's face it— the guy who goes out—he couldn't do it unless he had a guarantee from somebody like TIME Magazine who would say look we will give you a job for life. Then what do they do? He would go to a job at LIFE, and everyone would treat him like a pariah. He is in a very dangerous situation. These guys you know—the informers. Look what it did to Chambers. Chambers informed because he didn't give (expletive deleted). But then one of the most brilliant writers according to [Time Inc. president] Jim Shepley we have ever seen in this country—and I am not referring to the Communist issue—greatest writer of his time,—about 30 years ago, probably TIME'S best writer of the century —they finished him. Either way, the informer is not one in our society. Either way, that is the one thing people can't survive. They say no civilized (characterization deleted) informs.

*   *   *

The conversation moves on to the subject of news leaks and then to a discussion of White House strategy regarding the investigation of the Watergate break-in:

D. I have got to say one thing. There has never been a leak out of my office. There never will be a leak out of my office. I wouldn't begin to know how to leak and I don't want to learn how you leak . . .

P. This happens all the time. Well, you can follow these characters to their Gethsemane. I feel for those poor guys in jail, particularly for Hunt with his wife dead.

D. Well there is every indication they are hanging in tough right now.

P. What the hell do they expect though? Do they expect clemency in a reasonable time? What would you advise on that?

D. I think it is one of those things we will have to watch very closely. For example,—

P. You couldn't do it, say, in six months.

D. No, you couldn't. This thing may become so political as a result of these hearings that it is a vendetta. This judge [John Sirica] may go off the deep end in sentencing, and make it so absurd that its clearly injustice that they have been heavily—

P. Is there any kind of appeal left?

D. Right. Liddy and [former CRP security chief James] McCord, who sat through the trial, will both be on appeal and there is no telling how long that will last. It is one of these things we will just have to watch.

P. ... But the President should not become involved in any part of this case. Do you agree with that?

D. I agree totally, sir. Absolutely. That doesn't mean that quietly we are not going to be working around the office. You can rest assured that we are not going to be sitting quietly.

P. I don't know what we can do. The people who are most disturbed about this (unintelligible) are the (adjective deleted) Republicans. A lot of these Congressmen, financial contributors, et cetera, are highly moral. The Democrats are just sort of saying, "(expletive deleted) fun and games!"

D. Well, hopefully we can give them [political prankster Donald] Segretti.

P. (Expletive deleted) He was such a dumb figure, I don't see how our boys could have gone for him. But nevertheless, they did. It was really juvenile! But, nevertheless, what the hell did he do? What in the (characterization deleted) did he do? Shouldn't we be trying to get intelligence? Weren't they trying to get intelligence from us?

*   *   *

The President pauses to consider the state of the Democratic Party:

P. ... all this business is a battle and they are going to wage the battle. A lot of them have enormous frustrations about those elections, state of their party, etc. And their party has its problems. We think we have had problems, look at some of theirs. [Democratic chairman Robert] Strauss has had people and all the actors, and they haven't done that well you know.

D. Well, I was—we have come a long road on this thing now. I had thought it was an impossible task to hold together until after the election until things started falling out, but we have made it this far and I am convinced we are going to make it the whole road and put this thing in the funny pages of the history books rather than anything serious because actually—

P. It will be somewhat serious but the main thing, of course, is also the isolation of the President.

D. Absolutely! Totally true!

P. Because that, fortunately, is totally true.

D. I know that sir!

P. (expletive deleted) Of course, I am not dumb and I will never forget when I heard about this (adjective deleted) forced entry and bugging. I thought, what in the hell is this? What is the matter with these people? Are they crazy? I thought they were nuts! A prank! But it wasn't! It wasn't very funny. I think that our Democratic friends know that, too. They know what the hell it was. They don't think we'd be involved in such.

D. I think they do too.

P. Maybe they don't. They don't think I would be involved in such stuff. They think I have people capable of it. And they are correct, in that [former adviser Charles] Colson would do anything . . . now I will not talk to you again until you have something to report to me.

D. Alright, sir.

P. But I think it is very important that you have these talks with our good friend [Attorney General Richard] Kleindienst.

D. That will be done.

P. Tell him we have to get these things worked out. We have to work together on this thing. I would build him up. He is the man who can make the difference. Also point out to him what we have. (expletive deleted) Colson's got (characterization deleted), but I really, really,—this stuff here—let's forget this. But let's remember this was not done by the White House. This was done by the Committee to Re-Elect, and Mitchell was the Chairman, correct?

D. That's correct!

P. And Kleindienst owes Mitchell everything. Mitchell wanted him for Attorney General. Wanted him for Deputy, and here he is. Now, (expletive deleted). Baker's got to realize this, and that if he allows this thing to get out of hand he is going to potentially ruin John Mitchell. He won't. Mitchell won't allow himself to be ruined. He will put on his big stone face. But I hope he does and he will. There is no question what they are after. What the Committee is after is somebody at the White House. They would like to get Haldeman or Colson, Ehrlichman.

D. Or possible Dean.—You know, I am a small fish.

MARCH 13, 1973

The President and Dean confer again in the Oval Office. They discuss to what extent White House personnel should cooperate with the Federal prosecutors and the grand jury investigating Watergate:

D. Well, then you will get a barrage of questions probably, on will you supply—will Mr. Haldeman and Mr. Ehrlichman and Mr. Dean go up to the Committee and testify?

P. No, absolutely not.

D. Mr. Colson?

P. No. Absolutely not, It isn't a question of not—[Presidential press secretary Ronald] Ziegler or somebody had said that we in our executive privilege statement it was interpreted as meaning that we would not furnish information and all that. We said we will furnish information, but we are not going to be called to testify. That is the position. Dean and all the rest will grant you information. Won't you?

D. Yes. Indeed I will.

P. My feeling, John, is that I better hit it now rather than just let it build up where we are afraid of these questions and everybody, etc., and let Ziegler go out there and bob and weave around. I know the easy thing is to bug out, but it is not . . .

D. You're right. I was afraid. For the sake of debate, but I was having reservations. It is a bullet biter and you just have to do it. These questions are just not going to go away. Now the other thing that we talked about in the past, and I still have the same problem, is to have a "here it all is" approach. If we do that . . .

P. And let it all hang out.

D. And let it all hang out. Let's with a Segretti—etc.

P. We have passed that point.

D. Plus the fact, they are not going to believe the truth! That is the incredible thing!

* * *

The President and his counsel return to the question of the FBI bugging the Nixon campaign in 1968. Dean suggests that such a revelation would discredit the Democrats and help L. Patrick Gray in his confirmation hearings as the new director of the FBI:

D. . . . Let's say in the Gray hearings—where everything is cast that we are the political people and they are not—that Hoover was above reproach, which is just not accurate, total (expletive omitted). The person who would destroy Hoover's image is going to be this man Bill Sullivan. Also it is going to tarnish quite severely . . .

P. Some of the FBI.

D. . . . some of the FBI. And a former President. He is going to lay it out, and just all hell is going to break loose once he does it. It is going to change the atmosphere of the Gray hearings and it is going to change the atmosphere of the whole Watergate hearings. Now the risk . . .

P. How will it change?

D. Because it will put them in context of where government institutes were used in the past for the most flagrant political purposes.

P. How can that help us?

D. How does it help us?

P. I am being the devil's advocate . . .

D. I appreciate what you are doing. It is a red herring. It is what the public already believes. I think the people would react: (expletive deleted), more of that stuff! They are all bad down there! Because it is a one way street right now . . .

P. Do you think the press would use it? They may not play it.

D. It would be difficult not to. Ah, it would be difficult not to.

* * *

Getting back to the grand-jury investigation of Watergate, the two men discuss one of their most serious concerns—the testimony of Hugh Sloan, former deputy treasurer of the Committee to Re-elect the President:

P. Who is going to be the first witness up there?

D. Sloan.

P. Unfortunate.

D. No doubt about it—

P. He's scared?

D. He's scared, he's weak. He has a compulsion to cleanse his soul by confession. We are giving him a lot of stroking. Funny thing is this fellow goes down to the Court House here before [Judge John] Sirica, testifies as honestly as he can testify, and Sirica looks around and called him a liar. He just said —Sloan just can't win! So [Nixon personal attorney Herbert) Kalmbach has been dealing with Sloan. Sloan is like a child. Kalmbach has done a lot of that. The person who will have a greater problem as a result of Sloan's testimony is Kalmbach and [former CRP finance director Maurice] Stans. So they are working closely with him to make sure that he settles down . . .

P. Mitchell is now studying, is he?

D. He is studying. Sloan will be the worst witness. I think [former CRP deputy director Jeb Stuart] Magruder will be a good witness. This fellow, [campaign aide Herbert L.] Porter, will be a good witness. They have already been through Grand Jury . . . They did well . . .

P. None will be witnesses.

D. They won't be witnesses?

P. Hell, no. They will make statements. That will be the line which I think we have to get across to Ziegler in all his briefings where he is constantly saying we will provide information. That is not the question. It is how it is to be furnished. We will not furnish it in a formal session. That would be a break down of the privilege. Period. Do you agree with that?

D. I agree. I agree. I have always thought that's the bottom line, and I think that is the good thing that is happening in the Gray hearings right now. If they send a letter down with specific questions, I send back written interrogatories sworn. He knows, the lawyer, that you can handle written interrogatories, where cross examination is another ball game.

P. That's right.

*   *   *

The discussion continues on targets of the grand-jury investigation:

P. Let's face it, I think they are really after Haldeman.

D. Haldeman and Mitchell.

P. Colson is not a big enough name for them. He really isn't. He is, you know, he is on the government side, but Colson's name doesn't bother them so much. They are after Haldeman and after Mitchell. Don't you think so?

D. Sure . . .

P. In any event, Haldeman's problem is [Presidential appointments secretary Dwight] Chapin isn't it?

D. Bob's problem is circumstantial.

P. Why is that? Let's look at the circumstantial. I don't know, Bob didn't know any of those people like the Hunts and all that bunch. Colson did, but Bob didn't. OK?

D. That's right.

P. Now where the hell, or how much Chapin knew I will be (expletive deleted) if I know.

D. Chapin didn't know anything about the Watergate.

P. Don't you think so?

D. Absolutely not.

P. [Haldeman aide Gordon] Strachan?

D. Yes.

P. He knew?

D. Yes.

P. About the Watergate?

D. Yes.

P. Well, then, he probably told Bob. He may not have.

D. He was judicious in what he relayed, but Strachan is as tough as nails. He can go in and stonewall, and say, "I don't know anything about what you are talking about." He has already done it twice you know, in interviews.

P. I guess he should, shouldn't he? I suppose we can't call that justice, can we?

D. Well, it is a personal loyalty to him. He doesn't want it any other way. He didn't have to be told. He didn't have to be asked. It just is something that he found was the way he wanted to handle the situation.

P. But he knew? He knew about Watergate? Strachan did?

D. Yes.

P. I will be damned! Well that is the problem in Bob's case. Not Chapin then, but Strachan. Strachan worked for him, didn't he?

D. Yes. They would have one hell of a time proving that Strachan had knowledge of it, though.

P. Who knew better? Magruder?

D. Magruder and Liddy.

P. Oh, I see. The other weak link for Bob is Magruder. He hired him et cetera.

D. That applies to Mitchell, too.

P. Mitchell—Magruder. Where do you see Colson coming into it?

D. . . . I think that Chuck had knowledge that something was going on over there, but he didn't have any knowledge of the details of the specifics of the whole thing.

P. There must have been an indication of the fact that we had poor pickings. Because naturally anybody, either Chuck or Bob, were always reporting to me about what was going on. If they ever got any information they would certainly have told me that we got some information, but they never had a thing to report. What was the matter? Did they never get anything out of the damn thing?

D. I don't think they ever got anything, sir.

P. A dry hole?

D. That's right.

P. (Expletive deleted)

D. Well, they were just really getting started.

P. Yeah. Bob one time said something to me about something, this or that or something, about the fact we got some information about this, or that or the other but I think it was something about the Convention, I think it was about the convention problems they were planning something. I assume that must have been [Clark] MacGregor—not MacGregor, but Segretti.

D. No, Segretti wasn't involved in the intelligence gathering piece of it at all.

P. Oh, he wasn't? Who the hell was gathering intelligence?

D. That was Liddy and his outfit.

P. Apart from Watergate?

D. That's right. Well you see Watergate was part of intelligence gathering, and this was their first thing. What happened is—

P. That was such a stupid thing!

D. It was incredible—that's right. That was Hunt.

P. To think of Mitchell and Bob would have allowed—would have allowed—this kind of operation to be in the campaign committee!

P. . . . (Unintelligible) to think that Mitchell and Bob would allow, would have allowed this kind of operation to be in the Committee.

D. I don't think he knew it was there.

P. I don't think that Mitchell knew about this sort of thing.

P. You kidding?

D. I don't—

P. You don't think Mitchell knew about this thing?

D. Oh, no, no! Don't misunderstand me. I don't think that he knew the people. I think he knew that Liddy was out intelligence gathering. I don't think he knew that Liddy would use a fellow like [James] McCord, (expletive removed), who worked for the Committee. I can't believe that.

P. Hunt?

D. I don't think Mitchell knew about Hunt either.

P. Well Mitchell thought, well, gee, and I hired this fellow and I told him to gather intelligence. Maybe Magruder says the same thing.

D. Magruder says—as he did in the trial—well, of course, my name has been dragged in as the guy who sent Liddy over there, which is an interesting thing. Well what happened they said is that Magruder asked—he wanted to hire my deputy over there as Deputy Counsel and I said, "No way. I can't give him up."

P. Was Liddy your deputy?

D. No, Liddy never worked for me . . .

P. How the hell does Liddy stand up so well?

D. He's a strange man . . .

P. Strange or strong?

D. Strange and strong. His loyalty is—I think it is just beyond the pale . . .

P. He hates the other side too, doesn't he?

D. Oh, absolutely! He is strong. He really is.

MARCH 17, 1973

At this session, Dean and the President discuss two items that are only indirectly related to Watergate: (1) the activities of "dirty tricks" specialist Donald Segretti and (2) the break-in at the office of Daniel Ellsberg's psychiatrist. The President leads off:

P. Now on the Segretti thing, I think you've just got to—[Dwight] Chapin, all of them have just got to take the heat. Look, you've got to admit the facts, John, and—

D. That's right.

P. And that's our—and that's that. And [Herbert] Kalmbach paid him. And (unintelligible) a lot of people. I just think on Segretti, no matter how bad it is. It isn't nearly as bad as people think it was. Espionage, sabotage?

D. The intent, when Segretti was hired, was nothing evil nothing vicious, nothing bad, nothing. Not espionage, not sabotage. It was pranksterism that got out of hand and we know that. And I think we can lay our story out there. I have no problem with the Segretti thing. It's just not that serious. The other potential problem is Ehrlichman's and this is—

P. In connection with Hunt?

D. In connection with Hunt and Liddy both.

P. They worked for him?

D. They—these fellows had to be some idiots as we've learned after the fact. They went out and went into Dr. Ellsberg's doctor's office and they had, they were geared up with all this CIA equipment—cameras and the like. Well they turned the stuff back in to the CIA some point in time and left film in the camera. CIA has not put this together, and they don't know what it all means right now. But it wouldn't take a very sharp investigator very long because you've got pictures in the CIA files that they had to turn over to (unintelligible).

P. What in the world—what in the name of God was Ehrlichman having something (unintelligible) in the Ellsberg (unintelligible)?

D. They were trying to—this was a part of an operation that—in connection with the Pentagon papers. They were—the whole thing—they wanted to get Ellsberg's psychiatric records for some reason. I don't know.

P. This is the first I ever heard of this. I, I (unintelligible) care about Ellsberg was not our problem.

D. That's right.

P. (Expletive deleted) . . .

MARCH 20, 1973

As the effort to "contain" the scandal loses ground, the President decides to ask Dean for a formal report on his "investigation" of White House involvement in Watergate. They discuss the report over the telephone:

P. See, for example, I was even thinking if you could even talk to Cabinet, the leaders, you know, just orally and say, "I have looked into this, and this is that," so that people get sort of a feeling that—your own people have got to be reassured.

D. Uh, huh . . .

P. Could you do that?

D. Well, I think I can but I don't think you would want to make that decision until we have about a—

P. No, I want to know. I want to know where all the bodies are first.

D. And then, once you decide after that, we can program it anyway you want to do it.

P. Yeah. Because I think, for example, you could do it orally, even if you don't want to make the written statement. You could do it orally before the Cabinet, the leaders and the rest. Lay it all out. You see, I would not be present. You just lay it all out and I just—See what I mean?

D. Uh, huh . . .

P. What I mean is we need something to answer somebody, answer things, you know they say, "What are you basing this on", I can say, "Well, my counsel has advised me that"—Is that possible or not, or are—

D. Well, you know there is that—and there is always the FBI report which we have probably not relied upon enough. There is not one scintilla of evidence.

P. I know. But I mean, can't you say that? Or do you want to put it out?

D. Ah, it could be said, and it is something we haven't really emphasized.

MARCH 21, 1973

The most significant of all the transcripts records the meeting in the Oval Office between the President, Dean and Haldeman at which Dean lays out some of the unpleasant facts about Watergate and its aftermath:

D. The reason that I thought we ought to talk this morning is because in our conversations, I have the impression that you don't know everything I know and it makes it very difficult for you to make judgments that only you can make on some of these things and I thought that—

P. In other words, I have to know why you feel that we shouldn't unravel something?

D. Let me give you my overall first.

P. In other words, your judgment as to where it stands, and where we will go.

D. I think that there is no doubt about the seriousness of the problem we've got. We have a cancer within, close to the Presidency, that is growing. It is growing daily. It's compounded, growing geometrically now, because it compounds itself. That will be clear if I, you know, explain some of the details of why it is. Basically, it is because (1) we are being blackmailed; (2) people are going to start perjuring themselves very quickly that have not had to perjure themselves to protect other people in the line. And there is no assurance—

P. That that won't bust?

D. That that won't bust.

*   *   *

Dean proceeds to describe the beginnings of the Watergate affair. The original aim of the CRP, he says, was to set up "a perfectly legitimate campaign intelligence operation." The task was assigned to Gordon Liddy, who drew up "a million-dollar plan that was the most incredible thing I have ever laid my eyes on." When the plan was presented to John Mitchell, says Dean, he "just sat there puffing and laughing . . . so Liddy was told to go back to the drawing board and come up with something realistic." The second plan included bugging, and Dean says he thought that even this undertaking had been "turned off" by Mitchell. But yet a third plan followed, and it led to the break-in at Democratic National Committee headquarters:

D. . . . Apparently after they had initially broken in and bugged the DNC they were getting information. The information was coming over here to [Gordon] Strachan and some of it was given to Haldeman, there is no doubt about it.

P. Did he know where it was coming from?

D. I don't really know if he would.

P. Not necessarily?

D. Not necessarily. Strachan knew it. There is no doubt about it, and whether Strachan—I have never come to press these people on these points because it hurts them to give up that next inch, so I had to piece things together. Strachan was aware of receiving information, reporting to Bob. At one point Bob even gave instructions to change their capabilities from Muskie to McGovern, and passed this back through Strachan to [Jeb] Magruder and apparently to Liddy. And Liddy was starting to make arrangements to go in and bug . . . McGovern . . .

P. They had never bugged Muskie, though, did they?

D. No, they hadn't, but they had infiltrated it by a secretary.

P. By a secretary?

D. By a secretary and a chauffeur. There is nothing illegal about that. So the information was coming over here and then I, finally, after—. The next point in time that I became aware of anything was on June 17th when I got the word that there had been this break in at the DNC and somebody from our Committee had been caught in the DNC. And I said, "Oh, (expletive deleted)." You know, eventually putting the pieces together—

P. You knew what it was.

D. I knew who it was. So I called Liddy on Monday morning and said, "First, Gordon, I want to know whether anybody in the White House was involved in this." And he said, "No, they weren't." I said, "Well I want to know how in (adjective deleted) name this happened." He said, "Well, I was pushed without mercy by Magruder to get in there and to get more information. That the information was not satisfactory. That Magruder said, 'The White House is not happy with what we are getting.' "

P. The White House?

D. The White House. Yeah!

P. Who do you think was pushing him?

D. Well, I think it was probably Strachan thinking that Bob wanted things, because I have seen that happen on other occasions where things have said to have been of very prime importance when they really weren't.

P. Why at that point in time I wonder? I am just trying to think. We had just finished the Moscow trip. The Democrats had just nominated McGovern. I mean, (expletive deleted), what in the hell were these people doing? I can see their doing it earlier. I can see the pressures, but I don't see why all the pressure was on then.

D. I don't know, other than the fact that they might have been looking for information about the conventions.

P. That's right.

D. Because, I understand that after the fact that there was a plan to bug Larry O'Brien's suite down in Florida. So Liddy told me that this is what had happened and this is why it had happened.

P. Where did he learn . . . there were plans to bug Larry O'Brien's suite?

D. From Magruder, long after the fact.

P. Magruder is (unintelligible)

D. Yeah. Magruder is totally knowledgeable on the whole thing.

P. Yeah.

D. Alright now, we have gone through the trial. I don't know if Mitchell has perjured himself in the Grand Jury or not.

P. Who?

D. Mitchell, I don't know how much knowledge he actually had. I know that Magruder has perjured himself in the Grand Jury. I know that Porter has perjured himself in the Grand Jury.

P. Who is Porter? (unintelligible)

D. He is one of Magruder's deputies. They set up this scenario which they ran by me. They said, "How about this?" I said, "I don't know. If this is what you are going to hang on, fine."

P. What did they say in the Grand Jury?

D. They said, as they said before the trial in the Grand Jury, that Liddy had come over as Counsel and we knew he had these capacities to do legitimate intelligence. We had no idea what he was doing. He was given an authorization of $250,000 to collect information, because our surrogates were out on the road. They had no protection, and we had information that there were going to be demonstrations against them, and that we had to have a plan as to what liabilities they were going to be confronted with and Liddy was charged with doing this. We had no knowledge that he was going to bug the DNC.

P. The point is, that is not true?

D. That's right.

P. Magruder did know it was going to take place?

D. Magruder gave the instructions to be back in the DNC.

P. He did?

D. Yes.

P. You know that?

D. Yes.

P. I see. OK.

D. I honestly believe that no one over here knew that. I know that as God is my maker, I had no knowledge that they were going to do this.

P. Bob didn't either, or wouldn't have known that either. You are not the issue involved. Had Bob known, he would be.

D. Bob—I don't believe specifically knew that they were going in there . . .

P. Did Strachan know?

D. I think Strachan did know.

P. (unintelligible) Going back into the DNC—Hunt, etc.—this is not understandable! . . .

D. . . . this could have been disastrous on the electorate if all hell had broken loose. I worked on a theory of containment—

P. Sure.

D. To try to hold it right where it was.

P. Right.

D. There is no doubt that I was totally aware of what the Bureau was doing at all times. I was totally aware of what the Grand Jury was doing. I knew what witnesses were going to be called. I knew what they were asked, and I had to.

P. Why did [Assistant Attorney General Henry] Petersen play the game so straight with us?

D. Because Petersen is a soldier. He kept me informed. He told me when we had problems, where we had problems and the like. He believes in you and he believes in this Administration. This Administration has made him. I don't think he has done anything improper, but he did make sure that the investigation was narrowed down to the very, very fine criminal thing which was a break for us . . .

*   *   *

Next Dean turns to the payments that have been made to the Watergate burglars:

D. . . . Liddy said if they all got counsel instantly and said we will ride this thing out. Alright, then they started making demands. "We have to have attorneys fees. We don't have any money ourselves, and you are asking us to take this through the election." Alright, so arrangements were made through Mitchell, initiating it. And I was present in discussions where these guys had to be taken care of. Their attorneys fees had to be done. [Herbert] Kalmbach was brought in. Kalmbach raised some cash.

P. They put that under the cover of a Cuban Committee, I suppose?

D. Well, they had a Cuban Committee and they had—some of it was given to Hunt's lawyer, who in turn passed it out. You know, when Hunt's wife was flying to Chicago with $10,000 she was actually, I understand after the fact now, was going to pass that money to one of the Cubans—to meet him in Chicago and pass it to somebody there.

P. (unintelligible) but I would certainly keep that cover for whatever it is worth.

D. That's the most troublesome post-thing because (1) Bob is involved in that; (2) John is involved in that; (3) I am involved in that; (4) Mitchell is involved in that. And that is an obstruction of justice.

P. In other words the bad it does. You were taking care of witnesses. How did Bob get in it?

D. Well, they ran out of money over there. Bob had $350,000 in a safe over here that was really set aside for polling purposes. And there was no other source of money, so they came over and said you all have got to give us some money. I had to go to Bob and say, "Bob, they need some money over there." He said "What for." So I had to tell him what it was for because he wasn't just about to send money over there willy-nilly. And John was involved in those discussions. And then we decided there was no price too high to pay to let this thing blow up in front of the election.

P. I think we should be able to handle that issue pretty well. May be some lawsuits.

D. I think we can too. Here is what is happening right now. What sort of brings matters to the (unintelligible). One, this is going to be a continual blackmail operation by Hunt and Liddy and the Cubans. No doubt about it. And McCord, who is another one involved. McCord has asked for nothing. McCord did ask to meet with somebody, with [former CRP agent] Jack Caulfield who is his old friend who had gotten him hired over there. And when Caulfield had him hired, he was a perfectly legitimate security man. And he wanted to talk about commutation, and things like that. And as you know Colson has talked indirectly to Hunt about commutation. All of these things are bad, in that they are problems, they are promises, they are commitments. They are the very sort of thing that the Senate is going to be looking most for. I don't think they can find them, frankly.

P. Pretty hard.

D. Pretty hard. Damn hard. It's all cash.

P. Pretty hard I mean as far as the witnesses are concerned.

D. Alright, now, the blackmail is continuing. Hunt called one of lawyers from the Re-Election Committee on last Friday to leave it with him over the weekend. The guy came in to see me to give a message directly to me. From

Hunt to me . . . Hunt has now made a direct threat against Ehrlichman. As a result of this, this is his blackmail. He says, "I will bring John Ehrlichman down to his knees and put him in jail. I have done enough seamy things for he and [White House aid Bud] Krogh, they'll never survive it."

P. Was he talking about Ellsberg?

D. Ellsberg, and apparently some other things. I don't know the full extent of it.

P. I don't know about anything else.

D. I don't know either, and I hate to learn some of these things. So that is that situation. Now, where are at the soft points? How many people know about this? Well, let me go one step further in this whole thing. The Cubans that were used in the Watergate were also the same Cubans that Hunt and Liddy used for this California Ellsberg thing, for the break in out there. So they are aware of that. How high their knowledge is, is something else. Hunt and Liddy, of course, are totally aware of it, of the fact that it is right out of the White House.

P. I don't know what the hell we did that for!

D. I don't know either.

P. What in the (expletive deleted) caused this? (unintelligible)

D. Mr. President, there have been a couple of things around here that I have gotten wind of. At one time there was a desire to do a second story job on the Brookings Institute where they had the Pentagon papers. Now I flew to California because I was told that John had instructed it and he said, "I really hadn't. It is a mis-impression, but for (expletive deleted), turn it off." So I did. I came back and turned it off. The risk is minimal and the pain is fantastic. It is something with a (unintelligible) risk and no gain. It is just not worth it. But—who knows about all this now? You've got the Cubans' lawyer, a man by the name of Rothblatt, who is a no good, publicity seeking (characterization deleted), to be very frank with you. He has had to be pruned down and tuned off. He was canned by his own people because they didn't trust him. He didn't want them to plead guilty. He wants to represent them before the Senate. So F. Lee Bailey, who was a partner of one of the men representing McCord, got in and cooled Rothblatt down. So that means that F. Lee Bailey has knowledge. Hunt's lawyer, a man by the name of Bittmann, who is an excellent criminal lawyer from the Democratic era of Bobby Kennedy, he's got knowledge.

P. He's got some knowledge?

D. Well, all the direct knowledge that Hunt and Liddy have, as well as all the hearsay they have. You have these two lawyers over at the Re-Election Committee who did an investigation to find out the facts. Slowly, they got the whole picture. They are solid.

P. But they know?

D. But they know. You've got, then an awful lot of the principals involved who know. Some people's wives know. Mrs. Hunt was the savviest woman in the world. She had the whole picture together.

P. Did she?

D. Yes. Apparently, she was the pillar of strength in that family before the death.

P. Great sadness. As a matter of fact, there was a discussion with somebody about Hunt's problem on account of his wife and I said, of course commutation could be considered on the basis of his wife's death, and that is the only conversation I ever had in that light.

D. Right.

D. So that is it. That is the extent of the knowledge. So where are the soft spots on this? Well, first of all, there is the problem of the continued blackmail which will not only go on now, but it will go on while these people are in prison, and it will compound the obstruction of justice situation. It will cost money. It is dangerous. People around here are not pros at this sort of thing. This is the sort of thing Mafia people can do: washing money, getting clean money, and things like that. We just don't know about those things . . .

P. That's right.

D. It is a tough thing to know how to do.

P. Maybe it takes a gang to do that . . . How much money do you need?

D. I would say these people are going to cost a million dollars over the next two years.

P. We could get that. On the money, if you need the money you could get that. You could get a million dollars. You could get it in cash. I know where it could be gotten. It is not easy, but it could be done. But the question is who the hell would handle it? Any ideas on that?

D. That's right. Well, I think that is something that Mitchell ought to be charged with.

P. I would think so too.

D. And get some pros to help him . . .

D. Let me continue a little bit right here now. When I say this is a growing cancer, I say if for reasons like this. Bud Krogh, in his testimony before the Grand Jury, was forced to perjure himself. He is haunted by it. Bud said, "I have not had a pleasant day on my job." He said, "I told my wife all about this. The curtain may ring down one of these days, and I may have to face the music, which I am perfectly willing to do."

P. What did he perjure himself on, John?

D. Did he know the Cubans. He did.

P. He said he didn't?

D. That is right. They didn't press him hard.

P. He might be able to—I am just trying to think. Perjury is an awful hard rap to prove . . .

D. Well, so that is one perjury. Mitchell and Magruder are potential perjurers. There is always the possibility of any one of these individuals blowing. Hunt. Liddy. Liddy is in jail right now, serving his time and having a good time right now. I think Liddy in his own bizarre way the strongest of all of them. So there is that possibility.

P. Your major guy to keep under control is Hunt?

D. That is right.

P. I think. Does he know a lot?

D. He knows so much. He could sink Chuck Colson. Apparently he is quite distressed with Colson. He thinks Colson has abandoned him. Colson was to meet with him when he was out there after, you know, he had left the White House. He met with him through his lawyer. Hunt raised the question he wanted money. Colson's lawyer told him Colson wasn't doing anything with money. Hunt took offense with that immediately, and felt Colson had abandoned him.

P. Just looking at the immediate problem, don't you think you have to handle Hunt's financial situation damn soon?

D. I think that is— I talked with Mitchell about that last night and—

P. It seems to me we have to keep the cap on the bottle that much, or we don't have any options.

D. That's right.

P. Either that or it all blows right now?

D. That's the question . . . What really bothers me is this growing situation. As I say, it is growing because of the continued need to provide support for the Watergate people who are going to hold us up for everything we've got, and the need for some people to perjure themselves as they go down the road here. If this thing ever blows, then we are in a cover up situation. I think it would be extremely damaging to you and the—

P. Sure. The whole concept of Administration justice. Which we cannot have!

D. That is what really troubles me. For example, what happens if it starts breaking, and they do find a criminal case against a Haldeman, a Dean, a Mitchell, an Ehrlichman? That is—

P. If it really comes down to that, we would have to (unintelligible) some of the men.

D. That's right. I am coming down to what I really think, is that Bob and John and John Mitchell and I can sit down and spend a day, or however long, to figure out one, how this can be carved away from you, so that it does not damage you or the Presidency. It just can't! You are not involved in it and it is something you shouldn't—

P. That is true!

D. I know, sir. I can just tell from our conversation that these are things that you have no knowledge of.

P. You certainly can! Buggings, etc! Let me say I am keenly aware of the fact Colson, et al., were doing their best to get information as we went along. But they all knew very well they were supposed to comply with the law. There was no question about that! You feel that really the trigger man was really Colson on this then?

D. No. He was one of us. He was just in the chain. He helped push the thing . . .

P. Let's come back to this problem. What are your feelings yourself, John? You know what they are all saying. What are your feelings about the chances?

D. I am not confident that we can ride through this. I think there are soft spots.

P. You used to be—

D. I am not confortable for this reason. I have noticed of recent—since the publicity has increased on this thing again, with the Gray hearings, that everybody is now starting to watch after their behind. Everyone is getting their own counsel. More counsel are getting involved. How do I protect my ass.

P. They are scared . . .

P. So what you really come to is what we do. Let's suppose that you and Haldeman and Ehrlichman and Mitchell say we can't hold this? What then are you going to say? What are you going to put out after it. Complete disclosure, isn't that the best way to do it?

D. Well, one way to do it is—

P. That would be my view—

D. One way to do it is for you to tell the Attorney General that you finally know. Really, this is the first time you are getting all the pieces together.

P. Ask for another Grand Jury?

D. Ask for another Grand Jury. The way it should be done though, is a way—for example, I think that we could avoid criminal liability for countless people and the ones that did get it could be minimal.

P. How?

D. Well . . . You know, some people could be granted immunity.

P. Like Magruder?

D. Yeah. To come forward. But some people are going to have to go to jail. That is the long and short of it, also.

P. Who? Let's talk about—

D. Alright. I think I could. For one.

P. You go to jail?

D. That's right.

P. Oh, hell no! I can't see how you can.

D. Well, because—

P. I can't see how. Let me say I can't see how a legal case could be made against you, John.

D. It would be tough but, you know, I can see people pointing fingers. You know, to get it out of their own, put me in an impossible position. Just really give me a (unintelligible)

P. Oh, no! Let me say I got the impression here—but just looking at it from a cold legal standpoint: you are a lawyer, you were a counsel—doing what you did as counsel. You were not—What would you go to jail for?

D. The obstruction of justice.

P. The obstruction of justice?

D. That is the only one that bothers me.

P. Well, I don't know. I think that one. I feel it could be cut off at the pass, maybe, the obstruction of justice . . . Let me put it this way: let us suppose that you get the million bucks, and you get the proper way to handle it. You could hold that side?

D. Uh, huh.

P. It would seem to me that would be worthwhile.

D. Well, that's one problem.

P. I know you have a problem here. You have the problem with Hunt and his clemency.

D. That's right. And you are going to have a clemency problem with the others. They all are going to expect to be out and that may put you in a position that is just untenable at some point. You know, the Watergate Hearings just over, Hunt now demanding clemency or he is going to blow. And politically, it's impossible for you to do it. You know, after everybody—

P. That's right!

D. I am not sure that you will ever be able to deliver on the clemency. It may be just too hot.

P. You can't do it politically until after the '74 elections, that's for sure. Your point is that even then you couldn't do it.

D. That's right. It may further involve you in a way you should not be involved in this.

P. No—it is wrong that's for sure.

*　　*　　*

Dean and the President take stock of some grim options:

P. Suppose the worst—that Bob is indicted and Ehrlichman is indicted. And I must say, we just better then try to tough it through. You get the point.

D. That's right.

P. If they, for example, say lets cut our losses and you say we are going to go down the road to see if we can cut our losses and no more blackmail and all the rest. And then the thing blows cutting Bob and the rest to pieces. You would never recover from that, John.

D. That's right.

P. It is better to fight it out. Then you see that's the other thing. It's better to fight it out and not let people testify, and so forth. And now, on the other hand, we realize that we have these weaknesses . . . in terms of blackmail.

D. There are two routes. One is to figure out how to cut the losses and minimize the human impact and get you up and out and away from it in any way. In a way it would never come back to haunt you. That is one general alternative. The other is to go down the road, just hunker down, fight it at every corner, every turn, don't let people testify—cover it up is what we really are talking about. Just keep it buried, and just hope that we can do it, hope that we make good decisions at the right time, keep our heads cool, we make the right moves.

P. And just take the heat?

D. And just take the heat.

P. Now with the second line of attack. You can discuss this (unintelligible) the way you want to. Still consider my scheme of having you brief the Cabinet, just in very general terms and the leaders in very general terms and maybe some very general statement with regard to my investigation. Answer questions, basically on the basis of what they told you, not what you know. Haldeman is not involved. Ehrlichman is not involved.

D. If we go that route Sir, I can give a show we can sell them just like we were selling Wheaties on our position. There's no—

P. The problem that you have are these mine fields down the road. I think the most difficult problem are the guys who are going to jail. I think you are right about that.

D. I agree.

P. Now. And also the fact that we are not going to be able to give them clemency.

D. That's right. How long will they take? How long will they sit there? I don't know. We don't know what they will be sentenced to. There's always a chance—

P. Thirty years, isn't it?

D. It could be. You know, they haven't announced yet, but it—

P. Top is thirty years, isn't it?

D. It is even higher than that. It is about 50 years. It all—

P. So ridiculous!

D. And what is so incredible is, he is (unintelligible)

P. People break and enter, etc., and get two years. No weapons! No results! What the hell are they talking about?

*   *   *

Turning to the Ellsberg burglary, Dean, the President and Haldeman, who has joined them, search for a way to explain the affair:

D. You might put it on a national security grounds basis.

H. It absolutely was.

D. And say that this was—

H. (unintelligible)—CIA—

D. Ah—

H. Seriously.

P. National Security. We had to get information for national security . . .

D. Then the question is, why didn't the CIA do it or why didn't the FBI do it?

P. Because we had to do it on a confidential basis.

H. Because we were checking them.

P. Neither could be trusted.

H. It has basically never been proven. There was reason to question their position.

P. With the bombing thing coming out and everything coming out, the whole thing was national security.

D. I think we could get by on that.

P. On that one I think we should simply say this was a national security investigation that was conducted.

*   *   *

Next the three men discuss the tactics used by Charles Colson to keep the seven Watergate burglary defendants in line:

H. What's he planning on, money?

D. Money and—

H. Really?

P. It's about $120,000. That's what, Bob. That would be easy. It is not easy to deliver, but it is easy to get . . .

H. If the case is just that way, then the thing to do if the thing cranks out.

P. If, for example, you say look we are not going to continue to—let's say, frankly, on the assumption that if we continue to cut our losses, we are not going to win. But in the end, we are going to be bled to death. And in the end, it is all going to come out anyway. Then you get the worst of both worlds. We are going to lose, and people are going to—

H. And look like dopes!

P. And in effect, look like a cover-up. So that we can't do. Now the other line, however, if you take that line, that we are not going to continue to cut our losses, that means then we have to look square in the eye as to what the hell those losses are, and see which people can—so we can avoid criminal liability. Right?

D. Right.

P. And that means keeping it off you. Herb has started this Justice thing. We've got to keep it off Herb. You have to keep it, naturally off of Bob, off Chapin, if possible, Strachan, right?

D. Uh, huh

P. And Mitchell. Right?

D. Uh, huh

H. And Magruder, if you can.

P. John Dean's point is that if Magruder goes down, he will pull everybody with him.

H. That's my view. Yep, I think Jeb, I don't think he wants to. And I think he even would try not to, but I don't think he is able not to.

D. I don't think he is strong enough.

P. Another way to do it then Bob, and John realizes this, is to continue to try to cut our losses. Now we have to take a look at that course of action.

First it is going to require approximately a million dollars to take care of the jackasses who are in jail. That can be arranged. That could be arranged. But you realize that after we are gone, and assuming we can expend this money, then they are going to crack and it would be an unseemly story. Frankly, all the people aren't going to care that much.

D. That's right.

P. People won't care, but people are going to be talking about it, there is no question. And the second thing is, we are not going to be able to deliver on any of a clemency thing. You know Colson has gone around on this clemency thing with Hunt and the rest?

D. Hunt is now talking about being out by Christmas.

H. This year?

D. This year. He was told by [CRP attorney Paul] O'Brien, who is my conveyor of doom back and forth, that hell, he would be lucky if he were out a year from now, or after Ervin's hearings were over. He said how in the Lord's name could you be commuted that quickly? He said, "Well, that is my commitment from Colson."

H. By Christmas of this year?

D. Yeah.

H. See that, really, that is verbal evil. Colson is—That is your fatal flaw in Chuck. He is an operator in expediency, and he will pay at the time and where he is to accomplish whatever he is there to do. And that, and that's,— I would believe that he has made that commitment if Hunt says he has. I would believe he is capable of saying that.

P. The only thing we could do with him would be to parole him like the (unintelligible) situation. But you couldn't buy clemency.

D. Kleindienst has now got control of the Parole Board, and he said to tell me we could pull Paroles off now where we couldn't before. So—

H. Kleindienst always tells you that, but I never believe it.

P. Paroles—let the (unintelligible) worry about that. Parole, in appearance, etc., is something I think in Hunt's case, you could do Hunt, but you couldn't do the others. You understand.

*   *   *

The other defendants in the break-in seem to be cooperating with the White House. But Howard Hunt is a serious problem:

D. [The others are] going to stonewall it, as it now stands. Excepting Hunt. That's why his threat.

H. It's Hunt opportunity.

P. That's why for your immediate things you have no choice but to come up with the $120,000, or whatever it is. Right?

D. That's right.

P. Would you agree that that's the prime thing that you damn well better get that done?

D. Obviously he ought to be given some signal anyway . . .

P. Well look, what it is you need on that? When—I am not familiar with the money situation . . .

D. . . . You have to wash the money. You can get a $100,000 out of a bank, and it all comes in serialized bills.

P. I understand.

D. And that means you have to go to Vegas with it or a bookmaker in New York City. I have learned all these things after the fact. I will be in great shape for the next time around.

H. (Expletive deleted)?

CHAPTER 8

Congress

The United States Congress, exercising supreme legislative power, was at the beginning of the nineteenth century the most powerful political institution in the national government. It was feared by the framers of the Constitution, who felt that unless it was closely guarded and limited it would easily dominate both the presidency and the Supreme Court. Its powers were carefully enumerated, and it was made a bicameral body. This latter provision not only secured representation of different interests but also limited the power of the legislature which, when hobbled by two houses often working against each other, could not act as swiftly and forcefully as a single body could. Although still important, the power and prestige of Congress have declined while the powers of the President and the Supreme Court, not to mention those of the vast governmental bureaucracy, have increased. Congressional power, its basis, and the factors influencing the current position of Congress vis-à-vis coordinate governmental departments are discussed in this chapter.

CONSTITUTIONAL BACKGROUND: REPRESENTATION OF POPULAR, GROUP, AND NATIONAL INTERESTS

Article I, Section 1 of the Constitution states that "all legislative powers herein granted shall be vested in a Congress of the United States, which shall consist of a Senate and House of Representatives." Section 8 specifically enumerates Congressional powers, and provides that Congress shall have power "to make all laws which shall be necessary and proper for carrying into execution the foregoing powers, and all other powers vested by this Constitution in the government of the United States, or in any department or officer thereof."

Apart from delineating the powers of Congress, Article I provides that the House shall represent the people, and the Senate the states through appointment of members by the state legislatures. The representative function of Congress is written into the Constitution, and at the time of the framing of the Constitution much discussion centered on the nature of representation and what constituted adequate representation in a national legislative body. Further, relating in part to the question of representation, the framers of the Constitution had to determine what the appropriate tasks for each branch of the legislature were, and to what extent certain legislative activities should be within the exclusive or initial jurisdiction of the House or the Senate. All these questions depended to some extent upon the conceptualization the framers had of the House as representative of popular interests on a short-term basis and the Senate as a reflection of conservative interests on a long-term basis. These selections from *The Federalist* indicate the thinking of the framers about the House of Representatives and the Senate.

52

Alexander Hamilton or James Madison

FEDERALIST 53

... No man can be a competent legislator who does not add to an upright intention and a sound judgment a certain degree of knowledge of the subjects on which he is to legislate. A part of this knowledge may be acquired by means of information, which lie within the compass of men in private, as well as public stations. Another part can only be attained, or at least thoroughly attained, by actual experience in the station which requires the use of it. The period of service ought, therefore, in all such cases, to bear some proportion to the extent of practical knowledge requisite to the due performance of the service. ...

In a single state the requisite knowledge relates to the existing laws, which are uniform throughout the state, and with which all the citizens are more or less conversant. ... The great theater of the United States presents a very different scene. The laws are so far from being uniform that they vary in every state; whilst the public affairs of the union are spread throughout a very extensive region, and are extremely diversified by the local affairs connected with them, and can with difficulty be correctly learnt in any other place than in the central councils, to which a knowledge of them will be brought by representatives of every part of the empire. Yet some knowledge of the affairs, and even of the laws of all the states, ought to be possessed by the members from each of the states. ...

A branch of knowledge which belongs to the acquirements of a federal representative, and which has not been mentioned, is that of foreign affairs. In regulating our own commerce he ought to be not only acquainted with the treaties between the United States and other nations, but also with the commercial policy and laws of other nations. He ought not to be altogether ignorant of the law of nations; for that, as far as it is a proper object of municipal legislation, is submitted to the federal government. And although the House of Representatives is not immediately to participate in foreign negotiations and arrangements, yet from the necessary connection between the several branches of public affairs, those particular subjects will frequently deserve attention in the ordinary course of legislation, and will sometimes demand particular legislative sanction and cooperation. Some portion of this knowledge may, no doubt, be acquired in a man's closet; but some of it also can only be acquired to best effect, by a practical attention to the subject, during the period of actual service in the legislature. ...

FEDERALIST 56

The . . . charge against the House of Representatives is, that it will be too small to possess a due knowledge of the interests of its constituents.

As this objection evidently proceeds from a comparison of the proposed number of representatives, with the great extent of the United States, the number of their inhabitants, and the diversity of their interests, without taking into view, at the same time, the circumstances which will distinguish the Congress from other legislative bodies, the best answer that can be given to it, will be a brief explanation of these peculiarities.

It is a sound and important principle that the representative ought to be acquainted with the interests and circumstances of his constituents. But this principle can extend no farther than to those circumstances and interests to which the authority and care of the representative relate. An ignorance of a variety of minute and particular objects, which do not lie within the compass of legislation, is consistent with every attribute necessary to a due performance of the legislative trust. In determining the extent of information required in the exercise of a particular authority, recourse then must be had to the objects within the purview of that authority.

What are to be the objects of federal legislation? Those which are of most importance, and which seem most to require knowledge, are commerce, taxation, and the militia.

A proper regulation of commerce requires much information, as has been elsewhere remarked; but as far as this information relates to the laws, and local situation of each individual state, a very few representatives would be sufficient vehicles of it to the federal councils.

Taxation will consist, in great measure, of duties which will be involved in the regulation of commerce. So far the preceding remark is applicable to this object. As far as it may consist of internal collections, a more diffusive knowledge of the circumstances of the state may be necessary. But will not this also be possessed in sufficient degree by a very few intelligent men, diffusively elected within the state? . . .

With regard to the regulation of the militia there are scarcely any circumstances in reference to which local knowledge can be said to be necessary. . . . The art of war teaches general principles of organization, movement, and discipline, which apply universally.

The attentive reader will discern that the reasoning here used, to prove the sufficiency of a moderate number of representatives, does not, in any respect, contradict what was urged on another occasion, with regard to the extensive information which the representitives ought to possess, and the time that might be necessary for acquiring it. . . .

FEDERALIST 57

. . . The House of Representatives is so constituted as to support in the members an habitual recollection of their dependence on the people. Before the sentiments impressed on their minds by the mode of their elevation, can be effaced by the exercise of power, they will be compelled to anticipate the moment when their power is to cease, when their exercise of it is to be reviewed, and when they must descend to the level from which they were raised; there for ever to remain unless a faithful discharge of their trust shall have established their title to a renewal of it.

I will add, as a . . . circumstance in the situation of the House of Representatives, restraining them from oppressive measures, that they can make no law which will not have its full operation on themselves and their friends, as well as on the great mass of the society. This has always been deemed one of the strongest bonds by which human policy can connect the rulers and the people together. It creates between them that communion of interest, and sympathy of sentiments, of which few governments have furnished examples; but without which every government degenerates into tyranny. If it be asked, what is to restrain the House of Representatives from making legal discriminations in favor of themselves, and a particular class of the society? I answer, the genius of the whole system; the nature of just and constitutional laws; and, above all, the vigilant and manly spirit which actuates the people of America; a spirit which nourishes freedom, and in return is nourished by it.

If this spirit shall ever be so far debased as to tolerate a law not obligatory on the legislature, as well as on the people, the people will be prepared to tolerate anything but liberty.

Such will be the relation between the House of Representatives and their constituents. Duty, gratitude, interest, ambition itself, are the cords by which they will be bound to fidelity and sympathy with the great mass of the people. It is possible that these may all be insufficient to control the caprice and wickedness of men. But are they not all that government will admit, and that human prudence can devise? Are they not the genuine, and the characteristic means, by which republican government provides for the liberty and happiness of the people? . . .

FEDERALIST 58

. . . In this review of the constitution of the House of Representatives . . . one observation . . . I must be permitted to add . . . as claiming, in my judgment, a very serious attention. It is, that in all legislative assemblies, the greater the number composing them may be, the fewer will be the men who will in fact direct their proceedings. In the first place, the more numerous any assembly may be, of whatever characters composed, the greater is known to be the ascendancy of passion over reason. In the next place, the larger the number, the greater will be the proportion of members of limited information and of weak capacities. Now it is precisely on characters of this description that the eloquence and address of the few are known to act with all their force. In the ancient republics, where the whole body of the people assembled in person, a single orator, or an artful statesman, was generally seen to rule with as complete a sway as if a sceptre had been placed in his single hands. On the same principle, the more multitudinous a representative assembly may be rendered, the more it will partake of the infirmities incident to collective meetings of the people. Ignorance will be the dupe of cunning; and passion the slave of sophistry and declamation. The people can never err more than in supposing, that by multiplying their representatives beyond a certain list, they strengthen the barrier against the government of a few. Experience will for ever admonish them, that, on the contrary, after securing a sufficient number for the purposes of safety, of local information, and of diffusive sympathy with the whole society, they will counteract their own views by every addition to their representatives. The countenance of the government may become more democratic; but the soul that animates it will be more oligarchic. The machine will be enlarged, but the fewer, and often the more secret, will be the springs by which its motions are directed. . . .

FEDERALIST 62

Having examined the constitution of the House of Representatives . . . I enter next on the examination of the Senate.

The heads under which this member of the government may be considered are—I. The qualifications of senators; II. The appointment of them by the state legislatures; III. The equality of representation in the Senate; IV. The number of senators, and the term for which they are to be elected; V. The powers vested in the Senate.

I.

The qualifications proposed for senators, as distinguished from those of representatives, consist in a more advanced age and a longer period of citizenship. A senator must be thirty years of age at least; as a representative must be twenty-five. And the former must have been a citizen nine years; as seven years are required for the latter. The propriety of these distinctions is explained by the nature of the senatorial trust; which, requiring greater extent of information and stability of character, requires at the same time, that the senator should have reached a period of life most likely to supply these advantages. . . .

II.

It is equally unnecessary to dilate on the appointment of senators by the state legislators. Among the various modes which might have been devised for constituting this branch of the government, that which has been proposed by the convention is probably the most congenial with the public opinion. It is recommended by the double advantage of favoring a select appointment, and of giving to the state governments such an agency in the formation of the federal government, as must secure the authority of the former, and may form a convenient link between the two systems.

III.

The equality of representation in the Senate is another point, which, being evidently the result of compromise between the opposite pretensions of the large and the small states, does not call for much discussion. If indeed it be right, that among a people thoroughly incorporated into one nation, every district ought to have a *proportional* share in the government: and that among independent and sovereign states bound together by a simple league, the parties, however unequal in size, ought to have an *equal* share in the common councils, it does not appear to be without some reason, that in a compound republic, partaking both of the national and federal character, the government ought to be founded on a mixture of the principles of proportional [as found in the House of Representatives] and equal representation [in the Senate]. . . .

. . . [T]he equal vote allowed to each state, is at once a constitutional recognition of the portion of sovereignty remaining in the individual states, and an instrument for preserving that residuary sovereignty. So far the equality ought to be no less acceptable to the large than to the small states; since they are not less solicitous to guard by every possible expedient against an improper consolidation of the states into one simple republic.

Another advantage accruing from this ingredient in the constitution of the Senate is, the additional impediment it must prove against improper acts of legislation. No law or resolution can now be passed without the concurrence, first, of a majority of the people, and then, of a majority of the states. It must be acknowledged that this complicated check on legislation may, in some instances, be injurious as well as beneficial; and that the peculiar defense which it involves in favor of the smaller states, would be more rational, if any interests common to them, and distinct from those of the other states, would otherwise be exposed to peculiar danger. But as the larger states will always be able, by their power over the supplies, to defeat unreasonable exertions of this prerogative of the lesser states; and as the facility and excess of law-making seem to be the diseases to which our governments are most liable, it is not impossible, that this part of the constitution may be more convenient in practice than it appears to many in contemplation.

IV.

The number of senators, and the duration of their appointment, come next to be considered. In order to form an accurate judgment on both these points, it will be proper to inquire into the purposes which are to be answered by the Senate; and, in order to ascertain these, it will be necessary to review the inconveniences which a republic must suffer from the want of such an institution.

First. It is a misfortune incident to republican government, though in a less degree than to other governments, that those who administer it may forget their obligations to their constituents, and prove unfaithful to their important trust. In this point of view, a senate, as a second branch of the legislative assembly, distinct from, and dividing the power with, a first, must be in all cases a salutary check on the government. It doubles the security to the people by requiring the concurrence of two distinct bodies in schemes of usurpation or perfidy, where the ambition or corruption of one would otherwise be sufficient. . . . [A]s the improbability of sinister combinations will be in proportion to the dissimilarity in the genius of the two bodies, it must be politic to distinguish them from each other by every circumstance which will consist with a due harmony in all proper measures, and with the genuine principles of republican government.

Second. The necessity of a senate is not less indicated by the propensity of all single and numerous assemblies, to yield to the impulse of sudden and violent passions, and to be seduced by factious leaders into intemperate and pernicious resolutions. Examples on this subject might be cited without number; and from proceedings within the United States, as well as from the history of other nations. But a position that will not be contradicted need not be proved. All that need be remarked is, that a body which is to correct this infirmity ought itself to be free from it, and consequently ought to be less numerous. It ought, moreover, to possess great firmness, and consequently ought to hold its authority by a tenure of considerable duration.

Third. Another defect to be supplied by a senate lies in a want of due acquaintance with the objects and principles of legislation. It is not possible that an assembly of men, called, for the most part, from pursuits of a private nature, continued in appointments for a short time, and led by no permanent motive to devote the intervals of public occuption to a study of the laws, the affairs, and the comprehensive interests of their country, should, if left wholly to themselves, escape a variety of important errors in the exercise of their legislative trust. . . .

Fourth. The mutability in the public councils, arising from a rapid succession of new members, however qualified they may be, points out, in the strongest manner, the necessity of some stable institution in the government. Every new election in the states is found to change one-half of the representatives. From this change of men must proceed a change of opinions; and from a change of opinions, a change of measures. But a continual change even of good measures is inconsistent with every rule of prudence, and every prospect of success. . . .

FEDERALIST 63

A *fifth* desideratum, illustrating the utility of a senate, is the want of a due sense of national character. Without a select and stable member of the government, the esteem of foreign powers will not only be forfeited by an unenlightened and variably policy . . . ; but the national councils will not possess that sensibility to the opinion of the world, which is perhaps not less necessary in order to merit, than it is to obtain, its respect and confidence. . . .

I add, as a *sixth* defect, the want in some important cases of a due responsibility in the government to the people, arising from that frequency of elections, which in other cases produces this responsibility. . . .

Responsibility, in order to be reasonable, must be limited to objects within the power of the responsible party, and in order to be effectual, must relate to operations of that power, of which a ready and proper judgment can be formed by the constituents. The objects of government may be divided into two general classes; the one depending on measures, which have singly an immediate and sensible operation; the other depending on a succession of well chosen and well connected measures, which have a gradual and perhaps unobserved operation. The importance of the latter description to the collective and permanent welfare of every country, needs no explanation. And yet it is evident that an assembly elected for so short a term as to be unable to provide more than one or two links in a chain of measures, on which the general welfare may essentially depend, ought not to be answerable for the final result, any more than a steward or tenant, engaged for one year, could be justly made to answer for plans or improvements, which could not be accomplished in less than half a dozen years. Nor is it possible for the people to estimate the *share* of influence, which their annual assemblies may respectively have on events resulting from the mixed transactions of several years. It is sufficiently difficult, at any rate, to preserve a personal responsibility in the members of a *numerous* body, for such acts of the body as have an immediate, detached, and palpable operation on its constituents.

The proper remedy for this defect must be an additional body in the legislative department, which, having sufficient permanency to provide for such objects as require a continued attention, and a train of measures, may be justly and effectually answerable for the attainment of those objects.

Thus far I have considered the circumstances, which point out the necessity of a well constructed senate, only as they relate to the representatives of the people. To a people as little blinded by prejudice, or corrupted by flattery, as those whom I address, I shall not scruple to add, that such an institution may be sometimes necessary, as a defense to the people against their own temporary errors and delusions. As the cool and deliberate sense of the community ought, in all governments, and actually will, in all free governments, ultimately prevail over the views of its rulers; so there are particular moments in public affairs, when the people, stimulated by some irregular passion, or some illicit advantage, or misled by the artful misrepresentations of interested men, may call for measures which they themselves will afterwards be the most ready to lament and condemn. In these critical moments, how salutary will be the interference of some temperate and respectable body of citizens, in order to check the misguided career, and to suspend the blow meditated by the people against themselves, until reason, justice and truth can regain their authority over the public mind? What bitter anguish would not the people of Athens have often avoided, if their government had contained so provident a safeguard against the tyranny of their own passions? Popular liberty might then have escaped the indelible reproach of decreeing to the same citizens the hemlock on one day, and statues on the next.

It may be suggested that a people spread over an extensive region cannot, like the crowded inhabitants of a small district, be subject to the infection of violent passions; or to the danger of combining in the pursuit of unjust measures. I am far from denying that this is a distinction of peculiar importance. I have, on the contrary, endeavored in a former paper to show that it is one of the principal recommendations of a confederated republic. At the same time this advantage ought not to be considered as superseding the use of auxiliary precautions. It may even be remarked that the same extended situation, which will exempt the people of America from some of the dangers incident to lesser republics, will expose them to the inconveniency of remaining for a longer time under the influence of those misrepresentations which the combined industry of interested men may succeed in distributing among them. . . .

CONGRESS AND THE COMMITTEE SYSTEM

In 1885 Woodrow Wilson was able to state categorically in his famous work *Congressional Government:*

"The leaders of the House are the chairmen of the principal Standing Committees. Indeed, to be exactly accurate, the House has as many leaders as there are subjects of legislation; for there are as many Standing Committees as there are leading classes of legislation, and in the consideration of every topic of business the House is guided by a special leader in the person of the chairman of the Standing Committee, charged with the superintendence of measures of the particular class to which that topic belongs. It is this multiplicity of leaders, this many-headed leadership, which makes the organization of the House too complex to afford uninformed people and unskilled observers any easy clue to its methods of rule. For the chairmen of the Standing Committees do not constitute a cooperative body like a ministry. They do not consult and concur in the adoption of homogeneous and mutually helpful measures; there is no thought of acting in concert. Each Committee goes its own way at its own pace. It is impossible to discover any unity or method in the disconnected and therefore unsystematic, confused, and desultory action of the House, or any common purpose in the measures which its Committees from time to time recommend."

With regard to the Senate he noted:

"It has those same radical defects of organization which weaken the House. Its functions also, like those of the House, are segregated in the prerogatives of numerous Standing Committees. In this regard Congress is all of a piece. There is in the Senate no more opportunity than exists in the House for gaining such recognized party leadership as would be likely to enlarge a man by giving him a sense of power, and to steady and sober him by filling him with a grave sense of responsibility. So far as its organization controls it, the Senate . . . proceedings bear most of the characteristic features of committee rule."

The Legislative Reorganization Act of 1946 was designed to streamline Congressional committee structure and provide committees and individual Congressmen with increased expert staff; however, although the number of standing committees was reduced, subcommittees have increased so that the net numerical reduction is not as great as was originally intended. Further, because Congress still conducts its business through committees: (1) the senior members of the party with the majority in Congress dominate the formulation of public policy through the seniority rule; (2) policy formulation is fragmented with each committee maintaining relative dominance over policy areas within its jurisdiction; (3) stemming from this fragmentation, party control is weakened, especially when the President attempts to assume legislative dominance.

In the following selection Charles O. Jones discusses the contemporary committee system of Congress, and the ways in which committees and parties interact. He feels that the effectiveness of Congress can be increased by strengthening the role of parties to offset the decentralizing tendencies of committees. This selection was originally a working paper prepared for the House Select Committee on Committees in 1973. The Committee was investigating the operation of the committee system in the House to determine if improvements could be made. The Select Committee, chaired by Richard Bolling (D. Mo.), recommended major changes in the House committee system in 1974. The proposed plan would generally limit congressmen to one major committee assignment and curtail the jurisdiction of several powerful committees, including Ways and Means.

53
Charles O. Jones

CONGRESSIONAL COMMITTEES AND THE TWO-PARTY SYSTEM

During the early months of 1973 the halls of Congress reverberated with cries of anguish as the Administration presented bold budgetary proposals, impounded funds for programs popular on the Hill, reorganized the executive branch, and proposed an expansive interpretation of executive privilege. Buoyed by an incredible victory at the polls and final settlement in Vietnam, and skeptical of prospects for Congressional support, the President was testing his authority virtually to go it alone. Before Watergate broke, he clearly demonstrated that a President could go very far on his own—ignoring, even taunting, a Congress organized by the other party.

The President's actions were soon interpreted as commentary on the sad state of affairs in Congress. Many pictured Congress as immobilized—incapable of responding to presidential encroachments on legislative authority. As in the past, such direct threats to the power of Congress stimulated reform proposals both inside and outside the institution. And so here we are today, examining the heart of the legislative process in the House of Representatives.

The committee system is a logical place to begin any such examination but the diagnosis of congressional ills cannot be limited to those important legislative units. Political parties, in particular, also must be studied. Party and committee leaders have traditionally shared power in Congress—not always in happy accord. In this paper I will argue that the time has come to increase the authority, responsibility, and visibility of congressional party leaders. Inevitably any such increase comes partially at the expense of congressional committee leaders and therefore is not likely to be the most popular proposal set forth in these hearings. The proposal can be defended in two ways: (1) such reordering may, in fact, result in greater overall authority for Congress so that in absolute terms committee leaders may actually gain power; and (2) failure to make changes may jeopardize existing congressional authority and thereby threaten the whole democratic structure in this nation.

From Charles O. Jones, "Congressional Committees and the Two-Party System," Working paper for the Select Committee on Committees, U.S. House of Representatives, 1973.

PARTY OR COMMITTEE?

Always fearful of power, we have traditionally sought to disperse it where possible in this country. Nor have Americans ever been fond of political parties. In fact many attempts have been made through the years to destroy them. It should not surprise us, therefore, to find a weak party system in Congress. The rest of the world views this feature as quite curious, however. For example, in studying and observing the House of Representatives, Lord Bryce concluded that the "feature . . . Europeans find the strangest" is that the House "has parties, but they are headless."

> There is neither Government nor Opposition. There can hardly be said to be leaders . . . That the majority may be and often is opposed to the President and his cabinet, does not strike Americans as odd, because they proceed on the theory that the legislative ought to be distinct from the executive authority.

Yet both the House and Senate face what Bryce identifies as "the most abiding difficulty of free government"—i.e., *"to get large assemblies to work promptly and smoothly either for legislative or executive purposes."* Bryce notes that through history three methods have been employed to overcome this difficulty:

(1) "Leave very few and comparatively simple questions to the assembly . . ."

(2) "Organize the assemblies into well-defined parties, each recognizing and guided by one or more leaders . . . [which] move like battalions at the word of command."

(3) "Divide the assembly into a number of smaller bodies to which legislative and administrative questions may be referred . . ."

It is the third alternative that is "applied . . . most of all in the United States."

Though understanding its advantages, Lord Bryce found much to criticize in the congressional committee system. He spotted three results of the system that are particularly relevant today—so much so that they can serve as orienting purposes for this discussion.

(1) "It [the committee system] lessens the cohesion and harmony of legislation. Each committee goes on its own way with its own bills just as though it were legislating for one planet and the other committees for others. . . . The advance is haphazard; the parts have little relation to one another or to the whole."

(2) "It reduces responsibility. . . . In the United States the ministry cannot be blamed, for the cabinet officers do not sit in Congress; the House cannot be blamed because it has only followed the decision of its committee; the committee may be an obscure body, whose members are too insignificant to be worth blaming. The chairman is possibly a man of note, but the people have no leisure to watch sixty chairmen: they know Congress and Congress only; they cannot follow the acts of those to whom Congress chooses to delegate its

functions. No discredit attaches to the dominant party, because they could not control the acts of the . . . men in the committee room. This public displeasure rarely finds a victim . . .''

(3) "It lowers the interest of the nation in the proceedings of Congress. Except in exciting times, when large questions have to be settled, the bulk of real business is done not in the great hall of the House but in this labyrinth of committee rooms and the lobbies that surround them. . . . People cease to watch Congress with that sharp eye which every principal ought to keep fixed on his agent."

Of course, Congress did not settle on the third alternative (dividing "the assembly into a number of smaller bodies") just to give Lord Bryce something to criticize. There are perfectly sound reasons for a strong committee system associated with the political realities of congressional functions, structure, authority, and elections. The question before Congress today is whether the present system of strong committees-weak parties continues to accommodate political realities. I think it does not and the creation of this committee indicates that the members themselves are also questioning the existing structure.

NEW REALITIES FOR OLD PROCESSES

Perhaps the most obvious political reality today is that a Republican is in the White House while the Democrats continue to hold a majority in both houses of Congress. Further, that Republican was elected by one of the greatest landslides in history. After his inauguration for a second term, the President announced a bold design to reduce, not increase, federal programs. It seemed apparent earlier this year that he intended to govern with only very limited congressional participation.

The Watergate revelations have upset the President's plans, to be sure. But members of Congress should be mindful that Watergate only hurts the President—it has not cured the problems of the legislative branch. If the balance of power has been restored it has occurred momentarily while President Nixon recovers, not permanently as a result of Congress reestablishing its decision-making capacities. A balance in which the President is as immobile as Congress is not in the best interests of the nation, in my judgment.

So the tasks of this committee remain paramount. Indeed, one might argue that it must be even more diligent since the so-called "constitutional crisis" between the President and Congress seems to have abated. The temptation for Congress to settle back into the familiar patterns—constituency service, executive dependency, and diffuse responsibility—is certainly very real now that the President has been humbled before his countrymen.

Split party control between Congress and the White House serves to set Bryce's observations in sharp relief. Increased presidential authority has in the past tended to act as a corrective to the problems of cohesion, responsibility, and visibility of issues, with the President assuming the central leadership role in the national political system. With split control, however, the inadequacies of Congress are once again obvious to all. This would be less serious, perhaps, if split control were a rare phenomenon. That is, many scholars, pundits, and politicians are willing to accept presidential dominance of national policy-making as solving many of the problems raised by Bryce. As it is, however, split control is no longer exceptional. Indeed, the White House and Congress will have been under split party control for sixteen years during the post-World War II period, 1946–1976 (barring an unforseen Republican triumph in the 1974 congressional elections). And in the more recent period, 1954–1976, split control has (or will have) obtained nearly two-thirds of the time—fourteen of twenty-two years.

Apparently this condition is acceptable to the American public. First, they have given implicit approval by splitting their votes in huge numbers. Second, a recent Harris poll showed that 50 percent of the respondents thought that split control was a better way to govern and another 16 percent thought it made no difference.

WORK ASSIGNMENTS IN CONGRESS

It is in this context of confused responsibility that Lord Bryce's criticisms of the congressional committee system have relevance. One can make a logical argument in support of split control as an adversary process in which the public interest is ultimately served. As one of Harris' respondents observed: "Divided control keeps each branch of government in line." But how are we to determine responsibility, develop cohesion, and maintain interest in Congress if power is dispersed throughout the committee system? As Bryce says: "The people have no leisure to watch sixty chairmen." How is the ordinary citizen, or even the careful observer, to pinpoint responsibility in Congress today? It is not fair to assign it to the current group of party leaders for they have too little authority. And it is impossible to monitor the entire committee system. Though the number of standing committees was mercifully reduced by the Legislative Reorganization Act of 1946, federal government functions have increased many-fold and thus the congressional workload is greater than ever. As a result the total number of legislative work units continues to grow. My most recent count shows *57 standing and special committees* (House, Senate, Joint), and *288 standing and special subcommittees*—a total of 345 congressional work units for the 535 members. In the Senate alone there are 23 committees and 140 subcommittees—each requiring a chairman and ranking minority member. "Every member a leader" seems to be the operating principle in the Senate.

Even more dramatic is the number of work assignments involved in this division of labor. As indicated in Table 1, a total of *4,037 slots* are listed in the current directory of committees and subcommittees. Above all these figures demonstrate the staggering workload of the national legislature. It has been found necessary to create a fantastic array of specialized units which come to be demanding of a legislator's time and talents. As shown in Table 1, the 435 House members must fill 2,452 committee and subcommittee slots—an average of 5.6 per member (1.8 committee; 3.8 subcommittee). With less than one-fourth the membership of the House, the Senate has two-thirds of the committee and subcommittee positions of the lower chamber—1,585 slots for 100 Senators, an average of 15.9 per member (3.9 committee; 12 subcommittee).

THE PROBLEM OF ACCOUNTABILITY

How can the public possibly comprehend this maze of working units? Where is the accountability in this system? Each member must face reelection and in theory is accountable at that time. But the typical voter is unlikely to know very much about the member's committee and subcommittee assignments. Indeed, various polls and surveys show that most voters cannot even identify their representative (senators get somewhat more recognition). Further, most incumbents are re-elected—normally over 90 percent of those who seek another term. In summary, the available data from voting behavior studies do not suggest anything approaching the classic theoretical model of elections as "accountability" events.

What is the basis of voting in congressional elections, if it is not a weighing of an incumbent's record? Typically, in House races, it is party affiliation. Republicans vote for Republican candidates; Democrats for Democratic candidates; and Independents tend to split in the direction of the winner. For example, in districts where there are more Republicans than Democrats, the Republican candidate is elected over and over again. If redistricting occurs, or lots of Democrats move into a district, the incumbent may be defeated. But

Table 1.—TOTAL COMMITTEE AND SUBCOMMITTEE POSITIONS, 93D CONG., 1ST SESS.

	Committee positions	Subcommittee positions	Total
House of Representatives	732	1,581	2,313
House positions on Joint Committees	61	78	139
Total	793	1,659	2,452
Senate	328	1,113	1,441
Senate positions on Joint Committees	61	83	144
Total	389	1,196	1,585
Grand total	1,182	2,855	4,037

Source: Compiled from listings in "Congressional Quarterly Weekly Report," Apr. 28, 1973, pp. 957–1004.

then, typically, the Democrat is elected over and over again. Overall the trend has been in the direction of greater stability of the House, both in turnover of members and average length of terms served.

A party-based vote can, of course, be an accountability vote. That is, voters may be reaffirming support for a set of broad principles which they presume are the basis of policy action within the congressional party structure. Let's assume for the moment that this is what really happens—that the preceding statement is a rough approximation of what most voters believe. Holding the party and its candidate accountable depends on the visibility, responsibility, and cohesion of actions taken—those very traits Bryce warns are unlikely to characterize a legislature with a strong committee system. Though one cannot push assumptions about voter rationality too far, it surely can be said that there is more evidence in voting behavior data for a party accountability theory than a candidate accountability theory—at least for the House of Representatives. But the voter apparently relies on blind faith since he or she will not normally have available specific knowledge of the party's legislative record in Congress.

A RATIONALE FOR CHANGE

I propose strengthening political parties in Congress as a counterweight to the decentralizing tendencies of the committee system. It is the only move I can identify that will fix responsibility and promote unity and visibility for legislative issues. And, as indicated above, it is a move that bears some relationship to the voting basis of the American public—that is, party does seem to provide a general orientation for voters. To put it another way, surely neither the ordinary voter nor the sophisticated analyst has the "leisure to watch" 345 chairmen.

No institution with exclusive power to reform itself is likely to make change simply as an artful exercise. Either there must be direct payoffs or it must be apparent that continuing to do business in the same way will be harmful to the membership. Why should members support changes now? In the present circumstances of split party control, the Democrats have the incentive of developing alternative proposals to those offered by the Nixon Administration. But greater cohesion, responsibility, and visibility are prerequisites to any such offerings by the Congressional Democratic parties.

The House Republicans have made important changes in the last 15 years to facilitate development (or sometimes merely discovery) of party positions on policy questions. Since a minority party can never count on controlling the White House for very long, changes made now—when the Democrats also have a stake in the reform—can be of long-term significance by increasing the minority party's capacity to offer constructive opposition when a Democrat moves back into the White House.

This is the time to act. If the Democrats recapture the White House in 1976, there will be many fewer incentives for change. Democrats may be

Table 2.—REGIONAL DISTRIBUTION OF HOUSE AND SENATE SEATS BE-
TWEEN THE DEMOCRATS AND REPUBLICANS, 93D CONG. 1ST SESS.

	House seats				Senate seats			
	Democratic		Republican		Democratic		Republican	
Region	Number	Percent	Number	Percent	Number	Percent	Number	Percent
East	61	54	52	46	9	40	13[1]	60
South and Border	97	72	38	28	28	67[2]	10	33
Midwest	43	39	68	61	13	60	9	40
West	42	55	34	45	15	58	11	42
Total	243		192		57		43	

[1] Includes James Buckley (New York).
[2] Includes Harry Byrd, Jr. (Virginia).

expected to accept the leadership of their President, even in the fact of further
erosion of Congressional authority. The rewards of increased presidential
power are tempting and can be more easily shared within the majority party.
(Parenthetically one might observe that the "crisis" of presidential-congres-
sional relations came with a Republican in the White House—not so much
because he had more power than his Democratic predecessors but because in
exercising power he sought to undo programs supported by the Democratic
majority in Congress.)

At least one other argument in favor of reform can be offered. In the past,
a very persuasive case was made against any proposals which might bring more
than two members of Congress of the same party in the same room. Ours are
"umbrella-type" political parties, it is argued, and all points of view are accommodated. One cannot insist on a "party line," and maintain the two-party
system. The Democrats, in particular, have permitted widely divergent views
on fundamental issues—in part because their traditional strength in the South
provided a solid base for electing presidents and collecting majorities in Congress. Accepting the fact that both parties still allow for a broad spectrum of
ideologies, there is evidence to suggest that the parties are becoming "nationalized." No longer need either party feel so constrained by its base in a particular
region that it can never call a meeting of the membership. Thus, as indicated
in Table 2, the Republicans now have sizeable representation in both the House
and Senate from Southern and Border states. Just 10 years ago, in the 88th
Congress, Republicans had three Senators and 17 Representatives from Southern and Border states. The three Senators and 11 of the 17 Representatives
were from the Border South. The Democrats meanwhile have for some time
been building strength in traditionally Republican areas in the Midwest,
Northeast, and West. As indicated in Table 2, there are nearly as many
Democratic Senators from the West as from the South. And percentagewise,
Midwestern Democrats are capturing nearly as many Senate seats as their
Southern colleagues (60 percent compared to 67 percent).

AN AGENDA FOR CHANGE

Let me restate the principal purposes for suggested change: to improve the capacity of Congress for offering alternatives that are cohesive, visible, and for which responsibility can be fixed. I hope this committee will accept that charge and in doing so seek to balance the many advantages in dispersal of authority in the committee system with the advantages I have sought to identify in centralizing authority in party leaders for seeing to it that conclusions are reached in Congress.

In this context, I offer the following proposals for discussion by this committee. I have not limited proposals to those necessarily within the charge of this committee as specified in H. Res. 132. Rather I have included any suggestion affecting party-committee relationships, understanding that certain of these proposals would have to be implemented through existing party structure.

Party Leaders

Party leaders should be visibly responsible for policy action by their membership. They cannot legitimately be held responsible without an increase in authority, however. The following proposals are offered as means to increase leader visibility and authority.

1. Provide for more formal nomination and campaign procedures in electing party leaders—possibly holding two caucuses: the first for nominations; the second, a week later, for elections.

2. Permit the Speaker to appoint the Committee on Rules—consulting the Minority Floor Leader for filling minority party vacancies. (Requires a change in Rule X.)

3. Permit the Speaker to appoint the chairmen and the Minority Floor Leader to appoint the Ranking Minority Members of the Committees on Appropriations and Ways and Means. (Requires a change in Rule X.)

4. Require all privileged committee reports to be cleared through the Speaker's Office. (Requires a change in Rule XI.)

Party Apparatus

The majority and minority parties should increase their capacities for developing alternatives to the programs of a President of the other party. Efforts should be made to see to it that these alternatives receive consideration in Congress and are visible to the public.

1. Authorize policy research staffs for both political parties. These staffs would presumably support the caucus or conference and be under the direct control of a committee appointed by the party floor leaders (following the practice of the House Republicans).

2. Utilize the policy committees for developing party positions on proposals —those offered by the President, the other party, and the party's own

research staff—and for urging congressional committee consideration of the party's own proposals.

3. Establish a separate Committee-on-Committees in the Democratic Party, chaired by the Speaker, with the membership elected in caucus by region. The Floor Leader and Whip would serve ex officio on the committee.

4. Reduce the membership of the Republican Committee-on-Committees by having the membership elected in conference by region.

5. Institute an end-of-session caucus review of the party record in legislation, with reports from committee chairmen (or ranking minority members) and party leaders. Such a meeting should provide for debate and planning for the next session. It should be open to the press and the public.

Committees and Subcommittees

Other changes should be made that are less directly related to party-committee relationships but do involve the efficiency of committee operations, the potential for developing alternatives, and the power of committee leaders.

1. Survey existing staff functions and centralize where possible. For example, it may be feasible to establish an Office of Congressional Committee Organization and Administration which would handle routine matters such as scheduling hearings and executive sessions, arranging for witnesses, editing the hearings and reports, etc.

2. Increase the computer-based information capability of congressional committees and hire information retrieval specialists. This function could also be centralized—possibly in the Congressional Research Service.

3. Expand the Congressional Research Service's research capability (as distinct from its daily response capability for the thousands of inquiries it receives).

* * *

I am conscious of the fact that Congress reforms itself. If my comments in this paper do not strike a responsive chord among the members, then, of course, I have no place else to go. I have come to believe, however, that this Congress faces a unique opportunity. Changes made now could vastly increase Congress' decision-making capacities. I do not believe we should be forced to depend so heavily on the presidency for policy decisions—as important as that office is and should be. Congress has the potential through its political parties and their leaders to produce coordinated alternative proposals to those offered by the executive. This can be done without a return to Canonism or without losing the advantages of the most well-developed committee system in the world. It is to this end that the remarks and recommendations in this paper are directed.

The power of Congressional committee chairmen is a well known fact, and this article deals with a man who was once one of the most powerful chairmen in Congress—Wilbur Mills. He was Chairman of the House Ways and Means Committee, the most important committee in the House because it handles all matters pertaining to revenue-raising. The views that Mills held on taxation often conflicted with those of the President, and in such cases the Chairman of the Ways and Means Committee prevailed. Indeed, in 1971 when many proposed that Mills might consider running for President, some close associates suggested that gaining this office would, at most, be a lateral move in terms of political power. How Mills and the Ways and Means Committee worked is described in this selection from *Business Week*, with issues of public policy as examples.

54
WILBUR MILLS AND THE WAYS AND MEANS COMMITTEE

After endless weeks of hearings last year, Wilbur Mills leaned over to a colleague during a meeting of his House Ways and Means Committee and whispered: "I think we ought to go all the way with this welfare reform bill." It was the first indication that the formidable chairman would back one of President Nixon's top priority programs, and his assent meant that his committee would also support it and that so, probably, would the House of Representatives.

Ways and Means, the most powerful body in the House, currently has in its grasp more hot issues—from national health insurance and revenue sharing to trade policy and possible tax cuts—than it has had at any time in recent years. The trade issue is a case in point. Mills's committee is shaping the laws governing tariffs and import quotas in a watershed period for United States business: For the first time in twenty-five years, American enterprise is experiencing serious and widespread foreign competition in its domestic market. Ways and Means, traditionally manned by free traders, now must help decide how United States trade policy should adjust to meet these new conditions.

Mills's control over so much of Nixon's "new American revolution" has created a myth of Mills the Omnipotent. "What will Wilbur do?" is one of Washington's most frequently asked questions. Mills and his committee are often viewed as a private oligarchy, oblivious to the wishes of the White House. President Kennedy once complained: "Mills knows he was Chairman of Ways and Means before I got here and that he'll still be Chairman after I've gone, and he knows that I know it. I don't have any hold on him."

No wonder then that Nixon—like Presidents Kennedy and Johnson before him—has gone out of his way to curry Mills's favor. Before submitting final tax reform proposals, he dispatched Treasury Under Secretary Charles Walker to Mills's home in Arkansas to discuss them. To make dealings with the committee easier, the President has delegated enormous on-the-spot policy-making powers to top officials, such as Health, Education and Welfare Secretary Elliot Richardson, who participate in closed bill-writing sessions of the committee. That way, Mills is not kept waiting for an answer when he wants to know the nature of Administration reaction to a committee suggestion.

For all the committee's traditional independence of the White House, though, it would not have such tremendous influence if it strayed very far from the prevailing mood of the House. The liberal Education and Labor Committee, or Appropriations, a bastion of conservatism, will be overruled from time to time. But the Ways and Means Committee sits fairly well astride the center of political sentiment.

CONSENSUS COMMITTEE

If one accepts the proposition that the House, in all its variety and despite all its contradictions, represents the sense of the country, then Wilbur Mills and Ways and Means (they share common initials) is a consensus of the consensus. The fifteen Democrats and ten Republicans who make up the committee are literally a microcosm of the House, and it was designed that way. Members, at least on the Democratic side, are handpicked by party leaders in consultation with state delegations. Nominations are then sent to the party caucus that elects the committee's members.

As a result, the Democrats very broadly represent the nation's geographic areas and segments of party opinion. Oil has its say, and so do the Western timber and extractive industries. Several big city party organizations, Chicago, Cleveland, Detroit, and New York among them, have a claim to seats. There are no crusaders on Ways and Means; the leadership has always chosen good party men who have proved their willingness to compromise.

The Republicans, for their part, are not nearly so structured. Members are chosen by that party's House Committee on Committees, a large and broadly representative steering group whose only function is to make committee assignments and which is dominated by conservatives. With the possible exception of Barber B. Conable, Jr., of New York, who is relatively moderate, all the Ways and Means Republicans are conservatives themselves.

John F. Manley, a University of Wisconsin political scientist, writing in *The Politics of Finance,* a study of the committee, found that it is not the "autonomy" of Ways and Means that stands out but its "sensitivity to the House." The record shows, in fact, that the committee has taken a licking on major legislation only four times since Mills assumed the chairmanship in 1958. But on one of those four, a 1967 proposal to raise the debt limit, Mills implies he courted defeat. He deliberately brought the bill to the floor to demonstrate to Treasury Secretary Henry Fowler that the House was not ready for it.

It is not surprising that Ways and Means is not very strong on the philosophical aspects of taxation and revenue. Indeed, it is hard to tell what principles besides caution and consensus inform its efforts to shape key legislation. It is an action committee reflecting a Congress made up of politicians, not economists, social workers, or educators. Says Representative John Byrnes of Wisconsin, the ranking Republican on the committee: "You have to recognize that Mills is a political animal. He wants to make the Democrats shine a little brighter than the Administration."

RATIONALE

Mills, of course, does have stated reasons for the positions he takes. He opposes revenue sharing, for example, because he does not believe that state or local officials should have the privilege of spending money they do not have to raise, because Congress should not give out money without retaining control over what it is used for, and because he sees revenue sharing as a new, open-ended drain on the federal treasury that Congress might have to continually augment. Basically, the concept goes against his grain as a fiscal conservative.

A few weeks ago Mills agreed, at the President's personal request, to schedule hearings on revenue sharing after welfare reform, and ahead of health care. While he figures that the hearings will simply "justify killing it," his opposition has nothing to do with Nixon personally, with whom his relations are "not unfriendly." He claims he was "against revenue sharing long before Nixon became President," and the probability is that revenue sharing is no more popular in the House than in the committee.

Mills is much more sympathetic to Nixon's idea of bloc grants as a way of helping the cities. He tells mayors to forget no-strings revenue sharing and to concentrate on trying to get those grants—which are handled by other committees which deal with the subject matter involved, such as education, not by Ways and Means.

Some observers have attributed Mills's embrace of welfare reform to a calculated effort to enhance his standing with the urban wing of the Democratic Party, possibly out of ambition for a larger role in political affairs. A source close to Mills offers a more likely explanation, reflecting the committee's highly pragmatic approach to large issues: "Welfare just happened to be a problem his committee had to face up to. It falls in the lap of Ways and Means because it's all tied in with Social Security, aid to the blind, and things like that. The committee doesn't want to give revenue sharing to the states and still be confronted with this welfare problem. So they're taking the funds Nixon budgeted for revenue sharing and putting them into welfare."

This rationale fits Mills's own explanation of his surprise proposal for a $2 minimum wage by next February, a year earlier than the Democratic leaders of Congress recommended. The number of "working poor" who would come under his welfare plan would be sizable; a higher minimum wage would raise more of them out of the welfare category. "I don't see why some of the cost of helping the working poor shouldn't fall on the private sector."

Thus Mills is picking out what he likes about the Nixon program, shaping it his way, discarding the rest, or adding some of his own. For instance, he expects to start hearings in June that would produce a major health care program by this fall. But it will be neither Nixon's program nor the nationalized health insurance sought by labor and many Democrats. It will likely be something in between that preserves the concept of private health insurance.

POWER CENTER

If the committee wields its influence by maintaining a centrist position in the House, Mills wields his by doing the same in the committee. He is by no means an "iron chairman," as Carl Vinson or Mendel Rivers was in Armed Services. Mill's great success is his ability to forge consensus—and bend it a little his way. "Mills is like a river, wearing away stone," says Sam Gibbons (Democrat, Florida). "On the welfare bill, every suggestion by a member was aired. While Byrnes may occasionally get testy with other members or staff, Mills wears them out with patience."

"It's hard to tell whether Mills gets his way in the end, because you're never sure what it was when you started," says Charles A. Vanik (Democrat, Ohio), a liberal member of the committee. "His position just evolves." Adds New York's Conable: "Mills likes to shroud himself in mystery." A staff aide sees it a little differently: "People say he's inscrutable when he just hasn't made up his mind," he says.

The technique leaves all options open until the last and keeps members off balance. "I've never seen him lock a door yet," says Byrnes. He even avoids roll call votes in committee if he can, so that members can change their minds later. If one part of a bill gets sticky, he lets it drop; he likes to have as wide agreement as possible on any bill he takes to the floor. Usually a fairly clear consensus will emerge, though sometimes the "consensus" is what Mills finally decides it is. "We'll be talking at great length on some point," says Conable with some amusement, "when suddenly Mills will turn to the staff and say 'O.K., draft that up;' and we'll look at each other and say 'draft what up?' "

Last year he warned the Senate that if it raised the welfare base above $1,600 he would kill the bill, and nobody doubted that he could. This year the committee has had substantial disagreement over whether to pay part of a state's supplementary welfare payments—those in excess of the regular federal contribution. Mills, much more willing to compromise, raised the basic payment for a family of four from $2,200 (which now includes cash instead of food stamps) to $2,400 in lieu of supplementary payments.

In the end, the record shows, Mills is seldom at odds with the final committee decision. Of forty recorded votes in the committee since he became chairman, he has been with the losers only seven times.

No matter how democratic the committee may be, however, there is little doubt who wields the most influence. "Mills and Byrnes between them are 80 percent of the committee," says Conable, himself an influential member. The two are seldom far apart ideologically, and they are both masters of the complex tax, Social Security, and trade issues. They dominate by sheer knowledge and hard work. If only two members are left when everyone else has left a tedious hearing, it is most likely to be Mills and Byrnes.

Liberals feel strongly that the committee is a conservative drag on the House, partly because it grinds so slowly, waiting until opinion has already jelled on an issue before tackling it. "Ways and Means is 30 percent more conservative than the House," figures Vanik. Certainly conservative areas are more heavily represented than big cities. Since World War II, six or seven of the fifteen Democrats have come from the eleven Southern states; joined with the Republicans, they constitute a conservative majority. Says Vanik: "Mills can get a majority by starting with Byrnes and the other nine Republicans, who usually follow him faithfully. Then he needs only two of three Democrats and he's got it."

STILL CONSERVATIVE

While the committee's membership has turned over substantially (and gotten a little younger) in the past decade, not much else has changed. "The only difference in the make-up of the committee," says Manley, "is that the liberals have succeeded in getting a couple of 'shouters' on. But it's more a stylistic change than any shift in the conservative-liberal balance." In terms of "man-years," which takes account both of numbers of bodies and of years served, the South since 1947 has been represented by 118 "man-years"; the East 58; border states 32; the Midwest 46. So the South has twice as many man-years' service as any other section. And this roughly parallels the representation of the Democratic Party in the House.

As evidence of the committee's conservatism, liberals cite the long battle for medicare. During the early 1960s the Democratic leadership began granting Ways and Means seats only to those who favored medicare until by 1965 there was finally a thirteen-to-twelve majority for the program. And liberals claim that a tax reform package could have cleared Congress earlier than 1969; President Truman had proposed one in 1951. But the committee avoided the whole subject, partly out of fear that any reform would have to include cutting the oil depletion allowance, to which a substantial number of committee members were committed.

The committee is still highly protective of oil. For example, it has not touched intangible drilling benefits or deductions for foreign tax payments.

CRITICISM

Such lags in the legislative process lead to criticism that Mills follows rather than leads. Representative Richard Bolling (Democrat, Missouri), a member of the intellectually oriented Joint Economic Committee, charges Mills with "total lack of leadership" in letting the 10 percent surtax to pay for Vietnam languish a year while inflation built up.

Mills stoutly rebuts the charge that the committee is a Johnny-come-lately. There simply were not enough votes in the House to pass medicare before 1965, he says, and Manley's analysis supports him. Many times the chairman has taken bills to the floor "when early vote counts showed they might fail." Then he and the committee have swung into action to round up support. The tax surcharge, he feels, passed only after it was coupled with a spending limit and because debate had made clear that the dollar was in trouble. Tax reform became possible only after a "taxpayers' revolt."

Whether leading or following, the Ways and Means Committee is uniquely powerful. For one thing, its bills go before the House under a "closed rule" that permits no amendments. The closed rule is justified on the ground that revenue and social welfare are carefully balanced; opening them to amendments would tempt the House to add benefits without producing the revenue to pay for them. And trade bills would offer congressmen a field day in respect to quotas and tariffs benefitting constituents.

Another source of Ways and Means' power is the dual role of the Democratic majority. Ever since a House revolt in 1910 against the autocratic rule of Speaker Joseph Cannon, the Democratic contingent has been granted the power to make—or withold—committee assignments for other Democrats. There are good committees such as Appropriations and "dogs" such as District of Columbia. The committee's opportunities for horsetrading are therefore limitless.

Aside from this power over the House careers of other Democrats, the committee is in a position to do little favors in jiggering the tax code, an especial irony in the committee that has charge of tax reform.

Nearly every Congressman needs a special favor from Ways and Means from time to time. A leading corporation in a Congressional district may have a unique problem with the tax code; Ways and Means can fix it. Annually, on "members' day," the chairman goes around the table and lets each member offer two little private tax or tariff bills. If no other member, or the Treasury, objects, they go through. The bills are seldom of much import, but they can be terribly important to the beneficiary. The "Mayer Amendment" once saved MGM's Louis B. Mayer about $2 million in taxes on his retirement fund.

Of far greater moment, obviously, are the billions at stake in tax treatment of industries, which makes Ways and Means a focal point of intense industry pressure. The pressure pays off. The timber industry, for instance, pays an effective tax rate in the low 30s compared with 45 percent for manufacturing generally; Representative Al Ullman (Democrat, Oregon) helps see to that. Representative John C. Watts of Kentucky, top Democrat under Mills, looks after tobacco and liquor. Representative Martha Griffiths (Democrat, Michigan) fights automobile excise taxes. Farming and mineral resources generally get favored treatment because of the large number of Southern and Western members.

Still, the committee has been moving toward greater tax equity, especially with the reform bill of 1969. "I'm inclined to think it's harder for industries to come in and get a special tax break now," says a leading tax authority who deals frequently with the committee. Lobbyists generally fare better in the Senate, where any tax bill is freely open to amendments.

To a certain extent, the Ways and Means Committee is probably just facing up to the increased militancy of younger House members who have been bucking the "Establishment" generally, demanding that committees pay more attention to majority party policy. The committee felt, for instance, that it simply could not pass a tax reform bill without cutting the oil depletion allowance, which it finally did, from 27.5 percent to 22 percent.

TRADE POLICY

Likewise, in the trade fight last year, the committee was bending to House sentiment in passing textile and shoe quotas. Ways and Means has long been a free-trade outpost and, in his long reign as Speaker, Sam Rayburn would not assign anybody to the committee who was not a free trader. But increased foreign competition is making it harder for the committee to hold the line— especially when the Administration opens up the subject by proposing textile quotas. "The committee is still basically free trade," says Myer Rashish, a consultant to Congress on trade. "But it responds to the tone set by the Administration."

David Steinberg, executive director of the Committee for a National Trade Policy, sees free trade "in deep trouble in Congress as long as indecision continues at the White House." He feels that the Administration must come up with a comprehensive trade policy that includes adjustment assistance or tax or antitrust measures to help industries beset by imports.

Nor did Mills's private negotiations—outside normal diplomatic channels —with Japanese exporters solve very much. Byrnes, for one, does not think it solved anything at all.

Mills himself is under no illusions, and chances are the temporary detente with the Japanese, which is already beginning to fall apart in the fight over the return of Okinawa to Japan, was never considered by him as more than a way of putting off having to do anything about trade this year. At worst, Mills has bought some time.

He clearly sees a need for "some new approaches in the 1970s." It is increasingly difficult to bring up a trade bill "without getting it loaded down," he feels. He himself is still staunchly pro-trade. "I don't even like voluntary quotas if you can avoid them," he says.

NOT A CANDIDATE

The spotlight that has been focused on Mills and the committee with such intensity recently has helped spark a "Mills for President" boomlet, nurtured by Congressional friends. Other members of the committee do not take it seriously. They note that the traditionally publicity-shy Mills is "going public" a little more, even appearing on the Today show. But they think he is just mellowing and enjoying the attention for a change.

Mills, who will be sixty-two on May 24, says: "I'm not a candidate. I have no intention of becoming a candidate." He acknowledges that he could not turn down a nomination if it fell in his lap, "but that's such a remote possibility," he says, "I don't even consider it." The possibility is indeed remote. Mills's popularity is in the House, and political conventions are controlled by governors and local politicians. Whether Mills would like the presidency is hard to say, but he is realistic.

By and large, committee members are content with how Ways and Means operates, although liberal members, particularly, would like to see some changes. Uniquely, the committee has no subcommittees specializing in complex areas of its business, and its staff, though expert at drafting bills, is small and oriented away from thinking about policy. The staff has only one expert on trade, three on health and welfare. Thus, when a big bill comes up, the committee must rely heavily on experts in the Executive Branch, and on the knowledge and experience of Mills and Byrnes. Mills expects to be around quite a while, but Byrnes is "losing some sleep" over a decision whether to run again for Congress. Ways and Means is sometimes described as "the salt mine of Congress," because of the workload, and the last couple of years, says Byrnes, have been "hellish."

On problems of taxation, the committee is in better shape, or at least Mills is. He has first call on the twenty-man staff of the Joint Committee on Internal Revenue Taxation. Since the House is constitutionally the originator of revenue bills, the senate Finance Committee representatives are rather junior partners, and Mills dominates the joint committee.

Byrnes would like to see some investigating subcommittees set up to keep a closer watch on programs such as welfare and Social Security. But Mills feels that investigations are the province of the Government Operations Committee, and that Ways and Means, if anything, has too much to do already.

Although Congress is often pictured as powerless in confrontation with the executive branch, the fact is that the chairmen of powerful congressional committees often dominate administrative agencies over which they have jurisdiction. This is particularly true of the chairmen of appropriations committees and subcommittees, for they are able to wield far more influence over the bureaucracy because of their control of the purse strings than the chairmen of other committees. The appropriations committees have a direct weapon—money—that they can wield against administrative adversaries. And, the chairmen of all committees have seniority that often exceeds that of the bureaucrats with whom they are dealing. The secretaries and assistant secretaries of executive departments are political appointments who rarely stay in government more than two years, whereas powerful congressmen have been around for one or more decades. This gives the congressmen expertise that the political levels of the bureaucracy often lack. Political appointees in the bureaucracy must rely upon their professional staff in order to match the expertise of senior congressmen. The power of the chairmen of the appropriations committees often leads them to interfere directly in administrative operations. They become in effect part of the bureaucracy, often dominating it and determining what programs it will implement. The constant interaction between committee chairmen and agencies results in "government without passing laws," to use the phrase of Michael W. Kirst. (See Michael W. Kirst, *Government Without Passing Laws,* Capitol Hill: University of North Carolina Press, 1969.) The following selection deals with this process of legislative influence, and describes how one senior Southern congressman has established himself as the "permanent secretary of agriculture."

55
Nick Kotz

JAMIE WHITTEN, PERMANENT SECRETARY OF AGRICULTURE

With the sensitive instincts of a successful career bureaucrat, Dr. George Irving scanned the list of states scheduled for the National Nutrition Survey, which was to measure the extent of hunger in America. Halfway down the column his glance froze, and he quickly dialed Congressman Jamie Whitten, the man known in Washington as the "permanent secretary of agriculture."

"Mr. Chairman, they've got Mississippi on that malnutrition study list, and I thought you's want to know about it," dutifully reported Irving, Administrator of the Agriculture Department's Agricultural Research Service.

For the better part of eighteen years as chairman of the House Appropriations Subcommittee on Agriculture, dapper Jamie L. Whitten has held an iron hand over the budget of the Department of Agriculture (USDA). The entire 107,000-man department is tuned in to the Mississippi legislator's every whim.

"George, we're not going to have another smear campaign against Mississippi, are we?" declared Whitten to his informant. "You boys should be thinking about a *national* survey—and do some studies in Watts and Hough and Harlem!"

From Nick Kotz, *Let Them Eat Promises: The Politics of Hunger in America.* © 1969 by Nick Kotz. Published by Prentice-Hall, Inc., Englewood Cliffs, New Jersey.

Dr. Irving alerted the government's food aid network. "Mr. Whitten wants Mississippi taken off that list," he told Department of Agriculture food administrator Rodney Leonard.

Leonard, in turn, called Dr. George Silver, a Deputy Assistant Secretary of Health, Education, and Welfare, who was responsible for the joint USDA-HEW malnutrition survey.

"Jamie Whitten's found out Mississippi is on the list and is raising hell. I think we'd better drop it," Leonard said.

Silver, recalling HEW Secretary Wilbur Cohen's order to "avoid unnecessary political friction" in choosing the sample states for the hunger survey, called Dr. Arnold Schaefer, the project chief.

"Mississippi's out—politics!" Silver said curtly.

Back at the Department of Agriculture, food administrator Leonard snapped at Jamie Whitten's informant, "You couldn't have killed the project any better if you had planned it!"

Thus, in August, 1967, the Johnson Administration's first meaningful attempt to ascertain the facts about hunger in Mississippi was stopped cold by an executive department's fear of one congressman. This kind of bureaucratic-congressional maneuvering, exercised between the lines of the law, is little understood, seldom given public scrutiny, and far too infrequently challenged. In the quiet process of hidden power, a bureaucrat in the Agriculture Department reacts more quickly to a raised eyebow from Jamie Whitten than to a direct order from the Secretary himself. Time after time, a few words from Jamie Whitten can harden into gospel at the Department of Agriculture. Indeed, a casual Whitten statement may be so magnified, as it is whispered from official to offical, that the response is more subservient than even the Congressman had in mind.

The stocky, 59-year-old Congressman is not shy about his meteoric rise from a country store in Tallahatchie County to a key position in the nation's capital. And his record is impressive—trial lawyer and state legislator at 21, district attorney for five counties at 23, U.S. Congressman at 31 (in 1941), and chairman of an appropriations subcommittee at 36. His steely self-confidence, studied informality, and carefully conservative clothes suggest anything but the stereotype of country-lawyer-come-to-Washington. Only the beginning of a paunch detracts from a physical sense of strength and energy that radiates from Jamie Whitten.

For all his dynamic presence, Whitten has a way of confounding a listener —or potential critic—with silky Southern rhetoric. It is a test of mental agility to remember the original course of a conversation, as one high USDA official noted: "When you check on things with him, Whitten can go all around the barn with you. Often-times you don't fully understand what he meant. So you latch onto the most obvious point you can find and act on that."

With his implicit power, Whitten doesn't *have* to threaten or be specific. In fact, as George Irving pointed out about his conversation with the Congressman that led to dropping Mississippi from the national hunger survey, "He wasn't saying 'don't go to Mississippi,' he was just suggesting that we think about other places."

Bureaucratic officials who are familiar with Whitten's oblique way of expressing his ideas know also that the Mississippian can rattle off complicated economic statistics and arguments with precise logic and organized thought.

Whitten legally holds the power of the purse, and he exercises it shrewdly. His appropriations subcommittee doles out funds for every item in the Agriculture Department's $7 billion budget, and it does not take long for Washington bureaucrats to realize that the chairman's wrath can destroy precious projects and throw hundreds of people out of jobs.

"He's got the most phenomenal information and total recall," one Agriculture offical says of Whitten. "Once you full understand his do's and don't's and establish rapport with him, life is a whole lot easier!"

Jamie Whitten's considerable power is enhanced by his scholarship. He is a conscientious student of every line of the Agriculture budget, and his hawk's-eye is legendary among Department officials. They, in turn, anticipate his scrutiny by checking planned moves with him, thus extending to him a virtual veto on the most minute details. "A suggestion, that's all you have to have in this business," admitted Rodney Leonard.

The key to this phenomenal power—which goes beyond that of budget control—lies in Whitten's network of informants within the Department, and his skill directing their activities and operations. Executive branch officials learn to protect their own jobs, adjusting their loyalties to the legislative branch in a way the Founding Fathers may not have envisioned when they divised their splendid system of checks and balances. Bureaucratic allies of a particular congressman may be able to inject that congressman's political views (or their own) into laws or programs sponsored by the Administration without the consent, or even the knowledge, of the Department head. Secretaries of Agriculture come and go, but Jamie Whitten remains, a product of Mississippi's political oligarchy and the seniority system in Congress.

In theory, an appropriations subcommittee only considers requests for funds to finance programs already approved by Congress. Thus, Whitten shares some power with Bob Poage (D-Tex.), chairman of the House Agriculture Committee. In actuality, a skillful chairman such as Whitten can control policy, alter the original authorizing legislation, and wind up virtually controlling the administration of a department.

In addition to Chairman Whitten, the Agriculture Appropriations Subcommittee has seven members: Democrats William H. Natcher of Kentucky, W. R. Hull, Jr., of Missouri, George Shipley of Illinois, and Frank Evans of Colorado, and Republicans Odin Langen of Minnesota, Robert H. Michel of Illinois, and Jack Edwards of Alabama. Because a majority of these members share Whitten's outlook on agriculture and his arch-conservative view of social action, the chairman's will becomes the subcommittee's will. As chairman, he also has a hold over staff appointments.

Much of Whitten's power derives from the system within the House of

Representatives. Once a subcommittee makes a decision, the full House Appropriations Committee almost always backs it up. This is particularly true with agriculture appropriations, because House Appropriations Chairman George Mahon (D-Tex.) shares Whitten's views on farm policy, welfare spending, and racial issues. For years, Whitten has been in absolute control of all bills before his subcommittee, from the first markup session to the final House vote. "The lines in my face would be deeper except for you" Mahon inscribed on his own portrait in the Mississippian's office.

The House at large rarely has challenged Agriculture budgets because most non-farmbloc members find the subject too complex or dull and rarely take the trouble to inform themselves about it. If some members, or the public, are roused to the point where a challenge develops, the House's committee chairmen generally pull together to defeat the move. Committee members follow to ensure that they will have the chairman's support for their own pet bills—and to keep sacrosanct the whole system of mutual support and protection.

If a challenge happens to get out of hand, the first commandment of a subcommittee chairman is "Never let yourself in for a battle on the House floor if there is any chance for defeat." Part of the power of chairman stems from his apparent invincibility—and the image must be preserved! Therefore, Whitten went along with the Nixon Administration's full budget request for food aid in 1969, knowing there was sufficient pressure for a much bigger appropriation. Whitten responded here only to the politics of the issue, not the substance, for he still complained to Senator George McGovern that hunger was not a problem, that "Nigras won't work" if you give them free food, and that McGovern was promoting revolution by continuing to seek free food stamps for the poorest Americans.

Where agriculture legislation is concerned, Whitten must share power in some measure with Senator Spessard Holland, a Florida Democrat who chairs the Senate Appropriations Subcommittee on Agriculture. Holland is a blunt man who insists that Section 32 funds—food dollars from customs receipts—should be held in reserve to be used at the proper time to boost prices for his state's citrus, vegetable, and beef industries. When Whitten and Holland act in unison—as they often do—the results are predictable. After the School Lunch Act was liberalized in 1964, they managed to refuse funding free school lunches for more than two years. The Johnson administration had sought only $2–3 million to help some of the estimated 5 million poor children who got no benefits from the lunch program, but all the funds were held back in committee until Senator Philip Hart (D-Mich.) threatened to take the fight to the floor.

Jamie Whitten's power is greater than Holland's, however, not only because appropriations usually originate in the House, but also because in the smaller body of the Senate there is less hesitation to overturn subcommittee decisions than in the tradition-bound House of Representatives. The House system, therefore, assures more *inherent* power for its subcommittee chairmen, and Jamie Whitten has been vigorous and skillful in pursuing it.

GETTING ALONG WITH WHITTEN

Even the Secretary himself feels he must bend to the power of the "permanent secretary." When a delegation headed by Richard Boone of the Citizens' Crusade Against Poverty had asked Orville Freeman to provide free stamps and commodities to help the hungry in Mississippi, the Secretary told them: "I've got to get along with two people in Washington-the President and Jamie Whitten. How can you help me with Whitten?"

Just back from a study of hunger in Mississippi in April, 1967, Dr. Robert Coles and three other doctors also found out about Whitten's influence when they appealed to Orville Freeman. They walked into the Secretary's office feeling that they would be welcomed as helpful, authoritative reporters of the facts, and they left feeling that they had been tagged as troublemakers.

"We were told that we and all the hungry children we had examined and all the other hungry Americans would have to reckon with Mr. Jamie L. Whitten, as indeed must the Secretary of Agriculture, whose funds come to him through the kindness of the same Mr. Whitten. We were told of the problems that the Agriculture Department has with Congress, and we left feeling we ought to weigh those problems as somehow of the same order as the problems we had met in the South—and that we know from our work elsewhere existed all over the country," recalled Coles.

Whitten's power goes beyond the Secretary to the Presidency itself. In the last year of his Administration, President Johnson steadily refused to adopt proposals for broadened food aid that were drafted within his Administration. Johnson was then trying to get his income surtax bill through the Congress, and he needed the support of Whitten and the rest of the small group of Southern hierarchs. Johnson declined to risk possible loss of critical votes on the war- and inflation-related surtax.

When Senator Jacob Javits (R-N.Y.) asked Agriculture Secretary Freeman, "What are you afraid of in Mississippi?" (at a July, 1967, hearing on hunger in Mississippi), he wanted to know why Freeman would not modify the food program to reach more of the hungry in Mississippi and elsewhere. The only response he got was ex-marine Freeman's outthrust jaw and a growl that he was not afraid of anyone and would not be intimidated.

Nevertheless, faced with Jamie Whitten's power over his department, and fed information by a Whitten-conscious bureaucracy, Freeman had failed for two years to take measures to feed more of the hungry poor in America. Moreover, the Secretary had subbornly refused to acknowledge the chasm between his department's efforts and the real needs of the hungry.

From Freeman on down, every Agriculture Department official knew that hunger spelled "hound dog" to Jamie Whitten.

"You've got to understand how Jamie feels about 'hound dog' projects," a career official explained. (In Southern country jargon, a "hound dog" is always hanging around, useless, waiting to be thrown scraps.) Years before, the chairman had killed a small pilot project to teach unemployed Southern

Negroes how to drive tractors. "Now, that's a 'hound dog' project, and I don't want to see any more of them," he had said.

Whitten's opposition to any program resembling social welfare—or aid to Negroes—contributed to the failure of War on Poverty programs for rural America. When President Johnson signed an executive order, giving the Agriculture Department responsibility for coordinating the rural war on poverty, Secretary Freeman created a Rural Community Development Service (RCDS) to give the Department a focal point for helping the poor. It was designed to coordinate programs meeting all the needs of the rural poor—housing, education, water, food—not only within the Agriculture Department, but throughout the federal government.

Within a year, the Rural Community Development Service was dead. "Whitten thought the Service smacked of social experimentation and civil rights," a Department of Agriculture official said. In addition, Whitten's brother-in-law, one of many cronies who have filled Agriculture jobs over the years, had clashed with Robert G. Lewis, the idealistic Wisconsin progressive who headed the program. Whitten simply cut off the funds and pigeonholed the coordinating powers of RCDS by placing the responsibility with the docile, conservative Farmers Home Administration. Freeman never fought the issue. There were too many other matters, other appropriations, that were more important to him, so the embryonic effort to coordinate rural poverty programs through the Department of Agriculture ended as little more than a passing idea.

(By assigning the broad rural poverty responsibility to the Department of Agriculture, President Johnson, like President Nixon after him, indicated either a great naïveté about the Department or a lack of seriousness in his proposals. The four congressional committees with which Agriculture must deal undoubtedly are the least receptive of any in Congress to attempts to provide meaningful help to the hard-core rural poor.)

Jamie Whitten has wielded that kind of influence since the mid-1940's, when he killed an emerging Agriculture study that tried to anticipate the social and economic problems of Negro GI's returning from World War II to the feudal cotton South. At that time, the Mississippi Congressman was the youngest chairman of an appropriations subcommittee. By opposing all studies exploring the effects of a changing agriculture upon people, Whitten helped ensure that Agriculture's farm policy would never include serious consideration of the effects of its programs on sharecroppers or farm workers. Whitten and the other powerful Southern congressmen who share his views ensure that the Department would focus only on the cotton planter and his crop. As a result, farm policies that have consistently ignored their toll on millions of black poor have contributed to a rural-urban migration, to a civil rights revolution, and to the ruin of many Americans.

There is no doubt as to the motives of Whitten and the other congressmen who run the Agriculture Department. Testifying on the proposed food stamp law before the Senate Agriculture Committee in 1964, one Department official bodly suggested that it would not help those with little or no income. Committee Chairman Allen J. Ellender (D-La.) indignantly dismissed this complaint against the bill, revealing clearly his own legislative intent.

"I know that in my state we had a number of fisherman who were unable to catch fish," retorted Ellender. "Do you expect the government, because they cannot catch fish, to feed them until the fish are there? In other words, this food stamp program is not to be considered a program just simply to feed people because they cannot get work. This is not what it is supposed to be."

SURPLUS SERFS

What the food stamp program was "supposed to be" was a substitute for a free commodity program that had outlived its usefulness—to Southern plantation owners. Surplus commodities—barely enough to live on—were distributed in the winter when work ceased on the Mississippi plantation of Senator James Eastland (D-Miss.) and on the huge Texas ranches. In the spring, when the $3-a-day planting jobs opened up, the food aid ended. The federal government eased the planter's responsibility by keeping his workers alive during the winter, then permitted the counties that administered the program to withdraw that meager support during planting season—forcing the workers to accept near-starvation wages for survival. When the rural serfs were no longer needed, having been slowly replaced by machines, even that support vanished as the government stopped free commodities in favor of food stamps, which the poorest rural people could not afford. As counties throughout the nation changed from commodities to food stamps, participation fell off by 40 per cent; more than 1 million persons, including 100,000 in Mississippi, were forced to drop out of the food program. Whispers of "planned starvation" emerged from the economic crisis of 1967, when the combination of production cutbacks in cotton, automated machinery, and the end of free commodities left the Deep South with thousands of blacks who were unneeded—and hungry. The decisions of the white supremacists in Congress, supported by the subservient Department of Agriculture, contributed to that result.

Whitten's decisions are not always understood by the uninitiated. With his wily ability to juggle figures and cloud ideas, Whitten convinces officials unfamiliar with his technique (and lacking intimate knowledge of the facts) that he is quite a reasonable man—especially when the conversation turns to hunger and the food programs. As he tells it, he was a pioneer on the nutrition issue.

In 1950, he fought for funds for a Department of Agriculture cookbook, and he warned the House it had better concern itself with human as well as animal health. To this day, Whitten insists that the Agriculture Department keep the book in print; he sends a free copy to newlyweds in his district.

The subcommittee chairman also denies that he paralyzed Freeman on the hunger issue: "I *helped* the Secretary by making two points with him,"

Whitten insists. "I told him he had to charge people what they were accustomed to paying for food stamps because that's what the law says. And I pointed out to him that the law forbids selling food stamps and distributing commodities in the same counties." By making these two helpful points, Whitten blocked the most feasible emergency measures.

"Why, I gave him more money for those food programs than he could spend!" said Whitten.

Actually, the hopelessly inadequate $45 million for food programs Whitten "gave" to Freeman was fought, bought, and paid for by the Administration and congressional liberals; this was what was left after Whitten and Holland whittled down the original $100 million, three-year authorization won by liberals on the House floor.

Whitten's explanations of food programs may have appeared perfectly reasonable to Freeman, Sargent Shriver, and many members of Congress, but their total impact was to stop any reform that would get food to the hungry. His own strongly held view is that the food programs should serve the farm programs, not vice versa, and his actions over the years have halted any kind of aid the Agriculture Department might have directed toward the poor. In the early 1960's, when the Kennedy Administration was momentarily concerned for the poor of Appalachia, Agriculture found a way to provide housing grants to aid the hardest-core poor; but once Whitten discovered the grant program in operation, he killed all further appropriations for it.

A few years later, a new cotton program provided advance payments to cotton farmers for withdrawing some of their acreage from production. Sharecroppers, who provided most of the cotton labor force, were supposed to receive their "share" of government payments for idle land. With Whitten's inspiration or blessing, Agriculture adopted a regulation permitting the plantation owner to deduct from the sharecropper's government payments the amount he claimed was owed for the sharecropper's rent, farming expenses, etc. Under the feudal system of the plantation, however, the sharecropper *never* had any legal guarantee that he would receive his fair share of profit for the crop he produced. Blacks who declined to turn over their checks were kicked off hundreds of plantations. The Agriculture Department did not halt the practice.

One of Whitten's sharecropper constituents, trying desperately to find food for her family, gave her own intuitive view of her congressman's attitudes: "He's probably with the bossman's side, don't you know. He's with them. No one's with us but ourselves, and no matter how many of us there are, we don't have what they have."

WINE FOR MISSISSIPPI

Although much of the legislation he favors has enriched American agricultural business with government funds, Whitten's stock answer to any proposed liberalization of the Department of Agriculture food programs is that they are "food programs, not welfare programs." He is adamant about suggestions that food programs be moved to the more liberal Department of Health, Education, and Welfare, "Who'll see to it that [funds for food] don't go for frivolity and wine?" he asks.

Whitten's views on welfare, so strongly felt through the Department of Agriculture are shared by many Americans. Yet when viewed against the background of Tallahatchie County and its social history, these views, and their interpretations through Agriculture programs, take on a different meaning. Since hunger means poverty, and poverty in Mississippi usually means black, any expanded aid to the hungry means one more threat to the socioeconomic order in which the black worker has always been held in absolute dependency upon crumbs from the plantation owner.

The 100,000 or more black Mississippi farm workers who suddenly found themselves with nothing to hold onto in the winter of 1967 were little concerned with frivolity and wine. They had lost their sole supply of food, as Mississippi counties switched over from the inadequate but free surplus commodities to a food stamp program the poor could not afford. "No work, no money, and now, no food," was their outcry, and they desperately sought a reduction in the price of stamps at the very moment when Jamie Whitten was starting his annual review of the Department of Agriculture's budget, with its accompanying discourses on the nature of the poor man. He had heard, the chairman said, that "organized groups" sought to make food stamps free to the poor.

"This is one of the things you always run into," he said to Secretary Freeman. "You make stamps available at 30 percent discount; then they want them at 50, then 75. Now, I have heard reports that some of the organized minority groups are insisting they be provided free of charge. When you start giving people something for nothing, just giving them all they want for nothing, I wonder if you don't destroy character more than you might improve nutrition. I think more and more American people are coming to that conclusion."

They built a lot of character in Mississippi that winter, where the disruption caused by the abrupt changeover to food stamps contributed to the kind of wholesale distitution not seen in this country since the Great Depression.

But the chairman did not seem to think his black constituents were learning the character lesson well enough when it came to the school lunch and new school breakfast programs. Out of work and out of money, few Mississippi Negroes could afford to give their children 25 cents a day for a school lunch, and few schools provided the free lunches that the law technically required for the poor. Agriculture officials virtually begged that the special school lunch assistance budget be raised from $2 million to $10 million annually to give meals to an added 360,000 children in poor areas. Whitten expressed concern only about the impact of civil rights sanctions as he slashed the request by two-thirds.

When another project—a requested million dollars for a pilot school breakfast program to help the neediest youngsters—came up, Whitten's patience wore thin. "Do you contemplate having a pilot dinner program—evening meals—called supper where I grew up?" Whitten asked sarcastically.

When Agriculture Department officials explained that "a hungry child in the morning is not able to take full advantage of the schooling that is offered," Whitten wanted to know why the government should be supplying what the family should have supplied before the child left home.

"We all recognize that the type of home from which some children come effects them in many, many ways, but there is a problem always as to whether the federal government should start doing everything for the citizens. You may end up with a certain class of people doing nothing to help themselves. To strike a happy medium is always a real problem."

In this case, Whitten struck it by cutting all $6.5 million requested for breakfast funds from the budget.

Each time a group of doctors, team of reporters, or other investigators produced firsthand reports of hunger in the South, Whitten launched his own "investigation" and announced that parental neglect is largely responsible for any problems. In 1968, when the drive for a bigger food program began to gether steam nationally, Whitten sent out the FBI to disprove the evidence of the problem. The FBI men, who are assigned to the House Appropriations Committee, in effect intimidated people who had provided evidence of hunger.

When a private group investigating hunger, the Citizens' Board of Inquiry, reported after a lengthy investigation that "we have found concrete evidence of chronic hunger and malnutrition in every part of the United States where we have held hearings or conducted hearings," even the Pentagon rallied to the defense of Jamie Whitten's system. The Pentagon-financed Institute for Defense Analyses published an attack on the book *Hunger* USA,* which contained the Board of Inquiry report. The author of the Defense document, Dr. Herbert Pollack, took the position that ignorance was at the root of any hunger problems in the United States—the same position taken by Whitten and his congressional allies.

The Mississippi Congressman demands that the poor, if they are to get any benefits, must prove they are hungry on a case-by-case basis. "The doctors have not submitted any names," he wrote one concerned Northern lady, assuring her that he would be "most sympathetic and helpful in trying to work this matter out."

Time after time, Whitten has requested names and addresses of the poor who complain of ill-treatment in his home state. Yet in Jamie Whitten's home county, the thought of having their names known strikes terror among those who have had dealings with the local officials.

A news team from television's Public Broadcast Laboratory (PBL), inter-

---

*Citizen's Board of Inquiry. *Hunger* USA (Boston: Beacon Press, 1968.)

viewing a black housewife in Whitten's home town of Charleston, felt the danger involved in "naming names." As Mrs. Metcalf began to explain why the food stamp and school lunch programs were not helping her family, a task force of sedans and panel trucks began to cruise back and forth on the U.S. highway about 50 yards from her plantation shack. Suddenly the trucks lunged off the highway into the shack's front yard, surrounding the television crew's two station wagons. A rifle or shotgun was mounted in the rear window of each truck.

"You're trespassing. Git!" growled the plantation manager as he pushed his way past the TV reporter and ordered Mrs. Metcalf to get outside the shack if she knew what was good for her.

"You were trespassing when you crossed the Mississippi state line," shouted Deputy Sheriff Buck Shaw as he ordered the PBL crew to clear out.

In an attempt to ensure Mrs. Metcalf's safety from the local "law," the reporter phoned Congressman Whitten in Washington.

"You remember when Martin Luther King went through my town!" the Congressman answered. "You read the *Wall Street Journal?* It said that he went through there and everybody turned out to look at him. And as soon as he left, they just turned over and went back to sleep. I just know, I live down there and I know. Good God, Chicago, Washington, Detroit. Every one of them would give any amount of money if they could go to sleep feeling as safe —both races—as my folks will!"

It wasn't so peaceful about three o'clock that afternoon with those hard-eyed men threatening Mrs. Metcalf, the reporter explained.

"I suspect Deputy Shaw's like I am," Whitten snapped. "They recognized when you crossed that state line you had no good intention in your mind. I'm no kingfish. I just know my people and my people get along. Unfortunately, you folks and the folks up here don't know how to get along. I bet you money if I ran tomorrow, and nobody voted except the colored people, I'd get the majority. I grew up where five or six of my closest neighbors were Negroes. We played together as kids. We swapped vegetables. Why, I grew up hugging my Momma, and my Momma hugging them."

There were as many Negroes as whites at his father's funeral, Whitten asserts—and he keeps on his desk a yellowed 1936 newspaper editorial that praised District Attorney Jamie Whitten for successfully prosecuting the white man who burned some Mississippi Negroes to death.

Against Whitten's statements about how he is respected by Negroes and would get their vote, about how close his relationship and understanding with Negroes has been, about how quiet and peaceful life is in Charleston, another point of view appeared, as one of his black constituents spoke on the same subject—rambling much as Jamie Whitten does. An eloquent, middle-aged woman told Dr. Robert Coles about the plantation owner for whom her husband works, about his wife, about food, and about life in America:

He [the plantation owner] doesn't want us trying to vote and like that—and first I'd like to feed my kids, before I go trying to vote.

His wife—the boss man's—she'll come over here sometimes and give me some extra grits and once or twice in the year some good bacon. She tells me we get along fine down here and I says "yes" to her. What else would I be saying, I ask you?

But it's no good. The kids aren't eating enough, and you'd have to be wrong in the head, pure crazy to say they are. Sometimes we talk of leaving; but you know it's just no good up there either, we hear. They eat better, but they have bad things up there I hear, rats as big as raccoons I hear, and they bit my sister's kid real bad.

It's no kind of country to be proud of, with all this going on—the colored people still having it so bad, and the kids being sick and there's nothing you can do about it.*

AFFECTION, NOT CASH

Whitten's affection for black constituents like this woman does not extend to federal measures to assist their lot in life. Of the 24,081 residents of Tallahatchie County, 18,000 have family incomes less than $3,000 a year, and 15,197 make less than $2,000. Of these thousands legally defined as poor, only 2,367 qualify for public assistance, and 6,710 receive food stamps. Only a few blocks from Whitten's own white frame home, Negroes live in shacks without toilets, running water, electricity—or food.

Whitten and his fellow white Mississippians point with great pride to the economic progress their state has made in recent years. Improved farming methods, conversion of marginal cropland to timber and other uses, and a strong soil bank program have greatly enriched the commercial farmer in Mississippi. Other government programs, including state tax inducements, have promoted wide industrialization, and rural white workers have found a new affluence in the hundreds of factories and small shops that have sprung up.

But the new farming has eliminated thousands of jobs for Negro plantation workers while the segregated social system denies them factory jobs. The able-bodied usually head north, leaving the very young, the very old, and the unskilled to cope with "progress." The rural black does not share in the new prosperity of Mississippi, and some Negroes are worse off than at any time since the Depression. Indeed, in many parts of the Deep South the black man is literally being starved out by the new prosperity.

Perhaps the white Southern politician is no more to blame than are whites anywhere. But the white in the South could not afford to see the truth of the Negro's suffering, because to feel that truth would have shattered a whole way of life.

---

*Robert Coles and Harry Hughe, "We Need Help," *New Republic* March 8, 1969.

Jamie Whitten truly believes in his own fairness, his idea of good works, and the imagined affection he receives from Negroes back home. For fifty-nine years, he has anesthetized his soul to the human misery and indignity only a few yards from his own home and has refused to believe that the responsibility for that indignity lies on his white shoulders. His belief in the basic laziness, indifference, and unworthiness of the black poor is as strong as his belief in the virtues of a way of life that for three centuries has denied these same black poor any avenues of pursuing ambition, self-respect, or a better future for their children.

That Jamie Whitten should suffer from blindness to human need is one thing. But that he can use this blindness as an excuse to limit the destiny of millions of Americans is another matter, one which should concern anyone who believes in the basic strengths of this country's constitutional guarantees. The checks and balances of a reasonable democratic republic have gone completely awry when a hugh bureaucracy and the top officals of an Administration base their actions concerning deepest himan need on their fearful perception of what one rather limited man seems to want.

The system of seniority and temerity that gives a man such as Jamie Whitten such awesome power must come under more serious public scrutiny if the American system of government is ever to establish itself on the basis of moral concern about the individual human being.

THE SENATE: FOLKWAYS AND FOLK WISDOM

Reading *The Federalist,* students can see that the framers of the Constitution expected the Senate to be the most important conservative force in our government. To some extent the Seventeenth Amendment, which provided for the popular election of Senators, modified conservative expectations, but the long term of office, one of the most important provisions designed to ensure conservatism in this branch of the government, remains. Proportionately, of course, the less populous states are better represented in the Senate than in the House. This fact, combined with the seniority system, reliance on committees and Southern solidarity renders the Senate, in the words of one commentator, an "old Southern home." Its essential conservatism remains, and it is still an institution in which state and regional influence is dominant. The conservatism of the Senate is reflected in what Donald R. Matthews has called "the folkways of the Senate," informal patterns of behavior resulting from a lack of party organization and formal structure. (See Donald R. Matthews, *U.S. Senators and Their World,* Chapel Hill: University of North Carolina Press, 1960, chapter 5.) These "folkways" help to minimize conflict and make the Senate a viable decision-making body.

The folkways of the Senate described by Donald R. Matthews have been used to buttress the idea that the Senate is controlled by those who respect its procedurals norms. William S. White in his influential book *Citadel: The Story of the U.S. Senate* (New York: Harper & Row, 1956) suggested that the Senate is run by an "inner club," composed of those Senators who venerate the Senate as an institution and adhere to its folkways. Membership in the inner club is not confined, according to White, to those who have a particular political philosophy. Both liberals and conservatives are eligible to join. However, the Senate's rules and customs support a slow, deliberative legislative process dominated by senior members of powerful committees. The Cloture Rule (Rule 22) requires a two-thirds majority vote to cut off debate, thereby enabling a minority of Senators to filibuster in order to prevent legislation desired by the majority. Although filibusters are used by liberals as well as conservatives, the Cloture Rule has tended to defeat more liberal than conservative legislation. In 1963 former Senators Clark and Douglas, joined by other colleagues, charged that the Senate was run by an "establishment," which they described as a small minority of Southern conservative Democrats and conservative Republicans from other parts of the country. (See *The Congressional Record,* February 19, 20, 21, and 25, 1963.) Clark charged that the Senate establishment controlled the legislative process by determining who would be appointed to particular committees. In this way the establishment could give whatever cast it wanted to the committees, thereby controlling their legislative recommendations.

Nelson W. Polsby in the following selection discusses the concept of the "inner club," and suggests that although it might once have existed (which he doubts) it certainly no longer exists.

56
Nelson W. Polsby

GOODBYE TO THE INNER CLUB

At the opening of the 91st Congress in January [1969], Senator Edward M. Kennedy (D-Mass.) challenged Senator Russell Long (D-La.) for the position of Senate Democratic Whip. Long, chairman of the powerful Finance Committee and a Senator for twenty years, had held the Whip post nearly as long as Kennedy had been in the Senate.

The position is elective, by secret ballot in the caucus of Democratic Senators at the opening of each Congress, and, as readers of newspapers could hardly avoid noticing, Kennedy won handily.

A few days later, Senator Robert P. Griffin (R-Mich.) left the Committee on Labor and Public Welfare for an opening on the relatively low-ranked Committee of Government Operations, and Senator Eugene F. McCarthy

From Nelson W. Polsby, "Goodby to the Inner Club," *The Washington Monthly* (August 1969), pp. 30–34. Reprinted by permission.

(D-Minn.) voluntarily left the prestigious Foreign Relations Committee to take up a place on the same committee. His public explanation of the move consisted of a Delphic quote from Marshall McLuhan: "Operations is policy." When Senator Lee Metcalf (D-Mont.) removed himself from the Finance Committee that same week, in order to stay in Government Operations, he explained that the Finance Committee had become "just a rubber stamp for the House Ways and Means Committee. No matter what the Finance Committee or the Senate does," he said, "when we come back from conferences with the House we have given in to Wilbur Mills. He runs both committees." In part, Metcalf was protesting a decision of the Democratic Steering Committee, which had forced him to reduce his committee responsibilities from three to two (while permitting more senior Senators to hold three assignments). The Steering Committee also reduced the size of the Appropriations and Foreign Relations Committees in a move widely interpreted as an attempt to staunch the flow of power from senior to junior Senators who might otherwise have been able to go a long way toward out-voting the chairmen of these two committees.

To a generation of followers of the U.S. Senate, these were peculiar goings-on. Whoever heard of Senators leaving important committees to go on unimportant ones—voluntarily? Or committee chairmen worried about uprisings of the peasants? Or an agreeable young man of negligible accomplishments, one eye cocked on the Presidency, knocking off a senior Southern chairman running for a job tending the inner gears of the institution?

If this sort of thing can happen in broad daylight these days on Capitol Hill, there must be something seriously the matter with the ideas that have dominated conversation about the Senate for the last 15 years. For at least since the publication of William S. White's *Citadel: The Story of the U.S. Senate* (1956), the common assumption has been that the Senate has been run by an "inner club" of "Senate types." "The Senate type," White wrote, "is, speaking broadly, a man for whom the Institution is a career in itself, a life in itself, and an end in itself." Although others might belong to the inner club, "At the core of the Inner Club stand the Southerners, who with rare exceptions automatically assume membership almost with the taking of the oath of office."

"The Senate type," White continued, "makes the Institution his home in an almost literal sense, and certainly in a deeply emotional sense. His head swims with its history, its lore. . . . To him, precedent has an almost mystical meaning. . . . His concern for the preservation of Senate tradition is so great that he distrusts anything out of the ordinary. . . . As the Southern members of the Inner Club make the ultimate decisions as to what is proper in point of manner—these decisions then infallibly pervading the Outer Club—so the whole generality of the Inner Club makes the decisions as to what *in general* is proper in the Institution and what *in general* its conclusions should be on high issues."

White conceded, of course, that the Senate had its "public men," who made their way by inflaming or instructing public opinion. But he argued that it was not these grasshoppers but rather the ants of the Inner Club who got their way in the decision-making of the Senate.

Since the publication of *Citadel*, commentators on Senate affairs have routinely alluded to the Inner Club as though to something as palpable as an office building. No senatorial biography—or obituary—is now complete without solemn consideration of whether the subject was in or out. Discussions of senatorial business can hardly compete with dissections of the Inner Club's informal rules, tapping ceremonies, secret handshakes, and other signs and stigmata by which members are recognized. One writer, Clayton Fritchey in *Harper's*, took the further step—in 1967—of actually naming names.

By far the most zealous promoter of the whole idea was someone whose opinion on the matter must be given some weight. This is the way Joseph S. Clark described a lunch that Majority Leader Lyndon B. Johnson gave for Clark's "class" of freshman Democrats in 1957:

> As we sat down to our steaks at the long table in the office of Felton M. (Skeeter) Johnston, Secretary of the Senate, . . . we found at our places copies of *Citadel: The Story of the U.S. Senate*, autographed "with all good wishes" not only by its author William S. White . . . but by the Majority Leader as well. During the course of the lunch, which was attended by the other recently re-elected leaders, Senator Johnson encouraged us to consider Mr. White's book as a sort of *McGuffey's Reader* from which we could learn much about the "greatest deliberative body in the world" and how to mold ourselves into its way of life.

These days, somehow, the mold seems to have broken. Ten years after the Johnson lunch Clayton Fritchey's *Harper's* article named Russell Long as a "full-fledged member" of the Inner Club. Of Edward M. Kennedy, Fritchey said: "On his own, the amiable Teddy might some day have become at best a fringe member of the Club, but he is associated with Robert F., who like John F., is the archetype of the national kind of politician that the Club regards with suspicion. It believes (correctly) that the Kennedy family has always looked on the Senate as a means to an end, but not an end in itself." And yet, only two years later, Kennedy unseated Long.

POWER IN THE SENATE

Some time ago, in *Congress and the Presidency* (1964), I argued that the notion of an inner club misrepresented the distribution of power in the Senate in several ways. First, it vastly underplayed the extent to which *formal* position —committee chairmanships, great seniority, and official party leadership— conferred power and status on individual Senators almost regardless of their clubability. Second, it understated the extent to which power was spread by specialization and the need for cooperative effort. Fritchey's list bears this out; of the ninety-two nonfreshman Senators in 1967, he listed fifty-three as members or provisional members of the Inner Club. This suggests a third point: the existence of an inner club was no doubt in part incorrectly inferred from the existence of its opposite—a small number of mavericks and outsiders. The Senate has always had its share of these, going back at least as far as that superbly cranky diarist, Senator William Plumer of New Hampshire, who served from 1803 to 1807. But the undeniable existence of cranks and mavericks—uncooperative men with whom in a legislative body it is necessary (but impossible) to do business—does not an Inner Club make, except, of course, by simple subtraction.

To dispute that there is an all-powerful Inner Club is not, of course, to claim that no norms govern the behavior of Senators toward one another, or that this body of adults has no status system. Any group whose members interact frequently, and expect to continue to do so on into the indefinite future, usually develops norms. All groups having boundaries, a corporate history, a division of labor, and work to do may be expected to have folkways and an informal social organization. What was opened to question was whether, in the case of the U.S. Senate, the informal social organization was as restrictive or as unlike the formal organization as proponents of the Inner Club Theory believed.

To these observations I would now add a number of others, the most important of which would be to suggest that the role of the Senate in the political system has changed over the last twenty years in such a way as to decrease the impact of norms internal to the Senate on the behavior and the status of Senators.

One possible interpretation of what went on at the opening of the current Congress is that the Senate today is far less of a citadel than when William S. White first wrote it. It is a less insular body, and the fortunes of Senators are less and less tied to the smiles and frowns of their elders within the institution.

WHY OPERATIONS?

What is the great attraction, for example, of the Committee on Government Operations? It reports little legislation, has oversight over no specific part of the executive branch. Rather, it takes the operations of government in general as its bailiwick, splits into nearly autonomous sub-committees, and holds investigations. In short, it has the power to publicize—both issues and Senators. It takes less of a Senator's time away from the increasingly absorbing enterprise of cultivating national constituencies on substantive issues.

The claim that lack of ambition for the Presidency distinguishes members of the Inner Club could not have been correct even twenty years ago, considering the Presidential hankerings of such quintessentially old-style Senate types as Robert A. Taft of Ohio, Richard B. Russell of Georgia, and Robert Kerr of Oklahoma. Today, Presidential ambition seems to lurk everywhere in the Senate chamber.

Over the course of these last twenty years, the Senate has obviously improved as a base from which to launch a Presidential bid, while other bases —such as the governorships—have gone into decline. There has certainly, since World War II, been a general movement of political resources and of public attention toward Washington and away from local and regional arenas. Growth of national news media—especially television—has augmented this trend. The impact upon the Presidency of this nationalization of public awareness has been frequently noted. To a lesser extent, this public awareness has spread to all national political institutions. But of these, only the Senate has taken full advantage of its increased visibility. In the House, Sam Rayburn refused to allow televised coverage of any official House function, and Speaker John W. McCormack has continued this rule. The executive branch speaks through the President or an occasional Cabinet member, and the Supreme Court remains aloof. Thus, only Senators have had little constraint placed on their availability for national publicity. Senate committee hearings are frequently televised. Senators turn up often on the televised Washington quiz shows on Sunday afternoons. House members, even the powerful committee chairmen, rarely do. National exposure does not seem to be as important a political resource for them.

As senatorial names—Kefauver, McCarthy, Kennedy, Goldwater— became household words, Governors slipped into relative obscurity. Where once the Governor's control of his state party organization was the single overwhelming resource in deciding who was Presidential timber at a national party convention, television and the nationalization of resources began to erode gubernatorial power. Early Presidential primaries, with their massive national press coverage, made it harder and harder for the leaders of state parties to wait until the national party conventions to bargain and make commitments in Presidential contests. Proliferating federal programs, financed by the lucrative federal income tax, were distributed to the states, in part as senatorial patronage. Governors were not always ignored in this process, but their influence was on the whole much reduced. Meanwhile, at the state level, services lagged and taxes were often inequitable and unproductive. Responsible Governors of both parties have often tried to do something about this problem, but it has led to donnybrooks with state legislatures, great unpopularity, and, on some occasions, electoral defeat.

This decline of Governors and the shift of public attention to national politics and national politicians goes some distance in explaining how the Senate, in its role as an incubator of Presidential hopefuls, seems to have made it increasingly hard for a Senate inner club to monopolize power. As the stakes of the senatorial game have changed, so has the importance of informal norms and folkways internal to the Senate, in the life space of Senators.

TWO ACCIDENTS

In my view, two historical accidents also played a part. The first was the majority leadership of Lyndon B. Johnson. Ambitious for the Presidency, immensely skilled, Johnson sedulously perpetuated the myth of the Inner Club while destroying its substance.

If the idea of the Inner Club was collegiality among the fellowship of the elect, the essence of Johnson's Senate operation was the progressive centralization of power in the hands of the Majority Leader. By the time Johnson left the Senate, after eight years as Majority Leader, the "Inner Club" could command little of the power attributed to it. It had too long been merely a facade for Johnson's own activity—a polite and palatable explanation for the exercise of his own discretion in committee appointments, legislative priorities, and tactics. Under the loose rein of Majority Leader Mike Mansfield, the Senate has again become a much more collegial body whose corporate work has been pretty much determined by Presidential programs and priorities. But it has not recaptured the sense of cohesion, community, and separateness that is supposed to have existed "in the old days." Younger men have come in, and in the last few years liberal majorities on legislation mobilized by the executive departments were by no means uncommon.

The second historical accident that shaped the contemporary Senate was the style of service hit upon by several post-war Senators, but most notably pioneered by the late Arthur Vandenberg of Michigan, and, in the 1950s and 1960s, brought to full flower by Hubert Humphrey. This new style combined the concerns over national issues—formerly attributed mainly to outsiders—with patience and a mastery of internal procedure and strategy. Like Johnson, Humphrey entered the Senate in 1949. Unlike Johnson, Humphrey had a large and varied stock of interests in, and commitments to, public policy. These attuned him to demands from outside the Senate. Through his phenomenally retentive mind, insatiable curiosity, and unquenchable optimism, Humphrey could learn enough to hold his own on any issue. Invariably his name went on the bills that reached out for new national constituencies.

Much earlier than most members of his generation, Humphrey sensed the possibilities in the Senate for long-range political education. He spent the Eisenhower era incubating ideas that, in a better climate, could hatch into programs. In the early 1950s a flood of Humphrey bills (many of them co-sponsored by other liberal Senators) on civil rights, Medicare, housing, aid to farm workers, food stamps, Job Corps, area redevelopment, disarmament, and so on died in the Senate. A little over a decade later, most of them were law, and Humphrey had in the meantime become a political leader of national consequence.

By reconciling acceptance within the Senate with large public accomplishments, Humphrey set a new style—and it is a style that has grown in popularity among younger Senators as the role of the Senate as an appropriate place in the political system for the incubation of new policy and the building of national constituencies emerges more sharply.

Chapter 9

The Judiciary

An independent judicial system is an important part of constitutional government. The United States Supreme Court was created with this view, and its members were given life tenure and guaranteed compensation to maintain their independence. However, Congress was given power to structure the entire subordinate judicial system, including control over the appellate jurisdiction of the Supreme Court. Regardless of any initial lack of power and various attempts made by and through Congress to curb its power, the Supreme Court today occupies a predominant position in the governmental system. The evolution of the Court, its present powers, and their implications are analyzed in this chapter, along with selected problems in the administration of justice.

CONSTITUTIONAL BACKGROUND: JUDICIAL INDEPENDENCE AND JUDICIAL REVIEW

The Supreme Court and the judicial system play important roles in the intricate separation-of-powers scheme. Through judicial review, both legislative and executive decisions may be overruled by the courts for a number of reasons. To some extent, then, the judiciary acts as a check upon arbitrary action by governmental departments and agents. The intent of the framers of the Constitution regarding the role of the judiciary, particularly the Supreme Court, in our governmental system is examined in *Federalist* 78.

57

Alexander Hamilton

FEDERALIST 78

We proceed now to an examination of the judiciary department of the proposed government.

In unfolding the defects of the existing confederation, the utility and necessity of a federal judicature have been clearly pointed out. It is the less necessary to recapitulate the considerations there urged; as the propriety of the institution in the abstract is not disputed; the only questions which have been raised being relative to the manner of constituting it, and to its extent. To these points, therefore, our observations shall be confined.

The manner of constituting it seems to embrace these several objects: lst. The mode of appointing the judges; 2nd. the tenure by which they are to hold their places; 3rd. The partition of the judiciary authority between different courts, and their relations to each other.

First. As to the mode of appointing the judges: This is the same with that of appointing the officers of the union in general, and has been so fully discussed ... that nothing can be said here which would not be useless repetition.

Second. As to the tenure by which the judges are to hold their places: This chiefly concerns their duration in office; the provisions for their support; the precautions for their responsibility.

According to the plan of the convention, all the judges who may be appointed by the United States are to hold their offices *during good behavior;* which is conformable to the most approved of the state constitutions. . . . The standard of good behavior for the continuance in office of the judicial magistracy is certainly one of the most valuable of the modern improvements in the practice of government. In a monarchy, it is an excellent barrier to the despotism of the prince; in a republic, it is a no less excellent barrier to the encroachments and oppressions of the representative body. And it the best expedient which can be devised in any government, to secure a steady, upright, and impartial administration of the laws.

Whoever attentively considers the different departments of power must perceive, that, in a government in which they are separated from each other, the judiciary, from the nature of its functions, will always be the least dangerous to the political rights of the constitution; because it will be least in a capacity to annoy or injure them. The executive not only dispenses the honors, but holds the sword of the community. The legislature not only commands the purse, but prescribes the rules by which the duties and rights of every citizen are to be regulated. The judiciary, on the contrary, has no influence over either the sword or the purse; no direction either of the strength or of the wealth of the society; and can take no active resolution whatever. It may truly be said to have neither FORCE NOR WILL, but merely judgment; and must ultimately depend upon the aid of the executive arm for the efficacious exercise even of this faculty.

This simple view of the matter suggests several important consequences: It proves incontestably, that the judiciary is beyond comparison, the weakest of the three departments of power, that it can never attack with success either of the other two; and that all possible care is requisite to enable it to defend itself against their attacks. It equally proves, that, though individual oppression may now and then proceed from the courts of justice, the general liberty of the people can never be endangered from that quarter; I mean so long as the judiciary remains truly distinct from both the legislature and executive. For I agree, that "there is no liberty, if the power of judging be not separated from the legislative and executive powers." It proves, in the last place, that as liberty can have nothing to fear from the judiciary alone, but would have everything to fear from its union with either of the other departments; that, as all the effects of such a union must ensue from a dependence of the former on the latter, notwithstanding a nominal and apparent separation; that as, from the natural feebleness of the judiciary, it is in continual jeopardy of being overpowered, awed or influenced by its coordinate branches; that, as nothing can contribute so much to its firmness and independence as PERMANENCY IN OFFICE, this quality may therefore be justly regarded an an indispensable ingredient in its constitution; and, in a great measure, as the CITADEL of the public justice and the public security.

The complete independence of the courts of justice is peculiarly essential in a limited constitution. By a limited constitution, I understand one which contains certain specified exceptions to the legislative no *ex post facto* laws, and the like. Limitations of this kind can be preserved in practice no other way than through the medium of the courts of justice, whose duty it must be to declare all acts contrary to the manifest tenor of the constitution void. Without this, all the reservations of particular rights or privileges would amount to nothing.

Some perplexity respecting the right of the courts to pronounce legislative acts void, because contrary to the constitution, has arisen from an imagination that the doctrine would imply a superiority of the judiciary to the legislative power. It is urged that the authority which can declare the acts of another void, must necessarily be superior to the one whose acts may be declared void. As this doctrine is of great importance in all the American constitutions, a brief discussion of the grounds on which it rests cannot be unacceptable.

There is no position which depends on clearer principles than that every act of a delegated authority, contrary to the tenor of the commission under which it is exercised, it void. No legislative act, therefore, contrary to the constitution, can be valid. To deny this would be to affirm, that the deputy is greater than his principal; that the servant is above his master; that the representatives of the people are superior to the people themselves; that men, acting by virtue of powers, may do not only what their powers do not authorize, but what they forbid.

If it be said that that legislative body are themselves the constitutional judges of their own powers, and that the construction they put upon them is conclusive upon the other departments, it may be answered, that this cannot be the natural presumption, where it is not to be collected from any particular provisions in the constitution. It is not otherwise to be supposed that the constitution could intend to enable the representatives of the people to substitute their *will* to that of their constituents. It is far more rational to suppose that the courts were designed to be an intermediate body between the people and the legislature, in order, among other things, to keep the latter within the limits assigned to their authority. The interpretation of the laws is the proper and peculiar province of the courts. A constitution is, in fact, and must be, regarded by the judges as a fundamental law. It must therefore belong to them to ascertain its meaning, as well as the meaning of any particular act proceeding from the legislative body. If there should happen to be an irreconcilable variance between the two, that which has the superior obligation and validity ought, of course, to be preferred; in other words, the constitution ought to be preferred to the statute, the intention of the people to the intention of their agents.

Nor does his conclusion by any means suppose a superiority of the judicial to the legislative power. It only supposes that the power of the people is superior to both; and that where the will of the legislature declared in its statutes, stands in opposition to that of the people declared in the constitution, the judges ought to be governed by the latter, rather than the former. They ought to regulate their decisions by the fundamental laws, rather than by those which are not fundamental. . . .

It can be of no weight to say, that the courts, on the pretense of a repugnancy, may substitute their own pleasure to the constitutional intentions of the legislature. This might as well happen in the case of two contradictory statutes; or it might as well happen in every adjudication upon any single statute. The courts must declare the sense of the law; and if they should be disposed to exercise WILL instead of JUDGMENT, the consequence would equally be the substitution of their pleasure to that of the legislative body. The observation, if it proved anything, would prove that there ought to be no judges distinct from the body.

If then the courts of justice are to be considered as the bulwarks of a limited constitution, against legislative encroachments, this consideration will afford a strong argument for the permanent tenure of judicial officers, since nothing will contribute so much as this to that independent spirit in the judges, which must be essential to the faithful performance of so arduous a duty.

This independence of the judges is equally requisite to guard the constitution and the rights of individuals, from the effects of those ill-humors which the arts of designing men, or the influence of particular conjunctures, some-times disseminate among the people themselves, and which, though they speedily give place to better information, and more deliberate reflection, have a tendency, in the meantime, to occasion dangerous innovations in the govern-ment, and serious oppressions of the minor party in the community. . . . Until the people have, by some solemn and authoritative act, annulled or changed the established form, it is binding upon themselves collectively, as well as individually; and no presumption, or even knowledge of their sentiments, can warrent their representatives in a departure from it, prior to such an act. But it is easy to see, that it would require an uncommon portion of fortitude in the judges to do their duty as faithful guardians of the constitution, where legisla-tive invasions of it had been instigated by the major voice of the community.

But it is not with a view to infractions of the constitution only, that the independence of the judges may be an essential safeguard against the effects of occasional ill-humors in the society. These sometimes extend no farther than to the injury of the private rights of particular classes of citizens, by unjust and partial laws. Here also the firmness of the judicial magistracy is of vast impor-tance in mitigating the severity, and confining the operation of such laws. It not only serves to moderate the immediate mischiefs of those which may have been passed, but it operates as a check upon the legislative body in passing them; who, perceiving that obstacles to the success of an iniquitous intention are to be expected from the scruples of the courts, are in a manner com-pelled by the very motives of the injustice they mediate, to qualify their at-tempts. . . .

That inflexible and uniform adherence to the rights of the constitution, and of individuals, which we perceive to be indispensable in the courts of justice, can certainly not be expected from judges who hold their offices by a temporary commission. Periodical appointments, however regulated, or by whomsoever made, would, in some way or other, be fatal to their necessary independence. If the power of making them was committed either to the executive or legislature, there would be danger of an improper compliance to the branch which possessed it; if to both, there would be an unwillingness to hazard the displeasure of either; if to the people, or to persons chosen by them for the special purpose, there would be too great a disposition to consult popularity to justify a reliance that nothing would be consulted but the consti-tution and the laws.

There is yet a further and a weighty reason for the permanency of judicial offices, which is deducible from the nature of the qualifications they require. It has been frequently remarked, with great propriety, that a voluminous code of laws is one of the inconveniences necessarily connected with the advantages of a free government. To avoid an arbitrary discretion in the courts, it is indispensable that they should be bound down by strict rules and precedents, which serve to define and point out their duty in every particular case that comes before them; and it will readily be conceived, from the variety of controversies which grow out of the folly and wickedness of mankind, that the records of those precedents must unavoidably swell to a very considerable bulk, and must demand long and laborious study to acquire a competent knowledge of them. Hence it is, that there can be but few men in the society, who will have sufficient skill in the laws to qualify them for the stations of judges. And making the proper deductions for the ordinary depravity of human nature, the number must be still smaller, of those who unite the requisite integrity with the requisite knowledge. . . .

From *Federalist* 78 students can observe that the intent of the framers of the Constitution, at least as expressed and represented by Hamilton, was to give to the courts the power of judicial review, i.e., the power to declare legislative or executive acts unconstitutional. Students should note that this concept was not explicitly written into the Constitution. Although the cause of this omission is not known, it it reasonable to assume that the framers felt that judicial power implied judicial review. Further, it is possible that the framers did not expressly mention judicial review because they had to rely on the states for adoption of the Constitution; judicial power would extend to the states as well as to the coordinate departments of the national government.

The power of the Supreme Court to invalidate an act of Congress was stated by John Marshall in *Marbury* v. *Madison,* 1 Cranch 137 (1803). At issue was a provision in the Judiciary Act of 1789 which extended the *original jurisdiction* of the Supreme Court by authorizing it to issue writs of mandamus in cases involving public officers of the United States and private persons, a power not conferred upon the Court in the Constitution. Marbury had been appointed a justice of the peace by President John Adams under the Judiciary Act of 1801, passed by the Federalists after Jefferson and the Republican Party won the elections in the fall of 1800 so that President Adams could fill various newly created judicial posts with Federalists before he left office in March, 1801. Marbury was scheduled to receive one of these commissions, but when Jefferson took office on March 4, with Madison as his Secretary of State, it had not been delivered. Marbury filed a suit with the Supreme Court requesting it to exercise its original jurisdiction and issue a writ of mandamus (a writ to compel an administrative officer to perform his duty) to force Madison to deliver the commission, an act which both Jefferson and Madison were opposed to doing. In his decision, Marshall, a prominent Federalist, stated that although Marbury had a legal right to his commission, and although mandamus was the proper remedy, the Supreme Court could not extend its original jurisdiction beyond the limits specified in the Constitution; therefore, that section of the Judiciary Act of 1789 permitting the court to issue such writs to public officers was unconstitutional. Incidentally, the Republicans were so outraged at the last-minute appointments of Adams that there were threats that Marshall would be impeached if he issued a writ of mandamus directing Madison to deliver the commission. This is not to suggest that Marshall let such considerations influence him; however, from a political point of view his decision was thought to be a masterpiece of reconciling his position as a Federalist with the political tenor of the times.

58
MARBURY v. MADISON
1 Cranch 137 (1803)

Mr. Chief Justice Marshall delivered the opinion of the Court, saying in part:
... The authority, therefore, given to the Supreme Court, by the [Judiciary Act of 1789] ... establishing the judicial courts of the United States, to issue writs of mandamus to public officers, appears not to be warranted by the Constitution [because it adds to the original jurisdiction of the Court delineated by the framers of the Constitution in Article III; had they wished this power to be conferred upon the Court it would be so stated, in the same manner that the other parts of the Court's original jurisdiction are stated]; ... it becomes necessary to inquire whether a jurisdiction so conferred can be exercised.

The question whether an act repugnant to the Constitution can become the law of the land, is a question deeply interesting to the United States; but, happily, not of an intricacy proportioned to its interest. It seems only necessary to recognize certain principles supposed to have been long and well established, to decide it.

That the people have an original right to establish, for their future government, such principles as, in their opinion, shall most conduce to their own happiness, is the basis on which the whole American fabric has been erected. The exercise of this original right is a very great exertion; nor can it nor ought it to be frequently repeated. The principles, therefore, so established, are deemed fundamental. And as the authority from which they proceed is supreme, and can seldom act, they are designed to be permanent.

This original and supreme will organizes the government, and assigns to different departments their respective powers. It may either stop here, or establish certain limits not to be transcended by those departments.

The government of the United States is of the latter description. The powers of the legislature are defined and limited; and that those limits may not be mistaken, or forgotten, the Constitution is written. To what purpose are powers limited, and to what purpose is that limitation committed to writing, if these limits may, at any time, be passed by those intended to be restrained? The distinction between a government with limited and unlimited powers is abolished, if those limits do not confine the persons on whom they are imposed, and if acts prohibited and acts allowed, are of equal obligation. It is a proposition too plain to be contested, that the Constitution controls any legislative act repugnant to it; or, that the legislature may alter the Constitution by an ordinary act.

Between these alternatives there is no middle ground. The Constitution is either a superior paramount law, unchangeable by ordinary means, or it is on a level with ordinary legislative acts, and, like other acts, is alterable when the legislature shall please to alter it.

If the former part of the alternative be true, then a legislative act contrary to the Constitution, is not law; if the latter part be true, then written constitutions are absurd attempts, on the part of the people, to limit a power in its own nature illimitable.

Certainly all those who have framed written constitutions contemplate them as forming the fundamental and paramount law of the nation, and, consequently, the theory of every such government must be, that an act of the legislature, repugnant to the constitution, is void.

This theory is essentially attached to a written constitution, and is consequently to be considered, by this court, as one of the fundamental principles of our society. It is not, therefore, to be lost sight of in the further consideration of this subject.

If an act of the legislature, repugnant to the Constitution, is void, does it, notwithstanding its invalidity, bind the courts, and oblige them to give it effect? Or, in other words, though it be not law, does it constitute a rule as operative as if it was a law? This would be to overthrow in fact what was established in theory; and would seem, at first view, an absurdity too gross to be insisted on. It shall, however, receive a more attentive consideration.

It is emphatically the province and duty of the judicial department to say what the law is. Those who apply the rule to particular cases, must of necessity expound and interpret that rule. If two laws conflict with each other, the courts must decide on the operation of each.

So if the law be in opposition to the Constitution; if both the law and the Constitution apply to a particular case, so that the court must either decide that case conformably to the law, disregarding the Constitution, or conformably to the Constitution, disregarding the law, the court must determine which of these conflicting rules governs the case. This is of the very essence of judicial duty.

If, then, the courts are to regard the Constitution, and the Constitution is superior to any ordinary act of the legislature, the Constitution, and not such ordinary act, must govern the case to which they both apply.

Those, then, who controvert the principle that the Constitution is to be considered, in court, as a paramount law, are reduced to the necessaity of maintaining that courts must close their eyes on the Constitution, and see only the law.

This doctrine would subvert the very foundation of all written constitutions. It would declare that an act which, according to the principles and theory of our government, is entirely void, is yet, in practice, completely obligatory. It would declare that if the legislature shall do what is expressly forbidden, such act, notwithstanding the express prohibition, is in reality effectual. It would be giving to the legislature a practical and real omnipotence, with the same breath which professes to restrict their powers within narrow limits. It is prescribing limits, and declaring that those limits may be passed at pleasure.

That it thus reduces to nothing what we have deemed the greatest improvement on political institutions, a written constitution, would of itself be sufficient, in America, where written constitutions have been viewed with so much reverence, for rejecting the construction. But the peculiar expressions of the Constitution of the United States furnish additional arguments in favor of its rejection.

The judicial power of the United States is extended to all cases arising under the Constitution.

Could it be the intention of those who gave this power, to say that in using it the Constitution should not be looked into? That a case arising under the Constitution should be decided without examining the instrument under which it arises?

This is too extravagant to be maintained.

In some cases, then, the Constitution must be looked into by the judges. And if they can open it at all, what part of it are they forbidden to read or to obey?

There are many other parts of the Constitution which serve to illustrate this subject.

It is declared that "no tax or duty shall be laid on articles exported from any State." Suppose a duty on the export of cotton, of tobacco, or of flour; and a suit instituted to recover it. Ought judgment to be rendered in such a case? Ought the judges to close their eyes on the Constitution, and only see the law?

The Constitution declares "that no bill of attainder or *ex post facto* law shall be passed."

If, however, such a bill should be passed, and a person should be prosecuted under it, must the court condemn to death those victims whom the Constitution endeavors to preserve?

"No person," says the Constitution, "shall be convicted of treason unless on the testimony of two witnesses to the same overt act, or on confession in open court."

Here the language of the Constitution is addressed especially to the courts. It prescribes, directly for them, a rule of evidence not to be departed from. If the legislature should change that rule, and declare one witness, or a confession out of court, sufficient for conviction, must the constitutional principle yield to the legislative act?

From these, and many other selections which might be made, it is apparent that the framers of the Constitution contemplated that instrument as a rule for the government of courts, as well as of the legislature.

Why otherwise does it direct the judges to take an oath to support it? This oath certainly applies in an especial manner to this conduct in their official character. How immoral to impose it on them, if they were to be used as the instruments, and the knowing instruments, for violating what they swear to support!

The oath of office, too, imposed by the legislature, is completely demonstrative of the legislative opinion on this subject. It is in these words: "I do solemnly swear that I will administer justice without respect to persons, and do equal right to the poor and to the rich; and that I will faithfully and impartially discharge all the duties incumbent on me as _____, according to the best of my abilities and understanding, agreeably to the Constitution and laws of the United States."

Why does a judge swear to discharge his duties agreeably to the Constitution of the United States, if that Constitution forms no rule for his government —if it is closed upon him, and cannot be inspected by him?

If such be the real state of things, this is worse than solemn mockery. To prescribe, or to take this oath, becomes equally a crime.

It is also not entirely unworthy of observation, that in declaring what shall be the supreme law of the land, the Constitution itself is first mentioned; and not the laws of the United States generally, but those only which shall be made in pursuance of the Constitution, have that rank.

Thus, the particular phraseology of the Constitution of the United States confirms and strengthens the principle, supposed to be essential to all written constitutions, that a law repugnant to the Constitution is void; and that courts, as well as other departments, are bound by that instrument.

The rule must be discharged.

POWERS AND LIMITATIONS
OF THE SUPREME COURT

Paul A. Freund, in his book *On Understanding the Supreme Court* (1949), notes that the Supreme Court has a definite political role. He asks:

"Is the law of the Supreme Court a reflection of the notions of 'policy' held by its members? The question recalls the controversy over whether judges 'make' or 'find' the law. A generation or two ago it was thought rather daring to insist that judges make law. Old Jeremiah Smith, who began the teaching of law at Harvard after a career on the New Hampshire Supreme Court, properly deflated the issue. 'Do judges make law?' he repeated. 'Course they do. Made some myself.' Of course Supreme Court Justices decide cases on the basis of their ideas of policy."

To emphasize this point today is to repeat the familiar. The Court makes policy. It would be difficult to conceive how a Court having the power to interpret the Constitution could fail to make policy, i.e., could fail to make rulings that have *general* impact upon the community as a whole. The essential distinction between policy-making and adjudication is that the former has a general effect while the latter touches only a specifically designated person or group.

If the Supreme Court has this power of constitutional interpretation, how is it controlled by the other governmental departments and the community? Is it, as some have claimed, completely arbitrary in rendering many of its decisions? Is it potentially a dictatorial body? The Supreme Court and lower courts are limited to the consideration of cases and controversies brought before them by outside parties. Courts cannot initiate law. Moreover, all courts, and the Supreme Court in particular, exercise judicial self-restraint in certain cases to avoid difficult and controversial issues and to avoid outside pressure to limit the powers of the judiciary. The discussion by John P. Roche deals with the background, the nature, and the implications of judicial doctrines of self-restraint.

59
John P. Roche

JUDICIAL SELF-RESTRAINT

Every society, sociological research suggests, has its set of myths which incorporate and symbolize its political, economic, and social aspirations. Thus, as medieval society had the Quest for the Holy Grail and the cult of numerology, we, in our enlightened epoch, have as significant manifestations of our collective hopes the dream of impartial decision making and the cult of "behavioral science." While in my view these latter two are but different facets of the same fundamental drive, namely, the age-old effort to exercise human variables from human action, our concern here is with the first of them, the pervasive tendency in the American political and constitutional tradition directed toward taking the politics out of politics, and substituting some set of Platonic guardians for fallible politicians.

While this dream of objectivizing political Truth is in no sense a unique American phenomenon, it is surely true to say that in no other democratic nation has the effort been carried so far and with such persistance. Everywhere one turns in the United States, he finds institutionalized attempts to narrow the political sector and to substitute allegedly "independent" and "impartial" bodies for elected decision-makers. The so-called "independent regulatory commissions" are a classic example of this tendency in the area of administration, but unquestionably the greatest hopes for injecting pure Truth-serum into the body politic have been traditionally reserved for the federal judiciary, and particularly for the Supreme Court. The rationale for this viewpoint is simple: "The people must be protected from themselves, and no institution is better fitted for the role of chaperone than the federal judiciary, dedicated as it is to the supremacy of the rule of law."

From John P. Roche, "Judicial Self-Restraint, "*The American Political Science Review*, 49 (September 1955). Reprinted by permission.

Patently central to this function of social chaperonage is the right of the judiciary to review legislative and executive actions and nullify those measures which derogate from eternal principles of truth and justice as incarnated in the Constitution. Some authorities, enraged at what the Supreme Court has found the Constitution to mean, have essayed to demonstrate that the framers did not intend the Court to exercise this function, to have, as they put it, "the last word." I find no merit in this contention; indeed, it seems to me undeniable not only that the authors of the Constitution intended to create a federal government, but also that they assumed *sub silentio* that the Supreme Court would have the power to review both national and state legislation.

However, since the intention of the framers is essentially irrelevant except to antiquarians and polemicists, it is unnecessary to examine further the matter of origins. The fact is that the United States Supreme Court, and the inferior federal courts under the oversight of the high Court, have enormous policy-making functions. Unlike their British and French counterparts, federal judges are not merely technicians who live in the shadow of a supreme legislature, but are fully equipped to intervene in the process of political decision making. In theory, they are limited by the Constitution and the jurisdiction it confers, but, in practice, it would be a clumsy judge indeed who could not, by a little skillful exegesis, adapt the Constitution to a necessary end. This statement is in no sense intended as a condemnation; on the contrary, it has been this perpetual reinvigoration by reinterpretation, in which the legislature and the executive as well as the courts play a part, that has given the Constitution its survival power. Applying a Constitution which contains at key points inspired ambiguity, the courts have been able to pour the new wine in the old bottle. Note that the point at issue is not the legitimacy or wisdom of judicial legislation; it is simply the enormous scope that this prerogative gives to judges to substitute their views for those of past generations, or, more controversially, for those of a contemporary Congress and President.

Thus it is naive to assert that the Supreme Court is limited by the Constitution, and we must turn elsewhere for the sources of judicial restraint. The great power exercised by the Court has carried with it great risks, so it is not surprising that American political history has been sprinkled with demands that the judiciary be emasculated. The really startling thing is that, with the notable exception of the McCardle incident in 1869, the Supreme Court has emerged intact from each of these encounters. Despite the plenary power that Congress, under Article III of the Constitution, can exercise over the appellate jurisdiction of the high Court, the national legislature has never taken sustained and effective action against its House of Lords. It is beyond the purview of this analysis to examine the reasons for Congressional inaction; suffice it here to say that the most significant form of judicial limitation has remained self-limitation. This is not to suggest that such a development as statutory codification has not cut down the area of interpretive discretion, for it obviously has. It is rather to maintain that when the justices have held back from assaults on legislative or executive actions, they have done so on the basis of self-established rationalizations. . . .

The remainder of this paper is therefore concerned with two aspects of this auto-limitation: first, the techniques by which it is put into practice; and, second, the conditions under which it is exercised. . . .

TECHNIQUES OF JUDICIAL SELF-RESTRAINT

The major techniques of judicial self-restraint appear to fall under the two familiar rubrics: procedural and substantive. Under the former fall the various techniques by which the Court can avoid coming to grips with substantive issues, while under the latter would fall those methods by which the Court, in a substantive holding, finds that the matter at issue in the litigation is not properly one for judicial settlement. Let us examine these two categories in some detail.

PROCEDURAL SELF-RESTRAINT

Since the passage of the Judiciary Act of 1925, the Supreme Court has had almost complete control over its business. United States Supreme Court *Rule 38,* which governs the certiorari policy, states, (§ 5) that discretionary review will be granted only "where there are special and important reasons therefor." Professor Fowler Harper has suggested in a series of detailed and persuasive articles on the application of this discretion [*University of Pennsylvania Law Review,* vols. 99–101; 103] that the Court has used it in such a fashion as to duck certain significant but controversial problems. While one must be extremely careful about generalizing in this area, since the reasons for denying certiorari are many and complex, Harper's evidence does suggest that the Court in the period since 1949 has refused to review cases involving important civil liberties problems which on their merits appeared to warrant adjudication. As he states at one point: "It is disconcerting when the Court will review a controversy over a patent on a pin ball machine while one man is deprived of his citizenship and another of his liberty without Supreme Court review of a plausible challenge to the validity of government action." . . .

Furthermore, the Supreme Court can issue certiorari on its own terms. Thus in *Dennis* v. *United States,* appealing the Smith Act convictions of the American communist leadership, the Court accepted the evidential findings of the Second Circuit as final and limited its review to two narrow constitutional issues. This, in effect, burked the basic problem: whether the evidence was sufficient to demonstrate that the Communist Party, U.S.A., was *in fact* a clear and present danger to the security of the nation, or whether the communists were merely shouting "Fire!" in an empty theater.

Other related procedural techniques are applicable in some situations. Simple delay can be employed, perhaps in the spirit of the Croatian proverb that "delay is the handmaiden of justice." . . . However, the technique of procedural self-restraint is founded on the essentially simple gadget of refusing jurisdiction, or of procrastinating the acceptance of jurisdiction, and need not concern us further here.

SUBSTANTIVE SELF-RESTRAINT

Once a case has come before the Court on its merits, the justices are forced to give some explanation for whatever action they may take. Here self-restraint can take many forms, notably, the doctrine of political questions, the operation of judicial parsimony, and—particularly with respect to the actions of administrative officers of agencies—the theory of judicial inexpertise.

The doctrine of political questions is too familiar to require much elaboration here. Suffice it to say that if the Court feels that a question before it, e.g., the legitimacy of a state government, the validity of a legislative apportionment, or the correctness of executive action in the field of foreign relations, is one that is not properly amenable to judicial settlement, it will refer the plaintiff to the "political" organs of government for any possible relief. The extent to which this doctrine is applied seems to be a direct coefficient of judicial egotism, for the definition of a political question can be expanded or contracted in accordion-like fashion to meet the exigencies of the times. A juridical definition of the term is impossible, for at root the logic that supports it is circular: political questions are matters not soluble by the judicial process; matters not soluble by the judicial process are political questions. As an early dictionary explained, violins are small cellos, and cellos are large violins.

Nor do examples help much in definition. While it is certainly true that the Court cannot mandamus a legislature to apportion a state in equitable fashion, it seems equally true that the Court is without the authority to force state legislators to implement unsegregated public education. Yet in the former instance the Court genuflected to the "political" organs and took no action, while in the latter it struck down segregation as violative of the Constitution.

Judicial parsimony is another major technique of substantive self-restraint. In what is essentially a legal application of Occam's razor, the Court has held that it will not apply any more principles to the settlement of a case than are absolutely necessary, e.g., it will not discuss the constitutionality of a law if it can settle the instant case by statutory construction. Furthermore, if an action is found to rest on erroneous statutory construction, the review terminates at that point: the Court will not go on to discuss whether the statute, properly construed, would be constitutional. A variant form of this doctrine, and a most important one, employs the "case or controversy" approach, to wit, the Court, admitting the importance of the issue, inquires as to whether the litigant actually has standing to bring the matter up. . . .

A classic use of parsimony to escape from a dangerous situation occurred in connection with the evacuation of the Nisei from the West Coast in 1942. Gordon Hirabayashi, in an attempt to test the validity of the regulations clamped on the American-Japanese by the military, violated the curfew and refused to report to an evacuation center. He was convicted on both counts by the district court and sentenced to three months for each offense, the sentences to run *concurrently*. When the case came before the Supreme Court, the justices sustained his conviction for violating the *curfew*, but refused to examine the validity of the evacuation order on the ground that it would not make any difference to Hirabayashi anyway; he was in for ninety days no matter what the Court did with evacuation.

A third method of utilizing substantive self-restraint is particularly useful in connection with the activities of executive departments or regulatory agencies, both state and federal. I have entitled it the doctrine of judicial *inexpertise,* for it is founded on the unwillingness of the Court to revise the findings of experts. The earmarks of this form of restraint are great deference to the holdings of the expert agency usually coupled with such a statement as "It is not for the federal courts to supplant the [Texas Railroad] Commission's judgment even in the face of convincing proof that a different result would have been better." In this tradition, the Court has refused to question *some* exercises of discretion by the National Labor Relations Board, the Federal Trade Commission, and other federal and state agencies. But the emphasis on *some* gives the point away; in other cases, apparently on all fours with those in which it pleads its technical *inexpertise,* the Court feels free to assess evidence *de novo* and reach independent judgment on the technical issues involved. . . .

In short, with respect to expert agencies, the Court is equipped with both offensive and defensive gambits. If it chooses to intervene, one set of precedents is brought out, while if it decides to hold back, another set of equal validity is invoked. Perhaps the best summary of this point was made by Justice Harlan in 1910, when he stated bluntly that "the Courts have rarely, if ever, felt themselves so restrained by technical rules that they could not find some remedy, consistent with the law, for acts . . . that violated natural justice or were hostile to the fundamental principles devised for the protection of the essential rights of property."

This does not pretend to be an exhaustive analysis of the techniques of judicial self-restraint; on the contrary, others will probably find many which are not given adequate discussion here. The remainder of this paper, however, is devoted to the second area of concern: the conditions under which the Court refrains from acting.

THE CONDITIONS OF JUDICIAL SELF-RESTRAINT

The conditions which lead the Supreme Court to exercise auto-limitation are many and varied. In the great bulk of cases, this restraint is an outgrowth of sound and quasi-automatic legal maxims which defy teleological interpretation. It would take a master of the conspiracy theory of history to assign meaning, for example, to the great majority of certiorari denials; the simple fact is that these cases do not merit review. However, in a small proportion of cases, purpose does appear to enter the picture, sometimes with a vengeance. It is perhaps unjust to the Court to center our attention on this small proportion, but it should be said in extenuation that these cases often involve extremely significant political and social issues. In the broad picture, the refusal to grant certiorari in 1943 to the Minneapolis Trotskyites convicted under the Smith Act is far more meaningful than the similar refusal to grant five hundred petitions to prison "lawyers" who have suddenly discovered the writ of habeas corpus. Likewise, the holding that the legality of Congressional apportionment is a "political question" vitally affects the operation of the whole democratic process.

What we must therefore seek are the conditions under which the Court holds back *in this designated category of cases.* Furthermore, it is important to realize that there are positive consequences of negative action; as Charles Warren has implied, the post-Civil War Court's emphasis on self-restraint was a judicial concomitant of the resurgence of states' rights. Thus self-restraint may, as in wartime, be an outgrowth of judicial caution, or it may be part of a purposeful pattern of abdicating national power to the states.

Ever since the first political scientist discovered Mr. Dooley, the changes have been rung on the aphorism that the Supreme Court "follows the election returns," and I see no particular point in ringing my variation on this theme through again. Therefore, referring those who would like a more detailed explanation to earlier analyses, the discussion here will be confined to the bare bones of my hypothesis.

The power of the Supreme Court to invade the decision-making arena, I submit, is a consequence of that fragmentation of political power which is normal in the United States. No cohesive majority, such as normally exists in Britain, would permit a politically irresponsible judiciary to usurp decision-making functions, but, for complex social and institutional reasons, there are few issues in the United States on which cohesive majorities exist. The guerrilla warfare which usually rages between Congress and the President, as well as the internal civil wars which are endemic in both the legislature and the administration, give the judiciary considerable room for maneuver. If, for example, the Court strikes down a controversial decision of the Federal Power Commission, it will be supported by a substantial bloc of congressmen; if it supports the FPC's decision, it will also receive considerable congressional support. But the important point is that *either* way it decides the case, there is no possibility that Congress will exact any vengeance on the Court for its action. A disciplined majority would be necessary to clip the judicial wings, and such a majority does not exist on this issue.

On the other hand, when monolithic majorities do exist on issues, the Court is likely to resort to judicial self-restraint. A good case here is the current tidal wave of anti-communist legislation and administrative action, the latter particularly with regard to aliens, which the Court has treated most gingerly. About the only issues on which there can be found cohesive majorities are those relating to national defense, and the Court has, as Clinton Rossiter demonstrated in an incisive analysis [*The Supreme Court and the Commander-in-Chief,* Ithaca, 1951], traditionally avoided problems arising in this area irrespective of their constitutional merits. Like the slave who accompanied a Roman consul on his triumph whispering "You too are mortal," the shade of Thad Stevens haunts the Supreme Court chamber to remind the justices what an angry Congress can do.

To state the proposition in this brief compass is to oversimplify it considerably. I have, for instance, ignored the crucial question of how the Court knows when a majority *does* exist, and I recognize that certain aspects of judicial behavior cannot be jammed into my hypothesis without creating essentially spurious epicycles. However, I am not trying to establish a monistic theory of judicial action; group action, like that of individuals, is motivated by many factors, some often contradictory, and my objective is to elucidate what seems to be one tradition of judicial motivation. In short, judicial self-restraint and judicial power seem to be opposite sides of the same coin: it has been by judicious application of the former that the latter has been maintained. A tradition beginning with Marshall's *coup* in *Marbury* v. *Marshall* and running through *Mississippi* v. *Johnson* and *Ex Parte Vallandigham* to *Dennis* v. *United States* suggests that the Court's power has been maintained by a wise refusal to employ it in unequal combat.

What should be the proper role of the judiciary, and particularly the Supreme Court, in our system of government is a matter of much debate. The power of judicial review over national and state legislative and executive actions where federal questions are involved gives to the federal judiciary, and particularly to the ultimate spokesman of the judiciary—the Supreme Court—enormous potential power to shape public policies at all levels of government. The question is just how far the judiciary should be active in involving itself in matters of public policy that are normally within the jurisdiction of legislative bodies. Activist Supreme Courts have always brought down upon themselves the wrath of those who have opposing political philosophies, whether liberal or conservative. During the early New Deal, key legislation of President Franklin D. Roosevelt was declared unconstitutional by a conservative Supreme Court, which crippled the efforts of FDR to deal with the crisis of the depression. FDR responded by attempting to push through Congress a "court-packing" plan which would have given him the authority to appoint a new Supreme Court justice for each justice who was over 70 years of age. Since the majority of the Court at that time consisted of septuagenarian justices this bill would have given the President the authority to control the court. This attack of FDR upon the Supreme Court was the most open effort in American history to undermine judicial independence and place the Supreme Court under presidential domination. The Roosevelt plan failed, due in large part to strong support from conservative elements of the community which were in turn reflected in Congress. In the early part of Roosevelt's second term the court majority switched in favor of the President which diminished the strong liberal attacks upon the Court.

After the Roosevelt era the Supreme Court exercised judicial self-restraint and did not become deeply involved in controversial political issues. It exercised judicial self-restraint on such important issues as the incorporation of the Bill of Rights under the Due Process Clause of the 14th Amendment, carefully "nationalizing" only those parts of the Bill of Rights that it considered to be fundamental, historical, and essential to the maintenance of the democratic process. It also refused to involve itself in the question of equal apportionment of state and congressional legislative districts. However, an activist Supreme Court reasserted itself under the tutelage of Chief Justice Earl Warren, appointed by President Eisenhower in 1953. The Warren Court rendered the historic *Brown v. Board of Education* (1954) decision desegregating public education, nationalized most of the Bill of Rights, making its provisions applicable to the actions of state governments, established the one-man, one-vote rule in *Baker v. Carr* (1962), and strengthened the separation between church and state in *Engle v. Vitale* (1962). All of these decisions caused consternation and confusion within a broad cross-section of the community. Whereas liberals hailed the decisions of the Warren Court as necessary, justified, and long overdue, conservatives attacked the court for undermining the Constitution and engaging in unauthorized "judicial legislation." The tables were turned from the New Deal. It was now the conservatives who were attacking the Court, and the liberals supporting it.

President Nixon in his election campaign of 1968 promised that if elected he would restore a conservative balance on the Supreme Court by appointing "strict constructionists." These presumably would be men who would adhere to the letter of the law and not engage in far-ranging judicial legislation. President Nixon did just that, and the Burger Court, although not directly overruling the decisions of the Warren Court, is returning to the doctrine of judicial self-restraint in many areas of constitutional law. The following selection assesses the Warren Court and describes the reactions to many of its decisions.

60
Rexford G. Tugwell

REFLECTIONS ON THE WARREN COURT

When he resigned in 1968 Chief Justice Warren had presided over the Supreme Court through three Presidencies. It had been a time of extraordinary activity and its record was freely compared with that of the Court presided over by Chief Justice Marshall.

Marshall's tenure had lasted thirty-four years, Warren's only fifteen, and there had been issues of national importance in the earlier time; nevertheless

From Rexford G. Tugwell, "Reflections on the Warren Court," reprinted from the January/February, 1973, issue of *The Center Magazine,* a publication of the Center for the Study of Democratic Institutions, Santa Barbara, California.

the later regime was regarded as having had comparable significance. Certainly judicial impact on public policy had never been more extraordinary; also the Court had never had greater prestige.

The Marshall Court's objectives had been largely the upholding of national power against efforts during the Jefferson succession to weaken it. The Warren Court had seemed to rediscover the Bill of Rights; at least its most startling decisions were the enlarging of civil liberties, reforming criminal procedures, buttressing racial equality, carrying democratic representation to its ultimate, and reinforcing the separation of church and state. Also, especially in the apportionment cases, the Warren Court had brought the Fourteenth Amendment to the support of the First, as well as the Fourth and Fifth. "Equal protection of the laws" may have been given some unintended meanings by the Warren Court, but, if so, they became recognized precedents. In any event, there was no doubt that the Court had turned away from its long preoccupation with the protection of property rights.

Chief Justice Warren's own accomplishments were unexpected. He had been a district attorney and had risen to be governor of California, but he had not been a noted lawyer and he had not been regarded as a liberal. With the growth of his state he had become so prominent a Republican that he had aspired to the Presidency. But his ambitions had been checked by Eisenhower's popularity and by Nixon's control of the California delegation in a Republican convention. Nixon captured the Vice-Presidency on the Eisenhower ticket in 1952, but Warren was presently compensated by being appointed Chief Justice, something Eisenhower was known to have regretted as soon as Warren's predilections became apparent.

In the opinion of legal scholars, Warren's appointment was an affront to the profession. He would not have been eligible, it was said, for a professorship in any respectable law school. This opinion may have been due in part to the persistent tendency of scholars to forget that Supreme Court appointments are seldom made from law school faculties or even from the lower judiciary. No matter how often justices are chosen for reasons other than eminence in legal scholarship, the chorus of disapprobation arises from academicians when it happens again. Perhaps they hold a narrower view of the Court's mission than do Presidents. The scholars do argue for a living Constitution, but they think that only legalists ought to take part in making it live.

Soon after Warren's appointment these critics began to change their estimates of him in one respect; under Warren the Court began to exert its influence in the direction of their own preferences. Being generally of the Brandeis school, the legal scholars had long deplored the property-protection bias of previous Court majorities. Their ideas tended to coincide with those of their colleagues in the departments of economics who still pressed for a laissez-faire economy but one made tolerable by stricter enforcement of antitrust laws.

Neither regulation of business nor protection of individual rights had ever reached a satisfactory stage in a country whose proudest claim was that it was a model of equality for the world. The Warren Court set out to make good this unfulfilled claim. Its decisions rooted out some of the most offensive constrictions on the liberties of citizens. School systems were directed to desegregate; criminal procedures were reformed to protect the rights of the accused; religious dogmas were purged from public education; and reapportionment to secure the principle of one-man, one-vote was imposed on state legislatures traditionally dominated by rural minorities.

Appraisals by legal professionals at the time of Warren's retirement, except for those from the more extreme conservatives, approved expansions of the Bill of Rights. Apparently it was forgotten that, by adhering to the same theory, liberties could be contracted as well as expanded. During much of the Court's earlier existence that had, in fact, happened. For a long time the commerce and due process clauses had been interpreted to prevent the humanizing of working conditions and the legitimizing of collective bargaining. The Warren Court expanded the most notable characteristic of the Constitution— protection of the individual against the state. As such, the majority had what was regarded as a liberal bias; but that bias could be changed by new appointments to the Court, operating with the same view of the Constitution's elasticity and concern for the individual. That such theory produces satisfactory constitutional law has been questioned, the argument being that it lacks the legitimacy of popular creation and might be challenged by the Congress or reversed by a later majority opinion. But this important issue was seldom confronted with any degree of seriousness or insight. The arguments turned rather on libertarian issues and on that ground the Court was praised in legal circles for its courage.

Brown v. Board of Education (1954) was known and discussed widely by knowledgeable Americans. The emotions aroused by that and later decisions tended to become stronger on both sides of the issue. The liberal reaction was more academic and much quieter. Approval was more noticeable among those minorities who had worked so long for the causes supported by the Court's successive opinions. But "Impeach Earl Warren" billboards appeared in those areas where reactionary views prevailed, particularly in the South. The Court had violated a widespread prejudice. Congressmen from those regions used the most vituperative language heard in the Capitol since the Civil War. Paradoxically the reactionaries who would have asserted the supremacy of the legislative branch (as the Constitution gave them authority to do) ran into the same difficulty that President Roosevelt had once encountered. Both wanted to impose reforms, but both collided with a widely held protective feeling for the Court. This fondness for the Court did not originate in the certainty that it was always right or that it always dispensed equal justice under law. It simply recognized that there had to be a place for final decisions, that the Court was the best venue for such judgments, that the Congress was the worst place for them, and that the President must not interfere.

The libertarian bias of the Court did not end immediately on Warren's retirement. It takes more than one Court member, even a Chief Justice, to make a majority. Like-minded colleagues remained, but they grew old and were replaced. Now came the realization that even if the Warren period of constitutional expansionism was really comparable with that of Marshall it, too, had an end.

*   *   *

The difference in thrust between the Marshall and Warren Courts is interesting in itself. Marshall in his fierce strengthening of the Union, consolidated half a century later by the Civil War, was determined that the nation should survive intact and, in the process, that the pretensions of the state politicians should be deflated. The deflation was a slow, gradual accomplishment, protested and fought all the way by active interests. But by Warren's time the states were much closer than they had ever been to being simply administrative areas. They were almost ready, it seemed, for inevitable reorganization in the interest of national unity and administrative efficiency.

The demands of citizens in the new age must be met. They were often to be the cause of serious disturbances in the next decade. It was much more important that claims to justice and tranquillity should be satisfied than that artificial entities called states should be preserved intact.

Technological improvements in transport and communications, followed by industries inclined to look upon state boundaries merely as nuisances, made union inevitable. Warren had succeeded as Chief Justice when this process was so nearly complete that union was taken for granted. What seemed most necessary now was to protect individuals against the sinister results of consolidated bureaucratic administration. Curiously, this was most manifest in the states and cities. The national government, having become responsible for so much and eventually understanding so well that it could not do everything, began handing over to the states, inept and corrupt though many of them were, the tough tasks of managing the expanding system of welfare organizations.

State politicians were delighted to get control of funds furnished by federal aid, but their concepts of responsibility were too often those of an earlier era. It was in statehouses and city halls that liberties were being invaded and the indigent being wronged. But because the Congress, like the state legislatures, was local-minded, there was a persistent tendency to let local politicians have the autonomy they demanded; and so, recipients were treated as though they were unworthy petitioners. Their rights were ignored whenever it seemed necessary.

The troubles of the new poor came about largely because of changes beyond their control. They found themselves put off the land or out of factories because their work was taken over by machines. Slum inhabitants, both urban and rural, were the unfortunate but incidental casualties of vast forces moving toward the one-nation reality.

The agents of that movement, the big businesses, were not inclined to acknowledge, or even recognize, any responsibility for the small people caught in the movement that was eliminating their jobs. Only the federal government could do that. The states were impotent, and, when they were also corrupt, businesses found it cheaper to bribe state officials than to pay the incidental costs of being regulated.

States and cities, with increasing burdens piled on their weak administrative organizations, were not prepared to carry their new responsibilities, so the grievances of the poor became intolerable. The local governments either avoided their responsibilities or repressed those who brought grievances.

The Warren Court found even the Congress unresponsive to the anguish of the poor. The Court set about establishing equal representation, equal justice, and equal rights. It required that educational facilities for the children of the poor be comparable to those for the more fortunate. To make matters more difficult, the Court insisted that the schools should not be racially separate. Not only were the poor to be served, but old tensions were to be eliminated in the serving.

The Court became the hated symbol in less advanced statehouses of the pressures they resented. Public opinion was polarized. Reactionaries dreamed of disciplining the justices, beginning with Warren himself. And much was heard again, like an echo from the past, of interposition—the right of the states to refuse compliance when Court decisions threatened their local institutions. Naturally liberals were enthusiastic about the rediscovery of expandable amendments to outlaw the discriminatory and repressive behavior of the backward state bureaucracies.

The Warren Court was in this sense revolutionary. It sought to direct administration. It had large notions of its own powers; and, for the sake of those powers, it developed the exasperating habit, hitherto a congressional charge, of telling other agencies of government what they should do. Local officials who did not want to do what they were told to do, and who could also point out that no means were made available for the reforms, were often as furious as they were frustrated. Who, they asked, would pay for desegregation? Who would furnish public defenders for those accused of crimes? And if police were handicapped in coping with the increasing number of offenses resulting from wild urban growth and crowding, who would find the extra police who were satisfactorily humanized?

Of course, it could be answered that all this should have been done long ago and the fact that it had not was itself evidence of an intolerable insensitivity to distress. But the Court's aloof commands were quite differently made than those the Congress might have issued. The latter would have been statutes; they would have been deliberated about at some length; and the enforcement costs and difficulties would have been taken into account. The Court was above such considerations. That it was not an appropriate legislating body was evident.

*   *   *

Also in the Warren years the Court's opinions became more and more ambiguous as new meanings were found to flesh out sparsely worded constitutional clauses. To be fair it should be noted that this was not the first Court conveniently to avoid precision. "Affected with a public interest" went back even to the common law and, when applied, it had quite different meanings at different times. The "clear and present danger" rule was enunciated much closer to Warren's time. But the Warren Court's "all deliberate speed" language for school desegregation came close to meaninglessness. And there were other similar pronouncements. What did it mean to say that urban housing was "in the public domain"? Or, in reference to conscientious objection, what did it mean to say that beliefs must be "sincere and meaningful"? Also, decisions turned, or seemed to turn, on such words as "discretion," "unrestrained," "principles," even "morality." Clarifying such locutions meant that those admonished had to take the tiresome and costly path of appeal.

When Warren spoke of resigning, hitherto muted comments became audible. It was freely said that, however politically and socially significant the Court's opinions, they had been sloppily written. The ambiguity in the Court's rulings was not always the result of faulty preparation. The volume of work for the justices, most of whom were tiring after years of hard work, was crushing. Also, the ambiguity may often have been intended. A rule, comprehensive but vague, giving only general direction to public policy and requiring return whenever application was in question, would serve to keep the Court in the thick of things. Thus, the Court would continue to be an active, essential force whenever new initiatives were indicated.

This central position of the Court was the most notable general result of the Warren years. True, this was no more than an intensification of a tendency that had been developing for more than half a century. Chief Justice Hughes had openly acknowledged that the Constitution had become what the justices said it was. Taken literally, that statement was notice of judicial supremacy. The Constitution belonged to the Court and to the Court alone. If it "lived," it lived as the justices allowed it to live. Hughes was, above all, a man with a lucid and literal mind. He was simply reporting what seemed to him to be a fact.

Nor was it new for the Court to seize opportunities for shaping public policy. Since President Roosevelt had appointed the eight justices of his Presidency, the Court had had a distinctly liberal cast; the Warren majority could be said merely to have gone further in the same direction. It was a direction, however, that, taken to an extreme, was certain to arouse the opposition of conservatives even though conservatives no longer dominated American public opinion.

It must be added—though this is a strange turn of events in a democracy —that the Court, after Roosevelt's appointments, was nearer the people than were their elected representatives. The Congress, unreformed since its beginning, and adhering to its seniority system, had fallen into the control of its oldest members, reëlected term after term from safe and conservative districts. What should have been done was to have reformed the Congress, not acquiesced in the taking over of its most significant work by the Supreme Court.

*   *   *

The circumstances surrounding Warren's resignation were thought of as being part of a plan to hold the gains made by the liberal Roosevelt justices. President Johnson had announced in March, 1968, that he would not again be a candidate. This meant that he would not be able to appoint a successor if Warren postponed his retirement. The coming election might be won by a Republican, and, it seemed, a notably conservative one at that, whose appointee might well reverse the liberal direction of the preceding decades.

That this issue could cause national furor is a measure of the importance reached by the Court in the country's social and political life. Its composition seemed a vital matter in the continuous struggle between those with differing views about the Bill of Rights. Those who reacted so angrily to the prospect of a Johnson appointee were aroused because the Court had now become more a legislative than a judicial body and because its legislation was becoming more and more libertarian.

The blocking of Johnson's appointment of Abe Fortas as Chief Justice, ending in Fortas's resignation, was really an attempt by the conservative senators to get control for themselves and to destroy the Court's rapport with the electorate. If they could do that they would have less objection to the legislative nature of judicial decision-making. Of course, for some time the conservatives had been trying to intimidate the justices by proposing statutes that would have narrowed their jurisdiction and prevented further expansive interpretations of the Bill of Rights. This was, then, a struggle between two legislative bodies: the Court and the Congress. But the conservatives in the Congress could not assemble the necessary majority; they could only threaten, delay, and hope.

There did seem now to be a change of public opinion regarding the Court. Poll-takers had been asking the public for thirty years whether it approved the Court's behavior. There was now a sharp decline of support even before the publicity given to Warren's alleged attempt to pave the way for a like-minded successor. This unfavorable opinion was taken to mean that the public had been offended by the Court's persistent expansionism of the past ten or fifteen years, and even that the nation, concerned by inter-racial violence and a rising incidence of crime, was in a reactionary mood. Liberals feared this was so, that the mood was deepening, and that a conservative era might now follow four decades of liberalism.

By its use of the power granted it in Article III, the Congress could restrict the Court's jurisdiction. But that could only be done by a congressional majority. If there was such a majority, and a conflict were precipitated between the Court and the Congress, the ultimate decision would be made by the public. The liberties that were supposed to be protected by making constitutional amendment difficult could not be insured in that way. In the long run, the Constitution was not what the justices said it was; it was what the electorate would say it ought to be. After all, the Constitution's opening words were

"We, the people." If the Court continued to lose popular support, this would eventually be registered in the Congress, or, if not there, in civil disorder.

True, a mood—by definition temporary—might be prevented from registering itself if the amending process could be kept from operating. But if there should be a serious disaffection with the Supreme Court's behavior over a considerable period, no devices to prevent amendment would be able to obstruct the wishes of the electorate. It had not enabled Marshall to hold the line for union; it took a war between unionists and secessionists to do that. It might take another conflict to settle the issues the Warren Court believed it had resolved.

The contemporary dispute seemed to echo that of a former time. The enemies lined up as they had in the eighteen-forties and eighteen-fifties. The Court's decline in favor was most marked in the old secessionists region—the South—and among the more conservative citizens. According to the pollsters there was no marked opinion change among citizens under thirty, or among Northerners. So the hostility to the Court could be discounted, the liberals thought. Another civil war was unlikely. The Court's detractors could not keep it from going on as it had, even if Warren's successor encountered trouble in being confirmed.

*   *   *

But the liberals might well want to reconsider the Constitution without fear that this would open the door to a reactionary trend. They have reason to believe that the states' righters would not prevail in a new constitutional convention. It seems more than likely that the younger generation would prevail instead. And wise counsel would also prevail: for example, in response to a polling question in 1968, sixty-one per cent of the citizens responding supported the proposition that appointees to the Court should be selected from a list presented to the President by the American Bar Association. In other words, the Court is being rebuked not because its bias is libertarian, but because it has any bias at all—that is, because it is legislating rather than judging. The Court is generally recognized as a second legislature, something Americans in general do not feel they need.

There is, however, no likelihood that the Court will retreat from the position it has won in the battle of the governmental branches. This is why the Chief Justice and the President had concerted their actions to secure the successor they preferred, a maneuver which underlined the illegitimacy of the powers the Court had assumed. The question at hand is larger than the particular political philosophy preferred by a particular Court, Chief Justice, or President.

The point is that the history of the Warren Court is typical; it reveals a constitutional defect that should be repaired. The Court's responsibilities should be clarified in a national act of reconsideration similar to that of 1787.

What happened when President Nixon's appointees began to show their preferences was precisely what had been anticipated. A new era of what the President called "strict construction" had begun. The rights expanded by the Warren Court began to be contracted by the Burger Court. It remains to be seen what the effect will be on civil liberties. What is not obscure—indeed, what is most evident—is that the Court still regards itself as a maker of constitutional law, a kind of super-legislature, whose first duty is to bring the nation back to its views of justice and tranquillity.

JUDICIAL DECISION MAKING

The preceding selections should dissuade students from accepting the commonly held assumption that judicial decision making is quasi-scientific, based upon legal principles and precedent, with the judges set apart from the political process. The interpretation of law, whether constitutional or statutory, involves a large amount of discretion. The majority of the Court can always read its opinion into law if it so chooses.

Justice William J. Brennan, Jr., a current member of the Supreme Court, discusses below the general role of the Court and the procedures it follows in decision making.

61

William J. Brennan, Jr.

HOW THE SUPREME COURT ARRIVES AT DECISIONS

Throughout its history the Supreme Court has been called upon to face many of the dominant social, political, economic and even philosophical issues that confront the nation. But Solicitor General Cox only recently reminded us that this does not mean that the Court is charged with making social, political, economic or philosophical decisions.

Quite the contrary, The Court is not a council of Platonic guardians for deciding our most difficult and emotional questions according to the Justices' own notions of what is just or wise or politic. To the extent that this is a government function at all, it is the function of the people's elected representatives.

From William J. Brennan, Jr., "How the Supreme Court Comes to Arrive at Decision," *The New York Times Magazine* (October 12, 1963). © 1963, by The New York Times Company. Reprinted by permission.

The Justices are charged with deciding according to law. Because the issues arise in the framework of concrete litigation they must be decided on facts embalmed in a record made by some lower court or administrative agency. And while the Justices may and do consult history and the other disciplines as aids to constitutional decisions, the text of the Constitution and relevant precedents dealing with that text are their primary tools.

It is indeed true, as Judge Learned Hand once said, that the judge's authority

> depends upon the assumption that he speaks with the mouth of others: the momentum of his utterances must be greater than any which his personal reputation and character can command; if it is to do the work assigned to it—if it is to stand against the passionate resentments arising out of the interests he must frustrate—he must preserve his authority by cloaking himself in the majesty of an over-shadowing past, but he must discover some composition with the dominant trends of his times.

ANSWERS UNCLEAR

However, we must keep in mind that, while the words of the Constitution are binding, their application to specific problems is not often easy. The Founding Fathers knew better than to pin down their descendants too closely.

Enduring principles rather than petty details were what they sought.

Thus the Constitution does not take the form of a litany of specifics. There are, therefore, very few cases where the constitutional answers are clear, all one way or all the other, and this is also true of the current cases raising conflicts between the individual and governmental power—an area increasingly requiring the Court's attention.

Ultimately, of course, the Court must resolve the conflicts of competing interests in these cases, but all Americans should keep in mind how intense and troubling these conflicts can be.

Where one man claims a right to speak and the other man claims the right to be protected from abusive or dangerously provocative remarks the conflict is inescapable.

Where the police have ample external evidence of a man's guilt, but to be sure of their case put into evidence a confession obtained through coercion, the conflict arises between his right to a fair prosecution and society's right to protection against his depravity.

Where the orthodox Jew wishes to open his shop and do business on the day which non-Jews have chosen, and the Legislature has sanctioned, as a day of rest, the Court cannot escape a difficult problem of reconciling opposed interests.

Finally, the claims of the Negro citizen, to borrow Solicitor General Cox's words, present a "conflict between the ideal of liberty and equality expressed in the Declaration of Independence, on the one hand, and, on the other hand, a way of life rooted in the customs of many of our people."

SOCIETY IS DISTURBED

If all segments of our society can be made to appreciate that there are such conflicts, and that cases which involve constitutional rights often require difficult choices, if this alone is accomplished, we will have immeasurably enriched our common understanding of the meaning and significance of our freedoms. And we will have a better appreciation of the Court's function and its difficulties.

How conflicts such as these ought to be resolved constantly troubles our whole society. There should be no surprise, then, that how properly to resolve them often produces sharp division within the Court itself. When problems are so fundamental, the claims of the competing interests are often nicely balanced, and close divisions are almost inevitable.

Supreme Court cases are usually one of three kinds: the "original" action brought directly in the Court by one state against another state or states, or between a state or states and the federal government. Only a handful of such cases arise each year, but they are an important handful.

A recent example was the contest between Arizona and California over the waters of the lower basin of the Colorado River. Another was the contest between the federal government and the newest state of Hawaii over the ownership of lands in Hawaii.

The second kind of case seeks review of the decisions of a federal Court of Appeals—there are eleven such courts—or of a decision of a federal District Court—there is a federal District Court in each of the fifty states.

The third kind of case comes from a state court—the Court may review a state court judgment by the highest court of any of the fifty states, if the judgment rests on the decision of a federal question.

When I came to the Court seven years ago the aggregate of the cases in the three classes was 1,600. In the term just completed there were 2,800, an increase of 75 percent in seven years. Obviously, the volume will have doubled before I complete ten years of service.

How is it possible to manage such a huge volume of cases? The answer is that we have the authority to screen them and select for argument and decision only those which, in our judgment, guided by pertinent criteria, raise the most important and far-reaching questions. By that device we select annually around 6 percent—between 150 and 170 cases—for decision.

PETITION AND RESPONSE

That screening process works like this: When nine Justices sit, it takes five to decide a case on the merits. But it takes only the votes of four of the nine to put a case on the argument calendar for argument and decision. Those four votes are hard to come by—only an exceptional case raising a significant federal question commands them.

Each application for review is usually in the form of a short petition, attached to which are any opinions of the lower courts in the case. The adversary may file a response—also, in practice usually short. Both the petition and response identify the federal questions allegedly involved, argue their substantiality, and whether they were properly raised in the lower courts.

Each Justice receives copies of the petition and response and such parts of the record as the parties may submit. Each Justice then, without any consultation at this stage with the others, reaches his own tentative conclusion whether the application should be granted or denied.

The first consultation about the case comes at the Court conference at which the case is listed on the agenda for discussion. We sit in conference almost every Friday during the term. Conferences begin at ten in the morning and often continue until six, except for a half-hour recess for lunch.

Only the Justices are present. There are no law clerks, no stenographers, no secretaries, no pages—just the nine of us. The junior Justice acts as guardian of the door, receiving and delivering any messages that come in or go from the conference.

ORDER OF SEATING

The conference room is a beautifully oak-paneled chamber with one side lined with books from floor to ceiling. Over the mantel of the exquisite marble fireplace at one end hangs the only adornment in the chamber—a portrait of Chief Justice John Marshall. In the middle of the room stands a rectangular table, not too large but large enough for the nine of us comfortably to gather around it.

The Chief Justice sits at the south end and Mr. Justice Black, the senior Associate Justice, at the north end. Along the side to the left of the Chief Justice sit Justices Stewart, Goldberg, White and Harlan. On the right side sit Justice Clark, myself and Justice Douglas in that order.

We are summoned to conference by a buzzer which rings in our several chambers five minutes before the hour. Upon entering the conference room each of us shakes hands with his colleagues. The handshake tradition originated when Chief Justice Fuller presided many decades ago. It is a symbol that harmony of aims if not of views is the Court's guiding principle.

Each of us has his copy of the agenda of the day's cases before him. The agenda lists the cases applying for review. Each of us before coming to the conference has noted on his copy his tentative view whether or not review should be granted in each case.

The Chief Justice begins the discussion of each case. He then yields to the senior Associate Justice and discussion proceeds down the line in order of seniority until each Justice has spoken.

Voting goes the other way. The junior Justice votes first and voting then proceeds up the line to the Chief Justice, who votes last.

Each of us has a docket containing a sheet for each case with appropriate places for recording the votes. When any case receives four votes for review, that case is transferred to the oral argument list. Applications in which none of us sees merit may be passed over without discussion.

Now how do we process the decisions we agree to review?

There are rare occasions when the question is so clearly controlled by an earlier decision of the Court that a reversal of the lower court judgment is inevitable. In these rare instances we may summarily reverse without oral argument.

EACH SIDE GETS HOUR

The case must very clearly justify summary disposition, however, because our ordinary practice is not to reverse a decision without oral argument. Indeed, oral argument of cases taken for review, whether from the state or federal courts, is the usual practice. We rarely accept submissions of cases on briefs.

Oral argument ordinarily occurs about four months after the application for review is granted. Each party is usually allowed one hour, but in recent years we have limited oral argument to a half-hour in cases thought to involve issues not requiring longer arguments.

Counsel submit their briefs and record in sufficient time for the distribution of one set to each Justice two or three weeks before the oral argument. Most of the members of the present Court follow the practice of reading the briefs before the argument. Some of us often have a bench memorandum prepared before the argument. This memorandum digests the facts and the arguments of both sides, highlighting the matters about which we may want to question counsel at the argument.

Often I have independent research done in advance of argument and incorporate the results in the bench memorandum.

We follow a schedule of two weeks of argument from Monday through Thursday, followed by two weeks of recess for opinion writing and the study of petitions for review. The argued cases are listed on the conference agenda on the Friday following argument. Conference discussion follows the same procedure I have described for the discussions of certiorari petitions.

OPINION ASSIGNED

Of course, it is much more extended. Not infrequently discussion of particular cases may be spread over two or more conferences.

Not until the discussion is completed and a vote taken is the opinion assigned. The assignment is not made at the conference but formally in writing some few days after the conference.

The Chief Justice assigns the opinions in those cases in which he has voted with the majority. The senior Associate Justice voting with the majority assigns the opinions in the other cases. The dissenters agree among themselves who shall write the dissenting opinion. Of course, each Justice is free to write his own opinion, concurring or dissenting.

The writing of an opinion always takes weeks and sometimes months. The most painstaking research and care are involved.

Research, of course, concentrates on relevant legal materials—precedents particularly. But Supreme Court cases often require some familiarity with history, economics, the social and other sciences, and authorities in these areas, too, are consulted when necessary.

When the author of an opinion feels he has an unanswerable document he sends it to a print shop, which we maintain in our building. The printed draft may be revised several times before his proposed opinion is circulated among the other Justices. Copies are sent to each member of the Court, those in the dissent as well as those in the majority.

SOME CHANGE MINDS

Now the author often discovers that his work has only begun. He receives a return, ordinarily in writing, from each Justice who voted with him and sometimes also from the Justices who voted the other way. He learns who will write the dissent if one is to be written. But his particular concern is whether those who voted with him are still of his view and what they have to say about his proposed opinion.

Often some who voted with him at conference will advise that they reserve final judgment pending the circulation of the dissent. It is a common experience that dissents change votes, even enough votes to become the majority.

I have had to convert more than one of my proposed majority opinions into a dissent before the final decision was announced. I have also, however, had the more satisfying experience of rewriting a dissent as a majority opinion for the Court.

Before everyone has finally made up his mind a constant interchange by memoranda, by telephone, at the lunch table continues while we hammer out the final form of the opinion. I had one case during the past term in which I circulated ten printed drafts before one was approved as the Court opinion.

UNIFORM RULE

The point of this procedure is that each Justice, unless he disqualifies himself in a particular case, passes on every piece of business coming to the Court. The Court does not function by means of committees or panels. Each Justice passes on each petition, each time, no matter how drawn, in long hand, by typewriter, or on a press. Our Constitution vests the judicial power in only one Supreme

Court. This does not permit Supreme Court action by committees, panels, or sections.

The method that the Justices use in meeting an enormous caseload varies. There is one uniform rule: Judging is not delegated. Each Justice studies each case in sufficient detail to resolve the question for himself. In a very real sense, each decision is an individual decision of every Justice.

The process can be a lonely, troubling experience for fallible human beings conscious that their best may not be adequate to the challenge.

"We are not unaware," the late Justice Jackson said, "that we are not final because we are infallible; we know that we are infallible only because we are final."

One does not forget how much may depend on his decision. He knows that usually more than the litigants may be affected, that the course of vital social, economic and political currents may be directed.

This then is the decisional process in the Supreme Court. It is not without its tensions, of course—indeed, quite agonizing tensions at times.

I would particularly emphasize that, unlike the case of a Congressional or White House decision, Americans demand of their Supreme Court judges that they produce a written opinion, the collective expression of the judges subscribing to it, setting forth the reason which led them to the decision.

These opinions are the exposition, not just to lawyers, legal scholars and other judges, but to our whole society, of the bases upon which a particular result rests—why a problem, looked at as disinterestedly and dispassionately as nine human beings trained in a tradition of the disinterested and dispassionate approach can look at it, is answered as it is.

It is inevitable, however, that Supreme Court decisions—and the Justices themselves—should be caught up in public debate and be the subjects of bitter controversy.

An editorial in *The Washington Post* did not miss the mark by much in saying that this was so because

> one of the primary functions of the Supreme Court is to keep the people of the country from doing what they would like to do—at times when what they would like to do runs counter to the Constitution. . . . The function of the Supreme Court is not to count constituents; it is to interpret a fundamental charter which imposes restraints on constituents. Independence and integrity, not popularity, must be its standards.

FREUND'S VIEW

Certainly controversy over its work has attended the Court throughout its history. As Professor Paul A. Freund of Harvard remarked, this has been true almost since the Court's first decision:

> When the Court held, in 1793, that the state of Georgia could be sued on a contract in the federal courts, the outraged Assembly of that state passed a bill

declaring that any federal marshal who should try to collect the judgment would be guilty of a felony and would suffer death, without benefit of clergy, by being hanged. When the Court decided that state criminal convictions could be reviewed in the Supreme Court, Chief Justice Roane of Virginia exploded, calling it a "most monstrous and unexampled decision. It can only be accounted for by that love of power which history informs us infects and corrupts all who possess it, and from which even the eminent and upright judges are not exempt."

But public understanding has not always been lacking in the past. Perhaps it exists today. But surely a more informed knowledge of the decisional process should aid a better understanding.

It is not agreement with the Court's decisions that I urge. Our law is the richer and the wiser because academic and informed lay criticism is part of the stream of development.

CONSENSUS NEEDED

It is only a greater awareness of the nature and limits of the Supreme Court's function that I seek.

The ultimate resolution of questions fundamental to the whole community must be based on a common consensus of understanding of the unique responsibility assigned to the Supreme Court in our society.

The lack of that understanding led Mr. Justice Holmes to say fifty years ago:

We are very quiet there, but it is the quiet of a storm center, as we all know. Science has taught the world skepticism and has made it legitimate to put everything to the test of proof. Many beautiful and noble reverences are impaired, but in these days no one can complain if any institution, system, or belief is called on to justify its continuance in life. Of course we are not excepted and have not escaped.

PAINFUL ACCUSATION

Doubts are expressed that go to our very being. Not only are we told that when Marshall pronounced an Act of Congress unconstitutional he usurped a power that the Constitution did not give, but we are told that we are the representatives of a class—a tool of the money power.

I get letters, not always anonymous, intimating that we are corrupt. Well, gentlemen, I admit that it makes my heart ache. It is very painful, when one spends all the energies of one's soul in trying to do good work, with no thought but that of solving a problem according to the rules by which one is bound, to know that many see sinister motives and would be glad of evidence that one was consciously bad.

But we must take such things philosophically and try to see what we can learn from hatred and distrust and whether behind them there may not be a germ of inarticulate truth.

The attacks upon the Court are merely an expression of the unrest that seems to wonder vaguely whether law and order pay. When the ignorant are taught to doubt they do not know what they safely may believe. And it seems to me that at this time we need education in the obvious more than investigation of the obscure.

JUSTICE AND CRIMINAL LAW

A central component of the folklore of American democracy is the belief that the administration of justice is not affected by political considerations, but is impartial. With regard to criminal courts, people generally believe that alleged criminals are usually tried in the presence of an impartial judge before a jury of their peers, whose verdicts render justice to the accused. The judicial process is not nearly so simple and unbiased. Richard Quinney emphasizes the political character of the judicial process in the criminal realm and the large amount of discretion exercised by those involved in bringing cases to and trying cases in our courts.

62

Richard Quinney

THE ADMINISTRATION OF CRIMINAL JUSTICE

Justice is an ideal that abstractly pervades the value systems of most human societies. The American colonists, imbued with the liberal thought of the European enlightenment, made justice the basis of democratic government. The Massachusetts Bill of Rights of 1780 captured the essence of the ideal: "It is essential to the preservation of the rights of every individual, his life, liberty, property, and character, that there be an impartial interpretation of the laws and the administration of justice." A similar notion of justice was written into the Declaration of Independence and the Bill of Rights.

In symbolic form, justice weighs all men impartially on her scales. She represents our ideal of equality between all parties and classes. Law is thus to be administered according to an ideal, not according to the experiences of everyday life. Yet the administration of justice is full of devices for individual-

From Richard Quinney, *The Social Reality of Crime,* pp. 137–150. Copyright © 1970 by Little, Brown and Company (Inc.). Reprinted by permission. Some footnotes are omitted; all are renumbered.

izing the application of criminal law. The complicated machinery of the judicial system involves a series of mitigating practices whereby cases are necessarily individualized according to the numerous extralegal factors. However, the very structure of the judicial system tends to obscure from public view the operation of the criminal law. Partly by design, the decision-making activities of the judicial system are hidden behind the "purple curtain" of the law. The fiction of judicial objectivity is obscured by a system that administers the law according to its own rules.

From an idealistic standpoint, it is useful to analyze the administration of criminal law in reference to the concept of justice. Even from a standpoint of scientific inquiry, the concept of justice is appropriate. Whether or not we always maintain an explicit image of the good and the beautiful, our sociological interest in the administration of criminal law is directed to a goal that is consistent with—and aided by—considerations of justice: How is the criminal law actually administered? From personal experience we know that the criminal law is not administered uniformly. To understand the processes involved in the administration of the criminal law is thus our immediate interest. Nevertheless, in our moments of idealism, we are investigating the differentials in the administration of justice. Whether we use the phrase "administration of criminal law" or "administration of justice," our interest is a sociological investigation of the processes that result in the application of criminal definitions.

POLITICALITY OF JUSTICE

The administration of justice, contrary to common belief, is not "above politics" but is by its very nature political. That is, the administration of criminal law is political in that public policy is being made. The political nature of the judiciary is inherent in government itself. Wherever decisions are made—and that is what the judiciary is about—politics necessarily serves as the basis of the process.

In addition to being political in the general sense of policy making, the judicial system is a creature of the political community in more specific ways. The courts, for instance, are an essential part of the local political structure. To begin with, the kinds of criminal cases that enter the courts are influenced by the character of community politics. The prosecuting attorney, an elected official and often the key figure in the local political machine, determines according to his discretion what law is being violated. His actions result in either the release of suspects or their indictment; and if suspects are indicted, the prosecutor decides the character of the charge. Still later in the process, the fate of the accused depends upon the discretion of the judge, also an appointed or locally elected official. The extent to which the local political system and the administration of criminal laws are related is indicated in conclusions reached by two political scientists:

Thus, elected officials sensitive to the political process charge, prosecute, convict, and sentence criminal defendants. This means that such decisions are made in response to cues from the political structure; thereby the political system provides channels by which local claims and local interests can influence judicial outcomes. In this way, the judiciary helps create the conditions necessary for the reelection of court officials or for their frequent promotion to higher offices in the state or nation. In short, criminal prosecutions provide opportunities for the political system to affect judicial decisions and for the judicial process to provide favors which nourish political organizations.[1]

The politicality of local criminal justice is shaped considerably by the structure of the American party system. Political leadership in the country is dispersed among the political parties. Because of the decentralized nature of the parties, local politics is influenced by party considerations. Party leaders use the judiciary as a source of patronage. Elected judges usually owe their office to favors rendered to a political party. Specific party concerns inevitably enter into the content of public policy, including the decisions made in respect to criminal matters.

Since the judiciary is the focus of significant power, it is one of the principal points at which the claims of interest groups are aimed. Because courts serve as the arena where the conflicting claims of diverse groups are presented and resolved, some control over the courts is desired by the interest groups affected by judicial decisions. Interest groups utilize every resource at their command to ensure that decisions of the courts are made in the protection of their interests.

Because the judiciary operates within a fairly routinized legal structure, interest groups must rely primarily upon indirect means to gain access to the decision-making process. These indirect methods may be classified into three categories: (1) those influencing the selection of judges, (2) those influencing the content of decisions, and (3) those maximizing or minimizing the effects of decisions as they are implemented. By such methods, interest groups are able to have criminal statutes interpreted in their favor. The application of criminal definitions at the judicial level is largely a matter of selective interpretations of the law that favor the interests of some while negating the interests of others. Under the adversary system of justice, there is little compromise: someone wins while someone else loses.

The politicality of justice is by no means the sole result of the conflict between diverse interest groups. The political nature of the administration of criminal law is also affected by the interests of the government itself. In every society the wielders of governmental power use the criminal law to legitimate their assertions and the criminal courts to maintain their domination. Opposing political viewpoints and actions may be suppressed through the use of the

---

[1]. Herbert Jacob and Kenneth Vines, "The Role of the Judiciary in American State Politics," in Glendon Schubert (ed.), *Judicial Decision-Making* (New York: The Free Press of Glencoe, 1963), p. 250.

courts by the government. Through various forms of the *political trial,* political foes may be eliminated from political competition. In addition, the judicial system may be used by governments to repress certain groups in the society. Judges in the American south, for example, have tended to consistently make decisions that would maintain the domination of the white man over the black. In South Africa, the ruling minority has been able to successfully subjugate the rest of the population in large part by their use of the criminal courts. In these cases and others, the judiciary maintains the interests of the established government.

DISCRETION AND DECISION MAKING
IN THE JUDICIAL PROCESS

Justice is political because the administration of criminal law involves making decisions. Furthermore, whenever decisions are made, discretion necessarily occurs. Judicial decision making without the exercise of discretion is inconceivable.

Within the judicial process a number of types of decisions are made at various stages. Once a case is admitted to the judicial system, after an arrest, a series of decisions are made regarding the fate of the suspect. Some cases, on the basis of the decision reached during the first judicial appearance, may be removed entirely from the judicial system. The other cases, however, move sequentially from one stage to another before going out of the system. At each stage, the decision reached by certain officials limits the alternatives for the decisions in the subsequent stages.

Following the arrest, then, the suspect is usually brought before a court official (the magistrate) to determine the nature of the case. A preliminary hearing may follow to establish "probable cause." A decision is also made on the detention of the suspect, including the possible setting of bail. Between the time of the first judicial appearance and the indictment, the prosecution decides what charges to press or whether to press charges at all. Once formal charges are made, pretrial proceedings are established during the arraignment. Decisions are reached regarding such matters as the time of trial, the use of the plea, challenge of the formal charge, the nature of the evidence, and the defendant's mental or physical capacity. If a trial takes place, rather than a settlement through guilty plea proceedings, decisions are made by judge and jury in the courtroom. In arguing their cases, the prosecuting attorney and the lawyer for the defense make innumerable strategic decisions. The decision to convict the accused and the decision to impose a particular sentence are the consequences of the decisions from the time of the arrest.

The fate of the convicted person is still problematic to some extent, however, in that an appellate review may alter previous decisions. But most likely the convicted person must continue within the judicial system until the time when officials make decisions regarding his release. From the time the suspect enters the judicial process, the decisions of others determine whether or not he will be defined as criminal.

As in the use of discretion by the police, the boundaries of discretion in the administration of criminal law are not clearly defined. Obviously judicial decisions are not made uniformly. Decisions are made according to a host of extralegal factors, including the age of the offender, his race, and social class.

Perhaps the most obvious example of judicial discretion occurs in the handling of cases of persons from minority groups. Negroes, in comparison to whites, are convicted with lesser evidence and sentenced to more severe punishments. In a study of 821 homicides in several counties of North Carolina between 1930 and 1940, it was found that the fewest indictments were made when whites killed Negroes and the highest proportion when Negroes killed whites. The courts tended to regard the slaying of a white by a Negro as almost prima facie evidence of guilt, while the murder of a Negro by a white was believed to require mitigating circumstances such as provocation. Furthermore, prisoner statistics show that in most states Negroes are committed to prison longer than are whites for the same types of offenses.

Another source of variation in judicial decision making is found in the great variety of judicial systems. In the United States there are fifty-two separate court jurisdictions, consisting of the judicial systems of the fifty states, the District of Columbia, and the federal government. Furthermore, within the state jurisdictions there are several forms of courts, variously known as "police" courts, "special sessions" courts, and "quarter" courts. Some courts deal with minor criminal violations of local laws and ordinances and others with more serious offenses. While these courts have specialized functions, considerable confusion results from the overlapping of their jurisdictions.

The federal judicial system is also composed of several types of courts with diversified activities and functions. In addition, there are the federal circuit courts which are divided according to the geographical areas of the country. Because of the complexity and diversity of the judiciary in the United States, variations in judicial decision making are to be expected. The administration of the criminal law cannot be uniform, but necessarily involves the use of localized discretion in the course of individualized justice.

PROSECUTION AND NONTRIAL ADJUDICATION

By popular conception, the focal point of the administration of justice consists of the court trial, where the fate of the accused is decided by twelve of his peers. Not only is this conception incorrect about the *way* in which persons are convicted, but it is misleading in the implication that adjudication consists *only* of the decision of the judge or jury to convict or acquit. As we have seen, several judicial stages necessarily precede a trial. But it is most significant that in these pretrial proceedings the majority of criminal cases never reach the stage of the criminal trial. The decision to impose a criminal definition is usually made in the *pretrial* proceedings by *nontrial* adjudication.

Upon arrest, or following the issuance of a summons or on-the-spot citation, the suspect is supposed to be brought promptly before a magistrate, who reads the warrant to the suspect. If the offense is a minor one, triable by the magistrate, a summary trial may be held immediately. If the offense is more serious, not triable by the magistrate, the purpose of the initial appearance is more limited. The suspect will be given the opportunity of having a preliminary hearing to determine if there is sufficient evidence to justify being held for possible trial. If he waives a preliminary hearing, he is then bound over to a court of trial jurisdiction.

The principal function of the first judicial appearance is not, however, to determine whether there is sufficient evidence for trial. Neither the prosecuting attorney nor the defense lawyer is ready at this point to determine whether probable cause exists. The principal function of the first appearance is to provide for the defendant's release, pending further judicial proceedings. While release is a constitutional right, the bail procedure of temporarily forfeiting money for freedom has resulted in a number of unjust practices. Ideally the only criterion for the determination of the amount of bail is the amount necessary to ensure the reappearance of the defendant. In practice, however, the bail system discriminates against those who cannot afford to pay the bail fee, fosters a shady bail-bond business, and promotes the use of questionable judicial procedures in the setting of bail. Recent alternatives to the bail system, such as pretrial parole, are eliminating the deficiencies of bail, at the same time providing for both the constitutional release of the defendant and the assurance of his return for subsequent judicial processing.

Arraignment and the Plea

In some jurisdictions the suspect is arraigned immediately after being booked at the police station, thus bypassing the appearance before a magistrate. Whether arraignment is the first judicial appearance or a later one, the arraignment proceeding consists of an appearance before a judge of the trial court. There the judge reads the charge to the defendant and informs him of his right to counsel. The initial charge is based either upon the "information" or "indictment," depending upon the procedures used in the jurisdiction. Some jurisdictions rely upon a grand jury to return an indictment for felony cases with charges for misdemeanors being based on information filed by the prosecuting attorney.

Whatever procedure is used for reaching a charge, the judge then asks the defendant to plead to the charge. The defendant may plead guilty, not guilty, or may stand mute. With the permission of the judge, he may also have the option of pleading *nolo contendere,* which is the same as a plea of guilty except that it cannot be used as an admission in subsequent civil suits. If the defendant pleads guilty, the judge will ordinarily enter a judgment of conviction, postponing the sentence until a presentence investigation can be made by the probation department. If the defendant stands mute, the judge will enter a plea of not guilty, and a trial will follow. If the plea of the defendant is not guilty, the judge asks whether the defendant desires a jury trial or whether he prefers to be tried by the judge without the presence of a jury. A plea of not guilty places the burden on the state to prove every element of the offense beyond a reasonable doubt.

Guilty Plea Negotiation

Important as the trial is as an ideal in the administration of justice, it is far from the most commonly used method of convicting and acquitting defendants. Roughly 90 percent of criminal convictions are based on pleas of guilty which are adjudicated without a trial. Estimates on the percentage of cases disposed of by guilty pleas, however, are difficult to establish because of such matters as variations in use from one jurisdiction to another, fluctuations from time to time, and variations according to the kinds of crime being tabulated. Nevertheless, the statistics in Table 1 indicate the extent to which guilty plea convictions are used in the general trial jurisdictions of several states.

Our judicial system has come to depend upon the use of the guilty plea. If all criminal cases were to receive a trial upon a plea of not guilty, the courts simply could not handle the case load. There are not enough, and conceivably could never be enough, judges, prosecutors, and defense attorneys to operate a system in which most defendants would go to trial.

The judicial necessity of guilty pleas has given rise to the practice commonly known as "plea bargaining." A substantial portion of guilty pleas result from negotiations between the prosecutor and defense lawyer or between the prosecutor and the defendant. In addition to managing the case load, the negotiated plea accomplishes other purposes.

> As the term implies, plea negotiation involves an exchange of concessions and advantages between the state and the accused. The defendant who pleads guilty is treated less severely than he would be if he were convicted of the maximum charge and assessed the most severe penalty. At the same time, he waives his right to trial, thereby losing his chance, no matter how slight, for outright acquittal. The state, at the relatively small cost of charge reduction leniency, gains the numerous administrative advantages of the guilty plea over a long, costly, and always uncertain trial. In this way the negotiated plea in a real sense answers two important objectives of criminal justice administration: the individualization of justice and the maintenance of the guilty plea system.[2]

The negotiated guilty plea is thus a compromise conviction reached by the state and the accused for the benefit of both.

Having studied this informal conviction process, Newman reported in an article that plea bargaining occurred in more than half the felony cases stud-

---

2. Donald J. Newman, *Conviction: The Determination of Guilt or Innocence without Trial* (Boston: Little, Brown, 1966), p. 77.

Table 1 Guilty Plea Convictions in Several States

State	Total convictions	Guilty pleas Number	Guilty pleas Percentage
California (1965)	30,840	22,817	74.0
Connecticut	1,596	1,494	93.9
District of Columbia (yr. end. June 30, 1964)	1,115	817	73.3
Hawaii	393	360	91.5
Illinois	5,591	4,768	85.2
Kansas	3,025	2,727	90.2
Massachusetts (1963)	7,790	6,642	85.2
Minnesota (1965)	1,567	1,437	91.7
New York	17,249	16,464	95.5
U.S. District Courts	29,170	26,273	90.2
Average			87.0

Source: President's Commission on Law Enforcement and Administration of Justice, *Task Force Report: The Courts* (Washington, D.C.: U.S. Government Printing Office, p. 9.

ied.[3] During the process the accused, directly or through an attorney, offered to plead guilty providing the charge was reduced in kind or degree, or exchanged for a specific type or length of sentence. The subsequent conviction agreements followed several patterns according to the types of bargains involved:

1. Bargain Concerning the Charge. A plea of guilty was entered by the offenders in exchange for a reduction of the charge from the one alleged in the complaint. This ordinarily occurred in cases where the offense in question carried statutory degrees of severity such as homicide, assault, and sex offenses. This type was mentioned as a major issue in twenty percent of the cases in which bargaining occurred. The majority of offenders in these instances were represented by lawyers.

2. Bargain Concerning the Sentence. A plea of guilty was entered by the offenders in exchange for a promise that the offender would be placed on probation, although a less-than-maximum prison term was the basis in certain instances. All offenses except murder, serious assault, and robbery are represented in this type of bargaining process. This was by far the most frequent consideration given in exchange for guilty pleas, occurring in almost half (45.5 percent) of the cases in which any bargaining occurred. Again, most of these offenders were represented by attorneys.

3. Bargain for Concurrent Charges. This type of informal process occurred chiefly among offenders pleading without counsel. These men exchanged guilty pleas for the concurrent pressing of multiple charges, generally numerous counts of the same offense or related violations such as breaking and entering and larceny. This method, of course, has much the same effect as pleading for consideration in the sentence. The offender with concurrent convictions, however, may not be serving

3. Donald J. Newman, "Pleading Guilty for Considerations: A Study of Bargain Justice," *Journal of Criminal Law, Criminology and Police Science,* 46 (March-April, 1956), 780–790.

a reduced sentence; he is merely serving one sentence for many crimes. Altogether, concurrent convictions were reported by 21.8 percent of the men who were convicted by informal methods.

4. Bargain for Dropped Charges. This variation occurred in about an eighth of the cases who reported bargaining. It involved an agreement on the part of the prosecution not to press formally one or more charges against the offender if he in turn pleaded guilty to (usually) the major offense. The offenses dropped were extraneous law violations contained in, or accompanying armed robbery and violation of probation where a new crime had been committed. This informal method, like bargaining for concurrent charges, was reported chiefly by offenders without lawyers. It occurred in 12.6 percent of cases in which bargaining was claimed.[4]

Although most of the remainder of the sample pleaded guilty without considerations, in many of these cases the attorneys probably bargained, or attempted to bargain, without successfully achieving a conviction compromise.

The interactions and perceptions of the prosecutor and the defense are critical in the negotiation of a guilty plea. A student of the guilty plea process observed that the prosecutor (district attorney) and the defense (public defender) develop during their interactions a common orientation to the alteration of charges.[5] The negotiations are not able, for purposes of a suitable reduction in charge, to refer to a statutory definition of a particular offense, since the penal code does not provide the reference for deciding the correspondence between the conduct of the offender and the legal category. In the charge of burglary, for example, the prosecutor and defense negotiate about a nonstatutory type of "burglar." The reduction of a burglary charge to a charge of petty theft is accomplished because the negotiators are able to regard the reduction as reasonable and consistent with the kinds of behaviors that are normally associated with the specific charge. During their interaction and repeated negotiations, then, the prosecutor and defense develop unstated guides for reducing original charges to lesser charges.

Plea bargaining takes place between the prosecutor and the accused or his defense for reasons more immediate than those of the individualization of justice and the maintenance of the judicial system. The decision to reduce the charge is often made because the prosecutor realizes that his evidence is probably insufficient for conviction at trial. In other cases reduction may be necessary because of the reluctance of complainants, victims, or witnesses to testify. The prosecutor at other times may suggest a reduction in charge because he believes that the judge or jury is unlikely to convict the defendant. Judges themselves in some cases may favor charge reduction to avoid the necessity of imposing the mandatory sentence (either maximum or minimum)

4. *Ibid.*
5. David Sudnow, "Normal Crimes: Sociological Features of the Penal Code in a Public Defender Office," *Social Problems,* 12 (Winter, 1965), 255–276.

associated with the original charge. A parole sentence may only be possible if the original charge is reduced to a lesser charge. On the other hand, whatever the bargaining agreement, the judge may acquit the defendant for a number of reasons that grow out of an interest in individualized justice and judicial maintenance. Acquittals are made because (1) the conduct is regarded as a minor violation, (2) the offender is viewed as unaccountable for his behavior, (3) the conduct is considered normal to the subculture of the defendant, (4) the conduct is a matter of private morality, (5) specialized treatment may be deemed more appropriate than punishment, (6) restitution is otherwise made to the victim, and (7) the judge disagrees with the purpose of the law or with the law enforcement effort.

Whether the judge convicts according to the plea negotiated by the prosecutor and defense or acquits the defendant, he obviously has a personal interest in the outcome of each case. Technically the judge is not supposed to enter into the bargaining. However, by subtle cues and not so subtle demands, the judge has an influence on the negotiation of pleas. The advantages of plea negotiation for the judge have been indicated in a study of "Metropolitan Court":

> According to the ideology of the law, the judge is required to be not only impartial but active in seeking out and preserving the rights of all offenders. Nevertheless, he also has a vested interest in a high rate of negotiated pleas. He shares the prosecutor's earnest desire to avoid the time consuming, expensive, unpredictable snares and pitfalls of an adversary trial. He sees an impossible backlog of cases, with their mounting delays, as possible public evidence of his "inefficiency" and failure. The defendant's plea of guilty enables the judge to engage in a social-psychological fantasy—the accused becomes an already repentant individual who has "learned his lesson" and deserves lenient treatment. Indeed, as previously indicated, many judges give a less severe sentence to a defendant who has negotiated a plea than to one who has been convicted of the same offense after a trial.[6]

Whatever may be the reason for the negotiation of a guilty plea, be it the vested interest of the prosecutor, the defense, the judge, or an interest further removed, the resulting conviction is a criminal definition. Guilty plea negotiation ultimately amounts to the creation of crime. . . .

On October 10, 1973, Vice-President Spiro Agnew walked into the United States District Court in Baltimore and stated: "My decision to resign and enter a plea of *nolo contendere* [no contest] rests on my firm belief that the public interest requires swift disposition of the problems which are facing me." The plea of *nolo contendere* was made to the charge that he had received payments in 1967 which he had failed to report for the purposes of income taxation. Thus ended a dramatic

---

6. Abraham S. Blumberg, *Criminal Justice* (Chicago: Quadrangle Books, 1967), p. 65.

series of revelations concerning political pay-offs from Maryland contractors to the Vice-President while he was Governor of Maryland and even after he assumed the vice-presidency. Both the Vice-President's resignation and his plea were the result of "plea bargaining" between Attorney General Richardson and a four-man staff of Justice Department attorneys on the one hand, and Spiro Agnew's lawyers on the other. It was Richardson who essentially overruled the others on the justice Department team by agreeing to allow the Vice-President to resign and plead *nolo contendere* in return for dropping the serious charges that could have been used against him. The debate within the Justice Department team over what kind of a bargain, if any, should have been made with Vice-President Agnew was later to be echoed throughout the country. A particularly interesting issue in the Agnew case is the question of whether or not an elected or appointed official should be permitted to use his office as a trade-off in plea bargaining. The following selection, written just before the revelation of the deal that Vice-President Agnew made with Attorney General Richardson, discusses the role of plea bargaining in the court system and the problem of plea bargaining with public officials in particular.

63
Nathan Lewin

BARGAINING WITH
FEDERAL PROSECUTORS

While announcing publicly that "evidence regarding the VP" would be presented to a federal grand jury in Baltimore, Attorney General Elliot Richardson confirmed that during the two weeks preceding that statement, he, as well as the head of the Justice Department's Criminal Division and the US attorney in Baltimore had been meeting with Mr. Agnew's lawyers "to discuss procedural aspects of the case and options available to the Vice President." The words "plea bargaining" were not used but the announcement substantially confirmed earlier news stories that Mr. Agnew's attorneys had been negotiating with the prosecutors to work out a disposition of the possible criminal charges. *The Washington Post* reported on September 26 that the prosecutors had offered to allow the Vice President to plead guilty to a "minor offense," if he would resign and simultaneously issue a statement acknowledging that he was guilty of taking bribes. The Vice President's lawyers, it was said, had offered only a resignation.

The decision to start presenting proof to a grand jury does not end the negotiating process. Nor does a request for congressional investigation or even

From Nathan Lewin, "Bargaining with Federal Prosecutors," *The New Republic* (October 6, 1973), pp. 12–14. Reprinted by permission of *The New Republic,* © 1973 Harrison-Blaine of New Jersey, Inc.

an attempt to halt the grand jury mean that discussions with the prosecutors are at an end. If all other avenues fail, the Vice President may reconsider the refusal to do more than resign. If on the other hand Mr. Agnew were to succeed in delaying grand jury action (and possibly deferring any criminal charge until the federal five-year statute of limitation has expired), the prosecutors might soften their demands. In Agnew's case, as in any major criminal investigation and prosecution, feelers and proposals will probably continue to be exchanged among all counsel.

Plea bargaining is one of the hidden recesses of the law. It is, as the words indicate, a process by which a prosecutor and the lawyer for someone formally accused of crime haggle over the conditions under which the accused will agree to forego a trial and admit to the court that he was guilty. Since more than 90 percent of the criminal charges filed in the United States result in guilty pleas, and in almost all situations there has been some agreement struck before the plea is made, it is surprising that so little is known about the process. Deals are concluded between prosecutors and defense lawyers in the most informal ways, and each prosecutor's office—and, at times, each prosecutor within a single office—may have a peculiar and unique approach. Most criminal defendants are therefore better off with a tough negotiator as a lawyer, or with one who is attuned to the quirks of the particular prosecutor, than with a courtroom technician.

The usual carrot that a prosecutor offers in a plea bargain is a reduction of the charges. Federal indictments in particular are customarily drafted in multiple counts. That is why the first news reports of a federal indictment often say that the defendant, if convicted, "faces imprisonment for thirty-five years" or "sixty years"—totally unrealistic figures arrived at by multiplying the number of charges by the maximum possible jail term for each and assuming that the judge will sentence the accused, if he is guilty, to serve the sentences one after the other. In practice federal judges seldom impose consecutive sentences, and the maximum for any single charge is usually more than the judge would mete out even if all the allegations were sustained at trial.

Knowing this, the practice of federal prosecutors is to allow a defendant to plead guilty to one "count" of an indictment alleging many offenses and to drop the other "counts" when the defendant is sentenced. If the accused takes up this offer he is assured that no matter how seriously the judge views his crime or crimes, he will not be punished more than the maximum Congress specified in the law for the single violation. Prosecutors have, at times, been able to drive harder bargains—when their evidence is strong—sometimes requiring pleas of guilty to two or more charges or to a charge that carries a long maximum jail sentence. And there have been occasions when defendants' lawyers have wangled better deals for their clients, such as reduction of a felony charge (which in the federal system means potential imprisonment of more than one year) to a misdemeanor (less than one year maximum).

A second aspect of the bargaining process that the courts have legitimized has to do with the sentence actually imposed. In all the judicial systems in the United States, state or federal, a judge decides what punishment will be given a defendant who has admitted his guilt. In most federal courts—with a handful of exceptions—prosecutors make no specific recommendations as to what the sentence should be. But in the major metropolitan centers on the east coast, they follow the practice of "bringing to the sentencing court's attention" facts that they think should result in a lighter or heavier sentence. A criminal defendant who cooperates with an investigation, for example, can count on the prosecutor's informing the judge of his helpfulness before or at the time of sentence. A recalcitrant defendant, on the other hand, will find the prosecutor implying to the judge that there is no reason not to be severe.

In a most famous recent plea bargain, counsel for E. Howard Hunt and Prosecutor Earl Silbert agreed initially at the outset of the Watergate trial that the charges against Hunt could be disposed of if Hunt pleaded guilty to three counts of the six in the original Watergate indictment. At this point Judge Sirica stepped in and exercised the prerogative that a judge has, once there is an indictment before him, to reject even the terms that the prosecutor has agreed to. The judge refused to take the action needed to make the deal effective—that is formally dismiss those charges that the prosecutor agreed to drop in exchange for Hunt's guilty plea. Mr. Hunt finally had no choice but to plead guilty to *all* the charges against him or proceed to trial on all. He elected to plead and now has moved to vacate that plea.

Special Prosecutor Cox's lawyers have, in the bargains they have struck so far, avoided putting themselves into a position where Judge Sirica could undo their deals. Neither Fred LaRue nor Jeb Magruder was formally charged with all the federal offenses that their own testimony showed they had committed. Rather than make the plea bargain *after* indictment, when the court would have to approve dismissal of charges, Cox's office offered to LaRue and Magruder—as it is reputed to have offered to others—a deal that bypasses the grand jury and results in a lesser charge being filed at the outset. Under the federal court's criminal rules a defendant may choose to give up his right to have the grand jury hear the evidence and return an indictment; he may stand charged if he wishes on the prosecutor's allegation alone. The technical difference in terms is that a grand jury's charge is an "indictment"; a prosecutor's is an "information."

Both LaRue and Magruder agreed to plead guilty to one-count informations that carry maximum jail terms of five years. They stand charged with nothing else, and Judge Sirica is powerless, even is he were unhappy with the form of the accusation, to do anything about it.

Whether this is a desirable approach to take to prospective Watergate defendants is not beyond dispute. Is it fair that Hunt, Liddy, McCord and the four Cubans face extended jail terms because of their part in the Watergate break-in while the higher-ups risk no more than a five-year sentence? Is it not of some importance to history, at least, and possibly to a fair wrap-up of all the prosecutions that grow out of the break-in and cover-up for a grand jury to charge all those who deserve to be charged with all the crimes that have been committed and then leave it to the prosecutors to negotiate out all cases on an evenhanded basis, taking to trial those who refuse to accept a uniform offer?

If one views the Watergate prosecutions as just a means of putting away those who deserve incarceration, the bypassing of grand jury indictments probably does the job. Judge Sirica will, in all likelihood, reduce the extravagant sentences he has already imposed on those convicted and sentenced and will probably not give out prison terms of more than five years even to those on the LaRue-Magruder plateau. Even President Nixon, however, with his call to turn Watergate over to the courts, recognized that the process plays a greater national role than is served by bare punishment.

Several aspects of Mr. Agnew's case complicate his plea bargaining and suggest doubts about whether it should be going on at all. First there is the matter of his public office. Should an elected or appointed public official be permitted to offer his resignation as an element of a plea bargain? Obviously this gives public officials greater license to commit crimes than ordinary citizens who have nothing equivalent to give if they are caught. Did the Department of Justice remotely conceive of letting Judge Kerner of the Court of Appeals in Chicago quietly resign instead of facing trial on the charges made against him? Were such pre-indictment offers made to congressmen who have been formally accused such as John Dowdy or Bertram Podell? The only case one can think of in which criminal prosecution was fended off by a resignation was John Mitchell's successful removal of Abe Fortas from the Supreme Court. Whether there was really enough in that Justice Department file for the institution of a criminal investigation is, of course, uncertain.

On the other side is the unfairness to the public official of entangling his public status with the allegation of crime. Opening a criminal investigation and agreeing to shut it off in exchange for resignation could be a way of forcing one from public office. That concern is increased if there is any possibility that the individual negotiating the deal on the prosecution side may have reason other than the objective of law enforcement in securing the resignation. President Nixon's interest in his Vice President's departure is now the subject of only the faintest of denials, and if his Attorney General incorporates a resignation in a disposition of the criminal charges, Mr. Richardson's ringing promise before the American Bar Association to remove even the appearance of politics from Justice Department action will be broken while its echo still reverberates.

A second concern peculiar to the Agnew case, which did not apply to the LaRue and Magruder situations, is that neither the specific allegations nor the hard facts of Mr. Agnew's situation are known. The public is entitled to know them so long as they affect a vice president, and it plainly would not do if the Justice Department and Mr. Agnew's attorneys were to agree on a minor accusation, generally framed, to which guilt would be admitted. Given the rumor, denial, charge and counter-charge that have marked this case from the time it first broke into public notice, the public interest demands the full treatment by way of indictment (if there is evidence to return one) and full public awareness of all the elements that even enter into a plea bargain.

CHAPTER 10

The Bureaucracy

American bureaucracy today is an important fourth branch of the government. Too frequently the administrative branch is lumped under the heading of the "Executive" and is considered to be subordinate to the President. But the following selections will reveal that the bureaucracy is often autonomous, acting outside of the control of Congress, the President, and even the judiciary. This fact raises an important problem for our constitutional democracy: How can the bureaucracy be kept responsible if it does not fit into the constitutional framework that was designed to guarantee limited and responsible government?

CONSTITUTIONAL BACKGROUND

64

Peter Woll

CONSTITUTIONAL DEMOCRACY AND BUREAUCRATIC POWER

The administrative branch today stands at the very center of our governmental process; it is the keystone of the structure. And administrative agencies exercise legislative and judicial as well as executive functions—a fact that is often overlooked. . . .

How should we view American bureaucracy? Ultimately, the power of government comes to rest in the administrative branch. Agencies are given the responsibility of making concrete decisions carrying out vague policy initiated in Congress or by the President. The agencies can offer expert advice, closely attuned to the most interested pressure groups, and they often not only determine the policies that the legislature and executive recommend in the first place, but also decisively affect the policy-making process. Usually it is felt that the bureaucracy is politically "neutral," completely under the domination of the President, Congress, or the courts. We will see that this is not entirely the case, and that the President and Congress have only sporadic control over the administrative process.

The bureaucracy is a semi-autonomous branch of the government, often dominating Congress, exercising strong influence on the President, and only infrequently subject to review by the courts. If our constitutional democracy is to be fully analyzed, we must focus attention upon the administrative branch. What is the nature of public administration? How are administration and politics intertwined? How are administrative constituencies determined? What is the relationship between agencies and their constituencies? What role should the President assume in relation to the administrative branch? How far should Congress go in controlling agencies which in fact tend to dominate the legislative process? Should judicial review be expanded? What are the conditions of judicial review? How do administrative agencies perform judicial functions, and how do these activities affect the ability of courts to oversee their actions? These questions confront us with what is called the problem of administrative responsibility: that is, how can we control the activities of the adminis-.

From Peter Woll (ed.), *Public Administration and Policy* (Harper Torchbooks, 1966), pp. 1–14. Reprinted by permission.

trative branch? In order to approach an understanding of this difficult problem, it is necessary to appreciate the nature of the administrative process and how it interacts with other branches of the government and with the general public. It is also important to understand the nature of our constitutional system, and the political context within which agencies function.

We operate within the framework of a constitutional democracy. This means, first, that the government is to be limited by the separation of powers and Bill of Rights. Another component of the system, federalism, is designed in theory to provide states with a certain amount of authority when it is not implied at the national level. Our separation of powers, the system of checks and balances, and the federal system help to explain some of the differences between administrative organization here and in other countries. But the Constitution does not explicitly provide for the administrative branch, which has become a new fourth branch of government. This raises the question of how to control the bureaucracy when there are no clear constitutional limits upon it. The second aspect of our system, democracy, is of course implied in the Constitution itself, but has expanded greatly since it was adopted. We are confronted, very broadly speaking, first with the problem of constitutional limitation, and secondly with the problem of democratic participation in the activities of the bureaucracy. The bureaucracy must be accommodated within the framework of our system of constitutional democracy. This is the crux of the problem of administrative responsibility.

Even though the Constitution does not explicitly provide for the bureaucracy, it has had a profound impact upon the structure, functions, and general place that the bureaucracy occupies in government. The administrative process was incorporated into the constitutional system under the heading of "The Executive Branch." But the concept of "administration" at the time of the adoption of the Constitution was a very simple one, involving the "mere execution" of "executive details," to use the phrases of Hamilton in *The Federalist.* The idea, at that time, was simply that the President as Chief Executive would be able to control the Executive Branch in carrying out the mandates of Congress. In *Federalist 72,* after defining administration in this very narrow way, Hamilton stated:

> ... The persons, therefore, to whose immediate management the different administrative matters are committed ought to be considered as Assistants or Deputies of the Chief Magistrate, and on this account, they ought to derive their offices from his appointment, at least from his nomination, and ought to be subject to his superintendence.

It was clear that Hamilton felt the President would be responsible for administrative action as long as he was in office. This fact later turned up in what can be called the "presidential supremacy" school of thought, which held and still holds that the President is *constitutionally* responsible for the administrative branch, and that Congress should delegate to him all necessary authority for this purpose. Nevertheless, whatever the framers of the Constitution might have planned if they could have foreseen the nature of bureaucratic development, the fact is that the system they constructed in many ways supported bureaucratic organization and functions independent of the President. The role they assigned to Congress in relation to administration assured this result, as did the general position of Congress in the governmental system as a check or balance to the power of the President. Congress has a great deal of authority over the adminstrative process.

If we compare the powers of Congress and the President over the bureaucracy it becomes clear that they both have important constitutional responsibility. Congress retains primary control over the organization of the bureaucracy. It alone creates and destroys agencies, and determines whether they are to be located within the executive branch or outside it. This has enabled Congress to create a large number of *independent* agencies beyond presidential control. Congress has the authority to control appropriations and may thus exercise a great deal of power over the administrative arm, although increasingly the Bureau of the Budget and the President have the initial, and more often than not the final say over the budget. Congress also has the authority to define the jurisdiction of agencies. Finally, the Constitution gives to the legislature the power to interfere in high level presidential appointments, which must be "by and with the advice and consent of the Senate."

Congress may extend the sharing of the appointive power when it sets up new agencies. It may delegate to the President pervasive authority to control the bureaucracy. But one of the most important elements of the separation of powers is the electoral system, which gives to Congress a constituency which is different from and even conflicting with that of the President. This means that Congress often decides to set up agencies beyond presidential purview. Only rarely will it grant the President any kind of final authority to structure the bureaucracy. During World War II, on the basis of the War Powers Act, the President had the authority to reorganize the administrative branch. Today he has the same authority, provided that Congress does not veto presidential proposals within a certain time limit. In refusing to give the President permanent reorganization authority, Congress is jealously guarding one of its important prerogatives.

Turning to the constitutional authority of the President over the bureaucracy, it is somewhat puzzling to see that it gives him a relatively small role. He appoints certain officials by and with the advice and consent of the Senate. He has directive power over agencies that are placed within his jurisdiction by Congress. His control over patronage, once so important, has diminished sharply under the merit system. The President is Commander-in-Chief of all military forces, which puts him in a controlling position over the Defense Department and agencies involved in military matters. In the area of international relations, the President is by constitutional authority the "Chief Diplomat," to use Rossiter's phrase. This means that he appoints Ambassadors (by and with the advice and consent of the Senate), and generally directs national activites in the international arena—a crucially important executive function. But regardless of the apparent intentions of some of the framers of the Constitution as expressed by Hamilton in *The Federalist,* and in spite of the predominance of the Presidency in military and foreign affairs, the fact remains that we seek in vain for explicit constitutional authorization for the President to be "Chief Administrator."

This is not to say that the President does not have an important responsibility to act as chief of the bureaucracy, merely that there is no constitutional mandate for this. As our system evolved, the President was given more and more responsibility until he became, in practice, Chief Administrator. At the same time the constitutional system has often impeded progress in this direction. The President's Committee on Administrative Management in 1937, and later the Hoover Commissions of 1949 and 1955, called upon Congress to initiate a series of reforms increasing presidential authority over the administrative branch. It was felt that this was necessary to make democracy work. The President is the only official elected nationally, and if the administration is to be held democratically accountable, he alone can stand as its representative. But meaningful control from the White House requires that the President have a comprehensive program which encompasses the activities of the bureaucracy. He must be informed as to what they are doing, and be able to control them. He must understand the complex responsibilities of the bureaucracy. Moreover, he must be able to call on sufficient political support to balance the support which the agencies draw from private clientele groups and congressional committees. This has frequently proven a difficult and often impossible task for the President. He may have the *authority* to control the bureaucracy in many areas, but not enough *power.*

On the basis of the Constitution, Congress feels it quite proper that when it delegates legislative authority to administrative agencies it can relatively often place these groups outside the control of the President. For example, in the case of the Interstate Commerce Commission . . . Congress has delegated final authority to that agency to control railroad mergers and other aspects of transportation activity, without giving the President the right to veto. The President may feel that a particular merger is undesirable because it is in violation of the antitrust laws, but the Interstate Commerce Commission is likely to feel differently. In such a situation, the President can do nothing because he does not have the *legal authority* to take any action. If he could muster enough political support to exercise influence over the ICC, he would be able to control it, but the absence of legal authority is an important factor in such cases and diminishes presidential power. Moreover, the ICC draws strong support from the railroad industry, which has been able to counterbalance the political support possessed by the President and other groups that have wished to control it. Analogous situations exist with respect to other regulatory agencies.

Besides the problem of congressional and presidential control over the bureaucracy, there is the question of judicial review of administrative decisions. The rule of law is a central element in our Constitution. The rule of law means that decisions judicial in nature should be handled by common law courts, because of their expertise in rendering due process of law. When administrative agencies engage in adjudication their decisions should be subject to judicial review—at least, they should if one supports the idea of the supremacy of law. Judicial decisions are supposed to be rendered on an independent and impartial basis, through the use of tested procedures, in order to arrive at the accurate determination of the truth. Administrative adjudication should not be subject to presidential or congressional control, which would mean political determination of decisions that should be rendered in an objective manner. The idea of the rule of law, derived from the common law and adopted within the framework of our constitutional system, in theory limits legislative and executive control over the bureaucracy.

The nature of our constitutional system poses very serious difficulties to the development of a system of administrative responsibility. The Constitution postulates that the functions of government must be separated into different branches with differing constituencies and separate authority. The idea is that the departments should oppose each other, thereby preventing the arbitrary exercise of political power. Any combination of functions was considered to lead inevitably to arbitrary government. This is a debatable point, but the result of the Constitution is quite clear. The administrative process, on the other hand, often combines various functions of government in the same hands. Attempts are made, of course, to separate those who exercise judicial functions from these in the prosecuting arms of the agencies. But the fact remains that there is a far greater combination of functions in the administrative process than can be accommodated by strict adherence to the Constitution.

It has often been proposed, as a means of alleviating what may be considered the bad effects of combined powers in administrative agencies, to draw a line of control from the original branches of the government to those parts of the bureaucracy exercising similar functions. Congress would control the legislative activities of the agencies, the President the executive aspects, and the courts the judicial functions. This would maintain the symmetry of the constitutional system. But this solution is not feasible, because other parts of the Constitution, giving different authority to these three branches make symmetrical control of this kind almost impossible. The three branches of the government are not willing to give up whatever powers they may have over administrative agencies. For example, Congress is not willing to give the President complete control over all executive functions, nor to give the courts the authority to review all the decisions of the agencies. At present, judicial review takes place only if Congress authorizes it, except in those rare instances where constitutional issues are involved.

Another aspect of the problem of control is reflected in the apparent paradox that the three branches do not always use to the fullest extent their authority to regulate the bureaucracy, even though they wish to retain their power to do so. The courts, for example, have exercised considerable self-restraint in their review of administrative decisions. They are not willing to use all their power over the bureaucracy. Similarly, both Congress and the President will often limit their dealings with the administrative branch for political and practical reasons.

In the final analysis, we are left with a bureaucratic system that has been fragmented by the Constitution, and in which administrative discretion is inevitable. The bureaucracy reflects the general fragmentation of our political system. It is often the battleground for the three branches of government, and for outside pressure groups which seek to control it for their own purposes.

THE ROLE OF THE BUREAUCRACY IN POLICY MAKING

No man in recent decades has been a more powerful figure in foreign policy making than Henry Kissinger. Both as National Security Advisor to President Nixon and as Secretary of State, Kissinger almost singlehandedly shaped American foreign policy during the Nixon and Ford administrations. The following selection contains Kissinger's observations on the role of the bureaucracy in policy-making with particular emphasis upon the foreign policy field. It is excerpted from a seminar given by Kissinger on "Bureaucracy, Politics, and Strategy" at the University of California in 1968. Kissinger's views undoubtedly helped to shape his unique style and particularly the way in which he has handled the bureaucracy since assuming power. He felt that the bureaucracy often dominates the policy-making process, and that it reflects the differing orientations of the institutions that comprise it. He certainly does not feel that the bureaucracy is capable of innovation, nor blessed with "generosity and vision." Perhaps this is one reason why Kissinger's style is highly personal, often circumventing the traditional bureaucratic channels of decision-making.

As Kissinger himself recognizes, however, the problem with his style is that policy-making by government cannot always be allowed to depend upon the personal characteristics of those who are involved in the process. The institutionalization (bureaucratization) of the policy-making process should help to guarantee effective and responsive policy-making even when individuals less charismatic and capable than Kissinger are present. If the bureaucracy lacks the flexibility to take new directions in policy-making, and is locked into preconceived ways of doing things, perhaps some attempt should be made to change the orientation and style of administrative agencies rather than relying upon personalities to make the process work. The personal factor in decision-making will always be important, but it should be balanced with proper institutional arrangements.

65
Henry Kissinger

BUREAUCRACY AND POLICY

The most frequent question that one is asked when abroad, or by people who are concerned with international affairs and have not seen policy made, is "What is American policy?" Foreign policy is additionally complicated in the contemporary period by the fact that the actual decision-making process leads to a fragmentation of the decisions. Also, research and intelligence organizations, either foreign or national, attempt to give a rationality and consistency to foreign policy which it simply does not have. I have found it next to impossible to convince Frenchmen that there is no such thing as an American foreign policy, and that a series of moves that have produced a certain result may not have been planned to produce the result. . . .

Once the American decision-making process has disgorged an answer, it becomes technically very difficult to change the policy because even those who have serious doubts about it become reluctant to hazard those doubts in an international forum. There is no telling what would come out of a reevaluation of existing measures. If one wishes to influence American foreign policy, the time to do so is in the formative period, and the level is the middle level of the bureaucracy—that of the assistant secretary and his immediate advisers. That is the highest level in which people can still think. Above that, the day to day operation of the machine absorbs most of the energy, and the decisions that are made depend very much on internal pressures of the bureaucracy. . . .

When I first started advising at high levels of the government in the early days of the Kennedy administration, I had the illusion that all I had to do was walk into the President's office, convince him I was right, and he would then naturally do what I had recommended. There were a number of things wrong with this view. Most of the people who advise the President are plausible, so he constantly sees individuals who sound very convincing. His time is so budgeted and the pressures on him are so great that it is almost impossible for him to know whether he should listen to one convincing individual or the other.

Also, even if by chance I persuaded him that his whole bureaucracy was wrong and I was right, he would then have the next problem of going about implementing what had been suggested. And that is not a negligible issue. There is only so much that even the President can do against the wishes of the

From "Henry Kissinger—Bureaucracy and Policy," *The Washington Post* (September 17, 1973). Reprinted by permission.

bureaucracy, not because the bureaucracy would deliberately sabotage him but because every difficult issue is a closed one. The easy decisions are made at subordinate levels. A closed issue is characterized by the fact that the pros and cons seem fairly evenly divided and/or because the execution really depends on certain nuances of application. Unless you can get the willing support of your subordinates, simply giving an order does not get very far. . . .

When the bureaucracy is as large and fragmented as it is, decisions do not get made until they appear as an administrative issue. One cannot convince a high level official that he has a problem until it appears unambiguously in the form of an administrative conflict. There is no such thing, in my view, as a Vietnam policy; there is a series of programs of individual agencies concerned with Vietnam. These programs are reconciled or not, as the case may be, if there is a conflict between the operating agencies. In the areas where there is no conflict between agencies, it would be very unusual to get a high level consideration of a problem. When conflict exists, the environment becomes receptive. For example, when General Westmoreland asked for 200,000 troops, that forced a high level review. But the day to day operations of a war or of an alliance diplomacy will not generally engage the President and the Secretary of State. . . .

I think most policy planning staffs in our government are created as sops to administrative theory and spend their time projecting the familiar into the future. They are not used for real innovation or even for developing criteria by which one can judge progress properly. This creates considerable rigidities. The executives become extremely conscious of the morale of their staffs. . . .

Our governmental process works reasonably well in relation to specific technical issues and also when there is an adversary procedure. If one department is strongly for something and another department opposed, then the President or cabinet officer has a chance of elaborating an overall purpose. The system goes awry if you have a small, dedicated, unopposed group. . . .

Because of this gap between expertise and decision making, a great deal of communication occurs by means of a briefing. Now, briefings reward theartrical qualities. They put a premium on the ability to package information and to present a fore-ordained result. Every briefer worth his salt says, "Interrupt me at any point with a question." Usually the victim of the briefing is very proud if he can formulate a question. The briefer has heard the question a hundred times before, and it is like throwing a fast ball across the middle of the plate to Mickey Mantle. He gives a glib response which is overwhelming. All this creates a state of mind where the policymaker may have the uneasy feeling of knowing he is being taken, even though he doesn't quite know how. This magnifies the sense of insecurity.

Because management of the bureaucracy takes so much energy and precisely because changing course is so difficult, many of the most important decisions are taken by extra-bureaucratic means. Some of the key decisions are kept to a very small circle while the bureaucracy happily continues working away in ignorance of the fact that decisions are being made, or the fact that a decision is being made in a particular area. One reason for keeping the decisions to small groups is that when bureaucracies are so unwieldy and when their internal morale becomes a serious problem, an unpopular decision may be fought by brutal means, such as leaks to the press or to congressional committees. Thus, the only way secrecy can be kept is to exclude from the making of the decision all those who are theoretically charged with carrying it out. There is, thus, small wonder for the many allegations of deliberate sabotage of certain American efforts, or of great cynicism of American efforts because of inconsistent actions. In the majority of cases this was due to the ignorance of certain parts of the bureaucracy, rather than to malevolent intent. Another result is that the relevant part of the bureaucracy, because it is being excluded from the making of a particular decision, continues with great intensity sending out cables, thereby distorting the effort with the best intentions in the world. You cannot stop them from doing this because you do not tell them what is going on. . . .

It was easy under the Eisenhower administration to ridicule the formalism of the decision-making process. In effect, it was somewhat ridiculous—there were many documents which were really diplomatic treaties between the various departments, and which enabled each department to do what it had wanted to do in the first place. But it had the great advantage of a regular procedure for getting decisions made. Under Kennedy this procedure was dismantled, and he substituted for it a sort of nervous energy and great intellectual activity, which worked well because he was an enormously intelligent man, surrounded by a very lively group of people, so that all sorts of ideas were floating into the very receptive White House. The drawback under the Kennedy administration was that there really was no regular procedure to getting things done, except on crisis issues, because you never could be sure who was being heard in addition to the constituted people, who did not always present their cases in the presence of the others who disagreed with them. It was a somewhat amorphous process. Under Johnson you had the disorganization of Kennedy without the intellectual excitement, and with somewhat of a fear of the President superimposed on it. The organizational problem seems to be to combine the procedural regularity of Eisenhower with the intellectual excitement of Kennedy. Whether that is possible, I do not know. . . .

The tendency is to say that something is either a military problem or a diplomatic problem—and if it's a diplomatic problem, then it's the State Department's job. The State Department, probably for reasons of background of its personnel that one could go into, tends to approach it on a largely tactical level. They'll develop a position, they'll want to see what the other position is, then they'll see what is negotiable. The difference between what is negotiable and what is desirable may be very wide. And if you don't know what is desirable and operate only on the basis of what is negotiable, you really encourage the other side to take a very extreme position. . . .

I must say I hold the view that we are so overstaffed that it makes thinking almost impossible. When you have in embassies abroad individuals assigned to particular small groups, each of them filing endless reports, the result is that no senior official can possibly read everything that comes in—no new official in turn will say that he has nothing to report, so the machine keeps churning on. I've often been struck by the fact that when a U.S. embassy would use me to get people in that weren't easily accessible, there would be about twelve Americans hanging over these people taking down practically every word, so that they could include it in their reports the next day rather than to let it develop in a more normal way. I think the handling of all this material does make it more difficult to reflect. Which part you cut out is a big problem because the world has become more complicated and you have to know more things. On the whole, if we could get rid of the bottom half of the Foreign Service we might be better off.

Now about the State Department. There is a definite problem in the State Department, and it consists of many factors. One is that State Department training is in the direction of reporting and negotiation, not of thinking in terms of national policy. They are trained to give a very good account of what somebody said to them. They can give a much less good account of that this means. . . .

Another quality that is rewarded is a certain negotiation skill. But what is not encouraged in the State Department hierarchy, though it is in a military hierarchy, is an assumption of responsibility and the tendency to think of problems from the vantage point of a higher level. I think the first eight to 10 years of a State Department man's career tend to be such as to drive the more imaginative and more purpose-oriented people out of it. . . .

And finally, there is the inherent dynamism of the political and bureaucratic process itself. In that sense, there is a certain necessity about this. If you do not know how this process operates, it is very difficult to predict on the basis of abstract rationality how it is going to come out. The reason why this particular problem is magnified is, it seems to me, that only in the rarest cases is there a relationship between high position and great substantive knowledge. Most of our elective officials had to spend so much of their energy getting elected that they can give relatively little attention to the substance of what they are going to do when they get elected. And therefore you get the curious phenomenon of people deciding to run for high office first and then scrambling around for some intellectuals to tell them what their positions ought to be. In many cases it is not that the intellectuals are used merely as speech writers for positions that the policy makers already have; it is literally the case that you are starting with a *tabula rasa,* and that the position the political leader takes is much influenced by the type of intellectual that sometimes quite accidentally winds up in his entourage. . . .

The typical political leader of the contemporary managerial society is a man with a strong will, a high capacity to get himself elected, but no very great conception of what he is going to do when he gets into office. This is true of many of the cabinet officials as well, and in this sense . . . I am pessimistic about the ability of modern bureaucratic society to manage a world which is quite discontinuous with its previous experience, and especially to do so with generosity and vision. I am not saying it's technically impossible, but the challenges are so much greater.

THE BUREAUCRACY AS A CHECK ON THE PRESIDENT

The final staff report of the Senate Watergate Committee in 1974 recommended the dilution of White House powers by giving more independence to the permanent agencies of the bureaucracy, in particular the Justice Department, the Federal Bureau of Investigation, the Internal Revenue Service, and the Central Intelligence Agency. Essentially the report recommended strengthening the bureaucracy as a check upon the President. Before Watergate, and dating back to the New Deal, the trend in public administration was towards increasing executive power over administrative agencies rather than diminishing it. One of the principal recommendations of the President's Committee on Administrative Management in 1937, the Hoover Commissions of 1949 and 1955, and later management-oriented study groups, was that the independence of the bureaucracy constituted a major barrier in the path of efficient government. These groups recommended eliminating administrative independence and centralizing control over the bureaucracy in the White House. A major rethinking of the proper role of the bureaucracy in relation to the President has occurred as the result of Watergate. The following selection discusses the role of the bureaucracy as a check upon the President in light of the events of Watergate.

66

Peter Woll and Rochelle Jones

THE BUREAUCRACY: A BRAKE ON PRESIDENTIAL POWER

The Watergate hearings have intensified the debate over the growth—and proper limits—of presidential power. Among many concerned people in and out of government the feeling is that Richard Nixon was making an unprece-

From Peter Woll and Rochelle Jones, "Against One-Man Rule: Bureaucratic Defense in Dept," *The Nation* (September 17, 1973), pp. 229–232. Reprinted by permission.

dented attempt to concentrate political power in the White House. For evidence the critics point to Nixon's attempt to dismantle the Office of Economic Opportunity, an office created by Congress, his impoundment of funds appropriated by Congress for water pollution, highways and other programs, and his repeated disregard of congressional resolutions on the war in Southeast Asia. Only after he was pushed to the wall by congressional action that threatened to cut off funds for the entire federal government if he did not stop the bombing of Cambodia, did he agree to an August 15th deadline for a bombing halt. In a recent series of articles in *The New York Times* Henry Steele Commager said that the United States is closer to one-man rule than at any time in its history.

While there is no doubt that Nixon frequently thwarts the will and intent of Congress, it does not necessarily mean we are on the verge of one-man rule. Nixon apparently would like to retitle the federal government "U.S. Government, Inc.; President: Richard M. Nixon," but the federal bureaucracy, composed of the Cabinet, independent regulatory commissions and administrative agencies, puts important limits on the power of the President. Under the Nixon Administration the bureaucracy is turning into a vital although little noticed safeguard of the democratic system.

The bureaucracy, sometimes with Congress but often by itself, has frequently been able to resist and ignore presidential commands. Whether the President is FDR or Richard M. Nixon, bureaucratic frustration of White House policies is a fact of life. Furthermore, the bureaucracy often carries out its own policies which are at times the exact opposite of White House directives. A classic case occurred during the India-Pakistan war in 1971 when the State Department supported India while the White House backed Pakistan. The State Department's behind-the-scenes maneuvering in support of India prompted Henry Kissinger's famous enraged order "to tilt" toward Pakistan.

In a system marked by a weak Congress and a Supreme Court that is increasingly taking its direction from Nixon appointees, the bureaucracy is turning into the crucial check on presidential power. Under the Constitution Nixon is chief executive, but this does not mean he has legal authority or political power to control the bureaucracy. On the contrary, the bureaucracy has become a fourth branch of government, separate and independent of the President, Congress and the courts. There are limits to bureaucratic discretion, but these are set as much by Congress and the courts as by the President. Decisions of independent regulatory commissions may be overturned under certain circumstances by the courts. And while the administrative agencies created by Congress are delegated considerable discretionary authority, this authority must be exercised with broad guidelines that are set by the legislature. It is precisely this accountability of the bureaucracy to the courts and Congress that helps it to be a powerful constraint on Presidential power. For example, in *State Highway Commission of Missouri* v. *Volpe (1973)* the Eighth Circuit Court of Appeals ruled that the Secretary of Transportation could not legally follow Nixon's directives and impound highway funds. The court held that Congress had clearly specified in the Federal Highway Act that appropriated funds were to be apportioned among the states. In effect, the court was saying that the Department of Transportation, a Cabinet department presumably under Presidential control, must comply with the intent of Congress, as it is interpreted by the court, instead of following the orders of the President.

Ultimately the bureaucracy curbs the President because it has independent sources of political power. Nixon's attempt to cut back governmental programs and reduce spending conflicts with the vested interests of powerful groups in and out of government. Like Congress and the President, administrative agencies and regulatory commissions have constituencies that are relied on for political support. The Defense Department needs the armaments industry, Agriculture the farmers, Labor the AFL-CIO, the ICC the railroads and truckers, and the Food and Drug Administration the giant pharmaceutical companies.

Because the bureaucracy depends on the political support of these allies for its continued existence, and because this alliance survives the four or eight years a President is in office, the bureaucracy is apt to prefer its interests over the wishes of the President. This is not new. On numerous occasions, for instance, the independent regulatory agencies have adopted policies that directly opposed the programs of the President. In the early 1960s both the Interstate Commerce Commission and Civil Aeronautics Board ignored White House directives in approving railroad and airline mergers that reduced competition.

Outside political support enables agencies to act independently. The regulatory agencies have been able to resist, for the most part, attempts by presidents from Franklin D. Roosevelt to Richard Nixon to organize and bring them under presidential supervision. A number of presidents on a number of occasions have tried to transfer the regulatory functions of the Interstate Commerce Commission to a Cabinet department like the Department of Transportation, which is more capable to being controlled by the White House. But the railroads' support for the ICC has been felt in and reflected by Congress, and the ICC has retained its separate identity. With the help of equally strong support from their allies, other agencies have defeated attempts, most recently by Nixon, to reorganize them. In 1971 Nixon proposed a major reorganization of the Executive Branch that would have meant a major shift of authority. The Department of Agriculture, for example, would have lost control over a variety of programs to a proposed super Department of Natural Resources. But the Department of Agriculture rallied its constituency behind it, and the reorganization plan languished in Congress.

Agencies that lack independent political support in Congress and are not supported by private pressure groups are apt to be swayed by the President. There is a big difference between the Department of Transportation and the Department of State. The former is supported by a wide range of groups, from proponents of federal airport subsidies to groups connected with aviation safety, urban transit, highway safety, and the Coast Guard. The latter is without Congressional and interest group backing. When Nixon tried to create a "super-Cabinet" at the start of his second term, Secretary of Transportation Claude S. Brinegar announced loudly and repeatedly that he was not going to be subordinate to the super-Cabinet Secretary James Lynn, Secretary of the Department of Housing and Urban Development, who had been named his superior by Nixon. But Secretary of State William Rogers was upstaged from the very start of the Nixon Administration by Henry Kissinger. Kissinger has usurped the major foreign policy-making responsibilities of the State Department while serving as an unofficial ambassador at large and roving emissary to foreign governments, a pleasant duty that is traditionally the prerogative of the Secretary of State. Secretary of State John Foster Dulles played such a role in the Eisenhower administration. But this is possible only if the Secretary of State enjoys the confidence of the President as Dulles did. If he doesn't, the Secretary of State will be a mere figurehead in the foreign policy field because the State Department is exceedingly vulnerable to domination by the White House. Its lack of domestic allies enables it to win very little support from Congress. When Sen. Joseph McCarthy launched his witch hunt after subversives in government, he wisely tackled the State Department first. As long as he was battling the State Department, he was safe. When he turned on the Department of the Army with its close links to a powerful domestic constituency and hence to key Congressional committees, his downfall was imminent.

In addition to its political support the bureaucracy contains the President in other ways. The President has minimal influence within the bureaucracy because of its size, complexity, wide-ranging responsibilities and continuity. More than one-half of the 3 million civilian employees of the federal government work for the Defense Department, for one good example. Tens of thousands of them are in key policy-making positions. All recent Secretaries of Defense, with the possible exception of McNamara, have had difficulty keeping up with day-to-day shifts in policy that are the result of decisions made by subordinates. Obviously Nixon cannot keep up with the operations of this mammoth department. And this is true in every large department of government. The President must delegate authority, and by doing so tends to lose control. Admittedly Nixon has made a strong attempt to change this. Before Watergate heightened the debate over the limits of presidential power, Washington civil servants were operating in an atmosphere that was permeated with fear. Since the Watergate hearings started, however, bureaucrats have resumed their traditional independent stance.

Moreover, since Nixon can't know what is going on in every nook of the federal bureaucracy, he must rely on the information that is provided by it for his decision-making. By carefully controlling the information that reaches the President, the bureaucracy can control his decision-making. This is not necessarily Machiavellian. Very often administrators, even subordinate administrators, are the only ones who possess the background and arcane knowledge to fill in the details of vague Congressional legislation. The strength of the bureaucracy is magnified when the President and Congress must come to it for the necessary information and technical skills to formulate and implement public policy. In a highly technical and increasingly specialized society the power of bureaucracy grows because the bureaucracy is the domain of the specialist, while the Congress and President are necessarily generalists.

The use of bureaucratic expertise in congressional policy making will be facilitated through the Office of Technological Assessment (OTA), being formed under the sponsorship of Sen. Edward Kennedy (D., Mass.). The OTA, created by legislation in 1972, is a way of challenging the present power of the Office of Management and Budget to prevent agencies from going directly to Congress with policy-making proposals. Such administrative inputs to the legislative process must first be cleared by the OMB. But the OTA is authorized to use the technical resources of the bureaucracy to draft policies that reflect the priorities of Congress. With these outside sources of information Congress will be able to challenge the President in a way previously impossible. Because Congress will be relying on information that comes from the bureaucracy, the bureaucracy will have vastly increased influence in the policy-making process. And since agency personnel assigned to the OTA will be working for Congress, not the President, they can give substantial help in developing programs that may directly contradict the programs of the President. A new bureaucratic check on the President is emerging.

Presidents come and go; the bureaucracy stays. Even if the President's only concern were the control of the bureaucracy, he would find this extremely difficult to accomplish in eight years. Obviously the President has many other pressing concerns besides the bureaucracy. At the beginning of his first term he is concerned with making a good impression. With the election mandate behind him and the congressional honeymoon ahead of him, the President wants to charge ahead, to do great things which, if they don't win him a place in the history books, may at least win him a second term in office. But such great plans can be abruptly halted by the bureaucracy. The newly elected President can find that many top bureaucrats who were appointed by the previous President are entrenched in power, protected by civil service regulations or terms of office that are set by statutes. The President is reduced to watching helplessly as the bureaucracy stymies his key programs. By the start of his second term the President may decide to make a determined effort to control the bureaucracy in a final, valiant attempt to push through his program.

And in fact, Nixon tried exactly that, finding that it is easy to try to curb the bureaucracy but exceedingly difficult to succeed. Nixon created a super-Cabinet last January in an attempt to centralize power in the White House; it was a dismal failure. It never functioned as it was supposed to. Agencies ignored it and did as they pleased or bypassed it and went directly to the

President. Nixon finally junked the super-Cabinet four months after it was established.

In opposing presidential programs, the bureaucracy relies heavily on informal contacts with Congress. The White House may, and often does, try to muzzle administrators, but the bureaucracy has ways of getting necessary information to key Congressmen. Information flows back and forth among bureaucrats and Congressmen over the phone, at casual meetings and cocktail parties. Pressure groups also channel information from the agencies to Congressional committees.

For example, the President can order the Department of Agriculture to eliminate or reduce various agricultural programs, but these orders are likely to fail eventually because of the strong support for the department in Congress and among various agricultural interest groups. The department might have to go along with the President temporarily, but it would not have to wait long for congressional support to back up its policy favoring maintenance of such programs. This happened in 1972 when the Department of Agriculture abolished several key programs at the request of Nixon. An angry Congress overwhelmingly voted to restore the programs.

Many agencies are closer to Congress than to the President. The Securities and Exchange Commission (SEC) is a good example of an agency that has stronger ties to the House and Senate than to the White House. Rep. John Moss (D., Calif.), chairman of the House Subcommittee on Commerce and Finance, and Sen. Harrison Williams (D., N.J.), chairman of the Securities Subcommittee of the Senate Banking Committee, deal directly with the SEC on a continuous basis. The SEC supplies these legislators with information, and they, in turn, prod the agency to implement the policy positions that they favor. With the help of a strong professional staff, these men are directly involved in the regulation of the securities industry. Of course, the White House can wield a certain amount of power, as it did when it influenced the SEC staff to withhold important information on the financial dealings of financier Robert Vesco because the information might embarrass the Committee for the Re-election of the President. But this influence is sporadic and limited to specific issues, while Congress deals with the SEC and other agencies on an almost daily basis.

Nixon can exert some control over the bureaucracy through his power of appointment. The President directly controls the appointment of more than 2,000 top-level bureaucrats. These positions were filled during Nixon's first term with people considered "reliable." After the 1972 election all of these appointees were required to submit their resignations. Many have been fired, producing great disillusionment throughout the ranks. As a result of the insensitive behavior of Nixon's staff, the White House faced enormous difficulty in recruiting new people, and many positions remain vacant in the top echelons of departments and agencies.

Nixon has been appointing former White House aides and CREEP employees as an elite corps of "agents," numbering more than 100, to departments, independent regulatory commissions and agencies to find out what is going on and to carry out the Nixon philosophy. Such agents have been installed at the Under Secretary level in Treasury, Interior, Transportation and HEW. At lower levels agents were placed in Commerce (25), Interior (13), Agriculture (17), Treasury (11), the Environmental Protection Agency (20), Veterans Administration (11), FAA (5), and FTC (9). Nixon has filled twenty-eight of the thirty-eight positions on six major regulatory commissions and named the chairmen of all six. White House clearance has been required of many staff appointments. This attempt to control the independent regulatory commissions prompted the House Interstate and Foreign Commerce Committee to begin an investigation of what its chairman, Harley O. Staggers (D., W. Va), considers inappropriate White House pressure.

For a short time Nixon's appointees can undoubtedly influence administrative policy-making. But Nixon has failed more often than he has succeeded in changing the direction of the bureaucracy through the appointment process. He has created anxiety, frustration and disillusionment, and impeded independent policy-making by the bureaucrats in those limited number of agencies where he has placed his agents.

In the case of the independent regulatory commissions the President may be able to stack them in his favor, but this is only a temporary impediment to the commisions' inherent ability to limit Presidential power. Nixon's appointees will constitute a major limitation on the next President. From the standpoint of the presidency, the influence of one President on Regulatory agencies through appointments can lay the groundwork for future agency resistance to a new President. Similarly, the expansion of the bureaucracy in line with the philosophy of a President who believes in an activist government, such as FDR, limits future Presidents who believe in a concept of limited governmental intervention. Thus the appointment process is a two-edged sword, working against presidential power in the long run while giving short-term advantage.

Many of Nixon's appointees, even in his elite corps, were given jobs as a political payoff for their loyalty to him and their work in his campaigns. These strictly political types have been put in showcase jobs in many cases, often as assistants to top-echelon people, consultants, and in public affairs jobs. Even "deputy administrators" are often phony jobs with an impressive title but little clout. Moreover, most polical types know little or nothing about the agencies they are appointed to. They cannot rival the top-grade permanent civil servants in policy making. And while the political appointees often have short stays in their jobs, the civil servants tend to be permanent employees. In the final analysis the expertise, continuity and political ties of the permanent civil service severely limit the ability of any President to alter bureaucratic practices through his appointments.

The courts can help the bureaucracy in imposing limits on the President. In recent years, an active judiciary has forced administrative agencies to adhere closely to congressional intent, as defined by the courts, reinforcing the ability of the bureaucracy to resist presidential control. Within the last few months the courts declared *ultra vires* Nixon's actions to impound funds that would be appropriated to administrative agencies under normal circumstances. The courts also preserved, at least temporarily, the Office of Economic Opportunity which was in the process of being dismantled under orders from Nixon.

The Watergate affair clearly reveals the value of a semi-autonomous bureaucracy. A President who could direct the activities of all administrative agencies would threaten our constitutional system. If the White House had been able to use the FBI and CIA as it had planned, a far-flung political intelligence operation would now be operating in a way that would undermine basic guarantees of our constitutional system, such as the Fourth Amendment guarantees against unreasonable searches and seizures. It was because J. Edgar Hoover and the FBI resisted that the efforts of the White House to set up a secret police operation with the approval of Nixon were stymied. Asst. Atty. Gen. Henry Petersen, a career atorney, refused to go along with Ehrlichman's improper requests. Richard Helms and General Walters of the CIA likewise maintained their independence under pressure by Haldeman and Ehrlichman. And it seems evident that a number of career professionals at the FBI leaked information to the press in order to frustrate what they saw as a move to corrupt the bureau.

At the same time, however, bureaucrats need to be imbued with the values of our constitutional democracy because, for the most part, the limits on them are those they impose upon themselves. It is ironic that the independence of the FBI and J. Edgar Hoover, so often criticized as a potential threat to responsible government, turned out under the Nixon Administration to be a bulwark of freedom. Perhaps, in the final analysis, we are saved from tyranny by the pluralism of our system and even its inefficiency. The pluralistic and independent bureaucracy, although often inefficient and yielding to special-interest group pressure, helps to preserve the balance of powers among the branches of government that is necessary for the preservation of our system of constitutional democracy.

THE DILEMMAS OF THE NON-CONFORMING BUREAUCRAT

Ralph Nader was one of the first advocates of "whistle blowing" for public officials. He has encouraged lower echelon bureaucrats to "blow the whistle" on their superiors if they feel strongly that the superiors' actions are against the public interest. Effective whistle blowing requires public revelation of the questionable actions that have been taken, and public statements critical of those actions. Getting out of the bureaucracy and speaking out on actions with which one disagrees is not only the concern of lower echelon bureaucrats but also may involve high level political appointees. Indeed, the higher the level of criticism the more effective it is likely to be. While the mere act of resignation of a cabinet secretary may imply criticism of the incumbent administration in the minds of the public, such resignations should be accompanied by forthright statements of the reasons for the resignation if they are to be effective in bringing different points of view to the public. While getting out and speaking out may seem to be a simple matter, in fact it is a course of action surrounded by difficulties. These are provocatively discussed in the following selection.

67
James C. Thomson, Jr.

GETTING OUT
AND SPEAKING OUT

Among the issues brought to center stage by the Watergate crisis is the responsibility of the individual official when confronted by policies from which he strongly dissents. Hugh Sloan resigned in quiet disapproval. John Dean stayed on until he sensed a frame-up, then began to tell all. Others have lied or kept silent out of loyalty to their President. No one really blew the whistle. No one resigned and spoke out.

Before Watergate, on a parallel track, came the Indochina war. Questions about the responsibility of individual office-holders under Nixon on Watergate-related issues reopen questions about their predecessors, under Kennedy and Johnson, on the making of Indochina policy. I will explore only one of these questions: Why don't officials get out and speak out when they deeply disagree with the policies of their government?

In early June 1970, after the Cambodian invasion, I communicated to three highly-placed friends in the Nixon Administration my hope that they might at long last consider resigning and speaking out, individually or collectively, in order to help create a brake against further escalation. My plea fell, I knew, on somewhat fertile soil: all three were opposed to the Cambodia move. Two replied that I had raised an important question; the third, the most disaffected, soon moved with apparent relief to a government agency that had nothing to do with the war.

Eight months later, in February 1971, after the Laos "incursion," I tried out the idea more publicly. In the course of a Harvard Teach-In speech, I suggested the creation of a National Committee for the Regeneration of Con-

From James Thomson, "Getting Out and Speaking Out," *Foreign Policy* 13 (Winter 1973–1974). Reprinted from *Foreign Policy* 13. Copyright 1973 by National Affairs, Inc.

science in Government. Such a group should be composed, I thought, of antiwar former officials, diplomats, and military men, and, if possible, the college-age children of present officials. Its purpose should be to encourage individual and even collective resignations on the grounds of conscience— resignations to be followed by speaking tours to take their antiwar dissent to the public. The Committee might also provide between-jobs financial assistance.

My proposal elicited a handful of encouraging letters from local former bureaucrats, plus interested inquiries from one psychoanalyst and two clergymen. But from former Ambassador John Kenneth Galbraith came an important caveat. It would take artful wording, he said, for those of us who were former officials to explain why we were asking current officials to do what we had been unwilling to do ourselves over the Bay of Pigs, the Dominican intervention, and the earlier Indochina escalations.

Galbraith's point was hardly new to me, but it remains crucial. Why *hadn't* any of us resigned and gone public at once? Why hasn't anyone done so since on issues of foreign policy? Why, in the course of the longest and most unpopular war in American history, did no one exit and speak out right away? And why, over a longer time span, is it hard to find anyone at a Cabinet or sub-Cabinet or Assistant Secretary level who has left the U.S. government on an issue of foreign affairs *and said so at the time?*[1]

One major use of secrecy in the making of foreign policy is to conceal internal disagreement. Yet one major recourse of the dissenting official, in a democracy at least, should be to get out and take his case to that allegedly ultimate court, the voting public. So noisy resignations over issues—as opposed to genteel departures on other grounds—should be one antidote to secrecy, one means of preserving openness. And the tacit *threat* of such a recourse for dissenters should be a constraint on chief executives and an added strength to the dissenter's voice.

But that is not the way things work.

STAYING IN

Let me deal at once with the obvious and compelling grounds for alternative behavior: *not* getting out, but instead staying in—and fighting from within. That is the time-honored norm of individual behavior within all bureaucratic institutions, and it is a norm that is essential to the functioning of such inherently pluralistic bodies. If officials chose to resign each time a decision went against them, there would be scores of departures at all levels every day. More important, the "winners" would quickly "take all," since the temporary

---

[1]Interior Secretary Walter Hickel is a special case. He parted company with President Nixon over other issues as well as Vietnam. But his parting was politely staged, and he did not speak out.

"losers" had exited. And, most important for the dissenter, his effectiveness on all policy issues—his accumulated power, prestige, and alliances within government—would largely evaporate with his resignation. He would have lost what Albert Hirschman has called his "voice."[2]

So the perennially persuasive reasons for staying in are what sustain very large numbers of men and women of conscience when they disagree with prevailing administration policies. They may lose today, but they stay in to fight tomorrow. And if they were to leave, there is always the alarming prospect that their jobs might well be filled by the wrong-headed or the less competent.

What concerns me, then, is not the familiar arguments for staying in, but rather the reasons for silent departure once the break point is reached on issues of policy—once one decides to get out. Why, again, did no one leave government over Indochina policy *and* speak out at once?

It might be argued that, in the case of Vietnam, some did resign and eventually speak out. The key word here is "eventually"—one to which we will return—for it shows that constraints continue to operate after departure. As for some of the high-level resigners who were doubters on Vietnam (we know of their doubts either through their later public statements or the Pentagon Papers): Far East Assistant Secretary Roger Hilsman was told to find other employment fast, which he did (early 1964); Michael Forrestal of the White House staff silently slipped back to the practice of law in New York (1965–66); so did Under Secretary of State George Ball (1966); John Gardner departed as Secretary of HEW vigorously denying any disagreement over Vietnam (early 1968); Robert McNamara was removed as Secretary of Defense and allowed himself to be placed, mute, in the World Bank (early 1968); Chester Cooper of the White House staff quietly moved to the Institute for Defense Analyses (1968); Townsend Hoopes quietly resigned as Under Secretary of the Air Force (mid-1969). Others, including Clark Clifford, Averell Harriman, Chester Bowles, Cyrus Vance, and even Daniel Ellsberg, stayed on as full-time employees or periodic consultants to the government until Richard Nixon's inauguration in January 1969.

There are certainly more names that could be cited, but the point becomes obvious: *When you leave, you go quietly; and at the very least, you stay quiet for a while.* The question is, why? The answer is not simple. How people act on leaving government depends in part on why they left. And here one deals with a spectrum of possibilities.

---

[2]See Albert O. Hirschman, *Exit, Loyalty and Voice* (Cambridge, Mass., 1969). One troubling aspect of the felt need to preserve one's effectiveness is a bureaucratic constraint I have described elsewhere as the "effectiveness trap." This can militate not only against leaving and speaking out, but also against dissenting from within too often or too forcefully. See James C. Thomson, Jr., "How Could Vietnam Happen?—An Autopsy," *Atlantic Monthly,* April 1968, pp. 47–53.

WHYS AND WHEREFORES

There is, first of all, exit through a clear public firing. So, in a classic case, Truman got rid of Commerce Secretary Henry Wallace. That is a searing experience, but also potentially a liberating one in creating the immediate possibility of vocal opposition.

A more likely variant, however, is a concealed firing through apparently friendly resignation. Here the official—who may or may not have been a dissenter, as opposed to merely incompetent in the eyes of his superiors—is asked to leave (i.e., is fired) but given a period in which to find alternative employment, and perhaps even assistance in finding it, prior to the cordial exchange of letters of resignation and appreciation. Such solicitude not only eases the blow to the resigner's ego; it also creates, for a while at least, a sense of obligation to those who threw him out so gently.

A more common phenomenon is probably the muddled departure: the product not of firing but of frustration and fatigue. Mixed into the usually multiple reasons for this kind of resignation may be the following factors: simple exhaustion from long bureaucratic hours; a sense that one is losing more battles than one is winning; a sense that one has lost the ear of the powerful (perhaps never had it) and won't be advanced to a better spot; guilt about neglect of one's wife and children; concern about one's alternative career; and perhaps the financial limitations of government salaries. Included among such factors may be increasingly persistent and ineffective dissent on one or more issues, but it often gets blurred by the mix of other ingredients.

A further case of resignation may be quite simply the apparent availability of much greener pastures elsewhere. This can relate to the previous point and become an inducement to exit in the midst of frustration and fatigue, or it can suddenly confront an otherwise content official in the form of that legendary unrejectable job offer—a great foundation, or university, or corporate presidency. Such men obviously leave with a minimal desire to speak out since they have little to speak out about.

There are, of course, a few rare birds who follow the angry-fed-up-blow-your-top route. General Hurley resigned (and blew his top) as Ambassador to China in late 1945. Secretary Harold Ickes, under FDR, went through the motions repeatedly without being permitted to resign. Such impulsiveness is usually caught before it explodes in public. If the official cannot be dissuaded, a graceful departure is arranged, creating a sense of obligation (see above). If he does resign, the multiple pressures of bureaucratic life that have led up to the departure usually blur in his own mind, as well as in the minds of others, the clarity of his stand on the specific triggering issue. He becomes, in the eyes of others, perhaps in his own as well, a tired sorehead who couldn't play team ball.

The resignation spectrum includes, finally, the foul-up, or the ouster within (conventionally, the kicking upstairs, though it may often be sideways, or even down). Here recurrent dissent alerts one's superiors to one's disaffection, and therefore potential disloyalty, in time for the superiors to propose a new job—usually a respectable but non-sensitive ambassadorship, or perhaps the directorship of an international agency. At this point the would-be resigner is dually trapped—on the one hand, it is hard to cut one's ties entirely, and perhaps some good might be done in the new job; and on the other hand, resignation *now* would look like personal pique over a job reassignment (therefore selfish), not resignation on grounds of conscience.

So much for some of the reasons why people seem to resign or, in some cases, not quite resign.

For those who finally make the break, what are the factors that prevent, inhibit, or at least delay their speaking out?

A PERSONAL ACCOUNT

Before attempting an answer, let me first offer some evidence in the form of a highly unscientific case study, i.e., an account of my own experience as a resigner. My own experience is, of course, illustrative mainly of my own experience, and recounting it runs the risk of seeming trivial, or self-serving, or both. But it may nonetheless suggest some categories of constraints. So here is a capsulized account of one resigner's progression.

To begin with, I wasn't fired, but I didn't actually resign. By which I mean to say that though I told my National Security Council boss, Walt W. Rostow, that I would be leaving in the autumn (of 1966) to accept a teaching appointment at Harvard, I couldn't decide to whom I should send a letter of resignation and therefore never sent one. As a 34-year-old East Asianist who had spent six years in government, I was still on the payroll of the Department of State but had been assigned for two years to the NSC staff at the White House. I thought briefly of writing a thank-you-and-good-bye letter to Secretary Rusk, but since I had long regarded him as The Archenemy of wise East Asian policy, I decided to avoid any eleventh-hour hypocrisy. As for resigning to President Johnson, that seemed presumptuous, even perilous. ("Who the hell is *he?*" the President might ask, "and why is he quitting?") A friend did get him to inscribe a photograph to me, misspelled, but with best wishes. And except for collecting accumulated vacation and sick-leave pay, plus arranging at the last minute to have the National Archives cart off my six years of chaotic files for the Kennedy Library, that was that. On September 15, 1966, I walked out of the Executive Office Building a free man.

I must now explain a thing or two. My "resignation" belongs, in retrospect, to the category of the muddled departure—i.e., it derived from several concurrent factors. In no particular order: (1) I had come to Washington for two years and had stayed nearly seven—with Chester Bowles in the Congress and at State, through thick and thin; with Roger Hilsman and briefly William P. Bundy at State; and then with McGeorge Bundy and briefly Walt W. Rostow at the White House. (2) The policy frustration and defeats had long since outnumbered the victories. (3) I had recently lost my most stimulating and demanding employer with the departure of McGeorge Bundy for the Ford Foundation. (4) I was fatigued, and my family long since fed up, with endless bureaucratic days and evenings. (5) Harvard had made an offer, and it was nearing time to choose between a base in the academy or a long-term government career. (6) My own central hopes for Sino-American détente now seemed hopelessly obstructed by the Vietnam folly of the Johnson Administration.

Since speaking out is the subject at hand, I should say something about my Vietnam views as they had evolved by September 1966. As one whose real interest since childhood was China (I had grown up there, as the son of educational missionaries), I had largely ignored and disdained Indochina in the Kennedy years, hoping that the problem might simply go away. During 1964, I found myself counting on a neutralist *coup d'état* in Saigon that would politely invite us out of Vietnam. And once the decision was taken to escalate American involvement in 1965, I worked with others in a futile effort to bring about a speedy end to the bombing and a negotiated settlement. Throughout this period it was my view that the alleged illegality and immorality of the Vietnam war was not the issue, but that the issue was instead the war's semi-suicidal stupidity in terms of American national interests. For a while I had hoped that this view, for which I found quiet support in many parts of government, might soon prevail. But by the time of my departure, I had despaired of persuading Messrs. Johnson, Rusk, and McNamara to turn back from their chosen course. I felt, by then, totally alienated from the policy, but helpless as to how to change it.

THE EXIT SYNDROME, PHASE I: THE SNIPER

Tucked in my briefcase, as I left the Executive Office Building in September 1966, was a parody I had written on Cape Cod during a brief holiday earlier that summer. Entitled "Minutes of a White House Meeting, Summer 1967," it was a spleen-venting effort to satirize Walt W. Rostow, our Vietnam policy, and a few of my NSC colleagues. Officials, it seems, find diverse ways to relieve tensions and frustrations. Mr. McNamara is said to have read Homer. One of my White House colleagues constructed entire miniature three-ring circuses in his Chevy Chase basement. I tended to write parodies, all through my Washington years, and this was one of my best. On return to the job in August, I showed it privately to some NSC friends, and it evoked much glee.

That parody was to become my first vehicle for speaking out—but it took seven months for the voice to be heard. The point is instructive. One refuge of the inside dissenter is the covert expression of disapproval—through private sharing with confederates of outrage, witticisms, ridicule, or despair. Once outside, my first instinct was to do more of the same—to pass the piece around to antiwar former bureaucrats and academic colleagues. And inevitably two things happened: first, I was told it must certainly be published, and second, it fell, thanks to Xerox, into a wider public domain and was referred to, without attribution, in the press. A friend urged that I offer it at once to *Esquire* under a pseudonym. I finally did so, uneasily, but the editor, who liked it, said their lawyers judged it libelous with real names assigned to the characters. Robert Manning of *The Atlantic Monthly,* however, had more courage and ingenuity.

By March 1967, when the piece was in press in *The Atlantic,* I found myself both excited and nervous. I had spent the previous autumn "decompressing," which meant mainly sleeping late, finding out what Harvard students were like, and preparing a new lecture course. In my conversations with students I had been increasingly frank about my views on the war, but I had prudently stayed out of print. Meanwhile, in October, I had also been asked to do an Asian policy speech text for the President in Hawaii, which made me feel that I had not been forgotten or barred, despite my dovish inclinations.

Now, however, the parody was about to appear, with altered names—Herman Melville Breslau instead of Walt Whitman Rostow, for instance—but with my own real byline. (John Kenneth Galbraith, an enthusiast for the piece, had thoughtfully offered me his *nom-de-plume,* Marc Epernay, and I was deeply touched—until my canny wife pointed out that then Galbraith would get credit for the article.) The fears of the unknown and of possible retribution were gathering.

One Saturday night I came home late to discover that the White House switchboard (Mr. Rostow calling) had phoned close to midnight (he would call back). He didn't call back, but I wondered what was up and tried to practice telling him that the whole thing was a joke, didn't he see? On Monday came the follow-up: a call from one of my Harvard bosses who had been phoned by a Harvard professor on leave, who was still a member of the Rostow staff. My caller said he didn't think I should take the message too hard, but that the Rostow man had said that great damage would be done if my parody were printed, that I sure as hell would never get back into government under any administration, and that if Jim Thomson were declaring war on this Administration, they were ready for him. I responded weakly that I thought they had learned their lesson about nonessential, brushfire wars and then asked what my caller thought this all meant. I was told that it meant trouble but that maybe things would blow over in a few years.

When the parody finally appeared in the May 1967 *Atlantic,* there were no audible thunderbolts from Washington—though I did later learn that the President had finally had his chance to say, "Who the hell is *he?*"

THE EXIT SYNDROME, PHASE II:
THE EPISTOLARY BREAKTHROUGH

I had, then, gone public—but only rather snipingly, using the tool of mockery.

Yet confidence and indignation were gathering—thanks largely to the effect of some extraordinary Harvard undergraduates who were teaching me, by their example, to speak out on the war. (I was finding "community.") Their example was twofold: not merely the clarity and reasonableness with which they argued against Washington's policies, but the fact that *they* represented our cannon fodder, those numbers on Washington's charts.

Early in May I had talked with a high Yale administrator at a dinner in New Haven. He agreed that the war was a terrible thing, but he added that of course no "constructive alternatives" were now being offered in place of Washington's policies, nor had critics ever proposed such alternatives. These comments increasingly enraged me as I sped home on the train late that night, writing my final lecture in a course on American-East Asian relations for delivery the next morning. The result of the challenge from that Yale official was several pages of lecture notes in which I argued that constructive alternatives had in fact been available and offered at each stage of our Vietnam involvement from at least 1961 onward; that such alternatives had been repeatedly rejected on the grounds that the price of accepting them would be higher than the price of deeper and wider intervention; but that in retrospect the price of further intervention had been infinitely higher.

Late that month, as the war turned sharply upward—and nine months after I had left the government—I finally pulled myself together and transcribed these thoughts in the form of a letter to the *New York Times,* a letter in which I identified myself as a former State and NSC aide and argued that I knew from within that constructive alternatives to escalation had in fact been available but regularly rejected since 1961 when I entered government. My closing paragraphs read:

> For the greatest power on earth has the power denied to others: the power to take unilateral steps, and to keep taking them: the power to be as ingenious and relentless in the pursuit of peace as we are in the infliction of pain; the power to lose face; the power to admit error; and the power to act with magnanimity.

I had originally closed with the words, "and the power to lose wars," but was emphatically urged to delete them by another recent returnee from Washington.

The letter to the *Times* seemed to me, at the time, a large and perilous step: a move from ridicule to deadly serious stuff. I blew hot and cold, hoping at moments that the *Times* wouldn't use it or that no one would read it, at other moments that I would achieve at least minor fame though immediate public denunciation, or perhaps (a Walter Mitty daydream) that the President would be so moved and persuaded that he would stop the war at once. None of these things actually happened. The *Times* did run the letter prominently in its issue of Sunday, June 4, 1967. It simultaneously ran a substantial editorial commenting favorably on what I had written. That morning I felt exhilarated and scared. The phone soon rang, a long distance call, and for an instant fear prevailed. It turned out to be some man in Harrisburg, Pa., who had just read the letter and had to tell me right away how grateful he was. Other calls that day were from friends, saying well done. In the next week or so a score of letters arrived, many of them from former government officials, some known to me, some not. They were uniformly congratulatory. Meanwhile, from those inside there was silence. I began to breathe more easily.

Later that summer I slipped back into the State Department for the first time since my departure, at the invitation of a friend. There I encountered an assistant to one of my previous State employers who told me that the former boss was furious that my letter had "cast aspersions on his honor." I replied that it had only cast aspersions on his judgment. And there the matter rested until many months had passed and much had changed in me. In mid-March 1968, I received one further reaction to the *Times* letter, and maybe the parody as well, when McGeorge Bundy of the Ford Foundation preceded his Godkin Lectures at Harvard by a debate with Professor Stanley Hoffmann on the war. Bundy opened his remarks by setting some special ground rules: he would not talk about the past, period. He added, in rather vivid explanation, that those who had been entrusted with responsibility by a President had been handed a pistol along with that trust, and that those who later spoke out about their period of service not merely broke the trust, but turned that pistol on the man who had trusted them and shot him in the head. As Bundy said this, my wife elbowed me and said, "He's talking about you." "No, no," I whispered, "he's talking about Arthur Schlesinger." As a small footnote to the domino-effect in guilt, I should report that I ran into Schlesinger the next day and told him the story. "No, no," said Schlesinger, "he was talking about Ken Galbraith and Dick Goodwin." (Later evidence indicated that my wife, once again, was right.)

THE EXIT SYNDROME, PHASE III:
GOING (ALMOST) ALL THE WAY

By the time Bundy had delivered his grim injunction, my guilt, exhilaration, rage, and sense of impending doom had all reached a new height. Even as he spoke, *The Atlantic Monthly,* my wondrously supportive conduit, was already going to press with something that moved a good way beyond parody and letters to the editor. It was a longer piece of reflection, intuition, illustrative anecdotes, and analysis entitled "How Could Vietnam Happen?" (The editor had added a premature subtitle: "An Autopsy.") That piece would appear in the April 1968 issue, out on the newsstands the last days of March.

This Vietnam essay was a product of serendipitous intervention. In August 1967, the psychoanalyst and writer Robert Jay Lifton, a Cape Cod neighbor, had asked me to make the annual "outsider's presentation" to his Wellfleet seminar on psychohistory—a gathering of psychiatrists and historians who converse intensively about personality and history under the benevolent wing of Erik H. Erikson. Would I please think out loud, he asked, about how men and events had intersected to produce the Vietnam war? I agreed uneasily, free-associated for several days in the Truro sunshine, made extensive notes, and then held forth one evening. Things went quite well, and I felt stretched. You should really do an article, I was told: but I shrank from the thought. The *Times* letter had already strained me. Why take further risks?

And so things stood until the first weekend of December 1967, when I attended a very private conference on the war that was held in Bermuda and sponsored by the Carnegie Endowment for International Peace. There, from all sectors of the foreign policy establishment, were assembled sundry great men who pondered for two and a half days and prepared a confidential message to the President urging de-escalation. It must be recalled that the fear of the moment was further escalation, and that for the Democrats present there was an urgent desire to keep Johnson from handing the Republicans a victory in 1968. But that conference of decent and able but still cautious people, trying shrewdly to "work from within," took me right back to government days. (Of course none of us, our benign chairman had intoned, are for "withdrawal"— that then anathema word.) I suddenly realized the qualities of pomposity and constraint I had hated—and how far I had come, for better or worse. I found at least two who shared my itchiness at Bermuda—Frances Fitz-Gerald and Daniel Ellsberg. We became briefly a sort of token-Bolshevik cluster, and those two brilliant firsthand observers of the Vietnam scene reinforced my convictions and sense of community.

Bermuda sent me into a rage. The great men of the center, gathered in council, had come up with an obsequious, ameliorative (and private) petition to the White House.[3] Meanwhile, the best of my students (not conscientious objectors, within the then rigid confines of the legal definition) faced the intolerable alternatives decreed by that White House: service in an immoral war (I now agreed), or jail, or exile to Canada. On return to Cambridge I quickly and belatedly transformed my Cape notes into an article, tried to peddle it to *Life* (they said no), to *Look* (they said yes, then weeks later reneged), and finally to old faithful, *The Atlantic,* which had wanted it in the first place but had seemed to me a journal whose subscribers were already persuaded.

Time wasted on *Life* and *Look* meant that my piece didn't run till the April issue. On the eve of its publication, President Johnson announced his abdication—not, I fear, cause and effect. And with its publication I felt I had finally come clean—had finally spoken out. The response, again, was heartening—this time dozens of appreciative letters, from men inside government, former officials, and a great many others. Most astonishing was a handwritten note on official stationery from a Cabinet member I had never met, who agreed with what I had said but asked why I had not had the guts to add that Rusk

---

[3]The Bermuda message to the President was duly, and confidentially, presented at the White House, where our delegates were received by two junior assistants to Mr. Rostow.

and Rostow must go. But most saddening was one from a former boss I had much admired. I wonder, he wrote in his most searing sentence, what standards of personal decency can have caused a man to do what you have done.

THE EXIT SYNDROME, PHASE IV:
GOING ALL THE WAY

I never got to this phase, nor knew of it prior to the Ellsberg phenomenon. John Dean, in very different circumstances, has now reconfirmed its existence.

There is no immediate lesson to the foregoing account except that it took one foreign affairs resigner, whose departure was conventionally muddled, but who dissented on a central issue, approximately 18 months (including press time) to break through the multiple constraints that inhibit speaking out once one resigns from the U.S. government. The circumstances were special—both mine and those of the issue—as they are in every case. But perhaps it might be possible to extrapolate from my own experience, and observation of others, some more general conclusions about the factors that prevent, inhibit, or at least delay speaking out once one departs.

Here are factors that seem to be important, in no special order of priority:

1. A sense of duty or loyalty to the President and the Presidency. To those who have weathered the past decade, this thought will seem a bit archaic. Yet there does linger, in most exiting officials, a feeling that the Chief Executive is, for the time being, the only one we have (unlike parliamentary government, where ultimate national loyalty is not to the Prime Minister); a feeling, too, that you were in His Service, at his invitation, that he—or his agent—trusted you, and you owe him a debt of trust. It is simply ungrateful to bite the hand that gave you power and responsibility, and an attack on his policies is an attack on him, ergo betrayal.

2. The fear of immediate retribution. The post-World War II American Presidency is the world's most powerful institution of government. A former official is one lonely person—unless, of course, he has strong political roots of his own (as a previously elected official), or an influential constituency of colleagues in, say, business or banking or law, or can attach himself as a new recruit to an opposition movement on the outside. Even with such possible bases of support, he faces, on exit, the fact that the executive branch has instant and continued access to the media, has massive sources of support among its partisans throughout the country, and can make use, if necessary, of the FBI and the Justice Department (not to mention the Internal Revenue Service) to harass an opponent. Lest this sound overdrawn about pre-Watergate days, it should be noted that when Chester Bowles resisted his firing as Under Secretary of State in November 1961 and temporarily rejected an alternative job offer, preferring to get out and speak out, President Kennedy's White House staff intermediary warned him, "We will destroy you." A fear of retribution in an electronic age—the unknown, what they may have on you, what they might do to you if only through denunciation and ridicule—is certainly an inhibiting factor.

*3. The fear of barred return.*Most men who have worked in high positions in government would like, however disaffected, some day to return—at least for a while, if the circumstances are right. Most departing officials are therefore careful not to do things that might bar such a return—that might burn their bridges once and for all. To be asked back you must behave like a team player. You may well have dissented openly, even passionately, within the councils of government, and your colleagues may know why you really resigned, if it was really over dissent; but you owe it to the Club—and to your continued membership in the Club, though temporarily on leave—to abide by the unwritten rule: dissent inside (and within limits) is fine; dissent outside, and in public, is bad form. Furthermore, an internal dissenter who becomes an external dissenter inevitably suggests the existence of previous internal debates and thereby breaks another Club rule: revealing the Club's internal squabbles to nonmembers. One would think that a two-party system would have modified these rules, i.e., that an exiting internal critic would find welcome and refuge in the opposition party. Such is the nature of foreign policy issues, however, cutting as they do across both parties; such is the nature of one's political allegiance (a dissenter doesn't necessarily want to join the other party); and such is the nature of the Club itself, providing foreign affairs officials to administrations of *both* parties—that the barring of one's return usually means a barring of one's return *regardless* of party in power. The Club's grapevine crosses party lines, and once known as a rule-breaker under one administration, the *fear* is that one will be barred from all future administration.

*4. Anxiety over security regulations.*This may seem a fairly trivial factor, hardly worth citing. Yet a man who has worked for an extended period within the special constraints of a system of security classifications as well as the attendant political constraints, but without the harsh but clear guidelines of an Official Secrets Act, is very much at sea once he leaves government service. He has developed habits of discretion and prudence in his dealings with outsiders, though he may have indulged from time to time in the tradition of selective leakage to friends in the press. Once on the outside he is a bit unsure of the ground rules—of what to say to whom, where and when. However much he may have dissented within, he is automatically careful, still weighing his words lest he let slip information or ideas that might somehow be classified. (All right to say it in the classroom, for instance, but in print?) The syndrome undoubtedly lasts longer in some than in others. But it operates as a strong constraint against speaking out at once.

*5. The fear of intermediate ostracism.*This is a variant of the earlier point about fear of barred return. It has not to do with government but with those adjuncts of government, the friendly watering places of other departed officials—for instance, New York's Council on Foreign Relations, Washington's Brookings

Institution, and periodic conferences hosted by foundations with an international interest. Despite the jarring effect of Vietnam, intercourse between government and the institutions of the external foreign affairs establishment has continued. Former insiders oftern look forward to a continued relationship with present and former policy-makers—and a continued sense of involvement —through participation in such aspects of the extended Club. To speak out soon and bluntly, to be noisy or shrill or impassioned, to break the internal Club's rules—all this, one fears, may ostracize one from even the status of friendly auditor. Since the other friendly auditors are men who will probably staff, or recommend the staff for, future administrations, this fear reinforces the fear of barred return.

*6. Anxiety about community.*This is admittedly a subtle and highly speculative matter: the resigner's need for a sense of community once he has left the community of government officials and their associates. Once again, extended service in government can isolate a man from previous communities—his former constituents, if he earlier had been an elected official; his students and faculty colleagues, if he was a teacher; his former business or professional associates. Relocating yourself takes time—especially psychic time. If you have resigned over an issue of policy, you may find that your recent community (government) is not immediately replaced by your previous community (particularly if it doesn't share your dissent). To find a new community to encourage you and strengthen your voice takes time, hence time passes. Without question, the university is the best haven for the resigner—the turnaround time there is the shortest.

*7. Loyalty to the good guys still inside.*Here we deal with another subtle matter. Most dissenters eventually find fellow dissenters. Most stay on for a while— sometimes forever—"conspiring" with their co-dissenters to make a few good things happen, keep a few bad things from happening. Once a man leaves, he knows that he has left behind a network of fellow-believers who are still fighting the good fight. What is his responsibility to them? If he becomes an external nuisance to the administration, he may well harm their cause, if only because they have usually been identified with him and his views by the higher-ups. Sometimes his external assaults can help them. But it is a hard matter to judge—and for a while he may opt to keep quiet and merely wish them well.

*8. Desire for continued access, to influence even the bad guys.*No one ever quite gives up on trying to influence his President, Secretary of State, or other inside superiors. Despite a formal parting of the ways, there lingers the hope that one can still get across one's message—perhaps even do it better—from the outside: private letters or memoranda to one's former bosses; periodic visits; private collective efforts with other colleagues from the outside. The key here is access. Wouldn't it be foolish to destroy the possibility of access by (prematurely) speaking out?

9. And what good, after all, will it do? Here the issue is not "what will happen to me," or even "how can I retain influence," but simply "will anything I do by speaking out on the outside change anything at all?" Most noisy resignations at state and local levels are flashes in the pan. A man is a headline today, forgotten or a pariah tomorrow. Bad policy is seldom changed by assaults from those who jumped ship and then sang. Would it not be more constructive to work from inside and outside simultaneously—to stay in touch, perhaps on tap as a consultant, and to play the external role of a friendly analyst who doesn't exceed the bounds of permissible criticism?

What will happen to me? How can I retain influence? And what good, after all, will it do? Here are three central constraints on the exercise of individual conscience against the excesses of the national security apparatus, abroad or at home, against all that Indochina has meant and all that Watergate entails.

In the post-cold war era, the rehabilitation of the executive branch will take relentless work by courageous judges, journalists, congressmen, candidates, and voters. But it will take something else as well: the planting and rooting of a tradition of getting out and speaking out in a society and political system that have heretofore discouraged such behavior. Only through the development of such a tradition can the individual conscience be freed to act as a brake against the tyranny inherent in the American Presidential state and its ideology, the national security ethic.

The Constitution of the United States

We the People of the United States, in Order to form a more perfect Union, establish Justice, insure domestic Tranquility, provide for the common defence, promote the general Welfare, and secure the Blessings of Liberty to ourselves and our Posterity do ordain and establish this CONSTITUTION for the United States of America.

ARTICLE I

Section 1. All legislative Powers herein granted shall be vested in a Congress of the United States, which shall consist of a Senate and House of Representatives.

Section 2. (1) The House of Representatives shall be composed of members chosen every second Year by the People of the several States, and the Electors in each State shall have the Qualifications requisite for Electors of the most numerous Branch of the State Legislature.

(2) No Person shall be a Representative who shall not have attained to the Age of twenty-five Years, and been seven Years a Citizen of the United States, and who shall not, when elected, be an Inhabitant of that State in which he shall be chosen.

(3) [Representatives and direct Taxes[1] shall be apportioned among the several States which may be included within this Union, according to their respective Numbers, which shall be determined by adding to the whole Number of free Persons, including those bound to Service for a Term of Years, and excluding Indians not taxed, three fifths of all other Persons.][2] The actual Enumeration shall be made within three Years after the first Meeting of the Congress of the United States, and within every subsequent Term of ten years, in such Manner as they shall by Law direct. The

---

[1]The Sixteenth Amendment replaced this with respect to income taxes.
[2]Repealed by the Fourteenth Amendment.

Number of Representatives shall not exceed one for every thirty Thousand, but each State shall have at Least one Representative; and until such enumeration shall be made, the State of New Hampshire shall be entitled to choose three, Massachusetts eight, Rhode-Island and Providence Plantations one, Connecticut five, New-York six, New Jersey four, Pennsylvania eight, Delaware one, Maryland six, Virginia ten, North Carolina five, South Carolina five, and Georgia three.

(4) When vacancies happen in the Representation from any State, the Executive Authority thereof shall issue Writs of Election to fill such Vacancies.

(5) The House of Representatives shall choose their Speaker and other Officers; and shall have the sole Power of Impeachment.

Section 3. (1) The Senate of the United States shall be composed of two Senators from each State, [chosen by the Legislature][3] thereof, for six Years; and each Senator shall have one Vote.

(2) Immediately after they shall be assembled in Consequence of the first Election, they shall be divided as equally as may be into three Classes. The Seats of the Senators of the first Class shall be vacated at the Expiration of the second Year, of the second Class at the Expiration of the fourth Year, and of the third Class at the Expiration of the sixth Year, so that one-third may be chosen every second Year; [and if Vacancies happen by Resignation, or otherwise, during the Recess of the Legislature of any State, the Executive thereof may make temporary Appointments until the next Meeting of the Legislature, which shall then fill such Vacancies].[4]

(3) No person shall be a Senator who shall not have attained to the Age of thirty Years, and been nine Years a Citizen of the United States, and who shall not, when elected, be an Inhabitant of that State for which he shall be chosen.

(4) The Vice President of the United States shall be President of the Senate, but shall have no Vote, unless they be equally divided.

(5) The Senate shall choose their other Officers, and also a President pro tempore, in the absence of the Vice President, or when he shall exercise the Office of President of the United States.

(6) The Senate shall have the sole Power to try all Impeachments. When sitting for that Purpose, they shall be on Oath or Affirmation. When the President of the United States is tried, the Chief Justice shall preside: And no Person shall be convicted without the Concurrence of two thirds of the Members present.

(7) Judgment in Cases of Impeachment shall not extend further than to removal from Office, and disqualification to hold and enjoy any Office of

---

[3]Repealed by the Seventeenth Amendment, Section 1.
[4]Changed by the Seventeenth Amendment.

honor, Trust or Profit under the United States: but the Party convicted shall nevertheless be liable and subject to Indictment, Trial, Judgment and Punishment according to Law.

Section 4. (1) The Times, Places and Manner of holding Elections for Senators and Representatives, shall be prescribed in each State by the Legislature thereof; but the Congress may at any time by Law make or alter such Regulations, except as to the Places of Choosing Senators.

(2) The Congress shall assemble at least once in every Year, and such Meeting shall [be on the first Monday in December,][5] unless they shall by Law appoint a different Day.

Section 5. (1) Each House shall be the Judge of the Elections, Returns and Qualifications of its own Members, and a Majority of each shall constitute a Quorum to do Business; but a smaller number may adjourn from day to day, and may be authorized to compel the Attendance of absent Members, in such Manner, and under such Penalties as each House may provide.

(2) Each House may determine the Rules of its Proceedings, punish its Members for disorderly Behavior, and, with the Concurrence of two thirds, expel a Member.

(3) Each House shall keep a Journal of its Proceedings, and from time to time publish the same, excepting such Parts as may in their Judgment require Secrecy; and the Yeas and Nays of the Members of either House on any question shall, at the Desire of one fifth of those Present, be entered on the Journal.

(4) Neither House, during the Session of Congress, shall, without the Consent of the other, adjourn for more than three days, nor to any other Place than that in which the two Houses shall be sitting.

Section 6. (1) The Senators and Representatives shall receive a Compensation for their Services, to be ascertained by Law, and paid out of the Treasury of the United States. They shall in all Cases, except Treason, Felony and Breach of the Peace, be privileged from Arrest during their Attendance at the Session of their respective Houses, and in going to and returning from the same; and for any Speech or Debate in either House, they shall not be questioned in any other Place.

(2) No Senator or Representative shall, during the Time for which he was elected, be appointed to any civil Office under the Authority of the United States, which shall have been created, or the Emoluments whereof have been increased during such time; and no Person holding any Office under the United States, shall be a Member of either House during his Continuance in Office.

---

[5]Changed by the Twentieth Amendment, Section 2.

Section 7. (1) All Bills for raising Revenue shall originate in the House of Representatives; but the Senate may propose or concur with Amendments as on other Bills.

(2) Every Bill which shall have passed the House of Representatives and the Senate, shall, before it become a Law, be presented to the President of the United States; If he approve he shall sign it, but if not he shall return it, with his Objections to that House in which it shall have originated, who shall enter the Objections at large on their Journal, and proceed to reconsider it. If after such Reconsideration two thirds of that House shall agree to pass the Bill, it shall be sent, together with the Objections, to the other House, by which it shall likewise be reconsidered, and if approved by two thirds of that House, it shall become a Law. But in all such Cases the Votes of both Houses shall be determined by Yeas and Nays, and the Names of the Persons voting for and against the Bill shall be entered on the Journal of each House respectively. If any Bill shall not be returned by the President within ten Days (Sundays excepted) after it shall have been presented to him, the Same shall be a Law, in like Manner as if he had signed it, unless the Congress by their Adjournment prevent its Return, in which Case it shall not be a Law.

(3) Every Order, Resolution, or Vote to which the Concurrence of the Senate and House of Representatives may be necessary (except on a question of Adjournment) shall be presented to the President of the United States; and before the Same shall take Effect, shall be approved by him, or being disapproved by him, shall be repassed by two thirds of the Senate and House of Representatives, according to the Rules and Limitations prescribed in the Case of a Bill.

Section 8. (1) The Congress shall have Power To lay and collect Taxes, Duties, Imposts and Excises, to pay the Debts and provide for the common Defense and general Welfare of the United States; but all Duties, Imposts and Excises shall be uniform throughout the United States;

(2) To borrow money on the credit of the United States;

(3) To regulate Commerce with foreign Nations, and among the several States, and with the Indian Tribes;

(4) To establish an uniform Rule of Naturalization, and uniform Laws on the subject of Bankruptcies throughout the United States;

(5) To coin Money, regulate the Value thereof, and of foreign Coin, and fix the Standard of Weights and Measures;

(6) To provide for the Punishment of counterfeiting the Securities and current Coin of the United States;

(7) To establish Post Offices and post Roads;

(8) To promote the Progress of Science and useful Arts, by securing for

limited Times to Authors and Inventors the exclusive Right to their respective Writings and Discoveries;

(9) To constitute Tribunals inferior to the supreme Court;

(10) To define and punish Piracies and Felonies committed on the high Seas, and Offenses against the Law of Nations;

(11) To declare War, grant Letters of Marque and Reprisal, and make Rules concerning Captures on Land and Water;

(12) To raise and support Armies, but no Appropriation of Money to that Use shall be for a longer Term than two Years;

(13) To provide and maintain a Navy;

(14) To make Rules for the Government and Regulation of the land and naval Forces;

(15) To provide for calling forth the Militia to execute the Laws of the Union, suppress Insurrections and repel Invasions;

(16) To provide for organizing, arming, and disciplining the Militia, and for governing such Part of them as may be employed in the Service of the United States, reserving to the States respectively, the Appointment of the Officers, and the Authority of training the Militia according to the discipline prescribed by Congress;

(17) To exercise exclusive Legislation in all Cases whatsoever, over such District (not exceeding ten Miles square) as may, by Cession of particular States, and the acceptance of Congress, become the Seat of the Government of the United States, and to exercise like Authority over all Places purchased by the Consent of the Legislature of the State in which the Same shall be, for the Erection of Forts, Magazines, Arsenals, dock-Yards, and other needful Buildings;—And

(18) To make all Laws which shall be necessary and proper for carrying into Execution the foregoing Powers, and all other Powers vested by this Constitution in the Government of the United States, or in any Department or Officer thereof.

Section 9. (1) The Migration or Importation of such Persons as any of the States now existing shall think proper to admit, shall not be prohibited by the Congress prior to the Year one thousand eight hundred and eight, but a tax or duty may be imposed on such Importation, not exceeding ten dollars for each Person.

(2) The privilege of the Writ of Habeas Corpus shall not be suspended, unless when in Cases of Rebellion or Invasion the public Safety may require it.

(3) No Bill of Attainder or ex post facto Law shall be passed.

(4) No capitation, or other direct, Tax shall be laid, unless in Proportion to the Census or Enumeration herein before directed to be taken.[6]

---

[6]Changed by the Sixteenth Amendment.

(5) No Tax or Duty shall be laid on Articles exported from any State.

(6) No Preference shall be given by any Regulation of Commerce or Revenue to the Ports of one State over those of another: nor shall Vessels bound to, or from, one State, be obliged to enter, clear, or pay Duties in another.

(7) No Money shall be drawn from the Treasury, but in Consequence of Appropriations made by Law; and a regular Statement and Account of the Receipts and Expenditures of all public Money shall be published from time to time.

(8) No Title of Nobility shall be granted by the United States: And no Person holding any Office of Profit or Trust under them, shall, without the Consent of the Congress, accept of any present, Emolument, Office, or Title, of any kind whatever, from any King, Prince, or foreign State.

Section 10. (1) No State shall enter into any Treaty, Alliance, or Confederation; grant Letters of Marque and Reprisal; coin Money; emit Bills of Credit; make any Thing but gold and silver Coin a Tender in Payment of Debts; pass any Bill of Attainder, ex post facto Law, or Law impairing the Obligation of Contracts, or grant any Title of Nobility.

(2) No State shall, without the Consent of the Congress, lay any Imposts or Duties on Imports or Exports, except what may be absolutely necessary for executing its inspection Laws: and the net Produce of all Duties and Imposts, laid by any State on Imports or Exports, shall be for the Use of the Treasury of the United States; and all such Laws shall be subject to the Revision and Control of the Congress.

(3) No State shall, without the Consent of Congress, lay any duty of Tonnage, keep Troops, or Ships of War in time of Peace, enter into any Agreement or Compact with another State, or with a foreign Power, or engage in War, unless actually invaded, or in such imminent Danger as will not admit of delay.

ARTICLE II

Section 1. (1) The executive Power shall be vested in a President of the United States of America. He shall hold his Office during the Term of four Years, and, together with the Vice-President, chosen for the same Term, be elected, as follows

(2) Each State shall appoint, in such Manner as the Legislature thereof may direct, a Number of Electors, equal to the whole Number of Senators and Representatives to which the State may be entitled in the Congress; but no Senator or Representative, or Person holding an Office of Trust or Profit under the United States, shall be appointed an Elector.

[The Electors shall meet in their respective States, and vote by Ballot for two persons, of whom one at least shall not be an Inhabitant of the same State with themselves. And they shall make a List of all the Persons voted for, and of the Number of Votes for each; which List they shall sign and certify, and transmit sealed to the Seat of the Government of the United States, directed to the President of the Senate. The President of the Senate shall, in the Presence of the Senate and House of Representatives, open all the Certificates, and the Votes shall then be counted. The Person having the greatest Number of Votes shall be the President, if such Number be a Majority of the whole Number of Electors appointed; and if there be more than one who have such Majority, and have an equal Number of Votes, then the House of Representatives shall immediately choose by Ballot one of them for President; and if no Person have a Majority, then from the five highest on the List the said House shall in like Manner choose the President. But in choosing the President, the Votes shall be taken by States, the Representation from each State having one Vote; A quorum for this Purpose shall consist of a Member or Members from two-thirds of the States, and a Majority of all the States shall be necessary to a Choice. In every Case, after the Choice of the President, the Person having the greatest Number of Votes of the Electors shall be the Vice-President. But if there should remain two or more who have equal Votes, the Senate shall choose from them by Ballot the Vice-President.][7]

(3) The Congress may determine the Time of choosing the Electors, and the Day on which they shall give their Votes; which Day shall be the same throughout the United States.

(4) No person except a natural born Citizen, or a Citizen of the United States, at the time of the Adoption of this Constitution, shall be eligible to the Office of President; neither shall any Person be eligible to that Office who shall not have attained to the Age of thirty-five Years, and been fourteen Years a Resident within the United States.

(5) In case of the Removal of the President from Office, or of his Death, Resignation, or Inability to discharge the Powers and Duties of the said Office, the same shall devolve on the Vice-President, and the Congress may by Law provide for the Case of Removal, Death, Resignation or Inability, both of the President and Vice-President, declaring what Officer shall then act as President, and such Officer shall act accordingly, until the Disability be removed, or a President shall be elected.[8]

(6) The President shall, at stated Times, receive for his Services, a Compensation, which shall neither be increased nor diminished during the Period for which he shall have been elected, and he shall not receive within that Period any other Emolument from the United States, or any of them.

(7) Before he enter on the Execution of his Office, he shall take the following Oath or Affirmation:—"I do solemnly swear (or affirm) that I will faith-

---

[7] This paragraph was superseded in 1804 by the Twelfth Amendment.
[8] Changed by the Twenty-fifth Amendment.

fully execute the Office of President of the United States, and will to the best of my Ability, preserve, protect and defend the Constitution of the United States."

Section 2. (1) The President shall be Commander in Chief of the Army and Navy of the United States, and of the Militia of the several States, when called into the actual Service of the United States; he may require the Opinion in writing, of the principal Officer in each of the executive Departments, upon any subject relating to the Duties of their respective Offices, and he shall have Power to Grant Reprieves and Pardons for Offenses against the United States, except in Cases of Impeachment.

(2) He shall have Power, by and with the Advice and Consent of the Senate, to make Treaties, provided two-thirds of the Senators present concur; and he shall nominate, and by and with the Advice and Consent of the Senate, shall appoint Ambassadors, other public Ministers and Consuls, Judges of the supreme Court, and all other Officers of the United States, whose Appointments are not herein otherwise provided for, and which shall be established by Law: but the Congress may by Law vest the Appointment of such inferior Officers, as they think proper, in the President alone, in the Court of Law, or in the Heads of Departments.

(3) The President shall have Power to fill up all Vacancies that may happen during the Recess of the Senate, by granting Commissions which shall expire at the End of their next Session.

Section 3. He shall from time to time give to the Congress Information of the State of the Union, and recommend to their Consideration such Measures as he shall judge necessary and expedient; he may, on extraordinary Occasions, convene both Houses, or either of them, and in Case of Disagreement between them, with Respect to the Time of Adjournment, he may adjourn them to such Time as he shall think proper; he shall receive Ambassadors and other public Ministers; he shall take Care that the Laws be faithfully executed, and shall Commission all the Officers of the United States.

Section 4. The President, Vice President and all civil Officers of the United States, shall be removed from Office on Impeachment for, and Conviction of, Treason, Bribery, or other high Crimes and Misdemeanors.

ARTICLE III

Section 1. The judicial Power of the United States, shall be vested in one supreme Court, and in such inferior Courts as the Congress may from time to time ordain and establish. The Judges, both of the supreme and inferior Courts, shall hold their Offices during good Behavior, and shall, at stated Times, receive for their Services a Compensation which shall not be diminished during their Continuance in Office.

Section 2. (1) The judicial Power shall extend to all Cases, in Law and Equity, arising under this Constitution, the Laws of the United States, and Treaties made, or which shall be made, under their Authority;—to all Cases affecting Ambassadors, other public Ministers and Consuls;—to all Cases of admiralty and maritime Jurisdiction;—to Controversies to which the United States shall be a Party;—to Controversies between two or more States;—[between a State and Citizens of another State];[9] —between Citizens of different States;—between Citizens of the same State claiming Lands under Grants of different States, and [between a State, or the Citizens thereof, and foreign States, Citizens or Subjects].[10]

(2) In all Cases affecting Ambassadors, other public Ministers and Consuls, and those in which a State shall be Party, the supreme Court shall have original Jurisdiction. In all the other Cases before mentioned, the supreme Court shall have appellate Jurisdiction, both as to Law and Fact, with such Exceptions, and under such Regulations as the Congress shall make.

(3) The trial of all Crimes, except in Cases of Impeachment, shall be by Jury; and such Trial shall be held in the State where the said Crimes shall have been committed: but when not committed within any State, the Trial shall be at such Place or Places as the Congress may by Law have directed.

Section 3. (1) Treason against the United States, shall consist only in levying War against them, or in adhering to their Enemies, giving them Aid and Comfort. No Person shall be convicted of Treason unless on the Testimony of two Witnesses to the same overt Act, or on Confession in open Court.

(2) The Congress shall have power to declare the Punishment of Treason, but no Attainder of Treason shall work Corruption of Blood, or Forfeiture except during the Life of the Person attained.

ARTICLE IV

Section 1. Full Faith and Credit shall be given in each State to the public Acts, Records, and judicial Proceedings of every other State. And the Congress may by general Laws prescribe the Manner in which such Acts, Records and Proceedings shall be proved, and the Effect thereof.

Section 2. (1) The Citizens of each State shall be entitled to all Privileges and Immunities of Citizens in the several States.

(2) A Person charged in any State with Treason, Felony, or other Crime, who shall flee from Justice, and be found in another State, shall on demand of the executive Authority of the State from which he fled, be delivered up, to be removed to the State having Jurisdiction of the Crime.

[9]Restricted by the Eleventh Amendment.
[10]Restricted by the Eleventh Amendment

(3) [No Person held to Service or Labor in one State, under the Laws thereof, escaping into another, shall, in Consequence of any Law or Regulation therein, be discharged from such Service or Labor, but shall be delivered up on Claim of the Party to whom such Service or Labor may be due.][11]

Section 3. (1) New States may be admitted by the Congress into this Union; but no new State shall be formed or erected within the Jurisdiction of any other State; nor any State be formed by the Junction of two or more States, or parts of States, without the Consent of the Legislatures of the States concerned as well as of the Congress.

(2) The Congress shall have Power to dispose of and make all needful Rules and Regulations respecting the Territory or other Property belonging to the United States; and nothing in this Constitution shall be so construed as to Prejudice any Claims of the United States, or of any particular State.

Section 4. The United States shall guarantee to every State in this Union a Republican Form of Government, and shall protect each of them against Invasion; and on Application of the Legislature, or of the Executive (when the Legislature cannot be convened) against domestic Violence.

ARTICLE V

The Congress, whenever two-thirds of both Houses shall deem it necessary, shall propose Amendments to this Constitution, or, on the Application of the Legislatures of two-thirds of the several States, shall call a Convention for proposing Amendments, which, in either Case, shall be valid to all Intents and Purposes, as part of this Constitution, when ratified by the Legislature of three-fourths of the several States, or by Conventions in three-fourths thereof, as the one or the other Mode of Ratification may be proposed by the Congress; Provided that no Amendment which may be made prior to the Year One thousand eight hundred and eight shall in any Manner affect the first and fourth Clauses in the Ninth Section of the first Article; and that no State, without its Consent, shall be deprived of its equal Suffrage in the Senate.

ARTICLE VI

(1) All Debts contracted and Engagements entered into, before the Adoption of this Constitution, shall be as valid against the United States under this Constitution, as under the Confederation.

(2) This Constitution, and the Laws of the United States which shall be made in Pursuance thereof; and all Treaties made, or which shall be made, under the Authority of the United States, shall be the supreme Law of

---

[11]This paragraph has been superseded by the Thirteenth Amendment.

the Land; and the Judges in every State shall be bound thereby, any Thing in the Constitution or Laws of any State to the Contrary notwithstanding.

(3) The Senators and Representatives before mentioned, and the Members of the several State Legislatures, and all executive and judicial Officers, both of the United States and of the several States, shall be bound by Oath or Affirmation, to support this Constitution; but no religious Test shall ever be required as a Qualification to any Office or public Trust under the United States.

ARTICLE VII

The Ratification of the Conventions of nine States, shall be sufficient for the Establishment of this Constitution between the States so ratifying the Same.

DONE in Convention by the Unanimous Consent of the States present the Seventeenth Day of September in the Year of our Lord one thousand seven hundred and Eighty seven and the Independence of the United States of America the Twelfth. In Witness whereof We have hereunto subscribed our Names.

Go WASHINGTON
President and deputy from Virginia

ARTICLES IN ADDITION TO, AND AMENDMENT OF, THE CONSTITUTION OF THE UNITED SATES OF AMERICA, PROPOSED BY CONGRESS, AND RATIFIED BY THE LEGISLATURES OF THE SEVERAL STATES, PURSUANT TO THE FIFTH ARTICLE OF THE ORIGINAL CONSTITUTION.

ARTICLE I[12]

Congress shall make no law respecting an establishment of religion, or prohibiting the free exercise thereof; or abridging the freedom of speech, or of the press; or the right of the people peaceably to assemble, and to petition the Government for a redress of grievances.

ARTICLE II

A well regulated Militia, being necessary to the security of a free State, the right of the people to keep and bear Arms, shall not be infringed.

ARTICLE III

No Soldier shall, in time of peace be quartered in any house, without the consent of the Owner, nor in time of war, but in a manner to be prescribed by law.

---

[12]The first ten amendments were adopted in 1791.

ARTICLE IV

The right of the people to be secure in their persons, houses, papers, and effects, against unreasonable searches and seizures, shall not be violated, and no Warrants shall issue, but upon probable cause, supported by Oath or affirmation, and particularly describing the place to be searched, and the persons or things to be seized.

ARTICLE V

No person shall be held to answer for a capital, or otherwise infamous crime, unless on a presentment or indictment of a Grand Jury, except in cases arising in the land or naval forces, or in the Militia, when in actual service in time of War or public danger; nor shall any person be subject for the same offence to be twice put in jeopardy of life or limb; nor shall be compelled in any criminal case to be witness against himself, nor be deprived of life, liberty, or property, without due process of law; nor shall private property be taken for public use, without just compensation.

ARTICLE VI

In all criminal prosecutions, the accused shall enjoy the right to a speedy and public trial, by an impartial jury of the State and district wherein the crime shall have been committed, which district shall have been previously ascertained by law, and to be informed of the nature and cause of the accusation; to be confronted with the witnesses against him; to have compulsory process for obtaining witnesses in his favor, and to have the Assistance of Counsel for his defence.

ARTICLE VII

In suits at common law, where the value in controversy shall exceed twenty dollars, the right of trial by jury shall be preserved, and no fact tried by a jury, shall be otherwise reexamined in any Court of the United States, than according to the rules of the common law.

ARTICLE VIII

Excessive bail shall not be required, nor excessive fines imposed, nor cruel and unusual punishments inflicted.

ARTICLE IX

The enumeration in the Constitution, of certain rights, shall not be construed to deny or disparage others retained by the people.

ARTICLE X

The powers not delegated to the United States by the Constitution, nor prohibited by it to the States, are reserved to the States respectively, or to the people.

ARTICLE XI[13]

The Judicial power of the United States shall not be construed to extend to any suit in law or equity, commenced or prosecuted against one of the United States by Citizens of another State, or by Citizens or Subjects of any Foreign State.

ARTICLE XII[14]

The Electors shall meet in their respective states and vote by ballot for President and Vice-President, one of whom, at least, shall not be an inhabitant of the same state with themselves; they shall name in their ballots the person voted for as President, and in distinct ballots the person voted for as Vice-President, and they shall make distinct lists of all persons voted for as President, and of all persons voted for as Vice-President, and of the number of votes for each, which lists they shall sign and certify, and transmit sealed to the seat of the government of the United States, directed to the President of the Senate; —The President of the Senate shall, in presence of the Senate and House of Representatives, open all the certificates and the votes shall then be counted; —The person having the greatest number of votes for President, shall be the President, if such number be a majority of the whole number of Electors appointed; and if no person have such majority, then from the persons having the highest numbers not exceeding three on the list of those voted for as President, the House of Representatives shall choose immediately, by ballot, the President. But in choosing the President, the votes shall be taken by states, the representation from each state having one vote; a quorum for this purpose shall consist of a member or members from two-thirds of the states, and a majority of all the states shall be necessary to a choice. [And if the House of Representatives shall not choose a President whenever the right of choice shall devolve upon them, before the fourth day of March next following, then the Vice-President shall act as President, as in the case of the death or other constitutional disability of the President.][15] —The person having the greatest number of votes as Vice-President, shall be the Vice-President, if such number be a majority of the whole number of Electors appointed, and if no person have a majority, then from the two highest numbers on the list, the Senate shall

---

[13]Adopted in 1798.
[14]Adopted in 1804.
[15]Superseded by the Twentieth Amendment, Section 3.

choose the Vice-President; a quorum for the purpose shall consist of two-thirds of the whole number of Senators, and a majority of the whole number shall be necessary to a choice. But no person constitutionally ineligible to the office of President shall be eligible to that of Vice-President of the United States.

ARTICLE XIII[16]

Section 1. Neither slavery nor involuntary servitude, except as a punishment for crime whereof the party shall have been duly convicted, shall exist within the United States, or any place subject to their jurisdiction.

Section 2. Congress shall have power to enforce this article by appropriate legislation.

ARTICLE XIV[17]

Section 1. All persons born or naturalized in the United States, and subject to the jurisdiction thereof, are citizens of the United States and of the State wherein they reside. No state shall make or enforce any law which shall abridge the privileges or immunities of citizens of the United States; nor shall any State deprive any person of life, liberty, or property, without due process of law; nor deny to any person within its jurisdiction the equal protection of the laws.

Section 2. Representatives shall be apportioned among the several States according to their respective numbers, counting the whole number of persons in each State, excluding Indians not taxed. But when the right to vote at any election for the choice of electors for President and Vice-President of the United States, Representatives in Congress, the Executive and Judicial officers of a State, or the members of the Legislature thereof, is denied to any of the male inhabitants of such State, being twenty-one years of age, and citizens of the United States, or in any way abridged, except for participation in rebellion, or other crime, the basis of representation therein shall be reduced in the proportion which the number of such male citizens shall bear to the whole number of male citizens twenty-one years of age in such State.

Section 3. No person shall be a Senator or Representative in Congress, or elector of President and Vice-President, or hold any office, civil or military, under the United States, or under any State, who, having previously taken an oath, as a member of Congress, or as an officer of the United States, or as a member of any State legislature, or as an executive or judicial officer of any State, to support the Constitution of the United States, shall have engaged in insurrection or rebellion against the same, or given aid or comfort to the

---

[16]Adopted in 1865.
[17]Adopted in 1868.

enemies thereof. But Congress may by a vote of two-thirds of each House, remove such disability.

Section 4. The validity of the public debt of the United States, authorized by law, including debts incurred for payment of pensions and bounties for services in suppressing insurrection or rebellion, shall not be questioned. But neither the United States nor any State shall assume or pay any debt or obligation incurred in aid of insurrection or rebellion against the United States, or any claim for the loss or emancipation of any slave; but all such debts, obligations and claims shall be held illegal and void.

Section 5. The Congress shall have power to enforce, by appropriate legislation, the provisions of this article.

ARTICLE XV[18]

Section 1. The right of citizens of the United States to vote shall not be denied or abridged by the United States or by any State on account of race, color, or previous condition of servitude—

Section 2. The Congress shall have power to enforce this article by appropriate legislation.

ARTICLE XVI[19]

The Congress shall have power to lay and collect taxes on incomes, from whatever source derived, without apportionment among the several States, and without regard to any census or enumeration.

ARTICLE XVII[20]

The Senate of the United States shall be composed of two Senators from each State, elected by the people thereof, for six years; and each Senator shall have one vote. The electors in each State shall have the qualifications requisite for electors of the most numerous branch of the State legislatures.

When vacancies happen in the representation of any State in the Senate, the executive authority of such State shall issue writs of election to fill such vacancies: *Provided,* That the legislature of any State may empower the executive thereof to make temporary appointments until the people fill the vacancies by election as the legislature may direct.

This amendment shall not be so construed as to affect the election or term of any Senator chosen before it becomes valid as part of the Constitution.

---

[18]Adopted in 1870.
[19]Adopted in 1913.
[20]Adopted in 1913.

ARTICLE XVIII[21]

Section 1. After one year from the ratification of this article the manufacture, sale, or transportation of intoxicating liquors within, the importation thereof into, or the exportation thereof from the United States and all territory subject to the jurisdiction thereof for beverage purposes is hereby prohibited.

Section 2. The Congress and the several States shall have concurrent power to enforce this article by appropriate legislation.

Section 3. This article shall be inoperative unless it shall have been ratified as an amendment to the Constitution by the legislatures of the several States, as provided in the Constitution, within seven years from the date of the submission hereof to the State by the Congress.

ARTICLE XIX[22]

The right of citizens of the United States to vote shall not be denied or abridged by the United States or by any State on account of sex.

Congress shall have power to enforce this article by appropriate legislation.

ARTICLE XX[23]

Section 1. The terms of the President and Vice-President shall end at noon on the 20th day of January, and the terms of Senators and Representatives at noon on the 3d day of January, of the years in which such terms would have ended if this article had not been ratified; and the terms of their successors shall then begin.

Section 2. The Congress shall assemble at least once in every year, and such meeting shall begin at noon on the 3d day of January, unless they shall by law appoint a different day.

Section 3. If, at the time fixed for the beginning of the term of the President, the president elect shall have died, the Vice-President elect shall become President. If a President shall not have been chosen before the time fixed for the beginning of his term, or if the President elect shall have failed to qualify, then the Vice-President elect shall act as President until a President shall have qualified; and the Congress may by law provide for the case wherein neither a President elect nor a Vice-President elect shall have qualified, declaring who shall then act as President, or the manner in which one who is to act shall be selected, and such person shall act accordingly until a President or Vice-President shall have qualified.

---

[21]Adopted in 1919. Repealed by Section 1 of the Twenty-first Amendment.
[22]Adopted in 1920.
[23]Adopted in 1933.

Section 4. The Congress may by law provide for the case of the death of any of the persons from whom the House of Representatives may choose a President whenever the right of choice shall have devolved upon them, and for the case of the death of any of the persons from whom the Senate may choose a Vice-President whenever the right of choice shall have devolved upon them.

Section 5. Sections 1 and 2 shall take effect on the 15th day of October following the ratification of this article.

Section 6. This article shall be inoperative unless it shall have been ratified as an amendment to the Constitution by the legislatures of three-fourths of the several States within seven years from the date of its submission.

ARTICLE XXI[24]

Section 1. The eighteenth article of amendment to the Constitution of the United States is hereby repealed.

Section 2. The transportation or importation into any State, Territory, or possession of the United States for delivery or use therein of intoxicating liquors, in violation of the laws thereof, is hereby prohibited.

Section 3. This article shall be inoperative unless it shall have been ratified as an amendment to the Constitution by conventions in the several States, as provided in the Constitution, within seven years from the date of the submission hereof to the States by the Congress.

ARTICLE XXII[25]

Section 1. No person shall be elected to the office of the President more than twice, and no person who has held the office of President, or acted as President, for more than two years of a term to which some other person was elected President shall be elected to the office of the President more than once. But this Article shall not apply to any person holding the office of President when this Article was proposed by the Congress, and shall not prevent any person who may be holding the office of President, or acting as President, during the term within which this Article becomes operative from holding the office of President or acting as President during the remainder of such term.

Section 2. This article shall be inoperative unless it shall have been ratified as an amendment to the Constitution by the legislatures of three-fourths of the several States within seven years from the date of its submission to the States by the Congress.

---

[24]Adopted in 1933.
[25]Adopted in 1951.

ARTICLE XXIII[26]

Section 1. The District constituting the seat of Government of the United States shall appoint in such manner as the Congress may direct:

A number of electors of President and Vice-President equal to the whole number of Senators and Representatives in Congress to which the District would be entitled if it were a State, but in no event more than the least populous State; they shall be in addition to those appointed by the States, but they shall be considered, for the purposes of the election of President and Vice-President, to be electors appointed by a State; and they shall meet in the District and perform such duties as provided by the twelfth article of amendment.

Section 2. The Congress shall have power to enforce this article by appropriate legislation.

ARTICLE XXIV[27]

Section 1. The right of citizens of the United States to vote in any primary or other election for President or Vice-President, for electors for President or Vice-President, or for Senator or Representative in Congress, shall not be denied or abridged by the United States or any state by reasons of failure to pay any poll tax or other tax.

Section 2. The Congress shall have power to enforce this article by appropriate legislation.

ARTICLE XXV[28]

Section 1. In case of the removal of the President from office or of his death or resignation, the Vice-President shall become President.

Section 2. Whenever there is a vacancy in the office of the Vice-President, the President shall nominate a Vice-President who shall take office upon confirmation by a majority vote of both Houses of Congress.

Section 3. Whenever the President transmits to the President pro tempore of the Senate and the Speaker of the House of Representatives his written declaration that he is unable to discharge the powers and duties of his office, and until he transmits to them a written declaration to the contrary, such powers and duties shall be discharged by the Vice-President as Acting President.

Section 4. Whenever the Vice-President and a majority of either the principal officers of the Executive departments or of such other body as Congress may by law provide transmit to the President pro tempore of the Senate and the

---

[26]Adopted in 1961.
[27]Adopted in 1964.
[28]Adopted in 1967.

Speaker of the House of Representatives their written declaration that the President is unable to discharge the powers and duties of his office, the Vice-President shall immediately assume the powers and duties of the office as Acting President.

Thereafter, when the President transmits to the President pro tempore of the Senate and the Speaker of the House of Representatives his written declaration that no inability exists, he shall resume the powers and duties of his office unless the Vice-President and a majority of either the principal officers of the Executive departments or of such other body as Congress may by law provide transmit within four days to the President pro tempore of the Senate and the Speaker of the House of Representatives their written declaration that the President is unable to discharge the powers and duties of his office. Thereupon Congress shall decide the issue, assembling within forty-eight hours for that purpose if not in session. If the Congress, within twenty-one days after receipt of the latter written declaration, or, if Congress is not in session, within twenty-one days after Congress is required to assemble, determines by two-thirds vote of both houses that the President is unable to discharge the powers and duties of his office, the Vice-President shall continue to discharge the same as Acting President; otherwise, the President shall resume the powers and duties of his office.

ARTICLE XXVI[29]

Section 1. The right of citizens of the United States, who are 18 years of age or older, to vote shall not be denied or abridged by the United States or any state on account of age.

Section 2. The Congress shall have power to enforce this article by appropriate legislation.

ARTICLE XXVII[30]

Section 1. Equality of rights under the law shall not be denied or abridged by the United States or by any State on account of sex.

Section 2. The Congress shall have the power to enforce, by appropriate legislation, the provisions of this article.

Section 3. This amendment shall take effect two years after the date of ratification.

---

[29] Adopted in 1971.

[30] Approved by Congress in 1972 and sent to the states for ratification. As of November, 1974, 33 had ratified this "equal rights amendment," 5 short of the necessary 38 ratifications.